Social-Science Commentary on the Letters of Paul

Social-Science Commentary on the Letters of Paul

BRUCE J. MALINA

JOHN J. PILCH

Fortress Press
MINNEAPOLIS

SOCIAL-SCIENCE COMMENTARY ON THE LETTERS OF PAUL

Cover design: Ann Delgehausen

Cover image: Paul's Letter to the Galatians. Greek text on papyrus c. 180–200 C.E. © The Trustees of the Chester Beatty Library, Dublin.

Interior photos: Photos on pages 10, 16, 184, and 197 are © Erich Lessing/Art Resource, New York, and used by permission. All other photographs are from *Cities of Paul* © 2004 The President and Fellows of Harvard College. Map on page 6 by Lucidity Information Design.

Library of Congress Cataloging-in-Publication Data

Malina, Bruce J.

Social-science commentary on the Letters of Paul / Bruce J. Malina, John. J. Pilch.

p. cm.

Includes bibliographical references (p.).

ISBN 0-8006-3640-6 (alk. paper)

1. Bible. N.T. Epistles of Paul—Commentaries. 2. Bible. N.T. Epistles of Paul—Social scientific criticism. I. Pilch, John J. II. Title.

BS2650.53.M35 2006

227'.067—dc22

2005035389

The paper used in this publication meets the minimum requirements of American National Standard for Information Sciences—Permanence of Paper for Printed Library Materials, ANSI Z329.48-1984.

Manufactured in the U.S.A.

10 09 08 07 06 1 2 3 4 5 6 7 8 9 10

Contents

Abbreviations vii
Preface ix

Introduction 1

1 THESSALONIANS **27**
I. 1 Thess 1:1 Letter Opening (Superscription) 30
II. 1 Thess 1:2—3:13 About the Relationship between the Change Agents and the Jesus Group They Formed 33
III. 1 Thess 4:1—5:24 Directives and Exhortations 45
IV. 1 Thess 5:25-28 Letter Closing: Salutation and Blessing 55

1 CORINTHIANS **57**
I. 1 Cor 1:1-8 Letter Opening (Superscription) 60
II. 1 Cor 1:9—6:20 Reaction to a Report from Chloe's People 62
III. 1 Cor 7:1—15:58 Response to Corinthian Questions 85
IV. 1 Cor 16:5-24 Letter Closing: Salutations and Blessings 130

2 CORINTHIANS **133**
I. 2 Cor 2:14—6:13 Letter 1: Written before the Dispute 136
II. 2 Corinthians 10–13 Letter 2: Written during the Dispute 150
III. 2 Cor 1:1—2:13 [7:5-16] Letter 3: Written after the Dispute 162
IV. 2 Cor 8:1-24 Insert: Part of a Letter of Recommendation for Titus about the Collection for Jerusalem 171
V. 2 Cor 9:1-15 Insert: Part of a Letter about the Collection for Jerusalem 175

GALATIANS **177**
I. Gal 1:1-5 Letter Opening (Superscription) 180
II. Gal 1:6-9 Introduction 182
III. Gal 1:10—2:21 Paul Defends His Honor (Form: Encomium) 183
IV. Gal 3:1—6:10 Paul Defends His Gospel (Form: Public Argument) 201
V. Gal 6:11-18 Conclusion 217

ROMANS			**219**
I.	Rom 1:1-7	Letter Opening (Superscription)	222
II.	Rom 1:8-10	Letter Thanksgiving	224
III.	Rom 1:11-17	Introduction and Travel Plans	224
IV.	Rom 1:18-32	They and the Ten Commandments	227
V.	Rom 2:1-16	You Judeans and Judging Hellenists	232
VI.	Rom 2:17—3:20	Israelites	234
VII.	Rom 3:21—8:39	The Present Time: Now	239
VIII.	Rom 9:1—11:36	Recalcitrant Israel	263
IX.	Rom 12:1—13:14	You: Jesus-Group Values	275
X.	Rom 14:1—15:13	They (the Weak) and the Torah Commandments	282
XI.	Rom 15:15-32	Conclusion and Travel Plans	288
XII.	Rom 15:33	Letter Ending	290
XIII.	Rom 16:1-29	Appendix: Letter of Recommendation for Phoebe and Doxology	290

PHILIPPIANS			**295**
I.	Phil 1:1-11	Superscription	296
II.	Phil 1:12—2:15	Body A: Paul's Prison Circumstances and Its Significance for the Philippians	301
III.	Phil 2:16—3:21	Body B: Ingroup and Outgroup Relations	308
IV.	Phil 4:1-23	Concluding Remarks	316

PHILEMON			**321**
I.	Phlm 1-3	Superscription	322
II.	Phlm 4-7	Thanksgiving: The Exordium	323
III.	Phlm 8-16	Body of the Letter Part A: Probatio	326
IV.	Phlm 17-22	Body of the Letter Part B: Peroratio	328
V.	Phlm 23-25	Conclusion	328

Reading Scenarios for the (Authentic) Letters of Paul **331**

Bibliography 411
List of Reading Scenarios 419

Abbreviations

AB	Anchor Bible
Abr.	Philo, *On the Life of Abraham* (*De Abrahamo*)
Agr.	Philo, *Agriculture* (*De agricultura*)
Alleg. Interp.	Philo, *Allegorical Interpretation* (*Legum allegoriae*)
ANRW	*Aufstieg und Niedergang der römischen Welt*
Ant.	Josephus, *Antiquities of the Judeans* (*Antiquitates judaicae*)
b.	Babylonian Talmud
Ber.	*Berakhot*
BibInt	*Biblical Interpretation*
BibIntSer	Biblical Interpretation Series
Blass and Debrunner	F. Blass and A. Debrunner. A *Greek Grammar of the New Testament and Other Early Christian Literature.* Translated and edited by Robert W. Funk. Chicago: University of Chicago Press, 1961.
BTB	*Biblical Theology Bulletin*
CBQ	*Catholic Biblical Quarterly*
OGIS	*Orientis graeci inscriptiones selectae.* Edited by W. Dittenberger. 2 vols. Leipzig, 1903–1905.
HCNT	M. Eugene Boring, Klaus Berger, and Carsten Colpe, eds. *Hellenistic Commentary to the New Testament.* Nashville: Abingdon, 1995.
HTS	Harvard Theological Studies
HvTSt	*Hervormde teologiese studies*
JBL	*Journal of Biblical Literature*
JSNT	*Journal for the Study of the New Testament*
KJV	King James Version
LCL	Loeb Classical Library
Life	Josephus, *The Life* (*Vita*)
LSJ	Liddell, H. G., R. Scott, H. S. Jones, A *Greek-English Lexicon.* 9th ed. with revised supplement. Oxford: Oxford University Press, 1996.
LXX	Septuagint
Migr.	Philo, *Migration* (*De migratione Abrahami*)
mss.	manuscripts
NRSV	New Revised Standard Version
NTS	*New Testament Studies*
Post.	Philo, *On the Posterity of Cain* (*De posteritate Caini*)
RSV	Revised Standard Version
Sanh.	*Sanhedrin*
SHR	Studies in the History of Religions

Spec. Laws	Philo, *On the Special Laws* (*De specialibus legibus*)
Unchangeable	Philo, *That God Is Unchangeable* (*Quod Deus sit immutabilis*)
War	Josephus, *The Judean War* (*Bellum judaicum*)
WBC	Word Biblical Commentary
Worse	Philo, *That the Worse Attacks the Better* (*Quod deterius potiori insidari soleat*)
WUNT	Wissenschaftliche Untersuchungen zum Neuen Testament

Preface

Given the fact that there are hundreds, if not thousands, of commentaries on the letters of Paul, one might ask, Why another commentary? Most commentaries are theologically or religiously oriented, underscoring features of Paul's letters that might be of use in articulating contemporary denominational Christianity. Others are linguistically or philologically oriented, based on the belief that written documents can be best understood by literary, aesthetic criteria. The distinctive feature of this social-science commentary is that it draws insights from an array of social sciences such as anthropology, social psychology, sociolinguistics, and the like in order to determine the most culturally plausible interpretation of Paul's letters. The concerns considered here derive from first-century Eastern Mediterranean social systems, with the various social structures, cultural values, and understandings of what it meant to be a person that existed at that time and place. Our concern is to discover what Paul was up to within the social setting of his society by examining the typical Eastern Mediterranean social behaviors witnessed in his letters. What social interactions do the letters evidence? What sort of outcomes in his society did Paul expect?

The New Testament text that is authoritative in the churches is, of course, the critical edition of the Greek. There is no perfect version of the Bible, not even the King James Version, as the Revised Standard Version indicates. The New Testament translation printed in this book is the New Revised Standard Version (NRSV). We shall at times have occasion to question the accuracy of some renderings, for reasons that will be specified.

This book provides two types of interpretative material. First, by way of clarification, we offer short **Textual Notes** commenting on each letter. The letters are presented in historical sequence, following the common opinion of historically oriented biblical scholars. This sequence diverges from the canonical sequence printed in Bibles. These **Notes** draw the reader's attention to dimensions of the social system expressed in the language of each letter and provide a small-scale social-science commentary that supplements the traditional, more theologically oriented studies available on the authentic Pauline documents.

Second, later in this book we provide a collection of **Reading Scenarios** drawn from anthropological studies of the Mediterranean social system. This is the social system that has been encoded in the language of the letters in ways that are not always obvious to modern readers. Since most of the reading scenarios apply throughout Paul's letters, however, we have duly referenced them in the commentary for the convenience of the reader. Together with the **Textual Notes**, the **Reading Scenarios** offer clues for filling in the unspoken or implicit elements of the writing as a Mediterranean reader would certainly have done. The **Notes** and **Reading Scenarios** help the modern reader develop a considerate posture toward the ancient author and prevent imposing on that author's work interpretations that would be culturally incompatible. An index of reading scenarios is provided at the close of the book. On general introductory questions about the Pauline writings as well as on questions concerning the dating and sequence of these letters, we have followed Dennis C. Duling's *The New Testament: History, Literature, and Social Context* (4th ed.; Belmont, Calif.: Wadsworth/Thomson, 2003).

Finally, the illustrations, map, and charts included are intended to serve as a reminder that in reading the New Testament we are indeed in a different world. The scenarios that these and our written comments evoke and that we ask the reader to understand come from a time and place that for all of us remain foreign territory. It is unlike anything we are likely to imagine from our experience in the modern West. It is a world we invite you to enter as a thoughtful and considerate reader.

Bruce J. Malina, Creighton University
John J. Pilch, Georgetown University

Introduction

Toward a Considerate Reading

In this commentary we restrict our attention to the authentic letters of the Apostle Paul. In the New Testament collection fourteen letters have traditionally carried the title "Letter of St. Paul to. . . ." Of these fourteen documents, modern scholars, using philological methods and a critical sense of history, have determined that only seven of these letters are authentic, meaning that Paul was their author. The other letters are not authentic, meaning that Paul did not compose them. They were written by second- and third-generation members of Jesus groups who lived in the Pauline tradition. Historically, Christian churches have considered all these writings in the New Testament canonical, that is, inspired by God and therefore normative. It is important for Bible readers to understand that historical authenticity and canonicity are quite different. Similarly, it is important to realize that in the Christian tradition, an inspired writing is one coming from an author considered by the early Christian church to have been inspired by God. Inspiration, in this sense, has nothing to do with whether or not a contemporary reader feels inspired while reading such a writing.

Of these seven authentic letters, five deal with problems confronted by groups founded by Paul: 1 Thessalonians, 1 and 2 Corinthians, Galatians, and Philippians. Romans is motivated primarily by Paul's travel arrangements, while Philemon serves as a letter of recommendation on behalf of a runaway slave, asking his master to accept him back. Paul's writings are second-generation Jesus-group documents in which Paul interacts with persons in the Jesus groups that he founded. Other letters ascribed to Paul, such as Colossians and 2 Thessalonians, are third-generation Jesus-group productions by other authors in the Pauline tradition that deal with the concerns of the generation immediately following Paul's time and apply his teaching to that new situation. Finally, Ephesians (a sort of letter to non-Israelite Jesus-group members), Hebrews (a sort of letter to practicing Judean Jesus groups), and the letters to Timothy and Titus are fourth-generation Jesus-group documents in the Pauline tradition, dealing with different problems and situations in terms and perspectives of Pauline church members of the fourth-generation after Jesus (see Malina 2005). To repeat, our concern in this volume is with Paul's authentic letters.

In order to understand Paul and his concerns and behaviors, the first act is to read his letters. We offer this introduction as a "pre-reading," however, since without such an explicit pre-reading readers invariably supply a pre-reading of their own. Long before any words are read people actually begin their reading, just as people who converse with others begin their conversation before any words are spoken. People who engage in a conversation learn to "read the situation" through stereotypes provided by the culture. For example, they know what to expect when they speak with an uninvited or unannounced salesperson at the door, or with a couple of Jehovah's Witnesses canvassing their neighborhood, or with a pastor at church, another fan at a football game, and so on. These are called "contexts" of the use of language, and they largely limit what persons can say. The same is true with receiving an e-mail or a letter. As for "snail mail," people engage in a pre-reading by looking at the letter: is it handwritten or typed, is it a personal letter or a business letter, is it an official government letter or a non-government letter? Upon opening the envelope the reader finds more clues in the salutation for what will likely follow. "Dear Mom and Dad" from a college student away from home invariably, even if implicitly, will contain a request for funds. A "Dear Occupant" letter will engage the recipient in some sort of commercial interaction. Those uninterested in a commercial transaction will simply throw the letter away without reading it, without interpreting it. They do not wish to engage in this context of the use of language.

The same was true of Paul's letters. They had a context of use that enabled recipients to pre-read them. People receiving these letters in the first century knew what they generally were about before they had the letter read to them. (Only about 2 percent of the population was literate, that is, could read and write with some measure of proficiency; see Hopkins 1998.) This context of use in Paul's letters was largely determined by who people thought Paul was. Paul was a Jesus-group "apostle," authorized as such by the God of Israel. Readers also knew Paul's proclamation, "the gospel of God." The recipients' social status and how and when they received the letter also determined the context of use. The addressees of Paul's letters were his "clients," the first ones to receive and accept the Good News communicated by Paul.

All these points indicate that reading is fundamentally a social act. Readers and writers always participate in a social system that provides the clues for filling in implicit information or for reading between the lines. Meanings are embedded in a social system shared and understood by all participants in any communication process. While meanings not rooted in a shared social system can sometimes be communicated, such communication inevitably requires extended explanation because a writer cannot depend upon the reader to conjure up the proper sets of related images or concepts needed to complete what is left unsaid.

This understanding of the social moorings of the reading process is confirmed by contemporary studies of reading (see Sanford and Garrod 1981). A "scenario model" drawn from recent research in experimental psychology suggests that readers understand a written document as setting out a succession of implicit or explicit mental pictures consisting of culturally specific scenes or schemes sketched by an author. These in turn evoke corresponding scenes or schemes in the mind of the reader that are drawn from the reader's own experience in the culture. With the scenarios suggested by the author as a starting point, the reader then carries out appropriate alterations to the settings or episodes as directed by clues in the written document. In this way an author begins with the familiar and directs the reader to what is new and unfamiliar or unexpected. Because of the nature of this process, we might say that a kind of "agreement" exists between author and reader. Considerate authors attempt to accommodate their readers by beginning with scenarios those readers would readily understand. With such mutual understanding in place, an author can then proceed to the new or unfamiliar.

As modern readers, we do not enjoy such an author-reader agreement with Paul. Paul's letters neither begin with what we know about the world nor make any attempt to explain their ancient world settings in terms we might understand from our own contemporary experience. The letters presume that their readers are first-century, Eastern Mediterranean Israelites who are part of a particular social system. The letters further assume that their readers understand the intricacies of honor and shame, are fully aware of what daily life is like in a ruralized society and its pre-industrial cities, know how folk healers operate, believe in limited good, routinely experience interactions with patrons and brokers, and so on. The letters do not start with what is familiar to us in our present world. Another way of saying this is simply to remind ourselves that Paul, like other New Testament writers, did not have modern Americans in mind when he wrote.

In order to make this author-reader agreement work, therefore, modern readers of Paul will have to make the effort to be considerate readers. To this end, we will have to voluntarily—though temporarily—enter the world that existed when Paul was alive, the world that was very familiar to him and his readers. To be considerate, modern readers will have to be willing to do what is necessary in order to bring to their reading a set of mental scenarios proper to Paul's time, place, and culture instead of imposing the ones familiar to modern Americans, whether churchgoers or not. Modern Christianity in all its forms has little to do with its ancestral expressions in the Jesus groups of Paul's day, as we hope our commentary will demonstrate.

Of course, making the effort to be considerate readers has not always been a priority of American readers of the Bible. Consciously or unconsciously we have often used mental images or scenarios drawn from modern American experience and denominational church traditions to fill in the undescribed pictures that are necessary to understand the complete text and its context. Thus when we read in our modern English translations that in Christ there is neither "Jew nor Greek," it is not difficult for most Americans to construct a reference. We do it from our modern experience of Jews and non-Jews (or Gentiles). That such a "scenario" is completely inappropriate, however, never dawns on most American readers. They simply do not know that in the first-century Mediterranean there really were no "Greeks" since there was no Greek nation nor any state called Greece. "The idea of a Greek nation is alien to the thought of most Greeks at most periods throughout

Greek history" (Walbank 2002:254–55). In fact, the word "Greek" referred to a status, to persons who were "civilized," indicated by the fact that they spoke Greek and adopted Hellenic values and habits in interpersonal relations. Similarly, the reference to "Jews" in poorly conceived English translations actually refers to "Judeans," people who followed the customs of one group of people living in that section of the Roman province of Syria called Palestine. The Hebrew term *yehudim* and the Greek *Ioudaioi* are simply erroneously translated in English (not necessary in other languages). To "Greeks," including Israelite "Greeks," Judeans were barbarians. Roman elites, who were "Greeks," were poorly informed about Judeans. Cassius Dio, a late second-century Roman writer, observed:

> This was the course of events at that time [Pompey's conquest in 63 B.C.E.] in Palestine [Greek: *Palaistina*]; for this is the name that has been given from of old to the whole country extending from Phoenicia to Egypt along the inner sea. They have also another name that they have acquired: the country has been named Judea and the people themselves Judeans. I do not know how this title came to be given them, but it applies also to all the rest of mankind, although of alien race, who affect their customs. This class exists even among the Romans. (Cassius Dio, *Roman History*, 37, 17, LCL)

Thus Judeans were people who practiced the customs of Judea, while Greeks were people who practiced the customs of Hellenists, a broad configuration of "civilized" Mediterranean peoples characterized by their use of the common Greek language. Taking the phrase "Judean and Greek" to mean Jews and Greeks, or worse, Jews and Gentiles, is simply erroneous, as well as anachronistic and ethnocentric. **Jew and Greek/Judean and Hellenist**.

Such ethnocentric and anachronistic readings of Paul are nevertheless common enough in our society that they underscore our point that reading is a social act. Yet how can contemporary American Bible readers participate in that social act with Paul if for the most part they have been socialized and shaped by the experience of living in twentieth- and twenty-first century America rather than the first-century Mediterranean? Will we not continue to conjure up reading scenarios Paul and his first readers could never have imagined? If we do, of course, the inevitable result is misunderstanding. Too often we do not bother to fill in scenarios as Paul's audiences did simply because we do not bother to acquire some of the reservoir of experience on which the authors expected their audiences to draw. For better or worse, we read ourselves and our world back into the text in ways we do not suspect. In social interaction this process is called "selective exposure," defined as the tendency to attend to communication messages that are consistent with one's existing knowledge, attitudes, and beliefs.

Obviously, reading is always a risky business, especially for writers. The same holds for learning. Classroom learning is a risky business, notably for teachers. The reason for this is that whatever writers or teachers say will always be interpreted according to the presuppositions of their audiences. (The medieval philosopher and theologian Thomas Aquinas expressed it thus: *Quidquid recipitur per modum recipientis recipitur*; whatever one perceives is perceived in terms of one's presuppositions.) If this holds for modern writers and teachers, it holds all the more so for ancient writers and their modern readers. The problem is rooted in what social psychologists call "selective perception." Selective perception is the tendency to interpret what others say in terms of one's existing attitudes and beliefs. While selective perception is a problem for modern writers and classroom teachers, it looms as an insurmountable obstacle to the understanding of ancient authors, not excluding biblical authors. While in our social system we are expected to spell out clearly what we mean to audiences with whom we are unacquainted, the ancients presupposed that their audiences could always fill in the blanks and thus did not bother to articulate many of the dimensions of what they meant.

Paul's Context and Ours

The New Testament was written in what anthropologists call a "high context" culture. People who communicate with each other in high context societies presume a broadly shared, generally well-understood knowledge of the context of anything referred to in conversation or in writing. For example, all ancient Mediterranean farmers used the same implements, in the same way, for the same purposes, and at the same season of the year. An ancient might say, "I farmed this plot last year," and all would know that the person was a tenant farmer in debt to a patron for seed, using a similar shallow plow, planting right before rainy season (beginning in October in the Eastern Mediterranean), then plowing the field after the seeds were sown. Obviously all of this could not be understood by a modern U.S. city dweller, and much of it would be mysterious even to modern U.S. farmers, who do not plant seeds before plowing. The point here is that cultures differ in the degree to which people are required to fill in the blanks for the persons with whom they communicate. Thus writers in such high context cultures usually produce sketchy and impressionistic writings, leaving much to the reader's or hearer's socially attuned imagination in rather static societies. Documents from high context cultures encode much information in widely known and understood symbolic or stereotypical statements. For this reason, these documents require the reader to fill in large gaps in what is left unwritten. All readers are expected to know the context and therefore to understand what is only implicit in the writing.

In this way biblical authors, like authors of most documents written in the high context ancient Mediterranean world, presumed readers to have a broad and adequate knowledge of the social context presumed in what those documents describe. Biblical documents offer very little by way of extended explanation. When Paul, a Pharisaic Israelite, writes that he was sent to "the (other) peoples" (usual English translation: "Gentiles"), for example, he feels no necessity to explain for his readers what going to "the (other) peoples" might concretely mean. He makes no mention of the crucial and salient ethnocentric social boundaries in antiquity between ingroup and outgroup, between Israelites and Everyone Else. Members of the

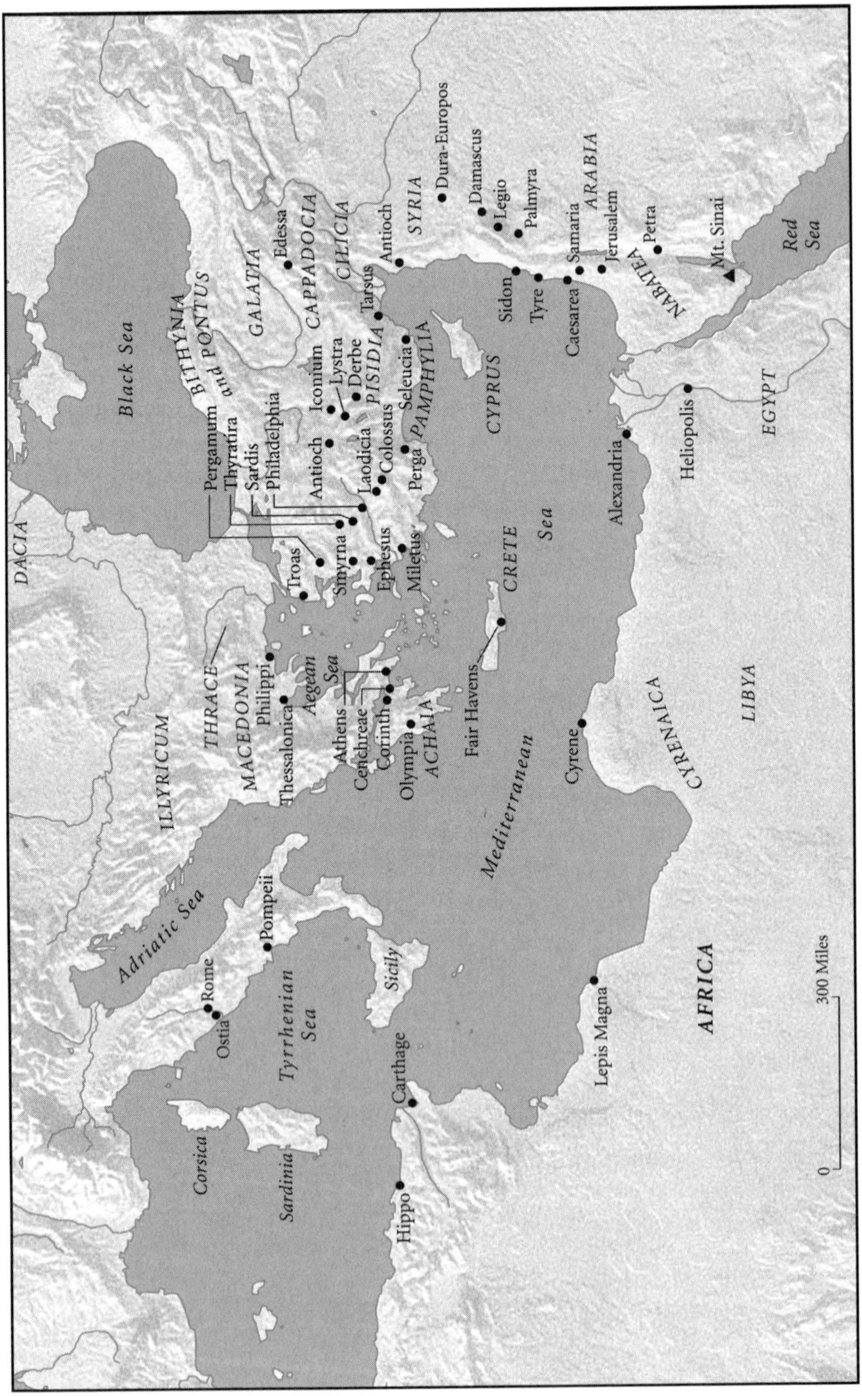
Black Sea
BITHYNIA and PONTUS
GALATIA
CAPPADOCIA
CILICIA
Edessa
SYRIA
Dura-Europos
Damascus
Legio
Palmyra
ARABIA
Antioch
Tarsus
Samaria
Jerusalem
Petra
NABATEA
Mt. Sinai
Red Sea
Sidon
Tyre
Caesarea
Iconium
Lystra
Derbe
PISIDIA
Seleucia
PAMPHYLIA
CYPRUS
Pergamum
Thyatira
Sardis
Philadelphia
Antioch
Laodicia
Colossus
Perga
EGYPT
Heliopolis
Alexandria
DACIA
Troas
Smyrna
Ephesus
Miletus
CRETE
Sea
THRACE
MACEDONIA
Philippi
Aegean Sea
Athens
Cenchreae
Corinth
Olympia
ACHAIA
Fair Havens
Thessalonica
ILLYRICUM
Mediterranean
CYRENAICA
LIBYA
Cyrene
Adriatic Sea
Pompeii
Rome
Ostia
Sicily
Tyrrhenian Sea
Carthage
Lepis Magna
AFRICA
0
300 Miles
Corsica
Sardinia
Hippo

house of Israel lumped all the rest of the world's population into that rubber-bag word, "the (other) peoples" (Gentiles). The Greek word *ethnē* (Gentiles) literally means "peoples," and when used by Israelites to set themselves off from other peoples, the word meant Everyone Else (other peoples, peoples other than us).

It is very important to reflect on a fact of social psychology that, in ingroup contexts, any Israelite "going to the other peoples" would be presumed to be going to Israelites resident among those other peoples. To take a modern example, when Israelis speak of "going to Americans" to sell U.S. tax-exempt Israeli bonds, they are presumed to be going to Jews resident in the U.S., not to non-Jewish Americans. Most American non-Jews are totally unaware of Israeli bonds. So too most first-century Mediterraneans were totally unaware of the Jesus-group gospel spread among Israelites living in non-Israelite regions. Paul believed that in a few short years he actually fulfilled his commission of proclaiming the gospel of God among Everyone Else, since "from Jerusalem and as far round as Illyricum I have *fully* preached the gospel of Christ, thus having made it a point of honor to proclaim the gospel, where Christ has not already been named" (Rom 15:19-20). The fact is, however, that perhaps 99.9 percent of the non-Israelite population of the regions Paul traversed fell far beyond the pale of Paul's outreach and were fully unaware of his activity. Paul was, in fact, apostle to Israelite minorities living among non-Israelite majority populations.

Paul does not have to explain this since all first-century Eastern Mediterraneans were ethnocentric and cared little, if anything, for outsiders; each group interpreted the whole world in terms of its values, its viewpoints, its worldview. Under most conditions what others thought about their group was inconsequential and totally unimportant. With their concern for preserving ingroup boundaries along with prevailing ethnocentrism, people hearing of Paul's going to the *ethnē*, that is, among other peoples of the Mediterranean, would understand that Paul went to Israelites resident among other peoples of the Mediterranean. These included Israelites located in Greco-Roman cities, that is, Israelites found in non-Israelite regions, where Israelites were a minority. All of this, of course, is critical to understanding Paul's statement about his being an "apostle to the Gentiles." Paul (and the author of the Acts of the Apostles) simply assumed that readers would understand.

By contrast, "low context" societies are those that produce highly specific and detailed documents that leave relatively little for the reader to fill in or supply. In general the United States and northern Europe are typical low context societies. Accordingly, Americans and northern Europeans expect writers to give the necessary background if they refer to something unusual or atypical. A computer operator, for example, learns a certain jargon and certain types of procedures (e.g., computer operating systems) that are not widely understood outside the circle of computer initiates. Within that specific circle these concepts can be used without explanation because they are easily supplied by any competent reader of technical computer manuals. But since they are not yet part of the experience of the general public, when writing for a nontechnical (low context) audience, a writer must explain the computer jargon and the technical information at some length if she or he wants to be understood.

A moment's reflection will make clear why modern industrial societies are low context and ancient ruralized ones were high context. Life today has complexified into a thousand spheres of experience the general public does not have in common. There are small worlds of experience in every corner of our society that the rest of us know nothing about. The worlds of the corporate CEO, the atomic or civil or electronic engineer, the plumber, the insurance salesperson, and the farmer, to name a few, are in large measure self-contained. Should any one of these people write for the "layperson" who is not a corporate CEO, engineer, plumber, insurance salesperson, or farmer, he or she would have much to explain. It was very different in antiquity, however, where change was slow and where the vast majority of the population had the common experience of farming the land and dealing with benefactors and patrons, with the Roman military, landlords, traders, merchants, and tax collectors. People had far more in common, and experience was far less discrepant. Thus writers could more nearly count on readers to fill in the gaps with some accuracy from behaviors into which Mediterraneans were socialized in their rather similar societies.

The obvious problem this creates for reading the Bible today is that low context readers in the United States frequently mistake biblical documents for low context documents and erroneously assume the authors have provided all of the contextual information needed to understand it. A survey by the Barda polling company found that in 2002, 76 percent of Americans believe the Bible is a perfectly adequate and thorough statement of Christian life and behavior that anyone can understand by just reading it (in English, of course, the language in which God "inspired" it). Such people assume they are free to fill in the gaps from their own experience because if that were not the case, the New Testament writers, like any considerate low context authors, would have provided the unfamiliar background a reader requires. Unfortunately, this is rarely the case because expectations of what an author will provide (or has provided) are markedly different in American and Mediterranean societies.

This point is not merely theoretical. When we consider the misery and suffering in the Middle East, for example, we are impressed that U.S. policies that we regard as particularly deleterious—in Palestine, Iraq, and elsewhere—nevertheless enjoy broad support among Americans, in part because they are so congenial to a particular Christian fundamentalist reading of the Bible. An insensitive, intolerant, and sometimes racist Christian Zionist perspective assents, in effect, in leaving millions of our fellow human beings at the mercy of broadly imperialist policies. Such misery-causing misunderstanding of the Bible derives from reading and interpreting a high context set of documents as though they were low context directives from God. While the foregoing example derives from U.S. civil religion (which now incorporates elements of Christian and Jewish Zionism), the same process has been going on in churches for centuries. People were little interested in what a writer like Paul said and wanted to say to his first-century Jesus groups. Rather, they were interested in finding Paul relevant and useful in their contemporary situations. They were not interested in an inspired author, but in an inspiring text for an inspired reader. To do this, they adopted a common misconception of the reading process.

Who Was Paul?

The question "Who was Paul?" can elicit a range of responses. Initially we can say that Paul was a second-generation Jesus-group member. Members of this second generation for the most part did not actually know Jesus personally, did not interact with him, did not actually hear him when he was alive on earth. In this they differed, of course, from Jesus' first followers, their wives and children, and all those others who heard and interacted with Jesus. The distinctive thing about the second generation was that they took up the witness of the first generation yet were largely not concerned with what Jesus said and did. The story of the life of Jesus was not a primary focus for the second generation (see Malina 2005).

Second-generation interest was focused, rather, on what the God of Israel did in Jesus of Nazareth's death and resurrection and on the fact that this act of God confirmed Jesus' proclamation of a forthcoming theocracy, a kingdom of the God of Israel. As Paul witnessed, the second-generation Jesus groups were to be found in Palestine as well as among Israelites resident outside of Palestine. In Palestine, second-generation Jesus groups, like the first, had political-religious interests (see Acts 1–9). They in fact formed a political-religious party in Israel, like other parties: the Pharisees, Sadducees, and Essenes. They believed that the kingdom of heaven, an Israelite theocracy, was coming, and they firmly believed that this would be ushered in with Jesus as Israel's Messiah. Very definitely this would happen soon. Jesus groups outside of Palestine shared identical beliefs in the forthcoming kingdom of God in Israel. While they nurtured this Israelite political-religious ideology, they were in fact resident in locations with their own political-religious institutions and their own citizenry. As resident aliens, their favored social structure followed kinship lines; they formed fictive kin groups of brothers and sisters meeting in domestic space, whether tenements or houses.

It was to such fictive kin Jesus groups that Paul directed his letters. In those letters, Paul explains who he was based on the context of language use in first-century C.E. expectations: "circumcised on the eighth day, of the people of Israel, of the tribe of Benjamin, a Hebrew born of Hebrews; as to the law a Pharisee, as to zeal a persecutor of the church, as to righteousness under the law blameless" (Phil 3:5-6). First-century persons defined themselves, as a rule, in terms of gender, genealogy, and geography (see Malina and Neyrey 1996). This was all that was required to know a person well. Here Paul implies gender and geography but specifies genealogy, first in terms of kinship—Israelite, Benjaminite, of a family practicing Judean customs devotedly (that is what "Hebrew" meant; see Harvey 1996)—then in terms of his associational or fictive kinship affiliation, namely, a Pharisee. He offers similar information in his Corinthian correspondence: "Are they Hebrews? So am I.

This stone inscription (Caesarea Maritima) honors Emperor Tiberius and Pontius Pilate, prefect of Judea (26–36 C.E.), where Paul reported he persecuted Jesus groups.

Are they Israelites? So am I. Are they descendants of Abraham? So am I" (2 Cor 11:22, with emphasis on genealogy and implicit geography). The geography in both instances is Judea (not Tarsus, as in Acts 9:30; 21:39; 22:3).

Paul was an Israelite. He was formed in the Pharisaic style of living the Mosaic Torah; hence he believed that "as to righteousness under the Law" he was "blameless." In terms of the values embodied by Pharisaic ideology (**Pharisaic Ideology**), his zeal moved him to become "a persecutor of the church," that is, of the members of the Jesus group he encountered in Judea. He refers to this phase of his life as follows: "For you have heard of my former life in Judaism, how I persecuted the church of God violently and tried to destroy it; and I advanced in Judaism beyond many of my own age among my people, so extremely zealous was I for the traditions of my fathers" (Gal 1:12-14) Paul intimates that his "violent" persecution of the "church of God" took place in Judea. After a period in "Arabia," three years in Damascus, and a period "in the regions of Syria and Cilicia," he specifies, "and I was still not known by sight to the churches of Christ in Judea," the members of which said: "He who once persecuted us is now preaching the faith he once tried to destroy" (Gal 1:22-23; Acts 7:48—8:3 similarly recalls that Paul was present at the stoning of Stephen in Jerusalem, then participated in doing violence to Jesus-group members in Judea and Samaria). The point to note from all this is that Paul was an Israelite who persecuted Jesus groups in Judea.

The significant event in his life that accounts for his letters is that he believed he was called by the God of Israel as an Israelite prophet, to proclaim the gospel of God to Israelites resident among non-Israelites (see Pilch 2003). Paul recalls, "But when God, who had set me apart before I was born and called me through his grace, was pleased to reveal his Son to me, so that I might proclaim him among the Gentiles, I did not confer with any human being, nor did I go up to Jerusalem to those who were already apostles before me" (Gal 1:15-17, NRSV). This passage underscores two important features about Paul: first, he believed he was called to be an Israelite prophet (the phrase "he who had set me apart before I was born and called me" traces back to the prophetic call of Jeremiah; Jer 1:5; see Isa 49:1). This means Paul did not "convert to Christianity" but rather continued to obey the God of Israel as he had previously done, this time with a prophetic mission. Second, in this call the God of Israel revealed his Son along with the task of proclaiming this "revelation." The "revelation" Paul refers to belongs to a category of human experiences called altered states of consciousness. Research into altered-state events has demonstrated that such experiences are always shaped by previous personal and social events. **Altered States of Consciousness.** That means that if Paul had a vision of the resurrected Jesus through whom the God of Israel authorized Paul to proclaim "the gospel of God," Paul must have known something about the Israelite Jesus, specifically as a person raised from the dead by the God of Israel.

What Was the Nature of Paul's Call?

Where did Paul learn about the Jesus he experienced in his altered state of consciousness experience? The answer is not difficult to find. After all, Paul tells us he persecuted Jesus-group members, those who believed the God of Israel had done something in and through Jesus of Nazareth. Unless we imagine Paul was a psychopathic murderer, we can presume that he persecuted them because he was aware of their agenda to some extent. He presumably knew what he was doing. What, then, did he know about Jesus?

What was distinctive about Jesus groups was that they had a new message for Israel. They were not simply revitalizing Israel. They had a gospel, Good News, something new, an innovation. If we assume that Paul was a rational person, and his letters indicate that he was, we may further assume that he had knowledge of what these Jesus-group members believed: that the God of Israel had raised the crucified Jesus from the dead, indicating that Jesus was Israel's Messiah to come and that an Israelite theocracy was in the offing. These people whom Paul persecuted were surely motivated or persuaded to believe what they did. Initially Paul found their ideas and arguments wanting, even preposterous, and this to such an extent that he felt their activities had to be suppressed.

Given his self-attested behavior, Paul rejected this Jesus-group innovation, and not only that: since he entered into conflict with Jesus-group members, we can be sure that their position made him feel aggrieved in some way. **Dispute Process**. He had a grievance against them. This meant at least that what they said about the

God of Israel and their proclamation of a forthcoming Israelite theocracy were blasphemous and insulting. It was a threat to Israel's political religion and dishonoring to the God of Israel. Thus if Paul persecuted "the church of God," he surely was exposed to the innovation proclaimed by Jesus-group members. He surely gained some understanding of the theoretical and practical significance of this innovation for Israel. At some point, he formed an unfavorable attitude toward the Jesus-group innovation. To develop such an attitude, he presumably discussed the existence and activity of Jesus groups with others sharing his Pharisee orientation, and they judged the Jesus movement's proclamation unfavorably.

Interpersonal channels are usually at work in the persuasion process. The result was that Paul was persuaded to implement his assessment of Jesus groups by engaging in activities that supported his choice to reject the Jesus group's innovation (see Rogers 1995). He sought out Jesus-group members to force them to discontinue the innovation they had adopted. His "persecution" sought to force the discontinuance of the Jesus group's innovation, specifically by punishing Jesus-group members for their decision to discontinue previous Israelite practices and for putting their fellow Israelites at risk. Obviously Paul sought out and received reinforcement from his fellow Pharisees for the decision he had made.

Since Paul previously knew about the gospel of God from the people he persecuted, when he had his "call" in an altered state of consciousness experience, he did not need to get any new knowledge about this gospel. Rather this revelation of Jesus by God led him to discontinue his previous position and replace it with a new posture. What followed in his life was implementation, putting his decision about God's gospel into practice. After a period he began to seek out Israelites in non-Israelite cities. His goal was to disseminate the innovation of what the God of Israel had done to Jesus, raising him from the dead as Israel's Messiah and cosmic Lord, with a view to a forthcoming theocracy for Israel. He believed that his task to inform his fellow Israelites of this innovation was God-given, hence God-driven and directed to regions where Israelites were a minority, that is, among non-Israelite majorities (the *ethnē*).

We think all would agree that if Paul's letters attest to anything, they indicate his concern to spread what he called the gospel of God. This gospel, the Good News, was that the God of Israel would soon establish a theocracy for Israelites, "the kingdom of God." The trigger event behind this news was that the God of Israel had raised Jesus (of Nazareth, a geographical reference Paul does not use), an Israelite, from the dead. Jesus would be Israel's Messiah with power, ushering in the forthcoming theocracy. It is quite significant to note that Paul's proclamation was Israelite-specific in all of its dimensions: in its means of transmission (Paul received it through a revelation ascribed to the God of Israel who calls prophets), in its origin (the God of Israel), in its medium (a revelation of Israel's Messiah, the crucified and resurrected Jesus), in its content (an Israelite theocracy), and in its rationale (spelled out according to Israel's scriptures). Hence it is fairly obvious that this proclamation was meant specifically for Israelites. There are other indications of the exclusively Israelite nature of Paul's task. Consider the following features:

- Paul's use of Israel's scriptures follows Israelite usage. These scriptures would hardly be authoritative or probative for non-Israelites. Wherever non-Israelites appear in these scriptures, it is only as supporting cast to applaud the God of Israel, who lavishes such benefits on his own people. Non-Israelites are expected to give a grant of honor to Israelites. This of course is the role of non-Israelites throughout the Bible, in all the books of the Bible including the allegedly universalistic outlooks of Second Isaiah.
- Paul's references to God are references to the God of Israel and of Israel's ancestors, the God who sent his son to Israel for Israel. This is Israel's henotheistic God of the Israelite confession of faith (Deut 6:4; "the Lord *our* God is one"). What characterized Israel is that it was a people with a single God. If this God were a monotheistic, universal, and sole God, there would be nothing special about Israel. Such a God would be the God of all people, not of a single chosen people. The creed would be "the Lord God is one," not "the Lord *our* God is one."
- Paul describes his call to be "apostle" as a prophetic call. That is typical of Israel's prophets, who were called by the God of Israel to proclaim God's message to Israel alone.
- The God of Israel is in covenant with his people Israel, and not with any other people in the rest of the world. There is really no biblical indication that Israel's God has any concern for those not in covenant with him.
- The God of Israel raised Jesus of Nazareth from the dead for the benefit of his people Israel, specifically with a view to a forthcoming "kingdom of heaven/God," an Israelite theocracy, centered in Jerusalem in the land of Israel, with Jesus as Israel's Messiah..
- Paul's use of the "we" versus "they" language sets Israelites off from Everyone Else. For Paul the population of the world consisted of two peoples: Israel and Everyone Else, that is, the other peoples (NRSV: "Gentiles"). For all practical purposes Everyone Else form an undifferentiated mass, all equal, all the same, all non-Israelites. Israel, on the other hand, has differentiation and graded distinctions of clean and unclean, sacred and profane. This is typically ethnocentric.
- Paul was punished by Israelite communities, that is, synagogues (2 Cor 11:24: "Five times I have received at the hands of the Judeans the forty lashes less one"). These events point to the fact that he perceived himself as a member of these communities and interacted with them as an ingroup member. Israelite communities would not bother to single out any Israelite member unless he belonged to their communities and was judged to be doing damage to their communities.
- Paul's clients were Jesus-group Israelites. But there were other types of Jesus-group Israelites seeking clients of their own. These were the traveling "Judaizers" who sought to have Paul's clients adopt one of their Judean versions of the gospel of God. Their goal was not to convert Paul's clients

to some uniform, basic Judaism but to direct them away from Paul's gospel of God, adapted as it was to Israelites living among majority non-Israelite populations.

- The difference in theology between Israelites and non-Israelites is that Israel worshiped one and only one God in monarchy, while non-Israelites worshiped many gods in hierarchy. Greeks, that is, civilized people, had no difficulty in identifying the God of Israel with Zeus or Jupiter, thus identifying the God of Israel with the most high god of their own systems. Israelites, on the other hand, while denying the reality of other gods in the forms of statues, nonetheless believed in entities with all the features of lesser deities, whom they called "archangels" and "angels" (see Barker 1992; Davidson 1992; Gieschen 1998). In other words, apart from different labels, we have the same sort of entities functioning in the world in the first-century Eastern Mediterranean world no matter in which cultural context—Greek or Israelite or other. While fights about labels might be significant, in practice, as Paul says, "there are many lords and many gods" (1 Cor 8:5). This is henotheism.

Israelite adherence to this monarchical, exclusive tribal god breaks downs as Israelites have recourse to angels and archangels (whom non-Israelites would call lesser deities) for specialized purposes. Clement of Rome quotes a Jesus-group document called the *Preaching of Peter* (*Kērygmata Petrou,* dating to the turn of the first century C.E.), which describes Judean customs as follows: "for the Judeans (*Ioudaioi*) [who] think that they only know God, do not know Him, adoring as they do angels and archangels, the month and the moon" (*Stromata* 6.1; Sources Chrétiennes 446, p. 145). And when colonial Israelites encountered these lesser deities with Greek and Roman names, they likewise felt free to have recourse to them and to build altars to them much as they did at home for their angels and ancestors (see Kant 1987).

Israelites among Non-Israelites: Paul's Audience

Because of the nature of his "gospel of God," according to which the God of Israel revealed his intention of establishing a theocracy for Israel by raising Jesus from the dead in Jerusalem, Paul's obvious addressees were his fellow Israelites. The question here is, What were these first-century Israelites like, these Israelites resident among non-Israelite majorities?

Cohen notes that Israelites and Everyone Else "were corporeally, visually, linguistically, and socially indistinguishable" (Cohen 1999:37). There were no genealogical records that would have proven who was an Israelite and who was not. And if Israelites in the first-century Mediterranean world "looked like everyone else, spoke like everyone else, were named like everyone else, and supported themselves like everyone else," then how would one know an Israelite when one saw one? (Cohen 1999:53). Many modern readers of Paul confuse twenty-first-century Jewishness, based on the sixth-century C.E.

Talmud, with the Judean customs of antiquity. Many think that in antiquity, the main infallible and usable marker distinguishing an Israelite from a non-Israelite was circumcision. **Circumcision.** But as Cohen further notes, such was not the case at all. As a matter of fact, infant genital mutilation as a distinguishing Judean marker was rather late in Palestine (ca. 150 B.C.E.), and perhaps several centuries later, if at all, among Yahweh worshipers far from the region of Judea. About this time Judea proper was a small part of Palestine almost identifiable with the territory of the city of Jerusalem, as we learn from Polybius in the middle of the second century B.C.E. (16, fragment 39). Samaria and Galilee were outside it (Momigliano 1975:88). The point is that one cannot presume Israelite identity was evident because of circumcision. Many Yahweh worshipers were spread around the Mediterranean centuries before the Maccabean reforms of 150 B.C.E. that introduced circumcision as a distinguishing marker of Judean identity.

Further, cultural boundaries between Israelites and non-Israelites were often quite blurred, indicating far more diversity than generally imagined, as for instance indicated by Aune and Kant (the following data are taken from Aune 1997 passim and Kant 1987:617–713). In their enclaves in Greco-Roman cities, Israelites were frequently indistinguishable from their non-Israelite neighbors in their religious customs. They inscribed many of their funerary monuments with the polytheistic D M (*diis manibus*, i.e., to the divine shades or spirits) to Roman ancestral deities, at other times to the spirit gods, the Junonian spirits. Israelite slaves were sold to Apollo, and an Israelite sold his slaves to Apollo. Israelites signed oaths to Jupiter, Gaia (Earth), Helius (Sun), as well as to the Highest God (presumably the God of Israel). One Israelite from Boeotia, upon being manumitted, set up an altar to the Greek gods Amphiaraus and Hygeia, after being commanded to do so in a dream (Kant 1987). In Upper Egypt, Israelite inscriptions are found in a temple dedicated to the god Pan, while another speaks of Moira (divine fate), of crossing the underworld river Lethe, with Hades as the final destination of the dead. In typical Hellenistic fashion (also characteristic of non-Judeans), the inscriptions speak of tears, grief, laments, and the swiftness of death. In Italy Israelites believed graves were imbued with divine power and were subjects of propitiation; they even considered graves as sacrificial altars, a place for funerary meals (see Jer 16:7; Ps 106:28; Tob 4:17: "place your bread on the grave of the righteous, but give none to sinners"). Graves were shrines for the dead, a place to worship the dead, a habitation of the dead. Those who tampered with graves would have to answer to God or the gods, and they and their families would be cursed.

There is even evidence that Israelites took part in Greek athletics and were spectators at Greek athletic events. These events were intimately bound up with rituals directed to various deities. A menorah incised on the wall of the gymnasium at Priene, a Hellenistic city on the Maeander southeast of Ephesus and a few miles downstream from Tralles, intimates Israelite presence. The Alexandrian Israelite Philo was familiar with the intimate details of athletic events and must frequently have been a spectator himself (Philo, *Agr.* 11.1–17). This is not very surprising, since even in Palestine, where Paul presumably grew up, literary evidence suggests that many young Israelite men participated in Greek athletics in Jerusalem when it was under the control of Antiochus Epiphanes, 175–163 B.C.E. (2 Macc 4:7-20; *Ant.* 12.241; 19.335–337). Greek games, held in specially constructed amphitheaters, hippodromes, and stadiums, are attested in Caesarea Maritima (*War* 1.415; *Ant.* 15.341) and Jerusalem (*Ant.* 15.268–273). Athletic buildings are also attested for Tiberias (*War* 2.618–619; 3.539; *Life* 92) and Tarichaeae, both on the shore of the sea of Galilee (*War* 2.599; *Life* 132). Stadiums (which had to be two hundred yards long) were outfitted with seating that typically accommodated ten thousand spectators. Since the population of Sepphoris and Tiberias was predominantly Israelite, the spectators at such events must have been predominantly Israelite (Harris 1972).

Guilds in Greco-Roman cities were generally under the patronage of deities and local patrons. Israelites had guilds of purple dyers and carpet weavers (Hierapolis, Phrygia), goldsmiths (Corycus, Cilicia), and fishermen (Joppa, Palestine). They also worked as merchants and traders of spices, perfume, wine, linen, cloth, and silk. Others were bakers, boot makers, physicians, and bankers. Several of the nearly one hundred inscriptions (three in Hebrew, the rest in Greek) discovered in connection with the excavation of the Sardis synagogue reveal that eight synagogue members were also members of the municipal council, which routinely involved oaths and prayers to the local protective gods. Such provincial councilors (*decuriones*) were hereditary positions held by people of wealth. Other elite members of Sardis included Aurelius Basileides, a former procurator, and Paulus, a *comes* (i.e., a

The ancient harbor of Caesarea, built by Herod the Great in 22–10 B.C.E., was the Roman administrative center of Judea. Paul was judged here.

ISRAELITES, YES, POSSIBLY —
BUT JEWS?

"count"). Other wealthy donors were citizens of Sardis, like Hippasios the Second.

Israelites also served in the Roman Army: an Israelite commander and officer are mentioned in Egypt; a centurion in Palestine and soldiers in the Roman army are mentioned in Italy. There were even a Judean military unit and one Israelite service in the Roman navy. Of course, all these military persons had to take an oath to their officers and a vow to the Roman deities. Other Israelites who paid homage to local deities included the city councilmen of Sardis, Acmonia (Phrygia), Corcyrus (Cilicia), Cyrene, and El Hamman (Palestine). Even Philo calls the Israelite God "the Supreme father of the gods" (*Spec. Laws* 2.165). Israelite associations (collegia, synagogues) were often modeled on Greco-Roman patterns of club organizations (collegia), with a set of offices bearing Greco-Roman names. In sum, all this suggests that Israelites both in Palestine and in Israelite colonies were far more enmeshed in Hellenistic culture than had been previously thought possible.

Israelites among Other Ethnocentrics

Genealogy rooted in geography was a fundamental marker of group identification in antiquity. Paul's Israelite ethnocentrism—his concern exclusively for Israelites—is no different from the viewpoint revealed by Jesus in his commissioning the apostles in Matthew (10:5: "Go nowhere except to the lost sheep of the house of Israel"), a commissioning taken up again at the close of the Gospel (Matt 28:16: "make disciples of all nations," meaning, of course, "of Israelites living among all nations." By our standards, ancient ethnic divisions clearly underscore the unsurprising ethnocentrism of learned ancient Mediterranean writers. A fundamental cultural presupposition of the culture area was the ingroup/outgroup perspective. Ingroup feelings are rooted in the perception of similarity with others, specifically with one's gender, family, extended family, neighborhood, town or city section, and ethnic group (see Esler 1998:29–57). Ingroup members are treated with loyalty, openness, solidarity, and support. Those falling outside the ingroup boundaries are the outgroup. With the outgroup, almost "anything goes." Dealings with outgroup persons are indifferent, even hostile. For practical purposes they are, again, a different species of being. Ingroup and outgroup lines were not entirely fixed. To an outsider they seem constantly shifting.

By way of comparison with Paul's focus on Israel, consider what elite Romans thought (see Malina 1992). Plutarch, for example, advised:

> When differences arise against brothers, we must be careful especially at such times to associate familiarly (*plēsiazein*) with our brothers' friends, but avoid and shun all intimacy with their enemies, imitating at this point, at least, the practice of Cretans, who, though they often quarreled with and warred against each other, made up their differences and united when outside enemies attacked; and this it was which they called "syncretism" (*sygkretismos*). (*On Brotherly Love* 19.490B LCL)

Being of similar genealogical and geographical origin meant to harbor ingroup feelings, especially when away from that place of origin and even when long departed from it, for it was the place of origin that endowed group members with particular characteristics. Pliny, for example, considered Europe the significant part of the world and Italy as the center of Europe. Rome, of course, was the center of Italy:

> To begin then with Europe, nurse of the race that has conquered all the nations, and by far the loveliest portion of the earth, which most authorities not without reason have reckoned to be not a third part, but a half of the world, dividing the whole circle into two portions by a line drawn from the river Don (Tanaus) to the Straits of Gibraltar (Gadatinum). (Pliny, *Natural History* 3.1.5)

And further on:

> I am well aware that I may with justice be considered ungrateful and lazy if I describe in this casual and cursory manner a land (Italia) which is at once the nursling and the mother of all other lands, chosen by the providence of the gods to make heaven itself more glorious, to unite scattered empires, to make manners gentle, to draw together in converse by community of language the jarring and uncouth tongues of so many nations, to give mankind civilization, and in a word to become throughout the world the single fatherland of all the races. But what am I to do? The great fame of all its places—who could touch upon them all? And the great renown of the various things and peoples in it give me pause. . . . The Greeks, themselves a people most prone to gushing self-praise, have pronounced sentence on the land by conferring on but a very small part of it the name of Great Greece! (Pliny, *Natural History* 3.5.39–42)

For Pliny, "The one race (*gens*) of outstanding eminence in virtue among all the races in the whole world is undoubtedly the Roman" (*Natural History* 7.40.130 LCL). This was not difficult to prove, in his view. "There is a countless series of Roman examples (of men of intellectual excellence), if one chose to pursue them, since a single race (*gens*) has produced more men of distinction in every branch whatever than the whole of the other lands (*terrae*)" (*Natural History* 7.30.116).

Two generations earlier, Cicero too noted that Rome's preeminence was due basically to the moral virtue of its inhabitants: "However good be our conceit of ourselves, conscript fathers, we have excelled neither Spain in population, nor Gaul in force (*robor*), nor Carthage in cleverness (*calliditas*), nor Greece in technology (*ars*), nor indeed Italy and Latium itself in the innate sensibility (*sensus*) characteristic of this land and its peoples; but in piety, in devotion to religion (*pietas et religio*), and in that special wisdom which consists in the recognition of the truth that the world is swayed and directed by the disposal of the gods, we have excelled every race and every nation" (Cicero, *De haruspicum responsis* 9.19 LCL).

This inscription is a copy of a plaque (called a tabula ansata*) that was part of a mosaic floor in an assembly hall (see photo on page 22). It reads, "Porphyrius, bishop, made the mosaic of the basilica of Paul in Christ," thus honoring Paul, who was the founder of the church in Philippi.*

Romans, like the other empire builders of antiquity, considered their empire as the only "state" in the world: there simply was no civilized, humanized world apart from Rome. Thus people did not come under Roman rule or Roman oppression. Rather to be "Romanized" was to be civilized, that is, to become "Greek," immersed in worldwide values and behaviors. The normative set of civilizing qualities derived from Hellenic civilization. As Veyne has observed,

> the words "Roman," "Latin," or "Pilgrim" indicate a status, not an ethnic origin: and no difference was made among Roman citizens of Italic origin and those of provincial origin. Ethnic differences counted so little for Romans that at the end of antiquity, they felt no repugnance in recruiting their soldiers and generals from among the Germani. . . . Republican Rome, that people who had had as its culture that of another people, the Greeks, did not feel this culture as strange, but simply as civilization. Likewise, in the Empire and outside its frontiers, Greco-Roman civilization was civilization itself; one did not Romanize or Hellenize, one civilized. (Veyne 1989:410–11)

In sum, as we shall see from Paul's usage, "Judean" and "Greek" indicated a status. To designate genealogy, the words "Israelites" and "(other) peoples" were used ("Jew and Gentile" was not an acceptable linguistic collocation).

What characterized the various Israelite groups and their Judaisms was a common "genealogical" story of mythical origin rooted in Abraham. Some of Paul's Israelite clients would know Israel's scriptures, but for Paul's audience these would be in Greek. When it came to Judaism, that is, the customs of Judea practiced by Israelites, there was little unity or commonality around the Mediterranean. In a world based on gossip and networking, such unity would simply be impossible. In his approach to Israelite residents among non-Israelites, Paul presumed, it seems, that his audience held Israel's story as sacred along with Israel's ancient sacred writings and that his essential task was to proclaim how the God of Israel was revealed in the resurrection of Jesus, thus appointing Jesus Israel's Messiah with a forthcoming Israelite theocracy. This presumption makes it quite clear that Paul's message was meant exclusively for Israelites. And because of the range of Israelites in the first century, the perception both of the message and of approaches to the message would follow the patterns of the recipients of this innovation spread by Paul, a change agent in Israel.

Paul the Apostle as Change Agent

Paul insists that he was an apostle. "Apostle" is a transliterated Greek word (*apostolos*). The Greek word refers to someone commissioned by someone else for some mission. Apostles can be sent for various reasons. Some philosophers thought themselves apostles of Zeus to make people aware of how to live. Paul believed he was an apostle of God because he was commissioned to proclaim the "gospel of God." Commissioning by one with authority is sufficient to constitute a person an apostle. But Paul was not simply authorized to make a proclamation on God's behalf but to proclaim something new, hitherto unheard of. People commissioned to make known something new are called change agents today. The task of a change agent is to communicate and diffuse some innovation. And this is precisely what Paul was about. The emphasis on the new aspect is what sets Paul apart from other apostles or commissioned messengers who communicate information from some authorizing agency about some ongoing agenda (tax rates, king's family, etc.). Such messengers really have nothing significantly new to communicate.

If the "gospel of God" proclaimed by Paul had any distinctive quality, it was the fact that it was something new, something unheard of, perhaps even something inconceivable. We believe all would agree that Paul was communicating an innovation to his fellow Israelites. Paul's letters are evidence of his attempts to diffuse the innovation revealed to him. Since the 1970s much research on the communication of innovation has been accomplished. To understand what the diffusion of an innovation entails, we shall employ such models from the social sciences that have been cross-culturally verified with a range of data drawn from all over the world. The diffusion of an innovation follows a rather fixed social pattern of interaction (the models come from Everett Rogers [1971, 1995]; see his bibliography for comparative data).

Paul was a Jesus-group change agent of a distinctive sort. As a rule, a change agent is an authorized person who influences innovation decisions in a direction deemed desirable by a change agency (the one who proposes the change, in this case the God of Israel). The change agent thus functions as a communication link between two or more social systems, that of the receivers of the communication (the clients) and that of the change agency (the ones sending). In the New Testament story, authorized change agents include the Twelve sent by Jesus during his career (Matthew 10); those sent by a Jesus-group agency, such as the Twelve in Jerusalem (Acts); and Israelite scribes sent by some Pharisee group (mentioned in Matt 22:16).

Paul was not sent by any such group. Rather, he insists that his authorization and commission came from the God of Israel through an altered state of consciousness experience. In this he was just like Jesus and John the Baptist, both of whom were authorized to proclaim God's Good News through altered states of consciousness experiences. **Altered States of Consciousness**. Since these change agents were not sponsored or authorized by any observable change agency, they had to face questions of authorization or authority by those who inquired about or rejected the innovation (see Matthew 11 relative to Jesus [vv. 2-6] and John [vv. 7-15]). Paul, like Jesus and John the Baptist, was a change agent, "unauthorized" (by human authorities); all three communicated information about an innovation and influenced innovation decisions in a direction deemed desirable in terms of his experience of God. The God of Israel was the change agency behind the symbol system that all three constructed on the basis of their experience of God. The urgency that Paul, like John and Jesus before him, intimates in his activities derives from the charge he had received from the change agency, the God of Israel.

This feature underscores the conviction of early Jesus-group members that the "founder" of the task and gatherings inaugurated by Jesus, as well as of the post-resurrection Jesus groups, was none other than the God of Israel. The innovation that Jesus proclaimed was a forthcoming Israelite theocracy or the kingdom of heaven/God. The innovation Paul proclaimed was that the God of Israel raised Jesus from the dead, thus revealing Jesus to be Israel's Messiah (Christ) and cosmic Lord, with a view to the forthcoming Israelite theocracy (1 Thessalonians and frequently). According to these New Testament witnesses, then, the founder or change agency of Jesus groups and their ideology is God, the God of Israel. God's directly authorized change agents were individuals, such as John the Baptist, Jesus, and Paul. All functioned for the same change agency, the God of Israel. To shift the thrust from the agency (God) to the agent (for example, Jesus or Paul) is to miss the thrust of early Jesus groups that emerge eventually as "Christianity." **Change Agent**.

Paul's Political Message for His Israelite Clients

As a change agent authorized by the God of Israel, Paul approached Israelite groups in majority non-Israelite cities throughout the northeastern Mediterranean. These Israelite groups were to be found largely in Israelite enclaves in Greco-Roman cities. We find valuable information about these groups and their locations offered by the author of the Acts of the Apostles. In this commentary we will use the book of Acts as a source for early Jesus-group memories. It would be anachronistic to expect them to be direct historical remembrances. Like other historical writings of the period, Acts surely offers compressed, telescoped, simplified, stripped-down stories of remembrances of the story of Paul. We do not believe the accounts of Acts are fictional, however, since the categories of fact and fiction are nineteenth-century etic inventions. Appropriately, in Luke's emic terms, he was interested in presenting the truth, as opposed to lies, a more appropriate first-century contrast (Luke 1:1-4). Perhaps what the author of Acts describes may not have happened in the way he says, but his way was exactly the way a first-century Mediterranean would describe what truly happened.

The Israelite innovation communicated by Paul to Israelite groups located in non-Israelite majority cities of the Eastern Mediterranean was a piece of radically

This Christian church of Philippi can be dated from approximately 313–350 C.E. *on the basis of the floor's foundational mosaic inscription (see photo on page 19). It is the earliest known public gathering place for Christians in Greece and Macedonia that can be dated with some certainty.*

new political-religious news of relevance to Israelites. The God of Israel was on the verge of instituting an Israelite theocracy. The harbinger of this event was the act by which this God raised a person named Jesus from the dead, thus constituting him Lord and Messiah—all with a view to the forthcoming theocracy.

First-century Mediterraneans were collectivistic persons. **Collectivistic Personality.** Group integrity was far more important than individual self-reliance. When collectivistic persons and their communities adopt an innovation, research indicates that adopting the innovation (the decision to accept an innovation) is far less significant than actually putting the innovation to use, that is, implementation. On this basis, we may suppose that upon hearing Paul's proclamation, a number of fellow Israelites (called "innovators and first adopters" here) would decide rather quickly that because of the events occurring in Jerusalem, Paul made sense and that God's "kingdom of heaven" was something soon to occur in Jerusalem and Judea. **Coworkers: Innovators and First Adopters.** What was required now was for those who accepted Paul's message to behave in a way that would conform to the implications of the proclamation, specifically by forming a support group (a local "church") and expressing their trust in the God of Israel by proper behavior toward one another and toward God. Thus a new moral posture and worship form indicated implementation, putting the innovation to use.

As a change agent focused upon Israelites living among non-Israelites, Paul proclaimed his gospel that the God of Israel was about to bring redemption or restoration of honor to Israel. The message was a solution to an Israelite problem. The problem was Israel's situation both in Judea as well as outside Judea. Paul was one of those who believed God's raising Jesus signaled Israel's forthcoming redemption. Hence the people Paul approached were an Israelite minority living in Hellenistic societies, and his message to his fellow Israelites was that God's redemption of Israel had dawned by means of Israel's Messiah raised by God. The Israelites who found this message a solution to their problem would fit this information into their traditional ancestral kinship religion. Paul (and others in Jesus groups) helped them make sense of how this experience or this event could fit into their ancestral kinship religion and its expanded political religion. Their ancestors (in Paul's estimation) included Abraham, Isaac, Jacob, Moses, and the Covenant and Torah.

Was Paul Winning Converts?

It may be useful at this point to make a distinction between conversion, that is, transfer from one group to another, already existing group, and innovation adoption. Paul was not converting Israelites in Thessalonika or Corinth to another group competing with Israel. Rather he announced a new stage in Israel's corporate history, a new development in Israel launched by the God of Israel. He was communicating an innovation. The adoption of an innovation by an existing group is not exactly what people mean by conversion. The problem with conversion studies applied to the New Testament, apart from the fact that they are anachronistically psychological (see Pilch 1997), is that they presume conversion similar to the modern experience associated with that label. In this anachronistic perspective, when Paul came to town, he was urging Israelites to join the local Jesus group, hence to change from one group to another, from Israelite groups to Jesus groups. This model is misplaced. There were no Jesus groups when Paul went to proclaim the innovation the God of Israel had wrought in Israel. Social conversion is a choice between this group or that one, either/or. In contrast, the innovation Paul presented was a choice to adopt or not to adopt a change within the same group, a yes or no, not a choice of this group or that group, since there was no other group to choose.

Among the authentic letters, Paul's missive to the Romans does not fit into this model of Paul's change-agent activity. The reason for this is that the letter to the Romans is really about travel arrangements. Paul writes to a Jesus group or collection of groups that he himself did not found. In this letter, in the process of requesting hospitality, Paul wishes to show Jesus-group members in Rome (none of whom seem to be Romans but rather Israelites living there) that he has lots in common with them. If there is anything they heard about him that was negative in their estimation, it really was either not true or not what he said or not what he meant. So he makes travel arrangements and intends to rectify the distorted gossip they may have heard about him.

Conclusion

Paul's letters lack any direct information about the initiation stage of his groups' innovation adoption, just as they lack direct information about the forming stage of his groups' establishment. **Small-Group Development**. We must presume, on the basis of the existence of those Jesus groups to which Paul wrote, that there was an initiation stage, a period of forming. Yet in Paul's letters there are all too brief hints of those early stages. For example, Paul states that his initial presence among the Corinthian Israelites was not marked by rhetorical niceties (we might say "advertising gimmicks") "in plausible words of wisdom, but in demonstration of the Spirit and power." Yet demonstrations of the Spirit and power are already part and parcel of group experience when Paul writes at the later phases of group formation, the phases of mutual accommodation and assimilation (1 Corinthians 12; Romans 14). **Small-Group Development**.

What the models we adopt underscore is that it was not Paul's theology that was of interest both to Paul and to his fellow Jesus-group Israelites, but rather the exchange relationship that his letters were meant to maintain with a view to group stability. To focus on Paul's "theology" rather than on the social interrelationship between the change agent and his clients is to miss the thrust of his letters.

In summary, we offer the following chart comparing the prevailing modes of interpreting Paul's letters and the viewpoints adopted here:

Received View	**Social-Science View**
Paul is the apostle to the Gentiles.	Paul is the apostle to Israelites living among non-Israelite peoples outside Judea.
Paul is an apostle with a ministry.	Paul is a change agent with an innovation to communicate to Israel.
Paul is the source of theology.	Paul is focused on interpersonal relations in Jesus-group formation.
Paul is the second founder of Christianity, after Jesus.	God is the founder of Christianity.
Paul is apostle to heterophilous groups, that is, non-Israelite Gentiles.	Paul is a change agent to homophilous groups, that is, Israelites living among non-Israelite peoples.
Paul's doctrine is eschatological, sometimes apocalyptic.	Paul's doctrine is political religion, proclaimed theocracy, for fictive kin groups.
Paul writes to religious groups.	Paul writes to fictive kin groups with a domestic religion, awaiting the kingdom of God (political religion in abeyance).
Paul is directly and immediately relevant to twenty-first-century churches.	Paul was directly and immediately relevant to first-century Jesus groups.
Paul is a monotheist.	Paul is a henotheist.
Paul is a universalist.	Paul is an ethnocentric particularist.

1 Thessalonians

I. 1 Thess 1:1
Letter Opening (Superscription)

II. 1 Thess 1:2—3:13
About the Relationship between the Change Agents and the Jesus Group They Formed

Section One: 1 Thess 1:2–2:16
Events Since the Formation of the Jesus Group at Thessalonika

1:2-3	Introduction
1:4-5	The Wondrous Quality of the Innovation-Communication Event at Thessalonika
1:6-10	The Marvelous Reception of the Innovation Communicated at Thessalonika
2:1-12	The Attitude of Paul and His Associates
2:13-16	The Attitude of First Adopters of the Innovation

Section Two: 1 Thess 2:17–3:13
After the Forming of the Jesus Group at Thessalonika

2:17-20	Paul's Desire to Visit the Group Once More
3:1-10	The Outcomes of Timothy's Visit
3:11-13	Conclusion: Best Wishes for Divine Favors

III. 1 Thess 4:1—5:24
Directives and Exhortations

Section One: 1 Thess 4:1-12
Conduct Pleasing to God

4:1-2	Introduction: A Solemn Appeal to Distinctive Conduct
4:3-8	About "Holiness"
4:9-12	About Proper Ingroup Behavior

Section Two: 1 Thess 4:13–5:11
Solutions to Problems about What Is Next

4:13-18	Concerning Group Members Who Have Died
5:1-11	Concerning the Time of God's Forthcoming Intervention

Section Three: 1 Thess 5:12-24
About Group Support

5:12-13	Respect Local Opinion Leaders
5:14-22	Group-Bolstering Advice
5:23-24	Invocation

IV. 1 Thess 5:25-28
Letter Closing: Salutation and Blessing

Why This Letter?

Paul was an "apostle," a change agent who communicated information about an innovation, information about what the God of Israel had recently done in raising Jesus from the dead and its implications for Israelites. **Change Agent**. He took up this change-agent task because, he says, he was commissioned by the God of Israel, the change agency. After making known the innovation and winning some clients in the Israelite community of Thessalonika, Paul's main task was to develop an information exchange relation with those clients. The purpose of this information exchange was to enable Paul to diagnose problems rising from the adoption of the innovation, to maintain the clients' intent to change, and to translate that intent into action. Finally, Paul sought to stabilize the client group and prevent discontinuance of the change if possible.

The letter to the Thessalonians is the first of the writings of Paul that have come down to us. The document evidences Paul's concern about his Thessalonian clients. Of course, every time Paul proclaims the gospel of God and some in the Israelite community accept and adopt this gospel, the new Jesus-group members inevitably aggrieve the local Israelite community and experience social pressure not to destabilize the status quo. The result for the innovation adopters (new Jesus-group members) is conflict, pressure to reject the innovation, and anxiety about whether accepting the proclamation was such a good idea. Paul's concern to inaugurate information exchange is evident in his sending Timothy, a fellow change agent, to find out what has happened in Thessalonika and to report back to him. It was after Timothy returned with a positive report that Paul wrote this letter, continuing the information exchange relation.

Presuppositions

To utilize the commentary that follows, it is important that one read the introduction to this volume. The authors work with a number of presuppositions, as specified in that introduction.

The first concerns Paul's self-identification as "the apostle to the Gentiles." Since his presentations and arguments make sense only to an Israelite audience, the phrase must be taken geographically: Paul traveled to proclaim his gospel of God exclusively to Israelites resident among majority non-Israelite populations in Greco-Roman cities.

Second, Paul's Jesus groups were formed of Israelites whose deity was the God of Israel. There is no evidence that Paul addressed non-Israelites in any of his letters directed to Jesus groups that he founded. Paul shows no interest in non-Israelites at all. The exception seems to be the letter to the Romans, but that letter is directed to Jesus groups in Rome that Paul did not found (hence the small segment about non-Israelites in Romans 11).

Third, it is an error in method to form images or scenarios of Israelite life and customs of Paul's day based on twenty-first-century Jewishness. Today's Jewish religion traces back structurally and ideologically to behaviors inculcated by rabbinism and the Talmud, an extensive compilation of opinions about the Torah. The Jewish religion known to most readers of this commentary has little, if any, connection with the Temple-based political religion of the Israel of Paul's day. Thus it would be simply erroneous to consider Paul either a Christian or a Jew in any modern sense of those labels.

This is a view of modern Thessalonika from the southwest, approaching the city from the sea. Thessalonika is in central Macedonia, today the northernmost part of the Greek Republic.

In Brief, What Does the Letter Say?

Upon Timothy's return from Thessalonika to Corinth with a favorable report of the situation there, Paul writes first of all recalling the past, underscoring the relationship between the change agents and the Jesus groups they formed. The letter is usually dated to about 51 C.E. He recalls events surrounding the formation of the Jesus group there: the wondrous quality of the innovation-communication event, the marvelous reception at the time, the attitudes of Paul and his associates as well as of the first adopters of the innovation. After the group had been formed, Paul desired to visit again but could not. So Timothy came instead and brought excellent news.

In a second section Paul begins with some exhortations about holiness and ingroup behavior. Then he deals with questions about Jesus-group members who have died and about the time of God's forthcoming intervention. Finally he exhorts the group about respecting their local opinion leaders and supporting one another. A significant feature of this letter is Paul's emphasis on the interpersonal dimensions of this communication. His use of emphatic pronouns (in Greek) fills the letter with a certain interpersonal closeness matched only by his letter to the Philippians.

I. 1 Thess 1:1
Letter Opening (Superscription)

1:1 Paul, Silvanus, and Timothy,
To the church of the Thessalonians in
God the Father and the Lord Jesus Christ:
Grace to you and peace.

Textual Notes: 1 Thess 1:1

Hellenistic letters opened with a formula consisting of the name of the sender(s), then the addressee(s) and a greeting. These three elements are called a superscription (or prescript). The next element, connecting the superscription with the body of the letter, is called a thanksgiving. The thanksgiving consists of a statement of gratitude to God for something done in the past, plus wishes for the proximate future. **Hellenistic Letter.**

1:1: The senders of this letter are Paul, Silvanus, and Timothy, although Jesus-group tradition ascribed the letter to Paul alone. Timothy was coauthor of four of Paul's letters (1 Thessalonians, 2 Corinthians, Philippians, and Philemon). As we learn from Paul's other letters and the third-generation recollections of the book of Acts, Paul, Silvanus, and Timothy were Jesus-group change agents. **Change Agent.** After initial group formation, change agents who move on have to set up an information exchange relation to be assured of the ongoing development of the group in the direction desired by the change agency. This letter, like all of Paul's letters, is an instance of the expected information exchange relationship. Paul has obviously had no information from the Thessalonians for some time—hence his satisfaction when Timothy returns with some news (3:1-5). This letter is a response to Timothy's report, thus continuing the required information exchange relation.

The senders' names here are Greek, although in Acts we find that Paul and Silvanus had Semitic names too. Paul was also called "Saul" and Silvanus "Silas." Timothy had a Hellenistic father (Acts 16:1), hence his Greek name. Why do Paul and Silas use Greek names if they had Semitic ones as well? Greek names point to civilized persons. It is important that modern readers of Paul's writings realize that the term "Greek" is not a national or ethnic designation. In the first century C.E. there was no "Greece" in our territorial and nationalistic sense of the word. To be a "Greek" basically meant to be Hellenized, a synonym for civilized. The opposite of Greek was barbarian, uncivilized. Along with a number of values, the common Greek language of the period was the language used by civilized people in the Mediterranean in the first century C.E. **Greeks and Israelites.**

1:1: "Church" translates the Greek *ekklēsia*, a much-used term found here for the first time in Jesus-group writings. ***Ekklēsia* (Gathering).** It is a word taken from the civilized Greek vocabulary to refer to a gathering of the entitled residents of a "polis," the Greek term for "city." **City.** Hence it refers to a gathering of citizens of a city (the word "citizen" referred solely to "cities"; there was no national citizenship before the nineteenth century) with the privilege of deciding matters of significance to the city and with the obligation to support what was of significance to the city. Moreover, *ekklēsia* was used in the Greek (hence civilized) version of Israel's sacred scriptures, called "the Septuagint," where it referred to those summoned or called by God in the wilderness to serve God in the folkloric story of the Exodus and God's constituting the people of Israel. Significantly, Paul now sees the gathering of Jesus-group members as God's new summoned people, the *ekklēsia* of God. In this way, the term serves as a label providing group members with social identity, identifying them with Israel of old, and distinguishing them from their proximate, conflicting outgroup, the *synagogē,* a general Greek term also meaning "gathering," used by Israelites for their meetings. **Social Identity.**

Since the word "church" today refers to institutional Christianity, Christian groups, and the buildings in which Christians meet, the use of the word in modern translations of the New Testament is rather anachronistic and confusing. We shall use the word "gathering," that is, "the gathering of those called by God," when referring to the Pauline *ekklēsia.*

1:1: "In God the Father." It is important to notice in this letter how Paul's perspectives are essentially theologically motivated. "Theologically" means God-motivated, with God as the main actor in Jesus-group formation, support, and activity, as well as the main focus and source of Jesus' activity. It is equally important to note that when Paul uses the word "God," he invariably means the God of Israel. After all, he lives in a world where "there are many gods and many lords—yet for us there is one God, the Father, from whom are all things and for whom we exist, and one Lord, Jesus Christ, through whom are all things and through whom we exist" (1 Cor 8:5-6). Paul calls the God of Israel "father," a word deriving from the kinship institution and often used in the kin-like relationship of social superior to inferior called patronage. For Paul, the God of Israel is most often described as "Father" or patron of the gathering summoned by God. **Patronage System.**

The role of "the Lord Jesus Christ" is that of an intermediary, of a broker, or go-between, between God and Paul's churches. Jesus' titles here are a mixture of Greek and Judean, that is, civilized and barbarian. The title "Lord" refers to Jesus as endowed with power, while "Christ" refers to Jesus as Israel's Messiah.

"Lord" (Greek: *kyrios*; Latin: *dominus*; Semitic: *'adon* or *baal*) is a Hellenistic word referring to a person having the most complete power over persons and things. The lord is the absolute owner of all persons and things in his domain. He is a person who has the power to dispose of persons and things as he likes and who holds this power by a title recognized as valid (by either ad hoc force, custom, or law). This power is lordship (Greek: *kyriotēs*, Latin: *dominium*). The lord was entitled to use any thing or person who was his, to enjoy all their products or properties, and to consume entirely whatever was capable of consumption. Because of

This theater, located in the lower part of the city of Ephesos, was used as the site of dramatic competitions under the divine patronage of Dionysos, a meeting place of the Ephesos city council, and an assembly place for the ekklēsia *of the city.*

the perception that Jesus was with the God of Israel in the sky, to call Jesus "lord" meant that he wielded supreme cosmic dominion, after God. Significantly, in this letter, the title "lord" is the main title for Jesus, used twenty-four times (1:3, 6, 8; 2:15, 19; 3:11, 12, 13; 4:3, 15, 16, 17; 5:9, 23, 27, 28; without article: 1:1; 4:6, 15, 17; 5:2; and in the phrase "in the Lord," 3:8; 4:1; 5:12).

Paul's gospel is ultimately about a forthcoming Israelite theocracy (kingdom of God, 2:21); thus it is noteworthy that the reigning emperor, Claudius, likewise bore the title "lord." The underlying clash of political-religious ideologies is not far below the surface of social interactions. **Kingdom of God.** Talk of a forthcoming

Israelite theocracy with the resurrected Jesus as living lord could only be interpreted by outsiders as a political challenge to Roman power.

"Messiah" (Greek: *christos*; Semitic: *mashiach*) is an Israelite word referring to a person chosen by the God of Israel to be his vice-regent on behalf of the people Israel. This person may be an Israelite or a non-Israelite (e.g., the Persian king, Cyrus, is called Messiah in Isa 45:1) chosen by the God of Israel to act on God's behalf for the people Israel. Literally, the term means "anointed," because traditionally Israel's significant elite office holders (priest, king, official prophet) took office by having oil poured on their heads. They were thus "oiled in" just as U.S. officials are "sworn in" by oath with hand on the Bible. The process of infusing oil symbolized the pouring in/on of power. It is a very small step to see how a person upon whom God's Wind or Spirit was poured was likewise "anointed" (as in Luke 4:18, following Isa 61:1). Recall that in first-century assessments, oil, water, fire, and wind were all liquids; people could be "anointed" with them as they could be dipped—that is, baptized—in them (see Matt 3:11; Luke 3:16).

Some hold that the gathering of Jesus-group members in Thessalonika (and elsewhere) probably took place in an *insula* or tenement building, since these first Thessalonian group members were low-status nonelites (see Jewett 1993). However, innovators and first adopters of innovations are rarely low-status persons. They presumably were of the same social level as their fellow Israelites. Of these nonelite Israelites in that city, the first adopters of Paul's gospel had to be of the higher social levels. See details in **Notes** on 1 Thess 2:13-16; this conclusion is based on the generalizations provided by Rogers (1971, 1995).

II. 1 Thess 1:2—3:13
About the Relationship between the Change Agents and the Jesus Group They Formed

After constituting the Thessalonian Jesus gathering on the basis of their acceptance of his gospel of God, Paul saw as his first task setting up an information exchange relation with this group. The sending of Timothy and this letter are instances of that information exchange relation. The process of exchanging information with the Thessalonians allows Paul the opportunity to diagnose the problems mentioned in the letter as well as to create in Jesus-group members a deeper commitment to the gospel of God to be made evident in their behavior. What Paul seeks is stability in the gathering marked by adherence to the ingroup boundaries that define the Jesus group, revealed in the norms he suggests. These norms are the demands on group members that indicate how those who belong to the group must live their lives. **Pauline Norms.**

Section One: 1 Thess 1:2—2:16
Events Since the Forming of the Jesus Group at Thessalonika

Introduction 1:2-3

1:2 We always give thanks to God for all of you and mention you in our prayers, constantly
3 remembering before our God and Father your work of faith and labor of love and steadfastness of hope in our Lord Jesus Christ.

Textual Notes: 1 Thess 1:2-3

The next section expected in a Hellenistic letter is called a thanksgiving. In the Middle East "thanks" intends to terminate a relationship; the Greek is better rendered "we acknowledge our indebtedness to God" for all of you (Pilch 2002c). This pattern of thanksgiving consists of two parts, the first of which deals with the past and the second with good wishes for the proximate future. First Thessalonians has an extensive "thanksgiving," running from 1:2—3:13, with focus on the past in 1:2—3:10 and the usual best wishes for the proximate future coming at 3:11-13. **Hellenistic Letter.**

In their analysis of linguistic communications, sociolinguists note that speakers express three features simultaneously in every utterance: they talk about something (the ideational feature) to someone (the interpersonal feature) using language (the modal function). Significantly, right from the outset, this letter is totally permeated with an interpersonal emphasis. What is foregrounded is not so much what Paul has to talk about as his attitude toward the persons to whom he talks. This feature points to Paul's style in establishing an information exchange relationship. Consider the constant presence of the pronouns "we, our" and "you, your [plural]" as these move in counterpoint almost from sentence to sentence. Interpersonal emphasis in language points to an insistence on mutual commitment and solidarity rather than any concern with power (authority) or influence (teaching). The teaching that Paul does provide in this letter is about practical attachment to fellow members of the Thessalonian Jesus group (4:9-12), about those who have died (4:13-18), and about the coming of Jesus (5:1-11). And the teaching is fully imbued with this interpersonal accent.

Faith, love, and hope are a trio of attitudes mentioned elsewhere by Paul (1 Thess 5:8; 1 Cor 13:13; Gal 5:5-6; and in the rest of the New Testament, see Eph 4:2-5; Col 1:4-5; Heb 6:10-12; 10:22-24; 1 Pet 1:3-8). Faith refers to the social value of one's trust in another person's reliability, the person one has faith in. The value is ascribed to persons as well as to objects and qualities. Relative to persons, faith is one's belief in another's reliability in interpersonal relations; it thus takes on the value of enduring personal trust in another's personal faithfulness. The nouns "faith," "belief," "fidelity," and "faithfulness" as well as the verbs "to have faith" and "to believe" refer to the social glue of trust that binds one person to another, trusted person. "Works of faith" refers to this bond when revealed in externally, emotionally rooted behavior of the trusting partner in this interpersonal relationship of commitment and solidarity. "Works of faith" are behaviors based on one's trust in another's reliability. As social bond, they function along with the two other values mentioned here. "Love" means personal attachment to one's group (family, association) and to God, revealed in one's actions. And "hope" means personal allegiance or abiding confidence in another. Here the trio would refer to enduring, personal, trusting loyalty to God, group attachment revealed in behavior to group members, and allegiance and abiding confidence in the Lord Jesus, who is soon to establish a theocracy. (For more on faith, hope, and love, see Pilch and Malina 1998.) It would seem that for Paul, these three features are the hallmark of the social identity of the Jesus-group membership. As Esler notes (2001:1202b), if asked who they were, Thessalonian Jesus-group members could have given the distinctive answer: "People characterized by faith (in the God who raised Jesus), love and hope." These form the groundwork norms marking off Jesus-group social identity.

The Wondrous Quality of the Innovation-Communication Event at Thessalonika 1:4-5

1:4 For we know, brothers and sisters beloved by God, that he has chosen you, 5 because our message of the gospel came to you not in word only, but also in power and in the Holy Spirit and with full conviction; just as you know what kind of persons we proved to be among you for your sake.

Textual Notes: 1 Thess 1:4-5

1:4: In antiquity, domestic religion was the order of the day. Households offered prayer and sacrifice to the deities who supported family members and saw to their well-being. Given that Paul addresses his audience as "brothers" (NRSV: and sisters), his Jesus groups were a type of domestic or household religion redefined and expanded to include non-family members. It was a sort of fictive household religion of brothers and sisters in Christ. The *polis* public religion was a sort of household religion outfitted for and expanded into the political realm, a political religion of and for the citizenry. Just as domestic religion entailed the embedding of religion in the kinship institution, so too, political religion involved religion embedded in the political institution of the *polis*, the first-century "city." **Political Religion.** The "kingdom of God" proclaimed by Paul (and Jesus before him) refers to a theocracy, a political system focused on a religious ideology that is embedded in a political system. The rules, roles, behaviors, and attitudes of the first-century Mediterranean Israelite monarchy provided the rules, roles, behaviors, and attitudes of the forthcoming rule of God in Israel. Terms such as "kingdom," "lord," "rule," "parousia," and the like are all political terms.

Since Paul's Jesus groups are located outside of Palestine, where the theocracy was to emerge, they in fact are a fictive domestic expression rooted in hope for the political religion of the forthcoming Israelite theocracy. As domestic religion (to disappear with the advent of the theocracy; see 1 Cor 15:23-25) Jesus-group rules, roles, behaviors, and attitudes derive from first-century Mediterranean kinship structures. Jesus-group members were like siblings, hence fictive kin. Paul addresses them here (and seventeen times more) as brothers (NRSV adds: and sisters) to whom God is notably attached; this is what "beloved" means.

1:5: Paul knows that God has chosen those in the Thessalonian church because they in fact have adopted the innovation he proclaimed and experienced the results of that adoption. The experience is attributed to God's Spirit or Wind, the Holy Spirit. "Holy Spirit" refers to God's power and activity, God's experienced presence in human life. Paul's communication of the good news about how the God of Israel raised Jesus from the dead normally resulted in manifestation of God's power in altered states of consciousness experiences, usually called "charismata," as in 1 Corinthians 12. The mutual interaction of change agents and clients has resulted in mutual solidarity. **Altered States of Consciousness.** Paul's knowledge of their being chosen is a sort of "after the fact" predestination. It was common Israelite belief that because something has happened, it was supposed to happen. Paul knows that the God of Israel has chosen his addressees, Thessalonian Jesus-group members, because they in fact belong to the Jesus group and have experienced the Holy Spirit.

Group members sharing a belief in being chosen greatly facilitates the development of a distinctive group identity, marking off the group from other, non-chosen groups. Group identity depends upon cognitive, emotive, and evaluative features: knowledge of being distinct ("you have been chosen and accepted the word"), undergoing distinctive emotive experiences (of "power and the Holy Spirit"), and being able to assess themselves positively ("beloved by God"). These three features draw social boundaries that mark off this group from others and make it distinctive, an "assembly or gathering." (See Esler 2001:1201–2; 1998:40–57.) Developing a distinctive group identity is crucial to the change agent's task to provide stability and prevent discontinuance of the innovation. Distinctive group identity sets the Thessalonian members apart as members of an ingroup, with the rest of society as well as their former Israelite co-believers forming an outgroup. **Social Identity.**

The Marvelous Reception of the Innovation Communicated at Thessalonika 1:6-10

1:6 And you became imitators of us and of the Lord, for in spite of persecution you received the word with joy inspired by the Holy Spirit, 7 so that you became an example to all the believers in Macedonia and in Achaia. 8 For the word of the Lord has sounded forth from you not only in Macedonia and Achaia, but in every place your faith in God has become known, so that we have no need to speak about it. 9 For the people of those regions report about us what kind of welcome we had among you, and how you turned to God from idols, to serve a living and true God, 10 and to wait for his Son from heaven, whom he raised from the dead—Jesus, who rescues us from the wrath that is coming.

Textual Notes: 1 Thess 1:6-10

1:6: The word translated "persecution" (*thlipsis*, also in 3:3.7 and the verb form in 3:4) means distress, anxiety. Distress implies an external and usually temporary cause of great physical or mental strain and stress, while anxiety refers to feelings of uncertainty in face of impending harm. Since Paul proclaimed his gospel of God among fellow Israelites and not all accepted this proclamation, those who did accept normally experienced distress resulting from adopting the innovation in face of those who rejected it in their Israelite communities. Their fellow Israelites, perhaps

Reporting on the deeds of an Egyptian god, this inscription is evidence that Thessalonika was a significant center for the propagation of the Egyptian associational religion. At about the same time Paul reported the Thessalonian Jesus group's promotion of the gospel of God throughout Macedonia and Achaia (1 Thess 1:7-8).

a local majority, were aggrieved because these new Jesus-group members discontinued their customary Israelite behavior and often split with the local Israelite group. Grievance quickly leads to conflict, and this is what distress entailed. **Conflict.** Social identity theory suggests "that external opposition and persecution will often encourage members to act in terms of their group membership, so that past suffering, now brought again to mind by Paul, probably strengthened their involvement with, and commitment to, the congregation" (Esler 2001:1203a).

1:7-8: Paul now gives a grant of honor to the Thessalonians by underscoring their proven worth among other Jesus groups in Macedonia and Achaia. Such a grant of honor wins the benevolence of the addressees of this letter, further enhancing interpersonal bonding.

1:9a: The phrase "the people of those regions" (NRSV) translates the Greek "they." These people of Macedonia and Achaia, of course, are not the whole populations of those regions. They emphatically are not "the Gentiles." In fact, the people of Macedonia and Achaia are solely and only members of Jesus groups who are attuned to the gossip network following Paul's activity. The information is ingroup information that ingroup members share, as opposed to outgroups who know little, if anything, about the honorable behavior of the Thessalonian Jesus-group members.

1:9b-10: Paul describes his Thessalonian clients as people who turned "from idols to serve the living and true God and to wait for his Son from the sky." The word translated "idols" (Greek: *eidōlōn*) means images. In contrast with "the living and true God," it probably means image of a deity. Those who turned away from these deity images are, of course, members of Paul's Israelite audience. The presumption that these were non-Israelites is simply misplaced for two reasons: Paul's target audience consisted of Israelites, and many Israelites resident among non-Israelites were far along the way of assimilation, including adopting local worship patterns.

On the basis of inscriptions, Kant (1987) has described how Israelites often inscribed their funerary monuments with the polytheistic D M (*diis manibus*, i.e., to the divine shades or spirits) to Roman ancestral deities, at other times to the spirit gods, the Junonian spirits. Israelite slaves were sold to Apollo, and an Israelite sold his slaves to Apollo. Israelites signed oaths to Jupiter, Gaia (earth), Helius (Sun) as well as to the Highest God (presumably the God of Israel). One Israelite from Boeotia, upon being manumitted, set up an altar to the Greek gods Amphiaraus and Hygeia, being commanded to do so in a dream.

Israelites served in the Roman Army: an Israelite commander and officer are noted in Egypt, an Israelite centurion in Palestine, and Israelite soldiers in the Roman army in Italy. There was even a Judean military unit, and there is mention of an Israelite serving in the Roman navy. Of course all these military persons had to take an oath to their officers and a vow to the Roman deities. Then there were other Israelites who paid homage to local deities, including the city councilmen of Sardis, Acmonia (Phrygia), Corcyrus (Cilicia), Cyrene, and El Hamman (Palestine). Even Philo calls the Israelite God "the Supreme father of the gods" (*Spec. Laws* 2, 165), acknowledging those other deities.

Thessalonika of Paul's day had a range of deities whose help was sought for the range of maladies that afflicted their adherents: Serapis and Isis, Zeus, Asclepius, Demeter, Dionysus, and a notable worship of Cabirus. Hence it is not so far-fetched to find Paul describing his fellow Israelites as turning away from idols to pledge their commitment to Israel's God and his plan to send his resurrected Son from the sky, soon, to establish an Israelite theocracy.

1:10b: Note that, for the first time in the Pauline writings, the God of Israel is described as "the one who raised Jesus from the dead," the new Jesus-group name for the God of Israel. The term "resurrection" was a technical term in Israel, to be distinguished from the resuscitation of a dead person or reviving a corpse. Resurrection meant the transformation of a dead person into a life marked by a radically different way of being a living human. Belief in such a resurrection was rooted in Israel's Persian experience and transmitted notably by that Judean group named after the Persians (Farsi), the Pharisees. This belief, held in Pharisee circles, was given clear expression in the second century B.C.E. (see Dan 12:2-3; 2 Macc 12:43-46; Wis 4:16; and in subsequent Israelite writings). **Death and Resurrection.** During the time of Paul, Pharisees continued their belief in such a resurrection, as did the Qumran covenanters; the Sadducees opposed the idea as contrary to Israel's sacred writings.

The resurrected Jesus' role is to "rescue us from the wrath that is coming." He does this when he comes down from the sky. "Wrath" is Paul's usual way of referring to God's defending his honor by taking satisfaction on those who shame the deity. Those who shame God, of course, are sinners, specifically Israelite sinners. Since only Israelites have a covenant with the God of Israel, only Israelites are obliged to defend this God's honor and are to serve this God alone. It is Israel's shaming its God that requires satisfaction or "wrath." God has to have satisfaction for Israel's acts of shaming him because otherwise other peoples (often called "the peoples" or in Greek *ta ethnē*, tendentiously translated as "the Gentiles") will believe Israel's God is no God at all. **Wrath.**

The Attitude of Paul and His Associates 2:1-12

2:1 You yourselves know, brothers and sisters, that our coming to you was not in vain, 2 but though we had already suffered and been shamefully mistreated at Philippi, as you know, we had courage in our God to declare to you the gospel of God in spite of great opposition. 3 For our appeal does not spring from deceit or impure motives or trickery, 4 but just as we have been approved by God to be entrusted with the message of the gospel, even so we speak, not to please mortals, but to please God who tests our hearts. 5 As you know and as God is our witness, we never came with words of flattery or with a pretext for greed; 6 nor did we seek praise from mortals, whether from you or from others, 7 though we might have made demands as apostles of Christ. But we were gentle among you, like a nurse tenderly caring for her own children. 8 So deeply do we care for you that we are determined to share with you not only the gospel of God but also our own selves, because you have become very dear to us.

9 You remember our labor and toil, brothers and sisters; we worked night and day, so that we might not burden any of you while we proclaimed to you the gospel of God. 10 You are witnesses, and God also, how pure, upright, and blameless our conduct was toward you believers. 11 As you know, we dealt with each one of you like a father with his children, 12 urging and encouraging you and pleading that you lead a life worthy of God, who calls you into his own kingdom and glory.

Textual Notes: 1 Thess 2:1-12

2:2: "Our God." The "our" in the phrase is inclusive since in context Paul is underscoring interpersonal commonalities and points of contact. The phrase is another indication that Paul shares the same deity as his audience; they are both Israelites. What Paul proclaims is "the gospel of God" (obviously the God of Israel). Paul attests to the opposition he faced in Thessalonika, briefly recalled in Acts 18, where the opposition was due to the Israelite community's feeling aggrieved by Paul's inroads among their members. Such opposition on the part of local vested interests is quite normal for change agents importing an innovation.

Local Israelite opponents of the innovation proclaimed by Paul shared the past as point of reference. If the good news were new, it automatically was to be suspect. Paul's opponents made their decisions in terms of what had been done in previous generations. Since the God of Israel already had a theocracy in Jerusalem, to which local Israelite communities subscribed, there was little hope of some new theocracy occurring in the near future. Characteristics of these opponents included (a) taking the past as normative (i.e., only the past as presented in Israelite tradition); (b) approving social interaction with others who have traditional values (even Roman traditionalists); and (c) open suspicion of innovations, innovators, and change agents (hence opposition to Paul).

To Paul's Israelite opposition, Paul clearly sounded like a false prophet, to be dealt with according to the directions of Deut 13:1-5, 12-18. Hence his insistence on his own positive qualities: "how pure, upright, and blameless our conduct was toward you believers" (2:10).

2:3-4: "deceit or impure motives or trickery" are characteristic of false prophets in Israel: "deceit"—Deut 4:19; 13:6; Isa 19:14; 30:10.20; Jer 23:13.32; Ezek 14:11; Mic 3:5; Jude 11; "impure motives"—Zech 13:2; Mark 3:30; Rev 16:13-14; "trickery"—Num 25:18; Isa 53:9; Dan 8:25; Acts 13:10.

2:7: Paul notes that "apostles of Christ" were allowed to demand support from the Jesus groups they set up. This is a sort of reciprocal obligation, a quid pro quo, mentioned elsewhere (e.g., 1 Cor 9:1-18). Yet to undergird the purity of his motivation, he bypasses such sustenance and instead supports himself.

2:12: "Glory" refers to the visible, manifest features that reveal a person's honor status. The goal of Jesus-group members is to participate in a new political system, the kingdom of God, which will reveal what God is really like.

The Attitude of First Adopters of the Innovation 2:13-16

2:13 We also constantly give thanks to God for this, that when you received the word of God that you heard from us, you accepted it not as a human word but as what it really is, God's word, which is also at work in you believers. 14 For you, brothers and sisters, became imitators of the churches of God in Christ Jesus that are in Judea, for you suffered the same things from your own compatriots as they did from the Jews, 15 who killed both the Lord Jesus and the prophets, and drove us out; they displease God and oppose everyone 16 by hindering us from speaking to the Gentiles so that they may be saved. Thus they have constantly been filling up the measure of their sins; but God's wrath has overtaken them at last.

Textual Notes: 1 Thess 2:13-16

For a change agent like Paul, the first people to adopt the innovation he disseminated are called innovators and first adopters. Cross-cultural studies of people who are first to adopt an innovation indicate that the innovator category has the following characteristics. Innovators control adequate material and personality resources to absorb the possible failure due to an unsuccessful innovation. They have the ability to understand and apply rather complex knowledge. And most especially, they espouse the salient value of venturesomeness, that is, a desire for the daring, the chancy, and the risky. Finally, innovators are cosmopolites; that means that they have contact with outsiders and most often have social relationships with them (Rogers 1971, 1995). This cosmopolite feature is indicated by the fact that they previously were devotees of sorts of various deities (1 Thess 1:9b-10).

Since an innovation like the gospel of God affected everyday behavior dealing with how the local Jesus group functioned, innovators had the material resources to absorb the risk of the innovation undertaking, that is, the ability to deal with conflict, to provide a place to meet, to support change agents, to assist others who might be cut off from community aid, and the like.

Early adopters, on the other hand, are a more integrated part of the local social system than are innovators; they tend to be locally focused people and frequently are opinion leaders with the following characteristics. In their social system they are not too far ahead of the average individual in innovativeness and serve as role models for other members of a social system in adopting the innovation. They are respected by their peers and are the embodiment of successful and discreet use of new ideas. Finally, they know that they must continue to earn the esteem and reputation of their colleagues if their position as opinion leaders in the social system is to be maintained (Rogers 1971, 1995).

In the Jesus groups Paul founded, these innovators and first adopters would consist of the higher levels of the various Israelite communities in which Paul proclaimed his gospel. Clearly, the highest and lowest ranks of synagogue members would not be among the first to adopt such an innovation. Presumably these social levels of Israelites would be quick to feel aggrieved by what Paul was up to as he tore the fabric of the local Israelite social group.

Paul describes the qualities of these Thessalonian first adopters. Proof of the Thessalonians' sincere adoption of the gospel of God is found in their endurance and perseverance in face of conflict with their fellow Thessalonian Israelites. Paul sees this conflict as a replication of what Judeans (v. 14 here anachronistically translated as "Jews" **Greeks and Israelites**) did to Jesus. Judeans are proverbial killers of prophets, as noted in such Israelite documents as *The Lives of the Prophets* and the *Martyrdom of Isaiah*; Jesus groups took up the idea since it applied to Jesus' death as well (see Luke 13:34; Matt 5:12; 23:31, 35, 37; Acts 7:52; Rom 11:3; Rev 11:8).

2:16a: A new datum noted by Paul is that these Judeans also sought to keep Paul from his change-agent task, directed to Israelites resident among non-Israelites. The Judeans in question seem to have been those who previously supported Paul in his Pharisaic zeal to put down Jesus groups. When Paul took on his new charge from the God of Israel to proclaim the gospel of God, that group turned to suppress Paul as well. **Establishment Violence.** Verse 16 is better translated: "they hindered us from speaking to Israelites among the Gentiles so that those Israelites may be saved." Obviously the salvation here is rescue from the wrath soon to come, a wrath directed to Judeans; after all, it is about Judeans that Paul notes that "God's wrath overtakes them at last" (the verb form is called a "proleptic aorist," describing a completed action soon to occur). **Wrath.**

Many authors believe the reference to "God's wrath" overtaking the Judeans refers to a massacre that occurred in Jerusalem in 48 C.E. consequent to a Judean riot (as noted by Josephus in *Ant.* 20.112 and *War* 2.224–27). It seems, however, that this massacre hardly measures up to the wrath that Paul has in mind. Because of the tenor of Paul's argument and other references to the wrath to come, it would seem that the reference here is to the forthcoming catastrophic action inaugurated by the God of Israel to maintain his honor in face of continued Israelite shaming challenges.

2:16b: Sin against God means shaming or dishonoring God. "Filling up the measure of their (the Judeans) sins" means reaching a point in shaming God so that God must take satisfaction in order to defend his honor (see Lev 26:3-42 for an understanding of God's wrath). Again, this is what "wrath" is about—obtaining satisfaction after being dishonored in order to defend one's honor. Paul does not need to specify the nature of this "wrath" focused on Judeans, since his Jesus-group members would know that God's wrath would emerge from the sky over Judea and onto Jerusalem (see comments at 4:15-17). Obviously the time of this event will coincide with the inauguration of the forthcoming theocracy.

Section Two: 2:17–3:13
After the Forming of the Jesus Group at Thessalonika

Paul's Desire to Visit the Group Once More 2:17-20

2:17 As for us, brothers and sisters, when, for a short time, we were made orphans by being separated from you—in person, not in heart—we longed with great eagerness to see you face to face. 18 For we wanted to come to you—certainly I, Paul, wanted to again and again—but Satan blocked our way. 19 For what is our hope or joy or crown of boasting before our Lord Jesus at his coming? Is it not you? 20 Yes, you are our glory and joy!

Textual Notes: 1 Thess 2:17-20

2:17: After the forming of the Jesus group at Thessalonika, one would expect a period of storming or conflict, followed by norming. **Small-Group Development.** Paul expresses how attached he is to the Thessalonian Jesus-group members, whom he considers part of his ingroup. His letter seeks to maintain this relation by sharing information.

2:18: Satan (in Greek: *diabolos*, English: devil, accuser) is a nonhuman person in charge of testing loyalty to God (see Job 1:1). The role derives by analogy from the secret service of the Persian emperor, who used such agents (Persian word: *satan*) to tempt or test the loyalty of his subjects. In Israelite cosmic theology and under Persian influence, from about the third century B.C.E., Satan broke with the service of God and sought to recruit his own loyal subjects by deception. Thus Satan's perennial task was to deceive. Just as in our own society (e.g., FBI, CIA), such deceiving secret police tactics were known in Paul's world. Consider the offhand remark of Epictetus, a first-century Stoic philosopher:

> When someone gives us the impression of having talked to us frankly about his personal affairs, somehow or other we are likewise led to tell him our own secrets. . . . In this fashion the rash are ensnared by the soldiers in Rome. A soldier, dressed like a civilian, sits down by your side, and begins to speak ill of Caesar, and then you too, just as though you had received from him some guarantee of good faith in the fact that he began the abuse, tell likewise everything you think. And the next thing is—you are led off to prison in chains. (*Discourses* IV.13.1,5)

Paul's way back to Thessalonika was blocked by some deception or ruse that he then attributed to the tricks of that cosmic secret service agent, Satan. The experience in some way involved testing Paul's loyalty to God, which is why Satan is mentioned. Otherwise attribution to some demonic force would have sufficed. **Demons/Demon Possession.**

2:19-20: Honor, a publicly acknowledged claim to worth, was the core value of the ancient Mediterranean. Concern for God's honor is what stands behind the references to the wrath of God—God defending his own honor. Here Paul specifies the motive behind his dedication as God's change agent: to be honored at the coming of the Lord Jesus! The Thessalonians who have adopted and persevered in the gospel of God communicated by Paul form the basis of his hope and joy soon to be experienced in a public honor acclamation (glory) at the Lord's coming. It is significant to note that Paul's belief that Jesus would single him out for this honor acclamation indicates Paul's assumption that he belonged in that small inner circle of apostles close enough to Jesus to be observed and singled out by the Lord. His change-agent commission placed him in that inner circle; hence his willingness to stand up to the other apostles (e.g., as described in Galatians).

The Outcomes of Timothy's Visit 3:1-10

3:1 Therefore when we could bear it
no longer, we decided to be left alone in
Athens; 2 and we sent Timothy, our brother
and co-worker for God in proclaiming the
gospel of Christ, to strengthen and encourage you for the sake of your faith, 3 so that
no one would be shaken by these persecutions. Indeed, you yourselves know that this
is what we are destined for. 4 In fact, when
we were with you, we told you beforehand
that we were to suffer persecution; so it
turned out, as you know. 5 For this reason,
when I could bear it no longer, I sent to
find out about your faith; I was afraid
that somehow the tempter had tempted
you and that our labor had been in vain.

6 But Timothy has just now come
to us from you, and has brought us the
good news of your faith and love. He has
told us also that you always remember us
kindly and long to see us—just as we long
to see you. 7 For this reason, brothers and
sisters, during all our distress and persecution we have been encouraged about
you through your faith. 8 For we now
live, if you continue to stand firm in the
Lord. 9 How can we thank God enough
for you in return for all the joy that we
feel before our God because of you? 10
Night and day we pray most earnestly
that we may see you face to face and
restore whatever is lacking in your faith.

Textual Notes: 1 Thess 3:1-10

3:1-5: These verses form a unit, marked off by the phrase "to bear it no longer." As change agent, Paul has to set up an information exchange relation. And he obviously had no information from the Thessalonians until Timothy returned with the news. This letter is a response to Timothy's report, thus continuing the required information exchange relation.

What he expected was that the Thessalonians would be distressed on account of the conflict that would emerge when their fellow Israelites expressed their grievance against these new Jesus-group members. The words translated "persecution" (*thlipsis,* here and v. 7; verb form in v. 4) means distress, anxiety. "Distress" implies an external and usually temporary cause of great physical or mental strain and stress. Undoubtedly the Thessalonians were harassed in a way to cause grief or social suffering due to their adoption of the gospel of God.

3:5: The social experience of persistent annoyance coupled with pleas and importunities from their fellow Israelites marked the temptation or loyalty test that Paul ascribes to the "tempter," that is, Satan. For Paul "to labor in vain" would be shameful, a mark against his honor as change agent.

3:6: Timothy brings information that dissolves Paul's anxieties. The Thessalonians have in fact persisted in the innovation they had adopted, relying upon God (faith) and continuing in their attachment to the ingroup (love) and still holding Paul in high esteem. The stereotypical presumption of being quickly forgotten by one's friends and acquaintances is a common Mediterranean quality (see 1 Cor 11:24-25; Luke 22:19).

3:7-9: Paul's own distress and anxiety have been allayed; he can now say that he is alive (again) since the Thessalonians are firm in their resolve "in the Lord." In fact he is filled with joy, as might be expected.

3:10: Paul concludes here by noting his constant prayer that he might come and see the Thessalonians again. His motive, to amend the shortcomings of their faith, is part and parcel of the change agent's role, for the process of exchanging information with the Thessalonians through Timothy allows Paul the opportunity to diagnose problems (some noted later in the letter) as well as to develop a deeper commitment to the gospel of God evidenced in behavior. Paul seeks to prevent discontinuance of the innovation he proclaimed as well as to support continued stability in the group marked by adherence to the ingroup boundaries that define the group, revealed in the norms he will suggest.

Conclusion: Best Wishes for Divine Favors 3:11-13

3:11 Now may our God and Father himself and our Lord Jesus direct our way to you. 12 And may the Lord make you increase and abound in love for one another and for all, just as we abound in love for you. 13 And may he so strengthen your hearts in holiness that you may be blameless before our God and Father at the coming of our Lord Jesus with all his saints.

Textual Notes: 1 Thess 3:11-13

Letter thanksgivings usually have two sections after a formula in which God is acknowledged or blessed. The first section looks to the past and present, while the second section looks to the forthcoming future. These verses mark the second part, the forthcoming future, still in the form of a thanksgiving prayer to God. They form a literary unit in chiastic form:

A God the Father . . . Our Lord Jesus
  B may the Lord make you . . . love
    C as we abound in love for you
  B' may he so strengthen your hearts
A' God and Father . . . Our Lord Jesus

The central emphasis, as in the whole previous passage, is Paul's attachment to the Thessalonians. This is actually the theme of the first three chapters of the letter. It underscores Paul's activity as change agent of the gospel of God, the process of his establishing an information exchange relation with the Thessalonians, and his abiding attachment and interest in them. Clearly the whole focus of this prayer for the forthcoming is love, that is, mutual attachment of all persons concerned in the innovation enterprise: God the Patron of the group, the cosmic Lord Jesus, intermediary between God and those who rely upon God, the change agent Paul, and the Thessalonian first adopters and innovators. The letter must substitute for Paul's presence until the God of Israel and our Lord "direct our way to you."

III. 1 Thess 4:1—5:24
Directives and Exhortations

Section One: 1 Thess 4:1-12 Conduct Pleasing to God

4:1-12 form a unit or mental paragraph since the passage is marked off by the word "to walk, walk around" (Greek: *peripatein*), translated in v. 1 "to live" and in v. 12 "to behave." A favorite Israelite metaphor for human deportment saw conduct as inevitably involving a person's walking along a pathway (Hebrew *halakah* means walking and is the word for Torah-compliant conduct; see the admonition about the Two Ways, Matt 7:13-14; *Didache* 1:1; and the Jesus group labeling itself "The Way," Acts 9:2; 19:9, 23; 24:14, 22).

Introduction: A Solemn Appeal to Distinctive Conduct 4:1-2

4:1 Finally, brothers and sisters, we ask and urge you in the Lord Jesus that, as you learned from us how you ought to live and to please God (as, in fact, you are doing), you should do so more and more. 2 For you know what instructions we gave you through the Lord Jesus.

Textual Notes: 1 Thess 4:1-2

Paul here urges the Thessalonians to adopt a line of conduct that might distinguish their group from others, an ingroup hallmark. "To walk and please God" refers to God-pleasing conduct, already a feature of this gathering. Such conduct serves as a group identity marker. At the end of the passage (v. 12) Paul wishes outsiders to be able to see their conduct and note its distinctive, honorable character. He notes that he previously spoke of this.

About "Holiness" 4:3-8

4:3 For this is the will of God, your sanctification: that you abstain from fornication; 4 that each one of you know how to control your own body in holiness and honor, 5 not with lustful passion, like the Gentiles who do not know God; 6 that no one wrong or exploit a brother or sister in this matter, because the Lord is an avenger in all these things, just as we have already told you beforehand and solemnly warned you. 7 For God did not call us to impurity but in holiness. 8 Therefore whoever rejects this rejects not human authority but God, who also gives his Holy Spirit to you.

Textual Notes: 1 Thess 4:3-8

4:3: Paul now specifies the conduct that pleases God, namely holiness. It is important not to fill this word with the moral overtones that it has in our society. **Sacred/Profane.** Holiness or sanctification means exclusivity. Persons, places, and things that belong to a person (e.g., family, house, car) are exclusive or holy to that person. What belongs to no one in particular belongs to the area called the profane, common, not exclusive or distinctive. Here Paul tells the Thessalonians that God wishes them to conduct themselves as persons belonging exclusively to God, in a way that mirrors the qualities of the God who called them and set them apart. In context the two features Paul specifies are desisting from deviant sexual behavior (vv. 3-8) and persisting in attachment to Jesus-group members (vv. 9-12).

4:3: The word translated "fornication" (Greek: *porneia*) is a general word referring to deviant sexual relations. What is deviant depends on the boundaries provided by the social system. In Israel, deviant sexual relations mostly involved sexual relations that transgressed Israel's interpersonal purity rules: marriages in forbidden degrees (uncles, aunts, parents, siblings), marriages with non-Israelites, sexual relations with cross-dressing males, sexual relations with animals (Leviticus 18), adultery since it dishonors the husband, the idolatry of sexual relations with a sacred prostitute, and the like. In the cultures of the day, the word did not refer to sexual relations between unmarried individuals. A fundamental reason for this was that apart from female slaves, unmarried post-pubescent females were simply not available if only because females were married off as soon after menarche as possible. Furthermore, sexual relations between a married male and an unmarried female (prostitute or slave) was not adultery because adultery meant dishonoring another male by having sexual relations with his wife.

4:4: The word translated "body" is the Greek word *skeuos* (Hebrew: *kly*). Literally, the Greek word means "vessel," and both in Greek (Aelianus, *De natura animalium* 17.11; *Anthologia Planudea* 16.243A) and in Hebrew (Qumran 4Q416 2 ii.21; 1 Sam 21:6) the word is a euphemism for the male sexual organ. Paul thus urges his Thessalonian males to engage in sexual conduct that is in line with the demands of God and that will bring honor to them.

4:5: Paul here contrasts his Israelite Jesus-group members with their surrounding majority population, which does not know the God of Israel; these may be non-Israelites as well as Israelites (the Greek word *ethnē* and translated "Gentiles" basically means a class or category of people, here those people who do not know God in practice).

4:6: The word "sister" does not appear in the Greek but has been added by the NRSV translators. The context is sexual deviance. The verbs here are *hyperbainein*, "to outdo," and *pleonektein*, "to gain advantage over." His directive is that Thessalonian Jesus-group members should not participate in contests of sexual prowess like others in the city, "for whom sexual conquests were a matter of pride and the more one achieved the more one had to boast about" (Esler 2001:1208a). God's honor is involved in the deviant behavior of those whom he set apart, hence "the Lord is an avenger in all these things, just as we have already told you beforehand and solemnly warned you."

4:7: "Impurity" and "holiness" are not opposites here. Rather, Paul notes that God called us in holiness, not for uncleanness. Uncleanness or impurity is behavior that puts or leaves a person out of social place, where he or she should be—just like dirt or the impure is matter out of place. The distinctive gathering of Jesus-group members is holy, exclusive to God, and hence should abstain from contests of sexual prowess.

4:8: The Spirit or power of God is given to the group ("you" is plural) and further underscores its distinctiveness; the rejection of the deviance in question is demanded by the presence of the Spirit, by divine authority.

About Proper Ingroup Behavior 4:9-12

4:9 Now concerning love of the brothers and sisters, you do not need to have anyone write to you, for you yourselves have been taught by God to love one another; 10 and indeed you do love all the brothers and sisters throughout Macedonia. But we urge you, beloved, to do so more and more, 11 to aspire to live quietly, to mind your own affairs, and to work with your hands, as we directed you, 12 so that you may behave properly toward outsiders and be dependent on no one.

Textual Notes: 1 Thess 4:9-12

4:9-10: "Love" means group attachment shown by behavior. The Thessalonians demonstrated their mutual support rather spontaneously, setting aside previous customary ingroup attitudes that keep outgroup members at a distance. Paul ascribes this love to the direct action of God, since Mediterranean human beings do not behave with spontaneous attachment toward members of an outgroup, here fellow believers "throughout Macedonia," that is, beyond Thessalonika.

4:11-12: Paul's exhortations consist in encouraging members of the Jesus group to conduct themselves in such a way that when their fellow city residents observe them, their distinctive conduct will be blameless and not challenge others, thus provoking a negative reaction (this is what being dependent here means). Such conduct pleases God (as in 4:1). That these Jesus-group members were regarded by their city peers, at least in Paul's view, as significant enough to call attention to themselves, hence as noteworthy personages in the city, further underscores the expected qualities of first adopters of an innovation.

Section Two: 1 Thess 4:13–5:11 Solutions to Problems about What Is Next

This section presents two related paragraphs clearly marked off with the same phrase, "about/concerning . . ." (4:13: about those who have fallen asleep [NRSV: have died]; and 5:1: about the times and seasons). And both end with the same phrase (4:18 and 5:11: encourage one another). It seems that the Thessalonians know Paul's teaching relative to the how and when of the arrival of the Lord Jesus Christ but need encouragement in face of the death of some of their group members. It seems they expected all in their group to be alive at the Lord Jesus' arrival that would usher in the Israelite theocracy. Paul's task as change agent is to solve these sorts of problems through further information and encouragement and thus facilitate group stability and perseverance. The remedy is hope, that is, continued allegiance to and abiding confidence in God and his Messiah, Jesus.

Concerning Group Members Who Have Died 4:13-18

4:13 But we do not want you to be uninformed, brothers and sisters, about those who have died, so that you may not grieve as others do who have no hope. 14 For since we believe that Jesus died and rose again, even so, through Jesus, God will bring with him those who have died. 15 For this we declare to you by the word of the Lord, that we who are alive, who are left until the coming of the Lord, will by no means precede those who have died. 16 For the Lord himself, with a cry of command, with the archangel's call and with the sound of God's trumpet, will descend from heaven, and the dead in Christ will rise first. 17 Then we who are alive, who are left, will be caught up in the clouds together with them to meet the Lord in the air; and so we will be with the Lord forever. 18 Therefore encourage one another with these words.

Textual Notes: 1 Thess 4:13-18

4:13: The frequently used phrase "we do not want you to be uninformed" marks a transition to a new topic (see Rom 1:13; 11:25; 1 Cor 10:1; 1 Cor 12:1; 2 Cor 1:8).

While the topic is "about those who have fallen asleep," the problem is the grieving of the Thessalonians.

The Greek word *koimaomai*, "to fall asleep" (also vv. 14, 15), translated here as "died," is used by Paul also in 1 Cor 7:39; 11:30; 15:6, 18, 51; it is also common in the Septuagint (LXX) (see Gen 47:30; Deut 31:16; 2 Sam 7:12; 1 Kings 2:10; 11:21.43; 14:31; 15:8, 24; 16:6, 28, 35). For people who believe in the resurrection of the dead, "to fall asleep" is not exactly a euphemism for "to die." The Greek word *koimētērion*, "cemetery," is related to the same word; it means a dormitory. In Jesus-group usage, a cemetery is a place where all are sleeping with a view to the resurrection.

4:13: "Those who have no hope" serves as a name for the outsider outgroups over against which Paul seeks to mark off Thessalonian Jesus-group members. To have hope is an ingroup value. The basis for their hope is stated again in the next verse.

4:14: Since they do in fact believe Jesus died and was raised by God, so by means of Jesus God will bring with Jesus those who have died to participate in the new theocracy. Again, God is in charge; Jesus is intermediary. With this role, Jesus-group members not only live in and through the Lord, but they also die in and through the Lord. Jesus' resurrection causes death to be for Jesus-group members an event full of hope, with certitude of resurrection and honor with God.

4:15: The "word of the Lord" means taught or instructed by the Lord. Here that "word" provides Paul's explanation that follows with authority and certainty, to allay the grief of the Thessalonians. The source of this instruction is probably an altered state experience by which Paul is "persuaded in the Lord Jesus" (Rom 14:14). **Altered States of Consciousness.**

4:16-17: The Lord's "coming" translates the Greek word *parousia*. *Parousia* means coming, arrival, or presence (it never means "return"). The early Jesus-group gospel proclaimed Jesus as the Messiah appointed for us; however, Jesus has actually not yet exercised the role of Messiah with the power accorded him at the resurrection (see Rom 1:4; Acts 1:6-7; 3:20; 17:31). Jesus' arrival would mark the beginning of the exercise of his Messiahship over Israel.

Along with the foregoing meanings, *parousia* also designates a fixed set of social behaviors. The word was used to designate a ceremonial rite that characterized participation in the official visit of an emperor or some other high-ranking official to a provincial city. The meaning of "ceremonial rite" is appropriate here because of all the details Paul provides about the *parousia*. This ceremony consisted of a solemn announcement of the advent of the dignitary and trumpet blast marking his proximate arrival (v. 16), heralding to city-dwellers that the emperor or official was near enough so that the populace should drop what they were doing and proceed through the main city gate to line either side of the road to meet and acclaim the noble personage as he and his entourage move down the road. This feature of the ceremony, marked by meeting and cheering as the visiting dignitary passed by, is called *apantesis*, translated in v. 17 as "meet." In the rite the noble personage enters the city while the populace follows in a swelling entourage. When all are in the city, festivities follow, often with gifts from the emperor or official for the city and its residents.

Paul uses this ceremonial rite, well-known to Hellenistic city dwellers in the Roman Empire, to describe the proximate arrival of the Lord Jesus from the sky. He offers this explanation to support his clients in their innovation decision, in the face of their grief at the death of their fellow group members. Modern readers might call Paul's use of the *parousia* ceremony an analogy. However, for first-century Thessalonian Jesus-group members, the fact that it came through "a word of the Lord" (v. 15) indicated how the Lord's coming would actually happen as a *parousia*.

What is left out is any specific mention of where this *parousia* would take place. Because of the high context culture shared by Paul and his Israelite audience, however, the location of this event was obvious to all. Since Jesus is Israel's Messiah and Lord, presently with God in the sky, he would come from the sky. And the opening in the sky to the celestial realm of the God of Israel is over Jerusalem. This opening in the sky is well attested in the Bible (1 Kgs 22:19; 2 Chron 18:18; Ezek 1:1; Mark 1:10; Matt 3:16; Rev 4:1). According to Mesopotamian lore, appropriated so well by Israel, to get to a deity's real home in his celestial temple and its attendant city, a person had to pass through the opening in the firmament that led to the other side of the vault of the sky, where the deity in question was enthroned. This opening was to be found directly over the deity's earthly temple. In Acts, for example, the sky opens above Jerusalem to allow the resurrected Jesus to ascend to God through the opening in the firmament (Acts 1:2-9). Likewise because of a sky opening, Stephen in Jerusalem can see the exalted Jesus standing by the throne of God (Acts 7:56). And in Revelation John frequently mentions this opening through which one can see the celestial altar (Rev 8:3; 9:13; 14:18) and the ark of the covenant in the celestial temple (Rev 11:19). The celestial Jerusalem descends through this opening ultimately to come to rest where the earthly Jerusalem is located (Rev 21:2, 10). This is consonant with Israel's tradition according to which certain people saw God's presence in the sky from earthly Jerusalem. God's "holy habitation," his "dwelling place," is in the sky (Deut 26:15; 1 Kings 8:43; 2 Chron 30:27), high in the sky (Job 22:12). The prophet Micaiah "saw the LORD sitting on his throne, and all the host of heaven standing on his right hand and on his left" (1 Kgs 22:19; 2 Chron 18:18). Clearly, his holy temple, his throne, is in the sky (Ps 11:4) although he does have a house below in Jerusalem (2 Chron 36:23; Ezra 1:2).

This was such common knowledge that even those Jesus-group members expecting the *parousia* of the Lord knew that "the signs of truth will appear: first the sign of an opening in the sky, then the sign of the sound of the trumpet, and thirdly the resurrection of the dead" (*Didache* 16:6).

4:17: The outcome for those with hope is that they will be with the Lord forever. Hence the need for continued allegiance to and abiding confidence in God and his Messiah, Jesus.

Concerning the Time of God's Forthcoming Intervention 5:1-11

5:1 Now concerning the times and the seasons, brothers and sisters, you do not need to have anything written to you. 2 For you yourselves know very well that the day of the Lord will come like a thief in the night. 3 When they say, "There is peace and security," then sudden destruction will come upon them, as labor pains come upon a pregnant woman, and there will be no escape! 4 But you, beloved, are not in darkness, for that day to surprise you like a thief; 5 for you are all children of light and children of the day; we are not of the night or of darkness. 6 So then let us not fall asleep as others do, but let us keep awake and be sober; 7 for those who sleep sleep at night, and those who are drunk get drunk at night. 8 But since we belong to the day, let us be sober, and put on the breastplate of faith and love, and for a helmet the hope of salvation. 9 For God has destined us not for wrath but for obtaining salvation through our Lord Jesus Christ, 10 who died for us, so that whether we are awake or asleep we may live with him. 11 Therefore encourage one another and build up each other, as indeed you are doing.

Textual Notes: 1 Thess 5:1-11

5:1: Paul now broaches another Thessalonian question, that of the time of Jesus' arrival from the sky. "Times and seasons" is a figure of speech for some specific time. The Thessalonians already knew from Paul's proclamation about when Jesus would arrive as Lord with power. The standard Jesus-group answer was "soon." The cultures of the first-century Mediterranean shared the perception of time focused on the present. The distant past and the abstract future were in the hands of God(s), and humans could not really know them. But what they could and did know was the proximate past, witnessed by living contemporaries, and the forthcoming. The forthcoming entails events that would soon happen because of their intimate connection with the present as part of an ongoing process with a foreseeable end. Examples of the forthcoming include: a woman pregnant now pointing to a forthcoming, proximate birth of a child; a sown field with its budding plants pointing to a forthcoming, proximate harvest. We might call this perception of the forthcoming rooted in the present a proximate future. Jesus-group members knew that since Jesus was raised in the rather proximate past, God outfitted him with power that he would exercise soon; his messianic role is forthcoming. While we must call him Lord and Messiah, we await his exercise of those roles. Thessalonians knew this, so there is nothing more Paul can tell them except to live in line with this knowledge. Furthermore, in this high context culture, everyone knew that "on time" meant when the most significant person arrives for some occasion (e.g., a groom at a wedding, a high official for a dinner). Jesus' arrival can never be late or delayed since whenever Jesus comes is on time.

5:2: Paul identifies the day of Jesus' coming with power as "the day of the Lord." In Israel's scriptures, this hoped-for day was to mark God's glorious restoration and final salvation of Israel (see Zeph 1:15; Ezekiel 30; 34; 36; Joel 2:2; 4:15; Isaiah 2; Mic 1:2-3; Joel 3:4; Zechariah 14). This day is not the opposite of night; the metaphor of a thief breaking in a house at night is about suddenness.

5:3-8: Paul now contrasts another set of characteristics that marks off the social identity of the Thessalonian Jesus group over against its opposition, "they." Since the only opposition mentioned in the letter are members of the Israelite group from whom these Thessalonian innovators and first adopters came, the contrast is between "us" (Jesus-group members) and "them" (Israelite rejecters of the innovation communicated by Paul).

Characteristics of "them" is, first of all, a belief in their present security and peace, much like ancient Israel berated by Jeremiah (6:14) and Ezekiel (13:10, 16). Their destruction will be as sudden as the Lord's arrival is sudden. The advent of birth pangs on a pregnant woman is another image of the forthcoming or proximate future (v. 3). "They" are in darkness, children of the night, of darkness (vv. 4-5), drunk and asleep (vv. 6-7).

This bronze coin, minted at the city of Thessalonika in the last third of the first century B.C.E., *displays the head of Julius Caesar and a legend indicating that he was acclaimed as a god of the city of Thessalonika, part of the empire's propaganda. Compare 1 Thess 5:3, in which Paul foretells the destruction of those who believe in the empire's peace and security.*

Characteristic of "us" is that we are sons (NRSV: "children") of light, sons (NRSV: "children") of the day (v. 5). So far "we" are awake and sober, and Paul urges that we stay that way since we do belong to the day (vv. 6, 8).

5:8: Paul now introduces another metaphor for readiness: a soldier's state of preparedness. With the presence of the Roman army in every city of the East, the image would be ready at hand. However, the image has its roots in Isa 59:17 (see Isa 11:5; Wis 5:17-20): "He put on righteousness as a breastplate, and a helmet of salvation upon his head; he put on garments of vengeance for clothing, and wrapped himself in fury as a mantle." In this Israelite tradition, God alone dons metaphorical war gear to take vengeance on those who dishonor him in order to restore his honor—a theme quite prominent in Paul, as we have seen. When God's satisfaction runs its course, the outcome will be justice, peace, and security. Paul's use of the metaphor, however, is not about God's honor but about the Thessalonians' readiness: they are to be ready by maintaining their ingroup characteristic of faith, love, and hope, just as Roman soldiers are ready for any contingency.

5:9-10: Three features in these lines link up with the opening of the letter: the mention of faith, love, and hope (1:3), of God destining us (1:4; "God has chosen you"), and of wrath (1:10). Wrath, of course, is Paul's usual way of referring to God's defending his honor by taking satisfaction on those who shame him. Those who shame him are sinners, specifically Israelite sinners. Since only Israelites have a covenant with the God of Israel, since only Israelites are obliged to defend this God's honor, and since only Israelites are obligated to serve this God, it is Israel's shaming its God that requires the satisfaction entailed in "wrath." The salvation that Jesus-group members have obtained through the Lord Jesus Christ refers to their rescue from this wrath. Although they may have dishonored God, thanks to Jesus' death for them (v. 10), they shall avoid the requirements of satisfaction. Forgiveness means the waiving of due satisfaction or revenge.

5:10-11: The goal of the innovation communicated by Paul is that "we may live with him," new life both now and in the forthcoming theocracy. Thessalonian Jesus-group members know this, and Paul acknowledges that they do in fact build up each other with this hope. He simply wishes to encourage them in their resolution. The phrase "encourage one another" marks the end of this section, as it did the conclusion of the previous section (4:18).

Section Three: 1 Thess 5:12-24
About Group Support

Respect Local Opinion Leaders 5:12-13

5:12 But we appeal to you, brothers and sisters, to respect those who labor among you, and have charge of you in the Lord and admonish you; 13 esteem them very highly in love because of their work. Be at peace among yourselves.

Textual Notes: 1 Thess 5:12-13

5:12: In studies of the communication of innovation, the persons referred to here, who labor and have charge and admonish, are called opinion leaders. **Opinion Leaders.** These are persons in the group capable of informally influencing the attitudes and overt behavior of group members in a desired way with relative frequency. Such persons normally possess some notable sanctioning ability (e.g., relatively higher status and wealth, patronage ties with many in the group, knowledge of Israel's traditions), but they had no formal power, i.e., they are not *the* authority. In terms of patriarchal family structure, these local leaders were like the males on the mother's side of the family (mother's brother, *Oheim* in German). They had no formal or jural authority, which followed the patriline. Authority means the ability to control the behavior of others. For Jesus-group opinion leaders, their authority came from their interpersonal ability and connections to the change agent, not from some law or set of entitlements. Formal authority belonged to Paul's role, for which he deserved remuneration. However, as he previously noted, he was like a nurse, gentle in his dealings with the Thessalonians (2:7), that is, "not insisting on the benefits which rightly belonged to such an honorable position" as an apostle with authority (Esler 2001:1204a), or like a father with his children (2:10) with the authority of a patriarchal head of the household.

5:13: Those who have charge over the group deserve to be honored with loyalty and solidarity because of their function. Their function is not an official office, but rather an unofficial management role that invariably emerges when a change agent takes leave of a recently founded group.

The peace Paul urges clearly refers to ingroup harmony. Esler (2001:1211a) makes note of "the antagonistic conduct common among unrelated males in this culture." Paul would have Jesus-group members relate to each other with the mutual care and concern of brothers (and sisters).

Group-Bolstering Advice 5:14-22

5:14 And we urge you, beloved, to admonish the idlers, encourage the faint hearted, help the weak, be patient with all of them. 15 See that none of you repays evil for evil, but always seek to do good to one another and to all. 16 Rejoice always, 17 pray without ceasing, 18 give thanks in all circumstances; for this is the will of God in Christ Jesus for you. 19 Do not quench the Spirit. 20 Do not despise the words of prophets, 21 but test everything; hold fast to what is good; 22 abstain from every form of evil.

Textual Notes: 1 Thess 5:14-22

As change agent on behalf of the God of Israel, who raised Jesus from the dead, Paul's initial task after proclaiming the gospel of God was to establish and maintain an information exchange relation. His letter to the Thessalonians is an instance of this relation. He now concludes the letter with a listing of attributes that are intended to mark off, define, and characterize the identity of the Thessalonian Jesus group. Such attributes are the values that are to typify the acceptable (and unacceptable) orientations and behaviors for members of the ingroup.

The advice Paul gives here is directed to all the members of the group, who are to admonish, encourage, help, and be patient with each other (v. 14); not seek revenge but forgive both insiders and outsiders (v. 15); and adopt a permanent pattern of joy (v. 16), prayer (v. 17), and acknowledgment of God's benefactions (v. 18) because this is what pleases God now that group members have accepted Paul's gospel and await the coming of the Lord Jesus. Group experiences of altered states of consciousness inspired by God's spirit are to be sustained (v. 19), and the prophetic speech that occurs in these experiences is to be cherished (v. 20). On the other hand, they are not to be gullible but must test everything, choosing what is good and avoiding what is evil (v. 21-22).

Invocation 5:23-24

5:23 May the God of peace himself sanctify you entirely; and may your spirit and soul and body be kept sound and blameless at the coming of our Lord Jesus Christ. 24 The one who calls you is faithful, and he will do this.

Textual Notes: 1 Thess 5:22-24

Paul states the good he wishes God to bestow on the Thessalonians: to remain totally exclusive to God (holy), in good physical (sound) and moral (blameless) health at the arrival of the Lord Jesus. Since their calling is from God, who is trustworthy and reliable, he will enable them to realize this condition.

This relief on the Arch of Galerius shows a ritual at an altar of Zeus and Herakles involving the rulers Augustus Diocletian and Galerius. Also featured are three female figures who represent the inhabited world, harmony, and peace—all part of typical imperial propaganda that proclaimed peace and security (compare 1 Thess 5:3-10).

IV. 1 Thess 5:25-28
Letter Closing: Salutation and Blessing

5:25 Beloved, pray for us.
26 Greet all the brothers and sisters with
a holy kiss. 27 I solemnly command you by
the Lord that this letter be read to all of them.
28 The grace of our Lord Jesus Christ
be with you.

Textual Notes: 1 Thess 5:25-28

5:25: Paul requests prayers on behalf of himself and his change agent colleagues, presumably to ask God for assistance and endurance in their task.

5:26: The "holy kiss" is an ingroup marker, a sign of fictive kinship in the Lord, of belonging to the Jesus group, a fictive kinship group "in Christ."

5:27: Paul, with the singular "I," invokes his authority to command the Thessalonians who receive this letter to have it read to any of the brothers (and sisters) who might not hear it at its first reading.

5:28: This wish for God's favor mediated by Jesus seems to have been a distinctive, conventional Jesus-group letter closing.

1 Corinthians

I. 1 Cor 1:1-8
Letter Opening (Superscription)

1:1-3	Superscription
1:4-8	Thanksgiving

II. 1 Cor 1:9—6:20
Reaction to a Report from Chloe's People

Section One: 1 Cor 1:9–3:23
Reported Ingroup Conflict and Reminders to Facilitate the Restoration of Harmony

1:9-16	Clique Formation
1:17-25	The Cross of Christ and Folly: Power and Wisdom
1:26-31	Reminder about Social Status
2:1-9	Reminder about the Circumstances of Their Innovation Adoption
2:10-16	Reminder about the Spirit
3:1-23	A Comparison Based on Feeding, Farming, and Construction
4:1-13	Reflections on the Role of Change Agents
4:14-21	Conclusion and Travel Plans

Section Two: 1 Cor 5:1–6:20
Reported Complacency with a Case of Ingroup Incest and Directives for Dealing with It

5:1-8	The Problem: Corinthian Complacency about Ingroup Incest
5:9-13	Reminder of Previous Admonitions about Interpersonal Relations
6:1-11	Censure of Ingroup Litigants and Their Litigiousness
6:12-20	Once More: Dealing with the Complacency about Ingroup Incest

III. 1 Cor 7:1—15:58
Response to Corinthian Questions

Part One: 1 Cor 7:1-40
About Marriage Now

7:1-16	About Sexual Relations in Marriage
7:17-24	General Principle: Stay in the State in Which You Were Called

7:25-35 About Arranging Marriages Now
7:36-38 About Levirate Marriages
7:39-40 About Widows and Marriage

Part Two: 1 Cor 8:1–11:1
About Foods and Dining
8:1-13 Food Presented before Images

Part Three: 1 Cor 9:1-27
About Jesus-Group Change Agents and Their Entitlements
9:1-14 Change Agents, Their Entitlements, and Waiving Entitlements
9:15-27 The Basis of Paul's Change-Agent Career and Waiving Entitlements

Part Four: 1 Cor 10:1–11:1
About Showing Respect for Images
10:1-13 Lessons from the History of Israel
10:14–11:1 Detailed Application of the Foregoing Story

Part Five: 1 Cor 11:2-34
About Behavior at Jesus-Group Gatherings
11:2-16 Jesus-Group Gatherings Are Not Domestic Gatherings
11:17-34 Proper Dining Behavior at Jesus-Group Gatherings

Part Six: 1 Cor 12:1–14:40
About Phenomena Induced by the Spirit
12:1-31a Phenomena Induced by the Spirit
12:31b–13:13 The Central Value of *Agapē* (Group Allegiance)
14:1-40 More about Spirit-Induced Phenomena

Part Seven: 1 Cor 15:1-58
A Reminder about Paul's Gospel and the Resurrection of the Dead
15:1-11 God Has Raised Jesus from the Dead: Significance and Witnesses
15:12-19 Corinthian Reinvention
15:20-28 What Paul's Proclamation Implies
15:29-34 Why the Dead Must Be Raised
15:35-58 How Are the Dead Raised?

Part Eight: 1 Cor 16:1-4
Questions about Collecting the Temple Tax and Travel Plans
16:1-4 About the Temple Tax 16:1-4

IV. 1 Cor 16:5-24
Letter Closing: Salutations and Blessing

16:5-11	Travel Plans
16:12	About Apollos
16:13-22	Salutations
16:23-24	Blessings

Paul's letters, aside from Romans and Philemon, are instances of an information exchange relation between Paul and his clients, now his fellow Jesus-group members. While the Thessalonian letter was a follow-up to such an information exchange relation set up by Timothy's visit to Jesus groups in that city, 1 Corinthians, sent from Ephesus between 53 and 56 C.E., attests to the fact that Paul was already situated in a well-set-up information exchange relation. There was an initial letter (which has not come down to us; see 1 Cor 5:9), to which the Corinthians reacted as reported by Timothy, thanks to his visit there (1 Cor 4:17). That report underscored the arrogance of some in the Corinthian Jesus group. Subsequently Chloe's people (perhaps slaves; 1 Cor 1:11) came to Paul with further information about the developing reactions to the innovation he communicated, and this information flow was capped off by a letter sent by some at Corinth (1 Cor 7:1). Our (first) letter to the Corinthians is Paul's response to all the information he has received through the previous channels.

What was happening at Corinth was a process of reinvention. The innovation proclaimed by Paul was changed or modified to some extent in the process of its adoption and implementation by Corinthian Jesus-group members. Jesus-group members from other areas visited the Corinthians as well. Invariably, the Corinthians' use of the new ideas about the God of Israel acting in Jesus of Nazareth departed to varying degrees from Paul's own version of the innovation. His letters demonstrate the fact that his gospel of God did not remain unvaried during the process of its diffusion. In fact, any innovation or the context connected with some innovation always changes when the innovation is introduced into new settings or situations. Such context-based change is called "refraction" (Rogers 1995:178–80). The reports and questions put to Paul in this letter derive from the reinventions occurring in Corinth.

In the first part of the letter, Paul responds to the information brought by Chloe's people. They reported about cliques that have developed and fractured the group (1:11ff), about a deviant conjugal union (5:1ff), and about ingroup lawsuits taken outside the group (6:1ff). In the second part covering questions put in the letter sent by some Corinthians, Paul deals with their concerns about having children (7:1ff), arranging marriage (7:25ff), eating foods set before images (8:1ff), and gifts of the Spirit (12:1ff); about his own idea of a collection for Jerusalem (16:1ff); and about Apollos (16:12).

Since 1 Corinthians is based on an established information exchange relation, its focus is to diagnose and to offer solutions to problems that have arisen from the

Corinthians' innovation adoption as well as to maintain their intent to adhere to the innovation they have accepted and to stabilize changes and prevent discontinuances. Hence the three main features of change-agent concern surface in the letter: Paul's attempts at problem solving for the Corinthians; the Corinthians' manner of reinventing and thus of not adhering to the innovation as Paul conceived it; the Corinthians' threatening or actually implementing discontinuance.

From the letters we can piece together the other side of this information exchange, in reality a conversation at a distance, since this is what this sort of letter is. To fill in this other side of the conversation, the reader might look for how Paul presented himself, who the recipients are, when and why they receive the letters, and the like.

This view of Corinth looks north from the Sanctuary of Demeter, on the slope of Acrocorinth. The Roman Forum is situated in front of Temple Hill to the right.

I. 1 Cor 1:1-8
Letter Opening

Superscription 1 Cor 1:1-3

1:1 Paul, called to be an apostle of Christ Jesus by the will of God, and our brother Sosthenes,

2 To the church of God that is in Corinth, to those who are sanctified in Christ Jesus, called to be saints, together with all those who in every place call on the name of our Lord Jesus Christ, both their Lord and ours:

3 Grace to you and peace from God our Father and the Lord Jesus Christ.

Textual Notes: 1 Cor 1:1-3

Hellenistic letters opened with a formula consisting of the name of the sender(s), then the addressee(s) and a greeting. These three elements are called a superscription (or prescript). The next element, connecting the superscription with the body of the letter, is called a thanksgiving. The thanksgiving was an expression of indebtedness to God for favors received. The thanksgiving consists of a statement of gratitude to God for something done in the past plus wishes by the writer for the proximate future. **Hellenistic Letter.**

1:1: "Called to be an apostle" is a grammatical construction in the passive voice. As a rule, passive voice constructions mean God is the agent of the action. IN ACCURATE Paul ascribes his change-agent role ("apostle") to the change agency of the God of Israel. See **Notes** at 1 Thess 1:1. Sosthenes is an associate and quite possibly an amanuensis of Paul in the writing of 1 Corinthians. It is difficult to determine whether this is the same person mentioned in Acts 18:17.

1:2: "Church" refers to the gathering of those summoned by God. ***Ekklēsia* (Gathering).** In this address, Paul describes the gathering of Jesus-group members in Corinth as part of the total gathering of all those called by the God of Israel, underscoring the cosmopolite quality of this gathering of Israelites. Corinthian localite behavior belongs in this broader framework, a feature the Corinthian Jesus group seems to have forgotten. Hence for Jesus-group members, there is one cosmopolite gathering with but one Lord Jesus Christ.

1:3: The usual Hellenistic greeting is "grace," while the usual Semitic greeting is "peace." Here Paul combines both, intimating the quality of the Jesus-group gathering, yet he also connects the greeting with the change agency he represents: God their Father or Patron and Messiah Jesus, whom they recognize as their Lord (see **Notes** at 1 Thess 1:1).

Thanksgiving 1 Cor 1:4-8

1:4 I give thanks to my God always for you because of the grace of God that has been given you in Christ Jesus,

5 for in every way you have been enriched in him, in speech and knowledge of every kind— 6 just as the testimony of Christ has been strengthened among you— 7 so that you are not lacking in any spiritual gift as you wait for the revealing of our Lord Jesus Christ. 8 He will also strengthen you to the end, so that you may be blameless on the day of our Lord Jesus Christ.

Textual Notes: 1 Cor 1:4-8

1:4-8: These verses form the thanksgiving and express indebtedness to God for favors received with wishes for the proximate future. The past is noted in vv. 5-6, the forthcoming in vv. 7-8.

1:6: The "testimony of Christ" is the gospel of God proclaimed by Paul. One of his primary concerns as change agent is to strengthen that adherence to this gospel, which is the innovation he communicates. Paul seeks not only to create the intent to adhere to the innovation but also to stabilize change and prevent discontinuance.

1:7-8: The gospel of God entails the proclamation of the forthcoming theocracy in Israel. The advent of that theocracy is marked by the "the revealing of our Lord Jesus Christ," the veritable "day of our Lord Jesus Christ." Paul, like Jesus, is a proclaimer of an Israelite political religion, religion embedded in a political system. Those who accepted Paul's proclamation, those who believed in Jesus Christ our Lord, formed associations for mutual support. They were support groups (not task groups) awaiting the forthcoming Israelite theocracy. The structure these associations adopted was that of the Greco-Roman household, a sort of fictive extended kin group. Yet with their faith in a forthcoming Israelite theocracy with Jesus as Lord Messiah, the values, norms, and standards of the prevailing political system of Corinth in the broader political system of the Roman Empire stood over against their hope and aspirations. This contrast between Jesus groups and society, Jesus-group gatherings and the world, is quite clear in this letter. **Political Religion.**

II. 1 Cor 1:9—6:20 Reaction to a Report from Chloe's People

This heading covers two topics, based on the report Paul received about the goings on in Jesus groups in Corinth. The first deals with cliques that have formed and thus divide the Corinthian Jesus group; this is an ingroup problem. The second topic deals with improprieties at the social border between the ingroup and the outgroup.

Section One: 1 Cor 1:9–3:23 Reported Ingroup Conflict and Reminders to Facilitate the Restoration of Harmony

Paul's treatment of this first topic is marked off as a unit by the repetition of the names of Paul, Apollos, Cephas, and Christ at the beginning and the end of the piece (an inclusion: 1:12 and 3:23). The problem Paul addresses is that of clique formation rooted in the social interactions surrounding the initiation of new members into the Jesus group of Corinth. The resulting cliques introduced division in the Corinthian gathering. **Cliques.** Paul presents a series of reminders to support unity and resolve the issue of divisions. The clustering of specific words in each part points to Paul's topics of interest, unfolding in a topical chiastic pattern:

A on baptismal clique formation (1:10-16);
  B on wisdom and baptism (1:17—2:9);
    C on the Spirit and baptism (2:10-16);
    C' on change-agent functions and baptism (3:1-15),

B' on wisdom and baptism (3:16-19);
A' on baptismal clique formation (3:20-23).

Clique Formation 1:9-16

1:9 God is faithful; by him you were called into the fellowship of his Son, Jesus Christ our Lord.

10 Now I appeal to you, brothers and sisters, by the name of our Lord Jesus Christ, that all of you be in agreement and that there be no divisions among you, but that you be united in the same mind and the same purpose. 11 For it has been reported to me by Chloe's people that there are quarrels among you, my brothers and sisters. 12 What I mean is that each of you says, "I belong to Paul," or "I belong to Apollos," or "I belong to Cephas," or "I belong to Christ." 13 Has Christ been divided? Was Paul crucified for you? Or were you baptized in the name of Paul? 14 I thank God that I baptized none of you except Crispus and Gaius, 15 so that no one can say that you were baptized in my name. 16 (I did baptize also the household of Stephanas; beyond that, I do not know whether I baptized anyone else.)

Textual Notes: 1 Cor 1:9-16

The opening verse (1:9) serves to tie in the thanksgiving with the body of the letter, thus serving as an introduction to this section, specifying the perspective through which Paul will deal with the problem he faces, the problem of divisions. Paul notes that Jesus-group membership derives from a call by the God of Israel; the gathering consists of those called (this is the meaning of *ekklēsia,* translated "church") by God, who is reliable and trustworthy. Jesus-group members are now in the "fellowship" of the resurrected Jesus and in Christ with one another. This fellowship should be characterized by agreement, by their being "united in the same mind and the same purpose." Yet there are divisions among them; they have formed cliques. **Cliques.**

A clique is a type of coalition, defined as a collection of people within some larger, encapsulating structure, consisting of distinct parties in temporary alliances for some limited purpose. Specifically, a clique is a coalition whose members associate regularly with each other on the basis of affection (shared commitment, for emotional, expressive reasons) and common interests (for pragmatic, instrumental reasons) and possess a marked sense of identity.

The problem Paul addresses is that of clique formation rooted in the social interactions surrounding the ritual introduction of members into the Jesus group of Corinth. The Corinthian membership, it seems, perceived the rite of baptism as establishing a bond between the one baptizing and those baptized. **Baptism.** The problem is the relationship between the one baptizing and the ones they baptized as well as the relationship among those baptized by the same person. In Pauline groups baptism was a ritualized symbolic action employed to put people in Christ. In this ritual new members passed from the outside into the inside of the group. The social outcome was characterized by mutual fellowship in Christ. To be "in Christ" was of the same social quality as being "in Israel." Just as one got to be "in Israel" through birth, so one gets to be "in Christ" through baptism. The focus in baptism therefore was not so much forgiveness of sin and repentance as it was in the Synoptics' story of John the Baptist.

Paul sets the theme of his argument by noting just what baptism does: it produces a belonging in Christ, who cannot be divided. It also results in sharing in the effects of Jesus' crucifixion, which is what Paul's proclamation is all about. As we learn at the conclusion of the section: "For all things are yours, whether Paul or Apollos or Cephas or the world or life or death or the present or the future—all belong to you, and you belong to Christ, and Christ belongs to God" (3:22-23). So through baptism, everything belongs to the baptized. They, in turn, belong to no one but Christ alone, who belongs to God.

1:11: Chloe was undoubtedly a Jesus-group opinion leader who could take the initiative and inform Paul of the situation at Corinth. Given Paul's description of Stephanas' activity at the close of this letter (16:15), we can assume that Stephanas too was a local opinion leader. **Opinion Leader.**

1:12: The new cast of persons introduced here include Apollos and Cephas. Apollos was a traveling Jesus-group member who was either prophet or teacher. The Corinthians explicitly asked about his coming: "Now concerning our brother Apollos, I strongly urged him to visit you with the other brothers, but he was not at all willing to come now. He will come when he has the opportunity" (16:12). "Cephas" (a transliteration of the Aramaic *Kepha'*) was the nickname given to Simon bar Jonah by Jesus (Matt 16:18; Mark 8:27-30; Luke 9:18-21). The Aramaic word was translated into Greek as "Petros." Paul almost always refers to Peter by his Aramaic nickname. This is an indication of how Paul perceives Cephas. Given Paul's ranking of Israelite Jesus-group members as either Judean or Greek (i.e., barbarian or civilized), Cephas (Peter) falls into the "Judean" category. **Jew and Greek/Judean and Hellenist.** Whether Cephas or persons authorized by Cephas were present at Corinth cannot be determined. But there were "the weak" (Judeans or uncivilized) and "the strong" (Greeks or civilized) in the Corinthian Jesus groups. It is equally possible, however, that Paul adds up the "I belong" phrases for rhetorical effect. "I belong to Christ" may be Paul's response to the first three contentions.

The Cross of Christ and Folly: Power and Wisdom 1:17–25

1:17 For Christ did not send me to baptize but to proclaim the gospel, and not with eloquent wisdom, so that the cross of Christ might not be emptied of its power.

18 For the message about the cross is foolishness to those who are perishing, but to us who are being saved it is the power of God. 19 For it is written,

"I will destroy the wisdom of the wise,
and the discernment of the
discerning I will thwart."

20 Where is the one who is wise? Where is the scribe? Where is the debater of this age? Has not God made foolish the wisdom of the world? 21 For since, in the wisdom of God, the world did not know God through wisdom, God decided, through the foolishness of our proclamation, to save those who believe.

22 For Jews demand signs and Greeks desire wisdom, 23 but we proclaim Christ crucified, a stumbling block to Jews and foolishness to Gentiles, 24 but to those who are the called, both Jews and Greeks, Christ the power of God and the wisdom of God. 25 For God's foolishness is wiser than human wisdom, and God's weakness is stronger than human strength.

Textual Notes: 1 Cor 1:17-25

The passage is marked off by the mention of wisdom and power. While power is noted a few times, the word "wisdom" in one form or another occurs some nineteen times in the passage running from 1:17–2:9. Such repetition indicates that wisdom is the concern throughout. A number of scholars hold that the relevance of the theme of wisdom here derives from the fact that the cliques in question used wisdom as a feature of their social identity. Paul does in fact demolish the value of the wisdom in question by contrasting it with the power of the cross, deriving from the wisdom of God.

Wisdom means a way of living based on and deriving from some rationale. This is what "philosophy" (Greek for "love of wisdom") was about in antiquity. Thus wisdom entailed a well-thought-out understanding of the significance of life with a plan of action about how to succeed in life. Obviously, various types of wisdom will depend on the range of life goals available in a given society. Ancient books of wisdom offer all sorts of details about how to understand and succeed in life in a meaningful, human way. So too in Israel (for example, the book of Proverbs, the Wisdom of Sirach, the Wisdom of Solomon, and the like). The Sermon on the Mount (Matthew 5–7) is a wisdom discourse that envisions success in life to derive from Torah righteousness as explained by Jesus.

The quick mention of wisdom after listing the cliques would have one think that in some way the cliques drew their boundaries on the basis of the wisdom position of their members. In context, Paul labels cliquish wisdom as the wisdom of the world, that is the wisdom available in Hellenistic society. Such ways of understanding life and living based on some philosophy were to be found in popular Stoicism, Platonism, and the like. Philosophical groups in antiquity were concerned with ways of living based on their understanding of the meaning of life.

1:17: Paul is a change agent sent to proclaim an innovation, not to preside at initiation rites of group formation (the ending of Matthew's gospel, Matt 28:16-20, presents a different scenario). In his gospel of God, Jesus was crucified by Judeans and raised by the God of Israel "for us," that is, in order to save from the "wrath of God," those who believe this divine intervention. The "wrath of God" refers to God's taking satisfaction to defend his honor in the face of repeated acts of shame and dishonor (sin) on the part of Israelites. **Wrath.** Given the collectivistic quality of first-century Mediterranean society, in the light of God's raising Jesus, it was rather obvious that Jesus' crucifixion was not just exclusive, personal, and individual with Jesus. Rather it had inclusive, communal, and collective dimensions for both Jesus and those who believed in the significance of that event, that is, the "holy ones" of Israel (see 1 Cor 1:2: the Corinthians and all Jesus-group members are "called to be saints," that is, holy ones). Jesus' crucifixion served to unleash the power of God in Jesus' resurrection that rescues all who believe in what God did from the forthcoming wrath. Paul's proclamation was straightforward, without any pretense of wisdom-filled rhetoric, so that the cross of Christ, that is, Jesus' crucifixion, might not be emptied of its significance. The point is that attraction to Paul's proclamation cannot be ascribed to communication techniques, called "rhetoric" in antiquity.

1:17: "Eloquent wisdom" (NRSV) here means "wordy wisdom," wisdom that has its effects because of its style of presentation (rhetoric) and not because of its actual content and meaning. Rhetoric in antiquity was much like advertising techniques of the twenty-first century. The goal of ancient rhetoric was to have some sort of persuasive effect on an audience.

1:18: The significance (NRSV: "message"; Greek: *logos*; signifies speech expressing meaning, reason, account) of the cross to outsiders is foolishness; to insiders it is power. Curiously, the opposite of folly or foolishness here is power, not wisdom. The concrete power of the cross is that it saves believing Israelites from God's necessary satisfaction, soon to take effect.

Folly or foolishness means lack of good sense or normal prudence. In an adult, it is a quality typical of persons without honor, persons who do not care about their reputation. Foolish persons are shameless. Folly or foolishness points to a lack of influence, a lack of the ability to have effect on others with appropriate knowledge, reasons, or information. For example, it is folly for a plumber to offer medical advice about cancer since a plumber lacks medical knowledge or pertinent medical information. Power, on the other hand, is the ability to produce some effect backed by a sanction of force; here it is the effect of disengaging and releasing persons from God's wrath.

1:19: Three times in this section Paul explicitly cites Israel's sacred scriptures to bolster his argument (here; 1:31; 2:9). Obviously his use of Israel's scriptures is meant to carry weight with his Corinthian Jesus group, indicating their Israelite socialization through which they appreciate Israel's scriptures as the word of God.

The first citation is from Isa 29:14, cited from the Greek version of Israel's sacred writings called the Septuagint (LXX). The passage indicates that the God of Israel has already acted in a way that nullifies the prevailing social wisdom. If God would not have wanted to confound the wisdom of the wise, he would not have chosen Jesus' crucifixion to trigger and access divine power.

1:20: The rhetorical question "where is X" to demonstrate the inability and impotence of some person or thing is common in Israel's scriptures. Isa 19:12: "Where are your wise men?" Isa 33:18: "Where is he who counted? Where is he who weighed the tribute? Where is he who counted the towers?" Baruch 3:16: "Where are the princes of the nations?" In this last passage, Israelite wisdom is identified with "the commandments of life," that is, the Torah. Here the persons judged to be incapable and impotent are the wise man (philosopher), the scribe (Torah expert), and the social critic or sophist of this age.

1:20: The words "age" (Greek: *aiōn*, time period) and "world" (Greek: *kosmos*, the created order) both refer to God's creation. The Hebrew world *'olam* covers both the temporal and the spatial qualities of God's creation, meaning "time period" or "world." In the New Testament the word "world" means both the physical world created by God, that is, the earth and the sky and all that inhabit them, and society, that is, first-century Mediterranean society, comprising all persons, human, demonic, and angelic. First-century Mediterranean people believed that the created order (this age, this world) was in a process of devolution; it was running down. **Devolution.** Israelites shared this perspective, but Israelites did not believe the world would end, since God created it good and as the scriptures taught, "the earth remains forever" (Eccles 1:4). After creation runs down, it will somehow start over again. Thus the phrase "this age," a temporal phrase, or "this world," a spatial phrase, referred to this running-down phase. The wise men, Torah interpreters, and sophists of this age pale in comparison with what the crucifixion of Jesus reveals and what it portends. God has reduced the wisdom available in society as we know it to an obvious lack of good sense or normal prudence. Hence those who pursue that wisdom are like dishonorable people, shameless and without concern for their reputation. That is quite significant in a society concerned with honor and shame. **Honor-Shame Societies.**

1:21: The word "for" almost always gives the reason for what was just said. The reason, then, for the scriptural assessment of prevailing social wisdom and for Paul's adopting this assessment is that it pleased God to save those who believe in Jesus crucified from the wrath that is coming soon. Paul's gospel proclaims the crucified Jesus, surely something foolish in terms of societal wisdom, yet this is the wisdom of God, which the philosophers and Torah experts could not possibly come to know by means of their wisdom.

1:22-23: These verses indicate that Paul has in mind the two types of Israelites that constitute the Corinthian gathering: Judeans and their Torah experts and Hellenists and their philosophical viewpoints. The NRSV translation of *Ioudaios* as "Jew" is totally misleading. The word means a person and/or social behavior deriving from Judea, hence Judean. "Greek" is likewise misleading since there was no Greek nation or Greece in the first century. To call a person a "Greek" meant that he or she was civilized. We translate the NRSV phrase "Jew and Greek" as "Judean and Hellenist," meaning barbarian and civilized Israelite. **Jew and Greek/ Judean and Hellenist.** The phrase covers the whole range of Israelites with whom Paul interacts. In the social stereotypes of the day, Judean Israelites are identified as barbarians, lacking in the refinements of Hellenistic culture, while Hellenistic Israelites are identified as civilized, Greek speakers, versed to some extent in the ways of Hellenism. Each has his or her own type of difficulty with Paul's gospel, since when it comes to the will of God, Judeans seek signs of power that would point to God's presence, while Hellenists seek philosophically cogent arguments to underpin a way of life that would make sense to any reasonable person. Christ crucified hardly provides either!

1:23: The crucified Jesus is surely not a sign of God's power, hence the crucifixion proves to be a stumbling block, a scandal or detour to Judean expectations. And it surely lacks good sense and is downright shameful for Hellenistic civilized tastes. The NRSV translates: "but we proclaim Christ crucified, a stumbling block to Jews and foolishness to Gentiles." However, coupling "Jews and Gentiles" disturbs the parallelism of the next sentence speaking of "Jews and Greeks." And "Greeks" does not mean "Gentiles." In fact the word *ethnē*—translated "Gentiles" in the NRSV—is not found in a number of good manuscripts, and from those manuscripts we adopt the reading "Judeans and Hellenists" thus:

"but we proclaim Christ crucified, a stumbling block to Judeans [barbarians] and foolishness to Hellenists [civilized]."

1:24-25: Those called by the God of Israel comprise both Judean and Hellenistic Israelites, for whom Jesus crucified is God's power to offset the wrath of God and God's wisdom pointing to a way of meaningful human living. Thus the paradox: the crucified Jesus is God's foolishness and God's weakness yet wiser and stronger than anything human society can offer. As change agent, Paul confronts the problem of ingroup cliques by demonstrating how power and wisdom actually derive from Christ crucified, whom he proclaims.

Paul continues his paradoxical thinking in the next consideration, the social status of the Corinthian Jesus group.

Reminder about Social Status 1:26-31

1:26 Consider your own call, brothers and sisters: not many of you were wise by human standards, not many were powerful, not many were of noble birth. 27 But God chose what is foolish in the world to shame the wise; God chose what is weak in the world to shame the strong; 28 God chose what is low and despised in the world, things that are not, to reduce to nothing things that are, 29 so that no one might boast in the presence of God. 30 He is the source of your life in Christ Jesus, who became for us wisdom from God, and righteousness and sanctification and redemption, 31 in order that, as it is written, "Let the one who boasts, boast in the Lord."

Textual Notes: 1 Cor 1:26-31

Paul now sets out a third category that served to mark off social distinction and hence serve as a basis for cliques. To the wisdom and power of the previous argument, he now introduces noble birth. Wisdom and power lead to acquired honor, while noble birth provides ascribed honor. **Honor-Shame Societies.** Among the Corinthian Israelites who adopted God's innovation proclaimed by Paul, "not many" shared in the outgroup honor ratings.

Paul's paragraph here is a refrain built on Jer 9:23-24: "Let not the wise man glory in his wisdom, let not the powerful man glory in his power, let not the wealthy man glory in his wealth; but let him who glories glory in this, that he understands and knows me, that I am the LORD who practices steadfast love, justice, and righteousness in the earth; for in these things I delight, says the LORD." Paul substitutes Jeremiah's third element, the wealthy, with noble born. And the three attributes practiced by God (steadfast love, justice, and righteousness), that is, God's wisdom, are ascribed to the crucified Jesus, the source of the Jesus group's living (that is, wisdom) in Christ! "Glory," a word that belongs to the semantic field of honor, refers to the external or outward features surrounding some person that reveal that person's honor ranking in the community. "To glory in" means to take some external or outward feature as indicator of one's honor ranking.

1:27: Again the "world" is society at large, here specifically, the Israelite community of Corinth. The Corinthian Israelites chosen by the God of Israel were rated foolish, weak, and low and were despised by other members of the Israelite community of Corinth. That only Israelites are at issue seems to be the case, since their joining the Jesus group led to God's dishonoring the wise, the strong, and the noble among their fellow Israelites. The God of Israel, as a rule, does not bother with outsiders and non-Israelites. They simply do not count, since they do not stand in the presence of God and cannot boast before God at all (1:29). Such behavior is typical of Israelites alone.

1:29: To boast refers to the acceptable Mediterranean practice of publicly making claims in relation to one's honor.

1:30-31: Paul's citation of Israel's scripture (Jer 9:23-24, also found in LXX 1 Kgs 2:10) again points to an Israelite audience that can appreciate such references. In that passage God's wisdom is revealed in God's practice of steadfast love, justice, and righteousness. Here the crucified Jesus, source of the life that human wisdom seeks, is God's wisdom for us. Paul makes no reference to Jesus' sayings and deeds as found in the Synoptics or John. For Paul, the crucified Jesus is not only wisdom but righteousness for us, sanctification for us, and redemption for us. "Righteousness" means the privileged social identity of being a Jesus-group member. The norms associated with righteousness defined proper interpersonal relationships between humans and God as well as between humans themselves; Jesus demonstrated such righteousness on our behalf on the cross. Further, sanctification means distinctiveness, the quality of being set apart, of being exclusive. It is in Christ that those who believe in him become holy, set apart for God, distinctive. Finally, redemption means the restoration of family or group honor, and it is this honor that Jesus restores through his dying for us and thus allaying the threat of God's just wrath.

Reminder about the Circumstances of Their Innovation Adoption 1 Cor 2:1-9

2:1 When I came to you, brothers and sisters, I did not come proclaiming the mystery of God to you in lofty words or wisdom. 2 For I decided to know nothing among you except Jesus Christ, and him crucified. 3 And I came to you in weakness and in fear and in much trembling. 4 My speech and my proclamation were not with plausible words of wisdom, but with a demonstration of the Spirit and of power, 5 so that your faith might rest not on human wisdom but on the power of God.

6 Yet among the mature we do speak wisdom, though it is not a wisdom of this age or of the rulers of this age, who are doomed to perish. 7 But we speak God's wisdom, secret and hidden, which God decreed before the ages for our glory. 8 None of the rulers of this age understood this; for if they had, they would not have crucified the Lord of glory. 9 But, as it is written,

"What no eye has seen, nor ear heard,
nor the human heart conceived,
what God has prepared for those who
love him."

Textual Notes: 1 Cor 2:1-9

2:1: Paul now reminds the Corinthians of how he approached them as change agent informing them of the innovation he wished them to adopt. That innovation is the gospel of God, here called the mystery of God. He brings up the point, it seems, to demonstrate that it was not as wisdom teacher of philosophy that he proclaimed this gospel, and it was not because of its wisdom potential, its philosophical rationale, that they adopted it. Rather their adoption of this innovation happened due to the remarkable altered state of consciousness experiences they had, that is, experiences of the Spirit. **Altered States of Consciousness.**

2:2-3: This description of Paul's communication style reflects Jesus crucified: weak, in fear, trembling, without persuasive wise words, but with tangible demonstration of God's Spirit and power (which God's raising of the crucified Jesus let loose on those who believe).

2:4: The result of this way of communicating the innovation wrought by the God of Israel was that the Corinthians' trust in God did not derive from human wisdom but from the power of God demonstrated in Jesus' resurrection and Corinthian altered states of consciousness experiences.

2:5-8: Paul now briefly describes the wisdom typical of committed believers. It is a way of life rooted in the fact that those who believe are in that situation because God decreed it, to our honor, before creation was complete. Paul knows that God decreed it because it has happened. One can be certain of what God decrees after the event, not before. Paul has this viewpoint from his Pharisee ideology, a sort of after-the-fact predestination. But this is not the wisdom available in contemporary society, controlled by the rulers of this age. These rulers (Greek: *archontes*) are those persons who produce the effects that make society to be the way it is. To understand this point, two cultural truisms of the time have to be taken into account. The first is that every significant effect in a person's or group's existence is caused by a personal cause, whether that person is human or nonhuman. The second truism is that the cosmos is populated with nonhuman persons, most often not even visible, who have an effect on human personal and social life. These nonhuman persons include stars (constellated or not), planets, and a range of demons, whom Semites called angels and spirits, Greek-speakers called demons, and Romans called genii. The rulers of this world are those human and nonhuman persons who effectively exert control on society as presently experienced. Of course, in the present devolutionary perspective, these rulers and the societies they control are devolving, doomed to perish.

2:8: Previously in his letter to the Thessalonian gathering, Paul noted that it was the Judeans who killed Jesus, as they did other prophets before him (1 Thess 2:15). Now he notes that it was the rulers of this age who were responsible for that action. There is no contradiction in this, since the rulers of this age rule by controlling people who do their bidding.

Yet these same rulers, human and cosmic, did not understand the implications of their actions in the plan of God decided before creation. To prove this point, Paul again has recourse to Israel's scriptures. The source of this citation is not clear, although it resonates with Isa 64:4. Paul's presentation of this citation makes it clear that what the gospel of God involves is what God has prepared, specifically for those who love God. It is love for God that is the linchpin of the rationale behind Jesus-group wisdom. And love or personal attachment requires loving actions that reveal that attachment, since in the ancient Mediterranean all the words describing internal states (for example, love, know, hate, desire) always entail some corresponding external actions (love = personal attachment; knowledge = concrete experience; hate = negative deeds; desire = taking something).

Reminder about the Spirit 1 Cor 2:10-16

2:10 These things God has revealed to us
through the Spirit; for the Spirit searches
everything, even the depths of God.
11 For what human being knows what is
truly human except the human spirit that is
within? So also no one comprehends what
is truly God's except the Spirit of God.
12 Now we have received not the spirit of the
world, but the Spirit that is from God, so that
we may understand the gifts bestowed on
us by God. 13 And we speak of these things
in words not taught by human wisdom but
taught by the Spirit, interpreting spiritual
things to those who are spiritual.
14 Those who are unspiritual do not
receive the gifts of God's Spirit, for they are
foolishness to them, and they are unable to
understand them because they are spiritually discerned. 15 Those who are spiritual
discern all things, and they are themselves
subject to no one else's scrutiny.
16 "For who has known the mind of
the Lord
so as to instruct him?"
But we have the mind of Christ.

Textual Notes: 1 Cor 2:10-16

Paul continues his discussion of wisdom, this time expanding on the means by which Jesus-group members come to understand the wisdom they have received. Note the repetition of terms here that deal with the process of investigating meanings: revealed, searches (investigates), knows, comprehends, understand, interpreting, taught, discern. The means afforded Jesus-group members in their interpretative task is God's Spirit, which they have received thanks to the outcome of Jesus' crucifixion. The word "spirit" (Greek: *pneuma*) means, literally, wind, blast of air, breeze; secondarily the word describes the wind proceeding from living beings, hence life-breath, breath. Given the lack of meteorological information, the ancients perceived the winds as having their effect in unknown and unknowable ways; they blow where and when they will and can produce unbelievably overwhelming effects (e.g., as cyclone or windstorm). For the ancients the wind was an uncontrollable and overwhelming force. This experience of the wind was applied by analogy to describe the activity of God. God's Wind, God's Spirit, is such an unbelievably overwhelming power producing incredible effects as God wills. God's Spirit refers to the divine activity. Invisible, personal forces that produced effects affecting human beings were ascribed to invisible persons, called demons in Greek but spirits in Semitic languages. One must be able to discern spirits, whether the Spirit of God or other spirits, and among these latter, whether good ones or not. The presence and quality of spirits are known by their effects. If there are no effects, there obviously are no spirits present. Finally, the spirit of human beings refers to their life-breath, the life that courses through their being.

2:10: The wisdom that Jesus-group members share comes through revelations effected by the Spirit of God. Such revelations take place in what we today call "altered states of consciousness," a human experience the ancients ascribed to the

Spirit or spirits. **Altered States of Consciousness.** And such revelations need to be interpreted.

2:11-12: Paul offers a comparison: just as human beings know what they experience through the human spirit or life-breath that courses through their being, so to know divine things the divine spirit must examine and clarify those things. Jesus gatherings have received this Spirit from God to assist them in living, to examine and clarify the significance of a meaningful life (wisdom), something that prevailing societal wisdom cannot do.

2:13-15: The main theme here is to explain how Jesus-group members come to their wisdom. Normally wisdom is the outcome of study, of investigation, of research put into daily practice and thus tested. The Spirit likewise examines and clarifies the significance of God's favors distributed among Jesus-group members in a range of practical deeds (see 1 Corinthians 12). Since revelations come through the Spirit (these are the spiritual things Paul speaks of) and since the interpretation of these revelations comes through the Spirit of God, Jesus-group members are in fact taught by the Spirit. Those who do not have altered states of consciousness experiences typical of Paul's gatherings are the unspiritual; they do not receive what the Spirit gives (the NRSV mentions "gifts" here, a word not in the Greek of v. 14). The unspiritual are considered foolish, incomprehensible, or, as we might say, irrational. Those who have altered states of consciousness experiences in Jesus-group group gatherings are capable of discerning what is going on; outsiders simply cannot understand.

2:16: Again Paul bolsters his contention with a scriptural citation from Isa 40:13: "For who has known the mind of the Lord so as to instruct him?" He then concludes with an emphatic: *we* (Jesus-group members) have the mind of Christ. As Paul often does, he selectively interprets the Old Testament word "Lord" as referring to the God of Israel or to the Lord Jesus Christ, as here. It is the mind of Christ, our wisdom and source of life, that the Spirit interprets for us.

A Comparison Based on Feeding, Farming, and Construction 3:1-23

3:1 And so, brothers and sisters, I could not speak to you as spiritual people, but rather as people of the flesh, as infants in Christ. 2 I fed you with milk, not solid food, for you were not ready for solid food. Even now you are still not ready, 3 for you are still of the flesh. For as long as there is jealousy and quarreling among you, are you not of the flesh, and behaving according to human inclinations? 4 For when one says, "I belong to Paul," and another, "I belong to Apollos," are you not merely human?

5 What then is Apollos? What is Paul? Servants through whom you came to believe, as the Lord assigned to each. 6 I planted, Apollos watered, but God gave the growth. 7 So neither the one who plants nor the one who waters is anything, but only God who gives the growth. 8 The one who plants and the one who waters have a common purpose, and each will receive wages according to the labor of each. 9 For we are God's servants, working together; you are God's field, God's building.

10 According to the grace of God given to me, like a skilled master builder I laid a foundation, and someone else is building on it. Each builder must choose with care how to build on it. 11 For no one can lay any foundation other than the one that has

been laid; that foundation is Jesus Christ.
12 Now if anyone builds on the foundation with gold, silver, precious stones,
wood, hay, straw— 13 the work of each
builder will become visible, for the Day
will disclose it, because it will be revealed
with fire, and the fire will test what sort
of work each has done. 14 If what has
been built on the foundation survives,
the builder will receive a reward. 15 If
the work is burned up, the builder will
suffer loss; the builder will be saved,
but only as through fire. 16 Do you not
know that you are God's temple and that
God's Spirit dwells in you? 17 If anyone
destroys God's temple, God will destroy
that person. For God's temple is holy, and
you are that temple. 18 Do not deceive
yourselves. If you think that you are wise
in this age, you should become fools so
that you may become wise. 19 For the
wisdom of this world is foolishness with
God. For it is written,

"He catches the wise in their craftiness,"

20 and again,

"The Lord knows the thoughts of
the wise,
that they are futile."

21 So let no one boast about human leaders.
For all things are yours, 22 whether Paul
or Apollos or Cephas or the world or life
or death or the present or the future—all
belong to you, 23 and you belong to Christ,
and Christ belongs to God.

Textual Notes: 1 Cor 3:1-23

Paul takes up the question of the cliques at Corinth, characterized by quarreling (1:11 and here 3:3) and here further expanded to include rivalry. With all the space he dedicates to wisdom, the bone of contention among the groups must relate to wisdom in some way. He has argued that Jesus-group wisdom comes solely from God, through Christ crucified, by means of the Spirit of God. All other wisdom, no matter to whom it may be ascribed, is outgroup wisdom, the wisdom of society at large, the wisdom of the world.

3:1-4: In Paul's analysis, this problem has arisen due to the Corinthians' lack of maturity in the ways of Jesus-group living. His contrast between being spiritual and being fleshly leads to an analogy from human development. When Paul came to them and proclaimed the innovation of the gospel of God, they were "flesh" people, like infants who could only ingest milk, not solid food. And their agonistic attitude revealed in ingroup envy and quarreling further reveals they are still "of the flesh." Paul describes the "flesh" as behaving in an entirely human way, rather than as open to God and the ramifications of the gospel of God. The contrast between flesh and spirit is a common one (see Gal 5:13-26 for a fuller explanation). "Flesh" frequently refers to human beings as weak, as mortal, hence as unlike God, even as closed to God and what God wishes. "Spirit," on the other hand, refers to human beings as full of the force of life, as strong and open to God and what pleases God. Paul, it seems, did not explain the ramifications of the gospel of God adequately. Further, the Corinthians did not comprehend the role of the various change agents and their assistants with whom they have had contact. The case in point has to do with Paul, the founding "father" of the Corinthian gathering, and Apollos, either a change agent himself or a follow-up prophet or teacher. In this passage, Paul clarifies the situation. In v. 4 Paul specifies the proof of his analysis: the clique formation among the Corinthians. To demonstrate that the conflicting Corinthians have it wrong, Paul presents two further analogies: from agriculture and from building construction.

3:5-9: Paul describes himself and Apollos as God's servants or middle men (*diakonoi*), with tasks assigned to each by God. Paul planted; he was the change agent who originally proclaimed the gospel of God. Apollos watered either as teacher or as prophet. The important point, though, is that it is God who gives growth. If life exists and thrives, that is God's doing. And that is paramount reality. For the Corinthians are God's field (a territory marked off by God) on which God's coworkers labor. At the end Paul attaches another image, that of a building.

Here four fragments of a letter from Emperor Claudius, arranged to represent their original positions in the inscription, include a mention of the proconsul Lucius Junius Gallio, who also appears in Acts 18:12-17. Scholars use this inscription, along with the account found in Acts 18:1-18, to date Paul's mission in Corinth to early 50 through 51, when he met Gallio.

3:10-16: With the analogy comparing the Corinthian Jesus group to a building, Paul seeks to demolish the very notion of clique. After all, thanks to God's commissioning him, Paul laid the building's foundation, none other than Jesus Christ. Others then build on it, but always on the selfsame foundation. Later construction is significant and will be assessed and rewarded when the Lord Jesus comes from the sky, "the Day will disclose it." Fire is a symbol of judgment; hence fire will test the value of the later construction. Good work will pass the fire test and be rewarded. Flimsy work will be destroyed. Significantly, Paul who lays the foundation stands outside this testing procedure.

3:16-17: These verses specify the quality of that building. It is a temple. The ancients believed that God (and the gods) actually dwelt in the sky, yet on occasion, God (gods) visited devotees at an exclusive place called a temple, which marked the earth end of a vertical axis between the realm of God and that of humans, where the divine and human touched and could interact. The Corinthian gathering now is that temple of God where God's power is to be found. Note that the word "you" here is plural (Greek *en hymin, hymeis*). The Corinthians need not be concerned about the Jerusalem Temple or pilgrimage or whatever is bound up with Israelite Temple worship, since what that temple offers can be experienced in their gathering. And just as destroying a temple is an offense against God's honor, a sacrilege, so too is the destruction of the Corinthian gathering. Such destruction is the outcome of cliques.

3:18-20: Paul now returns to the underlying theme of this whole discussion, wisdom, contrasting being wise in this age, the wisdom of the world, which is foolishness with God (as noted previously). Once more, proof comes from Israel's sacred scripture: Job 5:13 and Ps 94:11.

3:21-23: The fact is that through baptism, everything belongs to the Corinthian Jesus-group members. Consequently they belong to no one, but to Christ alone who belongs to God. The whole concept of cliques and of belonging to someone other than Christ is simply foolish.

These verses form an inclusion with the opening of the passage (1:10) and bring it to a close.

Reflections on the Role of Change Agents 4:1-13

4:1 Think of us in this way, as servants of Christ and stewards of God's mysteries. 2 Moreover, it is required of stewards that they be found trustworthy. 3 But with me it is a very small thing that I should be judged by you or by any human court. I do not even judge myself. 4 I am not aware of anything against myself, but I am not thereby acquitted. It is the Lord who judges me. 5 Therefore do not pronounce judgment before the time, before the Lord comes, who will bring to light the things now hidden in darkness and will disclose the purposes of the heart. Then each one will receive commendation from God.

6 I have applied all this to Apollos and myself for your benefit, brothers and sisters, so that you may learn through us the meaning of the saying, "Nothing beyond what is written," so that none of you will be puffed up in favor of one against another. 7 For who sees anything different in you? What do you have that you did not receive? And if you received it, why do you boast as if it were not a gift?

8 Already you have all you want! Already you have become rich! Quite apart from us you have become kings! Indeed, I wish that you had become kings, so that we might be kings with you! 9 For I think that God has exhibited us apostles as last of all, as though sentenced to death, because we have become a spectacle to the world, to angels and to mortals. 10 We are fools for the sake of Christ, but you are wise in Christ. We are weak, but you are strong. You are held in honor, but we in disrepute. 11 To the present hour we are hungry and thirsty, we are poorly clothed and beaten and homeless, 12 and we grow weary from the work of our own hands. When reviled, we bless; when persecuted, we endure; 13 when slandered, we speak kindly. We have become like the rubbish of the world, the dregs of all things, to this very day.

Textual Notes: 1 Cor 4:1-13

4:1: The opening sentence of this section presumes an implied clause such as "Instead of forming cliques in the name of various change agents and their assistants," think of us in this way. Paul again argues against Corinthian clique formation by explaining what is involved in being a change agent. He uses the analogy of a household manager or steward (Greek: *oikonomos*). Change agents and their assistants are like household managers (stewards) of the gospel of God, what Paul calls God's mysteries. As household managers, all that counts is that the owner of the household finds them trustworthy and capable in fulfilling their appointed tasks. What other people think really does not matter. So the Corinthians ought not to pass judgment on the relative merits of Paul or Apollos, a judgment that undergirds clique formation. That judgment belongs to God, the owner, and it will be rendered when the Lord comes (v. 5).

4:6: Minimally, Paul says he has used the foregoing analogies about himself and Apollos so that the Corinthians would see the truth of the saying "nothing beyond what is written." The meaning of the saying is disputed. Yet we know that it is meant to show that no one has any basis for claiming superiority over another. In the limited-goods society of Paul and the Corinthians, the statement would mean: don't make exaggerated claims, "nothing in excess." A further reason for this comes in the next sentence.

4:7: To prove that they are not really that different from one another, Paul cites a cultural truism: Everything we have comes from others. In the collectivistic society of Paul and his Jesus groups, the most significant determinants of who or what a person is derives from outside the individual person. It is these determinants that the ancients believed were worth knowing and noting. Everyone was an "other-made" man or woman. A person is never permitted to forget that everything in life that counts has been received from others in one's family, from patrons, and from neighbors. For the most part, what situates a person socially befalls the person or happens to the person. Achievements flow from ascribed status and are not produced by the individual achiever as we understand "self-made" persons. Instead of a "vanity wall" with plaques marking personal accomplishments such as we might see in our society, the first-century Mediterranean would feature masks, busts, and memorials of ancestors who made them to be who they were, thanks, of course, to the God(s) of these ancestors.

4:8-13: Paul moves on to put down Corinthian pretensions, moving from the singular "you" of the previous truism to the plural. The opening statement is rather derisive, ranking the Corinthians with societal elites and placing the change agents in the lowest possible social stratum. Like the 2 percent elites of the day, the Corinthians already have everything they want: they are rich; they have power; they are wise and strong and honorable. Yet in comparison, the gospel change agents are like the throwaway people at the very bottom of the status system: fools, weak, in disrepute, hungry, thirsty, shabbily dressed, beaten, homeless, weary, reviled, slandered, rubbish, dregs.

Conclusion and Travel Plans 4:14-21

14 I am not writing this to make you ashamed, but to admonish you as my beloved children. 15 For though you might have ten thousand guardians in Christ, you do not have many fathers. Indeed, in Christ Jesus I became your father through the gospel. 16 I appeal to you, then, be imitators of me. 17 For this reason I sent you Timothy, who is my beloved and faithful child in the Lord, to remind you of my ways in Christ Jesus, as I teach them everywhere in every church. 18 But some of you, thinking that I am not coming to you, have become arrogant. 19 But I will come to you soon, if the Lord wills, and I will find out not the talk of these arrogant people but their power. 20 For the kingdom of God depends not on talk but on power. 21 What would you prefer? Am I to come to you with a stick, or with love in a spirit of gentleness?

Textual Notes: 1 Cor 4:17-21

4:14-16: While Paul says he does not wish to shame the Corinthian clique adherents, he surely does so. We find out eventually why he does so—because they act arrogantly; hence they challenge Paul's honor and those of others in the group who are not "wise." Every challenge requires a riposte, and this is Paul's. **Challenge-Riposte.** And yet, since this is an ingroup interaction, the goal is not simply to shame the other person but to mend ingroup relations. As Paul notes, his real goal is to admonish his "beloved children." As the first change agent to proclaim the gospel of God to them, Paul is like their father, not like a guardian. A guardian (Greek: *paidagogos*) was a person, often a slave, whose task it was to accompany children and youths to and from their place of learning and to supervise their conduct in general. It was those who came after Paul who were like family guardians, that is, the traveling prophets and teachers. "Ten thousand" is "myriad" in Greek, the name for the largest number, like our million or billion used to be. There was no zero in ancient number systems yet. And so as a father, Paul would have his children imitate him and not reinvent the innovation he proclaimed to them.

4:16-17: In pursuing his change-agent task, Paul uses a letter (1 Cor 5:9) as well as his assistant, Timothy, in place of a letter to maintain the information exchange relation so necessary for the successful communication of an innovation. The problem is to deal with the reinventions that occur and to stabilize the Corinthians' intent to change while preventing discontinuance. Reinvention here has taken the form of clique formation with a refocusing on "wisdom." In Paul's diagnosis, the root of the problem is arrogance (vv. 18-19 and previously v. 6; also 5:2.). Arrogance is an exaggeration of one's own worth or importance in an overbearing manner. The Corinthians' presumptuous claims to wisdom are an indication of such arrogance. In an honor-shame society, arrogance is always a challenge to the honor of persons higher in social standing. In context, that person is Paul, God's authorized change agent.

4:18-19: Some Corinthians are willing to challenge Paul's honor since they do not believe he will come to them again. Such a challenge is really folly, since should Paul return as he hopes, the arrogant challenge will be deflated, and all involved will be utterly dishonored. **Honor-Shame Societies.**

4:20-21: What is at issue is power—having effect on other people through the sanction of force. And the forthcoming Israelite theocracy is about power, the power of God in and through Christ, already manifest in various altered states of consciousness phenomena. So Paul tells the Corinthians to back down and let him exercise his authority with the gentleness of one attached to group members, that is, love.

Section Two: 1 Cor 5:1–6:20
Reported Complacency with a Case of Ingroup Incest and Directives for Dealing with It

This section consists of three parts in an A-B-A' pattern. 5:1-13 deals with an instance of *porneia*, translated as "sexual immorality." ***Porneia.*** 6:2-13 deals with lawsuits; 6:14-20 returns to the case of sexual immorality with which the section opened.

The Problem: Corinthian Complacency about Ingroup Incest 5:1-8

5:1 It is actually reported that there is sexual immorality among you, and of a kind that is not found even among pagans; for a man is living with his father's wife. 2 And you are arrogant! Should you not rather have mourned, so that he who has done this would have been removed from among you? 3 For though absent in body, I am present in spirit; and as if present I have already pronounced judgment 4 in the name of the Lord Jesus on the man who has done such a thing. When you are assembled, and my spirit is present with the power of our Lord Jesus, 5 you are to hand this man over to Satan for the destruction of the flesh, so that his spirit may be saved in the day of the Lord. 6 Your boasting is not a good thing. Do you not know that a little yeast leavens the whole batch of dough? 7 Clean out the old yeast so that you may be a new batch, as you really are unleavened. For our paschal lamb, Christ, has been sacrificed. 8 Therefore, let us celebrate the festival, not with the old yeast, the yeast of malice and evil, but with the unleavened bread of sincerity and truth.

Textual Notes: 1 Cor 5:1-8

5:1: Paul has received a report about one of the Jesus-group members at Corinth having entered a conjugal union with his stepmother. Such behavior is clearly forbidden in the Israelite tradition (Lev 18:8; 20:11) in a list of sexual prohibitions that constitute *porneia* (Greek, translated "sexual immorality").

Paul's repetition of this word and its cognates make it obvious that the theme of this section is the problem of this *porneia* (see 5:1 twice, 9, 10, 11; 6:9, 13, 15, 16, 18 twice). Such a stepmother/stepson conjugal union was also forbidden by Roman law (Gaius, *Institutes* 1.63). However, the terms Paul uses to rid the group of the person in question (5:2, 5, 7, 13) all come from the Israelite tradition (Deut 17:7; 19:9; 22:24), so it seems Paul thinks in that context.

He mentions that this sort of behavior was not even found among non-Israelites (*ethnos*, NRSV: "pagans"; often "Gentiles"). The Greek word *ethnos* has a range of meanings but always refers to a group whose members have something in common: company of soldiers, a body of persons; a race, tribe; a people, a particular class or category of persons; a caste or status cohort; a province (outgroup, outsiders of city), association (of gravediggers), collegium. What all humans have in common relative to Israel is that they are not Israelites. Hence the translation "pagan" or "Gentile" should be dropped in favor of "non-Israelites." In Paul, the word is most often used to describe the counterfoil to Israel. The Greek term seems to be dependent on the Hebrew usage for non-Israelites, *goyim*, meaning "peoples (other than Israelites)" as a rule. Consequently it means a group whose members have this in common, that they are not Israelites. Perhaps the best translation of the word in such contexts is simply "non-Israelites." The translation "pagan" is quite off track, since the Latin *paganus* means villagers, people living outside cities, hence backward and boorish people; it was applied as an outgroup term to non-Christians only in the fourth century C.E. To retroject it to the first century with the meaning of non-Israelites is both anachronistic and erroneous.

Paul's labeling of the outgroup as *ethnē* (non-Israelites) further points to the Corinthians as Israelites, since the contrast is between Israelites and non-Israelites.

5:2: The Corinthians' allowing such *porneia* in their midst is ascribed to their arrogance. Paul would have them "mourn." Mourning is a ritualized process of self-humiliation, the opposite of arrogance. In the mourning ritual mourners protest the presence of evil before God by means of fasting, vigil, wearing sackcloth, and looking unkempt and unwashed. They take on the demeanor of beggars, begging God to remove the evil with which they are afflicted. Israelite custom included the practice of ritualized mourning in the face of social disaster, largely political in character (see Isa 58:3-6; Jer 14:12; Joel 1:14; also 1 Kgs 21:9, 12; 2 Chron 20:3; Ezra 8:21; Esther 4:16). The reasoning behind such behavior is that if a fellow human being would give assistance to me when I (and my family) humiliate myself, then all the more so will God give assistance.

Paul's command is that this person is to be removed from the community. That the problem is the presence of evil is indicated by the explicit allusion to scriptural directives calling for the removal of Torah transgressors by death ("to remove evil from the midst of you/from Israel"; Deut 17:7; 19:9; 21:21; 22:21, 22, 24; 24:7). Paul explicitly cites this passage in v. 13. In the Torah, the removal in question implies death by community stoning.

5:3-5: This passage describes a removal or purging ritual to take place when the Corinthians next gather. Paul, the authorized change agent, has passed judgment. In the New Testament, "to judge" normally connotes negative judgment, hence condemnation. Paul's task is to stabilize the group in behaviors desired by the change agency, God. To this end, he follows the scriptural injunction and would have the Corinthians expel the person in question. What is to happen is a sort of hexing, with Paul present "in spirit" and armed with the power of the Lord Jesus. Spirit and power are synonymous, and both imply some action, here handing over the guilty party to Satan (instead of stoning him as required in the Torah).

Concerning Satan, see **Notes** at 1 Thess 2:18. Satan (Greek: *diabolos*; English: devil, accuser) is a nonhuman person in charge of testing loyalty to God (see Job 1:1). Such common first-century loyalty testers were disguised Roman soldiers who used ruse and deception to apprehend disloyal subjects of the emperor. Once apprehended, the fate of the subjects was in the hands of their captors. So too here. Satan obviously found this Jesus-group member disloyal by his behavior and will see to his eventual destruction, perhaps through being shunned by Jesus-group members for the short period before the day of the Lord Jesus. At that time the punishment will allow the man to avoid the wrath of God, hence be saved with the rest of the Corinthians.

5:6-8: Once more Paul puts down the arrogance of the Corinthians. Boasting means the acceptable Mediterranean practice of publicly making claims in relation to one's honor. Paul now refers to the Feast of Unleavened Bread and the Passover, which they celebrate (v. 8). In the Israelite customary behavior for the Feast of Unleavened Bread, all old yeast must be removed from the house. Unleavened bread is used at the Passover meal. Leavened dough symbolizes what cannot remain within social boundaries, since leavened dough cannot be contained but simply expands. So too an evil person is like leaven that will expand into the whole group. To stop the process, the person must be cast out. By analogy the Jesus group must clean out the old yeast in preparation for the Passover; only they celebrate Christ as analogical Passover Lamb, whose death was understood to be like a sacrifice. Sacrifice is a ritual in which an offering (animal, vegetable, mineral) is rendered humanly irretrievable and ingestible and then directed to some controlling higher personage (usually a deity) by someone lower in social status in order to have some life-effect. Given the life-effect deriving from Jesus' death, it was easy for Paul and his fellow believers to see Jesus' death as a sacrifice. Paul now takes the occasion to pitch for sincerity and truth, as opposed to the malice and evil brought to the surface by the transgressor in their midst.

Reminder of Previous Admonitions about Interpersonal Relations 5:9-13

5:9 I wrote to you in my letter not to associate with sexually immoral persons— 10 not at all meaning the immoral of this world, or the greedy and robbers, or idolaters, since you would then need to go out of the world. 11 But now I am writing to you not to associate with anyone who bears the name of brother or sister who is sexually immoral or greedy, or is an idolater, reviler, drunkard, or robber. Do not even eat with such a one. 12 For what have I to do with judging those outside? Is it not those who are inside that you are to judge? 13 God will judge those outside. "Drive out the wicked person from among you."

Textual Notes: 1 Cor 5:9-13

This passage presents what might be called a Pauline purity rule. Purity rules maintain the distinctiveness of social groups by not permitting mixtures. Social groups are marked off from other groups by boundaries. These boundaries function as purity lines, with all persons and things within the boundaries as clean or pure, and all persons and things outside the boundaries as unclean or impure. Crossing boundaries produces mixtures of clean and unclean, of pure and impure. Such social mixtures are confusing in that ingroup members cannot tell who belongs and who does not belong to the group. All societies have such purity lines drawn around selves, others, animals and things, time and space. Kinship systems so basic to first-century Eastern Mediterranean societies demonstrate great concern with ingroup belonging of persons. The U.S. social system, focally concerned with property, shows great concern with property rights and ownership rules. Ancient Mediterranean purity rules, concerned almost exclusively with persons, seem quaint and antiquated in the United States. **Clean and Unclean.**

5:9: Paul mentions a previous letter, called here "the letter" (not "my letter" as in NRSV), in which he exhorted the Corinthians not to mix with those who commit *porneia* (Greek: *pornoi*). The verb translated "associate" (Greek: *synanamignymi*) means to mix in with, mingle with. Perhaps the word was chosen by association with the previous reference of getting rid of the (old) leaven, since a leavening agent such as yeast or baking soda is something mixed into dough. Pharisaic purity rules might be summed up with the phrase "No Mixtures." It is the unmixed quality of persons, foods, things, and events that express Israelite purity according to the Pharisee perspective.

5:10: Here Paul likewise calls for no mixture, but he makes a distinction. It is necessary to live in society (the world), hence necessary to mingle with all sorts of people, even evil ones. This holds for interacting with the outgroup. But it does not hold for ingroup interactions.

5:11: Paul would have the Corinthians not mix with any Jesus-group member who is a *pornos*, as in the case of the man who married his stepmother, just mentioned. Similarly, they ought not to associate with group members concerned about accumulating wealth in their limited-goods society (this is a greedy person), or one who goes to services in local temples (such a person worships alien deities), or one who is verbally abusive or who robs by swindling. Their "non-mixture" behavior should extend even to not eating with such persons. The outcome is to keep the ingroup pure, free of the "old yeast."

5:12: Again, the verb "to judge" normally means to pass negative judgment, hence "to condemn." As change agent charged by God to proclaim his gospel, Paul is not concerned with the outgroup. Nor should the Corinthians be so concerned. There is little concern for "evangelizing" the outgroup.

5:13: Paul repeats his scripturally based injunction to action with a scriptural verse repeatedly directed to Israel. This verse is an explicit quotation from a repeated refrain in Deuteronomy usually dealing with infractions of the Ten Commandments. **Ten Commandments.** The command calls for the communal execution of a transgressor (Deut 17:7; 19:9; 21:21; 22:21, 22, 24; 24:7 LXX) at times for *porneia* (Deut 22:21, 22, 24). Just as Israelite insiders were to pass judgment on the transgressions of their fellow Israelites, so too Jesus-group members are to attend to the behavior of ingroup members. The NRSV's "drive out," means to purge, to remove, and—in context—to execute. Paul changes the singular verb form in Deuteronomy to the plural, to involve the whole community.

Censure of Ingroup Litigants and Their Litigiousness 6:1-11

6:1 When any of you has a grievance against another, do you dare to take it to court before the unrighteous, instead of taking it before the saints? 2 Do you not know that the saints will judge the world? And if the world is to be judged by you, are you incompetent to try trivial cases? 3 Do you not know that we are to judge angels—to say nothing of ordinary matters? 4 If you have ordinary cases, then, do you appoint as judges those who have no standing in the church? 5 I say this to your shame. Can it be that there is no one among you wise enough to decide between one believer and another, 6 but a believer goes to court against a believer—and before unbelievers at that?

7 In fact, to have lawsuits at all with one another is already a defeat for you. Why not rather be wronged? Why not rather be defrauded? 8 But you yourselves wrong and defraud—and believers at that. 9 Do you not know that wrongdoers will not inherit the kingdom of God? Do not be deceived! Fornicators, idolaters, adulterers, male prostitutes, sodomites, 10 thieves, the greedy, drunkards, revilers, robbers—none of these will inherit the kingdom of God. 11 And this is what some of you used to be. But you were washed, you were sanctified, you were justified in the name of the Lord Jesus Christ and in the Spirit of our God.

Textual Notes: 1 Cor 6:1-11

This is the central panel of the A-B-A' composition of this section. It deals with cases requiring judgment and so ties in with Paul's previous mention of judgment.

6:1-4: Another point reported to Paul was that some Corinthians instituted insider lawsuits (Greek: *pragma*, as in Matt 18:19, for another procedure). The problem is that they sought out outsider wise men (see v. 5) as judges. These "unrighteous" outsiders are contrasted with insiders, the "saints" or holy ones. These judges would be those wise men among their previous Israelite acquaintances who were skilled in dealing with cases within the Israelite community. For Paul, these Israelites are "unrighteous," or unacceptable to God. Rather, Jesus-group members should go to their own, their fellow holy ones, to deal with their problems. As motive he notes that Jesus-group insiders will pass judgment on society (the world) as well as on invisible celestial beings (angels); hence anyone in their group is capable of judging everyday matters. There is no need to have recourse to those Israelites who have no standing in their gathering.

6:5-8: Paul now explicitly states that he intends to shame the Corinthians for behaving in this way, for they appeal to outsider Israelites—those to whom the gospel of God was proposed and who rejected it. To take another person to court is to shame them, and to do this before an outsider is very shameful. The underlying cause for Corinthian litigiousness is that the Corinthians in question wrong and defraud their fellow Jesus-group members. This behavior shames the ingroup members cited by their fellow Jesus-group members.

6:9-11: Paul's list of ten types of people whose behavior will cut them off from inheriting the forthcoming kingdom of God replicates the Ten Commandments and alludes to several of them. **Ten Commandments.** The pattern of the list is characteristic of Hellenistic descriptions of qualities in personified form. It consists of ten features of the quality in question, usually in the negative, followed by a conclusion marked by "all." (For examples, see *Testament of Issachar* IV on single-mindedness, *Testament of Benjamin* 6 on the good inclination, and 1 Cor 13:4-7 on group attachment). Here, instead of a personified quality, we have a category of person. Against God's honor: idolatry; against male honor: adulterers, male prostitutes, sodomites; against false witness: reviler; against coveting neighbor's wife: fornicator; against coveting neighbor's goods: thieves, greedy, swindlers. In the final verse, Paul changes the expected "all" to "some of you." This list takes up the listings in 5:9 and 5:11 and prepares for what follows.

6:11: In the Israelite tradition, all infractions of the Ten Commandments, aside from violating the prohibition on coveting one's neighbor's goods, require the death penalty. Some of the Corinthians were guilty of such behavior, but now they have been justified or made righteous. Each of the three verbs begins with a "but," taken out by the NRSV. The rhetorical effect is missing in English. The passive verbs point to God as the agent: God cleanses, sets apart, and makes righteous. Thus God purifies, moving a person into the ranks of the clean; only the clean are capable of standing before God. And God makes holy or exclusive, putting a person among those sacred to God. Finally, God bestows righteousness, a quality that entails the ascribed, privileged social identity entailing a blessed life and bright destiny (totally unlike the outsider unrighteous; see Proverbs 10–15). All this happens because of the Lord Jesus and God's Spirit. As Esler has noted, in terms of "the three dimensions of group identity, righteousness: (a) said something to Israelites about the substance of that identity (the cognitive dimensions); (b) made them feel good about belonging to it (the emotional dimension) and (c) gave them a criterion against which to make negative judgments concerning outgroups (the evaluative dimension)" (Esler 2003b:167; see Esler 1998:164–69).

Once More: Dealing with the Complacency about Ingroup Incest 6:12-20

6:12 "All things are lawful for me," but not all things are beneficial. "All things are lawful for me," but I will not be dominated by anything. 13 "Food is meant for the stomach and the stomach for food," and God will destroy both one and the other. The body is meant not for fornication but for the Lord, and the Lord for the body. 14 And God raised the Lord and will also raise us by his power. 15 Do you not know that your bodies are members of Christ? Should I therefore take the members of Christ and make them members of a prostitute? Never! 16 Do you not know that whoever is united to a prostitute becomes one body with her? For it is said, "The two shall be one flesh." 17 But anyone united to the Lord becomes one spirit with him. 18 Shun fornication! Every sin that a person commits is outside the body; but the fornicator sins against the body itself. 19 Or do you not know that your body is a temple of the Holy Spirit within you, which you have from God, and that you are not your own? 20 For you were bought with a price; therefore glorify God in your body.

Textual Notes: 1 Cor 6:12-20

Our interpretation of this passage is based on the fact that in Greek, the article is normally lacking with abstract nouns, hence the presence of the article has to be explained. In this context, the abstract noun "fornication" has the article in Greek (6:13.18; not accounted for in the NRSV). Hence the noun should be translated "the fornication (*porneia*) previously mentioned" (Blass and Debrunner, par. 258, in Zerwick 1966:40). What this means is that the whole passage actually takes up the problem of incest begun in 5:1 and forms the A' segments of the A-B-A' pattern.

6:12: The style of citing a statement and refuting it is called a diatribe. The statements cited are either the viewpoints of the Corinthians or the principles that Paul taught the Corinthians in face of their previous Israelite values. In any case, while the principle "all things are allowed" is correct, in practice one must consider whether one's intended behavior is beneficial or subjugating (this last phrase is based on a Greek pun: *exestin* = allow and *exousiasthesomai* = be subjected).

6:13-14: The statement on food is rebutted in order to get at the point at issue. The word "body" means both the self (as in nobody, somebody, anybody), the human person as physical entity, as well as a social entity, a social body. The range of meanings allows Paul punning room. Here Paul notes that the human person as physical entity is not meant for the incest he just spoke about, but for the Lord, who sustains human beings destined for resurrection.

6:15: Once a person becomes part of a Jesus group, he or she becomes a member of Christ, a point more fully described later (1 Corinthians 12). Paul's rhetorical question makes it obvious that a conjugal union with the prostitute (the one given to illicit marital relations) previously noted in the above mentioned case is unthinkable.

6:16: Again note that Paul does not speak of "a" prostitute but "the" prostitute (the woman given in illicit marital relations mentioned in 1 Cor 5:1), the Jesus-group member's stepmother. Paul does not intimate that she was a member of the Jesus gathering, yet he does presume the incestuous couple got married, as the verse from Gen 2:24 indicates. It is through marriage that the man becomes one body with his wife. In this case the marriage should not have taken place!

6:17: Joining the Jesus group is like marriage; the person joining becomes one spirit with the Lord.

6:18: Paul once more commands the Corinthians to distance themselves from this previously mentioned *porneia* (forbidden marital arrangements). "Sin" means some action that dishonors another. All dishonoring activities have others as their object. Through "sin" one seeks to dishonor another. Paul notes that this *porneia* dishonors the perpetrator himself. Focus is on the male because he is the Jesus-group member.

6:19: Now Paul uses the word "body" as the social body (see 1 Cor 12:17: "You [plural] are the body of Christ, and each one a member of it"). "Your" is plural, hence the social body. It is the Jesus-group gathering that is the temple of God's Spirit; hence group members do not really belong to themselves. The point is emphasized by the phrase "you were bought with a price," an idiom meaning "the deal was paid in full." The social body belongs to God; hence its members must glorify God. "Glorify" means to show honor by one's outward conduct.

III. 1 Cor 7:1—15:58 Response to Corinthian Questions

This part of the letter opens with the phrase "Now concerning the matters about which you wrote" (7:1) and is punctuated with the phrase "concerning . . ." as new topics are introduced (7:1, 25; 8:1; 12:1; 16:1; 16:12).

Part One: 1 Cor 7:1-40 About Marriage Now

About Sexual Relations in Marriage 7:1-16

7:1 Now concerning the matters about which you wrote: "It is well for a man not to touch a woman." 2 But because of cases of sexual immorality, each man should have his own wife and each woman her own husband. 3 The husband should give to his wife her conjugal rights, and likewise the wife to her husband. 4 For the wife does not have authority over her own body, but the husband does; likewise the husband does not have authority over his own body, but the wife does. 5 Do not deprive one another except perhaps by agreement for a set time, to devote yourselves to prayer, and then come together again, so that Satan may not tempt you because of your lack of self-control. 6 This I say by way of concession, not of command. 7 I wish that all were as I myself am. But each has a particular gift from God, one having one kind and another a different kind.

8 To the unmarried and the widows I say that it is well for them to remain unmarried as I am. 9 But if they are not practicing self-control, they should marry. For it is better to marry than to be aflame with passion.

10 To the married I give this command—not I but the Lord—that the wife should not separate from her husband 11 (but if she does separate, let her remain unmarried or else be reconciled to her husband), and that the husband should not divorce his wife.

12 To the rest I say—I and not the Lord—that if any believer has a wife who is an unbeliever, and she consents to live with him, he should not divorce her. 13 And if any woman has a husband who is an unbeliever, and he consents to live with her, she should not divorce him. 14 For the unbelieving husband is made holy through his wife, and the unbelieving wife is made holy through her husband. Otherwise, your children would be unclean, but as it is, they are holy. 15 But if the unbelieving partner separates, let it be so; in such a case the brother or sister is not bound. It is to peace that God has called you. 16 Wife, for all you know, you might save your husband. Husband, for all you know, you might save your wife.

Textual Notes: 1 Cor 7:1-16

The advice Paul offers in this section of his letter seems to derive from several governing principles. The first is: "the appointed time has grown short" (7:29). The arrival of the kingdom of God is forthcoming, and this perspective should govern decision making. The second principle is: "let each of you lead the life that the Lord has assigned, to which God called you" (7:17, 25). Paul urges Jesus-group members to remain in the social status in which God called them, whether married or unmarried, slave or free. The problems presented by the Corinthians are spin-offs from these principles.

The innovation that Paul proclaimed with his gospel of God left many dimensions of social life disjointed in the minds of those adopting the innovation. Paul now addresses some of those dimensions, responding to a series of questions about which the Corinthians wrote as part of the information exchange relationship he established (see Ford 1965). In this first passage he addresses the concerns of married Corinthian Jesus-group members (7:1-6), of the unmarried and widows (7:7-8), of the married group members thinking of divorce (7:9-11), and of group members married to an outsider (7:12-16).

7:1: This first statement is either a conclusion drawn by the Corinthians relative to sexual relations or Paul's own statement. In any event, to understand this very high context statement, several things must be understood that were obvious to Paul and his Corinthians. In the first place, the word for "wife" was "woman." Second, the perspective adopted is obviously the husband's viewpoint. "To touch a woman" meant "to have sexual relations with one's wife," and in both the Israelite and the non-Israelite value system, sexual relations with one's wife always took place with a view to having a child. The problem the Corinthians put to Paul here is not simply the question of sexual relations in marriage, as we might think. Since sexual relations in marriage in the first-century Mediterranean world was always about offspring, the statement might be better translated: "It is well for a married couple not to have children." Consider the viewpoint of Musonius Rufus: "Men who are not wanton or wicked are bound to consider sexual intercourse justified only when it occurs in marriage and is indulged in for the purpose of begetting children, since that is lawful, but unjust and unlawful when it is mere pleasure-seeking, even in marriage" (XI, 4–8, Lutz 86). Musonius, called a Stoic philosopher by Tacitus, articulated the popular, thoughtful outlook of the time. If the "civilized" view was that marital sexual relations are solely for begetting children, this would be Paul's view as well.

7:2-4: Paul's answer goes beyond the immediate question and places private sexual conduct within the public sphere of cases of sexual immorality (*porneia*). Lest Jesus-group members resort to public immorality, they must remain married and continue to have sexual intercourse with each other on an equal basis.

7:5: Refraining from sexual relations for prayer reasons is rooted in cultural purity rules. Purity refers to social rules defining how, where, when, and why a person is in proper condition to interact with other persons. Israel's purity rules were essentially about what went in and came out of the human body. Sexual relations and the fluids that exit the human body made a person unclean, meaning unfit for social intercourse. After a bath, persons returned to normal. **Clean and Unclean.**

In general, the behavior we call "prayer" refers to socially meaningful symbolic acts of communication, bearing directly upon persons perceived as somehow supporting, maintaining, and controlling the order of existence of the one praying, and performed with the purpose of getting results from or in the interaction of communication. Religious prayer is such communication addressed to God with the purpose of getting results.

Paul assumes here that people who have sexual intercourse are unfit to approach God in prayer without the proper interval of sexual abstinence. That such advice would make sense is another indication of the Israelite membership of Paul's audience.

Once more, concern for Satan enters consideration (as in 1 Cor 5:5). Satan, the cosmic secret service agent, specializes in deception to shake allegiance to God. Paul intimates that married couples depriving each other might assist Satan in this task.

7:7: The gift Paul speaks of is *charisma* in Greek, the topic of a later section of this letter (1 Corinthians 12). In this context, the status in which God called persons to Jesus groups is a dimension of God's gift. Hence no need to change.

7:8: The word "unmarried" (Greek masculine noun) may refer to bachelors and widowers. Paul's advice is to follow the principle of staying in the status in which one was called, but if these persons are not up to sexual continence, then they should get married. Again Paul specifies that other ancient purpose of marriage, to allay sexual passion. Non-Israelites believed sexual relations with prostitutes had as their purpose allaying sexual passion, which was not to occur with one's wife.

7:10-11: The next category includes married Jesus-group members contemplating divorce. Paul's solution here derives from a Jesus tradition: no divorce (Mark 10:2-9). If separation happens, then remarriage is not permitted.

7:12-14: This case looks to group members married to outsiders. If they live in peace, there is no reason for divorce. Paul again brings up purity concerns (see note 7:5). His argument is that the Jesus-group members sanctify, that is make pure and exclusive, those persons attached to them in marriage; their spouses and children are in proper condition to interact with other Jesus-group members and with the God who raised Jesus from the dead.

7:15-16: If the outsider spouse wants to divorce, that is fine. The main principle Paul cites here is that "It is to peace that God has called you." And peace means all that is necessary for a meaningful human existence.

7:16: The NRSV translates these sentences as statements, yet the Greek formation is an interrogative (as in the RSV): "Do you know, wife, whether you will save your husband? Husband, do you know whether you will save your wife?" The statement supports those ingroup members who have been divorced by outsider spouses.

General Principle: Stay in the State in Which You Were Called 7:17-24

7:17 However that may be, let each of you lead the life that the Lord has assigned, to which God called you. This is my rule in all the churches. 18 Was anyone at the time of his call already circumcised? Let him not seek to remove the marks of circumcision. Was anyone at the time of his call uncircumcised? Let him not seek circumcision. 19 Circumcision is nothing, and uncircumcision is nothing; but obeying the commandments of God is everything. 20 Let each of you remain in the condition in which you were called.

21 Were you a slave when called? Do not be concerned about it. Even if you can gain your freedom, make use of your present condition now more than ever. 22 For whoever was called in the Lord as a slave is a freed person belonging to the Lord, just as whoever was free when called is a slave of Christ. 23 You were bought with a price; do not become slaves of human masters. 24 In whatever condition you were called, brothers and sisters, there remain with God.

Textual Notes: 1 Cor 7:17-24

Paul turns to a treatment of the general principle that has governed much of his advice. This passage is marked off by a threefold repetition of this general principle: stay in the status in which you were called by God (vv. 17, 20, 24).

7:17: For Paul, it is the God of Israel who calls individuals to Jesus groups, while the Lord Jesus designates roles (see 1 Corinthians 12 about charisms). Paul now offers two example of statuses in which people were called.

7:18-19: The first example has to do with whether one was a truly devoted Israelite (also called "Hebrew") or an Israelite by descent. The former would follow the rather recent Judean symbolic custom (begun in Palestine in the Maccabean period) of male genital mutilation consisting of foreskin incision. **Circumcision.** They should not attempt to have the foreskin resewn. This was usually done to enable such circumcised Israelites to fit into broader Hellenistic society. To accept the gospel of God does not require foreskin reconstitution. On the other hand, those who were uncircumcised need not worry about circumcision since the gospel of God does not require what some would think to be recovering one's Israelite root. The point is that the practice of circumcision is insignificant. What counts is obeying the commandments of God. For Paul these are essentially the Ten Commandments. **Ten Commandments.**

7:21-22: The next example is that of slave or free status. A number of Israelite slaves did adopt Paul's innovation (see 1 Cor 12:13; Gal 3:28; Philemon 16). Whether slave or free, Jesus-group members have the Lord Jesus as their owner/master. Their current social status during this period before the coming of the Lord is insignificant.

7:23: Paul now repeats what he said previously (6:20): Jesus-group members were bought in a transaction paid in full; they belong to the Lord. Hence Paul's exhortation: do not become slaves of human masters. Paul could use the language of slavery because institutionalized slavery was fundamental to advanced agricultural economies, whether Roman or Israelite.

About Arranging Marriages Now 7:25-35

7:25 Now concerning virgins, I have no command of the Lord, but I give my opinion as one who by the Lord's mercy is trustworthy. 26 I think that, in view of the impending crisis, it is well for you to remain as you are. 27 Are you bound to a wife? Do not seek to be free. Are you free from a wife? Do not seek a wife. 28 But if you marry, you do not sin, and if a virgin marries, she does not sin. Yet those who marry will experience distress in this life, and I would spare you that. 29 I mean, brothers and sisters, the appointed time has grown short; from now on, let even those who have wives be as though they had none, 30 and those who mourn as though they were not mourning, and those who rejoice as though they were not rejoicing, and those who buy as though they had no possessions, 31 and those who deal with the world as though they had no dealings with it. For the present form of this world is passing away. 32 I want you to be free from anxieties. The unmarried man is anxious about the affairs of the Lord, how to please the Lord; 33 but the married man is anxious about the affairs of the world, how to please his wife, 34 and his interests are divided. And the unmarried woman and the virgin are anxious about the affairs of the Lord, so that they may be holy in body and spirit; but the married woman is anxious about the affairs of the world, how to please her husband. 35 I say this for your own benefit, not to put any restraint upon you, but to promote good order and unhindered devotion to the Lord.

Textual Notes: 1 Cor 7:25-35

The question dealt with in this passage is the question of whether or not Jesus-group members should proceed with arranging marriages for their children. The principle behind the answer are consistently the same: our present living is hemmed in by coercive conditions (v. 26) since "the appointed time has grown short" (v 29), so it is well for you to remain as you are (v. 29). The Lord is coming quite soon.

7:25: The word translated "virgin" means a female marriageable teenager who is not a widow. (At times it means a married young woman who did not yet bring forth male offspring; see 7:36.)

7:26-28: Paul offers his opinion on the basis of his call by God to be a prophetic change agent. And it is the same principle that governed the previous section: stay in the status in which you were called. But if one gets married, that is not shameful to God.

7:29-31: To further emphasize his principle, he runs through the contemporary Israelite steps to getting married, but in reverse order:

- the final married couple: "let those who have wives live as though they had none"
- the bride's family losing their daughter/sister: "and those who mourn as though they were not mourning"
- the groom's family and their gain: "and those who rejoice as though they were not rejoicing"
- the groom's family who must pay bridewealth at betrothal: "and those who buy as though they had no goods"
- the bride's family dealing at betrothal for suitable bridewealth: "and those who deal with the world as though they had no dealings with it"

We follow J. Duncan M. Derrett (1977) in this explanation.

7:31: Once more, Paul underscores the shortness of time before the coming of the Lord Jesus with power. The belief that the present form of this world is passing away was part of the common belief in social and physical devolution. **Devolution.**

7:32-35: The theme here is anxieties that come from family life. Given the shortness of time before the Lord's coming, it seemed better, in terms of orderly and devoted living, to bypass family problems. Similar advice was given by Stoic philosophers for those wishing to devote themselves to the pursuit of the Stoic way of life. Thus Epictetus writes:

> But in such an order of things as the present, which is like that of a state of war [a philosopher should not marry so as] to be free from distraction, wholly devoted to the service of God, free to go about among men, not tied down by the private duties of men, nor involved in relationships which such a person cannot violate and still maintain his role as a good and excellent man. . . . For see [if he got married] he must show certain service to his in-laws, to the rest of his wife's relatives and to his wife herself. Finally he is driven from his profession to act as a nurse in his own family and to provide for them. To make a long story short, he must get a kettle to heat water for the baby, for washing it in a bath-tub; wool for his wife when she has had a child, oil, a cot, a cup (the vessels get more and more numerous); to speak of the rest of his business and his distractions. . . . (*Discourses* III 22.69–72, LCL)

About Levirate Marriages 7:36-38

7:36 If anyone thinks that he is not behaving properly toward his fiancee, if his passions are strong, and so it has to be, let him marry as he wishes; it is no sin. Let them marry. 37 But if someone stands firm in his resolve, being under no necessity but having his own desire under control, and has determined in his own mind to keep her as his fiancee, he will do well. 38 So then, he who marries his fiancee does well; and he who refrains from marriage will do better.

Textual Notes: 1 Cor 7:36-38

The NRSV translation of this passage is not literal. It is based on the presumption that Paul is giving advice to a male regarding his virginal fiancee (the Greek is *parthenos*, "virgin," not virginal fiancee), something rather impossible in the first century, when families got married, not individuals. The choice ultimately is not the bridegroom's. Other translations (e.g., RSV) think it is advice to a father about a teenage daughter he wishes to marry off. We follow a third option, typically Israelite and in keeping with Paul's audience (see Ford 1964; 1966b). Literally the passage states:

> If anyone thinks of being shamed about the matter of his "virgin," in case she be close to menopause, and it must thus happen, let him do as he

desires (Greek: *thelei*); he does not sin. Let them marry. But if he is firm in his heart, not being compelled, for he has power over what he desires (Greek: *thelēmatos*), and he has judged this in his own heart to keep his "virgin" he does well. Therefore he does well to marry his own "virgin," but the one not marrying does better.

The problem looks to the Israelite custom and law obliging a brother-in-law to take his dead brother's wife and to raise an heir for that dead brother. This is called levirate (Latin: *levir* means brother-in-law) marriage. In this case, the word "virgin" refers to either a childless or a sonless previously married woman, and "his virgin" refers to a sister-in-law who has the right to have an offspring in the name of the dead brother. The law in Deut 25:5-10 requires the brother unwilling to perform this duty to be shamed in perpetuity. In the process the sister-in-law states before witnesses: "The brother of my husband does not desire (LXX: *thelei*) to raise up the name of his brother in Israel; the brother of my husband did not desire it (LXX: *ethelēsan*)" (Deut 25:7). Then she takes off one of his sandals and spits in his face—actions dishonoring him in public. The person Paul is talking about in this case did not wish to be publicly shamed.

About Widows and Marriage 7:39-40

7:39 A wife is bound as long as her husband lives. But if the husband dies, she is free to marry anyone she wishes, only in the Lord. 40 But in my judgment she is more blessed if she remains as she is. And I think that I too have the Spirit of God.

Textual Notes: 1 Cor 7:39-40

The final piece of advice in this section has to do with remarriage for widows. Paul begins with a principle ("A wife is bound as long as her husband lives"), which he then applies to the case in question. To this solution he adds further advice in line with the general tenor of the whole passage: stay in the state in which you were called and remain as you are. He ascribes this assessment to the Spirit of God, the basis for his role as Israelite change agent and prophet.

Part Two: 1 Cor 8:1—11:1
About Foods and Dining

This whole section deals with questions about food and eating. Eating is always a social act that makes sense according to culturally accepted patterns. These patterns form the "grammar" of a meal. In terms of this grammar, eating makes human sense. The elements of this grammar include: who eats what, with whom, when, where, how, and why. In this section these elements come to prominence as Paul attempts to correct the Corinthian grammar so that in their eating they would express the set of meanings proper to those in Christ. **Meals.**

Foods Presented before Images 8:1-13

8:1 Now concerning food sacrificed to
idols: we know that "all of us possess knowledge." Knowledge puffs up, but love builds
up. 2 Anyone who claims to know something
does not yet have the necessary knowledge; 3
but anyone who loves God is known by him.
4 Hence, as to the eating of food offered
to idols, we know that "no idol in the world
really exists," and that "there is no God but
one." 5 Indeed, even though there may be
so-called gods in heaven or on earth—as in
fact there are many gods and many lords— 6
yet for us there is one God, the Father, from
whom are all things and for whom we exist,
and one Lord, Jesus Christ, through whom
are all things and through whom we exist.
7 It is not everyone, however, who has
this knowledge. Since some have become
so accustomed to idols until now, they still
think of the food they eat as food offered to
an idol; and their conscience, being weak,
is defiled. 8 "Food will not bring us close to
God." We are no worse off if we do not eat,
and no better off if we do. 9 But take care
that this liberty of yours does not somehow
become a stumbling block to the weak.
10 For if others see you, who possess knowledge, eating in the temple of an idol, might
they not, since their conscience is weak,
be encouraged to the point of eating food
sacrificed to idols? 11 So by your knowledge
those weak believers for whom Christ died
are destroyed. 12 But when you thus sin
against members of your family, and wound
their conscience when it is weak, you sin
against Christ. 13 Therefore, if food is a
cause of their falling, I will never eat meat,
so that I may not cause one of them to fall.

Textual Notes: 1 Cor 8:1-13

8.1: The opening title refers to another topic about which the Corinthians wrote. Paul opens: "concerning idolothytes" (8:1), and more specifically "concerning eating idolothytes." The word "idolothyte" is a transliteration of the Greek. The word means: "that which has been offered before images" (the NRSV translation is traditional and wrong). The Greek word translated as "idol" here is *eidōlon*, a neutral term that refers to an image, likeness, appearance—in short, a visible shape of some sort. Tertullian (d. 220) transliterated the Greek into the Latin "idolum," causing the word to refer to "an image of a false god." During the time of Paul, however, the word *eidōlon* was a neutral term referring to an image. Images were certainly to be found in Greek and Roman temples as well as in households (busts, statues, death masks). In households images of ancestors were venerated and taken to burial places for periodic funerary celebrations involving eating and drinking as a show of respect for ancestors (see Kennedy 1987; 1994). Consequently, without further particulars, one cannot say whether Paul is referring to eating foods presented before statues of various deities or foods presented to household ancestors during periodic funerary celebrations. In both instances, images were venerated.

> The *eidōlon* as image, or likeness, or shadow was often believed to have the properties of a shadow. A shadow was a person's or animal's soul, life force, doppelganger or alter ego. One can do harm to another by doing violence to his shadow. And it can be dangerous or helpful to touch the shadow of certain people or animals. Shadows and life force are identical to such an extent that many feared the noon hour because then the shadow shrinks. And the shadow disappears when a person dies. Many magical practices are based upon these beliefs. (Van der Horst, 1979:27–28)

Concerning shadows, see RSV Num 14:9: "Only do not rebel against the Lord; and do not fear the people of the land, for they are bread for us; their protection is removed from them." This last sentence states literally, "their shadow is removed from them," referring to their power. To overshadow in the LXX and the New Testament means to exert power on behalf of (Deut 33:12 LXX; Luke 1:35). Peter's shadow has healing power (Acts 5:15). The point is that images have the positive and negative properties of shadows.

8:1-3: As change agent, Paul's underlying concern was to maintain group integrity, and it is from this point of view that he deals with the problems put to him. Group integrity requires Jesus-group members to have a social identity, a sense of ingroup identification and belonging. To this end, group-binding norms were necessary. The problem now is the significance of eating food items presented before images. Does a Jesus-group member's eating these items situate him or her outside the group, and thus compromise his or her social identity as a Jesus-group member? Before broaching the problem at all, Paul situates it within the perspectives shared by some of the Corinthian Jesus-group members. Obviously some group members believe eating food presented to images puts one outside the group; others believe such dining is insignificant. In other words, the problem is one of mixture again.

Hence what is involved is how one interprets images and their shadow power. Do these images actually exert interpersonal social force, or are they simply inert, powerless representations? Paul opens by admitting that we (inclusive: Paul and the Corinthians) all have an interpretation of what is involved ("all of us possess knowledge"), but the more learned the interpretations, the more arrogance ("puffs up") displayed by interpreters. On the other hand, group attachment and concern for ingroup members ("love") builds group integrity. Those who claim to have a special take on the issue in question that is not known by others do not have what it takes to be a proper group member. Instead of pushing their knowledge, those who are attached to God and try to do what pleases God are known by God. To be known by God means to be called, supported, and given the patronage of God.

8:4-6: Back to the topic at hand, Paul cites two statements of those who wrote. The statements would bolster the argument in favor of eating what has been presented before images. The first is that images are simply images, with no special force or impact. The second, perhaps more important than the first, is that none of the many images in Corinth or anywhere else represent the one God who alone actually exists and who alone has power. Paul agrees. For while the many gods and lords known in Corinth do indeed exist, these entities may have impact on outsiders, but for the Jesus ingroup, there is only one God and one Lord. **Many Gods and Many Lords.** Verse 6 looks like an early Jesus-group hymn that sets out early Jesus-group theology in brief (the words in brackets are not in the Greek):

> But for us [inclusive], [there is] one God the Patron
> from whom [comes] everything, and we [exist] for him
> And one Lord Jesus Christ,
> through whom [comes] everything and we [exist] through him.

With this hymn Paul emphasizes that our God is the celestial patron (Father), the creator of all, and the reason for the existence of all that exists. As celestial patron (Father), God has an intermediary, a broker, who puts us in contact with the patron. This broker or mediator is Jesus, sole Lord of all, hence cosmic Lord, through whom God has created and through whom all existence as God's is revealed and realized. The problem, of course, is how, in practical behavior, to maintain belief in one sole God and one sole Lord in the rather pluralistic cosmos of social experience in Corinth.

8:7-8: The specific problem with food presented before images is the residual belief held by some of the Corinthian Jesus-group members in the meaning of the images and the entities for which they stand. Even for us moderns, photos can conjure up all sorts of feelings in those who view them. What causes those feelings? In their anti-introspective perspective, the ancients attributed their reactions to images to the representations themselves. "Looking at an image has a power peculiar to itself; it takes possession of those who have attained to the sight of it and draws them along, even as men say that the magnet draws iron" (*Corpus Hermeticum* IV, 11b ed. Scott). A number of Corinthians now in the Jesus group once shared this customary belief and simply cannot shake it off. For them, eating foods presented out of respect to images means sharing in and consenting to the presence, impact, and influence of those gods and lords represented by the images. After all, even for those in the know, these gods and lords do exist, even though their images are truly inert. For example, the Judean Philo of Alexandria calls the Israelite God "the Supreme father of the gods" (*Spec. Laws* 2, 165), acknowledging the existence of those other deities.

The Hellenistic designation "weak" referred to persons untrained in the customs and amenities of the cultivated strata of society (*HCNT* 673–74). Driven by unwarranted fears, the "weak" behaved irrationally, guided by their dread rather than by rational knowledge. Paul calls some in the Corinthian group "the weak" since they do not share the social awareness of the total impotence and decrepit nature of these gods and lords in face of the God of Israel and the Lord Jesus. As a result, any participation in the foods set before their images was read by "the weak" as homage to those gods and lords. Such participation obfuscated group boundaries and ingroup social identity. For Paul, unconcern for "the weak" eradicated the group integrity ("holiness") that was to be its hallmark.

8:8-10: Another argument proposed by the Corinthians underscores the indifference to food that was to mark Jesus-group behavior. What one eats has no bearing on pleasing God. Paul agrees but argues that it is not what one eats but with whom one eats that fills what one eats with meaning. The Corinthian gathering included some who were previously accustomed to eating such foods and sharing in the power of the gods and lords thus represented. To see their fellows eating foods presented before images in places associated with image reverence (either a temple or a mausoleum—the term is not clear) might lead "the weak" to take up the practice again, since their group awareness, their group restraining sanctions, were weak.

8:11: Knowledge here is the experiential knowledge, the practical dimensions of knowing. Knowledge comes from experience, from doing. Those Corinthian Jesus-group members who choose to eat what was presented before images in a mausoleum- or temple-affiliated dining hall revive the addiction of the weak to the power and impact of gods and lords in such dining. In their estimation, such behavior would put them outside the Jesus group, thus leading to their destruction. Their presence in the Jesus group indicates that Jesus effectively died for their well-being, but their return to their prior habits would nullify that.

8:12: To revive the habits, feelings, and beliefs of the weak dishonors them as well as Christ. Sin is dishonoring or shaming another person. Because of the collectivistic quality of Jesus groups, shaming the weak also shames Christ, of whose body they are a part. **Collectivistic Personality.**

8:13: Paul's conclusion runs as follows: if it were up to him, he would not act according to his superior knowledge about the nature of food but refrain from eating so as to protect those previously addicted and less informed. In that way, of course, group integrity is maintained.

The dining couches that line the walls of the main room indicate that this structure, part of the Sanctuary of Demeter in Corinth, was a banquet hall, where cultic meals would have taken place. The diners, in intimate groups of fewer than a dozen people, would have consumed meat from sacrificial animals, the subject of one of the controversies addressed by Paul (see 1 Cor 8:7-9).

Part Three: 1 Cor 9:1-27
About Jesus-Group Change Agents and Their Entitlements

The argument in the previous passage implies that those in the Corinthian gathering who are aware of the true nature of images and of God may indeed be entitled to eating whatever they want, even with whom they want, wherever they want. But for the sake of some of their ingroup brothers and sisters, they ought to waive their entitlements. To make this point, Paul now proceeds to spell out exactly how he waived his entitlements for the sake of the Corinthian Jesus group.

Change Agents, Their Entitlements, and Waiving Entitlements 9:1-14

9:1 Am I not free? Am I not an apostle? Have I not seen Jesus our Lord? Are you not my work in the Lord? 2 If I am not an apostle to others, at least I am to you; for you are the seal of my apostleship in the Lord.

3 This is my defense to those who would examine me. 4 Do we not have the right to our food and drink? 5 Do we not have the right to be accompanied by a believing wife, as do the other apostles and the brothers of the Lord and Cephas? 6 Or is it only Barnabas and I who have no right to refrain from working for a living? 7 Who at any time pays the expenses for doing military service? Who plants a vineyard and does not eat any of its fruit? Or who tends a flock and does not get any of its milk?

8 Do I say this on human authority? Does not the law also say the same? 9 For it is written in the law of Moses, "You shall not muzzle an ox while it is treading out the grain." Is it for oxen that God is concerned? 10 Or does he not speak entirely for our sake? It was indeed written for our sake, for whoever plows should plow in hope and whoever threshes should thresh in hope of a share in the crop. 11 If we have sown spiritual good among you, is it too much if we reap your material benefits? 12 If others share this rightful claim on you, do not we still more?

Nevertheless, we have not made use of this right, but we endure anything rather than put an obstacle in the way of the gospel of Christ. 13 Do you not know that those who are employed in the temple service get their food from the temple, and those who serve at the altar share in what is sacrificed on the altar? 14 In the same way, the Lord commanded that those who proclaim the gospel should get their living by the gospel.

Textual Notes: 1 Cor 9:1-14

9:1-6: Paul argues that change agents commissioned by the God of Israel are entitled to be supported by those groups who have accepted the innovation. Not only are they entitled to sustenance, but they are also to be accompanied by their wives, who are likewise entitled to be supported. This was the behavior of those Judean Jesus-group change agents, including Jesus' family members and Cephas (Peter). On the other hand, Paul and Barnabas (a Judean name, here mentioned for the first time) have waived their entitlement to sustenance for themselves and an accompanying spouse so as not to "put an obstacle in the way of the gospel of Christ" (9:12). The implication is that Corinthian Jesus-group members should likewise waive their entitlement to eat any food so as not to put an obstacle in the way of their fellow group members.

9:7-12: Paul now offers a series of arguments demonstrating the basis for his entitlement to sustenance. The first argument is based on customary, common knowledge. Roman military service of the day, a type of mercenary army, was rewarded with pay deriving from the taxes that Romans collected. Likewise those engaged in tenant agriculture received part of the harvest and flock. The second argument is based on Israel's sacred scripture (citing Deut 25:4). Paul is not citing a Torah commandment to indicate that Jesus-group members are obliged by those commandments. Rather, Paul cites the passage as something the Corinthians might know (after all, they were Israelites), so that he can apply it in an a fortiori, metaphorical way. The rule about letting oxen eat as they thresh (the Torah commandment) should hold all the more so for humans as they work, as demonstrated by common human agricultural behavior (9:10). The conclusion to the argument compares change-agent activity to agricultural work (as Paul did in 1 Cor 3:6-9). Change agents are entitled to sustenance and support by the groups they establish. But Paul's point is that just as he has consistently waived his entitlement to such sustenance so as not to "put an obstacle in the way of the gospel of Christ," Corinthians ought to waive their entitlement to eat foods in contexts indicating those foods were presented to images so as not to block the "weak" from the gospel of Christ.

9:13-14: These verses repeat the previous theme demonstrating the entitlement of change agents to sustenance and support. Again Paul uses an analogy that Israelites would appreciate. Just as levitical and priestly temple service provide sustenance for those who serve the Jerusalem Temple and Temple altar (in fact and as directed by Num 18:8, 31, and Deut 18:1-8), so should change-agent service. This time Paul provides proof for his contention by citing an unspecified command of Jesus himself (perhaps as in Luke 10:7).

The Basis of Paul's Change-Agent Career and Waiving Entitlements 9:15-27

9:15 But I have made no use of any of these rights, nor am I writing this so that they may be applied in my case. Indeed, I would rather die than that—no one will deprive me of my ground for boasting! 16 If I proclaim the gospel, this gives me no ground for boasting, for an obligation is laid on me, and woe to me if I do not proclaim the gospel! 17 For if I do this of my own will, I have a reward; but if not of my own will, I am entrusted with a commission. 18 What then is my reward? Just this: that in my proclamation I may make the gospel free of charge, so as not to make full use of my rights in the gospel.

19 For though I am free with respect to all, I have made myself a slave to all, so that I might win more of them. 20 To the Jews I became as a Jew, in order to win Jews. To those under the law I became as one under the law (though I myself am not under the law) so that I might win those under the law. 21 To those outside the law I became as one outside the law (though I am not free from God's law but am under Christ's law) so that I might win those outside the law. 22 To the weak I became weak, so that I might win the weak. I have become all things to all people, that I might by all means save some. 23 I do it all for the sake of the gospel, so that I may share in its blessings.

24 Do you not know that in a race the runners all compete, but only one receives the prize? Run in such a way that you may win it. 25 Athletes exercise self-control in all things; they do it to receive a perishable wreath, but we an imperishable one. 26 So I do not run aimlessly, nor do I box as though beating the air; 27 but I punish my body and enslave it, so that after proclaiming to others I myself should not be disqualified.

Textual Notes: 1 Cor 9:15-27

9:15-18: The word "rights" in the NRSV is not found in Greek. Paul says he does not make use of any of these things. And as a good Mediterranean, he would never pass up a chance to boast (v. 15). "To boast" is to make a claim to honor, a claim to worth that one's audience will be motivated and impelled to acknowledge. And he deserves honor if he passes up an entitlement to the benefit of the Corinthians. However, he really does not decline any entitlement because he in fact has no choice about his task of proclaiming the gospel of God. Hence he cannot really boast since he has no choice. His role as change agent was not his choice. If it were, he could boast about his refusal of support. But his role was imposed upon him by the God of Israel, the change agency behind his activity.

The word "reward" (v. 18) in the NRSV ("What then is my reward?") is the Greek *misthos*. The word means "hire, pay" and here refers to Paul's state of being hired by God, hence "What then are the terms of my hire?" Now his answer to this rhetorical question makes sense: "that in proclaiming the gospel, I set it forth free of charge, so as to not make full use of my entitlement in the gospel."

9:19: Paul now underscores his strategy as change agent. Modern diffusion of innovation studies around the world have demonstrated the greater effectiveness of "homophilous" change agents. Homophily refers to the quality of being alike in social standing, values, and outlook. Paul shrewdly adopted a strategy of homophily. By attempting to be homophilous with the recipients of his gospel proclamation, Paul can overcome the social and psychological barriers of selective exposure, perception, and retention. The main possible effect is in the area of persuasion. Studies have shown that homophilous change agents can persuade the receiving individuals to form or change strongly held attitudes. Hence they have greater effectiveness in the face of resistance or apathy on the receiver's part. Paul can adopt a homophilous stance because he willingly subordinates ("enslaves") himself to those receiving his proclamation, and that includes the Corinthians as well.

9:20-22: The categories of persons listed here are not as neat as we might like. **Jew and Greek/Judean and Hellenist.** Paul begins with a geographically named category, Judeans. "Judean" was the name given by outgroups (i.e., non-Israelites) to members of the house of Israel, presumed to derive from Judea. For citizens of Rome, Corinth, Thessalonika, and so forth, a Judean was any member of the house of Israel. On the other hand, for a member of the house of Israel living outside Judea, a Judean meant a non-Greek Israelite, an Israelite given predominantly to the customs of "the old country," that is, a "barbarian" Israelite as opposed to a "civilized" Israelite.

Here Paul claims he has become like every type of those whom non-Israelites call "Judeans"—those following Torah prescriptions (under the Law, v. 20b), those not following Torah prescriptions (without the Law, v. 21), those scrupulous about mixing with non-Israelites (the weak, v. 22a), The goal of such accommodation on his part is "that I might by all means rescue some" (v. 22b). What motivates him? His imposed task of proclaiming the gospel of God, "so that I might have a share in it" (v. 23). The NRSV word "blessing" is not in the Greek. Paul wishes to share in the forthcoming event that he proclaims—the coming of the Lord that inaugurates God's rule over Israel.

9:24-27: Paul urges his Corinthians to strive for the single prize as athletes in the public city games do. As for himself, he too stays in shape (v. 27), focused on his task (v. 26) so that he might participate in the proclamation that he makes known in Israel.

Part Four: 1 Cor 10:1—11:1
About Showing Respect for Images

Lessons from the History of Israel 1 Cor 10:1-13

10:1 I do not want you to be unaware, brothers and sisters, that our ancestors were all under the cloud, and all passed through the sea, 2 and all were baptized into Moses in the cloud and in the sea, 3 and all ate the same spiritual food, 4 and all drank the same spiritual drink. For they drank from the spiritual rock that followed them, and the rock was Christ. 5 Nevertheless, God was not pleased with most of them, and they were struck down in the wilderness.

6 Now these things occurred as examples for us, so that we might not desire evil as they did. 7 Do not become idolaters as some of them did; as it is written, "The people sat down to eat and drink, and they rose up to play." 8 We must not indulge in sexual immorality as some of them did, and twenty-three thousand fell in a single day. 9 We must not put Christ to the test, as some of them did, and were destroyed by serpents. 10 And do not complain as some of them did, and were destroyed by the destroyer. 11 These things happened to them to serve as an example, and they were written down to instruct us, on whom the ends of the ages have come. 12 So if you think you are standing, watch out that you do not fall. 13 No testing has overtaken you that is not common to everyone. God is faithful, and he will not let you be tested beyond your strength, but with the testing he will also provide the way out so that you may be able to endure it.

Textual Notes: 1 Cor 10:1-13

10:1: The phrase "I do not want you to be unaware" is a disclosure formula that marks a transition to a new topic (see Rom 1:13; 11:25; 1 Cor 10:1; 12:1; 2 Cor 1:8; 1 Thess 4:13). The mention of *our* ancestors in the Exodus story once again underscores that Paul's audience consisted of members of the house of Israel. It was their mythical ancestors that figured in the story of events that happened in the wilderness after their mythical departure from Egypt. (Historically, the Exodus story was created by Judean scribes during the Persian period, modeled after their immigration from Persia.) Paul cites a tissue of passages from that story that serves his theme—food and service of images.

10:1-4a: The word "baptize" is not a translation but a transliteration, meaning that Paul's Greek word has been written in the Latin alphabet. The Greek word "baptize" means to dip in a liquid, to flood over with a liquid. **Baptism.** As a prophetic symbolic action in Israel, such dipping by another person (for example, by John the Baptist) might signify God's forgiving of offenses that required the satisfaction of divine honor. **Prophetic Symbolic Action.** Furthermore, in the first-century Mediterranean, such liquids or flooding agents included what we consider liquids (water, oil, wine) as well as wind and fire. Any substance that can be poured out or infused (for example, Holy Spirit) is liquid.

In Paul's story all of the ancestor Israelites were dipped in the cloud and sea, symbolizing that they were embedded "into Moses" (see Exod 13:21; 14:22). All of them similarly ate the divinely provided food (the manna, Exodus 16), and all drank the divinely provided drink (water from a rock, Exodus 17). Paul will contrast the positive experience of "all" (vv. 1-4) with the range of negative actions in which most engaged (vv. 5-10).

10:4b: That water was provided to the Israelites in the wilderness by a rock or mini-cliff that followed the group was a well-known piece of Israelite lore. Paul distinctively identifies this life-sustaining rock with Jesus the Messiah. This follows his principle that "for us there is one God, the Father, from whom are all things and for whom we exist, and one Lord, Jesus Christ, through whom are all things and through whom we exist" (1 Cor 8:6).

10:5: The destruction of the wilderness generation of Israelites was due to its dishonoring God by making an image, a molten calf of gold (Exodus 32). The Golden Calf was to serve as a place for the apparition of God wherever the people might carry it. With the Golden Calf, the people could say "This is your god, O Israel who brought you up out of the land of Egypt" (Exod 32:4) and steer it to lead wherever they wished to go. The Ark of the Covenant served a similar purpose, and there too Israel's God "sat" on the cherubim (winged bulls).

Specifically, the Golden Calf borne in procession served as a device for controlling God. The Israelites sought to return to Egypt, thus reversing the act of God that freed them from Egypt. With the controllable Golden Calf, the leaders could control the flow of people back to Egypt as they wanted, and they could ascribe it to the God of Israel situated over the Calf. In Israelite lore the incident of the Golden Calf occurred right after the God of Israel announced the Ten Commandments to all Israel from Mount Sinai and while Moses was still on the mountain, receiving those Ten Words from God, engraved by the "finger" of God on steles (Exod 31:18; 32:15-16). It was these stone steles that Moses threw down and broke upon seeing the Israelites' attempt to control God (Exod 32:19). According to the presentation of the story in the Old Testament, Moses then returned up the mountain to receive the Ten Words again, but now with God's other commandments for Israel. Later Jesus groups called these other, additional commandments God's second law (Greek: *deuterōsis*; most clearly articulated in the *Didascalia Apostolorum*, also Irenaeus, *Heresies* IV, 24–29; see also Pseudo-Barnabas 4 for the same idea). From the Jesus group's perspective, these additional commandments of Moses were given specifically to prevent Israel from attempting to control God again. It was this second law that Jesus-group members were no longer obliged to observe, since, through Jesus, Israel's wilderness sin of attempting to control God was taken away. Idolatry is always about attempting to control God.

In the story Paul cites, God was not pleased with most of the Israelites, "and they were struck down in the wilderness" (Num 14:16, 23, 30). Paul now proceeds to point out the meaning of this story of their ancestors for his Jesus group.

10:6: Paul takes the experience of the Exodus generation as applicable to what the Corinthians are experiencing. Note the refrain "as they/some of them did" (vv. 7, 8, 9, 10). In Paul's perspective, it is because of what God did to Jesus that Israel's scriptures are still of value for Jesus groups; here they provide a warning for Jesus-group members. The purpose of citing the past events in the Bible was in fact to demonstrate points of value to contemporary believers in the God of Israel, who raised Jesus from the dead.

The principle Paul cites from the wilderness behavior of ancient Israel is that people in Jesus groups ought not to "desire evil as they did." Paul's collectivistic culture was anti-introspective and not psychologically minded. This means that terms describing internal states always imply corresponding external behavior. "To desire" means to desire and demonstrate that desire in some behavior, to express a desire in word and deed. For example, to desire (synonym: covet, lust after) some item entails preparing to steal it and actually stealing it. In the Ten Commandments the final words on coveting are actually about stealing, amounting to "thou shalt not steal" (the commandment on stealing refers to stealing a free adult male, that is kidnapping). Hence to desire evil as they did means to plan and actually do evil. Paul now offers instances of this evildoing.

10:7: The word translated "idolaters" (NRSV) means to show respect to deities revealed in the presence of images. Notice that this respect for these deities entailed eating, drinking, and "play," a euphemism for sexual promiscuity. Presumably this behavior is what makes the behavior of those who respect images reprehensible. Paul quotes Exodus: "The people sat down to eat and drink, and they rose up to play" (Exod 32:6).

10:8: Another instance of the wilderness generation's desiring evil is *porneia* (NRSV: "sexual immorality"), that is, sexual behavior prohibited in the Torah. Again in the Israelite instance, the context is respecting images, where people ate and then "played." The verb "to play" or "be merry" (as in "Eat, drink, and be merry") refers to sexual merrymaking. Paul quotes this instance from Num 25:1, 9, according to which the number killed was twenty-four thousand. Perhaps at this point it is useful to note that numerals in the Bible for the most part are qualitative not quantitative. They describe the sort or type of event rather than the number of instances involved. There are several reasons for this. Ancient numeral systems had no efficient method of writing numbers and doing arithmetic. Those systems had no zero (invented by Arabs), and their large numbers were written out in full (for example, six hundred sixty-six). It was only the Hindu-Arabic numeral system (ca. 700 C.E.) that could write "666" or "23,000." That system was eventually adopted and employed in Europe only in the thirteenth century. Whether it was twenty-three thousand or twenty-four thousand, the number used means "very, very many."

10:9: The next instance Paul mentions refers to the incident in Num 21:5-6: "And the people spoke against God and against Moses, 'Why have you brought us up out of Egypt to die in the wilderness? For there is no food and no water, and we loathe this worthless food.' Then the LORD sent fiery serpents among the people, and they bit the people, so that many people of Israel died." "To put to the test" or "to tempt" always means to test one's loyalty. Since for Paul Christ is the agent through whom the God of Israel effects his will on behalf of his people, Israel tested Christ's loyalty to God by doubting his effectiveness on their behalf. Hence for Paul the Old Testament passage actually meant: "And the people spoke against God and against his Christ. . . ." Moses drops out of the picture.

10:10: The theme of "murmuring" or "complaining" against God's plan for Israel as the people trekked through the trackless wilderness runs throughout the story. The story in Numbers 14 describes those destroyed for such complaining.

10:11: Israel's behavior followed by God's punishment was a warning for latter Israelites. These include Paul's Jesus gatherings. What happened to Israel in the past serves as an instance of what is in store for Jesus-group members in similar circumstances. These events instruct and forewarn. Israel was on the verge of entering God's promised land to serve God; Paul's Jesus-group members are on the verge of experiencing the end of the ages with the advent of Jesus as Christ with power.

10:12-13: Paul relates standing and falling to testing. The test (the Greek is often translated "temptation") in question always refers to a test of loyalty to God, a loyalty test. God allows those in some relationship with God (e.g., by covenant, by being "in Christ") to have their loyalty tested. Paul assures the Corinthians that those tests never exceed the God-given means to withstand and pass the test. Hence Jesus-group members have the ability to remain loyal to God in the face of any tests they might face.

Detailed Application of the Foregoing Story 10:14—11:1

10:14 Therefore, my dear friends, flee from the worship of idols. 15 I speak as to sensible people; judge for yourselves what I say. 16 The cup of blessing that we bless, is it not a sharing in the blood of Christ? The bread that we break, is it not a sharing in the body of Christ? 17 Because there is one bread, we who are many are one body, for we all partake of the one bread. 18 Consider the people of Israel; are not those who eat the sacrifices partners in the altar? 19 What do I imply then? That food sacrificed to idols is anything, or that an idol is anything? 20 No, I imply that what pagans sacrifice, they sacrifice to demons and not to God. I do not want you to be partners with demons. 21 You cannot drink the cup of the Lord and the cup of demons. You cannot partake of the table of the Lord and the table of demons. 22 Or are we provoking the Lord to jealousy? Are we stronger than he? 23 "All things are lawful," but not all things are beneficial. "All things are lawful," but not all things build up. 24 Do not seek your own advantage, but that of the other. 25 Eat whatever is sold in the meat market without raising any question on the ground of conscience, 26 for "the earth and its fullness are the Lord's." 27 If an unbeliever invites you to a meal and you are disposed to go, eat whatever is set before you without raising any question on the ground of conscience. 28 But if someone says to you, "This has been offered in sacrifice," then do not eat it, out of consideration for the one who informed you, and for.

the sake of conscience— 29 I mean the other's conscience, not your own. For why should my liberty be subject to the judgment of someone else's conscience? 30 If I partake with thankfulness, why should I be denounced because of that for which I give thanks? 31 So, whether you eat or drink, or whatever you do, do everything for the glory of God. 32 Give no offense to Jews or to Greeks or to the church of God, 33 just as I try to please everyone in everything I do, not seeking my own advantage, but that of many, so that they may be saved. 11:1 Be imitators of me, as I am of Christ

Textual Notes: 1 Cor 10:15–11:1

10:12: As in the case of *porneia* in 6:18, since the article is normally lacking with abstract nouns in Greek, the presence of the article has to be explained here (Greek: *apo tēs eidōlolatreias*, = "from this service of images"). Hence the noun should be translated "the service of images (*eidōlolateria*) previously mentioned" (Blass and Debrunner, par. 258, in Zerwick 1966:40). The service of images previously mentioned is that of the Israelites in the wilderness and its Golden Calf. This entailed its desire for evil, service of images proper (eating, drinking, merrymaking), sexual promiscuity, putting Christ's loyalty to the test, and constant complaining about what God has decided and provided.

10:15-18: To make his point, Paul first refers to the significance of the Corinthians' ritual sharing of the blood and body of Christ, underscoring the fact that the one bread stands for one body, without division.

10:18: Paul cites a truism of Mediterranean sacrificial practice: those who eat of what is sacrificed are partners in the altar, that is, partners in the sacrifice linking worshipers with the deity and to one another. Such is the case with the God of Israel and the Israelites who sacrifice.

10:19-20: Such is not the case with non-Israelites, since the entities to which they offer sacrifice are not deities but demons. Demons were those nonhuman persons who inhabited areas of the sky and land and often impinged upon humans in their daily life. In the Semitic world such entities were called spirits or angels, while the proper Roman name for them was "genius" (female: "juno"). Philo, for example, notes:

> It is Moses' custom to give the name of angels to those whom other philosophers call demons, souls that is which fly and hover in the air. . . . For the universe must needs be filled through and through with life, and each of its primary elementary divisions contains the forms of life which are akin and suited to it. The earth has the creatures of the land, the sea and the rivers those that live in water, fire the fire-born which are said to be found especially in Macedonia, and heaven has the stars. For the stars are souls divine and without blemish throughout, and therefore as each of them is mind in its purest form, they move in the line most akin to mind—the circle. And so the other element, the air, must needs be filled with living beings, though indeed they are invisible to us, since even the air itself is not visible to our senses." (*On the Giants* II, 6–8, §263 LCL II 449)

> They are consecrated and devoted to the service of the Father and Creator whose wont it is to employ them as ministers and helpers, to have charge and care of mortal man. (*On the Giants* III, 12, §264, LCL II 451)

NRSV translates *ta ethnē* as "pagans," but the term "paganus" (Latin for village dweller, rustic, boor) was not applied to outsider unbelievers until after Constantine (see O'Donnell 1974). As previously noted, the term *ethnos* means "a people," and *ethnē* refers to "the other peoples, others, non-Israelites, outsiders," depending on context.

10:21: Temple dining on what was presented to images meant interacting with demons. It meant crossing social boundaries. For Jesus-group members, ingroup affiliation rooted in the Lord required breaking affiliations with any other nonhuman source of power and control. Provoking the Lord to jealousy with what is not a god (Deut 32:21) is what ancient Israel did. Jealousy refers to the feelings a person has toward persons and things exclusive or set apart to them. The emotion humans feel when "their" son or daughter, "their" parents, or "their" property is hurt or damaged is this feeling of jealousy. By analogy, jealousy is that protective, attached feeling God has toward persons set apart to God, exclusive to God, God's "holy" people. Only persons stronger than we are can trifle with persons and things that are "ours." Since God is stronger than any human or demon, no one can trifle with what is God's.

10:23-24: As in 6:12, Paul cites the position of some at Corinth who either held the slogan or misinterpreted a slogan that Paul taught. Again, Paul repeats his position that Corinthians must choose what is beneficial to others, what builds up others, what is advantageous to others, even if it means yielding their entitlements.

10:25-26: Yet one may eat whatever is sold in the market (the word *makellon* means food market in general, not meat market as in NRSV), in line with the Israelite tradition expressed in Ps 23:1. All foods derive from the Lord.

10:27: Paul now presents a concrete case. If a non-Jesus-group member invites a Corinthian Jesus-group member for a meal, presumably to his house (since temple dining rooms were dealt with previously), then the Corinthian should feel free to eat what is set before him. The scenario entails relative high-status personages, since ordinary people would not have the wherewithal to invite others to a meal at home.

10:28: Now a complication arises. If someone tells the Jesus-group member that the food offered to him has been offered in temple sacrifice, what should he do? Paul does not specify who the "someone" is, whether fellow Jesus-group member or not. Paul advises the Jesus-group guest to yield his entitlement to socialize and not eat. This refusal to eat is for the sake of the one telling the Jesus-group member that the food comes from the "table of demons." It deals with "conscience" or group awareness, since not eating draws the social line between outsider and insider social identity.

10:29-30: Now follow two rhetorical questions: Why should the informer's group awareness curtail my presumed liberty? Why should I be called down if I give thanks and eat with gratitude? The implied and unspecified answer is: for the sake of the other, for the sake of group integrity.

10:31: Paul now concludes this section with an exhortation to do everything for God's glory, including eating and drinking. "Glory," in an honor and shame context, refers to the outward things one does, the visible behavior one follows, that reveal one's social standing or honor. To glorify God means to act in a way that honors God. In context, yielding one's entitlements glorifies God.

10:32-33: Individual group members are not to offend the people with whom they live. The categories: Judean, Greeks, and the gathering of God indicate the categories of persons with whom Jesus-group members usually interact. Judeans and Greeks are Israelites of traditional and Hellenistic bent respectively. The gathering of God covers Paul's Jesus-group members. **Jew and Greek/Judean and Hellenist; *Ekklēsia* (Gathering).** Again, the theme is not to seek one's own entitlements but to seek what benefits the many so that the many be saved. Passive voice implies God is the saving agent.

11:1: In this behavior, focused on the well-being of others, Paul imitates Christ and urges his Corinthians to do the same.

Part Five: 1 Cor 11:2-34
About Behavior at Jesus Group Gatherings

This section deals with problems arising from confusion about the social quality of Jesus-group gatherings: Were they to be like domestic gatherings or like public ones? If Jesus groups are associations of fictive domestic kin (brothers and sisters in Christ), are these gatherings to be like those of household members with each other in an extended kinship setting, or are these gatherings of a public nature even if held in a household setting? The customary behaviors of husbands and wives in a household setting, either alone or with kin, are quite different from those in a non-household situation. Similarly, gatherings in a household setting involved the host's serving food of different quality depending on the social status of the guests. While there were public distributions of food, there was no egalitarian public dining. Nothing about the ancient world presumed egalitarianism in any arena. Now Paul presents his solution to these sorts of questions.

Jesus Group Gatherings Are Not Domestic Gatherings: 1 Cor 11:2-16

11:2 I commend you because you remember me in everything and maintain the traditions just as I handed them on to you. 3 But I want you to understand that Christ is the head of every man, and the husband is the head of his wife, and God is the head of Christ. 4 Any man who prays or prophesies with something on his head disgraces his head, 5 but any woman who prays or prophesies with her head unveiled disgraces her head—it is one and the same thing as having her head shaved. 6 For if a woman will not veil herself, then she should cut off her hair; but if it is disgraceful for a woman to have her hair cut off or to be shaved, she should wear a veil. 7 For a man ought not to have his head veiled, since he is the image and reflection of God; but woman is the reflection of man. 8 Indeed, man was not made from woman, but woman from man. 9 Neither was man created for the sake of woman, but woman for the sake of man. 10 For this reason a woman ought to have a symbol of authority on her head, because of the angels. 11 Nevertheless, in the Lord woman is not independent of man or man independent of woman. 12 For just as woman came from man, so man comes through woman; but all things come from God. 13 Judge for yourselves: is it proper for a woman to pray to God with her head unveiled? 14 Does not nature itself teach you that if a man wears long hair, it is degrading to him, 15 but if a woman has long hair, it is her glory? For her hair is given to her for a covering. 16 But if anyone is disposed to be contentious—we have no such custom, nor do the churches of God.

Textual Notes: 1 Cor 11:2-16

11:2-16: This section deals with the behavior of wives and husbands at Jesus-group gatherings. The situation describes women acting as they would in private. This makes sense if the gatherings were in a domestic setting among brothers and sisters. But Paul's advice indicates that while Jesus-group members are one in Christ, their gatherings are of a public nature. Hence wives and husbands at Jesus-group gatherings must act according to the social norms of public behavior.

11:2 and 16 form an inclusion or literary bracket marking off the piece. These statements refer to traditions about behavior that Paul handed on and that the Corinthians accepted. But there is this case about which, it seems, Paul has handed on nothing, although Jesus groups regularly follow the practice he will now examine (v. 16).

11:3: The word "head" in this passage is made to serve double duty, referring both to one in charge and to one's physical head. This is possible because the human body is always a sort of portable road map of the social body. The physical head is symbol of honor—personal honor and social honor. As symbol of honor, the head may be viewed as the source and public locus of honor. In the principle Paul enunciates here, Christ is Lord and source of honor of every Jesus-group husband, while the husband is lord and source of honor of every wife. In this hierarchy, the God of Israel is the Lord and source of honor of his Christ. In their behavior Jesus-group husbands and wives are expected to honor the source of their honor. To honor another is to show respect, to behave in a way that brings honor to another.

11:4: In Israelite circles any male who communicates with God or imparts some message from God to others must have his head uncovered to show respect for God. A covered head in these circumstances dishonors or shames God. Male head covering at prayer was not a Judean custom among Israelites during Paul's day, as it was to become in later Jewish religion.

11:5-6: In Israelite circles any female who communicates with God or imparts some message from God to others with head uncovered acts disrespectfully. The word translated "uncovered" may also mean "unbraided." Mediterranean married women of antiquity were to have their hair braided, signifying their married status. A married woman in public with unbraided hair surely shamed her husband. It was as shameful as having her head shaved. The behavior expected of married women at Jesus-group gatherings where they pray and prophesy is the same as that expected of them in public. Since in public they would not be seen with hair cut off or shaved, neither should they attend Jesus-group gatherings with hair unbraided.

11:7-8: Paul roots social gender roles in Israel's creation story. Men are the image and reflection of God the creator, so they must not cover their head; their honor is public and is directed to the outside of the family. Women, on the other hand, are the likeness of their husbands, and their honor is private, facing the inside of the family.

This statue (dated 12–14 C.E.) of Emperor Augustus performing a sacrifice shows that for Romans the veiling of a man's head could well have been a show of piety. Compare Paul's criticism of men who covered their heads (1 Cor 11:4).

11:9-10: As the Genesis story tells it, woman was made from man (Gen 2:22-23) and for the sake of man (Gen 2:18). According to the same story, unattached women were preyed on by angels (Gen 6:2), and an unveiled or unbraided female appears as unattached.

11:11: Nevertheless, in Jesus groups husbands and wives are mutually dependent. Paul's scriptural argument, again, is Genesis (2:18 and following): just as the first female was taken from the first male, all subsequent males come through women.

11:14-15: In first-century Hellenism the Greek word for "nature" (*physis*) referred, first of all, to what was customary and usual, hence the *ethos* of a given *ethnos* or people, or a given species of animals, or even of a given person or animal. In this sense, the natural stood opposed to the conventional or legal; the conventional or legal was behavior decided upon by a person or group with legal power. "Nature" also referred to what was usual in the qualities of all that existed, all creation—what is instinctive, species-specific. What happened customarily and recurrently was natural, traceable to origins, to creation. Planets naturally moved erratically. Honey naturally tasted sweet.

For Paul and his contemporaries, the word "nature" when applied to people referred to what we call "culture" today. While there is no word for "nature" in Hebrew, yet Israelites believed that their cultural arrangements derived directly from the commands of the God of Israel, the creator of all nature. In typical ethnocentric fashion, Israelites believed that those who did not follow Israelite culture were, to a greater or lesser extent, deviants and acted unnaturally. They deviated from the intentions of the creator God as fully realized in Israelite society rooted in Torah. Males with long hair in Paul's society were male transsexuals (see Philo, *Spec. Laws* III.7.37–42), a role that in Israelite perspective degraded men. Women, on the other hand, had long hair, a covering for their heads.

11:16: Paul's conclusion takes up the opening statement of this passage and further states that all Jesus groups follow this assessment of their gatherings as public, with wives expected to follow the customary behavior appropriate in public gatherings.

Proper Dining Behavior at Jesus-Group Gatherings 1 Cor 11:17-34

11:17 Now in the following instructions I do not commend you, because when you come together it is not for the better but for the worse. 18 For, to begin with, when you come together as a church, I hear that there are divisions among you; and to some extent I believe it. 19 Indeed, there have to be factions among you, for only so will it become clear who among you are genuine. 20 When you come together, it is not really to eat the Lord's supper. 21 For when the time comes to eat, each of you goes ahead with your own supper, and one goes hungry and another becomes drunk. 22 What! Do you not have homes to eat and drink in? Or do you show contempt for the church of God and humiliate those who have nothing? What should I say to you? Should I commend you? In this matter I do not commend you!

23 For I received from the Lord what I also handed on to you, that the Lord Jesus on the night when he was betrayed took a loaf of bread, 24 and when he had given

thanks, he broke it and said, "This is my body that is for you. Do this in remembrance of me." 25 In the same way he took the cup also, after supper, saying, "This cup is the new covenant in my blood. Do this, as often as you drink it, in remembrance of me." 26 For as often as you eat this bread and drink the cup, you proclaim the Lord's death until he comes.

27 Whoever, therefore, eats the bread or drinks the cup of the Lord in an unworthy manner will be answerable for the body and blood of the Lord. 28 Examine yourselves, and only then eat of the bread and drink of the cup. 29 For all who eat and drink without discerning the body, eat and drink judgment against themselves. 30 For this reason many of you are weak and ill, and some have died. 31 But if we judged ourselves, we would not be judged. 32 But when we are judged by the Lord, we are disciplined so that we may not be condemned along with the world.

33 So then, my brothers and sisters, when you come together to eat, wait for one another. 34 If you are hungry, eat at home, so that when you come together, it will not be for your condemnation. About the other things I will give instructions when I come.

Textual Notes: 1 Cor 11:17-34

11:17: Paul praised the Corinthians for their previous behavior, indicating their adherence to Jesus-group customs and Paul's instruction (11:2-16). But he now faces another facet of their group behavior that is not deserving of praise, specifically the question of cliques (note the report from Chloe's people about this matter treated in 1:9-16). **Cliques.** The critical importance of table fellowship as both reality and symbol of social cohesion and shared values cannot be overestimated in this passage.

11:18-19: The gathering of the Corinthian Jesus group is a negative experience as far as Paul is concerned because, rather than unity, cliques take up adversarial positions. But the divisions reveal group members who are genuine and those who are not. Paul's presumption is that the boundaries surrounding the Jesus group are rather porous, and experiences of divisiveness are required to test who really is in and who does not belong.

11:20: If the Corinthians gather at all, the purpose of their gathering is to eat the Lord's supper. Paul does not explain what that means, thus presuming the recipients of this letter know very well what he means. When they gather, however, they are not sufficiently aware of the purpose of their gathering, for the focus of their attention is not the Lord's supper but their own supper. If one goes hungry and another becomes drunk, it is obvious that group members bring their own food for themselves, with the better off eating apart from those with less or nothing. Such status-specific dining was well known in Greco-Roman society.

> It would be a long story, and of no importance, were I to recount too particularly by what accident I (who am not fond at all of society) supped lately with a person, who in his own opinion lives in splendor combined with economy; but according to mine, in a sordid but expensive manner. Some very elegant dishes were served up to himself and a few more of the company; while those which were placed before the rest were cheap and paltry. He had apportioned in small flagons three different sorts of wine; but you are not to suppose it was that the guests might take their choice: on

> the contrary, that they might not choose at all. One was for himself and me; the next for his friends of a lower order (for you must know, he measures out his friendship according to the degrees of quality); and the third for his own freed-men and mine. One who sat next to me took notice of this, and asked me if I approved of it. "Not at all," I told him. "Pray, then," said he, "what is your method on such occasions?" "Mine," I returned, "is to give all my company the same fare; for when I make an invitation, it is to sup, not to be censoring. Every man whom I have placed on an equality with myself by admitting him to my table, I treat as an equal in all particulars." "Even freed-men?" he asked. "Even them," I said; "for on those occasions I regard them not as freed-men, but boon companions." "This must put you to great expense," says he. I assured him not at all; and on his asking how that could be, I said, "Why you must know my freedmen do not drink the same wine I do—but I drink what they do." (Pliny the Younger, *Letters* II, 6, LCL 109–13; see also Martial, *Epigrams*, I, 20; III, 60, LCL 43, 201; Juvenal, *Satires* V, LCL 69–83)

11:22: Paul's mentioning that Corinthian Jesus-group members have their own houses in which to eat and drink implies that their gathering is not in a house but in some sort of meeting place, like the buildings Israelites used for their synagogues (that is, gatherings) or some other associational community center. Obviously, in a group professing unity in Christ, status-specific dining is a denial of unity. The behavior of some better-off group members in the presence of their poorly provisioned fellows is both contemptuous for the whole gathering and surely dishonoring to "those who have nothing." Such behavior on the part of the better-off is simply shameless and dishonorable.

11:23: Since the Jesus-group gathering comes together for the express purpose of participating in the Lord's supper, Paul reminds them of what the Lord's supper is about by citing the account of that supper that he "received from the Lord." Both the terms "receive" and "hand on" are technical terms referring to authoritative traditions in later Pharisaic documents, notably traditions from Moses. Their use here mirrors Paul's Pharisaic background. However, to "receive from the Lord" is a high context phrase meaning to receive as authoritative tradition in the Jesus group. As part of his role as change agent, one of Paul's tasks is to hand on authentic Jesus-group tradition.

11:23-25: Paul describes the action that presumably characterized the central ritual of the gathering. In later Jesus-group documents, we find an account of this action in the wider context of Jesus' final meal with his disciples (Matt 26:26-28; Mark 14:22-24; Luke 22:19-20). Jesus' action in breaking the bread and sharing the cup of wine would readily be perceived as a prophetic symbolic action. For example, in Ezekiel 5 the prophet is commanded to cut his hair and variously destroy and save what he cut; the behavior is clarified by the prophet with the statement: "This is Jerusalem" (Ezek 5:5). The prophet Jesus clarified what he was doing with "This is my body . . . the cup of my blood." **Prophetic Symbolic Action.**

Such an action consists of some symbolic action (usually commanded by God) performed by a prophet, then followed by words that clarify the meaning of the action. A symbolic action is an action that conveys meaning and feeling and invariably effects what it symbolizes by the power of God, who commands it. Here the action is eating bread and drinking a cup of wine. The first part of the action is explained as Jesus' body, that is, Jesus himself (or extended self), "for you." The second part of the action marks the separation of self from blood, the locus of life, indicating death. The blood is new covenant blood. Israel's old covenant blood, the Mosaic covenant, set up a special relationship of mutual obligation between the God of Israel and God's people with forgiveness of sins and reconciliation (see Exod 24:8 and its context). Forgiveness meant no satisfaction or revenge would be taken for their dishonoring God, thus allowing for reconciliation. Now those who participate in Jesus' prophetic symbolic action are sharers in the new covenant made effective by Jesus' death, specifically by his blood (as locus of life). It was Jesus' actual death on the cross that effected the new covenant, while subsequent Jesus groups repeat his final prophetic symbolic action at his command, in remembrance of Jesus (vv. 24 and 25). This remembrance fits within the reverence for ancestors common in ancient Israel. As inaugurating ancestor of all who believe in what the God of Israel did in raising him, Jesus himself merits the ancestor reverence previously proper to Israel's great ancestors, Abraham, Isaac, and Jacob. In this sense, reverence for Jesus is a form of ancestor reverence, in remembrance of what Jesus did for us.

11:26-27: What then do Jesus groups who share in the Lord's supper actually do? First of all, they proclaim the significance of the Lord's death, that is, the effects and outcomes of Jesus' death for us. These include God's waiving of satisfaction due to dishonor (called "forgiveness of sin"), the giving of God's spirit to Jesus-group members, the inauguration of a new covenant with God, and access to the forthcoming theocracy to be founded with the coming of Jesus as Lord and Messiah. Hence unworthy participants in the ceremony of the prophetic symbolic action, which is performed in remembrance of Jesus until he comes, will be answerable for the dishonor perpetrated.

11:28-34: If a person does not "discern the body" and participates in the Lord's supper, that person stands condemned. Evidence of such lack of discerning the body among the Corinthians is that many are weak and ill and some have fallen asleep. As indicated in vv. 33-34, the condemnation in context is due to not waiting for one another and eating while others have nothing to eat. Hence to "discern the body" refers to group awareness, to being attentive to one's fellow Jesus-group members, who together form "the body of Christ," as Paul will shortly explain (12:12). The point is that to avoid condemnation, Jesus-group members must be attentive to how they treat others in the group; otherwise the Lord will discipline us in order to form us in the proper ways to behave (the meaning of *paideuo* in v. 32) so that we will not be condemned with "the world," that is, the rest of society.

Paul concludes, stating he will put the remaining affairs in order when he comes to Corinth. What these other things might entail he does not say.

The inscription on this marble column, found in a Roman basilica in Athens, records the development and rules of the Iobacchoi, an organization of devotees of the god Dionysos. The regulations include membership dues, prohibitions against fighting and insulting other members, and fines for rule violations.

Part Six: 1 Cor 12:1–14:40
About Phenomena Induced by the Spirit

This section consists of three passages, in an A-B-A' pattern. The first deals with something the Corinthians wrote about, specifically phenomena induced by the Spirit (12:1-31a). The second sets out a rather well-composed description of a core central value that Paul calls *agapē* (most often translated "love" or "charity") (12:31b—13:13). The final passage deals again with Jesus-group gatherings (14:1-40).

Phenomena Induced by the Spirit 1 Cor 12:1-31a

12:1 Now concerning spiritual gifts,
brothers and sisters, I do not want you to
be uninformed. 2 You know that when
you were pagans, you were enticed and
led astray to idols that could not speak.
3 Therefore I want you to understand that
no one speaking by the Spirit of God ever
says "Let Jesus be cursed!" and no one can
say "Jesus is Lord" except by the Holy Spirit.
4 Now there are varieties of gifts, but
the same Spirit; 5 and there are varieties
of services, but the same Lord; 6 and there

are varieties of activities, but it is the same God who activates all of them in everyone. 7 To each is given the manifestation of the Spirit for the common good. 8 To one is given through the Spirit the utterance of wisdom, and to another the utterance of knowledge according to the same Spirit, 9 to another faith by the same Spirit, to another gifts of healing by the one Spirit, 10 to another the working of miracles, to another prophecy, to another the discernment of spirits, to another various kinds of tongues, to another the interpretation of tongues. 11 All these are activated by one and the same Spirit, who allots to each one individually just as the Spirit chooses.

12 For just as the body is one and has many members, and all the members of the body, though many, are one body, so it is with Christ. 13 For in the one Spirit we were all baptized into one body—Jews or Greeks, slaves or free—and we were all made to drink of one Spirit.

14 Indeed, the body does not consist of one member but of many. 15 If the foot would say, "Because I am not a hand, I do not belong to the body," that would not make it any less a part of the body. 16 And if the ear would say, "Because I am not an eye, I do not belong to the body," that would not make it any less a part of the body. 17 If the whole body were an eye, where would the hearing be? If the whole body were hearing, where would the sense of smell be? 18 But as it is, God arranged the members in the body, each one of them, as he chose. 19 If all were a single member, where would the body be? 20 As it is, there are many members, yet one body. 21 The eye cannot say to the hand, "I have no need of you," nor again the head to the feet, "I have no need of you." 22 On the contrary, the members of the body that seem to be weaker are indispensable, 23 and those members of the body that we think less honorable we clothe with greater honor, and our less respectable members are treated with greater respect; 24 whereas our more respectable members do not need this. But God has so arranged the body, giving the greater honor to the inferior member, 25 that there may be no dissension within the body, but the members may have the same care for one another. 26 If one member suffers, all suffer together with it; if one member is honored, all rejoice together with it.

27 Now you are the body of Christ and individually members of it. 28 And God has appointed in the church first apostles, second prophets, third teachers; then deeds of power, then gifts of healing, forms of assistance, forms of leadership, various kinds of tongues. 29 Are all apostles? Are all prophets? Are all teachers? Do all work miracles? 30 Do all possess gifts of healing? Do all speak in tongues? Do all interpret? 31 But strive for the greater gifts.

Textual Notes: 1 Cor 12:1-31

12:1: Paul once again turns to respond to a subject about which the Corinthians wrote. This time the subject is "spiritual gifts" (NRSV; Greek: *pneumatika*). The English translation is rather misleading, since the Greek means "spirit induced phenomena," "phenomena ascribable to a spirit." Aside from the fact that there is no word here meaning "gift," use of the word "gift" leaves the English reader with the wrong impression. In our society, we experience actual free gifts (free samples, no-strings-attached donations, etc.). However, in first-century experience where all goods were perceived as limited, nothing was free. Anything one accepted from another required some sort of reciprocity at some time. (An Arab proverb says, "Don't thank me. You will repay me.") Again, the term *pneumatika* does not have the connotation of gift at all. The topic the Corinthians presented Paul with was that of Spirit-induced phenomena, or phenomena ascribable to the spirit. As the context indicates, the spirit in question is the Spirit of God. **Altered States of Consciousness.**

12:2: Another problem introduced by modern translations is the word "pagans," a category that was nonexistent in the first century C.E. (see **Notes** on 1 Cor 5:1). The Greek word is *ethnē*. When contrasted with Israel, the term usually means "peoples other than Israel." This cannot be the meaning of the word here, since one cannot change one's ancestry or genealogy. The Corinthians were not former non-Israelites who changed into being Israelites. One's ancestry derives from birth, like one's biological sex. The fact is that the word *ethnē* has a range of meanings always referring to a group whose members have something in common (see **Notes** on 1 Cor 5:1). In context, what Corinthian Jesus-group members had in common was that before joining the Jesus group, they were outsiders, members of the out-group. The word *ethnē* here does not refer to ancestry or genealogy but to social standing. Hence the statement describes members of the Corinthian Jesus group when they were still outsiders. Like other Israelites resident among a non-Israelite majority, they too had recourse to local deities whose presence was mediated by mute images. It seems gatherings of devotees of local deities also experienced Spirit-induced phenomena, altered states of consciousness of various sorts.

12:3: The problem, of course, was which spirit was behind the altered states of consciousness people experienced. Paul underscores the fact that the Spirit of the God of Israel, the Holy Spirit, could only urge people to say "Jesus is Lord." To say "Let Jesus be cursed" is a phenomenon induced by some alien spirit.

12:4: Once more, the NRSV and its predecessors introduce the word "gift." In fact the Greek word here, *charisma*, seems to be a Pauline coinage that does not exactly mean "gift." Nor does it have anything in common with the modern sociological term "charism" popularized in sociology by Max Weber (for example, a charismatic presidential candidate, a charismatic preacher). *Charisma* refers to the various outcomes of God's patronage revealed in the favors God bestows on those who believe in the Jesus-group gospel of God. A favor (Greek: *charis*; Latin: *gratia*) is something given or done by a patron for a client that is either not available at all or not available at a particular time. Clients go to patrons for favors. Those accepting favors are obliged, in turn, to obey the patron, defend the patron's honor in public, glorify the patron, and remain loyal to the patron. Accepting a favor entails all these reciprocal obligations. The *charismata* (plural of *charisma*) are phenomena connected with God's favor bestowed on Jesus groups. In context, God's favor in fact is Christ himself, and it is Jesus-group members, each with his or her *charisma*, who together are Christ in society. **Patronage System.**

12:4-7: With this threefold contrast between variety and unity, Paul begins his argument about the variety of *charismata* and the unity of their source: the same Spirit, the same Lord, the same God. The *charismata* are given to everyone in the Jesus group. They are identified as services and activities. In what follows, these services and activities have a collectivistic function, to support and upbuild the Jesus group. In other words, they are not given for the good of the individual who possesses a *charisma*. Rather, for *charismata* to emerge, persons are required to be of service or to act on behalf of another. They are phenomena experienced by each person in the group and induced by God's Spirit for the common good of the group.

12:8-11: Paul now lists the phenomena in question: utterance of wisdom, utterance of knowledge, ability to inspire confidence, healing, working of power, prophecy, discernment of spirits, kinds of tongues, interpretation of tongues. What ties these phenomena together is that they are rooted in altered states of consciousness experiences. **Altered States of Consciousness.** Paul ascribes such phenomena to the presence of the Spirit of God, who activates them in each Jesus-group member as it pleases God.

12:12-13: Now Paul enunciates his great principle that fuses his understanding of the presence of Christ and of the nature of the Jesus assembly. Christ present is like a body consisting of many members and realized in the social body of Jesus-group members. The way this body that is Christ has been constituted is by means of the Spirit. To follow Paul's analogy, one must realize that in terms of first-century "physics," wind, fire, and water are liquids. Hence one can be dipped (that is, baptized) in the Spirit to form one body, and one can drink of the one Spirit. Paul notes that the social categories constituting the Corinthian Jesus groups through being dipped in the Spirit include Judean and Hellenistic Israelites, both those enslaved and those who are free or freed.

12:14-26: Paul now makes his case for unity in diversity in the Corinthian Jesus group as he unfolds his analogy of Christ as body in greater detail. His main point is that just as God arranged the human body as he chose, so too the social body of Christ at Corinth. In his description Paul seems to make several social criticisms. First of all, the weaker members are indispensable (v. 22); those clothed with greater honor are the less honorable; those treated with greater respect are in fact less respectable. In sum those given greater honor are inferior members. Second, regardless of honor ranking, members must have mutual care for one another: if one suffers, all suffer; if one is honored, all rejoice.

12:27-30: Here Paul once more states his understanding of the presence of Christ and develops its import for the Jesus group. Group members are the body of Christ, singly members of that body. The assembly of those called by God has its structure from God himself: "first apostles, second prophets, third teachers; then deeds of power, then gifts of healing, forms of assistance, forms of leadership, various kinds of tongues." All these outcomes of God's favor, like Christ himself, exist as they do at God's bidding. In practice they are made known in altered states of consciousness experienced by the group, upon whom the "Spirit has been poured." Why does Paul list them in the order that he does? His final admonition (12:31: "But strive for the greater *charismata*") indicates several things. First of all, the listing indicates that one can exchange his or her part in the body that is Christ for a greater one. Moreover, one ought to endeavor to take on the services or activities that Paul lists as greater. Obviously the *charismata* are not permanent but flexible, presumably alterable for the common good of the Jesus group.

The Central Value of *Agapē* (Group Allegiance) 12:31b–13:13

12:31b: And I will show you a still more excellent way.

13:1 If I speak in the tongues of mortals and of angels, but do not have love, I am a noisy gong or a clanging cymbal. 2 And if I have prophetic powers, and understand all mysteries and all knowledge, and if I have all faith, so as to remove mountains, but do not have love, I am nothing. 3 If I give away all my possessions, and if I hand over my body so that I may boast, but do not have love, I gain nothing.

4 Love is patient; love is kind; love is not envious or boastful or arrogant 5 or rude. It does not insist on its own way; it is not irritable or resentful; 6 it does not rejoice in wrongdoing, but rejoices in the truth. 7 It bears all things, believes all things, hopes all things, endures all things.

8 Love never ends. But as for prophecies, they will come to an end; as for tongues, they will cease; as for knowledge, 9 For we know only in part, and we prophesy only in part; 10 but when the complete comes, the partial will come to an end. 11 When I was a child, I spoke like a child, I thought like a child, I reasoned like a child; when I became an adult, I put an end to childish ways. 12 For now we see in a mirror, dimly, but then we will see face to face. Now I know only in part; then I will know fully, even as I have been fully known. 13 And now faith, hope, and love abide, these three; and the greatest of these is love.

Textual Notes: 1 Cor 12:31b–13:13

This passage breaks the flow of the argument about Spirit-induced phenomena in Jesus-group gatherings. The argument is taken up again in 1 Cor 14:1 and continues to the end of that chapter. This passage about *agapē* (NRSV: "love") is an insertion, of sorts. In an anti-introspective, nonpsychologically minded, collectivistic society, the word *agapē* is best translated "group allegiance." **Collectivistic Personality.** Such allegiance is the social bond of group members to each other individually and to the group as a whole. Group allegiance is a quality and direction of behavior that inheres in what group members do to and for each other and in how they do it. Paul admiringly describes this particular quality and direction of behavior, making the point that if such *agapē* does not characterize the exercise of Spirit-induced phenomena, then such phenomena are of little use to the individual Jesus-group member. Of course, those phenomena may be of great use to others, as *charismata* are wont to be.

The passage is well structured into three distinct parts:

- vv. 1-3: a progressive comparison of *charismata* and *agapē*
- vv. 4-7: a description of *agapē*
- vv. 8-13: a series of antitheses underlining the excellence and staying power of *agapē*

12:31b: This introductory statement describes *agapē* as a more excellent way. In Hellenism, the word "way" labeled moral teaching as well as the behavior that conformed to such teaching. Paul does not employ this usage, although it is used elsewhere in the New Testament (e.g., Acts 16:4: way of salvation; Acts 18:25: way of the Lord; Acts 18:26: the way of God; Heb 3:20: my ways (of God); Heb 10:20: a new and living way; 2 Pet 2:2: way of truth; 2 Pet 2:15: the right way, the way of Balaam; Heb 2:21: way of righteousness; Jude 1:11: way of Cain). Acts even reports that "the Way" was the pristine name for the distinctive Jesus-group teaching and behavior (Acts 9:2; 19:9, 23; 22:4; 24:14, 22).

13:1-3: These verses present a progressive comparison of *charismata* and *agapē*.

13:1: The language of men and angels means all possible languages, including the languages of those in altered states of consciousness, one of the *charismata* listed by Paul. Angels were thought to have their own language of worship (as in Isa 6:3; and often in Revelation). Gonging bass and clanging cymbals were used in temple worship around the Mediterranean. The verbal arrogance of public speakers was also labeled as the sound of a gong or cymbal. For a Jesus-group member to speak in tongues without group allegiance is like the noise made by an inarticulate musical instrument (see 1 Cor 14:2, 9, 11, 28).

13:2: In Paul's previous listing (12:28) the *charismata* of tongues and administration rank the lowest. With prophecy, knowledge, and faith, we come to a higher *charismata*. "Prophecy" refers to utterances deriving from altered states of consciousness experiences that apply the gospel of God to new situations. Prophecy indicates what has to be done in the here and now in line with the experience of Jesus. To know mysteries is to know the secrets of God, to know God's will for the here and now. To have knowledge is to penetrate into the depth and meaning of God's ways in human society, a sort of theology flowing from an altered state of consciousness experience. Finally, "faith" means trust in the God of Israel, that is, unwavering reliance on God; hence the word refers to the social, externally manifested behavior of loyalty and commitment to God, solidarity with God. To move or uproot a mountain, as much later rabbinic sources indicate, is an idiom for to make what is impossible possible (see *b. Sanh.* 24a; *b. Ber.* 64a). The phrase was applied to the intellectual prowess of those who were able to explain the knotty difficulties of moral problems (as in the intellectual context here).

The threefold repetition of "all" points to the possession of these *charismata* in their most perfect form. Without *agapē*, these *charismata* are nothing. While the prophecy of the prophet or the teachings of a theologian or moralist can and do produce good effects for the upbuilding of the Jesus group, without *agapē* they are of no value to the person having these *charismata*.

13:3: Once more, note the emphatic "all." To distribute all one's wealth for the benefit of one's poorer fellows is a heroic gesture (in the story of Jesus, see Matt 19:16-30; Mark 10:17-31; Luke 18:18-30). On the other hand, to hand oneself over to be burned for the sake of one's community was well-known courageous behavior in Asia Minor. In Corinth itself, tradition told of a certain Hellotis and one of his young sisters throwing themselves into the burning temple of Athena rather than surrender to the Dorians (circa 1000 B.C.E.). The Corinthians celebrated this noble deed in the feast of the Hellotia, a deed of supreme sacrifice in face of atrocious torment. Thus the Spirit-inspired impulses to give away one's goods on behalf of others and to die for the good of others are the noblest of *charismata*, yet without *agapē* even such noble deeds on behalf of others are useless to the one performing them.

13:4-7: This section sets out the characteristics of *agapē*, following one of the characteristic patterns used by Hellenists to describe a quality. The pattern consists of ten features characterizing some abstract personified quality, usually in negative statements, followed by a conclusion marked by "all." (Again, for examples, see *Testament of Issachar* IV on single-mindedness, *Testament of Benjamin* VI on the good inclination, and 1 Cor 6:9-11 on the inheritors of the kingdom.) The variant here opens with a positive statement in chiastic form (ABB'A'). The choice of ten features is not exhaustive but stylistic.

13:8-12: After describing the quality and direction of behavior encompassed by the value of group allegiance, the author of this piece now considers the lastingness of *agapē*. There is something imperishable about it. To demonstrate the point, there is a series of five antitheses meant to underscore the superior excellence and permanence of *agapē*: never . . . at some time (v. 8), in part . . . (entirely) (vv. 9-10), time of childhood . . . adulthood (v. 11), now . . . then (v. 12), now three . . . best of all (v. 13).

13:12: The often-repeated statement "now we see in a mirror dimly" (KJV: "darkly") refers to first-century mirrors, which were much like the top of a polished tin can rather than the silver-backed glass we call mirrors. The word "dimly" or "darkly" translates the Greek *en ainigmati*, literally "in a riddle." The allusion is probably to Israel's intertext, for in Num 12:8 God says that he will speak to Moses face to face (see also v. 12b), not through riddles (LXX), that is, obscurely. The mention of "face to face," that is person to person, here further bolsters this point.

13:13: The concluding statement notes that faith, hope, and *agapē* all perdure—they are all lasting. This trio of attitudes is mentioned elsewhere by Paul (1 Thess 1:3; 5:8; Gal 5:5-6; and in the rest of the New Testament, see Eph 4:2-5; Col 1:4-5; Heb 6:10-12; 10:22-24; 1 Pet 1:3-8). For Paul these three values are the hallmark of the social identity of the Jesus-group membership. (See **Notes** on 1 Thess 1:2-3.) However, of these abiding values, the greatest is group allegiance.

More about Spirit-Induced Phenomena 14:1-40

14:1 Pursue love and strive for the spiritual gifts, and especially that you may prophesy. 2 For those who speak in a tongue do not speak to other people but to God; for nobody understands them, since they are speaking mysteries in the Spirit. 3 On the other hand, those who prophesy speak to other people for their upbuilding and encouragement and consolation. 4 Those who speak in a tongue build up themselves, but those who prophesy build up the church. 5 Now I would like all of you to speak in tongues, but even more to prophesy. One who prophesies is greater than one who speaks in tongues, unless someone interprets, so that the church may be built up.

6 Now, brothers and sisters, if I come to you speaking in tongues, how will I benefit you unless I speak to you in some revelation or knowledge or prophecy or teaching? 7 It is the same way with lifeless instruments that produce sound, such as the flute or the harp. If they do not give distinct notes, how will anyone know what is being played? 8 And if the bugle gives an indistinct sound, who will get ready for battle? 9 So with yourselves; if in a tongue you utter speech that is not intelligible, how will anyone know what is being said? For you will be speaking into the air. 10 There are doubtless many different kinds of sounds in the world, and nothing is without sound. 11 If then I do not know the meaning of a sound, I will be a foreigner to the speaker and the speaker a foreigner to me. 12 So with yourselves; since you are eager for spiritual gifts,

strive to excel in them for building up the
church.
13 Therefore, one who speaks in a
tongue should pray for the power to interpret. 14 For if I pray in a tongue, my
spirit prays but my mind is unproductive.
15 What should I do then? I will pray with
the spirit, but I will pray with the mind also;
I will sing praise with the spirit, but I will
sing praise with the mind also. 16 Otherwise,
if you say a blessing with the spirit, how can
anyone in the position of an outsider say
the "Amen" to your thanksgiving, since
the outsider does not know what you are
saying? 17 For you may give thanks well
enough, but the other person is not built
up. 18 I thank God that I speak in tongues
more than all of you; 19 nevertheless, in
church I would rather speak five words
with my mind, in order to instruct others
also, than ten thousand words in a tongue.
20 Brothers and sisters, do not be children in your thinking; rather, be infants in
evil, but in thinking be adults. 21 In the law
it is written,

"By people of strange tongues
and by the lips of foreigners
I will speak to this people;
yet even then they will not listen
to me,"

says the Lord. 22 Tongues, then, are a sign
not for believers but for unbelievers, while
prophecy is not for unbelievers but for
believers. 23 If, therefore, the whole church
comes together and all speak in tongues,
and outsiders or unbelievers enter, will
they not say that you are out of your mind?
24 But if all prophesy, an unbeliever or outsider who enters is reproved by all and called
to account by all. 25 After the secrets of the
unbeliever's heart are disclosed, that person
will bow down before God and worship
him, declaring, "God is really among you."
26 What should be done then, my
friends? When you come together, each
one has a hymn, a lesson, a revelation, a
tongue, or an interpretation. Let all things
be done for building up. 27 If anyone
speaks in a tongue, let there be only two
or at most three, and each in turn; and let
one interpret. 28 But if there is no one to
interpret, let them be silent in church and
speak to themselves and to God. 29 Let
two or three prophets speak, and let the
others weigh what is said. 30 If a revelation
is made to someone else sitting nearby, let
the first person be silent. 31 For you can all
prophesy one by one, so that all may learn
and all be encouraged. 32 And the spirits of
prophets are subject to the prophets, 33 for
God is a God not of disorder but of peace.
(As in all the churches of the saints,
34 women should be silent in the churches.
For they are not permitted to speak, but
should be subordinate, as the law also says.
35 If there is anything they desire to know,
let them ask their husbands at home. For it
is shameful for a woman to speak in church.
36 Or did the word of God originate with
you? Or are you the only ones it has reached?)
37 Anyone who claims to be a prophet,
or to have spiritual powers, must acknowledge that what I am writing to you is a
command of the Lord. 38 Anyone who does
not recognize this is not to be recognized.
39 So, my friends, be eager to prophesy, and
do not forbid speaking in tongues; 40 but all
things should be done decently and in order.

Textual Notes: 1 Cor 14:1-40

The whole passage is about the *charisma* of speaking in tongues (Greek: *glossōlalia*) except for an insertion relative to married women's behavior (vv. 33b-36). In terms of our preferred cultural reality, anthropologists describe speaking in tongues as an act of vocalization, of uttering sounds while the person is in a trance state. **Altered States of Consciousness.** The syllables uttered are empty of semantic content. Paul and his Corinthian Jesus-group members believed that when people speak in tongues, what they utter is a language that could be understood if someone who spoke that language was present (*xenoglossia*). However, modern linguists studying the phenomenon indicate that the syllables produced do not conform to the characteristics of a natural language. Felicitas Goodman notes: "The confusion dissolves if we define speaking in tongues not as language but as communication. In this sense, it is communication between the Holy Spirit and the speaker, and between the speaker and the congregation." She goes on to explain:

> Speaking in tongues is not one single behavior but rather a behavioral complex. First of all, the supplicants learn to go into trance with the help of the strong rhythmic stimulation provided by the congregation in the form of music, clapping, punctuated shouting, and singing. This removes them from the awareness of ordinary reality. . . . After supplicants learn to go into trance, they learn to utter sounds: there is vocalization. Some people, especially those who acquire the behavior spontaneously, learn both the trance and the vocalization simultaneously. The trance now acts as a substratum to this speech, producing or generating a number of its features. One of these is its strong rhythmic quality, a regular alternation of consonants and vowels that evinces all the hallmarks of involuntary bodily functions such as heartbeat or breathing. Another feature, a very mysterious one, is a characteristic intonation pattern: there is an onset of a unit utterance (like a sentence in ordinary speech) in the medium range of the speaker; then it rises to a peak at the end of the first third of the curve, and this is perceivable as being louder or simply much faster. Finally, the voice of the speaker drops, but this drop is usually much lower than that at the end of a declarative sentence in English. A curve of a unit utterance registered by the level recorder in the phonetics lab clearly shows this pattern. . . . This complex pattern cannot be mimicked in ordinary consciousness, thus obviating the contention sometimes heard that the behavior is "faked"; however, the longer a person has been speaking in tongues, the less pronounced these patterns become. After falling silent, many supplicants do not instantly become aware of ordinary reality. They might appear confused; their speech seems slow before they return fully to ordinary consciousness. Once this happens, they remember very little of their actions during the trance. In particular, they cannot judge how long they spoke in tongues. They may not even be sure that they uttered anything at all, and if they are, they cannot repeat their utterance. Characteristically, however, once they are in trance again, their utterance is the same. (Goodman 2001:9; see also Goodman 1972, 1973)

14:1: This verse serves as conclusion to the foregoing description of *agapē* and as introduction to what follows. Again, the Greek article before the noun *agapē* indicates: "pursue this *agapē* we have been speaking about." It is a command to put it into practice after a description of what it is like. Spirit-induced phenomena (Greek: *pneumatika*) cannot be pursued like *agapē*, since they are given by the Spirit, but they can be earnestly desired and strived for. Of all the Spirit-induced phenomena available to the Corinthians in their trance experiences, Paul would have them strive after prophecy.

14:2-6: In terms of his culture's consensual reality, Paul describes speaking in tongues as communication addressed to God, speaking mysteries in the Spirit. Its outcome is self-upbuilding. This communication is not understandable by other human beings without interpretation, and without interpretation speaking in tongues is of no use to the Jesus group. Prophecy, in turn, is directed to others, serving to upbuild, encourage, and console members of the Jesus-group gathering. Prophecy, like items of revelation, knowledge, or teaching, is of great use to the Jesus group.

14:7-11: In sum, speaking in tongues is like noise, "lifeless sounds," to use Paul's phrase, that come from flute or lute or war trumpets that are not played for musical effect. Unintelligible speaking in tongues is simply speaking into the air, one of the myriad sounds in the world that make no sense unless one knows "the meaning of a sound" (Greek: *dynamis tēs phōnēs*, "the force of the sound"), much like local languages sound to foreigners.

14:12-17: Again Paul urges *charismata* that serve to build up group members. Those who pray in tongues need the power to interpret, to make sense to others, so that others can at least affirm the prayer with an "Amen." Speaking in tongues is the outcome of the presence of the Spirit and takes place in trance. But such speech does not involve the mind, that is, ordinary human awareness, and so cannot be interpreted for others.

14:18-19: Paul observes that he too has the altered state of consciousness experiences of speaking in tongues, but he sees more value in a few communicable words than in speaking in tongues.

14:20-25: Paul now takes a new tack in his argument about the social disvalue of speaking in tongues. The scriptural citation of Isa 28:11-12, perhaps resonating with Deut 28:49, forms the basis of his argument. Paul here offers a scenario in which the Corinthian Jesus group is gathered in prayer while those not in the group wander in. He presumes the gathering is not closed to curious outsiders. The curious observers are called non-group members and unbelievers. In social context these would be neighborhood residents, hence Israelites. The final sentence of the paragraph refers to the God of Israel.

Speaking in tongues is a sign for Israelite unbelievers, while prophecy is meant for ingroup believers. If unbelievers were to stumble upon a Jesus-group gathering with all speaking in tongues, outsiders and unbelievers would conclude all were mad—deviants of some sort. On the other hand, if all prophesy, any outsiders or an unbelievers would be prophetically reprimanded and called to account by all, since such prophecy will disclose the secrets of the unbeliever's heart, causing the unbelieving Israelite to fall down and reverence the God of Israel, while quoting Israel's scriptures and declaring "God is really among you" (Zech 8:23).

14:26-33a: Now Paul gives his practical advice based on the principle that all *charismata* are to be focused on building up the community. In altered states of consciousness, the experience of group members results in hymns, lessons, revelations, tongues, and interpretation of tongues. According to Paul's principle, only a few are to speak in tongues, and this while taking turns, but if no interpreter is present, then silence is the order of the day. Those who speak in tongues can simply communicate with God in silence. Similarly with prophets and their revelations, only a few are to speak in order, while others are to assess what is said, since the goal of prophecy is "that all may learn and be encouraged." Such orderly behavior replicates an attribute of God who is a God of peace, not disorder (similarly in 1 Cor 7:15: "It is to peace that God has called you").

14:33b-36: These verses are considered by many to be an insertion, considering that the subject of Spirit-induced phenomena is taken up again in v. 37. The NRSV sets these verses in brackets, indicating the same judgment. Here the Corinthian Jesus-group members are berated for permitting married women to speak in group gatherings presumably with their husbands present, contrary to Israelite custom ("the law," v. 34). Such public behavior of wives shames the husbands in whom they are socially embedded. Once more (as in 1 Cor 5:1-4) the Corinthians have chosen an improper line of conduct, in this case a behavior not practiced "in all the gatherings of the saints."

14:37-40: Paul expects that some Jesus-group members who have trance experiences as prophets and the like are able to discern that his position, that "all things should be done decently and in order," is a "command of the Lord." As he stated at the outset of this section, group members should be eager to prophesy, and speaking in tongues is permitted.

Part Seven: 15:1-58
A Reminder about Paul's Gospel and the Resurrection of the Dead

This section deals with the greatest of the phenomena effected by the Spirit of God, the raising of the dead. The way Paul broaches the topic here indicates that the Corinthian Jesus-group members either did not understand Paul's proclamation or misunderstood it rather thoroughly. In the process of the diffusion of an innovation, refraction and reinvention often occur. Refraction refers to the degree to which an innovation or the context of the innovation is changed when it is introduced into a new setting or situation. The innovation proclaimed by Paul in his gospel of God was refracted by the Corinthians. A key feature of this gospel was that those who believe in what the God of Israel did in the death and resurrection of Jesus will likewise be raised by the God of Israel. The Corinthian Jesus-group members reinvented or modified the significance of this forthcoming event and thus departed from Paul's mainline version of the innovation promoted by the change agency, the God of Israel who revealed it to Paul. As evidenced by the history of Jesus-movement groups, an innovation is not invariant during the process of its diffusion.

Paul proceeds in three stages. His first point is that God has in fact raised Jesus from the dead for us and proof of this comes from witnesses (1-11). Second, he describes how some Corinthian Jesus-group members have reinvented or modified this proclamation (12-19). Third, he unpacks the implications of his proclamation, presumably filling in what the Corinthians have either not known or overlooked (20-28). After an aside about "if the dead are not raised . . ." (29-34), Paul concludes with a description of how the dead are to be raised (35-58).

God Has Raised Jesus from the Dead: Significance and Witnesses 1 Cor 15:1-11

15:1 Now I would remind you, brothers and sisters, of the good news that I proclaimed to you, which you in turn received, in which also you stand, 2 through which also you are being saved, if you hold firmly to the message that I proclaimed to you—unless you have come to believe in vain.

3 For I handed on to you as of first importance what I in turn had received: that Christ died for our sins in accordance with the scriptures, 4 and that he was buried, and that he was raised on the third day in accordance with the scriptures, 5 and that he appeared to Cephas, then to the twelve. 6 Then he appeared to more than five hundred brothers and sisters at one time, most of whom are still alive, though some have died. 7 Then he appeared to James, then to all the apostles. 8 Last of all, as to one untimely born, he appeared also to me. 9 For I am the least of the apostles, unfit to be called an apostle, because I persecuted the church of God. 10 But by the grace of God I am what I am, and his grace toward me has not been in vain. On the contrary, I worked harder than any of them—though it was not I, but the grace of God that is with me. 11 Whether then it was I or they, so we proclaim and so you have come to believe.

Textual Notes: 1 Cor 15:1-11

15:1-2: Paul's recalling of his initial proclamation to the Jesus group at Corinth seeks to halt any discontinuance of the innovation it adopted. Even as Paul writes, they "are being saved." The passive voice form of the verb means God is the one saving, that is, excluding them from the group to whom God's punitive action to achieve satisfaction will be directed. That is what God's salvation entails.

15:3-4: Again Paul uses the technical terms for passing on traditions then in vogue in Israel: I handed on what I received (just as in 1 Cor 11:23). Both Jesus' death and his resurrection occurred "for us." Jesus' death is related to sin. Sin against God means shaming God. God, like any honorable, exalted person, must get satisfaction after being dishonored in order to defend his honor, lest he be made a mockery both to Israelites and to non-Israelites. This sort of satisfaction is God's wrath. Thanks to Jesus' death and resurrection, the God of Israel waives this requisite satisfaction for those who believe that the God of Israel raised Jesus from the dead. Given the collectivistic culture of the first-century Mediterranean, Jesus-group members understood Jesus' death not as something exclusive, personal, and individual to Jesus, but as inclusive, communal, and collective for both Jesus and God-fearing Israelites past and present. The same was true of God's raising Jesus. It was a communal and collective event so that the ancient promises of vindication and exaltation for God-fearing Israelites of earlier generations might be realized.

To make sense of Jesus' death and resurrection, Jesus-group members early in the chain of tradition had recourse to the sacred writings of Israel (see Isa 54:7; Hos 6:2; Jonah 1:17). Everything happened "according to the scriptures."

The Greek term for Jesus' being raised (*egeirō*) was the ordinary word for "getting up" or "being lifted up." It is invested with special theological meaning in the Israelite social system, first of all by its being used in the passive voice (used eighteen times in this section). Passive voice statements in the New Testament imply God is the agent or doer (it is God who raised Jesus). Second, the word was invested with the specific cultural meaning of being raised by the God of Israel from the dead. This action of being raised implies a transformation in one's way of being, a qualitative change in one's humanity, as Paul attempts to describe at the close of this section. The action is not about resuscitation of a corpse or a clinically dead person. These actions done by healers, both ancient and modern, do not entail a qualitative change in a person. Resuscitated persons still have to die.

15:5-7: Paul now presents a list of witnesses who interacted with the resurrected Jesus. The Greek word "appeared" (*ōphthē*), repeated four times in this passage, is passive voice again. That means God made Jesus to be seen by the people to whom Jesus "appeared." Again it was not Jesus' initiative that was involved, but the action of the God of Israel. God both raised Jesus from the dead and made Jesus appear to Cephas; the Twelve; more than five hundred Jesus-group members, many still alive; to James the brother of the Lord; to all the change agents whose task was to inform Israel of what the God of Israel had done; and finally to Paul himself, similarly to inform Israelites living in non-Israelite territories about what the God of Israel had done.

15:8-9: Paul variously mentions that he persecuted members of Jesus-group gatherings, although he gives no details. The fact that he persecuted them implies that he knew what they believed about Jesus, the stories they told about Jesus, and what they claimed the God of Israel did through and to Jesus.

15:10: Paul attributes his call and commission to the agency of God, specifically as God's patronage toward him. "Grace" means the favor given by a patron to a client. It was God's favor that impelled Paul.

15:11: Paul is aware that other change agents have been commissioned by God to proclaim the gospel of God with a view to developing believers in God's intervention on Israel's behalf in Jesus' death and resurrection and in the forthcoming Israelite theocracy.

Corinthian Reinvention 1 Cor 15:12-19

15:12 Now if Christ is proclaimed as raised from the dead, how can some of you say there is no resurrection of the dead? 13 If there is no resurrection of the dead, then Christ has not been raised; 14 and if Christ has not been raised, then our proclamation has been in vain and your faith has been in vain. 15 We are even found to be misrepresenting God, because we testified of God that he raised Christ—whom he did not raise if it is true that the dead are not raised. 16 For if the dead are not raised, then Christ has not been raised. 17 If Christ has not been raised, your faith is futile and you are still in your sins. 18 Then those also who have died in Christ have perished. 19 If for this life only we have hoped in Christ, we are of all people most to be pitied.

Textual Notes: 1 Cor 15:12-19

15:12: The contention of some Corinthian Jesus-group members is that there is no forthcoming resurrection of the dead because the dead are not raised. Our hope in Christ is for this life only (v. 19). This position taken in the face of Paul's proclamation of his gospel of God is a type of reinvention of Paul's proclaimed innovation.

15:13-16: Paul rebuts this view by noting that if it were true, it would also hold for Jesus, who would not have been raised from the dead by the God of Israel. Those change agents who proclaim the gospel of God as he did would have done so in vain; witnesses to the resurrection of Jesus would be false witnesses, dishonoring God.

15:17-18: Without God's raising Jesus, faith in Christ is futile, salvation from God's wrath is a chimera, and those who have died in Christ are simply dead. Hence Jesus-group members' faith merits pity rather than admiration.

What Paul's Proclamation Implies 1 Cor 15:20-28

15:20 But in fact Christ has been raised from the dead, the first fruits of those who have died. 21 For since death came through a human being, the resurrection of the dead has also come through a human being; 22 for as all die in Adam, so all will be made alive in Christ. 23 But each in his own order: Christ the first fruits, then at his coming those who belong to Christ. 24 Then comes the end, when he hands over the kingdom to God the Father, after he has destroyed every ruler and every authority and power. 25 For he must reign until he has put all his enemies under his feet. 26 The last enemy to be destroyed is death. 27 For "God has put all things in subjection under his feet." But when it says, "All things are put in subjection," it is plain that this does not include the one who put all things in subjection under him. 28 When all things are subjected to him, then the Son himself will also be subjected to the one who put all things in subjection under him, so that God may be all in all.

Textual Notes: 1 Cor 15:20-28

15:20: Paul now unpacks the significance of God's raising Jesus from the dead. The mention of the event leads to unraveling the nature of death. First of all, Jesus' resurrection marks the first fruits of the dead, that is, the first in a long series of persons to be raised by God. Death inaugurated by one person has its counter in the transformation of the dead into new life by one person. The earthling (this is what "Adam" means in Hebrew) of Genesis brought about death for all his descendants, while in Christ all who belong to Christ will be made alive.

15:23-24: This process too will be orderly: first Christ was raised, enabling all who belong to Christ to be raised eventually at his coming, then the end of the process marked by Christ handing over theocratic rule to God the Patron, and the destruction of hostile cosmic forces.

15:25: The rulers, authorities, and powers are hostile cosmic forces, types of demonic or angelic beings that affect the lives of human beings while working against God's plans. Paul, along with other early Jesus-group members, believe those cosmic entities have been inimical to Christ; they are his enemies. These cosmic forces include death, since Jesus has been raised from the dead; hence Jesus vanquished it. A passage from Israel's scriptures is cited to demonstrate that such cosmic subjection must takes place (Ps 109:1). Of course the Christ is not superior to God. Hence when all things and persons are subject to Christ through the action of God, then the Son himself will be subject to God. Then God will be all in all.

Why the Dead Must Be Raised 1 Cor 15:29-34

15:29 Otherwise, what will those people do who receive baptism on behalf of the dead? If the dead are not raised at all, why are people baptized on their behalf?

30 And why are we putting ourselves in danger every hour? 31 I die every day! That is as certain, brothers and sisters, as my boasting of you—a boast that I make in Christ Jesus our Lord.

32 If with merely human hopes I fought with wild animals at Ephesus, what would I have gained by it? If the dead are not raised,

"Let us eat and drink,
for tomorrow we die."

33 Do not be deceived:

"Bad company ruins good morals."

34 Come to a sober and right mind, and sin no more; for some people have no knowledge of God. I say this to your shame.

Textual Notes: 1 Cor 15:29-34

15:29: With the refrain "if the dead are not raised," Paul again returns to debunk the Corinthian reinvention of his proclaimed innovation. The Corinthian practice of "receiving baptism on behalf of the dead" seems to refer either to substitute baptism on behalf of dead family members or friends or to a sort of collectivistic baptism in which the baptism of the single person embraced all their deceased ancestors. In either case the baptism in question is to enable the dearly departed to take part in the resurrection. This *ad hominem* argument underscores the senselessness of the practice if there is no resurrection of the dead.

15:30-32: As an aside, Paul argues why he should put up with all the life-threatening difficulties he continues to experience in the task of proclaiming the gospel of God if there is no resurrection of the dead. If the dead are not raised, then why not live for this present life alone?

15:33-34: Paul concludes with the frequent admonition to be aware of deception. Things are never what they seem. In this case, his citing a Greek proverb (attributed by scholars to the Attic poet Menander) about bad company would be an allusion to those Jesus-group members who deny a forthcoming resurrection of the dead—hence his conclusion about some people having no knowledge. He says this to dishonor them, to deny them credibility.

How Are the Dead Raised? 1 Cor 15:35-58

15:35 But someone will ask, "How are the dead raised? With what kind of body do they come?" 36 Fool! What you sow does not come to life unless it dies. 37 And as for what you sow, you do not sow the body that is to be, but a bare seed, perhaps of wheat or of some other grain. 38 But God gives it a body as he has chosen, and to each kind of seed its own body. 39 Not all flesh is alike, but there is one flesh for human beings,

another for animals, another for birds, and
another for fish. 40 There are both heavenly
bodies and earthly bodies, but the glory of
the heavenly is one thing, and that of the
earthly is another. 41 There is one glory
of the sun, and another glory of the moon,
and another glory of the stars; indeed, star
differs from star in glory.

42 So it is with the resurrection of the
dead. What is sown is perishable, what
is raised is imperishable. 43 It is sown in
dishonor, it is raised in glory. It is sown in
weakness, it is raised in power. 44 It is sown
a physical body, it is raised a spiritual body.
If there is a physical body, there is also a
spiritual body. 45 Thus it is written, "The
first man, Adam, became a living being";
the last Adam became a life-giving spirit.
46 But it is not the spiritual that is first, but
the physical, and then the spiritual. 47 The
first man was from the earth, a man of dust;
the second man is from heaven. 48 As was
the man of dust, so are those who are of the
dust; and as is the man of heaven, so are
those who are of heaven. 49 Just as we have
borne the image of the man of dust, we will
also bear the image of the man of heaven.

50 What I am saying, brothers and sisters, is this: flesh and blood cannot inherit
the kingdom of God, nor does the perishable
inherit the imperishable. 51 Listen, I will
tell you a mystery! We will not all die, but
we will all be changed, 52 in a moment, in
the twinkling of an eye, at the last trumpet.
For the trumpet will sound, and the dead
will be raised imperishable, and we will be
changed. 53 For this perishable body must
put on imperishability, and this mortal body
must put on immortality. 54 When this perishable body puts on imperishability, and
this mortal body puts on immortality, then
the saying that is written will be fulfilled:

"Death has been swallowed up
in victory."
55 "Where, O death, is your victory?
Where, O death, is your sting?"

56 The sting of death is sin, and the power
of sin is the law. 57 But thanks be to God,
who gives us the victory through our Lord
Jesus Christ. 58 Therefore, my beloved, be
steadfast, immovable, always excelling in
the work of the Lord, because you know
that in the Lord your labor is not in vain.

Textual Notes: 1 Cor 15:35-58

15:35-40: The questions here, "How are the dead raised? With what kind of body do they come?" were posed to Paul by some of the Corinthians, notably those who believe there is no further resurrection of the dead. Paul's argument is based on analogies from first-century biology and astronomy. His point is that the resurrection of the dead entails a rather radical transformation, like that of a seed that dies to come to life. The type of body that comes from each vegetable seed is determined by God. The same is true of the seeds that produce human, animal, bird, and fish flesh. The same holds for celestial bodies when contrasted with the various terrestrial bodies just considered.

15:40: Paul now recounts the glory of celestial bodies. "Glory" means the external features that reveal the honor standing of a person. The skies tell the glory of God because God created them, and so they outwardly reveal God's preeminent honor standing. Paul now contrasts the honor of a range of celestial bodies: sun, moon, stars, and stars when compared with one another. Perhaps it is significant to note that celestial bodies were considered living entities in Paul's day:

> Aside from the Epicureans, all the major philosophical schools in the Hellenistic era believed in the divinity of the stars. Even the notorious atheist Euhemerus (fl. 300 B.C.) acknowledged that they (at least) were gods. . . . If one supposes, as later Platonism usually did, that stars were composed of

> soul and body, of sensible and intelligible, of superior and inferior, of ruling and ruled, one would think that only the soul of the star would be divine, and not its body. One response was to say that in the case of the stars, soul was perfectly adapted to body, and the lower and visible part to a higher intelligible part. The "secondary" gods exist through the higher invisible gods, depending on them as the star's radiance depends on the star. In the star the divine soul exercises a perfect supremacy. (Scott 1991:55, 57)

15:42: The previous excursus into the processes and sights of earth and sky now serve as analogy to describe the process and outcomes of the resurrection of dead human beings. What is sown is perishable, in dishonor, in weakness, an animate body; what emerges is imperishable, in glory, in power, a spirit body. The Greek term *psychikos* means "animate," "with soul"; the Greek term *pneumatikos* means "spiritual," "with spirit." Paul contrasts soul and spirit.

15:45-49: Paul now contrasts the first man, Adam as living soul (animate life), with the last Adam as life-giving spirit (spiritual life force). According to the scriptures, the soul comes first in creation, while the spirit comes later with the resurrection. The first man (called Adam; the word means "earthling") is from the earth, of dust; the second man is from the sky. Those of dust are from the man of dust; those of the sky are from the man of the sky. As earthlings all are in the image of the first earthling, so we who are in Christ will bear the image of the "skyman."

15:50-53: Now Paul concludes: the forthcoming Israelite theocracy, something imperishable, belongs to those who are transformed, not to ordinary human beings. This is the secret Paul imparts to the Corinthians. While with the coming of Christ all will not die, yet all will be transformed. Those who are asleep in the Lord will be raised as transformed beings. This transformation signifies the perishable putting on imperishability, the mortal putting on immortality. And all will take place in a moment, in the twinkling of an eye, at the last trumpet (see the analogies derived from social ritual attending the visit of an emperor to a city, a *parousia,* in 1 Thess 4:16-17).

15:54-57: Paul now cites a string of pertinent scriptural quotations (Isa 25:8; Hos 13:14) that will, of course, have probative effect for his Israelite Jesus group. He interprets the quotations in a chiastic way (ABCC'B'A'): the sting of death is sin, the power of sin is the law, and victory over death comes from God through the Lord Jesus Christ. He offers nothing by way of further explanation in this letter.

15:58: Paul concludes with an exhortation to constancy and greater excellence, since as they know, in the Lord they do not labor for nothing.

Part Eight: 1 Cor 16:1-4
Questions about Collecting the Temple Tax and Travel Plans

About the Temple Tax 16:1-4

16:1 Now concerning the collection for the saints: you should follow the directions I gave to the churches of Galatia. 2 On the first day of every week, each of you is to put aside and save whatever extra you earn, so that collections need not be taken when I come. 3 And when I arrive, I will send any whom you approve with letters to take your gift to Jerusalem. 4 If it seems advisable that I should go also, they will accompany me.

Textual Notes: 1 Cor 16:1-4

16:1: This is the last instance of the phrase "concerning . . ." that indicates a topic about which the Corinthian Jesus-group members wrote to Paul. The topic is the collection of money "for the saints." The word "collection" refers to a type of alms and offerings collected in coin (money used as standard of payment in the political economy; see Oakman 2002). If the collection is obligatory, as it seems to be here, then it is a tax. Tithing in Israel was a form of such obligatory tax. The idea behind tithing was that all Israel was to eat of the produce of God's land. Yet priests and levites were not allowed to own land, and the poor had their land taken from them. Tithing was meant to see to the needs of Israelites who had no land for income. In Israelite practice, within a seven-year cycle the first tithe, to be given annually apart from the seventh year, was eventually reserved for priests, whether poor or not, and could be collected by them wherever they might be. The second tithe, to be brought in the first, second, fourth, and fifth years, was to accompany its owners and provide for common feasting when on pilgrimage to Jerusalem. Finally, the tithe for the poor, collected in the third and sixth years, was to maintain the needy in the land. It seems Paul agreed with the Jerusalem pillars (Gal 2:10) that Jesus-group members living in non-Israelite territory should pay the Israelite tithe for the poor, specifically their poor fellow Jesus-group members in Jerusalem. (See Ford 1966a, who sees it as a Temple tax; note Acts 24:17-18, where it may well be the tithe for the poor). Because of his agreement with the Jerusalem pillars, Paul made precise arrangements about this collection; he expected such payment from all his Jesus-group gatherings (here he mentions the gatherings of Galatia and now Corinth; see 2 Corinthians 8 and 9; Gal 2:10; Rom 16:26). He expects each person to make such a payment; hence it was an obligatory payment. The payment is collected on the first day of the week, since in an Israelite group the collection could not be done on the Sabbath. And he specifically requires the gathering to approve those who are to carry the collection with letters of approval or credentials to be presented in Jerusalem. Obviously, as in Gal 2:10, the goal of the giving is Jerusalem. These features all fit some Israelite obligatory tithe. Non-Israelites are not obligated to pay Israelite tithes.

IV. 1 Cor 16:5-24
Letter Closing: Salutations and Blessings

Travel Plans 16:5-11

16:5 I will visit you after passing through Macedonia—for I intend to pass through Macedonia— 6 and perhaps I will stay with you or even spend the winter, so that you may send me on my way, wherever I go. 7 I do not want to see you now just in passing, for I hope to spend some time with you, if the Lord permits. 8 But I will stay in Ephesus until Pentecost, 9 for a wide door for effective work has opened to me, and there are many adversaries.

10 If Timothy comes, see that he has nothing to fear among you, for he is doing the work of the Lord just as I am; 11 therefore let no one despise him. Send him on his way in peace, so that he may come to me; for I am expecting him with the brothers.

Textual Notes: 1 Cor 16:5-11

Paul now discloses his travel plans to the Corinthians. This passage offers a fine glimpse of the way Paul planned his change-agent task.

16:5-7: Paul plans to go to Macedonia first, and then come back by way of Corinth, to spend the winter (the rainy season), when land and sea travel become rather difficult (except on Roman roads). What determines Paul's plans are the two seasons of the Eastern Mediterranean: the dry season (from March to October) and the rainy season (from October to March). Paul wishes to spend some time with the Corinthians, for unspecified reasons. But apart from any affection he might have toward them, as change agent he must still deal with diagnosing their problems and helping them translate their intent to action. As this letter indicates, he must continue working at stabilizing their ways of dealing with the innovation he communicated and preventing discontinuance.

16:8-9: The statement indicates that Paul is in Ephesus, the main city of the Roman province of Asia Minor. He presumes the Corinthians will understand his reference to the Israelite calendar with his reference to Pentecost—another indication that they are Israelites. Non-Israelites would not know Pentecost. Interestingly, Paul knows that wherever he finds the opportunity of proclaiming his gospel to his fellow Israelites, there will be adversaries. This implied conflict is normal since new Jesus-group members will break from previous allegiances and cause grievances among their previous associates.

16:10-11: Paul is not sure whether Timothy, who obviously is not with him in Ephesus, will pass through Corinth on his way back to Ephesus. Timothy is fundamental to Paul's information exchange relation with the various Jesus groups that Paul has founded. So with these few lines Paul offers a sort of letter of recommendation for Timothy.

About Apollos 16:12

16:12 Now concerning our brother Apollos, I strongly urged him to visit you with the other brothers, but he was not at all willing to come now. He will come when he has the opportunity.

Textual Notes: 1 Cor 16:12

The Corinthians must have asked for Apollos, since the phrase "concerning . . ." deals with topics about which they wrote and some of them attribute allegiance to Apollos (as noted initially in the letter in chapters 3 and 4). It seems that Apollos did not initiate the clique named after him, since he is not willing to come to Corinth. Yet Paul indicates he would be pleased if Apollos visited them—undoubtedly to stabilize their commitment to the gospel of God and prevent any discontinuance.

Salutations 16:13-22

16:13 Keep alert, stand firm in your faith, be courageous, be strong. 14 Let all that you do be done in love.

15 Now, brothers and sisters, you know that members of the household of Stephanas were the first converts in Achaia, and they have devoted themselves to the service of the saints; 16 I urge you to put yourselves at the service of such people, and of everyone who works and toils with them. 17 I rejoice at the coming of Stephanas and Fortunatus and Achaicus, because they have made up for your absence; 18 for they refreshed my spirit as well as yours. So give recognition to such persons.

19 The churches of Asia send greetings. Aquila and Prisca, together with the church in their house, greet you warmly in the Lord. 20 All the brothers and sisters send greetings. Greet one another with a holy kiss. 21 I, Paul, write this greeting with my own hand. 22 Let anyone be accursed who has no love for the Lord. Our Lord, come!

Textual Notes: 1 Cor 16:13-22

16:13-14: These verses mark Paul's final exhortation, typical of his letter conclusions.

16:15-18: Some persons presumably from Corinth, located in Achaia, are with Paul in Ephesus. Those mentioned include Stephanas and members of his household, Fortunatus and Achaicus. NRSV calls them "converts," but that word is not in the Greek. Rather, Paul calls them "first fruits" (Greek: *aparchē*). In Israelite tradition, the first fruits of any harvest are consecrated to God in a special way. And the first fruits enable what follows to arrive at maturity (just like the first-born enables all other offspring to be born). Acceptance of God's revelation in Christ articulated by Paul in his gospel is not a "conversion" but simply continued obedience to the God of Israel, to whom those who accept Paul's gospel have been obedient all along! Paul gives a grant of honor to these people—and through them to the Corinthian Jesus groups as well.

16:19: Aquila and Prisca, a Jesus-group couple known from Acts, have a house in Ephesus where the Jesus group meets. They, along with other Jesus groups in the Roman province of Asia, send their greetings to the Corinthians; this practice indicates the social attachment of Jesus-group members, who thus also get to become aware of the diffusion of their group members.

16:21: At the end Paul autographs the letter, perhaps written by Sosthenes, mentioned at the opening of the letter.

16:22: Paul concludes with a curse leveled at any group member who is not attached to the Lord. The Lord here is Jesus rather than God because the Aramaic prayer at the close (*Marana tha*) is addressed to Jesus as Lord. Paul's curse in defense of Jesus' honor underscores a dimension of his change-agent dedication. A curse refers to a statement and/or action intended to influence by superhuman means the welfare or behavior of animate entities (persons, animals, spirits, enspirited beings like winds, seas, etc.) against their will or normal modes of activity. What the curse is to effect is not specified. Presumably it will result in the unattached person leaving the Jesus group.

With the curse Paul looks to getting the person(s) in question outside. With the final Aramaic invocation, he looks to the Lord's coming to the group with the advent of the kingdom. *Marana tha* means "Come, our Lord" (the letters of the phrase may be divided as *Maran atha*; then the meaning is "Our Lord is coming"). The NRSV translates the Aramaic and does not include it (although it never translates the Hebrew "Amen"). *Maran atha* ("Our Lord is coming") seems to have been a Jesus-group greeting, while *Marana tha* ("Come, our Lord") was part of Jesus-group prayer, even when the congregation used Greek.

Blessing 16:23-24

6:23 The grace of the Lord Jesus be with you. 24 My love be with all of you in Christ Jesus.

Textual Notes: 1 Cor 16:23-24

The letter concludes with a "blessing," a sort of acknowledgment and wish for well-being. There is no verb "to be" in the Greek of either statement. So one may supply "is" as well as "be." With all that Paul has said about God's favor given to the Corinthians throughout the letter, his final words would just as well acknowledge the fact that God's favor that comes thanks to the Lord Jesus is in fact with them, just as his love or attachment to all of them in Christ Jesus actually exists. The blessing then is an affirmation of the good things the Corinthians have experienced from God along with an affirmation that Paul remains attached to them all.

2 Corinthians

I. 2 Cor 2:14—6:13
Letter 1: Written before the Dispute

2:14-17	Letter Thanksgiving

2 Cor 3:1–7:4
Body of Letter 1

3:1-3	Paul Has No Need to Commend Himself
3:4-18	Paul's Service Is Devoted to a New Covenant
4:1-6	Paul's Gospel of the Glory of Christ
4:7-15	The Qualities of Paul the Change Agent
4:16—5:10	Not Disheartened by Death
5:11-21	Representatives of Christ
Part I: 6:1-13	Plea for Openness [Part II: 7:2-4]
6:14—7:1	Insert: Fragment of a Letter
Part II: 7:2-4	Plea for Openness [Part I: 6:1-13]

II. 2 Corinthians 10–13
Letter 2: Written during the Dispute

2 Cor 10:1–13:10
Body of Letter 2

10:1-6	Paul's Plea Not to Force His Hand
10:7-18	He Will Not Be Put to Shame
11:1—12:13	Boasting like Fools [General Section]
11:1-6	Paul's Opening Ploy
11:7-11	Further Satirical Comments
11:12-21a	Comparisons with Opponents
11:22—12:13	In Defense of Honor: Rhetorical Comparison
12:14—13:4	Plans for a Third Visit
13:5-10	Test Your Loyalties

2 Cor 13:11-14
Letter Closing: Salutations and Blessings

III. 2 Cor 1:1—2:13 [7:5-16]
Letter 3: Written after the Dispute

2 Cor 1:1-2
Letter Opening (Superscription)

2 Cor 1:3-7
Letter Thanksgiving

2 Cor 1:8–2:13 [7:5-16]
Body of the Letter

1:8-11	Perils in Asia
1:12-14	Paul's Claim to Honor
1:15—2:13	Narratives of Events, Part I
7:5-12	Narratives of Events, Part II
7:13b-16	Resulting Comfort for Titus

IV. 2 Cor 8:1-24
Insert: Part of a Letter of Recommendation for Titus about the Collection for Jerusalem

V. 2 Cor 9:1-15
Insert: Part of a Letter about the Collection for Jerusalem

Most scholars consider 2 Corinthians to be a collection of fragments of perhaps five of Paul's letters to the Corinthians dealing in one way or another with a situation of dispute. The Corinthian correspondence dates to about 54–57 C.E. In the following outline, we present the fragments in chronological order based on the presumption of times before, during, and after the dispute, with other insertions as noted:

— Letter 1: 2 Cor 2:14—6:13; 7:2-4 (Written before the Dispute)
— Letter 2: 2 Cor 10:1—13:14 (Written during the Dispute)
— Letter 3: 2 Cor 1:1—2:13; 7:5-16 (Written after the Dispute)
— Insert: Part of a Letter of Recommendation for Titus about the Collection for Jerusalem 8:1-24
— Insert: Part of a Letter about the Collection for Jerusalem 9:1-15
— Insert: Non-Pauline Fragment 6:14—7:1

Commentaries usually follow the sequence of texts as they are now found in the biblical form of 2 Corinthians. A social-science commentary is interested in the social dynamics accompanying the dispute at Corinth to which these letters and letter fragments attest. In what follows we will discuss each letter or fragment according to its role in the flow of events, as in the following table:

Before the Dispute Letter 1 (what is now 2 Cor 2:14–6:13; 7:2-4)	**During the Dispute Letter 2 (what is now 2 Cor 10:1–13:14)**	**After the Dispute Letter 3 (what is now 2 Cor 1:1–2:13; 7:5-16)**	**Later Insertions**
I. 2:14-17 Letter Thanksgiving	I. 2 Cor 10:1–13:10 Body of Letter 2	I. 2 Cor 1:1-2 Letter Opening	**Insert: 6:14–7:1 (Non-Pauline letter fragment)**
II. 2 Cor 3:1–7:4 Body of Letter 1 3:1-3 Paul Has No Need to Commend Himself; 3:4-18 Paul's Service Is Devoted to a New Covenant; 4:1-6 Paul's Gospel of the Glory of Christ; 4:7-15 The Qualities of Paul the Change Agent; 4:16—5:10 Not Disheartened by Death; 5:11-21, Representatives of Christ; 6:1-13 Plea for Openness, Part I; 7:2-4 Plea for Openness, Part II	10:1-16 Paul's Plea Not to Force His Hand; 10:7-18 He Will Not Be Put to Shame; 11:1—12:13 Boasting Like Fools [General Section]; 11:1-6 Paul's Opening Ploy; 11:7-11 Further Satirical Comments; 11:12-21a Comparisons with Opponents; 11:22—12:13 In Defense of Honor: Rhetorical Comparison; 12:14—13:4 Plans for a Third Visit; 13:5-10 Test Your Loyalties	II. 2 Cor 1:3-7 Letter Thanksgiving	**Insert: 8:1-24 (Part of a letter of recommendation for Titus)**
	II. 2 Cor 13:11-14 Letter Closing: Salutations and Blessings	III. 2 Cor 1:8–2:13 [7:5-16] Body of the Letter 1:8-11 Perils in Asia; 1:12-14 Paul's Claim to Honor; 1:15—2:13 Narratives of Events, Part 1 [7:5-12 Narratives of Events, Part II; 7:13b-16 Resulting Comfort for Titus]	**Insert: 9:1-15 (Part of a Letter about the Collection)**

Since 2 Corinthians deals with a dispute, it might be useful at the outset to describe what a dispute is. Disputes emerge through a series of stages:

grievance ⟶ conflict ⟶ dispute.

From the perspective of social dynamics the stages entail first a single person (or group), then two persons (or groups), then three or more persons (or groups). At the origin of every dispute is a grievance perceived by a single person or a single group. As 2 Corinthians reveals, Paul was the initially aggrieved person. Conflict follows if the aggrieved person or group chooses to confront the person(s) thought to be responsible for the grievance. Paul's initial letter to the Corinthians relative to the grievance (2 Cor 2:14—6:13) bypasses this two-party phase; he does not write to the person responsible for the grievance. Instead he writes to the Corinthian Jesus group, thus making the conflict public. Three parties are now involved, and that is characteristic of a dispute. **Dispute Process**.

To understand what exactly has happened, we begin with the first letter, written before the dispute, now found in 2 Cor 2:14—6:13. Note that we will *return* to what now appears as the beginning of 2 Corinthians, which actually came from a later stage of the dispute process.

I. 2 Cor 2:14—6:13
Letter 1: Written before the Dispute

2:14-17 Letter Thanksgiving

2:14 But thanks be to God, who in
Christ always leads us in triumphal procession, and through us spreads in every place the fragrance that comes from knowing him.
15 For we are the aroma of
Christ to God among those who are being saved and among those who are perishing;
16 to the one a fragrance from death to death, to the other a fragrance from life to life. Who is sufficient for these things?
17 For we are not peddlers of God's word like so many; but in Christ we speak as persons of sincerity, as persons sent from God and standing in his presence.

Textual Notes: 2 Cor 2:14-17

The form of this passage is a thanksgiving that normally comes after the superscription of a Hellenistic letter. This second thanksgiving (after 1:3-4) belonged to the pre-dispute letter to the Corinthians.

2:14: Paul here acknowledges the activity of the God of Israel who is leading us in Christ like victors in a Roman victory parade. Incense was used in these parades. "Triumph" is the name of that victory parade in which vanquished prisoners of war were forced to march. Duling notes:

> In 71 C.E., for example, the Romans forced seven hundred captured Israelite warriors carrying confiscated Jerusalem temple vessels to march through the streets of Rome to mark the victory of the Romans over the

Israelites (Josephus Wars 7.5.3-6). This triumphal procession culminated in the execution of the "popular messiah" Simon ben Giora, one of the Israelite leaders of the revolt. A representation of the forced march can be seen today on an inside facade of the famous victory Arch of Titus in the Roman Forum, erected in 81 C.E. (Duling 2003:206–7)

2:15-16: Paul's reference to Jesus-group members as the aroma of Christ may allude to the sweet odor of sacrifice that is so pleasing to God in Israelite lore. On the other hand, because of the mention of death and life, he may be alluding to another bit of Israelite lore. When death comes to the righteous, there is a discernible sweet odor, but when death comes to sinners, the odor is fetid (*Testament of Abraham*, 16:7-8; 17:16-18; first-century Israelite). In this perspective, Jesus-group members as fragrance to God would allude to this tradition both since they are righteous and since their death will be followed by a resurrection like that of Christ's, a fragrance from life to life. Even those who are perishing can notice this, although their lot is the fetid fragrance from death to death.

In the *Testament of Abraham* death comes "in pleasing shape and glory," and "in youthful beauty and very quietly and with soft speech I come to the righteous, but to sinners I come in much decay and ferocity and the greatest bitterness and with a fierce and merciless look" (*Testament of Abraham* 1:7-8).

2:17: The mention of peddlers of God's word brings us to the crux of the dispute around which the letters cluster. It seems Paul was aggrieved that some accused him of being such a peddler, performing his change-agent function for gain, adulterating the product for the sake of more sales. Paul insists (and will go on to demonstrate) that he speaks sincerely, as one commissioned as change agent by God, the true change agency, and as one responsible to God. Like a peddler, he is accused by his opponents of commending himself rather than having others commend him (3:1-3). These opponents are people who endorse the covenant between God and Moses and Israel (3:4-18).

2 Cor 3:1–7:4 Body of Letter 1

Paul Has No Need to Commend Himself 3:1-3

3:1 Are we beginning to commend ourselves again? Surely we do not need, as some do, letters of recommendation to you or from you, do we? 2 You yourselves are our letter, written on our hearts, to be known and read by all; 3 and you show that you are a letter of Christ, prepared by us, written not with ink but with the Spirit of the living God, not on tablets of stone but on tablets of human hearts.

Textual Notes: 2 Cor 3:1-3

Paul's previous mention of his being described as a self-commending peddler (2:17) points up what is going on in Corinth now. As these verses indicate, in taking up his defense, Paul enters into conflict with those who have come to Corinth with letters of recommendation from other Jesus groups in which they were active (3:1). They seem to have taken up positions of authority in Corinth. Paul later labels them sarcastically as "super-apostles" (11:5; 12:11).

The only reason Paul might have for commending himself *again* is that Corinthian Jesus-group members, in their quest for reinforcement of the innovation decision they have made, have been exposed by the super-apostles to conflicting messages about the innovation proclaimed by Paul. As a result the Corinthians might reverse their previous decision. Persons who have made an innovation decision and are presented with another version of the innovation will seek to avoid a state of cognitive dissonance or to reduce it if it occurs. And the initial change agent's task is to confirm those individuals in their original decision by making their behavior consonant with their attitudes so as not to discontinue, misuse, or circumvent their adoption decision.

3:1: As initial change agent and founder of Corinthian Jesus groups, Paul obviously did not come with letters of recommendation to them. But the person(s) who grieve Paul did, in order to gain a hearing among them. In turn, they seek letters of recommendation from the Corinthians as they move elsewhere. The purpose of these letters is to obtain hospitality, which entailed patronage along with the usual favors of food and shelter.

3:2: After all their interactions, Paul considers the Corinthians as living letters of recommendation on his behalf, written by God's Spirit on their hearts.

Paul's Service Is Devoted to a New Covenant 3:4-18

4 Such is the confidence that we have through Christ toward God. 5 Not that we are competent of ourselves to claim anything as coming from us; our competence is from God, 6 who has made us competent to be ministers of a new covenant, not of letter but of spirit; for the letter kills, but the Spirit gives life.

7 Now if the ministry of death, chiseled in letters on stone tablets, came in glory so that the people of Israel could not gaze at Moses' face because of the glory of his face, a glory now set aside, 8 how much more will the ministry of the Spirit come in glory? 9 For if there was glory in the ministry of condemnation, much more does the ministry of justification abound in glory! 10 Indeed, what once had glory has lost its glory because of the greater glory; 11 for if what was set aside came through glory, much more has the permanent come in glory!

12 Since, then, we have such a hope, we act with great boldness, 13 not like Moses, who put a veil over his face to keep the people of Israel from gazing at the end of the glory that was being set aside. 14 But their minds were hardened. Indeed, to this very day, when they hear the reading of the old covenant, that same veil is still there, since only in Christ is it set aside. 15 Indeed, to this very day whenever Moses is read, a veil lies over their minds; 16 but when one turns to the Lord, the veil is removed. 17 Now the Lord is the Spirit, and where the Spirit of the Lord is, there is freedom. 18 And all of us, with unveiled faces, seeing the glory of the Lord as though reflected in a mirror, are being transformed into the same image from one degree of glory to another; for this comes from the Lord, the Spirit.

Textual Notes: 2 Cor 3:7-18

This whole passage has the story in Exodus 34 (explicitly cited in v. 16) as its intertext. Once more, Paul presumes his Corinthian Jesus-group members know this passage, a good indication that they are indeed Israelites. Exodus 34 is a story of Moses' going up Mount Sinai a second time, after the Golden Calf incident. He goes with newly cut tablets to receive another Ten Words from God (the Ten Words cited here are quite different from the popular Ten Commandments; read Exod 34:11-26). Moses himself inscribes the stones, and God makes a covenant with both Moses and the sons of Israel atop the mountain. Upon his descent, Moses appears as a divine entity, his countenance totally aglow as an effect of his interaction with the God of Mount Sinai. In order to interact with the Israelites he has to put a veil over his head, since they could not stand the intensity of his shining face.

3:4-18: In this passage Paul contrasts the Exodus incident and its residue among contemporary Israelites with the situation of Jesus-group members. It would seem that those who grieve Paul in this letter adopted a gospel that required taking the Mosaic covenant seriously. Paul's gospel proclaimed a new covenant entailing much more than the old covenant could deliver.

The two-part contrasts are quite typical of modes of perception of antiquity. Until the middle of the seventeenth century, perception was always in terms of *sic et non*, "yes or no," "for or against," "hot or cold." There was no middle ground. Indifference was so much out of the question that those who were not against us may be presumed to be for us; indifference or neutrality was simply not a perceived option! Such "either/or" constructs took on social reality in the perception of the world in terms of "us" and "them," ingroup and outgroup. In line with this viewpoint Paul now sets out the following contrasting categories:

- covenant of the letter, covenants of the spirit (v. 6)
- letter that kills, Spirit that gives life (v.6)
- the ministry of death, ministry of the Spirit (v. 7-8)
- the ministry of condemnation, ministry of justification (v. 9)
- lesser glory lost, due to greater glory (v. 9-10)
- impermanent glory, permanent glory (v.11)
- veiled, fading glory, unveiled permanent glory (v. 13-16)

In sum, the post–Golden Calf covenant is the old covenant, a covenant in writing that kills marked by condemnation and death with veiled, faded, and impermanent glory. The new covenant with the God of Israel is marked by spirit, life, approval by God, unveiled greater and permanent glory. Given that honor is the core value of Mediterranean society, to have one's honor permanently revealed to all (that is what glory does; see v. 7) is an unbelievable and immeasurable quality.

3:4-6: Those who aggrieve Paul seem to have accused him of being incompetent. In response he insists that he is quite competent, with the competence with which God has endowed him. The purpose of this divine favor was to make Paul a change agent in the service of an innovation here described as a new, God-initiated covenant or agreement between God and God's people. The word translated "ministers" is the Greek *diakonos*. In the Hellenistic world the word normally means someone functioning as an agent of a higher-ranking person, either as an intermediary in commercial transactions or as a messenger or a diplomat. Hence the Greek word *diakonos* is better translated as "a person in the service of." Here it means "persons in the service of the new covenant."

3:7: The word "glory" that appears frequently in the whole passage refers to the external, outward features or characteristics of some entity that reveal the true, lofty status or value of a person or thing. Marvelous external traits and lofty internal qualities go together, the visible being indicative of the invisible. Thus: "The heavens are telling the glory of God" (Ps 19:1), or "The wife is the glory of her husband" (1 Cor 11:7).

3:12: The gospel of the God of Israel who raised Jesus from the dead in order to inaugurate a theocracy soon fills believers with confidence (v. 4) and hope (v. 12). Paul (and Jesus-group members) then can act freely (v. 17) relative to the old covenant, with a boldness greater than that of Moses who encountered God on Mount Sinai.

3:13-17: Moses' face was aglow because he saw God; he put a veil on his head so as not to terrorize the Israelites to whom he imparted the covenant. Paul reinterprets the reason for the veil, saying Moses put it on because the initial splendor was fading. What was fading was the initial splendor of the covenant God struck up with both Moses and the people. Unaware of what was happening with this covenant, Israelites continued to read that covenant with veiled, hardened minds, although its splendor has faded. Because they have veiled minds, they still believe in the initial splendor of that older covenant. But now when an Israelite turns to God through Christ, the veil is taken away, and what they can now behold with their new covenant is the very glory of the Lord that increasingly transforms Jesus-group members thanks to God's activity, God's Spirit.

Paul's Gospel of the Glory of Christ 4:1-6

4:1 Therefore, since it is by God's mercy that we are engaged in this ministry, we do not lose heart. 2 We have renounced the shameful things that one hides; we refuse to practice cunning or to falsify God's word; but by the open statement of the truth we commend ourselves to the conscience of everyone in the sight of God. 3 And even if our gospel is veiled, it is veiled to those who are perishing. 4 In their case the god of this world has blinded the minds of the unbelievers, to keep them from seeing the light of the gospel of the glory of Christ, who is the image of God. 5 For we do not proclaim ourselves; we proclaim Jesus Christ as Lord and ourselves as your slaves for Jesus' sake. 6 For it is the God who said, "Let light shine out of darkness," who has shone in our hearts to give the light of the knowledge of the glory of God in the face of Jesus Christ.

Textual Notes: 2 Cor 4:1-6

Paul now draws some further conclusions from his previous reflections on Exodus 34, in the face of the accusation that his gospel is veiled! He intimates some more of the accusations leveled against him by the super-apostles: that he engages in his change-agent service on his own (v. 1); that he does things secretly, with guile and cunning (v. 2); that his gospel is something hidden and veiled (v. 3); and ultimately that he proclaims himself (v. 5).

To the contrary, he argues: God engaged him as change agent (v. 1), and he carries on the task without cunning or lying. He proclaims the gospel truthfully (v. 2). While the gospel might appear to be veiled, it is actually veiled only to unbelievers, who in fact are perishing (v. 3). He proclaims Jesus as Lord, while he behaves as a community slave for Jesus' sake (v. 5). It is God the creator of light in darkness (alluding to Gen 1:3) who has illumined his heart so that he sees the unveiled face of Jesus Christ that reveals the knowledge of the glory of God (v. 6).

4:1: The verb "obtain mercy" here is equivalent to "receive a favor." It is another way of expressing how one obtains favor from a patron. For Paul, the God of Israel is patron, and the favor he receives is the service task of being a change agent, communicating the innovation about God's raising Jesus from the dead with a view to the forthcoming Israelite theocracy.

4:2: "Conscience" refers to group awareness. (The Latin *conscientia* combines *cum + scientia*, that is, knowledge held in common.) As a collectivistic person, Paul is more concerned about group integrity than anything else. The group in question is Israel in general but his Jesus groups in particular. It is to these Israelite Jesus groups that he must make sense as person and as change agent for God's gospel.

These terra cotta votives (fifth to fourth century B.C.E.*) were offered to the god Asklepios, probably in gratitude for curing an ailment, and are evidence of how in the ancient Mediterranean world gods were seen as patrons. See 2 Cor 4:1.*

4:4: The reality of the "god of this world" (Greek: *aiōn* = social time span, this age) is rooted in the perception of personal causality. Ancient Mediterraneans believed that every effect that counted was caused by a person, visible or invisible. This perception was rooted in the belief that all good things in life were limited and that by one's own efforts one could hardly cope with the negative events in life (sickness, death, bad harvest). The only solution to such problems was to have recourse to better situated persons with resources, that is, to patrons. Some persons were more powerful than others, as can readily be proved by the effects caused by various persons. When effects were overwhelming, beyond the ability of any single human being, such events were ascribed to superhuman entities: invisible gods, spirits, demons, and the like. Paul has a rich vocabulary for such invisible, extremely potent entities. Here he claims the agency responsible for veiling the gospel from Israelites is "the god of this world." This entity blinds the eyes of unbelievers so they cannot behold the light of the gospel of the glory of Christ, the image of God.

Paul now calls the resurrected Jesus "the image of God." An image is that which has the same form as something else. In this case it is a living image. The title "image of God" is used in Genesis for human beings, male and female (Gen 1:26-27). However, it occurs frequently in Paul's time as a designation of emperors, gods less than the highest God, and righteous human beings (Danker 2000:282). The point here is that the resurrected Christ has glory that reflects the incomprehensible glory of God. To behold the glory of Christ is to behold the glory of the God of Israel.

4:6: Paul now describes his initial altered state of consciousness experiences as one in which God the creator of light shone in his heart to give the light of the knowledge of the glory of God in the face of Jesus Christ. Paul, as prophet, is just like Moses, who saw the glory of God. But his vision of God's glory took place through an experience of the resurrected Jesus.

The Qualities of Paul the Change Agent 4:7-15

4:7 But we have this treasure in clay
jars, so that it may be made clear that this
extraordinary power belongs to God and
does not come from us. 8 We are afflicted in
every way, but not crushed; perplexed, but
not driven to despair; 9 persecuted, but not
forsaken; struck down, but not destroyed;
10 always carrying in the body the death
of Jesus, so that the life of Jesus may also
be made visible in our bodies. 11 For while
we live, we are always being given up to
death for Jesus' sake, so that the life of Jesus
may be made visible in our mortal flesh.
12 So death is at work in us, but life in you.

13 But just as we have the same spirit
of faith that is in accordance with scripture—"I believed, and so I spoke"—we
also believe, and so we speak, 14 because
we know that the one who raised the Lord
Jesus will raise us also with Jesus and will
bring us with you into his presence. 15 Yes,
everything is for your sake, so that grace, as
it extends to more and more people, may
increase thanksgiving, to the glory of God.

Textual Notes: 2 Cor 4:7-15

Paul again turns to address the accusations that grieve him—that he is somehow a wanting change agent of the God of Israel, who raised Jesus from the dead. He now proudly sets out the range of distresses that have faced him and his response to them.

4:7: Paul is quite aware that his vision of God's glory through Christ derives from God himself. He has no resources to produce such an event, even for himself. He is like a fragile jar.

4:8-11: Now follows a list of the hardships bound up with his activity as change agent, with every distress matched by some upbeat counter attitude. Philosophers of the period used to list the trials they had overcome as proof of the excellence of their teaching. Paul lists his hardships as proof of the excellence of the gospel of God. The deeds of ill fortune he experiences are proof of his ultimate good fortune and favor from God:

— afflicted in every way, but not crushed (v. 8);
— perplexed, but not driven to despair (v. 8);
— persecuted, but not forsaken (v. 9);
— struck down, but not destroyed (v. 9);
— always bearing the death of Jesus, but with the life of Jesus visible (v. 10)
— alive, but given up to death for Jesus' sake (v. 11)
— so that the life of Jesus is visible in his dying flesh (v. 11)

4:12-13: While death is at work in him, life emerges among the Corinthians who have accepted the innovation he has communicated to them. Paul's proclamation is rooted in his trust in God, the basis for his willingness to proclaim his gospel. He quotes Ps 116:10 (LXX) to connect his faith with his proclamation activity.

4:14: Ultimately his whole activity is rooted in the God of Israel, who raised the Lord Jesus. This God will also raise Paul and his Corinthians and usher them into his glory-filled presence.

4:15: In sum, Paul's activity is for the sake of the Corinthian Jesus-group members, so that God's patronage or favor, as it increasingly spreads among Israelites who accept the gospel of God (the many), will lead to the greater acknowledgment of God's activity and thus further increase God's glory.

Not Disheartened by Death 4:16–5:10

4:16 So we do not lose heart. Even though our outer nature is wasting away, our inner nature is being renewed day by day. 17 For this slight momentary affliction is preparing us for an eternal weight of glory beyond all measure, 18 because we look not at what can be seen but at what cannot be seen; for what can be seen is temporary, but what cannot be seen is eternal.

5:1 For we know that if the earthly tent we live in is destroyed, we have a building from God, a house not made with hands, eternal in the heavens. 2 For in this tent we groan, longing to be clothed with our heavenly dwelling— 3 if indeed, when we have taken it off we will not be found naked. 4 For while we are still in this tent, we groan under our burden, because we wish not to be unclothed but to be further clothed, so that what is mortal may be swallowed up by life. 5 He who has prepared us for this very thing is God, who has given us the Spirit as a guarantee.

6 So we are always confident; even though we know that while we are at home in the body we are away from the Lord— 7 for we walk by faith, not by sight. 8 Yes, we do have confidence, and we would rather be away from the body and at home with the Lord. 9 So whether we are at home or away, we make it our aim to please him. 10 For all of us must appear before the judgment seat of Christ, so that each may receive recompense for what has been done in the body, whether good or evil.

Textual Notes: 2 Cor 4:16–5:10

From the vantage point of his gospel of God, Paul sets forth a list of contrasts between the present and the forthcoming. While the contrasts are listed to lay out his attitudes in face of his being aggrieved, his focus on the forthcoming is something he expects his clients to share as well. Evidence of the forthcoming can be found in the way that the inner person of Jesus-group members is increasingly renewed in the face of the ravages of social experience over time. Thus:

outer human being wasting away	*inner human being increasingly renewed* (4:16)
present trivial annoyances	*forthcoming considerable glory without measure* (4:17)
what can be seen—temporary	*what cannot be seen—endless* (4:18)
present house: a destructible tent on earth	*forthcoming house: indestructible in the sky* (5:1)
present tent that clothes with mortality	*forthcoming sky that clothes with life* (5:2)

5:3: To be found naked is to be ashamed. Paul hopes that when the present tent is taken away, Jesus-group members will not be found ashamed about the deeds they performed in this expanded present.

5:4: At present Jesus-group members groan and long for the forthcoming, life with God. With the metaphor of clothing, they long not to be unclothed—that is, to die—but rather to be further clothed with forthcoming life.

5:5: God has prepared Jesus-group members for the transition to life in the forthcoming, guaranteeing it with a down payment or first installment (Semitic loan word: *arrabon*) verifiable in experiences of the spirit of God in altered states of consciousness.

5:6-8: Another set of metaphors that situate Jesus-group members in the present condition:

at present we are at home in the body	*really away from home with the Lord*
now we live by faith	*then by sight*
and so to be away from body	*means to be at home with the Lord*

5:9: Paul concludes that for Jesus-group members,

whether at home (in the body)	*or away (from home) with the Lord,*

their goal is to please the Lord, since they will ultimately be rewarded by Christ for what they have done at home in the body, whether good or evil.

Representatives of Christ 5:11-21

5:11 Therefore, knowing the fear of the Lord, we try to persuade others; but we ourselves are well known to God, and I hope that we are also well known to your consciences. 12 We are not commending ourselves to you again, but giving you an opportunity to boast about us, so that you may be able to answer those who boast in outward appearance and not in the heart. 13 For if we are beside ourselves, it is for God; if we are in our right mind, it is for you. 14 For the love of Christ urges us on, because we are convinced that one has died for all; therefore all have died. 15 And he died for all, so that those who live might live no longer for themselves, but for him who died and was raised for them.

16 From now on, therefore, we regard no one from a human point of view; even though we once knew Christ from a human point of view, we know him no longer in that way. 17 So if anyone is in Christ, there is a new creation: everything old has passed away; see, everything has become new! 18 All this is from God, who reconciled us to himself through Christ, and has given us the ministry of reconciliation; 19 that is, in Christ God was reconciling the world to himself, not counting their trespasses against them, and entrusting the message of reconciliation to us. 20 So we are ambassadors for Christ, since God is making his appeal through us; we entreat you on behalf of Christ, be reconciled to God. 21 For our sake he made him to be sin who knew no sin, so that in him we might become the righteousness of God.

Textual Notes: 2 Cor 5:11-21

5:11: The phrase "fear of the Lord" has little or nothing to do with being afraid. It usually means reverence, awe, and respectfulness. Paul's respect for the God of Israel is rooted in his experience of God in his call, and that call demonstrated to him how well known he is to God. On the basis of this experience, Paul has taken up his change-agent task and attempts to persuade fellow Israelites of what the God of Israel has done in the death and resurrection of Jesus. Paul expresses his hope that the Corinthians might communally know him as well as God does.

5:12: Paul wishes that the Corinthians might really know him so that they might take his side in the smoldering conflict with his opponents. These opponents make claims based on outward appearances (Greek: literally, "the face"), not the inward person (the heart). In this context, Corinthians boasting about Paul are in fact defending him against the opposition.

5:13: The opposition, it seems, accuses Paul of being out of his mind! If he in fact is, he says, well, that is God's affair. On the other hand, if he is in his right mind, that is for the sake of Corinthians.

5:14-15: Paul insists that his change-agent activity is rooted in his being bonded with and attached to Jesus, Israel's Messiah soon to come. He is convinced (and presumes the Corinthians are as well) that Jesus has died for all Israelites and all who believe have in fact also died. This perspective is rooted in the perception of human beings as collective persons. As a collective person intent upon group integrity and group solidarity, Jesus died, and his death was for the sake of the group in which he was embedded, the house of Israel. On the other hand, the benefits of this death are for those who live, that is, for those who believe in Paul's gospel of God and what God has done for Israel. It is "those who live" whom Paul urges to live for the new collectivity, not for themselves. The "self" in this culture would be the individual and his or her family in a particular neighborhood, the kinship unit. Paul would have the individual's focus move from his or her kin group to the Jesus group whose members they are. In this way, Jesus-group members—"those who live"—will live "for him who died" and was raised by the God of Israel for them.

5:16: Henceforth Paul (and his clients) adopt a new perspective shaped by the gospel of God. In his old Israelite perspective as zealous Pharisee, Paul saw Jesus as a deceitful teacher and false Messiah who had led Israel astray (see Gal 1:13; Phil 3:5). Of course he no longer shares this viewpoint, which he calls "according to the flesh."

5:17: In terms of the gospel of God and what God has accomplished in the death and resurrection of Jesus, something entirely new has occurred. All who belong to Jesus groups, persons "in Christ," are a new creation; for them everything has become new.

5:18-19: Of course, all of this derives from the God of Israel. By means of what God has done through Christ, God has set aside his "wrath," that is, the satisfaction required by honor in face of repeated shameful acts. Through his Christ the God of Israel has waived the requirements of satisfaction; in Christ the God of Israel has reconciled "the world," that is, Israelite society, to himself. The process involves God not counting trespasses against God's honor. Paul and his fellow Jesus-group change agents are in the service of this reconciliation, proclaiming this reconciliation of God and Israel for those Israelites who accept the gospel of God.

5:20: Paul, as change agent, serves as legate or ambassador for God (the change agency), communicating the innovation of the gospel of God and the reconciliation with God that this entails. Those who believe in Christ believe in God's gospel and are reconciled to God. What is Jesus' role in all this? For the sake of Israel, the God of Israel made Jesus part and parcel of the prevailing culture of willingness to shame God (that is the meaning of sin: *hamartia*), even though Jesus never shamed God, so that in Jesus we might be acceptable to and approved by God.

Plea for Openness, Part I: 6:1-13 [Part II: 7:2-4]

6:1 As we work together with him, we urge you also not to accept the grace of God in vain. 2 For he says,

"At an acceptable time I have listened to you,
and on a day of salvation I have helped you."

See, now is the acceptable time; see, now is the day of salvation! 3 We are putting no obstacle in anyone's way, so that no fault may be found with our ministry, 4 but as servants of God we have commended ourselves in every way: through great endurance, in afflictions, hardships, calamities, 5 beatings, imprisonments, riots, labors, sleepless nights, hunger; 6 by purity, knowledge, patience, kindness, holiness of spirit, genuine love, 7 truthful speech, and the power of God; with the weapons of righteousness for the right hand and for the left; 8 in honor and dishonor, in ill repute and good repute. We are treated as impostors, and yet are true; 9 as unknown, and yet are well known; as dying, and see—we are alive; as punished, and yet not killed; 10 as sorrowful, yet always rejoicing; as poor, yet making many rich; as having nothing, and yet possessing everything.

11 We have spoken frankly to you Corinthians; our heart is wide open to you. 12 There is no restriction in our affections, but only in yours. 13 In return—I speak as to children—open wide your hearts also.

Textual Notes: 2 Cor 6:1-13

This passage again sets out reasons for Paul's credibility. It opens (vv. 1-2) with a note of present urgency, followed by an argument for his own credibility based on a list of obstacles that Paul has overcome in his change-agent task (vv. 3-10), and concludes with a plea for openness (vv. 11-13).

6:1-2: Paul's main problem as change agent is to keep the Corinthian Jesus-group members from discontinuing the innovation he proclaimed in his gospel of God. He insists that he labors on behalf of a change agency, the God of Israel. He urges his Corinthians not to set aside the favor offered by this cosmic patron, since the present time is all important. He underscores his focus on the present with a citation from Isaiah (49:8), with a sort of "either now or never" urgency.

6:3-10: Secondarily Paul must diminish the credibility of the unspecified opponents who have aggrieved him by their accusations. In the process Paul must further bolster his own credibility. He does this in a way well-known from public moral teachers in the Hellenistic world, that is, philosophers. Philosophers taught a way of living. To prove the excellence of their teaching, they would list their hardships, describe their courage and discipline in overcoming those hardships, and attribute their success to their teaching. Paul takes up this well-known approach by listing nine hardships (vv. 4-5), nine virtues (vv. 6-7), and seven moral antitheses (vv. 8-10)—all of which demonstrate his credibility and fundamental sincerity.

6:11-13: An open heart entails far more in Paul's culture than in ours. An open heart involves sincerity, affection, good will, honesty—in sum a totally welcoming attitude bereft of all deceit and deception (see 7:2). Paul would like his open heart to be matched by a like attitude on the part of the Corinthians. This discussion of the heart continues at 7:2-4. For this reason most scholars consider 2 Cor 6:14—7:1 to be an insertion. **Eyes-Heart.**

At this point in 2 Corinthians, Letter 1 is interrupted by the insertion of a non-Pauline fragment at 6:14—7:1; Letter 1 resumes at 7:2-4. We turn here to discuss the non-Pauline insertion.

Insert: Fragment of a Letter 6:14—7:1

6:14 Do not be mismatched with unbelievers. For what partnership is there between righteousness and lawlessness? Or what fellowship is there between light and darkness? 15 What agreement does Christ have with Beliar? Or what does a believer share with an unbeliever? 16 What agreement has the temple of God with idols? For we are the temple of the living God; as God said,

"I will live in them and walk among them,
and I will be their God,
and they shall be my people.
17 Therefore come out from them,
and be separate from them, says the Lord,
and touch nothing unclean;
then I will welcome you,
18 and I will be your father,
and you shall be my sons and daughters,
says the Lord Almighty."

7:1 Since we have these promises, beloved, let us cleanse ourselves from every defilement of body and of spirit, making holiness perfect in the fear of God.

Textual Notes: 2 Cor 6:14—7:1

There is much discussion about the origin and placement of this passage. This discussion need not deter us here, since as its stands, the passage is an insertion that makes a plea for ingroup purity, a significant dimension of social identity. Purity, of course, refers to the system of social boundaries that mark off one group from another. If read in the context of Paul's interaction with the Corinthians, this passage urges Corinthian Jesus-group members to keep their social boundaries clear and live socially and harmoniously within the ingroup. There must be no contamination from the outside through cooperation, agreement, sharing, or partnership with outsiders. As a plea for ingroup purity, the passage provides motivation for social identity.

Such social identity would have Jesus-group members at Corinth stay aware that they are fellow members of the same social category (believers in the gospel of God), share some emotional involvement in this common definition of themselves (by means of love or group attachment), and achieve some degree of social consensus about the evaluation of their group and of their membership in it (they are righteous or God-approved).

In fact the boundary markers Paul lists here are evaluative labels, underscoring the positive value of Jesus-group membership over against the negative qualities of the outgroup:

Ingroup	**Outgroup**
Jesus-group Members	*Unbelievers or Nonmembers*
righteousness	*lawlessness*
light	*darkness*

Christ	*Beliar (literally, worthlessness; Satan)*
believers	*unbelievers*
temple of God	*temple of idols*

Of course, the obvious question is, who are the outsiders? The negative outsider labels surely point to persons who do not accept the gospel of God proclaimed by Paul. In the Corinthian context, these would be Paul's opponents and the clients they might have gathered who take a stance against the innovation that had been proclaimed. The label "unbelievers" points to those who have heard the gospel of God and either rejected it or discontinued it. These unbelievers would not be non-Israelites, since non-Israelites were ignorant of the gospel of the God of Israel proclaimed by Paul and other early Jesus-group change agents. Everything would indicate that these unbelievers are all Israelites, a point further underscored by the following series of scriptural quotations, ascribed to God himself (v. 16b). The God of Israel has made these promises in the past and now fulfills them in Paul's Jesus groups.

6:16b-18: These verses form a chain of scriptural citations (as in Rom 3:10-18; 15:9-12). 6:16b cites Lev 26:11-12 and Ezek 37:27; 6:17 cites Isa 52:11 and Ezek 20:34 LXX; 6:18 cites 2 Sam 7:14; Isa 43:6. How to explain such chains? Some scholars say this reflects the knowledge and skill of the author, in this instance Paul. It was a mark of manliness to demonstrate mastery of the tradition and the ability to interweave it into an argument. Another explanation is that early Jesus-group teachers compiled a collection of citations to consult on given topics. Whatever the case, Paul has marshaled a fine collection of citations to make a point.

6:16b: That Jesus groups form a temple of the living God is a viewpoint previously expressed by Paul (1 Cor 3:16); the citation of Lev 26:11-12 indicates that a temple is a place where God dwells and acts. This is the Jesus-group experience. The citation from Ezek 37:27 is a covenant formula: Jesus groups form a people in covenant with God.

6:17: The citations from Isa 52:11 and Ezek 20:34 LXX urge ingroup purity and withdrawal from the outgroup.

6:18: Finally, the citation from 2 Sam 7:14 and Isa 43:6 underscores God's role as father (patron) of the sons and daughters who make up the Jesus-group membership.

7:1: This verse forms the conclusion to the whole, urging "cleansing from defilement," withdrawal from outgroup interaction, with emphasis on "holiness," that is, ingroup exclusivity, based on respect and reverence for the God of Israel.

In sum, whether the passage derives from Paul himself or was inserted by some later scribe, it does admirably fit Paul's insistence on ingroup unity and distancing from outgroup Israelite unbelievers.

At 7:2 the text of Letter 1, written *before* the dispute involving Paul and the Corinthians, resumes.

Plea for Openness, Part II: 7:2-4 [Part I: 6:1-13]

7:2 Make room in your hearts for us; we have wronged no one, we have corrupted no one, we have taken advantage of no one. 3 I do not say this to condemn you, for I said before that you are in our hearts, to die together and to live together. 4 I often boast about you; I have great pride in you; I am filled with consolation; I am overjoyed in all our affliction.

Textual Notes: 2 Cor 7:2-4

These verses take up Paul's plea at 2 Cor 6:1-13.

7:2: This verse describes further dimensions of Paul's open heart: he has wronged no one, corrupted no one, taken advantage of no one. Such behaviors derive from a "closed" heart.

7:3: "To die together and to live together" point to the relationship of friendship (see 2 Sam 15:21). In Paul's heart, Corinthian Jesus-group members are his friends.

7:4: As for his friends, he has only a positive evaluation and attitude toward them and finds in this relationship consolation in the face of any afflictions he might undergo.

At this point in the canonical 2 Corinthians, two letter fragments have been inserted: a letter of recommendation for Titus (at 8:1-24) and a letter concerning the collection (at 9:1-15). We will return to discuss these letter fragments later. For now, we move over them to discuss the second letter Paul wrote, during the dispute with the Corinthians, which now appears as 2 Corinthians 10–13.

II. 2 Corinthians 10–13
Letter 2: Written during the Dispute

Some of the Corinthian Jesus-group members discontinued Paul's innovative gospel of God. This discontinuance was triggered by some interlopers whom Paul calls "super-apostles." Whether Paul faced off with these super-apostles is never specified; that would have been the conflict phase of the interaction. In this letter (we call it Letter 2, often called "the tearful letter" by commentators) Paul brings the Corinthians into his conflict. The result is a dispute, a three-party interaction. His resorting to the Corinthians looks to resolving the dispute by means of adjudication, that is, by recourse to the court of Jesus-group opinion. Paul had other options in dealing with the dispute: "lumping it," avoidance, coercion, negotiation, mediation, and arbitration. Lumping it involved acquiescing in the opponents' opinion of Paul, while avoidance meant ignoring and keeping quiet about the problem. Both of these solutions would be dishonorable, hence out of the question. Coercion entails getting a group of Corinthians together to physically force the super-apostles and their supporters out of the city. Negotiation involves face-to-face interaction with the opponents to come to some amicable compromise. Mediation would have a third party, a mediator, resolve the dispute, while arbitration would likewise involve a third party making a decision binding on both parties. All of these dispute resolution procedures were out of the question for Paul. The letter indicates Paul has opted for adjudication; hence the context of the letter is one of Paul pleading for Corinthian loyalty and choosing to recognize Paul and his gospel of God. **Dispute Process.**

The problem provoking the conflict, of course, was the decision on the part of some Corinthian Jesus-group members to reject the innovation proclaimed by Paul after it had previously been adopted. The cause of the discontinuance was the replacement of this gospel by a new set of ideas and practices as well as dissatisfaction with Paul fomented by the super-apostles. At various stages of his career, Paul witnessed the threat of discontinuance due to "Judaizers," persons insisting that accepting the gospel of God required full observance of Judean customs. Paul's constant problem was that previous decisions in favor of the gospel of God may be reversed if adopters are exposed to conflicting messages about the innovation and, in this case, about the change agent. Hence Paul's urgent task here is one of confirmation, providing the Corinthians with reinforcement for the innovation decision they had already made. He hoped to provide this confirmation by having the Corinthians adjudicate in his favor over the claims of the super-apostles.

2 Cor 10:1–13:10
Body of Letter 2

Paul's Plea Not to Force His Hand 10:1-6

10:1 I myself, Paul, appeal to you by the meekness and gentleness of Christ—I who am humble when face to face with you, but bold toward you when I am away!— 2 I ask that when I am present I need not show boldness by daring to oppose those who think we are acting according to human standards. 3 Indeed, we live as human beings, but we do not wage war according to human standards; 4 for the weapons of our warfare are not merely human, but they have divine power to destroy strongholds. We destroy arguments 5 and every proud obstacle raised up against the knowledge of God, and we take every thought captive to obey Christ. 6 We are ready to punish every disobedience when your obedience is complete.

Textual Notes: 2 Cor 10:1-6

10:1-2: This passage mentions two accusations against Paul: he is gentle in face-to-face contact but bold when he writes (v. 1); he acts according to human standards (Greek: according to the flesh) (v. 2). These accusations attack Paul's character, intimating that he lacks manly virtues, that he lacks courage and openness to God. Paul thus opens the letter fragment with an appeal based on the non-manly virtues of Christ, kindness (NRSV: "meekness") and gentleness. His gentle appeal to the Corinthians asks them to put a halt to their discontinuance of his gospel of God and to stabilize their adoption of this gospel. The change agent's task is to stabilize adoption and prevent discontinuance.

10:3-6: Should the appeal be fruitless, he promises he will be bold when face-to-face. And he will take up the task of rectifying the situation not in terms of human standards but in terms of divine power. He describes what that entails with a military analogy: destruction of arguments, of arrogance that serves as obstacle against the knowledge of God, capturing wayward thinking, punishing disobedience. Savage destruction, capture for slavery, and vicious punishment for disobedience were all typical of the Roman army. The Hellenistic world was a world of violence. From the Roman military point of view, such violence was triggered only because people opposed Roman patronage and rejected Roman favor. Roman military violence was a type of "wrath," or satisfaction for dishonoring Romans and their patronage. Paul's analogy is not about physical violence but about annihilating ideas and arguments raised in opposition to his gospel of God. His goal is complete obedience to the gospel of God. People in Corinth, a Roman colony, would appreciate the analogy.

He Will Not Be Put to Shame 10:7-18

10:7 Look at what is before your eyes. If you are confident that you belong to Christ, remind yourself of this, that just as you belong to Christ, so also do we. 8 Now, even if I boast a little too much of our authority, which the Lord gave for building you up and not for tearing you down, I will not be ashamed of it. 9 I do not want to seem as though I am trying to frighten you with my letters. 10 For they say, "His letters are weighty and strong, but his bodily presence is weak, and his speech contemptible." 11 Let such people understand that what we say by letter when absent, we will also do when present.

12 We do not dare to classify or compare ourselves with some of those who commend themselves. But when they measure themselves by one another, and compare themselves with one another, they do not show good sense. 13 We, however, will not boast beyond limits, but will keep within the field that God has assigned to us, to reach out even as far as you. 14 For we were not overstepping our limits when we reached you; we were the first to come all the way to you with the good news of Christ. 15 We do not boast beyond limits, that is, in the labors of others; but our hope is that, as your faith increases, our sphere of action among you may be greatly enlarged, 16 so that we may proclaim the good news in lands beyond you, without boasting of work already done in someone else's sphere of action. 17 "Let the one who boasts, boast in the Lord." 18 For it is not those who commend themselves that are approved, but those whom the Lord commends.

Textual Notes: 2 Cor 10:7-18

10:7-11: This passage continues the point of the previous one, this time based on the slur against Paul cited in v. 10: "His letters are weighty and strong, but his bodily presence is weak, and his speech contemptible." Paul asks the Corinthians to look at the matter more closely (v. 7). He and the Corinthian Jesus-group members are both in Christ (v. 8), yet Paul has authority from the Lord to build up Jesus groups. He sees no dishonor in this (v. 9). Given his authority, his purpose in writing is not to frighten anyone (v. 10), even though they might say that when physically present, he cuts a poor figure and speaks poorly. Paul's point is that when he comes to Corinth again, he will act in the same way he writes to them, in a way that is "weighty and strong" (against the accusation of 2 Cor 10:1).

10:8: "To commend oneself" means to strive for the good opinion and good will of others by setting out one's merits and accomplishments. A proper rhetorical way to do this is to classify oneself with others who are well thought of (name dropping) or to compare oneself with others either positively or negatively. Paul intimates that his opponents do in fact commend themselves in this way, demonstrating how silly they are (v. 12). By accusing his opponents of a "lack of good sense," he impugns their honor. He says he will refrain from such self-commendation. And his reason for doing so is that what counts for Jesus groups is not persons who commend themselves but those commended by the Lord (v. 18).

10:13-14: "To boast" is to make an honor claim. As an honorable person, Paul must make honor claims; however he does so within proper limits. Specifically the limits are replicated by the social groups assigned to him by God. His change-agent task is totally governed by the change agency of the God of Israel. Thanks to God, Paul was the first to proclaim God's gospel of the significance of the death and resurrection of Jesus, Israel's Messiah, with a view to the coming kingdom of God. Paul claims honor from fulfilling his task as first change agent to the Corinthians.

10:15-18: The problem with the super-apostles is that they make honor claims over their reputed successes among persons who have already adopted the innovation of God's gospel. Because they take credit for what has already been accomplished by others, they must commend themselves rather than be commended by the Lord, who assigns social groups to change agents. Paul's citing Jer 9:23-24 in v. 17 serves to accuse his opponents of making honor claims not because of what God does but because of what they themselves do.

10:16: Paul notes that he plans to proclaim his gospel of God to Israelites dwelling beyond Corinth, who have not yet been contacted by any other Jesus-group change agent. His super-apostle opponents do not venture into Israelite communities untouched by others proclaiming the gospel of God. In other words, they encroach on the work of others.

Boasting like Fools 11:1–12:13 [General Section]

While Paul pleads his case against his opponents before the Corinthians, he also seeks to have them discontinue any innovation suggested to them by those opponents. Paul's ploy to effect this discontinuance in 2 Cor 11:1-21a is to use the rhetorical figure of satire on the Corinthian community. He ridicules their interactions with the opponents with a view to censure and reprove them. He has too much affection and respect for the Corinthians to be sarcastic. Sarcasm implies the intent to inflict pain by deriding, taunting, or ridiculing. Paul makes no mention of any intent to inflict pain. If anything, Paul is the one who is pained.

Paul's Opening Ploy 11:1-6

11:1 I wish you would bear with me in a little foolishness. Do bear with me! 2 I feel a divine jealousy for you, for I promised you in marriage to one husband, to present you as a chaste virgin to Christ. 3 But I am afraid that as the serpent deceived Eve by its cunning, your thoughts will be led astray from a sincere and pure devotion to Christ. 4 For if someone comes and proclaims another Jesus than the one we proclaimed, or if you receive a different spirit from the one you received, or a different gospel from the one you accepted, you submit to it readily enough. 5 I think that I am not in the least inferior to these super-apostles. 6 I may be untrained in speech, but not in knowledge; certainly in every way and in all things we have made this evident to you.

Textual Notes: 2 Cor 11:1-6

11:1-2: "Foolishness" usually means unconcern for honor, shameless behavior. Paul requests the Corinthians to put up with his shameless language, to not take it seriously (although Paul is quite serious, as becomes apparent; this is satire).

"Jealousy" is the feeling of attachment to persons and things that stand in some exclusive relation to a person. The feelings one experiences when one's house is broken into, when one's mother or father is hurt, when one's car is vandalized—all these feelings fall under the category of "jealousy." God is called a jealous God because of his attachment to persons who are exclusively his. The Greek of v. 2 states literally: "I am jealous about you with the jealousy of God." Paul thus expresses his attachment to the Corinthian Jesus groups and his deeply rooted, personal sense of concern for their well-being.

11:2b-3: Paul now describes his change-agent task in terms of an analogy. Like a jealous father with his daughter's well-being in mind, Paul has given the Corinthians in marriage to one husband, Christ, as a chaste virgin. The problem, of course, is that should the Corinthians yield to the innovations offered by Paul's opponents, they would no longer be faithful to their one husband, Christ. Hence his reference to the serpent's deception of Eve in Gen 3:13. The implication is that the opponents, like the serpent in Genesis, deceive by their cunning. The outcome is the Corinthians' being led astray from sincere and total devotedness to Christ.

11:4-5: Paul here sets out what he believes the opponents have been doing: proclaiming another Jesus, another spirit, and another gospel, all different from what Paul proclaimed and imparted. And the Corinthians yielded to those opponents.

11:6: While his oratorical skills may not be up to par, Paul admits, what he has experienced and knows is superior to what the super-apostles offer, as has been evident to the Corinthians. For this reason, Paul has greater credibility and trustworthiness than his opponents.

Further Satirical Comments 11:7-11

11:7 Did I commit a sin by humbling myself so that you might be exalted, because I proclaimed God's good news to you free of charge? 8 I robbed other churches by accepting support from them in order to serve you. 9 And when I was with you and was in need, I did not burden anyone, for my needs were supplied by the friends who came from Macedonia. So I refrained and will continue to refrain from burdening you in any way. 10 As the truth of Christ is in me, this boast of mine will not be silenced in the regions of Achaia. 11 And why? Because I do not love you? God knows I do!

Textual Notes: 2 Cor 11:7-11

The passage makes clear that Paul did not accept any subvention from the Corinthians when he arrived, or after he proclaimed his gospel of God and stayed with that Jesus group for a time. In terms of ancient Mediterranean culture, he declined their hospitality. Hospitality is a process in which a total stranger is taken in for a time by a local person or group that adopts the stranger as client in a patron-client relationship. At the end of the time period, the stranger leaves either as client/friend or enemy. Since Paul did not accept any such patronage favors from the Corinthians, he was not obliged to any of them by obligations of clientship or friendship. As a number of authors have noted, this gambit by Paul may have been perceived by local Corinthians as a challenge to their honor—and it surely was.

In such a scenario, Paul acted as he did in order to turn the tables, that is, to make the Corinthian Jesus-group members obliged to him, rather than vice versa. In point of fact, by their accepting his gospel of God, the Corinthians did owe Paul material sustenance and support. In the culture of the period, material and immaterial goods were still goods in limited supply and readily interchangeable. Those who proclaim the gospel are entitled to physical support (see Matt 10:10; Luke 10:7; and the discussion in 1 Cor 9:1-27).

11:7: Paul begins a series of satirical comments, first with a rhetorical question. Did he dishonor God by putting the Corinthians ahead of himself, proclaiming the gospel of the God of Israel without accepting anything in return? "To sin" means to dishonor or shame God or some person; "to humble oneself" means to remain in one's perceived social standing and be treated as such; "to exalt" means to attribute greater honor and treat the person in that way.

11:8-9: These verses provide the zinger: other Jesus groups paid Paul for his services to the Corinthians, specifically brothers (that is, fellow Jesus-group members; NRSV: "friends") from Macedonia. Corinth is in the Roman province of Achaia. There is no "Greece" at this time. Since other Jesus groups support Paul, he will not accept reciprocal support from the Corinthians, and thus he keeps them in his debt.

11:10-11: Paul finds his strategy quite worthy of honor, worthy of being broadcast throughout Achaia. Why does he act this way? The negative rhetorical question ("Because I do not love you?") requires an answer of "of course not." Paul is attached to the Corinthian Jesus group and shows this attachment by his behavior. God is his witness.

Comparisons with Opponents 11:12-21a

11:12 And what I do I will also continue to do, in order to deny an opportunity to those who want an opportunity to be recognized as our equals in what they boast about. 13 For such boasters are false apostles, deceitful workers, disguising themselves as apostles of Christ. 14 And no wonder! Even Satan disguises himself as an angel of light. 15 So it is not strange if his ministers also disguise themselves as ministers of righteousness. Their end will match their deeds.

16 I repeat, let no one think that I am a fool; but if you do, then accept me as a fool, so that I too may boast a little. 17 What I am saying in regard to this boastful confidence, I am saying not with the Lord's authority, but as a fool; 18 since many boast according to human standards, I will also boast. 19 For you gladly put up with fools, being wise yourselves! 20 For you put up with it when someone makes slaves of you, or preys upon you, or takes advantage of you, or puts on airs, or gives you a slap in the face. 21 To my shame, I must say, we were too weak for that!

Textual Notes: 2 Cor 11:12-21a

11:12: Paul's opponents were quick to accept material support. By not taking anything from the Corinthians, Paul reveals the hand of these opponents and gains honor over them, demonstrating they are no equals in this regard as well.

11:13-15: Here follows a tissue of weighty and shaming accusations: Paul's opponents are "false apostles," that is, change agents working for an agency other than the God of Israel. They deceive and disguise themselves just like that well-known cosmic deceiver and tester of loyalty, Satan. Their behavior will eventually reveal their true nature.

11:14: That Satan can and does disguise himself as an angel of light is known in Israelite lore (*Life of Adam and Eve* 9). In ancient Mediterranean culture it was believed that "all beings of higher rank than earthly humans can change into whatever form they choose" (*HCNT* #749 with references to Porphyry, *On Abstinence* 2.40,42; Pseudo-Clement, *Homilies* 9.13).

11:16-20: Paul once again takes up his satiric self-designation as "fool," that is, as a shameless person, a person without honor. His point is that the Corinthians have in fact accepted true fools and put up with their shameless and dishonorable behavior. If they are willing to accept shameless fools, Paul can play that role as well. However, his sense of honor ("he is too weak" in v. 21) does not allow him to go all the way in this role. He cannot enslave, deceive, put on airs, and insult as his opponents have done to the Corinthians! The passage is a heavy put-down both of his opponents and of the Corinthians who have taken those insulting opponents seriously.

In Defense of Honor: Rhetorical Comparison 11:22—12:13

11:21b But whatever anyone dares to boast of—I am speaking as a fool—I also dare to boast of that. 22 Are they Hebrews? So am I. Are they Israelites? So am I. Are they descendants of Abraham? So am I. 23 Are they ministers of Christ? I am talking like a madman—I am a better one: with far greater labors, far more imprisonments, with countless floggings, and often near death. 24 Five times I have received from the Jews the forty lashes minus one. 25 Three times I was beaten with rods. Once I received a stoning. Three times I was shipwrecked; for a night and a day I was adrift at sea; 26 on frequent journeys, in danger from rivers, danger from bandits, danger from my own people, danger from Gentiles, danger in the city, danger in the wilderness, danger at sea, danger from false brothers and sisters; 27 in toil and hardship, through many a sleepless night, hungry and thirsty, often without food, cold and naked. 28 And, besides other things, I am under daily pressure because of my anxiety for all the churches. 29 Who is weak, and I am not weak? Who is made to stumble, and I am not indignant?

30 If I must boast, I will boast of the things that show my weakness. 31 The God and Father of the Lord Jesus (blessed be he forever!) knows that I do not lie. 32 In Damascus, the governor under King Aretas guarded the city of Damascus in order to seize me, 33 but I was let down in a basket through a window in the wall, and escaped from his hands.

12:1 It is necessary to boast; nothing is to be gained by it, but I will go on to visions and revelations of the Lord. 2 I know a person in Christ who fourteen years ago was caught up to the third heaven—whether in the body or out of the body I do not know; God knows. 3 And I know that such a person—whether in the body or out of the body I do not know; God knows— 4 was caught up into Paradise and heard things that are not to be told, that no mortal is permitted to repeat. 5 On behalf of such a one I will boast, but on my own behalf I will not boast, except of my weaknesses. 6 But if I wish to boast, I will not be a fool, for I will be speaking the truth. But I refrain from it, so that no one may think better of me than what is seen in me or heard from me, 7 even considering the exceptional character of the revelations. Therefore, to keep me from being too elated, a thorn was given me in the flesh, a messenger of Satan to torment me, to keep me from being too elated. 8 Three times I appealed to the Lord about this, that it would leave me, 9 but he said to me, "My grace is sufficient for you, for power is made perfect in weakness." So, I will boast all the more gladly of my weaknesses, so that the power of Christ may dwell in me. 10 Therefore I am content with weaknesses, insults, hardships, persecutions, and calamities for the sake of Christ; for whenever I am weak, then I am strong.

11 I have been a fool! You forced me to it. Indeed you should have been the ones commending me, for I am not at all inferior to these super-apostles, even though I am nothing. 12 The signs of a true apostle were performed among you with utmost patience, signs and wonders and mighty works. 13 How have you been worse off than the other churches, except that I myself did not burden you? Forgive me this wrong!

Textual Notes: 2 Cor 11:22–12:13

This section of 2 Corinthians has the features of a segment of the Hellenistic encomium called comparison (*sygkrisis*). The encomium was a stereotypical speech pattern for praising a person or group of persons. In Galatians Paul employed that pattern for "self-praise" for defending his honor. He does much the same here with his comparison of himself and his opponents. **Encomium.** The comparison normally covers the items that comprise the encomium in general: origin and birth, nurture and training, accomplishments and deeds. These deeds may pertain to the body (strength, endurance) and the soul (virtues, such as piety, faithfulness, justice, and courage), as well as fortune (gifts of heavenly power, favor, revelation, protection). Here 11:22 presents origin and birth; nurture and training are omitted; accomplishments listed include deeds of the body with underlying deeds of the soul (11:23-29); deeds of fortune are mentioned (11:32-33; 12:1-6).

11:22: As for ascribed honor, honor rooted in origin and birth, Paul shares as much honor as his opponents.

11:23: But now Paul claims superiority over the super-apostles, being a better person in the service of Christ. The word "servant" here is the Greek *diakonos*. In the Hellenistic world the word normally means someone functioning as an agent of a higher-ranking person, either as an intermediary in commercial transactions or as a messenger or diplomat. Hence the Greek word *diakonos* is better translated as "a person in the service of." And that is exactly what Paul is: a change agent of God. As agent of God Paul claims he has been proven to be a loyal and steadfast agent, in fact more loyal and more honorable because of his faithful service. This service is described now with a listing of his accomplishments in terms of "deeds of the body."

11:23-33: He begins his account of his deeds of the body with a list of the generic hardships he has endured: labors (*kopois*), imprisonments (*phylakais*), beatings (*plēgeis*), and dangers of death (*thanatois*). This list seems to function as a type of topical statement that is subsequently developed point-by-point. First, he catalogs his beatings (vv. 24-25a), then his near death experiences (v. 25b). But he spends most of his time enumerating his labors (vv. 26-28). Finally, he mentions an imprisonment by the king of Damascus (vv. 31-33).

In terms of the comparison developed by Paul, while he admittedly was equal to his rivals in terms of ancestral and ethnic origin, he claims superiority to them in terms of his deeds of the body ("far greater . . . far more . . . countless . . . often"). He actually numbers his beatings ("five times . . . three times"), his stonings ("once"), his shipwrecks ("three times") to emphasize strength and endurance. He makes "frequent" journeys, during which he faces "dangers" from rivers, seas, deserts, and cities, from robbers and false brethren, and from Judeans and foreigners as well. The people, locale, and terrain to which he refers bespeak his broad experience in the wide world as well as the challenges from the whole world that he has been forced to face in obedience to God's mandate. Whatever and wherever the crisis, Paul has successfully endured. And it is precisely on this point that he contrasts his own experiences with those of his rivals.

11:30-31: Paul makes honor claims for experiences that demonstrate his weakness. How is such weakness praiseworthy in a culture that admires strength and power? With his weakness in face of such hardships, the fact that he survives is a demonstration of his endurance and strength of resolve, characteristics of the virtue of courage. In ancient perception, virtues belong to deeds of the soul. Thus Paul's physical endurance (deeds of the body) is rooted in his courage (deed of the soul). Paul claims he has demonstrated that he is far more courageous in the service of God than his opponents.

12:1-7a: Paul now lists another deed of fortune that has befallen him: altered states of consciousness experiences. **Altered States of Consciousness.** Paul describes these experiences in first-century Israelite terms as "visions and revelations of the Lord." He experienced the ineffable in "Paradise." Paradise in Israelite lore, of course, was the name of the garden of pleasure created by God for the first human beings (Genesis 2). However, by Paul's day this place of blessedness was transposed into the sky (see Luke 24:43), often referred to as the third or highest level of the sky, where the righteous dead dwelt awaiting the resurrection of the dead. Paul's reticence about speaking of this sort of altered state of consciousness experience indicates his Pharisaic enculturation among those who claimed one should not speak openly to others about such experiences. He wishes to make no honor claims on his own behalf on the basis of the exceptional character of these experiences.

12:7b-9: There is insufficient contextual information to determine what Paul's "thorn in the flesh" was. It surely was some sort of personal annoyance that kept him from finding a source of great pleasure in his altered states of consciousness experiences. He found the annoyance to be a sort of test of his loyalty to God (Satan tests a person's loyalty to God). Such loyalty tests come from personal or personified testing agents. Hence there is good reason to think this "thorn in the flesh" refers to persons in the groups Paul himself founded who opposed him for various reasons. As change agent he always had to deal with problems of misunderstanding, alteration, or discontinuance of the gospel of God he proclaimed. This made him and those around him aware that the successes of his activities on behalf of God's gospel simply made God's favor visible in face of his own weakness (v. 9). He asked God to remove this annoyance, undoubtedly in an altered state experience, since he received a quotable statement from God about it. Hence his conviction based on God's word: "power is made perfect in weakness."

12:10: On the basis of God's interpretation of events, Paul brags of his weakness, noted here, since that is how his power is made perfect. Power is the ability to have effect through the sanction of force. Paul's power is that of Christ correlating with the weaknesses he bears for the sake of Christ.

12:11: Paul now brings his rhetorical comparison to a close. While he previously seemed outraged to find himself the object of anyone else's comparison and disclaims practicing such a ploy (10:12a), he even shames those who seek honor by doing so (10:12b). But now as he concludes his own comparison, he admits that by doing this he too is a "fool" (v. 11). It is the Corinthians who forced him into this because they did not commend Paul but chose to discontinue the innovation Paul proclaimed in favor of the super-apostles' gospel. With typical satirical irony, Paul insists that he is nothing, yet the nothing that he is is far more than anything the super-apostles might be!

12:12-13: Now the conclusion: God enabled Paul to perform before the Corinthians the signs of a true apostle, God's own change agent. In this they were like other Jesus groups. The only thing Paul did not insist on is that they give him material support. He sarcastically concludes: "forgive me this wrong!"

Plans for a Third Visit 12:14–13:4

12:14 Here I am, ready to come to you this third time. And I will not be a burden, because I do not want what is yours but you; for children ought not to lay up for their parents, but parents for their children. 15 I will most gladly spend and be spent for you. If I love you more, am I to be loved less? 16 Let it be assumed that I did not burden you. Nevertheless (you say) since I was crafty, I took you in by deceit. 17 Did I take advantage of you through any of those whom I sent to you? 18 I urged Titus to go, and sent the brother with him. Titus did not take advantage of you, did he? Did we not conduct ourselves with the same spirit? Did we not take the same steps?

19 Have you been thinking all along that we have been defending ourselves before you? We are speaking in Christ before God. Everything we do, beloved, is for the sake of building you up. 20 For I fear that when I come, I may find you not as I wish, and that you may find me not as you wish; I fear that there may perhaps be quarreling, jealousy, anger, selfishness, slander, gossip, conceit, and disorder. 21 I fear that when I come again, my God may humble me before you, and that I may have to mourn over many who previously sinned and have not repented of the impurity, sexual immorality, and licentiousness that they have practiced.

13:1 This is the third time I am coming to you. "Any charge must be sustained by the evidence of two or three witnesses." 2 I warned those who sinned previously and all the others, and I warn them now while absent, as I did when present on my second visit, that if I come again, I will not be lenient— 3 since you desire proof that Christ is speaking in me. He is not weak in dealing with you, but is powerful in you. 4 For he was crucified in weakness, but lives by the power of God. For we are weak in him, but in dealing with you we will live with him by the power of God.

Textual Notes: 2 Cor 12:14–13:4

12:14-17: As Paul informs the Corinthian Jesus group that he plans to come for a third time, his attention once more falls on what the Corinthians found to be a challenge to their honor: that Paul will take care of his own material needs. By acting in this way, Paul incurred a riposte from the Corinthians in the accusation that he was crafty and deceitful and sought to take advantage of the Corinthians (vv. 16-17a), something with which his opponents agreed. Whatever his motive, Paul insists he is like a parent, and he quotes the truism of the culture: "children ought not lay up for their parents, but parents for their children." Since Paul willingly spends himself for the Corinthians, demonstrating his loving attachment to them, are they to pull back from him because of this? (v. 15).

12:17-19a: None of Paul's associates took material advantage of the Corinthians either. Hence Paul asks rhetorically: did Titus or the fellow Jesus-group member he brought with him to Corinth take advantage of them? Paul and all associated with him behaved quite properly. Their refusal of material support was not to defend themselves from other, nefarious pursuits. The implied fact is they did not wish to be obligated to anyone at Corinth.

12:19b-21: While Paul's expressed intention is to build up the Corinthian Jesus group, its attitude toward him might be symptomatic of other social problems. These include the usual behaviors typical of city residents in the first-century Mediterranean: quarreling, jealousy, anger, selfishness, slander, gossip, conceit, disorder, impurity, *porneia*, and licentiousness (vv. 20-21). Paul may have to "humble himself " and "mourn." Mourning is a ritualized process of self-humiliation (a translation of the Hebrew name for "fasting"; see 1 Cor 5:2). In the Israelite mourning ritual, mourners protest the presence of evil before God by means of fasting, vigil, wearing sackcloth, and looking unkempt and unwashed. They take on the demeanor of beggars, begging from God to remove the evil with which they are afflicted. Israelite custom included the practice of ritualized mourning in the face of social disaster, largely political in character (see Isa 58:3-6; Jer 14:12; Joel 1:14; also 1 Kings 21:9, 12; 2 Chron 20:3; Ezra 8:21; Esther 4:16). The reasoning behind such behavior is that if a fellow human being would give assistance when I (and my family) humiliate myself, then all the more so will God give assistance as we humiliate ourselves before God. The behaviors listed by Paul would require him to implore God's benevolence on behalf of the Corinthian Jesus group in face of these evils. The goal is repentance or integration into the group.

13:1-4: Paul's use of Deut 19:15 in his warning to the Corinthians is interesting. The passage from Israel's scriptures that he quotes states: "Any charge must be sustained by the evidence of two or three witnesses." Here the two or three witnesses are his second and third stay with the Corinthians. If their behavior has not changed at this third visit, the charge against them is sustained, and he will have to take steps to demonstrate that Christ speaks in him. Such a demonstration of the power of Christ acting in Paul is what the Corinthians want, yet Paul is weak and cannot claim fame on the basis of power. Nevertheless, the weak and crucified Christ lives now by the power of God, and it will be the power of God mediated by Christ in the weak Paul that will deal with Jesus-group problems at Corinth.

Test Your Loyalties 13:5-10

13:5 Examine yourselves to see whether you are living in the faith. Test yourselves. Do you not realize that Jesus Christ is in you?—unless, indeed, you fail to meet the test! 6 I hope you will find out that we have not failed. 7 But we pray to God that you may not do anything wrong—not that we may appear to have met the test, but that you may do what is right, though we may seem to have failed.

8 For we cannot do anything against the truth, but only for the truth. 9 For we rejoice when we are weak and you are strong. This is what we pray for, that you may become perfect. 10 So I write these things while I am away from you, so that when I come, I may not have to be severe in using the authority that the Lord has given me for building up and not for tearing down.

Textual Notes: 2 Cor 13:5-10

13:5-7: The NRSV "examine" is better translated "test your own loyalties" (Greek: *peirazō,* the word used for "test," "tempt"). And the next verb "test" (NRSV) is the usual word for "examine," "discern" (Greek: *dokimazō*). In any event, Paul would have the Corinthian Jesus-group members check each other out, since Jesus Christ is "in you" (plural, in the group). If they fail to meet the test, then of course Jesus Christ is not in them; they are no longer the body of Christ. And Paul's activity among them was in vain.

13:7-9: Again, Paul notes that the advantage of the Corinthians is always his priority. He prays to God that the Corinthians pass their self-examination not for his sake but for their own sake, even if Paul does fail. "Truth" here means what is true. Things are what they are. Paul is weak, but he rejoices in his weakness if only the Corinthians were powerful. He wishes the Corinthians to be perfect, that is, mature in their activity and attitudes in the Jesus group.

13:10: Letters were meant to substitute for the physical presence of the letter writer. Paul has the authority from the Lord to build up Jesus groups. He hopes he need not be severe in tearing down when he appears among the Corinthian Jesus-group members.

2 Cor 13:11-14 Letter Closing: Salutations and Blessings

13:11 Finally, brothers and sisters, farewell. Put things in order, listen to my appeal, agree with one another, live in peace; and the God of love and peace will be with you.
12 Greet one another with a holy kiss.
13 (12) All the saints greet you.
14 (13) The grace of the Lord Jesus Christ, the love of God, and the communion of the Holy Spirit be with all of you.

Textual Notes: 2 Cor 13:12-14

This conclusion to the letter written during the dispute consists of a series of general good wishes and exhortations. The final verse is much like the opening greeting, wishing divine favor, attachment, and benefit on all.

III. 2 Cor 1:1—2:13 [7:5-16] Letter 3: Written after the Dispute

2 Cor 1:1-2 Letter Opening (Superscription)

1:1 Paul, an apostle of Christ Jesus by the will of God, and Timothy our brother,
To the church of God that is in Corinth, including all the saints throughout Achaia;
2 Grace to you and peace from God our Father and the Lord Jesus Christ.

Textual Notes: 2 Cor 1:1-2

This is the usual Hellenistic letter opening, naming the sender, addressee, and greeting. This perhaps is the original opening of the letter written after the dispute at Corinth has been resolved. Note that the sender is plural: Paul and Timothy.

Timothy was a change agent, like Paul. **Change Agent.** He is co-sender with Paul of several of the letters (1 Thessalonians, the earliest, and 2 Corinthians and Philippians). He often travels on Paul's behalf (see 1 Cor 4:17; 16:10; 1 Thess 3:2, 6), thus assisting in the information exchange relation basic to the change agent's task (Phil 2:19). Paul relates to him like father to son (Phil 2:22), perhaps as elder to younger person, in a very close Mediterranean relationship. More important, Paul believes Timothy is genuinely concerned for the welfare of the Jesus groups Paul founded. For this reason, Timothy did more than simply transmit information from and to Paul. Such change-agent concern would be manifest in his change-agent tasks of diagnosing problems, solidifying the clients' intent to change, stabilizing the membership, and preventing discontinuance.

The letter is addressed not only to Jesus groups in Corinth but likewise to groups in Achaia. Achaia was the name of the Roman province in which Corinth was located. Notice that there is no usage of the word "Greece" to designate the territory of some collection of peoples called Greeks. "Greek" in Paul's time referred to people considered civilized, cultivated, well-bred.

2 Cor 1:3-7 Letter Thanksgiving

1:3 Blessed be the God and Father of our Lord Jesus Christ, the Father of mercies and the God of all consolation, 4 who consoles us in all our affliction, so that we may be able to console those who are in any affliction with the consolation with which we ourselves are consoled by God. 5 For just as the sufferings of Christ are abundant for us, so also our consolation is abundant through Christ. 6 If we are being afflicted, it is for your consolation and salvation; if we are being consoled, it is for your consolation, which you experience when you patiently endure the same sufferings that we are also suffering. 7 Our hope for you is unshaken; for we know that as you share in our sufferings, so also you share in our consolation.

Textual Notes: 2 Cor 1:3-7

1:3-4: In a Hellenistic letter, the letter opening is followed by a blessing. A blessing is a statement that acknowledges some divine benefaction. Here Paul acknowledges God's consolation in his affliction, presumably deriving from the recently resolved dispute situation. Consolation is the alleviation of some person's grief, sense of loss, or trouble. While God alleviates Paul's grief, Paul sees the purpose of this divine consolation to enable him to console other Jesus-group members so afflicted. Consoling others thus serves as a sort of group adhesive, facilitating Jesus-group bonding. The theme of consolation looms large in this post-dispute letter segment that presumes the problem leading to the dispute has been resolved.

1:5-7: The divine benefaction of abundant consolation acknowledged by Paul replicates the abundant benefactions of Christ's sufferings. The word for suffering (Greek: *pathemata*) refers to physical suffering, while the word for affliction (Greek: *thlipsis*) refers to trouble that causes distress. For Paul, reference to Christ's sufferings is a shorthand term that stands for the crucifixion and all that it means. Just as the significance of Jesus' death on the cross entailed so very much for Jesus-group members who believe, so too through Christ the alleviation of their troubling distress is very great. If Paul and his associates face difficulties, it is so that the Corinthians' troubles might be alleviated and that they might be rescued from their troubling situation (that is what "salvation" means here). Moreover, if Paul and his associates experience the alleviation of their difficulties, the purpose of their positive experience is to provide the Corinthians with the hope of experiencing similar alleviation in face of similar sufferings. Paul's forward-looking hope is that as the Corinthian Jesus-group members share sufferings similar to those of Paul and his associates, they would also share in the alleviation of those sufferings.

In this passage no specifics are yet mentioned. So the reader/hearer of the letter must look forward to some clarification. This comes in the next passage.

2 Cor 1:8–2:13 [7:5-16]
Body of the Letter

Perils in Asia 1:8-11

1:8 We do not want you to be unaware, brothers and sisters, of the affliction we experienced in Asia; for we were so utterly, unbearably crushed that we despaired of life itself. 9 Indeed, we felt that we had received the sentence of death so that we would rely not on ourselves but on God who raises the dead. 10 He who rescued us from so deadly a peril will continue to rescue us; on him we have set our hope that he will rescue us again, 11 as you also join in helping us by your prayers, so that many will give thanks on our behalf for the blessing granted us through the prayers of many.

Textual Notes: 2 Cor 1:8-11

1:8a: The body of the letter opens with the frequent disclosure formula, "we do not want you to be unaware," which usually marks a transition to a new topic (see Rom 1:13; 11:25; 1 Cor 10:1; 1 Cor 12:1; 2 Cor 1:8; 1 Thess 4:13). What Paul informs the Corinthians about here is his reason for not visiting them. In the letter written during the dispute (2 Cor 10:1—13:14; see below) Paul insisted he would be making a third visit to Corinth. Obviously that visit never materialized. This passage explains why.

1:8b-9: The problem was some life-threatening, troubling distress (Greek: *thlipsis*) that befell Paul and Timothy. Paul often speaks of troubling distress without specifying the source or circumstance of the trouble. Here all he says is that it occurred in the Roman province of Asia, without further specifics. Some have suggested that the riot in Ephesus recounted in Acts 19:23ff. or something similar might be the life-threatening distress to which he refers. Insofar as this letter was written from Ephesus, that suggestion is plausible. In any event, this is the first time in his letters that he expresses a sense that he might die before the return of the Lord Jesus (compare 1 Thess 4:15; 1 Cor 15:51). Paul and Timothy, however, did come out unscathed from this life-threatening situation, and Paul ascribes the positive outcome to the God "who raises the dead." This last phrase, a truly theological statement, refers, of course, to an attribute of the God of Israel, who raised Jesus from the dead—the central point of Paul's gospel of the God of Israel.

1:10: As God's change agents Paul and Timothy not only attribute this rescue to their change agency but expect divine support in the service they perform for God. They also attribute God's gift (Greek: *charisma*) of rescue to the prayers of the Corinthians. In Greek these prayers proceeded "from/by the faces of many" (Greek: *ek pollōn prosōpōn*), referring to the faces of the ones praying turned to God. The image is that of a person standing and looking up to God, undoubtedly with arms raised as in the well-known *Orans* (one praying) posture.

A view of the hill of the Areopagos in Athens. In Christian tradition it is the place of Paul's appearance before the Council of the Areopagites, in which he defended his "new teaching" (Acts 17:19) *and gained new Jesus-group members, including Dionysius the Areopagite* (Acts 17:34).

Prayer (Greek: *deesis*) to God is a type of human social behavior applied by analogy to interaction with God. By that we mean that most people actually pray to other people (compare the medieval English phrase "I pray thee" for "please"). Just as people pray to other people to have effect, so by analogy people pray to God to have effect. The behavior we call "prayer" is in fact a socially meaningful symbolic act of communication. This communication is invariably directed to persons perceived as somehow supporting, maintaining, and controlling the order of existence of the one praying. And the one praying prays in order to have some intended effect. People learn to pray to God in terms of how they pray to human beings who support, maintain, or control their existence (e.g., initially parents, adults, then other people in charge). **Prayer.**

Paul believes that the *charisma* of rescue given by God to him and Timothy is due to the prayer of the Corinthians; this in turn triggers a response of acknowledgment of God's action by many more Jesus-group members.

Paul's Claim to Honor 1:12-14

1:12 Indeed, this is our boast, the testimony of our conscience: we have behaved in the world with frankness and godly sincerity, not by earthly wisdom but by the grace of God—and all the more toward you. 13 For we write you nothing other than what you can read and also understand; I hope you will understand until the end— 14 as you have already understood us in part—that on the day of the Lord Jesus we are your boast even as you are our boast.

Textual Notes: 2 Cor 1:12-14

1:12: The NRSV "indeed" is the Greek *gar,* usually translated "for." *Gar* introduces a statement that gives the reason for a preceding statement. Here the word introduces the reason Paul believes he can expect such assistance from the Corinthians. The reason is his frank and sincere behavior in society ("the world") in general and especially among the Corinthians. His behavior has been guided by God's patronage or favor (NRSV: "grace"), not by human shrewdness. It is his behavior that is his "boast," that is, his claim to honor, to an acknowledgment of worth in the eyes of others. And, of course, the social awareness he shares with the Corinthians (his conscience) attests to this.

1:13-14: Paul insists that his previous and present letters are not intended to obfuscate matters. He hopes his Corinthian addressees will understand them fully (Greek *heōs telous*: the phrase can be taken either as adjectival phrase meaning "fully," as contrasted with "in part" in the next sentence as in the RSV; or the phrase can be taken temporally, as in NRSV "until the end"). He knows they understood him partially when he was with them, as the topics in 1 Corinthians indicate. The situation points to the usual change-agent need to establish an information exchange relationship to ascertain how the adopters of an innovation have begun implementing it. His stated purpose is that "on the day of the Lord Jesus," at the forthcoming establishment of the kingdom of God, the Corinthians might feel honored by their relationship with Paul just as he is honored by his relationship with them.

Narratives of Events, Part I 1:15–2:13 [Part II: 7:5-12]

1:15 Since I was sure of this, I wanted
to come to you first, so that you might have
a double favor; 16 I wanted to visit you on
my way to Macedonia, and to come back
to you from Macedonia and have you send
me on to Judea. 17 Was I vacillating when
I wanted to do this? Do I make my plans
according to ordinary human standards,
ready to say "Yes, yes" and "No, no" at the
same time? 18 As surely as God is faithful, our word to you has not been "Yes
and No." 19 For the Son of God, Jesus
Christ, whom we proclaimed among you,
Silvanus and Timothy and I, was not "Yes
and No"; but in him it is always "Yes."
20 For in him every one of God's promises
is a "Yes." For this reason it is through him
that we say the "Amen," to the glory of
God. 21 But it is God who establishes us
with you in Christ and has anointed us,
22 by putting his seal on us and giving us
his Spirit in our hearts as a first installment.
23 But I call on God as witness against
me: it was to spare you that I did not
come again to Corinth. 24 I do not mean
to imply that we lord it over your faith;
rather, we are workers with you for your
joy, because you stand firm in the faith.

2:1 So I made up my mind not to make
you another painful visit. 2 For if I cause
you pain, who is there to make me glad
but the one whom I have pained? 3 And I
wrote as I did, so that when I came, I might
not suffer pain from those who should have
made me rejoice; for I am confident about
all of you, that my joy would be the joy of
all of you. 4 For I wrote you out of much distress and anguish of heart and with many
tears, not to cause you pain, but to let you
know the abundant love that I have for you

5 But if anyone has caused pain, he has
caused it not to me, but to some extent—not
to exaggerate it—to all of you. 6 This
punishment by the majority is enough for

such a person; 7 so now instead you should forgive and console him, so that he may not be overwhelmed by excessive sorrow. 8 So I urge you to reaffirm your love for him. 9 I wrote for this reason: to test you and to know whether you are obedient in everything. 10 Anyone whom you forgive, I also forgive. What I have forgiven, if I have forgiven anything, has been for your sake in the presence of Christ. 11 And we do this so that we may not be outwitted by Satan; for we are not ignorant of his designs.

12 When I came to Troas to proclaim the good news of Christ, a door was opened for me in the Lord; 13 but my mind could not rest because I did not find my brother Titus there. So I said farewell to them and went on to Macedonia.

Textual Notes: 2 Cor 1:15–2:13

1:15: Paul is a present-oriented person, taking his cues more often than not from altered states of consciousness experiences, that is, revelations from God, rather than from forward planning. He often makes travel plans (as here) but rarely seems to have followed through with them (see 1 Thess 2:17-18; 1 Cor 4:18). Paul states that he planned to go to Corinth in Achaia on his way to Macedonia, then stop back in Corinth on his way to Judea. Presumably this trip entailed collecting tithes for the poor among Jesus groups in Jerusalem.

1:17: Since Paul did not follow through with his travel plans, he states two rhetorical questions that are meant to dodge accusations of hesitant uncertainty and inconsistency on his part. Such accusations may have been bruited around, given the fact that he never made the promised third visit to Corinth. Such uncertainty and inconsistency cast aspersions on a person's honor and character.

1:18: The phrase "As surely as God is faithful" is a word of honor. To demonstrate sincerity of intention and steadfastness of purpose, a person can give a word of honor. Giving a word of honor functions like making an oath or swearing. But such oath-making or swearing only engages the individual him- or herself, not God or others. A word of honor is only necessary for those who find what a person says or does ambiguous or incredible. It is this ambiguity and loss of credibility that Paul seeks to remove.

1:19-20: To remove any shadow of ambiguity and untrustworthiness from himself, he adopts the procedure of identifying himself with his proclamation to the Corinthians. Jesus Christ, the son of God, is always an unambiguous and credible "Yes," God's promises in Christ are unambiguously "Yes," so that we say "Amen," that is, they are fully credible. Thus Paul's master status as change agent of the God of Israel is to cover and embrace any other roles (for example, Paul the traveler, Paul the Israelite, and the like) he might play.

1:21-22: "To anoint" is to apply some liquid unguent, such as oil, on a person's hair or skin. Anointing, like applying insect repellent or skin cream, may have a practical purpose. Olive oil was used in this way in antiquity. However, anointing also served a symbolic purpose. In Israel, kings, priests, and prophets were anointed at their inauguration in office, much like our politicians are sworn in. Anointing to office in antiquity took place by pouring a liquid on the inductee's head. By analogy other liquids poured on a person's head in certain circumstances might be called anointing. Liquids in antiquity included the usually pourable liquids we know (water, oil, perfume) as well as fire and wind. Water, fire, and wind were considered liquids that could be poured out on a person (the Latin word "infuse" means to pour out on). Since God's spirit was wind-like (Greek: *pneuma*; Latin: *spiritus*; Hebrew *ruah*, mean wind), God's spirit was poured out on the heads or hearts of believers. Jesus was Messiah, Anointed One, because he was anointed with the spirit of God.

Here Paul notes that what he has in common with the Corinthians is that they have all been founded by God in Christ, all anointed with God's Spirit as down payment of what is to come. They have God's seal or brand on them. Whether this is a physical seal or a metaphorical one is not clear. Branding and tattooing on the forehead and hand to indicate group affiliation and dedication to a deity were known in Hellenism. The practice is noted in Rev 7:3; 9:4; 14:1; 22:4; and is well known in Israel from Ezek 9:1-11. In later Jesus-group practice, the initiation rite of dipping in water (baptism) was called the seal (Greek: *sphragis*).

1:23–2:2: "To call God as witness" is stronger than a word of honor; it is an oath requiring God to witness something to which there were no human witnesses. Here Paul is willing to have God witness his intention (only God knows the human heart; see 1 Sam 16:7). What follows is another attempt on Paul's part to excuse himself honorably for not making the third, promised visit: he did not come so as to spare Jesus-group Corinthians pain, which would have pained him as well, since he only wants joy for them. Next follow further reasons for why he wrote the way he did during the dispute.

2:3: The phrase "I wrote . . ." occurs four times (2:3; 2:4; 2:9; 7:12) in this post-dispute letter. His first reason for writing, specified here, was to head off the pain he would have felt by taking the Corinthians to task in a face-to-face setting. He would rather share in their joy.

2:4: Furthermore, he wrote because of his thorough sense of attachment to the Corinthian Jesus group, although the process of writing filled him with "much distress and anguish of heart and with many tears." He did not wish to cause them the pain of dishonor and breaches of interpersonal relations.

2:5-8: Paul now alludes to some unnamed person who aggrieved him and the Jesus group as well. But they have taken care of this deviant, and Paul urges reconciliation with the group.

2:9-11: A third reason for writing: Paul wishes to test the loyalties of his Jesus-group clients, to check out their obedience, presumably to the gospel of God and all it entails. Paul forgives deviants if they forgive them, and he does so for their sake in the presence of Christ. The reason for this is that he will not be outwitted by Satan, of whose designs he is aware. The frequent mention of Satan (here as well as 6:15; 11:14; and 12:7 in this letter, along with 1 Cor 5:5; 7:5; Rom 16:20; 1 Thess 2:18) is indicative of the perception of the world that Paul shares with his fellow first-century Mediterraneans. The word "Satan" comes from Persia, where it designated the role of a secret service agent who worked undercover testing people's loyalty to the king. This role was borrowed by analogy to describe the origin of tests of loyalty to God in Israel. For example, in Job 1 Satan is God's loyalty tester. In that book Satan is still part of God's council, but by about the third century B.C.E., the Pharisees ascribed an anti-God role to this Satan. He was seen as a rogue secret service agent who recruited anti-God persons on his own behalf (see Luke 10:18; Rev 12:9). His temptations became both a testing and a recruiting device (see 1 Peter 5:8).

In the Israelite tradition of the period, Satan (Greek: *diabolos*, devil, accuser—not to be confused with demon, an invisible, person-like entity much like an angel or spirit in Israel) was considered the great deceiver in a society in which deception abounded. The Roman military likewise had its secret service agents who "tempted" or tested the loyalty of the population. (See **Notes** on 1 Thess 2:18.) However, Satan was a celestial being, a cosmic being. The sky evidenced warring cosmic forces. Human experience, too, proved that suffering and misfortune come unjustly upon human beings, often as a result of the attacks of evil against the good. As a result, life in society was seen as profoundly ambiguous; disguise and deception were everywhere. Hostile intent on the part of the outgroup is presumed until otherwise proven. Like the celestial realm, human living is full of conflict amid competing forces.

Anthropologists designate societies with such traits as "witchcraft societies." Thanks to Paul's altered states of consciousness experiences, he is well aware of what is going on in the alternate reality in which Satan functions.

2:12: Note how 2:12-13 perfectly fits the syntax and flow of ideas of 7:5-7. It seems rather obvious that this section of 2 Corinthians was split into the two parts we now find in the document. We read them as a connected whole, forming the final, post-dispute letter, although we leave 7:5-12 in its present position below.

The point is that 2:12—7:7 provide an indication of why Paul moved on to Macedonia without visiting Corinth. At Troas he could not find Titus, whom he sorely wished to see, so he went on directly to Macedonia. Titus eventually arrived in Macedonia (specifically where in Macedonia Paul does not say) and told Paul that even during his dispute provoked by opponents in Corinth, the Jesus groups that Titus encountered came down fully on Paul's side. Those groups maintained their attachment to him, and this was a great source of joy for Paul.

Letter 3 continues at 7:5, that is, *following* the insertion of a non-Pauline letter fragment that now appears as 2 Cor 6:14—7:1 and the final fragment of Letter 1 at 2 Cor 7:2-4.

Narratives of Events, Part II: 7:5-12 [Part I: 1:15–2:13]

7:5 For even when we came into Macedonia, our bodies had no rest, but we were afflicted in every way—disputes without and fears within. 6 But God, who consoles the downcast, consoled us by the arrival of Titus, 7 and not only by his coming, but also by the consolation with which he was consoled about you, as he told us of your longing, your mourning, your zeal for me, so that I rejoiced still more. 8 For even if I made you sorry with my letter, I do not regret it (though I did regret it, for I see that I grieved you with that letter, though only briefly). 9 Now I rejoice, not because you were grieved, but because your grief led to repentance; for you felt a godly grief, so that you were not harmed in any way by us. 10 For godly grief produces a repentance that leads to salvation and brings no regret, but worldly grief produces death. 11 For see what earnestness this godly grief has produced in you, what eagerness to clear yourselves, what indignation, what alarm, what longing, what zeal, what punishment! At every point you have proved yourselves guiltless in the matter. 12 So although I wrote to you, it was not on account of the one who did the wrong, nor on account of the one who was wronged, but in order that your zeal for us might be made known to you before God. 13 In this we find comfort.

Textual Notes: 2 Cor 7:5-13a

7:5: This verse continues the statement that presently concludes at 2 Cor 2:12.

7:7: For the meaning of "mourning," see notes at 2 Cor 12:19b-21 below. The word refers to a rite of protesting the presence of social evil.

7:8-11a: Paul aggrieved the Corinthians with his pointed letter (what we call Letter 2, 2 Corinthians 10–13). But they did not perceive their being aggrieved as a challenge to honor (as Paul did when aggrieved by the super-apostles); rather they "lumped it." This colloquial phrase means that they simply absorbed it and dealt with it. They changed their viewpoints and put their affairs in order as indicated by their earnestness, eagerness to clear themselves, indignation, alarm, longing, zeal, and punishment (presumably of the culprits). The comment in v. 10 refers to what generally happens in society when one is aggrieved by another person or group and takes it as a challenge to honor. To riposte to such a challenge can lead to death.

7:11b-12: Thanks to Titus's report, Paul knows that Corinthian Jesus-group members did not side with the super-apostles. Thus once more Paul explains that he wrote so that the Corinthians might reveal before God their extraordinary commitment to Paul and his gospel. The Greek word translated as "zeal" (NRSV; Greek: *spoudē*) means "extraordinary commitment to civic and religious responsibilities which were frequently intertwined, and also of concern for personal moral excellence or optimum devotion to the interest of others" (Danker 2000:939).

7:13a: This verse, of course, restates the obvious. All this comforts Paul in the risky business of taking on the super-apostles and their presumed Corinthian supporters.

Resulting Comfort for Titus 7:13b-16

7:13b In addition to our own consolation, we rejoiced still more at the joy of Titus, because his mind has been set at rest by all of you. 14 For if I have been somewhat boastful about you to him, I was not disgraced; but just as everything we said to you was true, so our boasting to Titus has proved true as well. 15 And his heart goes out all the more to you, as he remembers the obedience of all of you, and how you welcomed him with fear and trembling. 16 I rejoice, because I have complete confidence in you.

Textual Notes: 2 Cor 7:13-16

7:13b-14: Along with his demonstrated attachment to his fellow change agent Titus, Paul notes in this post-dispute letter how much Titus has been comforted by what happened at Corinth. Titus was Paul's hatchet man with the task of informing the Corinthians of Paul's position against the super-apostles, whom Paul believed the Corinthians supported. But quite the contrary. The Corinthians showed Titus hospitality with respect. Thus Paul's honor claims about the excellent sort of Jesus group he founded in Corinth proved correct; Paul was not shamed.

7:15: Titus, too, feels attached to the Corinthian Jesus group and their kindnesses to him.

7:16: In sum Paul can rejoice in his verified sense of confidence in the members of Corinth's Jesus group.

IV. 2 Cor 8:1-24 Insert: Part of a Letter of Recommendation for Titus about the Collection for Jerusalem

8:1 We want you to know, brothers and sisters, about the grace of God that has been granted to the churches of Macedonia; 2 for during a severe ordeal of affliction, their abundant joy and their extreme poverty have overflowed in a wealth of generosity on their part. 3 For, as I can testify, they voluntarily gave according to their means, and even beyond their means, 4 begging us earnestly for the privilege of sharing in this ministry to the saints— 5 and this, not merely as we expected; they gave themselves first to the Lord and, by the will of God, to us, 6 so that we might urge Titus that, as he had already made a beginning, so he should also complete this generous undertaking among you. 7 Now as you excel in everything—in faith, in speech, in knowledge, in utmost eagerness, and in our love for you—so we want you to excel also in this generous undertaking.

8 I do not say this as a command, but I am testing the genuineness of your love against the earnestness of others. 9 For you know the generous act of our Lord Jesus Christ, that though he was rich, yet for your sakes he became poor, so that by his poverty you might become rich. 10 And in this matter I am giving my advice: it is appropriate for you who began last year not only to do something but even to desire to do something— 11 now finish doing it, so that your eagerness may be matched by completing it according to your means. 12 For if the eagerness is there, the gift is acceptable according to what one has—not according to what one does not have. 13 I do not mean that there should be relief for others and pressure on you, but it is a question of a fair balance between 14 your present abundance and their need, so that their abundance

may be for your need, in order that there may be a fair balance. 15 As it is written,
"The one who had much did not have
too much,
and the one who had little did not
have too little."
16 But thanks be to God who put in the heart of Titus the same eagerness for you that I myself have. 17 For he not only accepted our appeal, but since he is more eager than ever, he is going to you of his own accord. 18 With him we are sending the brother who is famous among all the churches for his proclaiming the good news;
19 and not only that, but he has also been appointed by the churches to travel with us while we are administering this generous undertaking for the glory of the Lord himself and to show our goodwill. 20 We intend that no one should blame us about this generous gift that we are administering, 21 for we intend to do what is right not only in the Lord's sight but also in the sight of others. 22 And with them we are sending our brother whom we have often tested and found eager in many matters, but who is now more eager than ever because of his great confidence in you.
23 As for Titus, he is my partner and coworker in your service; as for our brothers, they are messengers of the churches, the glory of Christ. 24 Therefore openly before the churches, show them the proof of your love and of our reason for boasting about you.

Textual Notes: 2 Cor 8:1-24

This passage (2 Cor 8:1-24) and the next one (2 Cor 9:1-15) are fragments of Paul's letters dealing with a collection of funds (coins) to be taken up among Jesus-group members in Achaia on behalf of Jesus-group members in Jerusalem. This collection was like the customary Israelite tithe collected for the poor. This particular passage recommends Titus to the Corinthians in this task of fund collecting; the second passage (2 Cor 9:1-5) may be part of a separate letter addressed to other Jesus-group members in Achaia, for example, at Cenchreae (see Rom 16:1). Paul solicits these funds first of all because the pillars of Jerusalem asked him to (Gal 2:10) and, second, because these Israelite Jesus groups knew about tithing and supporting the poor.

The underlying problems for Jerusalemite Jesus-group members would derive from their being displaced to Jerusalem from Galilee as they awaited the forthcoming kingdom of God—as promised by Jesus. The social context of first- and second-generation Jesus-group members in Jerusalem unable to support themselves seems to be where Paul's collection on their behalf fits. Paul himself mentioned the Galileans to be found in Jerusalem: Peter, John, James, and perhaps others along with Judeans from the countryside. In Jerusalem they would have no means of support; no one there would contribute to or support them. Hence they became worthy of the tithe for the poor, and they were dependent on help from outside of Jerusalem. The example of Barnabas in Acts may be one instance of what was necessary as Jesus groups clustered in Jerusalem. Paul's collections among Jesus-group members located in non-Israelite cities served to alleviate the situation. Of course once Jerusalem fell to the Romans and Judeans were dispersed (circa 70 C.E.), Jesus-group members in Judea would have to go elsewhere to await the forthcoming kingdom of God.

On what basis would it make sense for Jesus-group members in Corinth or Cenchreae or Philippi, for example, to give money to Jesus-group members in Jerusalem? Hellenistic associations were centripetal, each seeing to its own needs. Such associations did not form intercity organizations. The basic precedent for such intercity fund transfer from Hellenistic cities to Jerusalem was the Temple tax and tithes collected among Israelites and carried, with Roman approval, to Jerusalem. As Israelites Jesus-group members in Macedonia and Achaia would have no problem in making such a transfer of funds. This collection was very much like a tithe for the Israelite poor who could not support themselves from the produce of God's land, destined for all Israel. Thus the tithe for the poor in Israel was in fact a form of generalized reciprocity. Paul, too, considers the money collected for the Jesus-group members in Jerusalem as a type of payback in terms of generalized reciprocity. Paul calls it "a fair balance" (vv. 13-14 Greek: *isotes*, equality, political justice, fairness). Reciprocal relations, typical of small-scale, face-to-face social groups (for example, villages or neighborhoods in cities), involved back-and-forth exchanges that frequently followed the pattern of generalized reciprocity: open sharing based on generosity or need. Return was often postponed or forgotten. The expectation of some returned assistance is always implied, but left indefinite and open-ended. As a rule this sort of reciprocity characterized family relations and those with whom one had fictive kin relationships, for example, friends or fellow members of associations. Paul presumes upon this well-known pattern of behavior and extends it to even distant Jesus groups. **Reciprocity.**

Indications that such generalized reciprocity are involved are found in two terms that emerge frequently in this passage. The first is *charis* in vv. 1, 4, 6, 9, 16, 19 (NRSV translates variously: "grace," "privilege," "generous undertaking" [twice], "generous act," "thanks"). The word *charis* means "favor," something another person needs because it is either not available at all or not available now. Patrons are the usual dispensers of favor, thereby setting up relations of generalized reciprocity. But family members and friends do endless "favors" within their social groups. And the God of Israel, like a patron, dispenses favors on his people, most notably through the death and resurrection of Israel's Messiah, Jesus. The first witnesses to this divine benefaction were to be found in the Jerusalem Jesus groups, from whom the gospel of God was transmitted.

The other term is *spoudē* and cognates in vv. 7, 8, 16, 17, 22 (NRSV: "eagerness," "earnestness"). As noted above, however, the word denotes "extraordinary commitment to civic and religious responsibilities which were frequently intertwined, and also of concern for personal moral excellence or optimum devotion to the interest of others" (Danker 2000:939). Hence the best translation is "commitment." And in v. 8 Paul ascribes such extraordinary commitment to the Corinthians. Commitment is fundamental to group solidarity and is at the core of willingness to repay debts of gratitude behind generalized reciprocity. It is chiefly Paul's agents who reveal this extraordinary commitment to their task; however, by soliciting funds for the Jesus-group Jerusalemites, Paul implies that his Jesus groups, Israelites living among the non-Israelite majorities, having accepted his gospel of God, owe some sort of obligation to the Jerusalemite Jesus-group members. Hence the collection funds are for them.

8:1-2: This section opens with the usual disclosure formula, "we want you to know . . . ," which marks a new section. The patronage favor of God to the Jesus groups of Macedonia (for example, in Thessalonika, Philippi, Beroea) has produced a wealth of generosity for the Jerusalem Jesus group, in spite of conflict with fellow Israelites (see 1 Thess 1:6; 2:14; Phil 1:29-30). This was the fate of Jerusalem Jesus groups (1 Thess 2:14).

8:3-4: The Macedonians believed it was a "favor" (NRSV: "privilege") to be of service (NRSV: "ministry") to the Jerusalem Jesus group. While Paul calls all members of Jesus groups "saints" (those set apart, persons exclusive to the God of Israel), he often uses the term for members of the Jerusalem Jesus group (see 2 Cor 1:1; 9:1; 13:12; also 1 Cor 1:2; 6:2; 16:1, 15; Rom 1:7; Phil 1:1; 1 Thess 3:13).

8:5-6: The Macedonians, in accepting the gospel of the God of Israel, gave themselves to the Lord. However, a number of them chose to assist Paul (Acts recalls the Macedonians among Paul's collaborators: Jason, Acts 17:6; Gaius, Acts 19:29; Sopater, Aristarchus, Secundus, Acts 20:4), and Paul ascribes this behavior to God's good pleasure. These Macedonians had Paul urge Titus to complete the "favor" he had begun in Corinth (1 Cor 16:1-5). This introductory explanation allows the passage to sound like a letter of recommendation for Titus, Paul's agent in this activity.

8:7: Paul now recalls what the Corinthians had received from the Lord as they adopted the gospel of God, that is, their spiritual endowments: faith, speech, knowledge, extraordinary commitment, group attachment (1 Cor 1:5; 12:8-10; 13:1-2, 8). Because of what they have received, they should feel obliged to excel in this favor, which is part of generalized reciprocity.

8:8-9: While Paul does not command them to make a payback, he puts them on the spot by asking them to compare what they are about to do with the extraordinary commitment of others. In this way he seeks to activate their commitment obligations. The first one he asks them to consider is the Lord Jesus himself, whose "favor" involved becoming poor, even though he was unbelievably rich, so that the Corinthians, who were poor, could become rich. The worship-rooted hymn in Phil 2:6-8, perhaps a Jesus-group hymn known to the Corinthians, would remind them of this "favor" and imply a reminder of their own obligations.

8:10-12: The Corinthians began accumulating funds for the Jerusalemite Jesus groups a year earlier. Paul asks them to bring that collection to fruitful conclusion with the same eagerness with which they began.

8:13-14: In the process of generalized reciprocity, the goal is fair balance from the perspective of the giver, that is, the giver should not be made to suffer loss. Paul makes his point with a quotation from Exod 16:18 (LXX), in the story of God's providing for Israel in the wilderness with "bread from the sky."

8:16-19: Back to Titus: Paul ascribes Titus's extraordinary commitment to the Corinthians to God's "favor." Titus needs no command from Paul to fulfill the task at hand. He will be accompanied by a "brother" (anonymous here) well-known for proclaiming the gospel of God among various Jesus groups and designated by these Jesus groups to serve as a sort of accountant in the collection and delivery process. Of course, the "favor" done to the Jerusalem Jesus group is done to display God's honor and Paul's own willingness (NRSV: "good-will").

8:20-23: Along with that brother, Paul sends another (v. 22) so that these committed Jesus-group members can accompany Titus and serve as guarantors of Paul's good intention and actual accomplishment of delivering the funds. Paul clearly suspects accusations of absconding with or skimming funds (after all, he refused to take any support from the Corinthians!), so he wants to be transparent in his dealings both before God and before his fellow Jesus-group members.

8:23: Paul, then, concludes with a plea to the Corinthians to demonstrate their attachment to the Jerusalem Jesus group by their generosity and to make evident to all that Paul's boasting about them is not empty.

V. 2 Cor 9:1-15
Insert: Part of a Letter about the Collection for Jerusalem

9:1 Now it is not necessary for me to write you about the ministry to the saints,
2 for I know your eagerness, which is the subject of my boasting about you to the people of Macedonia, saying that Achaia has been ready since last year; and your zeal has stirred up most of them. 3 But I
am sending the brothers in order that our boasting about you may not prove to have been empty in this case, so that you may be ready, as I said you would be; 4 otherwise,
if some Macedonians come with me and find that you are not ready, we would be humiliated—to say nothing of you—in this undertaking. 5 So I thought it necessary to
urge the brothers to go on ahead to you, and arrange in advance for this bountiful gift that you have promised, so that it may be ready as a voluntary gift and not as an extortion.
6 The point is this: the one who sows sparingly will also reap sparingly, and the one who sows bountifully will also reap bountifully. 7 Each of you must give as you have
made up your mind, not reluctantly or under compulsion, for God loves a cheerful giver.
8 And God is able to provide you with every blessing in abundance, so that by always having enough of everything, you may share abundantly in every good work. 9 As
it is written,

> "He scatters abroad, he gives to the poor;
> his righteousness endures forever."

10 He who supplies seed to the sower and bread for food will supply and multiply your seed for sowing and increase the harvest of your righteousness. 11 You will
be enriched in every way for your great generosity, which will produce thanksgiving to God through us; 12 for the render-
ing of this ministry not only supplies the needs of the saints but also overflows with many thanksgivings to God. 13 Through
the testing of this ministry you glorify God by your obedience to the confession of the gospel of Christ and by the generosity of your sharing with them and with all others, 14 while they long for you and pray for you because of the surpassing grace of God that he has given you. 15 Thanks be
to God for his indescribable gift!

Textual Notes: 2 Cor 9:1-15

This fragmentary passage may be part of a separate letter addressed not to the Corinthians as in the previous passage but to other Jesus-group members in Achaia, for example, at Cenchreae (see Rom 16:1).

9:1: The passage begins with the phrase "Concerning the service of the saints" (NRSV is quite different). This type of phrase ("Concerning . . .") is quite frequent as a topic marker in 1 Corinthians.

9:2-3: As with the Corinthians, Paul brags about these Achaians to the Macedonians as well, reminding them that it is a year already since they made plans to send funds to the Jerusalemite Jesus group.

9:4-5: Paul states that he is sending some brothers for the funds and expects them to fulfill the task, lest Paul be shamed among the Macedonians on account of the Achaians. Of course, if Paul were to be shamed by them, he would have to do something to defend his honor. By sending the brothers on ahead, Paul is also saved the painful confrontation with the Achaians should the funds not be forthcoming. It is a free gift on their part, not extortion, yet Paul's honor is on the line.

9:6-10: Paul now presents some arguments to motivate the donors. One receives as much as one gives. One must give freely, for "God loves a cheerful giver" (free citation of Prov 22:8 LXX). God's patronage ("favor") is abundant, so one can give abundantly. Again another scriptural proof: "He scatters abroad, he gives to the poor; his righteousness endures forever" (citing Ps 112:9 LXX). Further evidence of God's ready patronage is the providence with which God supplies seed to the sower and bread for food. In like manner will God do for the Achaians, with the outcome being a "harvest of your righteousness" (see Hos 10:12 LXX). Righteousness means God's acceptance and approval.

9:11-12: In sum, the generosity of the Achaians, which both enrich them in every way and provide occasion for God's benefaction, is being acknowledged through Paul's activity. The NRSV "thanksgivings" is the Greek *eucharistēo*, which means to acknowledge a favor and express indebtedness. This activity is a managerial task (Greek: *diakonia*; NRSV: "ministry") facilitating a *leitourgia* (NRSV: "service"). The term *leitourgia* denotes a public service that private citizens performed at their own expense (see Rom 15:27). The outcome of this public service is the support of the "saints" and the acknowledgment of God's benefaction.

9:13: Again the NRSV of this statement is not as clear as the Greek would have it. Paul actually says: "Through your experience of this service you manifest honor to God by your profession of obedience to the gospel about Christ and by the generosity of your sharing."

The word "glorify" means to give honor to someone by something visible or some action or activity. The Achaians who have the experience of being of service to the Jerusalemite Jesus group thus give honor to God. That experience is a spin-off from their profession of obedience to the gospel of God, which is about Christ's death and resurrection. It is also a spin-off from their generosity. Paul sees this *leitourgia* as fully bound up with God's glory, God's gospel, and a person's virtue.

9:14-15: Further, an unspecified "all others," that is, other Jesus groups, pray for the Achaians because of God's "favor" bestowed on them. In sum, Paul, undoubtedly in the name of all his Jesus groups, acknowledges God's indescribable gift with gratitude.

Galatians

I. Gal 1:1-5
Letter Opening (Superscription)

1:1-5	The Salutation

II. Gal 1:6-9
Introduction

1:6-9	The Charges: Accepting a Different Gospel

III. Gal 1:10—2:21
Paul Defends His Honor (Form: Encomium)

1:10-12	Opening (*Prooimion*): Origin of Paul's Gospel—Divine Revelation
1:13-17	Paul's Lifestyle (*Anastrophē*)
1:13-14	Part 1: Paul, Persecutor of Jesus Groups
1:15-17	Part 2: Paul, Change Agent of the Gospel of God
1:18—2:10	Paul's Conduct (*Praxeis*)
1:18-20	Part 1: In Jerusalem
1:21-24	Part 2: In Syria and Cilicia
2:1-10	Part 3: Again in Jerusalem
2:11-21	Comparison of Paul and Others (*Sygkrisis*)
2:11-14	Part 1: Comparison of Paul and Cephas at Antioch
2:15-20	Part 2: Comparison of Paul and Judean Jesus-Group Leaders
2:21	Epilogue (*Epilogos*)

IV. Gal 3:1—6:10
Paul Defends His Gospel (Form: Public Argument)

Section One:
Gal 3:1–4:31 Proofs

3:1-5	Galatians Hexed: Made Oblivious to What Faith Effected
3:6-9	A Scriptural Argument Based on the Case of Abraham
3:10-14	A Scriptural Argument on How Israel's Honor Is Restored by Christ
3:15-16	A Scriptural Argument on Who Is Heir to God's Promises to Abraham

3:17-22 A Scriptural Argument on the Relationship of God's Promises to Abraham to God's Law through Moses
3:23—4:11 Further Clarification Comparing the Period of the Law and the Present Period of Faith: Slaves and Heirs
4:12-20 An Exhortatory Interlude
4:21-31 A Scriptural Argument Based on the Relationship between the Mothers of Abraham's Children, Sarah and Hagar

Section Two:
Exhortations Gal 5:1—6:10

5:1-12 First Focus: Circumcision
5:13-26 Second Focus: Flesh and Spirit
6:1-10 General Exhortations

V. Gal 6:11-18
Conclusion

6:11 Writing
6:12-17 Summary Observations: About Honor
6:18 Closing Wish

What's Going on in Galatia?

A significant dimension of a change agent's task is to prevent discontinuance after individuals adopt the innovation. **Change Agent.** One way to prevent discontinuance is by forming support groups—small groups of people who support each other in the realization of the innovation they have adopted. For Paul these small groups are called *ekklēsiai* (usually translated "churches"); in this commentary we call them Jesus groups. ***Ekklēsia* (Gathering).** For Jesus groups to cohere and to develop a sense of integrity is a continual concern of Paul, the change agent of the God of Israel. The basis of coherence and integrity maintenance is the development of a group identity, of social identity. This dimension features quite prominently in Paul's letter to the Galatians, written from Ephesus about Galatians 54–56 C.E. In fact as the letter indicates, it is specifically the social identity of the Jesus group as established by Paul that comes under attack, and the attacking agency is a group of people, called "Judaizers," with another form of the gospel of God.

The term "Judaizer" describes someone intent on making people into Judeans by insisting they accept Judean observances as practiced in Judea. Israelites living among non-Israelites, outside Judea, did not necessarily practice these same Judean customs. As we learn from Romans 1 (and other sources cited by Aune 1997 and Kant 1987:617–713), in the Hellenistic world Judeans could be considered barbarians, uncivilized, little concerned with the values and behaviors characteristic of that class of people called Greeks. "Greeks" meant civilized. **Jew and Greek/Judean and Hellenist.**

Paul's outreach to Israelites living among non-Israelites necessarily put him in contact with a large number of Greeks. It seems that the majority of Israelites whom Paul recruited as innovators and first adopters were indeed Greeks, that is, "civilized" Israelites. In Galatia Judaizers emerged, and their task was to strip these new Jesus-group members of specifically Greek features in favor of Judean features. This step would make sense to persons from Judea, such as Jesus' original witnesses, also called apostles, for Jesus had been raised by the God of Israel and designated Israel's Messiah. Jesus' crucifixion and resurrection took place in Jerusalem, in Judea, the center of Israel's political religion. And Jesus' promised that the kingdom of heaven would also emerge in Jerusalem, in Judea. In the eyes of these "Judaizers," then, it seemed only sensible that Judaism, the customs of the Israelite people of Judea, should be the fundamental orientation of Jesus-group members who have faith in Israel's Messiah.

In the eyes of these "Judaizers," Jesus-group members outside Judea would nevertheless need to adopt specific Judean practices in order to be true Israelites. These practices included circumcision, kosher laws, calendrical features practiced in Judea, and the like. Paul will argue that in order to be a true Israelite (True Israel) the Judean features are totally unnecessary. One can be an Israelite Greek and be a proper Israelite, True Israel. In order to understand the social dimensions of what is happening, following Philip Esler (1998) we employ a model of social identity. **Social Identity.** The social identity model in question includes three salient dimensions. One dimension is cognitive, that is, knowledge and awareness of the fact that "we" do indeed form a group over against "them," including knowledge of the characteristics of our group as opposed to theirs. A second dimension is evaluative, that is, our way of doing things is good, and our values are good, certainly better than theirs. A third dimension is emotional: we love one another, we bond with each other, we support one another, we are attached to the Lord Jesus and to one another. Thus, bonding, attachment, and affection for fellow group members are typical of this dimension. The three dimensions together characterize social group identity. Throughout this letter we see these features intertwined as Paul seeks to maintain group integrity and reaffirm the social identity of the Galatians among whom he proclaimed his gospel of God.

It is a common mistake in scholarship to consider first-century Israelites around the Mediterranean basin as the type of single-voiced entity one finds in the forms of modern Ashkenazi Jewishness in the United States and northern Europe. The Khazars were a Turkic people who converted to rabbinic Judaism in the ninth century C.E., to eventually settle in largely Slavic lands. Eighty-four percent of all Jews before World War II lived in Poland, and they were Khazar Jews (see the website www.khazaria.com). Most Christians derive their image of ancient Semitic

Judeans from images of contemporary non-Semitic Khazar Jews. The point is there was no lineal development from early Israel to contemporary Khazar Jewishness.

For centuries before the time of Paul people had drifted from Judea to what was called the "Dispersion," without a view to returning to Judea. After over five hundred years of emigration from Palestine, the Israelites Paul met among non-Israelites had a version of Israel-in-the-Bible that had assimilated, accommodated, and absorbed dimensions of the people among whom they lived, not unlike the assimilated, accommodated, and absorbed Euro-Judaism found today in the United States after two hundred years of immigration (see Barclay 1996). As Diane Jacobs-Malina (manuscript in progress) has written:

> Cutting through layers of Jewish image-management to get at the facts of Jews-in-relation-to-Everyone Else is a daunting procedure. The propensity to substitute flattering stories for the unvarnished historical kernels has emerged as the unifying element from the creation of Israel-in-the-Bible, through the Hellenistic revisions which produced instant antiquity, to writers like Josephus. This tendency manifested itself in the creation of the Oral Torah and its many interpretations culminating in the Bavli [the Babylonian Talmud]. A greater challenge presented itself with the descendants of Central Asians living in Khazaria (southern Russia) who converted to Rabbinic Judaism in the ninth century. These Khazars had to be recast not only as a Semitic people, but as the biological heirs of the Old Testament's literary characters. This mythical transformation has been accepted as a fait accompli by many Zionist Jews and Christians. From Israel-in-the-Bible to Hollywood, from marketing to the contemporary media; story-telling and image-management are the core values of Jewish group identity which characterize their relations with Everyone Else.

The point is, for readers of Paul interested in understanding Israelites in the first century C.E., the accretions of the past two thousand years have to be removed. Ancient Israelites have little in common with the Jews of today aside from Israel's scriptures, which Christians share as well.

I. Gal 1:1-5
Letter Opening (Superscription)

The Salutation 1:1-5

1:1 Paul an apostle—sent neither by human commission nor from human authorities, but through Jesus Christ and God the Father, who raised him from the dead— 2 and all the members of God's family who are with me,

To the churches of Galatia:

3 Grace to you and peace from God our Father and the Lord Jesus Christ, 4 who gave himself for our sins to set us free from the present evil age, according to the will of our God and Father, 5 to whom be the glory forever and ever. Amen.

Textual Notes: Gal 1:1-5

1:1: In the very superscription of this letter, Paul anticipates the accusation that he took up his task of change agent ("apostle") on behalf of some human agency. He insists that the change agency behind his activity is none other than the God of Israel directly, and this through a revelation of Jesus raised by the God of Israel.

1:1: Paul's distinctive name for the God of Israel is "he who raised Jesus from the dead," a name that he employs here.

1:1 and 1:3: For Paul, God is "Father," that is, patron. **Patronage System.** As "Father," the God of Israel initiated a patron-client relationship through the brokerage of Jesus, whom this God raised from the dead. The Greek word *mesites*, often translated "mediator," means broker, a person who puts others in contact with a patron. Patrons form kinship-type relations with their clients. Patronage "kinifies" interpersonal relations, with the patron showing concern for his or her clients and their families. In their turn, clients are obliged to honor the patron and diffuse the patron's praises. What patrons provide is favor (Greek: *charis*; Latin: *gratia*), that is, something necessary to a client that the client either does not have at all or cannot obtain at this time. For Paul this favor is salvation. **Salvation.** The patronage analogy was inaugurated by Jesus and is fundamental to the New Testament understanding of the God of Israel. Since all theology is rooted in analogy, the patronage analogy is basic in New Testament theology.

1:2: The NRSV translation "and all the members of God's family who are with me" reads in Greek "all the brothers who are with me." Paul indicates that his viewpoint is also shared by his fellow Jesus-group members.

1:3: As previously noted, we refer to Paul's *ekklēsiai* (NRSV: "churches") as Jesus groups. ***Ekklēsia* (Gathering).** Paul writes to a number of Jesus groups consisting of Galatians, people who live in or come from Galatia (just as Judeans are people who live in or come from Judea). The Roman province of Galatia, founded in 25 B.C.E., gets its name from the Celtic tribes that inhabited the region. There is much discussion among scholars concerning the precise location of the addressees of this letter, based largely on attempts to reconcile data in Paul's letter with the description of his journeys through Galatia presented in the Acts of the Apostles. Following Esler (1998) and Murphy-O'Connor (1996), we believe the first major town Paul and companions would have come to in Galatia (based on Acts 16:6-7 and Gal 4:13) was Pessinus (modern Balahissar). Pessinus was an important port of trade, a center of imperial cult with temple banquets, sacrifices, and gladiatorial combat (see inscriptions from 31–37 C.E.) and with a temple to Cybele and to the divine Augustus and the goddess Roma. It was to Israelite groups in this city and adjacent cities that Paul proclaimed his gospel of God and formed several Jesus groups (see Esler 1998:32–36).

1:3: Paul's usual salutation included the Hellenistic "grace" and the Semitic "peace." He wishes these upon the Galatians from God our patron and from our Lord Jesus Christ.

1:4: Paul now describes Jesus as one who gave himself "for our sins." In a collectivistic social system, anything Jesus did or that God did to Jesus was "for us."

Here specifically, he gave himself for "our sins." A sin is a word or deed that dishonors and shames another. To sin against God means to dishonor or shame God. Persons who are so dishonored are socially obliged to defend their honor by taking satisfaction. Paul calls God's taking satisfaction "wrath." For Jesus to save us from "our sins" against God means that in some way Jesus had God waive the social need of satisfaction for dishonors done to him (that is, sin). Thus freed from the present social situation of Israelites over whom the wrath of God looms large, Jesus-group members can confidently look forward to an Israelite theocracy "according to the will of our God and Father."

II. Gal 1:6-9
Introduction

In a usual letter at this point, there should be a "blessing"—an acknowledgment of God's past activity on behalf of the addressees, with a hope for God's future favor. This blessing is lacking. Most scholars would attribute this lack to Paul's highly incensed state of mind over the situation among the Galatians. In an honor-shame society, however, Paul's omission of any mention of God's past benefactions among the Galatians and hope for future divine favor would be taken as an attack against the collective honor of the Galatians.

Instead of the blessing, Paul provides an introduction to his self-defense and defense of his gospel. The introduction primarily states the case, but it also gets the listeners' attention as well. The normal means for gaining the allegiance of the audience was an appeal to the character of the speaker, the opponents' lack of character, the nature of the audiences, or the facts of the case.

The Charges: Accepting a Different Gospel 1:6-9

1:6 I am astonished that you are so quickly deserting the one who called you in the grace of Christ and are turning to a different gospel— 7 not that there is another gospel, but there are some who are confusing you and want to pervert the gospel of Christ. 8 But even if we or an angel from heaven should proclaim to you a gospel contrary to what we proclaimed to you, let that one be accursed! 9 As we have said before, so now I repeat, if anyone proclaims to you a gospel contrary to what you received, let that one be accursed!

Textual Notes: Gal 1:6-9

1:6-9: This passage sets forth the general situation that provoked this letter. Paul's opponents have accused him of tailoring his "gospel of God" in order to please and win the approval of his Israelite Galatian audiences, his innovators and first adopters. This implies that Paul's opponents find Paul's gospel to be attractive and pleasing to Israelites in non-Israelite cities, a gospel that might win ready approval. A question that arises, then, is what was so unattractive about the gospel proclaimed by Paul's opponents? What made it abhorrent or displeasing to Israelites outside of Palestine if Paul's gospel pleases others? Perhaps the gospel of Paul's opponents required Israelite Hellenists to live like Judeans, hence to distance themselves from their way of living in Hellenistic cities with the accommodation and acculturation that was traditional in those settings. In other words, from a Greek point of view, Hellenistic Jesus-group members would be expected to live like barbarians rather than like the civilized persons they were—that is, to adopt Judean practices—in order to be "true Israelites."

Paul insists that the gospel he proclaims, the innovation that he diffuses, is from the change agency of the God of Israel. Paul opens the argument by insisting that if his gospel is from the God of Israel, there simply cannot be another. Yet opponents would insist that their gospel is from the God of Israel, hence that Paul's is merely a human concoction. To discredit Paul by claiming it rested on solely human authorization implies that his gospel would be of the same quality. Thus the change agent and his innovation, the proclaimer and the proclamation, are closely linked.

1:6: It is important to note that Paul actually addresses the Galatians, and not his opponents or defamers. For Paul, the one who calls persons to join Jesus groups is the God of Israel. The one who called the Galatians in grace, that is, by favor (Greek: *charis*; Latin: *gratia*) is the God of Israel freely bestowing his patronage. Many ancient manuscripts omit the word "Christ," added under the assumption that the Galatians were turning away from Paul. In Paul's point of view, the Galatians were turning away from the God of Israel who called them, and this very quickly.

1:7: Paul's insistence that there is no other gospel intimates that what the Galatians had been offered was a gospel indeed, hence some form of proclamation about Christ. This means that the innovation competing with Paul's is likewise an Israelite innovation proclaimed by other Jesus-group members, equally concerned about proclaiming Jesus the Messiah.

1:8-9: A curse refers to a statement and/or action intended to influence by superhuman means the welfare or behavior of animate entities (persons, animals, spirits, enspirited beings like winds, seas, etc.), against their will or normal modes of activity. Paul's twofold curse here underscores a dimension of his change-agent role. For a dedicated change agent, the saying "love me, love my message" applied. Paul's honor and proclaimed innovation were mutually embedded. To attack him was to attack his message, and vice versa. Paul now proceeds to defend his honor.

III. Gal 1:10—2:21
Paul Defends His Honor (Form: Encomium)

Scholars have indicated that this section of Galatians has the features of a Hellenistic encomium (see Malina and Neyrey 1996). An encomium is a stereotypical speech

This detail of a fourteenth-century icon is a Byzantine portrayal of Paul's "conversion" on the road to Damascus. Compare **Notes** *to Gal 1:15-17.*

pattern employed for praising a person or group of persons. Paul employs that pattern here for "self-praise," that is for defending his honor. **Encomium.** The pattern of such an encomium has the following features, easily recognizable here:

I. Opening (*prooimion*) 1:10-12
II. Lifestyle (*anastrophē*) 1:13-17
III. Deeds (*praxeis*) 1:18—2:10
IV. Comparison (*sygkrisis*) 2:11-20
V. Conclusion (*epilogos*) 2:21

Opening (*Prooimion*): Origin of Paul's Gospel—Divine Revelation 1:10-12

1:10 Am I now seeking human approval, or God's approval? Or am I trying to please people? If I were still pleasing people, I would not be a servant of Christ.

11 For I want you to know, brothers and sisters, that the gospel that was proclaimed by me is not of human origin; 12 for I did not receive it from a human source, nor was I taught it, but I received it through a revelation of Jesus Christ.

Textual Notes: Gal 1:10-12

1:10: After leveling a curse against those who proclaim a gospel different from his, Paul obviously is not concerned with their approval; he does not care to please them or their followers. Paul thus opens his self-defense by insisting his goal is to continue to be a servant of Christ, not a servant of other people to get their approval. With this statement Paul anticipates a topic that will surface later in this letter.

1:11-12: Paul now opens his defense by laying out the source of the innovation he proclaimed, the change agency behind his activity. While his opponents might claim that the gospel of God he proclaims is of human origin, perhaps Paul himself, Paul insists that he received that gospel through a revelation. The Greek for revelation is *apokalypsis*. The word normally refers to making public something unknown about a person. Since what is being made known here has to do with something unknown about the God of Israel and his Messiah, the Lord Jesus, Paul's revelation is rooted in some altered state of consciousness experience in which the God of Israel revealed Jesus the Messiah to Paul. That is Paul's claim here. **Altered States of Consciousness.**

Paul's Lifestyle (*Anastrophē*) 1:13-17

Paul describes his way of life in two phases: as persecutor of Jesus groups (vv. 13-14) and as change agent of the gospel of God (vv. 15-17).

Part 1: Paul, Persecutor of Jesus Groups 1:13-14

1:13 You have heard, no doubt, of my earlier life in Judaism. I was violently persecuting the church of God and was trying to destroy it. 14 I advanced in Judaism beyond many among my people of the same age, for I was far more zealous for the traditions of my ancestors.

Textual Notes: Gal 1:13-14

Paul talks first about "my former (way of) life" (*tēn emēn anastrophēn*). The Greek for "way of life" here is *anastrophē*, the technical term we have observed in the list of elements in an encomium for "manner of life." When he tells us that "I advanced in Judaism beyond many among my people of the same age" (1:14), he indicates his native group, *ethnos* ("among my own people"), Israel. The Israelite worldview and customary behavior based on that worldview were called "Judaism," after the Roman-run kingdom of Judea. Non-Israelites, as a rule, believed all Israelites came from Judea; hence they called them "Judeans" and their customs "Judaism."

Be that as it may, wherever Paul was, he was trained in the behavior and customs typical of people from Judea (*en tōi Ioudaismōi*). He boasts that he was preeminent in his manner of life, which was rooted in respect for ancestors: "for I was far more zealous for the traditions of my ancestors" (1:15). This zeal showed itself in his uncompromising devotedness to the Israelite status quo, which accounted for his authorized persecution and destruction of "the churches of God" (see Malina 1994a:51–78). Thus three terms with emphatic placement quickly tell us of the unsurpassed excellence of Paul's manner of life: (a) "violently" (*kata hyperbolēn*), (b) "advanced" (*proekopton*), and (c) "extremely zealous" (*perissoterōs zēlōtēs*).

The further description of his "manner of life" would create problems for ancient readers, however, since the mention of change in his manner of life would normally be viewed with suspicion. The culture valued stability and constancy of character. Hence "change" of character was neither expected nor praiseworthy. Normally, adult persons were portrayed as living out the manner of life that had always characterized them: all that is in the mighty oak was already in the acorn. In certain philosophical circles, such as the Stoics, change and repentance were negatively viewed. He cites Cicero, quoting the Stoic view: "The philosopher surmises nothing, repents of nothing, is never wrong, and never changes his opinion" (*Pro Murena* 61 LCL; see Aesop, *Fable* 48). Some clever explanation would be needed to indicate why it would not be shameful for Paul to change his manner of living from "the customary behavior of Judeans" to that of the "churches of God." Of course, the explanation is forthcoming and duly exonerates Paul, because the God of Israel himself is responsible for the change!

Part 2: Paul, Change Agent of the Gospel of God 1:15-17

1:15 But when God, who had set me apart before I was born and called me through his grace, was pleased 16 to reveal his Son to me, so that I might proclaim him among the Gentiles, I did not confer with any human being, 17 nor did I go up to Jerusalem to those who were already apostles before me, but I went away at once into Arabia, and afterwards I returned to Damascus.

Textual Notes: Gal 1:15-17

Paul now goes on to tell something about his birth (*genesis*) that might explain the change in his manner of life. As was well known in Paul's time, the birth of Jesus had been accompanied with customary marks of the birth of a noble person (signs in the sky: Matt 2:2, 7-10; visions and dreams: Matt 1:20-23; 2:12, 13, 19; and other strange events: Matt 2:16-18). Paul, on the other hand, notes his birth more simply, yet in a way not without significance for this reading. He points up his unusual qualities by indicating the special role of God in that event: "From my mother's womb," he says, God both "set me apart" and "called me through his favor." He was, then, beloved of God ("called through his grace"), favored by God ("it pleased God"), and ascribed distinction by God ("he set me apart"). These features constitute a very powerful claim to honor. In fact they account for the change in Paul's behavior in a very positive way.

To begin with, these features identify Paul as a person to whom God ascribed the specific role of a prophet (Betz 1979:69–70).

Paul's Version	**Prophet's Version**
1. . . . who had set me apart	Jer 1:5 Before I formed you in the womb, I knew you; before you were born, I consecrated you. Isa 49:1b . . . from the body of my mother he named my name.
2. and had called me	Isa 49:1c The Lord called me though his grace from the womb.
3. to reveal his son to me	See Isaiah 6; Ezekiel 1.
4. in order that I might preach to the nations	Isa 49:6 I will give you as a light to the nations. Jer 1:6 I appoint you a prophet to the nations.

Paul describes his birth, then, in terms of the conventions of a prophetic calling, thus claiming a unique role and status in the house of Israel, thanks to the God of Israel.

But Paul did not initially act as God's prophet. As he now understands it, the first part of his life was marked by deviation from God's intent, undoubtedly because of what he learned in Israel. Specifically, he came to accept authorized violence on behalf of the status quo, Judean customary behavior, and the tradition of his ancestors. With the hindsight accompanying his new point of view, he could clearly see that his previous way of life was itself the change or "conversion" from what God originally intended for him. Hence his present change was simply a return to where he originally should have been. Since (as he now believes) his former "manner of life" set him against God's purposes, it was incumbent upon him finally to take up what God intended for him. Thus he was not an opportunist, a fickle person, or a flatterer! By invoking God as the agent of change, Paul claims that his new "manner of life" was ordained by God and thus should be regarded as highly honorable. God's "revealing" to him again marks Paul as a person of high standing even as it confirms him in the role of a prophet. He always was a prophet, even from his mother's womb, although previous circumstances thwarted the emergence of this dimension of his way of life. His prophetic calling was ascribed to him by the very God "who raised Jesus from the dead" (Gal 1:1; Rom 8:11). All of his subsequent actions, then, are to be viewed as the legitimate fulfillment of his divinely ascribed role, not as an alteration or deviation indicative of inconstancy.

This reference to Paul's prophetic status seems to be rooted in a conflict over roles intimated in this letter. There are evidently "apostles" in Jesus groups, certainly in the central Jerusalem Jesus group (Gal 1:17, 18-19). But in the Jesus groups of the Galatians a controversy raged over whether Paul qualified as an apostle with those Jesus-chosen witnesses in Jerusalem (1:1). His claim to be a prophet might well position Paul in a role higher than that of apostle. Prophets had immediate experience of God, whereas apostles were commissioned by the man Jesus. Further, Paul uses "immediacy" of revelation later to rank Abraham's covenant over that of Moses, which was "ordained by angels through an intermediary" (3:19). "Revelations" from God, moreover, must count as more honorable than the experience of merely seeing and hearing Jesus. Thus in 1:15-16 Paul shows how change in his "manner of life" (*anastrophē*) is no deviation but something quite expected, given his "birth" (*genesis*). His compliance with God's will for him is eminently honorable, because it is ordained by God. And so his divinely ascribed role as prophet must likewise be respected.

1:16-17: Using the rhetorical device of anticipation, Paul counters adverse criticism by taking up an earlier accusation that after his calling by God, he really learned his proclamation from the apostles in Jerusalem—hence he was taught it. If his gospel were human, then it stood on par with the gospel proclaimed by the Judaizing change agents in Galatia.

If we take our cue from the encomium conventions for describing a "life" (*bios*), these verses have to do with typical observations about a person's education (*paideia*), an important element in describing a "manner of life." The Acts of the Apostles relate that Paul studied his Pharisaic lore under Gamaliel (22:3), yet as regards his "knowledge" of Christ and God's ways, Paul claims here that he did not have a human teacher. In effect, he was taught by God, who "revealed his Son to me" (1:16a). While the truism indicated that a disciple cannot exceed his teacher, there was no such saying about the relative standing of teachers, but since Paul has God as teacher, surely he can exceed any other human teacher!

He thus begins his account of his life by disclaiming having any human teachers in his formation. He insists that "the gospel proclaimed by me is not of human origin (*kata anthrōpon*), for I did not receive it from a human source (*para anthrōpon*), nor was I taught it" (1:12). No human teachers were involved since he received it "through a revelation" (*di' apokalypseōs*), that is, he was instructed, informed, and formed exclusively by God. This would likewise seem to be the force of the disclaimer in 1:16-17 that after the "revelation of his Son to me" (literally in Greek, "in me"), Paul did not confer with flesh and blood, nor did he even go up to Jerusalem to those who were already apostles before him. There simply was no need, because he had no human teachers. He knew what he knew because of God's "revelation" (1:12,15).

In John's Gospel (6:45), being "taught by God" serves as a mark of divine selection or special status; there the expression is rooted in Isa 54:11. In 1 Cor 2:13 Paul boasts that he imparts knowledge "not taught by human wisdom but taught by the Spirit." Paul himself seems to have coined a term for "taught by God" (*theodidaktos*), which he used in 1 Thess 4:9. Considerable attention has been given to this term in recent Pauline scholarship, with specific reference to Philo's discussion of persons who are taught by others or self-taught. We are thus apprised of the cultural importance attached to education by a teacher or education by another and higher source. We suggest that when Paul claims that "I did not confer with flesh and blood" (1:16b), he is informing his readers of the source of his education. He has been formed in his Messianist way of life not by human teachers such as "the apostles before me," but by a higher teacher, namely, the God of Israel. Hence he stands above others, given the standing of his teacher!

Paul's Conduct (*Praxeis*) 1:18–2:10

Paul divides this segment into three parts: in Jerusalem (vv. 18-20), in Syria and Cilicia (vv. 21-24), and again in Jerusalem (2:1-10), forming a chiasm.

Part 1: In Jerusalem 1:18-20

1:18 Then after three years I did go up to Jerusalem to visit Cephas and stayed with him fifteen days; 19 but I did not see any other apostle except James the Lord's brother. 20 In what I am writing to you, before God, I do not lie!

Textual Notes: Gal 1:18-20

Next Paul claims that after three years he went up to Jerusalem to "visit" Cephas (1:18). It is significant that Paul refers to Cephas, known elsewhere as Peter or Simon Peter, by his Aramaic name. The Aramaic name points to Judean cultural preference, that is, to barbarian ways. Paul, a Greek name, points to civilized ways. This encounter with Cephas, Paul's first, marked his first trip to meet the central personages of the Jesus group in Jerusalem. He also met with James, Jesus' brother. It has been argued that this term "visit" (*historēsai*) means much more than just "talk about the weather" for two weeks. Dictionaries translate this word as "to visit a person for the purpose of inquiry" (LSJ 842; Dunn 1985:138–39). In this sense, Paul would have come to Jerusalem to make inquiries, to get informed, to find out things from Cephas. However the word also has a more common, neutral meaning: "to get to know a person." From the perspective of the encomium's directives on "education," we would have to opt for the more neutral meaning of the term. Paul was already the type of person God intended him to be, with knowledge of everything he needed to know. In that light Paul insists that he was *not* taught by any earthly teachers (Acts 22:3), for he was formed, informed, and taught by God.

If he really had nothing to learn from them, why would a Mediterranean such as Paul want to visit the central personages of the Jerusalem Jesus group? We can be sure of one thing: his purpose did not derive from a social system like that of modern westerners and their experience of ready mobility, travel, and keeping family ties alive over long distances. Paul's mention of the timing of the encounter may offer a clue to his motivation. Having been previously been taught by God and being absent from Israel's central place, Jerusalem, Paul already knows what he knows about God's plan for Israel rooted in Jesus the Messiah. Hence it is not information that is involved in his decision to go to Jerusalem; he had nothing to "inquire" about of Cephas. Nevertheless, by Mediterranean cultural standards his claim to having been "taught by God" needs to be acknowledged by others if it is to be a valid claim to honor and status. What seems important in Gal 1:18-19 is Paul's positioning himself on par with Cephas and James, the Lord's brother. He meets only with the leaders of the group, both as their peer and as a person acknowledged to have been taught by God—at least these seem to be Paul's own rhetorical claims. Thus his studied insistence on his absence from Judea and Jerusalem is indication of his independence and acknowledged divine "education" in matters pertaining to his gospel and Christ Jesus.

Part 2: In Syria and Cilicia 1:21-24

1:21 Then I went into the regions of Syria and Cilicia, 22 and I was still unknown by sight to the churches of Judea that are in Christ; 23 they only heard it said, "The one who formerly was persecuting us is now proclaiming the faith he once tried to destroy." 24 And they glorified God because of me.

Textual Notes: Gal 1:21-24

1:21: "The churches of Judea that are in Christ" were located in the Roman province of Syro-Palestine. That is why Judea falls under the mention of the regions of Syria.

1:23: The Jesus groups of Judea are very significant since it was from the members of these Jesus groups that Paul first learned about their beliefs and behaviors. At first, Paul had found their belief in Jesus of Nazareth as Israel's Messiah, in the God of Israel having raised Jesus from the dead, and in a forthcoming Israelite theocracy to be reprehensible in terms of his Pharisaic orientation and dangerous in terms of repercussions for Judea from the Roman presence. Without his interaction with the Jesus-group members whom he persecuted he would have known nothing about the Jesus movement and the groups that espoused it.

At this point in an encomium, an author would begin to discourse on a person's "accomplishments" (*epitēdeumata*) and "deeds" (*praxeis*). Many rhetorical authors indicate that in praising a person's deeds and accomplishments we may present them either chronologically or thematically. Quintillian states:

> It has sometimes proved the more effective course to trace a man's life and deeds in due chronological order, praising his natural gifts as a child, then his progress at school, and finally the whole course of his life, including words as well as deeds. At times on the other hand it is well to divide our praises, dealing separately with the various virtues, fortitude, justice, self-control and the rest of them and to assign to each virtue the deeds performed under its influence. (*Institutio Oratoria* 3.7.15 LCL)

These modes of presentation were not mutually exclusive, for even a chronological sequence is to contain indication that the person's "accomplishments" illustrate the four conventional virtues. Evidently, Paul presents a chronology of his labors ("immediately," v. 16b; "then after three years," v. 18; "then," v. 20). The chronology, however, ought to illustrate the more important issue of virtue, for Paul must demonstrate that his life is lived in accord with one or another of the conventional virtues, such as justice, wisdom, temperance, courage, and the like. Such are the requirements of the formal conventions of an encomium.

Modern readers need to pause and reflect on how the ancients defined the four cardinal virtues: prudence, justice, temperance, and fortitude. Occasionally a fifth or sixth virtue might be listed, such as "piety." But over time the famous four held pride of place. Depending on the rhetorical situation of a given author, one or another of the four cardinal virtues might be said to be the chief or primary virtue. Josephus, for example, makes "religion" or "piety" (*eusebeia*) the virtue that includes the rest (*Life* 14 LCL). Philo, reading Gen 15:6, cited "faithfulness" as the queen of the virtues (*Abr.* 270 LCL) and the most perfect of them (*Heres* 91 LCL). In 4 Macc 1:18, it is "wisdom."

Of particular interest to our examination of Galatians are Hellenistic discussions of "justice" or "righteousness" (*dikaiosynē*). Aristotle described *dikaiosynē* as follows:

> To righteousness it belongs to be ready to distribute according to desert, and to preserve ancestral customs and institutions and the established laws, and to tell the truth when interest is at stake, and to keep agreements. First among the claims of righteousness are our duties to the gods, then our duties to the spirits, then those to country and parents, then those to the departed; among these claims is piety [*eusebeia*], which is either a part of righteousness or a concomitant of it. Righteousness is also accompanied by holiness and truth and loyalty [*pistis*] and hatred of wickedness. (*Virtues and Vices* 5.2–3, 1250b LCL)

Thus, Aristotle defined "justice" or "righteousness" (*dikaiosynē*) and treated it as a genus, with species of "piety" and "loyalty." Moreover, he likewise believed that when one thinks of "justice," one should think of one's duties and the obligation of piety to perform them.

"Justice" or "righteousness" (*dikaiosynē*), then, is about proper interpersonal relations and the obligations entailed in these relations. It refers to the keeping of agreements and the performance of duties. "Piety" or "religion" describes the practical respect for those who control one's existence. Thus as part of justice, piety means loyalty and faithfulness to the gods. Aristotle's broad definition can be clarified by the comments of one of the authors of the *progymnasmata*, Menander Rhetor.

> The parts of justice are piety, fair dealing, and reverence: piety towards the gods, fair dealings towards men, reverence towards the departed. Piety to the gods consists of two elements: being god-loved (*theophilotēs*) and god-loving (*philotheotēs*). The former means being loved by the gods and

> receiving many blessings from them, the latter consists of loving the gods and having a relationship of friendship with them. (1.361.17–25)

Not only does Menander confirm piety as a part of justice, he speaks of a reciprocity between gods and mortals: benefaction from the gods to mortals and respect and honor from mortals to the gods. As with patrons in general, the patronage of the gods establishes a duty of loyalty and faithfulness in the one receiving patronage. Thus piety means that one shows respect, obedience, and loyalty to one's patron.

This attempt to understand the Hellenistic native meaning of "justice" and its relationship to "piety" and "loyalty" should have a bearing on how we might understand Paul's remarks in Gal 1:21-24. Paul states that he spent fourteen years (2:1) "proclaiming the faith he once tried to destroy" (1:23). We would classify this consistent and habitual behavior as an illustration of "piety" (*eusebeia*), which is a part of justice (*dikaiosynē*). When Paul twice notes that God "revealed" mysteries to him (1:12, 15), this should surely be taken to mean that he is god-loved or *theophilotēs*. To a sinner who persecuted the followers of God's designated Messiah, the God of Israel showed incomparable benefaction by giving Paul a revelation of God's exclusive plan, knowledge of his "Son." Moreover, this revelation did not simply alter Paul's awareness from being ignorant of some bit of information to one who was now informed about it. Rather, the revelation proved to be a formative event: it served as a sort of ritual of status transformation whereby the persecutor of people committed to the gospel about Jesus became its herald, "so that I might proclaim him among the [minority Israelite groups living among the] Gentiles" (1:16). Paul thus demonstrates that he was blessed indeed, one "loved by God." For his part, Paul now had a duty to be God-loving. He had received both a benefaction and a commission. He owed God loyalty to fulfill the gracious commission entrusted to him.

When he went first to Arabia and Damascus and then to the regions of Syria and Cilicia, he tells the Galatians that he spent three and then fourteen years fulfilling God's commission (1:18; 2:1). His later visit to Jerusalem indicates continued loyalty to the God of Israel, as does his present situation as the defender of the faith of the Galatians. He has, then, demonstrated remarkable piety and loyalty toward God. Note also his concern that "he not run in vain" (2:2), that is, that he not fail in his commission as change agent.

In the foregoing quote from Aristotle on the parts of "justice," the philosopher mentioned not only piety (*eusebeia*) but also loyalty or faithfulness (*pistis*): "Righteousness is also accompanied by holiness and truth and loyalty (*pistis*)." Significantly, Paul likewise shows concern to note his loyalty in his obedience to God's commission. Inasmuch as he was ascribed the authority and role of being an official herald "that I might preach him among the [minority Israelite groups living among the] Gentiles" (1:16), he faithfully fulfilled that commission by his labors in "Syria and Cilicia" (1:21).

Part 3: Again in Jerusalem 2:1-10

2:1 Then after fourteen years I went up again to Jerusalem with Barnabas, taking Titus along with me. 2 I went up in response to a revelation. Then I laid before them (though only in a private meeting with the acknowledged leaders) the gospel that I proclaim among the Gentiles, in order to make sure that I was not running, or had not run, in vain. 3 But even Titus, who was with me, was not compelled to be circumcised, though he was a Greek. 4 But because of false believers secretly brought in, who slipped in to spy on the freedom we have in Christ Jesus, so that they might enslave us— 5 we did not submit to them even for a moment, so that the truth of the gospel might always remain with you. 6 And from those who were supposed to be acknowledged leaders (what they actually were makes no difference to me; God shows no partiality)—those leaders contributed nothing to me. 7 On the contrary, when they saw that I had been entrusted with the gospel for the uncircumcised, just as Peter had been entrusted with the gospel for the circumcised 8 (for he who worked through Peter making him an apostle to the circumcised also worked through me in sending me to the Gentiles), 9 and when James and Cephas and John, who were acknowledged pillars, recognized the grace that had been given to me, they gave to Barnabas and me the right hand of fellowship, agreeing that we should go to the Gentiles and they to the circumcised. 10 They asked only one thing, that we remember the poor, which was actually what I was eager to do.

Textual Notes: Gal 2:1-10

2:1: After fourteen years, Paul has an altered state of consciousness experience ("revelation") directing him to go to Jerusalem and meet with the pillars of the Jesus group there. **Altered State of Consciousness.** On this second trip to Jerusalem he once more meets Cephas and James as well as John. Paul comes with Barnabas and Titus, who must have been persons well-known to the Galatian Jesus groups since Paul does not describe them at all.

2:2: Titus was a Greek (Greek: *Hellēn*). During Paul's time, the word "Greek" meant civilized. Titus, undoubtedly an Israelite, followed Hellenistic customs, spoke Greek well, and perhaps had a Hellenistic education. The opposite of Greek was some native name, for example, "Judean." The native name usually meant uncivilized or barbarian.

2:3: Paul calls local Judean Jesus-group members who oppose his gospel of God "false brothers." Paul insists that the gospel of God he proclaimed to the Galatians is true and that he never acceded to the "false brothers." He fully clarifies this point in what follows.

2:7: Just as Israelites viewed themselves divided between their fellows living in the land of Israel and those in the Dispersion, here we find another Israelite division of the world into the Circumcised and the Foreskins (NRSV: "uncircumcised"). Circumcision became an Israelite marker only during the Maccabee period (circa 150 B.C.E.) in Judea and vicinity. Obviously the hundreds of thousands of Israelites living in the Diaspora either knew nothing of this Maccabee innovation or did not practice it as a barbarian (that is, Judean) custom. **Circumcision.** The Israelite world of Judea and vicinity formed the territory of the Circumcised, while the rest of the non-Judean world was the territory of the Foreskins, ethnocentrically called "the peoples," or from Latin, "the Gentiles." Both Peter (Paul uses his Greek name now) and Paul had as their concern to proclaim the gospel of God to Israelites.

In the context of an encomium, this second trip to Jerusalem (2:1-10) further illustrates several of Paul's conventional virtues. He again acts obediently to God's "revelation" (2:1), demonstrating his "piety" both as one God-loved and as loving God, to whom he proved loyal.

What sort of virtue might be signaled by his desire to avoid error and misrepresentation of God's gospel, "lest somehow I should be running or had run in vain" (2:2)? His behavior in Jerusalem demonstrates his pious loyalty to his patron, the God of Israel. Yet he staunchly defends certain principles he learned from having been "taught by God." The point in question is circumcision. Titus was not required to be circumcised (2:3), although it is not clear that this is upon Paul's insistence. But it does show that others in Jerusalem acknowledged Paul's not requiring circumcision of Israelites living among non-Israelites, that is Greek, Israelites.

However it is clear that Paul's decision to go to Israelites living among the "Foreskins" (the Judean ingroup name for non-Israelites; NRSV: "uncircumcised") constitutes part of his commissioning by God (1:16). And perhaps the majority of those Israelites were themselves uncircumcised since the custom was begun in Palestine only in the Maccabean period. **Circumcision.** On the other hand, it may be properly implied that the decision not to circumcise the uncircumcised Israelites is likewise part of that "revelation." It is to be expected that Paul has enemies in Jerusalem, but he shows "courage" (*andreia*) by "not yielding submission even for a moment" (2:5). Thus Paul presents himself as a man of virtue, in particular as someone who possesses *dikaiosynē* in all its forms. He is both "beloved by God" and "God loving" in return; he excels in faithfulness and loyalty, and so in piety (*eusebeia*). He claims to be nothing less than a regular holy man.

Besides deeds of the soul, the encomiast is instructed to discourse also on deeds of fortune. Under deeds of fortune the rhetoricians regularly list all those important features that befall a person: power, wealth, friends, children, fame, fortune, and the like. In one sense Paul was always a well-known personage, with fame of sorts. For his new Jesus ingroup, that fame initially had to do with something negative, his persecution of the disciples of Jesus. But his reputation changed and his fame grew as a result of God's favor shown to him. "The churches of Christ in Judea heard about it," that is, about his proclaiming of the gospel of God (1:23), and they "glorified God because of me" (1:24). His reputation, moreover, could only be enhanced by his first meeting with Cephas and James (1:18-19). It grew to the point that he was privileged with a face-to-face meeting with the Jerusalem leaders (2:2). They truly enjoyed fame and a good reputation, for they were known as "the pillars" and "those of repute" (*hoi dokountes*), even if this term is taken ironically. By appearing in the company of famous people and by being treated as an equal to Cephas in terms of mission (2:7-9), Paul can be said ultimately to have fame and to enjoy a very good reputation.

In regard to friends, Paul claims that Cephas and the other pillars of the Jerusalem church extended the right hand of fellowship to him (*dexias . . . koinōnias*, 2:9). The high context phrase has been best explained by Esler:

> The actual source for the arrangement in Gal 2:9 lies elsewhere, in the Septuagint, where in 1 and 2 Maccabees, the precise expression "give right hands" occurs eleven times. In almost all of these cases a person who is in a superior position, usually in a military context, gives the right hand to people who are virtually suppliants, who "take it," as a way of bringing peace to a conflict. It is not a gesture made between equals, as claimed by Betz (1979:100). This context brings out some surprising dimensions to Gal 2:9. We should not read this verse as an expression of balance and amity between the parties. Rather James, Cephas and John condescend to Paul and Barnabas by acting as if they are in a superior position to them in a conflict and are graciously offering a cessation of hostilities. This is the force of "giving right hands." Paul and Barnabas clearly took the hands that were proffered to them, but Paul expressly dissents from the superiority implied in the gesture by describing the three Jerusalem leaders, in the same verse, as (only) seeming to be pillars. (Esler 1998:133)

2:9: What the three reputed pillars deigned to grant Paul was a peace or cessation of hostilities. The hostilities had previously to do with fellowship (*koinōnia* in Greek), a term that in Paul's letters always has the connotation of sharing or common participation. Its specific implications, however, vary by social context. Here it obviously is not sharing in the Spirit (1 Cor 1:9; 2 Cor 13:13; Phil 2:1; 3:10; Philemon 6) or in some material goods (Rom 15:26; 2 Cor 8:4; 9:13). Nor is it simply cooperation in some common enterprise (2 Cor 6:14; Phil 1:5). What is left is the common Hellenistic meaning of sharing in table fellowship (as in 1 Cor 10:16), even in Temple meals, a piece of behavior that fell under Judean kosher laws as well as calendrical features practiced in Judea. Given Titus' non-circumcision noted above, this right hand of fellowship also entailed cessation of hostilities relative to the Judean custom of circumcision. The implications of this peace surface in what follows in the letter, when Paul recalls how Cephas in Antioch engaged in non-kosher table fellowship with Israelite non-Judeans and then abruptly discontinued the practice. That was a breach of the fellowship agreement bestowed on Paul.

As regards fortune, we have already noted how Paul proclaims that he is blessed by God. He received not only mercy for persecuting God's church but also benefactions of "revelation" and commissioning. As regards honor, Paul's role and status are publicly acknowledged by the elite of Jerusalem. In an honor-shame society, such as the one in which Paul lives, claims to honor and precedence always require public acknowledgment, lest they be vain claims, ridiculed and leading to shame. Paul is acknowledged by the most important figures in his orbit, "those of repute," whose judgment carries great weight. Even Paul's sarcastic labeling of these figures in no way diminishes the importance of their acknowledgment of him: "They saw that I was entrusted with the gospel to the Foreskins" (2:7). And he proudly parades his legitimation by them: "They gave me and Barnabas the right hand of fellowship" (2:9). Thus his claim to honor is confirmed in a backhanded sort of way: as superior opponents in the conflict, Cephas and colleagues graciously call a halt to hostilities against Paul and his Hellenistic Jesus-group members. While Paul and his groups were certainly not on par with Cephas and the Twelve, nevertheless these superior personages condescended to tolerate Paul's version of the gospel.

As the foregoing indicates, Paul described this part of his career in terms that would be easily and readily appreciated in a culture in which the contents of an encomium were commonplace categories for organizing information about a person. He has high-ranking associates; he enjoys considerable good fortune in terms of God's benefactions; he possesses an excellent reputation, which has been publicly acknowledged by the elite of the group. Thus he is an eminently honorable person.

2:10: The implication here is that Jerusalem Jesus-group members had a notable number of needy persons. The assistance for the poor in Jerusalem fell within the categories of the Israelite tithing system. (See **Notes** to 1 Cor 16:1-4.) Paul agrees to have his Israelite Jesus-group members direct their tithe for the poor to assist these needy Jesus-group members.

Comparison of Paul and Others (*Sygkrisis*) 2:11-21

This comparative section of the encomium has two parts: a comparison of Paul and Cephas at Antioch (2:11-14) and a comparison of Paul and Judean Jesus-group leaders (2:15-21).

Part 1: Comparison of Paul and Cephas at Antioch 2:11-14

2:11 But when Cephas came to Antioch, I opposed him to his face, because he stood self-condemned; 12 for until certain people came from James, he used to eat with the Gentiles. But after they came, he drew back and kept himself separate for fear of the circumcision faction. 13 And the other Jews joined him in this hypocrisy, so that even Barnabas was led astray by their hypocrisy. 14 But when I saw that they were not acting consistently with the truth of the gospel, I said to Cephas before them all, "If you, though a Jew, live like a Gentile and not like a Jew, how can you compel the Gentiles to live like Jews?"

Textual Notes: Gal 2:11-14

After the exposition of the "accomplishments" of a person, the encomia indicate that it is appropriate to include a *sygkrisis* or "comparison." We might examine Gal 2:11-14 in this light. Hermogenes offers us a succinct definition of a "comparison": "Now sometimes we draw out comparisons by equality, showing the things which we compare as equal either in all respects or in several; sometimes we put the one ahead, praising also the other to which we prefer it; sometimes we blame the one utterly and praise the other, as in a comparison of justice and wealth" (Malina and

Neyrey 1996:48, citing Baldwin 1928). The "comparison," then, may elevate the status of a less honorable person to the level of a recognized and honorable person. Or it may praise the one and blame the other.

This fourth-century bas relief portrays the apostles Peter and Paul face to face. See **Notes** *to Gal 2:11.*

In this regard, we might reconsider the meeting of Paul with "those of repute" in 2:1-10. On the one hand, he earlier maintained that he did not "confer (about his gospel) with flesh and blood" (1:16) but now he does so: "I laid the gospel before them" (2:2). The two events may be "compared" in that the second one is directed by God ("I went up by a revelation," 2:2a), whereas previously Paul was under no such constraint. The latter, then, is not an indication of inconsistency and instability. Once more Paul indicates superior and praiseworthy behavior, since it was at God's direction that he behaved as he did.

At that meeting, moreover, Paul met privately with the elite of the Jerusalem group, "those of repute" (2:3,6) and "those reputed to be pillars" (2:9). On that occasion, the higher-ranking persons, James, Cephas, and John, agreed not to hassle Paul because of behaviors that followed from his gospel of God. And in their own way they judged that Paul was equal to Peter in that, "just as Peter was entrusted with the gospel to the circumcised," so too they acknowledged that Paul was comparably "entrusted with the gospel to the Foreskins" (2:6-7). Whether such outreach to Israelites in non-Israelite locations was of any merit is not discussed. Paul's mention of the meeting, however, served the rhetorical function of comparing Paul with Peter and putting him on a parallel track with the person commonly acknowledged to have the top management role. The world was ethnocentrically divided into two equal parts (Israelites in Judea and Israelites among non-Israelites), and Paul was credited as being in charge of Israelites living in the non-Israelite world. His honor claim is not simply acknowledged; he is also elevated in status through this comparison of being ranked on par with Peter.

The "comparison" seems most evident, however, in the narration of the encounter at Antioch in 2:11-14.

2:11: The expression "to oppose someone to their face" is a biblical one used to describe when people resist a determined military assault, usually without success. It means to stand up to an opponent in conflict even though one loses. Accordingly, Paul intimates that Cephas "made a frontal attack, in other words, that the hostilities previously settled in Jerusalem had now been resumed, and that he had resisted" (Esler 1998:135). The idiom intimates that he was ultimately unsuccessful against Cephas.

The controversy is about living styles in a context that presumes there is a Judean way of living and a non-Judean one. Paul previously was told that the non-Judean lifestyle of his Jesus-group Israelites living among non-Israelites is quite acceptable to the Jerusalem management group. Even Cephas dines in non-Judean style with his fellow Jesus-group Israelites in Antioch. Yet when called down by those Jesus-group members espousing the Judean lifestyle as the only one allowable for Jesus-group members, Cephas backs down. Paul calls this "hypocrisy," that is, playacting. Consider now what rhetorical comparison underscores about the character of Paul. Here it will be helpful to cite the rules of Theon on comparison:

> A comparison is a speech which shows what is better or what is worse. There are comparisons of characters and subjects: of characters: for example, Ajax, Odysseus; of subjects: for example, wisdom and courage. But since we prefer one of the characters over another in view of their actions, as well as whatever else about them is good, there can be one method for both. First, let it be established that comparisons are made not with matters that differ greatly from one another . . . but with matters that are similar and concerning which we disagree about which of the two we must prefer because we see no superiority of one over the other. So then, when we compare characters, we will first set side by side their noble birth, their education, their children, their public offices, their reputation, their bodily health. . . . After these items, we will compare their actions by choosing those which are more noble and the reasons for the numerous and greater blessings, those actions that are more reliable, those that are more enduring, those that were done at the proper time, those from which great harm resulted when they have not been done, those that were done with a motive rather than those done because of compulsion or chance, those which few have done rather than those that many have done (for the common and hackneyed are not at all praiseworthy), those we have done with effort rather than easily, and

> those we have performed that were beyond our age and ability, rather than those which we performed when it was possible. (10.1–26, in Malina and Neyrey 1996:49, citing Butts 1986)

The context of comparison, Theon says, is praise and blame: "what is better and what is worse." Two similar characters are compared: two warriors or two proclaimers of the gospel. Then their actions are compared, whether reliable and enduring, beneficial or harmful, free or under compulsion, requiring courage or not, or rare or commonplace. This more extended view of "comparison" greatly aids our reading of 2:11-14. At the very least we can say that in 2:11-14 one person is blamed and another praised, just as Hermogenes and Theon indicate should be the case. Paul blames Peter: "I opposed him to his face. . . . He stood condemned" (2:11). If Peter is blamed, then Paul is to be praised. Second, Peter is blamed for inconsistency and unreliability, hence "insincerity," which infected others in the group (*synypekrithēsan*, 2:13a; *hypokrisei*, 2:13b).

In contrast, when Paul claims that Peter and others were "not acting consistently with the truth of the gospel" (2:14), he positions himself as one who is "sincere" and who acts straightforwardly. Peter, moreover, acted out of "fear" of the circumcision party (2:12). "Fear" is one of the cardinal vices, a term sure to draw blame upon Peter. In contrast, Paul demonstrated "courage" by boldly challenging Peter in public and by steadfastly defending the truth. In this Paul can be seen to engage in "comparison" in which he first puts him on par with Peter (2:1-10) and then exalts himself over Peter (2:11-14). His gospel and his manner of living are "straightforward," "approved by the church," and "consistent." If Peter might be charged with "pleasing men" by returning to his kosher obligations and once more not eating with non-Judean Jesus-group members, Paul can claim consistency in his approach and boast that he was not "pleasing men." Otherwise, he would never have publicly challenged Peter. **Meals.**

From the foregoing considerations, it seems that the encomium looms large as the model according to which Paul cast his remarks about himself in this passage from Galatians. Most of the prescribed elements of an encomium are present: (a) birth and attendant divine ascription of honor (1:15-16); (b) manner of life as an advanced and observant Pharisee (1:13-14); (c) education not by mortals but "taught by God" (1:16-19); (d) accomplishments and deeds: deeds of the soul, for example, righteousness demonstrated by piety and faithfulness (1:21-24; 2:1-10) and courage (2:11-14), and deeds of fortune, for example, friends, fame, fortune, and honor; and (e) comparison between Paul's consistency and correctness and Peter's inconsistency (2:11-14). Further, the function of 1:13—2:14 is fully in accord with the aims of an encomium, to praise and to blame. "Praise" is analogous to apology or defense, just as "blame" corresponds to polemic. These observations on the encomiastic shape of Galatians 1–2 are not at all in conflict with other arguments about the larger rhetorical shape of the letter. But it is essential to note the presence and function of encomium features in this part of Paul's argument.

Part 2: Comparison of Paul and Judean Jesus-Group Leaders 2:15-20

2:15 We ourselves are Jews by birth and not Gentile sinners; 16 yet we know that a person is justified not by the works of the law but through faith in Jesus Christ. And we have come to believe in Christ Jesus, so that we might be justified by faith in Christ, and not by doing the works of the law, because no one will be justified by the works of the law. 17 But if, in our effort to be justified in Christ, we ourselves have been found to be sinners, is Christ then a servant of sin? Certainly not! 18 But if I build up again the very things that I once tore down, then I demonstrate that I am a transgressor. 19 For through the law I died to the law, so that I might live to God. I have been crucified with Christ; 20 and it is no longer I who live, but it is Christ who lives in me. And the life I now live in the flesh I live by faith in the Son of God, who loved me and gave himself for me.

Textual Notes: Gal 2:15-20

2:15: Paul now turns to his Galatians with the usual either/or division typical of antiquity. In this case Jesus-group Galatians are "Judeans by nature" and not sinners of non-Israelite origin. (The NRSV is inaccurate.) This, again, is another indication that Paul is not concerned about Gentiles. For first-century Mediterraneans, nature (*physis*) referred first of all to what was customary and usual: either for a given *ethnos* or people, for a given species of animals, or even for a given person or animal. The natural stood opposed to the conventional or legal, that is, the behavior decided upon by a person or group with legal power. What happened customarily and recurrently was natural, traceable to origins, to creation. Given this understanding of nature, it should be apparent that non-Israelites could not "convert" to Judaism, the customary and usual qualities and behaviors of Judeans. Non-Israelites (NRSV: "Gentiles") are sinners by nature, that is, hostile to the God of Israel. As noted previously, Paul did not "convert" to Christianity—there was no Christianity during his lifetime. Rather he maintained his reverence for and obedience to the God of Israel, who raised Jesus from the dead.

Here Paul calls Galatians "Judeans by nature," using the usual non-Israelite name for Israelites. Non-Israelites, such as Romans or Corinthians, called all Israelites "Judeans," believing that all of them traced back to an ancestral homeland of Judea. Israelites, on the other hand, called themselves "Israelites," distinguishing between Judean Israelites (barbarian) resident in Judea or adherents of Judean customs and Greek Israelites (civilized) either resident in the Diaspora or assimilated to Hellenistic customs.

2:16: The phrase, "a person is justified, refers, of course, to Israelites. Justification is not a central theme for Paul, although it is a central concern in Paul's defense of his gospel to the Galatians. As previously noted (1:23), the Greek word translated "justice" or "righteousness" (*dikaiosynē*) is also translated "justification," "piety," and even "religion." We previously considered this word and its range of meanings as used in Hellenistic philosophy.

However, in first-century Israelite ingroup usage the word *dikaiosynē* was considered a characteristic of Israelites by nature, something that made Israelites to be who they are. Perhaps the closest English equivalent to this usage is "acceptability," specifically "divine acceptability, acceptable to the God of Israel." In other words, from an Israelite ingroup perspective, what was it that made Israelites unique? It was divine acceptability, having been chosen by the God of Israel. And how was this acceptable condition maintained? Through observance of the directives of the God of Israel, the Torah or Law. To be "justified by Law" means to be acceptable to the God of Israel by obeying God's directives. Paul will oppose this position by insisting that "justification comes through faith," that is, one becomes acceptable to the God of Israel by showing trust and loyalty to God, who raised Jesus from the dead. In Paul's view, while God's Torah is very good, Torah observance alone is insufficient to maintain divine acceptability. This theme pervades the arguments that follow.

Epilogue (*Epilogos*) 2:21

2:21 I do not nullify the grace of God;
for if justification comes through the law,
then Christ died for nothing.

Textual Notes: Gal 2:21

2:21: This statement marks the end of Paul's defense of his honor. He insists that he does not devalue and reject God's favor, specifically the favor tendered Israel through the death and resurrection of Jesus. And so he concludes that if Israelite acceptability to God derives from doing Torah commandments, then Jesus' death makes no sense. With this concluding observation, he turns to the topic of the following section, in which he defends his gospel against its detractors.

IV. Gal 3:1—6:10 Paul Defends His Gospel (Form: Public Argument)

Paul's gospel entails the proclamation of the action of the God of Israel in raising Jesus from the dead with a view to a forthcoming theocracy for those who believe in what God had begun. Faith in the God of Israel, who is revealed as "he who raised Jesus from the dead," results in God's acceptance of those Israelites who thus believe in what God has done, purely and simply. This acceptance by God does not require the fulfillment of special rules or the performance of specific deeds. God accepts those Israelites who believe in his new revelation of himself. Those Israelites who believe, then, are not required to live according to the Torah of Israel given by Moses with its special requirements of circumcision, food prescriptions, and calendric regulations. Excluded from the Mosaic Torah are those commandments given by God directly to Israel in the wilderness, when "The Lord spoke to you face to face at the mountain, out of the fire" (Deut 5:4). What the Lord spoke was the Ten Commandments, the stipulation of the Israelite covenant with the God of Israel (see Exod 20:1, in which "God spoke all these words," at the end of which the people do not wish to hear God speak again lest they die, Exod 20:19). Moses eventually came down the mountain with a copy of those words the people heard, but found the people engaged in idolatry, so "he threw the tablets from his hands and broke them at the foot of the mountain" (Exod 32:19; the tablets contained the Ten Words only; see Exod 34:28). The rest of the commandments in the Mosaic Law came from God through angelic intermediaries (see Acts 7:53; Josephus, *Ant.* 15.136, and below, Gal 3:19-20) to Moses to Israel and included both written and unwritten commandments. Paul did not include the Ten Commandments in his reference to the Law given through Moses.

In this next part of the letter, Paul takes up the defense of his gospel, using the cultural device of rhetorical argument. In deliberative rhetoric, the argument clarifies the issues by showing the points agreed on by the two parties and those that separate them. This part consists of two sections. Section One (Gal 3:1—4:31) sets out proofs, a series of arguments establishing the truth of the speaker's point of view. Section Two (Gal 5:1-6:10) consists of exhortations to the addressees to comply with the truth of the gospel just demonstrated.

Section One: Gal 3:1—4:31
Proofs

The proofs establish the truth of the speaker's point of view by a series of arguments, usually proceeding from the strongest to the weakest. This would be the longest and most important part of the speech. Sometimes combined with this, occasionally given as a separate point, and sometimes even omitted was the refutation of the proofs offered by the opposing side.

Galatians Hexed: Made Oblivious to What Faith Effected 3:1-5

3:1 You foolish Galatians! Who has bewitched you? It was before your eyes that Jesus Christ was publicly exhibited as crucified! 2 The only thing I want to learn from you is this: Did you receive the Spirit by doing the works of the law or by believing what you heard? 3 Are you so foolish? Having started with the Spirit, are you now ending with the flesh? 4 Did you experience so much for nothing? —if it really was for nothing. 5 Well then, does God supply you with the Spirit and work miracles among you by your doing the works of the law, or by your believing what you heard?

Textual Notes: Gal 3:1-5

3:1: "Who has bewitched you?" translates a Greek verb (*baskainō*) for casting the evil eye. Paul continues the evil eye allusion by noting that it was before the Galatians' eyes "that Jesus Christ was publicly exhibited as crucified." This sight should have forearmed them against the evil eye of others. These others are those who would have the Galatians follow Mosaic Torah. They are envious of the gospel that the Galatians have accepted and the behavior entailed by that proclamation.

3:2-5: Paul opens his argument with an appeal to the actual experience of the Galatians. Their experience of the Spirit of the God of Israel, in altered states of consciousness, obviously derived from their acceptance of Paul's proclamation, not from doing any deeds prescribed by Israel's Torah. Yet somehow they have been made oblivious to what faith in God who raised Jesus effected, something that an evil eye hexing can obviously do!

A Scriptural Argument Based on the Case of Abraham 3:6-9

3:6 Just as Abraham "believed God, and it was reckoned to him as righteousness," 7 so, you see, those who believe are the descendants of Abraham. 8 And the scripture, foreseeing that God would justify the Gentiles by faith, declared the gospel beforehand to Abraham, saying, "All the Gentiles shall be blessed in you." 9 For this reason, those who believe are blessed with Abraham who believed.

Textual Notes: Gal 3:6-9

3:6: Paul quotes Gen 15:6 in the Septuagint version. With this appeal to Abraham, he reaches to the very roots of Israel's story. This ancestor of all Israelites was acceptable to God without following any Torah prescriptions at all. So too those rooted in this ancestor, namely, Israelites living among non-Israelites, can be acceptable to God without following any Torah prescriptions. What makes them acceptable is the same thing that made Abraham acceptable, faith in God revealing himself. Just as Abraham believed in the God who revealed himself to him, so too the Israelite recipients of Paul's gospel believe in the God revealed in the resurrection of Jesus.

3:7: He now draws a momentous conclusion from the passage in Gen 15:6: the authentic and legitimate descendants of Abraham are "those who believe." This high context phrase, of course, means "those who believe in God who raised Jesus from the dead." The point Paul makes is very significant in a society in which self-definition comes from genealogy (along with gender and geography). Abrahamic ancestry is most prestigious in Israel, but this ancestry really derives from believing in the God of Israel and his raising Jesus from the dead. Obviously, without this belief, any other claim to Abrahamic ancestry is spurious.

3:6-7: Paul now chooses another scriptural passage (Gen 18:18) to prove that acceptance by God comes from faith. Most commentators take this passage as emphasizing God's acceptance of Gentiles into Paul's community, but in this context, that is far from Paul's argument. His point is to prove that acceptance by the God of Israel depends on faith in God's raising Jesus from the dead and all this entails. First of all, he notes that the non-Israelite (Gentile) Abraham was the first to exhibit faith in the God of Israel and this made him a non-Israelite (Gentile) acceptable to the God of Israel. Thus to be a son of Abraham, the true requisite is not Abrahamic genealogy but faith like his that in fact made him acceptable to God. And it is this faith that so many of Abraham's progeny lack. This is Paul's first point.

3:8: As was common in Israel, Israel's scriptures are personified; they can see into the future. And with this foresight, Paul says, Israel's scriptures saw and proclaimed as good news that the God of Israel makes *ta ethnē* acceptable to him through faith. This is obvious for Paul from Gen 18:18: "All the *ethnē* will bless themselves in you." The problem for interpreters here is the meaning of *ta ethnē*. Again, the word is usually translated "Gentiles," usually with the connotation of non-Israelites. However while the word often does mean "people other than Israel" in Israelite ethnocentric perspective, the word cannot have that meaning here since there was no Israel yet in the time of Abraham's call by God. The word might better be translated "peoples." The peoples Paul has in mind in this letter are Hellenistic Israelites and Judean Israelites. For Paul in this context the word "*ta ethnē*" obviously meant all Israelites who believe as Abraham did. That he has Israelites in view is clear from his mode of argumentation, from Israel's sacred scriptures and Judean custom. What appears to non-Israelite readers as a random association of citations from Israel's sacred traditions is rather understood and appreciated by Israelites as a masterful arrangement of scriptural passages. This strategy is called *haruzin* in Hebrew (from the verb *hrz*), meaning "stringing pearls."

3:9: Paul's point, of course, is that the God of Israel finds acceptable through their faith all Israelites who are blessed with the faith of their ancestor Abraham.

A Scriptural Argument on How Israel's Honor Is Restored by Christ 3:10-14

3:10 For all who rely on the works of the law are under a curse; for it is written, "Cursed is everyone who does not observe and obey all the things written in the book of the law." 11 Now it is evident that no one is justified before God by the law; for "The one who is righteous will live by faith." 12 But the law does not rest on faith; on the contrary, "Whoever does the works of the law will live by them." 13 Christ redeemed us from the curse of the law by becoming a curse for us—for it is written, "Cursed is everyone who hangs on a tree"— 14 in order that in Christ Jesus the blessing of Abraham might come to the Gentiles, so that we might receive the promise of the Spirit through faith.

Textual Notes: Gal 3:10-14

3:10: Further indication that Paul's argument looks to Israelites is indicated by the "us" in verse 13 who are redeemed from the curse of the law. A curse refers to a statement and/or action intended to influence by superhuman means the welfare or behavior of animate entities (persons, animals, spirits, enspirited beings like winds, seas, etc.), against their will or normal modes of activity. The law functions as such a curse, and only Israelites have this law. The opening statement here notes that all who rely on works of the law, namely, devoted Judean Israelites, are accursed by God. Proof of this is another scriptural citation from Deut 27:26. Paul's presumption is that no one in Israel actually observes and obeys all the things written in the book of the law, and consequently they are accursed by the law itself.

3:11-12: Besides, divine acceptability derives not from observance of the law, from doing the law, but from faith in what God has done, as the citation from Hab 2:4 is meant to demonstrate. On the other hand, divine acceptability based on fulfilling the law does not rest on faith but on performance, as the citation from Lev

18:5 (LXX) is meant to demonstrate. Hence being accepted by the God of Israel derives from faith in God and what God does, not in doing items of the law.

3:13-14: Jesus, too, was accursed by the law by the very act of his being crucified, since the law states, "Cursed is everyone who hangs on a tree" (Deut 27:26; 21:23). Yet in the process he redeems Israelites under the law. Redemption means restoring the honor and status of one's group. As an act of redemption, Jesus' crucifixion restores the honor of those accursed by the law since the crucified Jesus was raised by the God of Israel. He was raised "for us," thus restoring Israel's honor. The final goal of this act of honor restoration was that we might receive the promise of the Spirit through faith in the God of Israel, who raised Jesus. In this way the blessing of Abraham has come to us, *ta ethnē*.

Once more, notice how throughout this passage the word translated "Gentiles" (Greek: *ta ethnē*) refers to the group Paul calls "us" ("redeemed us," "become a curse for us," "we might receive the promise") and to whom he addresses his argument, that is, fellow Israelites! "Gentiles" is simply a faulty translation. Paul takes up the term "*ta ethnē*" here because of his citation of Gen 12:3, and it is the usage in Gen 12:3 that surfaces throughout the passage. For an Israelite like Paul, Abraham's blessing is for all the posterity of Abraham, all Israelites, but this posterity is actually all Israelites who believe in what the God of Israel has done in the resurrection of Jesus.

3:14: Paul's reference to the promise leads to another discussion about who are Abraham's actual heirs, since what Abraham received from God was a promise of posterity and land. Who in fact are Abraham's heirs? Once more, faith in God who raised Jesus will serve as key to answering this question.

A Scriptural Argument on Who Is Heir to God's Promises to Abraham 3:15-16

3:15 Brothers and sisters, I give an example from daily life: once a person's will has been ratified, no one adds to it or annuls it. 16 Now the promises were made to Abraham and to his offspring; it does not say, "And to offsprings," as of many; but it says, "And to your offspring," that is, to one person, who is Christ.

Textual Notes: Gal 3:15-16

3:15-16: Paul presents an a fortiori (or "all the more so") argument. A will or testament or covenant (Greek: *diathēkē*) is a type of promise. If a human being's duly ratified will cannot be altered, a fortiori God's will or promise cannot be altered. God gave duly ratified promises, and the promises were duly specified as Abraham and his offspring (Gen 13:15; 17:8). Paul's point is that the scriptural document reads the singular: "offspring" (Greek: *sperma*, seed, in the singular), not "offsprings" (or seeds, in the plural). Hence God's irrevocable promise is to Abraham and an individual, single heir of Abraham. This individual, single heir is Israel's Messiah or Christ, revealed by God to be Jesus whom God raised from the dead.

(Incidentally, one might note here that Christian Zionists who support the Israeli state because they consider it the fulfillment of God's promises to Abraham and his seed publicly and officiously deny what Paul says here. One wonders how they understand the basis for their Christian allegiances.)

A Scriptural Argument on the Relationship of God's Promises to Abraham to God's Law through Moses 3:17-22

3:17 My point is this: the law, which came four hundred thirty years later, does not annul a covenant previously ratified by God, so as to nullify the promise. 18 For if the inheritance comes from the law, it no longer comes from the promise; but God granted it to Abraham through the promise.

19 Why then the law? It was added because of transgressions, until the offspring would come to whom the promise had been made; and it was ordained through angels by a mediator. 20 Now a mediator involves more than one party; but God is one.

21 Is the law then opposed to the promises of God? Certainly not! For if a law had been given that could make alive, then righteousness would indeed come through the law. 22 But the scripture has imprisoned all things under the power of sin, so that what was promised through faith in Jesus Christ might be given to those who believe.

Textual Notes: Gal 3:17-22

3:17: Paul once more repeats his major point: once God's covenant or will (Greek *diathēkē*, the same word as in 3:1) has been ratified, the promises made in this covenant or will cannot be annulled—even by the law of Moses, which by popular Israelite accounting came "four hundred thirty years later."

3:18-21: God granted the inheritance in question to Abraham's "seed." This inheritance did not come through the law but through God's promise made centuries before the giving of the law. This leads to the question, Why the law at all? Paul's answer is that the law was given because of Israel's transgressions. The law in question, "ordained through angels by a mediator," is the law given through angels to the mediator Moses (see Acts 7:53; Josephus, *Ant.* 15.136). And the transgressions in question provoking the law are those of Israel in the wilderness launched with the idolatrous episode of the Golden Calf (Exod 32:1-35). The period of the law thus runs from the time of Moses "until the offspring would come to whom the promise had been made," that is, the time of Jesus the Messiah.

As previously noted (in the introduction to Gal 3:1), the Ten Commandments were given to the wilderness generation without a mediator and before the incident of the Golden Calf. God himself spoke those words, without a mediator, just as God's promise to Abraham was given directly to the patriarch, without a mediator. Both events underscore the fact that the God of Israel is alone in taking the initiative in offering Abraham the promises and Israel the covenant. The law, on the other hand, is mediated, hence deflects from the oneness of God. But the law is not opposed to the promises; only the law could not give life to transgressors. Hence Israel's acceptability to God (here called "righteousness") does not derive from the observance of the law.

3:22: The previous contrast between promise and law gives way to another contrast between law and faith. The period between law and the advent of faith, as the scriptures indicate, was a period when Israelites (the "we" imprisoned and guarded) were imprisoned under the power of sin, and the imprisoning agent was Israel's scripture, a synonym for the Law. The word translated "sin" (Greek: *hamartia*) means disgracing or dishonoring another person. In the context of God's interaction with Israel, "sin" means Israel's dishonoring or disgracing God. The power of sin points to a culture of willingness to dishonor God. In Israel's scripture this culture of willingness to dishonor God emerged with the first humans (see Rom 5:12-20). And in the context of Israel's story, the power of sin emerged in the willingness to dishonor God through idolatry, notably the incident of the Golden Calf.

Further Clarification Comparing the Period of the Law and the Present Period of Faith: Slaves and Heirs Gal 3:23–4:11

3:23 Now before faith came, we were imprisoned and guarded under the law until faith would be revealed. 24 Therefore the law was our disciplinarian until Christ came, so that we might be justified by faith. 25 But now that faith has come, we are no longer subject to a disciplinarian, 26 for in Christ Jesus you are all children of God through faith. 27 As many of you as were baptized into Christ have clothed yourselves with Christ. 28 There is no longer Jew or Greek, there is no longer slave or free, there is no longer male and female; for all of you are one in Christ Jesus. 29 And if you belong to Christ, then you are Abraham's offspring, heirs according to the promise.

4:1 My point is this: heirs, as long as they are minors, are no better than slaves, though they are the owners of all the property; 2 but they remain under guardians and trustees until the date set by the father. 3 So with us; while we were minors, we were enslaved to the elemental spirits of the world. 4 But when the fullness of time had come, God sent his Son, born of a woman, born under the law, 5 in order to redeem those who were under the law, so that we might receive adoption as children. 6 And because you are children, God has sent the Spirit of his Son into our hearts, crying, "Abba! Father!" 7 So you are no longer a slave but a child, and if a child then also an heir, through God.

8 Formerly, when you did not know God, you were enslaved to beings that by nature are not gods. 9 Now, however, that you have come to know God, or rather to be known by God, how can you turn back again to the weak and beggarly elemental spirits? How can you want to be enslaved to them again? 10 You are observing special days, and months, and seasons, and years. 11 I am afraid that my work for you may have been wasted.

Textual Notes: Gal 3:23–4:11

3:23-24: The power of sin points to the condition of willingness to dishonor God. This helps to understand the comparison of the Law and the household guardian in charge of the formation of children. Such formation or pedagogy had as its goal the shaping of children into adult humans fit for civil society. During the period from Moses to Christ, the Law had played that role, namely, to form Israelites into persons acceptable to God through faith in what God effected in the resurrection of Jesus, marking the coming of Christ.

3:25-26: "In Christ Jesus" all who have faith in God, who raised Jesus from the dead, are now formed by God, not the Law, hence are children of God. The "children of God" label contrasts with the children under the tutelage of the Law.

3:27-29: Paul now concludes his argument about Christ Jesus as Abraham's offspring, heir of God's promise thanks to faith in God, without works of the Law. All who have been baptized into Christ have undergone a transformative event, a social "putting on" of Christ. Jesus-group members have become one in Christ.

Hence Israelites of whatever social rank, whether Judean or Hellenist, whether slave or free, and regardless of gender, are one in Christ Jesus. The bottom line, then, is that by belonging in Christ, the sole heir of Abraham, the collectivistic persons making up Jesus groups become the true offspring of Abraham, hence heirs of God's promise to Abraham.

(Once more, it bears repeating that Christian Zionists who regard the modern state of Israel as the fulfillment of God's promises to Abraham and his seed hold a position that clearly is at odds with what Paul says here.)

4:1-2: Paul takes up the analogy of the Law as guardian again. Israelites living before God raised Jesus were like minors under the tutelage of a guardian. Minors, even though they were heirs, could behave only within the social parameters of the slave (see, e.g., Sir 3:6-7). In fact Israelites (note the "us" and "we" again) had the social status of slaves, subject to the guardian tutelage of "the elements of the cosmos." (NRSV expands this to "elemental spirits of the world.") The phrase refers to celestial bodies such as comets or stars, whether constellated or not. These sky entities were considered living beings that influenced the people living on the lands over which they passed. One could not avoid their influence.

4:4: The phrase "the fullness of time" points once again to celestial calculations. God sends his Son at the appropriate time determined by God's creative designs for the cosmos. His Son was born as an Israelite human being, that is, subject to the Mosaic Law.

4:5: And the purpose for God's sending his Son to Israel ("those under the law") was to restore the honor of Israelites. This is what "to redeem those who were under the law" means. Again, there is no concern for non-Israelites or "Gentiles." This restoration of honor status had as its goal that Israelites under the Law might become adopted children of God. Adoption was not a Judean custom. Rather, it was typical of Hellenism; hence the analogy would make sense to Israelite Hellenists, Paul's audience in Galatians.

4:6-7: The Aramaic title "Abba" is duly translated as "Father." The term does not mean "Daddy." Rather, it is a respectful title proper to a patron, "O Father." (See Pilch 1999:2–3.) Patronage "kinifies" relationships between patron and client. Paul's analogy of adoption applied to the God of Israel and those who believe in God's raising Jesus from the dead enables Jesus-group members to address the God of Israel as "Father," or Patron. They in fact do this because of the presence of the Spirit of the Son, experienced in their gatherings in altered states of consciousness. The result, again, is that Jesus-group members, those who believe in God's having raised Jesus, no longer live as slaves "under the law," but as children and heirs of the promises to Abraham.

4:8-10: Because of the influence of the Judean Jesus-group members proclaiming another gospel, the Galatian Israelite Jesus-group members have returned to "observing special days, and months, and seasons, and years" (4:10; see Gen 1:14). These observances are typical of the Torah calendar rooted in the zodiacal almanac and horoscopes bound up with this calendar (see the *Treatise of Shem* in Malina 1995: 272–75; 1 Enoch 72–82; astrological documents in Qumran). Of course Israel's calendrical observances, like those of other peoples, are rooted in the study of the sky and its denizens: planets, stars, constellations, comets. Paul considers these to be "weak and beggarly elements" (NRSV translated *stoicheia* as "elemental spirits"), not divine "by nature." It was commonly believed, however, that stars and other light-emitting entities in the sky were living beings. (See **Notes** to 1 Cor 15:40.) The calendrical regulations of the Mosaic law were rooted in God's celestial creation (Gen 1:14). But human beings took these celestial creatures to be divine "by nature," since they were presumed to govern human living. To observe such regulations in social life was to be subject to the guardian slave, this time subjecting oneself to the determination of celestial beings.

4:9: To have become a Jesus-group member is to have come to know the God who raised Jesus from the dead. Conversely, to be known by this God as a client means that one is a client of a powerful and munificent patron (opposed to the weak and poor elements in the sky). To submit to these celestial entities is to recognize them as deities (which they are not by nature) and therefore insult the God of Israel, who raised Jesus. As change agent, Paul states that he fears his Galatians will discontinue the innovation he proclaimed among them; hence he will lose honor himself.

An Exhortatory Interlude Gal 4:12-20

4:12 Friends, I beg you, become as I am, for I also have become as you are. You have done me no wrong. 13 You know that it was because of a physical infirmity that I first announced the gospel to you; 14 though my condition put you to the test, you did not scorn or despise me, but welcomed me as an angel of God, as Christ Jesus. 15 What has become of the good will you felt? For I testify that, had it been possible, you would have torn out your eyes and given them to me. 16 Have I now become your enemy by telling you the truth? 17 They make much of you, but for no good purpose; they want to exclude you, so that you may make much of them. 18 It is good to be made much of for a good purpose at all times, and not only when I am present with you. 19 My little children, for whom I am again in the pain of childbirth until Christ is formed in you, 20 I wish I were present with you now and could change my tone, for I am perplexed about you.

Textual Notes: Gal 4:12-20

4:12-13: Paul urges the Galatians, as fellow Israelites who have accepted the innovation revealed by the God of Israel to Paul, God's change agent, to accept the innovation just as he did and to imitate him in faithfulness to his gospel (2:5, 14; 4:16b; see also 1:6-9), which was their original agreement. In the process Paul notes that the Galatians did nothing wrong toward Paul, as he recalls the time he first proclaimed his gospel to them. He was held up in their region because he fell sick, and it was then that he proclaimed his gospel to them.

4:14-16: His illness "put them to the test"—that is, it tried their loyalty to God—yet they did not scorn or spit (NRSV translates "despise"). Spitting was a way to protect oneself from the evil eye and its deleterious effect. The Acts of Paul and Thecla describe Paul as having joined eyebrows. In the ancient world it was believed that such people would cast the evil eye, that is, harm whomever they might look at. Not only did the Galatians not fear Paul's gaze, but they showed him hospitality (this is the meaning of the Greek *dechesthai*, "to welcome," in 4:14).

Hospitality is a social process by means of which an unknown person is given favors (food, shelter, assistance) by a local patron, and then leaves as friend (or enemy). The Galatian welcome, Paul says, was like that described in the Torah as given to an angel of God, here in apposition with Christ Jesus, full of good will. Instead of treating him as a person with the evil eye, Paul attests they would have given their eyes if Paul needed them.

4:16-18: As he did at the outset of this letter, Paul again asks, Why have the Galatians changed toward him and the innovation he proclaimed? Does his gospel make him their enemy? They have clearly befriended those proclaiming a Judean gospel. These make much of the Galatians and their discontinuance of Paul's gospel. But Paul believes those who preach a Judean gospel do so for human motives, to withdraw the Galatians from Paul and instead to focus their interests on these Judean change agents. Paul admits that it is always good when people show interest for a good purpose, but he wishes they showed such support for Paul in his absence.

4:19-20: Paul wishes he were present, indeed, and that he might not have to write so harshly, since as initial change agent in Galatia, he feels affection for the Galatians, along with parental pain and anxiety involved in seeing one's children grow up, "until Christ is formed in you [plural]." As it is, Paul remains perplexed about the situation.

After this interlude of exhortation, Paul picks up the thread of his main argument, the defense of his gospel.

A Scriptural Argument Based on the Relationship between the Mothers of Abraham's Children, Sarah and Hagar Gal 4:21-31

4:21 Tell me, you who desire to be subject to the law, will you not listen to the law?
22 For it is written that Abraham had two
sons, one by a slave woman and the other
by a free woman. 23 One, the child of the
slave, was born according to the flesh; the
other, the child of the free woman, was born
through the promise. 24 Now this is an allegory: these women are two covenants. One
woman, in fact, is Hagar, from Mount Sinai,
bearing children for slavery. 25 Now Hagar
is Mount Sinai in Arabia and corresponds to
the present Jerusalem, for she is in slavery
with her children. 26 But the other woman
corresponds to the Jerusalem above; she is
free, and she is our mother. 27 For it is written,

"Rejoice, you childless one, you who
bear no children,
burst into song and shout, you
who endure no birth pangs;
for the children of the desolate woman
are more numerous
than the children of the one who
is married."

28 Now you, my friends, are children
of the promise, like Isaac. 29 But just as at
that time the child who was born according to the flesh persecuted the child who
was born according to the Spirit, so it is
now also. 30 But what does the scripture
say? "Drive out the slave and her child;
for the child of the slave will not share
the inheritance with the child of the
free woman." 31 So then, friends, we are
children, not of the slave but of the free
woman.

Textual Notes: Gal 4:21-31

After the foregoing interlude, Paul returns to his main argument to demonstrate that Jesus-group members exist in a post-Law situation. He began his argument with reference to the patriarch Abraham and how he won acceptance by God thanks to his faith in God, a process like what Jesus-group members undergo now. Jesus-group members are no longer under the Law. To further demonstrate this point, Paul has recourse to the story of the children of Abraham and their mothers. His interpretation of these scriptural stories is allegorical, as he explicitly notes (4:24).

Allegory is a literary form of a narrative in which the story and its features refer to something other than what a hearer or reader might think based on his or her normal understanding of the world and how it works. Among Israelite scribes, such allegory was called "midrash." In other words, the story of the children of Sarah and Hagar in Genesis as any reader can understand is really not about the children of Sarah and Hagar but about something else. This "something else" comes from the allegorical interpreter, whose interpretation makes specific sense in a new cultural setting. Paul here takes the story of Abraham's children and makes specific sense in the new cultural setting of Jesus groups.

4:21: Paul again confronts those in Galatia who "desire to be subject to the law." These are Paul's Jesus-group members who have now accepted the innovation of the gospel of God, but in its Judean version. In context, the Judean version of the gospel is that supported by Cephas, John, and James. This version presumes that Jesus-group members will observe the Law of Moses as their fellow Israelites do in Judea. In Galatians the features of the Law that are highlighted are food rules, calendars observances, and circumcision. In this passage Paul includes Israel's scriptural stories as part of the Law.

4:22-23: The story in question is that of Abraham's sons, the older born of the slave woman, Hagar, born according to the flesh, and the younger born of the free woman, Sarah, born according to God's promise. Paul presumes his audience knows this story, since he provides very little detail. This is another strong indication that his audience is exclusively Israelite, aware of Israel's major stories.

4:24-27: Paul allegorizes: Hagar stands for the Sinai covenant (originally a mountain in Arabia that stands now for the present Jerusalem and its Judaic customs and practices); Hagar (Jerusalem) is in slavery, bearing children for slavery. Sarah presumably stands for a celestial covenant (standing for the celestial Jerusalem) and is in freedom, bearing free children. She in fact is the true Israelite mother. The point is demonstrated by a scriptural quote from LXX applied to the allegorical Sarah: "Rejoice, you childless one, you who bear no children, burst into song and shout, you who endure no birth pangs; for the children of the desolate woman are more numerous than the children of the one who is married" (Isa 54:1).

4:28: Paul now applies the allegory to the Galatian Jesus groups. As previously demonstrated, through their faith in God, who raised Jesus from the dead, they are "children of the promise, like Isaac." They are in conflict with Judean Jesus-group leaders just as Ishmael ("the child according to the flesh") was in conflict with Isaac ("the child according to the Spirit"). And scripture says: ""Drive out the slave and her child; for the child of the slave will not share the inheritance with the child of the free woman" (Gen 21:10 LXX). This goes to demonstrate that Paul's Jesus-group members are in fact children of the free woman, not of the slave, hence subject not to the enslaving covenant of Sinai but to the liberating covenant of the Jerusalem in the sky. The slave and her child—Judean Jesus-group leaders—must be turned away.

This allegory concludes Paul's defense of his gospel begun in 3:1. The defense consists largely of a consideration of the significance of the non-Israelite patriarch of all Israel, Abraham, who became acceptable to the God of Israel not through fulfilling the Torah but through faith in God's promise of offspring and land. The Moses-mediated Torah in fact was given after Israel dishonored God with idolatry in the wilderness; the purpose of this Torah was clearly "because of transgressions," that is, with a view to fending off God's satisfaction for that idolatry and to obviating such transgressions in the future. Now, according to Paul, those Judean Jesus-group members who wish the Galatians to take up these anti-transgression Torah practices in order to be good Jesus-group members are quite misguided. Jesus-group members are free from these anti-transgression Torah prescriptions because with his death on the cross Jesus somehow caused God to waive the required satisfaction of the wilderness offense; there is thus no need to worry about fending off that satisfaction (God's wrath) by means for carrying out the anti-transgression Torah prescriptions. And the allegory of Hagar and Sarah clearly demonstrate this. Paul thus utilizes Israel's scriptures to make his case among his Israelite Jesus-group members. For these Galatian Israelites, scriptural proofs would be quite convincing.

Section Two: Exhortations Gal 5:1–6:10

The topics of this exhortation section have two focuses. The first focus is on circumcision; the second is on behaviors and their sources: the flesh and Spirit. These conclude with a set of general exhortations.

First Focus: Circumcision Gal 5:1-12

5:1 For freedom Christ has set us free. Stand firm, therefore, and do not submit again to a yoke of slavery.

2 Listen! I, Paul, am telling you that if you let yourselves be circumcised, Christ will be of no benefit to you. 3 Once again I testify to every man who lets himself be circumcised that he is obliged to obey the entire law. 4 You who want to be justified by the law have cut yourselves off from Christ; you have fallen away from grace. 5 For through the Spirit, by faith, we eagerly wait for the hope of righteousness. 6 For in Christ Jesus neither circumcision nor uncircumcision counts for anything; the only thing that counts is faith working through love.

7 You were running well; who prevented you from obeying the truth? 8 Such persuasion does not come from the one who calls you. 9 A little yeast leavens the whole batch of dough. 10 I am confident about you in the Lord that you will not think otherwise. But whoever it is that is confusing you will pay the penalty. 11 But my friends, why am I still being persecuted if I am still preaching circumcision? In that case the offense of the cross has been removed. 12 I wish those who unsettle you would castrate themselves!

Textual Notes: Gal 5:1-12

5:1: Both this passage and the one that follows (5:13) open with emphasis on freedom. In the first century, the word "freedom" referred to being physically and socially unbound, untied, unfettered. It thus meant freedom from external constraints. In Israel's mythical—that is, sacred—history, the parade example of this freedom is God's liberating Israel from the external constraints of Egyptian slavery in the Exodus. This was a freedom from Egyptian slavery effected with the purpose of a new bondage to the God of Israel, exhibited in serving this God. However, Israel quickly surrendered this freedom by submitting to the service of the Golden Calf, idolatry in the wilderness. The logic of Paul's thought in Galatians is that the Law, given by angels and mediated by Moses, was the outcome of this idolatry and given to prevent Israel from further dishonoring the God of Israel. Now, thanks to the cross of Jesus and God's raising him from the dead, the wrath of God has been waived along with the remedial law of Moses. Thus for Paul, the freedom in question is freedom from the Law. "Law" here refers to the prescriptions of the Law given by God to Moses after the incident of the Golden Calf. The innovation Paul proclaimed to his fellow Israelites was rooted in God's raising Jesus from the dead. This even entailed freedom from the prescriptions of the Law of Moses, since acceptance by God came from faith in God, who raised Jesus, not from doing the prescriptions of the law. Paul then considers submission to the Law of Moses as submission to the yoke of slavery.

5:2-3: For Judeans since the time of the Maccabees (circa 150 B.C.E.) the main marker of Israelite exclusivity was the male genital mutilation called circumcision. **Circumcision.** It is important to realize that not all Israelites spread around the Mediterranean adopted this Judean practice. Through a revelation given by the God of Israel, Paul proclaimed his gospel of God among Israelites in non-Israelite regions. According to that revelation, Paul believed that the elaborate, presumably Torah-based customs developed by various Judean political-religious groups were not divinely required or necessary for Israelites living among non-Israelites who had faith in God who raised Jesus. Hence Paul argues that adopting Judean practices, even at the insistence of Judean Jesus-group leaders, will annul the benefits accrued by faith in the God who raised Jesus from the dead. Adopting Judean practices would mark a return to the condition of Israel before Jesus' death and resurrection, to the period of Israel's requisite submission to the remedial Law of Moses. For Judeans, circumcision marked a Judean male's inauguration into submission to the whole Law of Moses. For Paul it also targeted a person for the curse of the law, as he noted previously (see 3:10: "For all who rely on the works of the law are under a curse; for it is written, 'Cursed is everyone who does not observe and obey all the things written in the book of the law'"). To be circumcised means to be obliged to obedience to the whole Law of Moses, a step back into the slavery that Israel brought upon itself with its idolatry in the Sinai wilderness.

5:4: As Paul previously argued at length, divine acceptance comes from faith in the God of Israel who raised Jesus from the dead, not from performing works of the Law. And this acceptance by God is "grace," the favor given by a patron. In this case the patron is the Father, the God of Israel. To submit to works of the Law as a way to divine acceptance is to reject God's favor. For Paul's Galatian Israelites, along with the penis foreskin cut of circumcision (the "nick") comes the cutting off of self from Christ.

5:5: The ultimate realization of God's acceptance thanks to faith in God will come through God's power, the Spirit. At present in the Jesus group, which is existence "in Christ Jesus," it does not matter whether Israelite believers had been previously circumcised or have not been circumcised. The only thing that counts is faith in God, who raised Jesus from the dead, along with behavior marked by "love," that is, group attachment. This sort of behavior marked by love is considered in Paul's final exhortation, below.

5:7-12: Paul now briefly considers his competitors, those who sought to prevent the Galatians from obeying the truth of Paul's gospel. Their persuasiveness did not come from God, "the one who calls you." For Paul the call to join a Jesus group is always a call from the God of Israel. The proverb "A little yeast leavens the whole batch of dough" describes the nefarious activity of the few who are "confusing you." Paul believes that they are answerable to God and will be penalized accordingly. Among the other points previously mentioned in the letter, these competing confusers accused Paul of preaching circumcision and therefore of acting hypocritically in opposing circumcision for his Galatian Jesus-group members. From Paul's point of view, the contrary is the case. And if he were to require Israelite covenantal circumcision, he would be removing the offense of the cross, the focal event in the redemption wrought by Jesus. Mediterraneans typically consider the male genitals as symbolic of male honor. And as a typical Mediterranean, Paul shows contempt for his competitors, wishing that instead of a foreskin cut on others, they would cut off their own genitals.

Second Focus: Flesh and Spirit Gal 5:13-26

5:13 For you were called to freedom, brothers and sisters; only do not use your freedom as an opportunity for self-indulgence, but through love become slaves to one another. 14 For the whole law is summed up in a single commandment, "You shall love your neighbor as yourself." 15 If, however, you bite and devour one another, take care that you are not consumed by one another.

16 Live by the Spirit, I say, and do not gratify the desires of the flesh. 17 For what the flesh desires is opposed to the Spirit, and what the Spirit desires is opposed to the flesh; for these are opposed to each other, to prevent you from doing what you want. 18 But if you are led by the Spirit, you are not subject to the law. 19 Now the works of the flesh are obvious: fornication, impurity, licentiousness, 20 idolatry, sorcery, enmities, strife, jealousy, anger, quarrels, dissensions, factions, 21 envy, drunkenness, carousing, and things like these. I am warning you, as I warned you before: those who do such things will not inherit the kingdom of God.

22 By contrast, the fruit of the Spirit is love, joy, peace, patience, kindness, generosity, faithfulness, 23 gentleness, and self-control. There is no law against such things. 24 And those who belong to Christ Jesus have crucified the flesh with its passions and desires. 25 If we live by the Spirit, let us also be guided by the Spirit. 26 Let us not become conceited, competing against one another, envying one another.

Textual Notes: Gal 5:13-26

5:13-15: Israelite Jesus-group members, once under the law of Moses, are now free of those constraints. But this freedom is for a new slave service to fellow Jesus-group members, a service motivated by "love," that is, group attachment and concern for group integrity. There really was no "freedom from" in the ancient world without a "freedom for." The God of Israel freed Israel from Egyptian slavery so that Israelites would be freed for the service of God in God's land. Similarly, Jesus-group members freed from slave service to the Law were now free for slave service to fellow Jesus-group members. In fact, group attachment and concern for group integrity are what the whole Mosaic Law is about anyway, as summed up in the single commandment "You shall love your neighbor as yourself" (Lev 19:18). For Paul here, "neighbor" is fellow Jesus-group member.

5:16: Since Paul's concern is about "love," he now sets out a list of negative qualities and directions of behavior that if followed by group members would lead to group dissolution and social decay. He follows this list with another positive list of qualities and the directions of behavior those qualities would take. These values, if followed by group members, support group attachment and concern for group integrity. He ascribes the former group-withering qualities and behaviors to the flesh, the fundamental impotence characteristic of human beings. He ascribes the latter group-enhancing qualities and behaviors to the Spirit, the power of God at work in Jesus groups thanks to the Lord Jesus. Through the flesh, persons throw up obstacles to God and their own well-being. **Flesh and Spirit.** In order for Jesus groups to maintain their integrity, group members must adopt certain behaviors and attitudes. They must attempt to shape their characters in such a way as to be proper ingroup brothers and sisters "in Christ." Group members characterized by "flesh" disvalues would necessarily be a source of instability and conflict. The reason for this is that "what the flesh desires is opposed to the Spirit, and what the Spirit desires is opposed to the flesh." Through the Spirit, Jesus-group members become open to God. Paul would have his Galatians live by and follow the Spirit. If they did that faithfully and exclusively, then they certainly would not be subject to the Law at all.

5:19-21: Paul now lists the behaviors characteristic of the flesh. This list of disvalues describes a selection of the demands of the Ten Commandments in disguise, while punctuating ten areas: (1) fornication, impurity, licentiousness, (2) idolatry, (3) sorcery, (4) enmities, strife, (5) competitiveness (NRSV: "jealousy"), (6) anger, (7) ambitiousness (NRSV: "quarrels"), (8) dissensions, factionalism, (9) envy (and other mss.: "murder"), (10) drunkenness, carousing. **Ten Commandments.** Paul recalls that he previously told the Galatians that such behaviors exclude a person from the forthcoming Israelite theocracy to be inaugurated by the coming of the Lord Jesus (as he did in his Corinthian correspondence, 1 Cor 6:9-11).

5:22-23: The behaviors that characterize the Spirit have the following qualities: love, joy, peace, patience, kindness, generosity, faithfulness, gentleness, and self-control. Paul would have Galatian Jesus-group members form their character in terms of these values. As he previously noted, for persons embodying such qualities, the Law is beside the point.

5:24-26: These concluding remarks further underscore Paul's perspective. The flesh is driven by passions and desires, obviously for what the God of Israel does not wish. That is why persons impelled by the flesh show their human impotence as they throw up obstacles to a proper relationship with God, to their Jesus group, and to their own well-being. Those of the Spirit are guided by the Spirit, through which they live. Presumably the main obstacles to this end are those Mediterranean male qualities: arrogance, challenging others, and envy. Paul, of course, would have his Galatians reject these cultural values in favor of another—that foundation of collectivistic personality, group integrity. But the group in question is not a kin group from whom the Galatians would originally have learned about group integrity, but rather a fictive or surrogate kin group comprised of Jesus-group members.

General Exhortations Gal 6:1-10

6:1 My friends, if anyone is detected in a transgression, you who have received the Spirit should restore such a one in a spirit of gentleness. Take care that you yourselves are not tempted. 2 Bear one another's burdens, and in this way you will fulfill the law of Christ.

3 For if those who are nothing think they are something, they deceive themselves. 4 All must test their own work; then that work, rather than their neighbor's work, will become a cause for pride. 5 For all must carry their own loads.

6 Those who are taught the word must share in all good things with their teacher. 7 Do not be deceived; God is not mocked, for you reap whatever you sow. 8 If you sow to your own flesh, you will reap corruption from the flesh; but if you sow to the Spirit, you will reap eternal life from the Spirit. 9 So let us not grow weary in doing what is right, for we will reap at harvest-time, if we do not give up.

10 So then, whenever we have an opportunity, let us work for the good of all, and especially for those of the family of faith.

Textual Notes: Gal 6:1-10

6:1-2: This final medley of exhortations looks to group integrity and group support. It opens with urging those with the charism of correcting group members to perform the task in a spirit of gentleness. The word "transgression" means behaving contrary to some norm. It differs from the word "sin," which means shaming or dishonoring another person. In this context, the transgression in question does not seem to be anything generic, but something specifically related to temptation. A temptation is a test of loyalty to God, who has raised Jesus from the dead. By supporting each other in face of such loyalty tests, the Galatians will fulfill "the law of Christ." This last phrase is a metaphor, a figure of speech in which an expression is used to refer to something that it does not literally denote in order to suggest a similarity. That something is the Law, that is, the Law of Moses. Jesus-group members' support for each other is a dimension of "love" or group attachment and concern for group integrity.

6:3-5: Persons who support others and are motivated by arrogance deceive themselves. They would do better to evaluate their own character and "carry their own loads."

6:6: Jesus-group members who teach their fellows are deserving of material support.

6:7-8: Paul's exhortation not to be deceived points to a common feature of Mediterranean outgroup social interaction, that is, deception. Deception in the defense or pursuit of honor was well known. The presumption is that the God of Israel cannot be deceived, hence mocked. The proverb Paul cites is a truism: people reap what they sow (a sort of Mediterranean principle of karma—one receives what one gives). Again, the contrasting principles of flesh and spirit emerge. The daily life of Jesus-group members as they await the coming of the Lord Jesus and the concomitant Israelite theocracy is much like the life of an agriculturalist. God will judge fairly, with people reaping what they sow, whether it is corruption from the flesh or endless life from the Spirit. Hence Paul's encouragement to constancy in what is right, for the good of all, especially for fellow Jesus-group members, described as a fictive kin group, "the family of faith."

V. Gal 6:11-18
Conclusion

The conclusion sums up the earlier arguments and makes an impassioned plea to persuade the listeners to accept the speaker's point of view.

Writing 6:11

6:11 See what large letters I make when I am writing in my own hand!

Textual Notes: Gal 6:11

Paul was apparently among the 1 to 2 percent of the population who was literate, that is, who could read and write. It seems that he wrote some letters himself, others he dictated, and still others he might have given notes or ideas to an amanuensis who wrote the letter. Galatians seems to have been a dictated letter. At this point, however, Paul wrote in his own hand.

Summary Observations: About Honor 6:12-17

6:12 It is those who want to make a good showing in the flesh that try to compel you to be circumcised—only that they may not be persecuted for the cross of Christ. 13 Even the circumcised do not themselves obey the law, but they want you to be circumcised so that they may boast about your flesh. 14 May I never boast of anything except the cross of our Lord Jesus Christ, by which the world has been crucified to me, and I to the world. 15 For neither circumcision nor uncircumcision is anything; but a new creation is everything! 16 As for those who will follow this rule—peace be upon them, and mercy, and upon the Israel of God. 17 From now on, let no one make trouble for me; for I carry the marks of Jesus branded on my body.

Textual Notes: Gal 6:12-17

6:12-13: At the very close of the letter, Paul attacks his competitors by accusing them of insisting on Judean circumcision practices so as to avoid conflict (presumably in Judean communities, such as Jerusalem) with their fellow Israelites. In other words, their requirement of circumcision is not motivated by prerequisites specified by the gospel of God but by their own unwillingness to confront those who reject the significance of what the God of Israel has done in raising Jesus. This is a strong accusation against Cephas, John, James, and their followers. Paul insists as well that they do not obey the law but strive for the honor of including the Galatians among the ranks of those following their form of Judean Jesus-group living.

6:14-15: Paul would have his honor derive from the cross of the Lord Jesus Christ, which has effected a waiver of God's honor satisfaction, that is, God's wrath. For Paul, Israelite society that rejects God's saving act in Jesus Christ is shamefully dead, and Paul in turn is shamefully dead to that society. Hence their mutual antagonism. Consequently, the inaugurating Israelite male rite or the presence of a foreskin (NRSV: "uncircumcision") do not matter. What matters is the new creation, effected by God's raising Jesus.

6:16: To those who live according to this viewpoint, as well as to God's Israel, Paul wishes peace and mercy, as he did in the salutation of this letter. Presumably, this Israel of God is comprised of those Israelites who accept the gospel of God that Paul and his colleagues proclaim.

6:17: Paul does not wish to engage in conflict with anyone. After all, he has been branded like a slave, with the marks of Jesus, to whom he belongs and to whom he owes slave service. The tenor of the statement is that if anyone has problems with what Paul is saying and doing, they ought to take it up with his master and leave him alone.

Closing Wish 6:18

6:18 May the grace of our Lord Jesus Christ be with your spirit, brothers and sisters. Amen.

Romans

I. Rom 1:1-7
Letter Opening (Superscription)

II. Rom 1:8-10
Letter Thanksgiving

A III. Rom 1:11-17
Introduction and Travel Plans

B IV. Rom 1:18-32
They and the Ten Commandments

1:18-23	The First Commandments
1:24-27	Another Commandment
1:28-32	The Ten Commandments

C V. Rom 2:1-16
You Judeans and Judging Hellenists

2:1-10	Judeans and Hellenists
2:11-16	God Shows No Partiality

D VI. Rom 2:17—3:20
Israelites

2:17-24	About the Law and the Ten Commandments
2:25-29	About Circumcision
3:1-20	About Judean Advantage: The Law

E VII. Rom 3:21—8:39
The Present Time: Now

3:21-30	Introduction to What Has Now Happened— A New Revelation [for Israel]
3:31—4:25	Proof of the New Righteousness: The Case of Abraham

A We (Inclusive: I and You)
and Reconciliation Rom 5:1–6:10

5:1-11	We Are Reconciled with God
5:12-21	Why and How of Reconciliation with God
6:1-10	Reconciliation Means New Living

B You Romans Rom 6:11–7:25

6:11-23	Freed from Sin and Slaves to God

Three Examples of Freedom
from Legally Controlling Authorities Rom 7:1-25

7:1-4	Example 1: The Dead Husband and His Widow
7:5-14	Example 2: The Freed Slave
7:15-25	Example 3: The Successfully Exorcized

A' We (Inclusive: I and You)
and the Spirit Rom 8:1-39

8:1-15	Living in/with the Spirit
8:16-18	Children of God
8:19-30	Children of God: Creation Awaits and We Await
8:31-39	Conclusion: God's Role

D' VIII. Rom 9:1—11:36
Recalcitrant Israel

Question 1: Why Haven't All Israelites Believed
in Their God's Raising Jesus from the Dead? 9:1–10:4

9:1-5	Paul's Assessment of His Fellow Israelites
9:6-13	True Israel
9:14-29	God Elects True Israel Alone
9:30—10:4	True Israel Is Rooted in Faith

A Description of Law-Observant Israel's Unbelief Rom 10:5-21

10:5-15	The Fault Lies with Israelite Unbelievers, Not with God
10:16-21	Law Observant Israel's Disobedience

Question 2: Has God Rejected Law-Observant Israel? 11:1-36

11:1-12	Has God Rejected Israel?
11:13-24	Non-Israelite Jesus-Group Members in Rome
11:25-36	Conclusion

C' IX. Rom 12:1—13:14
You: Jesus-Group Values

12:1-8	Basic Jesus Group Analogies: Sacrifice and One Body
12:9-21	Generic Admonitions
13:1-6	Attitude toward Civil Authorities
13:7-14	Conclusion: Final Admonition and Motivation

B' X. Rom 14:1—15:13
They (the Weak) and the Torah Commandments

14:1-6	The Weak and Their Observances
14:7-13	Exhortation to the Strong
14:14-23	Again, the Weak and Their Observances
15:1-7	The Strong and Their Attitudes
15:8-14	Concluding Admonition

A' XI. Rom 15:15-32
Conclusion and Travel Plans

XII. Rom 15:33
Letter Ending

XIII. Rom 16:1-29
Appendix: Letter of Recommendation for Phoebe and Doxology

16:1-23	Letter of Recommendation for Phoebe and Assorted Greetings
16:25-27	Doxology

Paul writes his letter to the Romans as part of his travel plans for his planned trip to Spain. He did not found any Jesus group in Rome; hence with this letter he treads on ground previously worked by other Jesus-group change agents. It is generally held that he wrote this letter from Corinth about 56–58 C.E. Because Paul was a present-oriented person in a collectivistic society, the time dimensions envisioned in the foregoing outline are interesting: sections I–VI look to a period from the past to the present, section VII is about the present, while sections VIII–XI deal with the forthcoming based on the present. As is usual in Paul, there is no future orientation in any modern sense of the word. He sets forth his gospel and its implications lest Roman Jesus-group members believe any other views they might have heard about Paul (see Rohrbaugh 2001).

I. Rom 1:1-7
Letter Opening (Superscription)

1:1 Paul, a servant of Jesus Christ, called to be an apostle, set apart for the gospel of God, 2 which he promised beforehand through his prophets in the holy scriptures, 3 the gospel concerning his Son, who was descended from David according to the flesh 4 and was declared to be Son of God with power according to the spirit of holiness by resurrection from the dead, Jesus Christ our Lord, 5 through whom we have received grace and apostleship to bring about the obedience of faith among all the Gentiles for the sake of his name, 6 including yourselves who are called to belong to Jesus Christ,

7 To all God's beloved in Rome, who are called to be saints:

Grace to you and peace from God our Father and the Lord Jesus Christ.

Textual Notes: Rom 1:1-7

Hellenistic letters opened with a formula consisting of the name of the sender(s), then the addressee(s) and a greeting. These three elements are called a "superscription" (or prescript). The next element, connecting the superscription with the body of the letter, is called a "thanksgiving." The thanksgiving is a statement of indebtedness to God for something done in the past plus wishes for the proximate future. **Hellenistic Letter.** What is distinctive of Romans is the lengthy description presented in the sender element.

1:1: Literally the opening verse states: Paul, slave of Christ Jesus, called apostle, set apart for the gospel of God. "Slave" focuses on his role of being controlled by and dependent on a higher personage, Messiah Jesus—an Israelite designation. "Apostle" refers to his role as change agent, "called" by the God of Israel, the change agency for his project. It is the God of Israel who set him apart for the task of proclaiming the "gospel of God," the news of what the God of Israel did on behalf of Israel in raising Jesus from the dead and settling on a forthcoming theocracy.

1:2: Again, literally the second verse begins with "who" (not NRSV "which") proclaimed beforehand through his prophets in the holy scriptures. These "holy scriptures," of course, are the sacred scriptures of Israel.

1:3-4: The gospel of the God of Israel proclaimed beforehand by this God of Israel was about his Son. Who exactly this personage might be is defined by what many scholars see as a song or hymn:

> He who was descended from David according to the flesh
> was declared to be Son of God with power
> according to the spirit of holiness by the resurrection from the dead,
> Jesus Christ our Lord.

Jesus the Messiah is now given a Hellenistic title, "Lord." The hymn tells of his Israelite origins "according to the flesh" and of his designation as Son of God with power by the spirit or action of the God of Israel "according to the Holy Spirit" (which is the opposite of "according to the flesh") by his being raised by the God of Israel from among the dead. Resurrection from the dead was one of the many features of Persian religion adopted by the Judean exile immigrants who arrived in Judah (Yehud) in the fifth century B.C.E. These immigrants assimilated as much as possible of the language and history of Judah as they could, to really make the claim against the Judeans who never left the land, that they were really "Israel" (Isaiah 40–55 reflects this kind of issue, speaking of Zion's welcoming back her daughters). A group of these immigrants developed into an Israelite "Persian" party, the Pharisees (in Persian, "Farsi" means Persian). Traditionalist YHWH worshipers who never left the land did not share Persian beliefs (for example, exemplified in the traditionalist Sadducee party).

1:5-6: Through Jesus, Messiah and Lord, Paul and his other Jesus-group change agents ("we") have received God's favor as well as their task. As change agents their goal is to communicate the innovation of God's raising Jesus from the dead with a view to a forthcoming Israelite theocracy. Those Israelites accepting the innovation are not "converts" but simply Israelites obedient to this revelation of God in the event of Jesus' death-resurrection. Hence as change agents Paul and those like him seek to bring about obedience to God that consists in faith in the God of Israel who raised Jesus from the dead. This is the object of their task. Their field of activity is Israelites resident in the non-Israelite world. As we know from Paul's letters, this field of activity consisted of non-Israelite cities, where his fellow Israelites formed a small minority. The nature of the gospel of the God of Israel means that it is a proclamation meant for Israelites. And these Israelites are indeed his addressees, "called" by the God of Israel to belong to Jesus Christ. For Paul it is always God who does the calling to Jesus-group membership. In this sense, it is the God of Israel who is the founder of Jesus-group gatherings (or "churches").

1:7a: This verse specifies the addressees: God's beloved in Rome, called by the God of Israel to be "saints," that is, set apart, chosen, elect. As we discover in reading this letter, Paul will deal with two major groups (Israelites and non-Israelites), each with two subsets. The Israelites among the vast majority of Roman non-Israelites consisted of (1) Israelite groups that rejected the news of God's activity in raising Jesus and (2) Israelite groups that accepted the news of God's activity in raising Jesus (and both of these groups have Judean and Hellenistic Israelite members). Roman non-Israelites consisted of (3) a few non-Israelites who joined Jesus groups and (4) the vast majority of the population of Rome, non-Israelite people who stood in contrast with Israelites. Paul's main concern, of course, is with the largely Israelite Jesus groups, although he will deal with the other groups as well.

1:7b: The greeting here is typical of Paul's letters (Gal 1:3; 1 Cor 1:3; 2 Cor 1:2; Phlm 1). The wish for the favor (grace) of the gods or—in Paul's case—of God along with peace is very common in Hellenistic letters. The special feature in Pauline letters is the assignment of this grace and peace as coming from God our Father and the Lord Jesus Christ. God, of course, is the God of Israel, our patron who provides favor (grace); Jesus Christ in turn is Lord, the person raised by God, now with authority and dominion.

II. Rom 1:8-10
Letter Thanksgiving

1:8 First, I thank my God through Jesus Christ for all of you, because your faith is proclaimed throughout the world. 9 For God, whom I serve with my spirit by announcing the gospel of his Son, is my witness that without ceasing I remember you always in my prayers, 10 asking that by God's will I may somehow at last succeed in coming to you.

Textual Notes: Rom 1:8-10

1:8: Hellenistic letters usually follow the salutation with a "thanksgiving," an acknowledgment of God's past and present beneficial activity, concluding with a hope for the forthcoming. Here Paul notes the well-known faith of all the Romans whom he addresses. "Thanksgiving" is preferably understood as a statement of indebtedness to a benefactor. Paul expresses a debt for favors received and still being received with a hope for continuing benefaction. Faith in Paul's context means faith in the God of Israel, who raised Jesus from the dead, an abiding trust in and commitment to this God. Paul makes his acknowledgment through Jesus Christ, intermediary or broker for Jesus groups to God the Father-patron.

1:9-10: Paul believes his change-agent activity, proclaiming the gospel of the God of Israel, forms his service or worship of God. The Greek word *latris* connotes service or worship that entails a reward of sorts. This is a sort of balanced reciprocity. **Reciprocity.** He notes that he has always had the Roman Jesus groups in mind with a view to actually visiting them, if that might be God's good pleasure. "The will of God" refers to what pleases God (as in "Thy will be done," Matt 6:10). The phrase expresses submission to God's will, identical in usage as in the Islamic usage of adding "Insha' allah" (if God wills) to statements of human planning (the same idea is to be found in James 4:15).

III. Rom 1:11-17
Introduction and Travel Plans

1:11 For I am longing to see you so that I may share with you some spiritual gift to strengthen you— 12 or rather so that we may be mutually encouraged by each other's faith, both yours and mine. 13 I want you to know, brothers and sisters, that I have often intended to come to you (but thus far have been prevented), in order that I may reap some harvest among you as I have among the rest of the Gentiles. 14 I am a debtor both to Greeks and to barbarians, both to the wise and to the foolish— 15 hence my eagerness to proclaim the gospel to you also who are in Rome.

16 For I am not ashamed of the gospel; it is the power of God for salvation to everyone who has faith, to the Jew first and also to the Greek. 17 For in it the righteousness of God is revealed through faith for faith; as it is written, "The one who is righteous will live by faith."

Textual Notes: Rom 1:11-17

1:11-12: After opening with a flattering thanksgiving with his statement of indebtedness to God for all the specific good things he has experienced with the believers in Rome, Paul now specifies his plans for a forthcoming visit to the Roman Jesus groups with a view to sharing spiritual gifts for the purpose of mutual encouragement. (He takes up the topic of his travel plans in a parallel passage at the conclusion of the letter, Rom 15:15-32.) The focus is on what "we" have in common. Paul places himself squarely in the ingroup of Roman Jesus-group members.

1:13: With the formula "I want you to know, brothers," Paul marks the opening of his concerns in this letter. He begins by somewhat apologizing for not having proclaimed his gospel of God to Israelites in Rome. After all, if any Israelites find themselves a minority in the world of non-Israelites, surely the Israelites in Rome did. And Paul's charge is to proclaim this gospel of the God of Israel to Israelites living among non-Israelites. Someone has already done so in Rome, so that there is this Jesus group he can address with his letter.

When one reads this letter, it is important to realize that Paul is addressing fellow Jesus-group members not related to him in any way. He did not lay the foundation of their gathering. He had no say in how they are organized and who might belong to their group. He is a total outsider. Yet "in Christ," he can presume to be an insider and request ingroup assistance.

1:14: Some might find it curious that in this whole letter "to the Romans," Paul never mentions Romans! The Greek of this verse begins by directly noting the social groupings to whom Paul is indebted: Greeks and barbarians, the wise and the foolish. They form the categories of people in the Israelite quarter of Rome and the other Gentile cities Paul visited. In the first century C.E. there was no country called Greece and no nation called the Greeks. The word "Greek" (or the alternate translation: "the Hellenized") meant "civilized." "Greeks" were people of various social and/or genealogical origins who spoke Greek and adopted civilized social customs. The presumption is that these social groupings existed in Rome as well. Barbarians were the uncivilized, those who adhered to native languages and local customs. Rome adopted the language and many of the cultural forms of the cities they conquered in Macedonia, Thessaly, and Achaia (for example, Corinth, Philippi, Thessalonika, Athens). Romans were "Greeks." Rome, like the other empire builders of antiquity, considered its empire as the only state in the world. There simply was no civilized, humanized world apart from Rome. Thus people did not come under Roman rule or Roman oppression. Rather to be "Romanized" was to be civilized, immersed in worldwide, Hellenic civilization. Veyne (1993:411) has noted: "Republican Rome, that people who had had as its culture that of another people, Greece, did not feel this culture as strange, but simply as civilization. Likewise, in the Empire and outside its frontiers, Greco-Roman civilization was civilization itself; one did not Romanize or Hellenize, one civilized."

And so, for example, the Israelite author, Philo of Alexandria, when writing of Caesar Augustus's conquests in the Alps and in Illyria, stated how the *princeps* "had healed the disease common to Greeks and barbarians" (*Embassy to Gaius* 145, LCL 72–73). What in fact had Augustus done? "This is he who reclaimed every state (*polis*) to liberty, who led disorder into order, and brought gentle manners and harmony to all unsociable and brutish nations, who enlarges Greece (*Hellas*) with numerous new Greeces and hellenizes (*aphellēnisas*) the outside world (*barbaroi*) in its important regions" (*Embassy to Gaius* 147; LCL 74–75).

Israelites, too, consisted of "Greeks," civilized people who adopted Greek language and social customs, as well as "barbarians," people who kept to the languages and customs of Judea. In other words, Paul's phrase "Judeans and Greeks" (Rom 3:9; 10:12; so often poorly translated as "Jew and Greek," or even "Jew and Gentile") actually means "barbarian (or Judean) Israelite and civilized Israelite."

This bronze coin (first century C.E.) shows the head of Caesar with an inscription that refers to the full name of Roman Corinth—Colonia Laus Iulia Corinthiensis—the city that was refounded as a Roman colony by Julius Caesar in the year 44 B.C.E.

To be wise meant to know how to succeed in life (although there were philosophical arguments about what true success might be). The foolish, on the other hand, were people who lost their social status and did not care about social success.

1:16: Paul will frequently mention the fact that he (along with Jesus-group members) is not ashamed of God's gospel. Shame means loss of honor in face of a claim to worth. Paul's insistence on the worth of God's gospel, even if rejected, does not entail any loss of honor. The reason behind this is that the gospel is the source of divine power. This power is usually manifested in the activity of God's spirit (or activity) in Jesus groups. In this commentary we refer to this activity of the spirit as altered states of consciousness experiences. **Altered States of Consciousness.** But the gospel of God does even more than unleash the spirit; it leads to salvation. Salvation means rescue from a threatening situation. And the salvation Paul has in mind is rescue from the effects of God's wrath, God maintaining his honor by demolishing those who have shamed him.

For Paul this salvation is the hallmark of those who have faith in God's having raised Jesus from the dead. This salvation has come first to the Judeans, since the resurrection event took place in Judea and news of it spread among Judeans. But eventually this gospel of God was spread to Israelites outside of Judea who have adopted the values and customs of Hellenism. These latter are "Greeks."

1:17: Paul now articulates the point that forms the theme, as it were, of the whole letter. The point is that in this gospel of God, of the God of Israel raising Jesus from the dead, one finds the revelation of God's righteousness. God's righteousness is the interpersonal behavior proper to the God of Israel, through which God manifests his approval and acceptance of the persons with whom he interacts. More tersely, God's righteousness is God's approval and acceptance. First of all, there is Jesus of Nazareth; God's raising Jesus makes known that God approves and accepts Jesus as Israel's Messiah and Lord (as in the opening hymn above). This righteousness of God now embraces those who through faith in God, who raised Jesus from the dead, attain what faith in God entails, divine acceptance and rescue from God's wrath. Paul quotes Hab 2:4, "The one who is righteous will live by faith." In this Pauline context, the verse means that a person approved and accepted by God, a righteous person, will live by faith in the God of Israel, who raised Jesus from the dead.

IV. Rom 1:18-32
They and the Ten Commandments

Paul previously set himself firmly within the ingroup of Roman Jesus-group members. As ingroup member, he would see his group marked off from two major outgroups. The first is the overall society of Roman non-Israelites, the "they" of the first part of the letter. At the close of the letter there is a corresponding parallel section (14:1—15:13). The second major outgroup consists of Israelites in Rome who have rejected God's innovation of having raised Jesus from the dead. Paul will eventually speak of this outgroup (2:17—3:20), again with a corresponding parallel section in the second half of this letter (9:1—11:36).

Paul's treatment of the first major outgroup, Roman non-Israelites, touches upon features characteristic of the Ten Commandments. **Ten Commandments.** In Israelite lore the belief was that the whole population of the world could hear, hence learn about, the Ten Commandments because they were spoken directly by God alone—not through Moses. If the Israelites could hear the words from the mountain top (as in the following Exodus passages), so could the whole world. "And the LORD said to Moses, 'Lo, I am coming to you in a thick cloud, that the people may hear when I speak with you, and may also believe you for ever'" (Exod 19:9). "And

God spoke all these words, saying, 'I am the LORD your God, who brought you out of the land of Egypt, out of the house of bondage'" (Exod 20:1-2).

Furthermore, since these were the direct words of God, which all could hear and not just the prophet, to repeat them verbatim in Israel was taboo. Josephus reports that in the Israel of his day, just as it was forbidden to utter the sacred Tetragrammaton, YHWH, the most sacred name of the God of Israel, so, too, it was forbidden to utter the "Ten Words" given on Sinai to Israel. While these are the very Ten Words "which Moses has left inscribed on the two tables," yet "these words it is not permitted us to state explicitly, to the letter." Nevertheless, Josephus indicates their "power" [*hous ou themiton estin hēmin legein phanerōs pros lexin, tas de dynameis auton dēlōsomen*] (*Ant.* 3.90 LCL). After all, as the Alexandrian Israelite Philo notes, these very words, "the ten commandments which God himself gave to his people without employing the agency of any prophet or interpreter" (*Spec. Laws* III, 2, 7) were the direct words of the God of Israel, hence full of power. They must not be repeated verbatim.

The First Commandments 1:18-23

1:18 For the wrath of God is revealed from heaven against all ungodliness and wickedness of those who by their wickedness suppress the truth. 19 For what can be known about God is plain to them, because God has shown it to them. 20 Ever since the creation of the world his eternal power and divine nature, invisible though they are, have been understood and seen through the things he has made. So they are without excuse; 21 for though they knew God, they did not honor him as God or give thanks to him, but they became futile in their thinking, and their senseless minds were darkened. 22 Claiming to be wise, they became fools; 23 and they exchanged the glory of the immortal God for images resembling a mortal human being or birds or four-footed animals or reptiles.

Textual Notes: Rom 1:18-23

1:18: With the Greek *gar* (translated "for"), Paul states the reason for what he previously just said, namely, that God's proper interpersonal behavior of granting approval and acceptance of people is revealed in faith in the gospel of God's raising Jesus for those who share this faith. The event that marks the burden of this gospel serves to reveal that the God who raised Jesus is on the verge of demonstrating his "wrath" from the sky. God's "wrath" means God is prepared to get satisfaction for actions of public dishonor—that is, vengeance for being publicly dishonored—so as to maintain his honor. What triggers this divine activity is the ungodliness and wickedness of "them." "Ungodliness and wickedness" are Israelite Hellenistic buzz words or tropes for those who dishonor God by giving other gods precedence over the God of Israel and by making images of nonexistent deities. These activities violate the first two commandments of the Decalogue.

The idolatry in question is wickedness and suppressing the truth, meaning the behavior required by God, creator and maintainer of the universe.

1:19-20: Referring to the traditions of Israel, notably Genesis 1–2, Paul affirms that the God of Israel has created and maintained creation. Through what God has made, God has shown everyone, plainly, his eternal power and divinity, invisible though they are.

1:21-23: These people have inexcusably dishonored or shamed Israel's creator God. They did so, first of all, by their deviant ways of thinking about creation and their experiences as God's created beings. The outcome was folly rather than wisdom, as can be demonstrated by the fact that their images of the incorruptible (meaning: unchanging, immortal) deity took the shape of a corruptible (changing, mortal) human being or birds or quadrupeds or reptiles. Such images dishonor God the creator not only because they are images of creatures but also because all such imaged entities whether humans or creatures of the air, land, and under the land are controllable by human beings. The attitude underlying idolatry is the belief that a human can control God. That is most shameful and dishonoring.

In sum, what is wrong with non-Israelites is that they do not worship the God of Israel, whom Israelites claim created the world (with Judea and Jerusalem at its center).

Another Commandment 1:24-27

1:24 Therefore God gave them up in the lusts of their hearts to impurity, to the degrading of their bodies among themselves, 25 because they exchanged the truth about God for a lie and worshiped and served the creature rather than the Creator, who is blessed forever! Amen.

26 For this reason God gave them up to degrading passions. Their women exchanged natural intercourse for unnatural, 27 and in the same way also the men, giving up natural intercourse with women, were consumed with passion for one another. Men committed shameless acts with men and received in their own persons the due penalty for their error.

Textual Notes: Rom 1:24-27

1:24-25: Paul now moves on to describe the behavior typical of these idolaters, presumably not found among Israelites. It is this line of behavior that reveals them as idolaters, since their behavior is a direct tit-for-tat outcome of idolatry (God "gave them up" to it: 1:24, 26, 28). First of all, they who shame God come to dishonor and shame themselves. The reason for this is that they subvert interpersonal relations: they exchange God's demands for human behavior for a lie, and they worship creatures rather than the Creator.

1:26-27: Further, since they shame God, "God gave them up" to shameless passions and actions, both males and females. The "degrading" passions to which idolaters have been delivered by God include: (1) females (*thēleiai*) exchanging natural (*physikē*) sexual intercourse for what is against nature (*para physin*), and males (*arsenes*) giving up natural sexual (*physikē*) intercourse with females, consumed with passion for one another and receiving in themselves their due penalty for their error; and (2) debased minds, revealed in a list of deviant behaviors. Such shameless behaviors are "against nature" or "natural use."

For first-century Mediterraneans, nature (*physis*) referred first of all to what was customary and usual: either for a given *ethnos* or people, a given species of animals, or even a given person or animal. In this sense, the natural stood opposed to the conventional or legal, that is, the behavior decided upon by a person or group with legal power. The term also referred to what was usual in the qualities of all that existed, all creation—what is instinctive, species-specific. What happened customarily and recurrently was natural, traceable to origins, to creation. Planets naturally moved erratically. Honey naturally tasted sweet. The Greek word translated as "nature" could also refer to the genitals, male or female (see LSJ *ad verbum*).

What is natural is "what is instilled by nature in all creatures. It is not proper to the human species alone but to all animate beings of the sky, earth and sea. From it comes intercourse between male and female, which we call marriage, also the bearing and bringing up of children. Observation shows that other animals also acknowledge its force" (Justinian, *Institutes* I.1.2).

Ancient Romans call this *ius naturale* (often poorly translated as "natural law"). *Ius* stands opposed to *lex*. *Ius* is an innate entitlement or empowerment deriving from creation; it is what determines what is "natural" and "according to nature." *Lex* is a decision by some rational authority, such as the emperor, senate, or king. In antiquity nature did not mean, as it does for us, the autonomous area of concern of the contemporary "natural" sciences, the 100 percent sameness of all reality known through experimentation and laws of "nature" in physics, chemistry, and biology and by analogy in sociology and psychology. This is "nature" as conceived by Descartes (1596–1650) and the "new science" of Francis Bacon (1561–1626) and Giambattista Vico (1668–1744). This perspective separated the empirical from the personal or spiritual. Laws of nature were the regularities of the empirical world, observable and testable and formulated, if possible, in the univocal language of mathematics. The category was then applied by analogy (based on a perception of God as legislator) to laws of nature.

1:27: What did people in Paul's world mean by natural and unnatural sexual intercourse? There is an interesting passage in Artemidorus's *Oneirocritica* that offers a set of categories typical of early second-century Hellenism, perhaps earlier as well: "In the section on sexual intercourse *(synousia)*, the best method of arrangement will be to consider firstly examples of sexual intercourse that is natural (*kata physin*), legal *(kata nomon)* and customary (*kat'ethos*); secondly examples of sexual intercourse that is illegal (*para nomon*); and thirdly examples of sexual intercourse that is unnatural (*para physin*)" (*Oneirocritica* I.78, White 1975:58). The groupings are pertinent, since in Romans Paul begins his categories with intercourse against nature, followed by a list of behaviors, including intercourse, against law, in context of the law of Israel. What would such intercourse against nature include? While Paul specifies only two instances, Artemidorus observes that the sexual intercourse that is against nature is any sexual position apart from the frontal position, which is the only one "taught them (humans) by nature" (*to de sygchrēta monon hypo tēs physeōs didachthentes*). The reason for this is that all species have a sexual position proper to themselves, and "humans have the frontal position as their proper one [*anthropous to men oikeion schēma to proschrēta echein*]; they have devised the others when they gave in to insolence, dissipation and debauchery" (*Oneirocritica* I.79, White 1975:63).

Thus a female's sexual intercourse against nature, as Artemidorus notes, includes all other positions, specifically those in which the female role is not passive. This is in line with the Mediterranean gender concern that males are active and forceful, while females are passive and controlled. In this perspective, since males cannot engage in the frontal position with each other, their sexual relations have to be against nature.

If we follow Artemidorus, intercourse against convention or law (*para nomon*) is essentially incest of various types. Similarly oral sex is considered "doing the unmentionable" (*arretopoiesthai*). The Hellenistic sensibility was that persons doing oral sex cannot "share mouths," that is, kiss or eat together (*Oneirocritica* I.79, White 1975:63–64). Paul, too, knows an unmentionable sexual relation, that of a male who marries his father's wife (1 Cor 5:1-2).

People in Paul's world offered various explanations for anomalies such as females behaving like males or males behaving like females. An explanation in Phaedrus's *Fables* (4.15) accounts for "tribadic females and effeminate males" by recounting that Prometheus got drunk when making human beings and attached some male genitals to female people and some female genitals to male people by mistake.

Philo offers the view that apart from boys used in pederasty, the passive partners in male sexual relations are actually androgynous persons who got that way either by birth or continual same-gender sexual relations to the point of castrating themselves (*Spec. Laws* III.7.37–42). These passive partners demean male honor. For Romans and Israelites of the period, these passive partners demeaned male honor, and it was precisely this denigration of male status that made the passive male partner reprehensible. For Philo the active male partner in same-gender male sexual contact was usually a married male seeking sexual titillation from just such a passive partner—to the Hellenistic and Roman way of thinking just described, a "transexual." The passage from Philo suggests that this was the usual same-gender male sexual contact that Paul knew from his culture as well.

Paul, in turn, shares a similar view, although he explicitly ascribes same-gender sexual relations to idolatry. While Paul may have shared Hellenistic sensibilities, his *ethnos* (people) had its own *ethos* (customs) that supported the us-against-them boundary that controlled Paul and that Paul articulates. It seems this was the common viewpoint of first-century Israelites.

The Ten Commandments 1:28-32

1:28 And since they did not see fit to acknowledge God, God gave them up to a debased mind and to things that should not be done. 29 They were filled with every kind of wickedness, evil, covetousness, malice. Full of envy, murder, strife, deceit, craftiness, they are gossips, 30 slanderers, God-haters, insolent, haughty, boastful, inventors of evil, rebellious toward parents, 31 foolish, faithless, heartless, ruthless. 32 They know God's decree, that those who practice such things deserve to die—yet they not only do them but even applaud others who practice them.

Textual Notes: Rom 1:28-32

After demonstrating how God is dishonored by non-Israelites because of their "unnatural" sexual behavior contrary to Israel's conventions and customs revealed in the Torah, Paul goes on to list typical non-Israelite wickedness that likewise dishonors God in terms of the Ten Commandments. While it was forbidden to recite the Ten Words in the exact wording and order as found in the Torah passage recounting the Sinai incident, first-century Israelites did not refrain from quoting them. They simply disguised them or re-ordered them. **Ten Commandments.** In the Synoptic tradition, for example, Jesus offers a listing to the greedy young man as follows: "You shall not kill, You shall not commit adultery, You shall not steal, You shall not bear false witness, Honor your father and mother, and, You shall love your neighbor as yourself" (Matt 19:18-19; Mark 10:19 omits love of neighbor, as does Luke 18:20, which inverts adultery and killing). The passage here in Romans is also a disguised version of the commandments: "They were filled with all manner of wickedness: (1) evil, covetousness, (2) malice , envy, (3) murder, strife, (4) deceit, malignity, (5) gossips, slanderers, (6) haters of God, (7) insolent, haughty, (8) boastful inventors of evil, disobedient to parents, (9) foolish, faithless, (10) heartless, ruthless" (1:29-32).

1:32: As noted previously, for Paul and those in the scribal Pharisaic tradition, the whole world heard God's Ten Commandments, although only Israel was God's covenant partner and although it was only for Israel that the Ten Commandments and all the other commandments delivered to Moses formed the stipulations of the covenant.

V. Rom 2:1-16
You Judeans and Judging Hellenists

Judeans and Hellenists 2:1-10

2:1 Therefore you have no excuse, whoever you are, when you judge others; for in passing judgment on another you condemn yourself, because you, the judge, are doing the very same things. 2 You say, "We know that God's judgment on those who do such things is in accordance with truth." 3 Do you imagine, whoever you are, that when you judge those who do such things and yet do them yourself, you will escape the judgment of God? 4 Or do you despise the riches of his kindness and forbearance and patience? Do you not realize that God's kindness is meant to lead you to repentance? 5 But by your hard and impenitent heart you are storing up wrath for yourself on the day of wrath, when God's righteous judgment will be revealed. 6 For he will repay according to each one's deeds: 7 to those who by patiently doing good seek for glory and honor and immortality, he will give eternal life; 8 while for those who are self-seeking and who obey not the truth but wickedness, there will be wrath and fury. 9 There will be anguish and distress for everyone who does evil, the Jew first and also the Greek, 10 but glory and honor and peace for everyone who does good, the Jew first and also the Greek.

Textual Notes: Rom 2:1-10

In this short section Paul turns from "they," the non-Israelite outgroup, to address a generic "you" (singular). The "you" in question, then, is one or another Roman Jesus-group member, as indicated by the parallel passage Rom 12:1—13:14.

2:1-2: These verses address those who would agree with Paul's assessment of "them." "We know that God's judgment on those who do such things is in accordance with truth." Paul warns those who agree with him not to pass judgment on "them" if "you" do the very same things. Presumably Paul knows the behavior of Israelites in non-Israelite cities, which often was not very different from the majority community. And he knows of the behavior of some Jesus-group members who continued to act like persons in the majority population (see 1 Thess 4:3-8).

2:3-8: For those ingroup members who act like the non-Israelite outgroup and still condemn them, Paul explains that the only reason God's wrath has not been manifested yet is to allow repentance. Wrath, again, means the activity of taking satisfaction on those who have dishonored or shamed a person; in this case the person is the God of Israel. To dishonor God requires God to take satisfaction so as to demonstrate that he is an honorable and worthy God. Paul states that God is putting off taking satisfaction because God is rich in kindness, forbearance, and patience. But impenitence can only lead to God's fitting judgment depending on one's deeds. For those who honor God by doing good, the outcome is endless life. For those who dishonor God by self-seeking and wickedness (a general term usually referring to idolatrous behavior), the outcome is wrath.

2:9-10: Judeans and Hellenists (NRSV: "Jew and Greek") are two categories of Israelites mentioned frequently by Paul. The Judeans were the conservative, "weak" Israelites who closely followed the customs of Judea. These were considered barbarians by "civilized" Hellenists, perhaps including their own fellow Israelites and Jesus-group members. The Hellenists were Israelites who lived in line with their Hellenistic inculturation: civilized because they spoke Greek and followed Greek customs and public behaviors. The passage intimates that the Roman Jesus groups consisted largely of Israelites, both Judeans and Hellenists. Judean Jesus-group members come first because of the obvious precedence and preeminence of Judea and Jerusalem in Jesus-group origins and development. The cultural truism is that the first-born deserves ascribed honor simply for being the first-born, and thereby allowing all following births to occur. In this sense, all family (here group) members owe a debt of gratitude to the first-born, a sort of generalized reciprocal obligation. Hence Judean Jesus groups come first; Hellenistic Israelite Jesus groups among non-Israelites come after that. So even for Jesus-group members, evil doers will reap the due rewards of their behavior, while good doers will receive appropriate recompense.

God Shows No Partiality 2:11-16

2:11 For God shows no partiality.

12 All who have sinned apart from the law will also perish apart from the law, and all who have sinned under the law will be judged by the law. 13 For it is not the hearers of the law who are righteous in God's sight, but the doers of the law who will be justified. 14 When Gentiles, who do not possess the law, do instinctively what the law requires, these, though not having the law, are a law to themselves. 15 They show that what the law requires is written on their hearts, to which their own conscience also bears witness; and their conflicting thoughts will accuse or perhaps excuse them 16 on the day when, according to my gospel, God, through Jesus Christ, will judge the secret thoughts of all.

Textual Notes: Rom 2:12-16

2:11: This famous principle of God's impartiality does not mean that God does not favor certain people over others. It surely does not mean that God's chosen people are equal to other peoples. Literally, the phrase translates the word: "acceptance of the face" (Greek: *prosōpolēmpsia*). A first meaning is that God cannot be deceived, specifically by a person's reliance on the ascribed honor deriving from birth (= face). God will punish people for their evil actions, regardless of their group or "chosen" affiliation. The mere fact of being a descendant of Abraham or a Jesus-group member will not obviate divine judgment.

2:12-13: "To sin" means to dishonor God. Given the previous principle of God's impartiality, those who dishonor God will have to be treated in terms of how they have shamed God, with the Law of Moses or without it. Israelites know what pleases God from the Law of Moses. God's acceptance ("to be justified") requires doing what pleases God, not simply hearing about what pleases God.

2:14: Non-Israelites know what pleases God "by nature" (Greek: *physei*), since the requirements of the Law of Moses are "written on their hearts." This is an allusion to Jer 31:33, often applied to Jesus-group members. Paul here applies it either to non-Israelites in general or to non-Israelites who have joined Jesus groups in Rome. This latter seems to be the case, since according to Paul's gospel the God of Israel, through Jesus the Messiah, "will judge the secret thoughts of all" (2:16), and God's judgments look to those who are bound to God through covenant obligations of a sort. Non-Israelites in general are not so bound to God, except as Jesus-group members. The reason for this: God shows no partiality.

VI. Rom 2:17—3:20
Israelites

This section stands in parallel to 9:1—11:36, which deals with Israelites who have rejected the gospel of God. The topics treated here deal with the features of Israelite social identity: the Law and the Ten Commandments (2:17-24); circumcision (2:25-29); and Judean advantages (3:1-20).

About the Law and the Ten Commandments 2:17-24

2:17 But if you call yourself a Jew and rely on the law and boast of your relation to God 18 and know his will and determine what is best because you are instructed in the law, 19 and if you are sure that you are a guide to the blind, a light to those who are in darkness, 20 a corrector of the foolish, a teacher of children, having in the law the embodiment of knowledge and truth, 21 you, then, that teach others, will you not teach yourself? While you preach against stealing, do you steal? 22 You that forbid adultery, do you commit adultery? You that abhor idols, do you rob temples? 23 You that boast in the law, do you dishonor God by breaking the law? 24 For, as it is written, "The name of God is blasphemed among the Gentiles because of you."

Textual Notes: Rom 2:17-24

2:17-18: Paul now notes that Judeans "boast in the God of Israel," obviously because of their covenant relation (as the NRSV makes explicit). They know what pleases God since these features are specified in the Law of Moses and Judeans "are instructed in the Law." It seems that it is their being instructed in the Law that separates Judean Jesus-group members from Hellenistic members, Israelites who have accommodated to Hellenistic culture.

2:19-20: Judean social identity, in their estimation, ranks Judeans as "a guide to the blind, a light to those who are in darkness, a corrector of the foolish, a teacher of children, having in the law the embodiment of knowledge and truth." Compare these features of Judean social identity with those listed by Paul in Rom 9:4-5 about Israelites in general. In the Judean view, then, outgroup non-Israelites are blind, in darkness, foolish, children, ignorant, and living in falsehood. Perhaps the same is true of Hellenistic Jesus-group members.

2:21-23: Paul now accuses Judeans in Rome of acting contrary to the values they believe constitute their self-identity. They steal, commit adultery, rob temples; they dishonor God by transgressing the precepts of the Law.

2:24: For Paul, this has always been the case, as the prophets of Israel have stated. He quotes Isa 52:5 (LXX): "The name of God is blasphemed among the Gentiles because of you" (NRSV). The word "name" means person; "blaspheme" means to dishonor a person by words. That non-Israelites dishonor the person of the God of Israel is due to Israelites living among non-Israelites. It is those Israelites living among non-Israelites who have been Paul's target audience of the innovation he proclaimed.

About Circumcision 2:25-29

2:25 Circumcision indeed is of value if you obey the law; but if you break the law, your circumcision has become uncircumcision. 26 So, if those who are uncircumcised keep the requirements of the law, will not their uncircumcision be regarded as circumcision? 27 Then those who are physically uncircumcised but keep the law will condemn you that have the written code and circumcision but break the law. 28 For a person is not a Jew who is one outwardly, nor is true circumcision something external and physical. 29 Rather, a person is a Jew who is one inwardly, and real circumcision is a matter of the heart—it is spiritual and not literal. Such a person receives praise not from others but from God.

Textual Notes: Rom 2:25-29

2:25: This is the first time we come across the word "circumcision" in this letter. There seems to be as much modern confusion about the word "circumcision" as there is with the word "Judean." Circumcision was introduced as a marker by which non-Judeans could become Judeans by the Maccabees about 165 B.C.E. in Judea. We cannot tell to what extent it was practiced by the many Israelites who left Palestine often centuries before the Maccabees. What this circumcision entailed was cutting a nick in the foreskin of an infant male's penis. This practice was not the removal of the foreskin as it is today. The reason we know this is that Josephus reports how a number of Israelites had their foreskins resewn (called in Greek: *epispasmos*) so they might appear whole when present in the baths of the period. Of course, this resewing was done by Judeans who sought to follow the lifestyle of Hellenism. In order to prevent such "concealment" of Israelite affiliation, about 150 C.E. Pharisaic scribes determined that the whole foreskin must be removed to fulfill the requirements of the Law. How many Israelites outside the rather small and limited Pharisee circles might have followed their determination is quite difficult to determine. Apparently, before 150 C.E. the removal of the foreskin was not the practice. **Circumcision.**

Paul's argument with the Judeans here is rather obvious: snipping the foreskin as fulfillment of Torah requirement is of no value if one transgresses the Torah. Again, such snipping does not result in acceptance by the God of Israel regardless of one's behavior.

2:27: Given our view that Paul's readers are usually Israelites, we read the physically uncircumcised as a reference to uncircumcised Israelites, undoubtedly the majority outside Palestine and large Israelite population centers (e.g., Alexandria, Damascus, Antioch, and points East).

2:28-29: So who is a true "Judean"? For Paul (and a number of Israelite Jesus-group members), a true Judean is one marked on the heart, inwardly, who obeys God's directives (see 2:15 and Paul's allusion to Jer 31:33, which speaks of a circumcised heart **Eyes-Heart**). He obviously does not receive a grant of honor from fellow Israelites simply for being physically circumcised. A person is not a "Judean" who is one outwardly, nor is true circumcision something external and physical. These persons receive their grant of honor from the God of Israel.

About Judean Advantage: The Law 3:1-20

3:1 Then what advantage has the Jew? Or what is the value of circumcision? 2 Much, in every way. For in the first place the Jews were entrusted with the oracles of God. 3 What if some were unfaithful? Will their faithlessness nullify the faithfulness of God? 4 By no means! Although everyone is a liar, let God be proved true, as it is written,

"So that you may be justified in your words,
and prevail in your judging."

5 But if our injustice serves to confirm the justice of God, what should we say? That God is unjust to inflict wrath on us? (I speak in a human way.) 6 By no means! For then how could God judge the world? 7 But if through my falsehood God's truthfulness abounds to his glory, why am I still being condemned as a sinner? 8 And why not say (as some people slander us by saying that we say), "Let us do evil so that good may come"? Their condemnation is deserved!

9 What then? Are we any better off?
No, not at all; for we have already charged
that all, both Jews and Greeks, are under
the power of sin, 10 as it is written:
"There is no one who is righteous, not
even one;
11 there is no one who has understanding,
there is no one who seeks God.
12 All have turned aside, together they
have become worthless;
there is no one who shows kindness, there is not even one."
13 "Their throats are opened graves;
they use their tongues to deceive."
"The venom of vipers is under their
lips."
14 "Their mouths are full of cursing and bitterness."
15 "Their feet are swift to shed blood;
16 ruin and misery are in their
paths,
17 and the way of peace they have not
known."
18 "There is no fear of God before
their eyes."
19 Now we know that whatever the law
says, it speaks to those who are under the
law, so that every mouth may be silenced,
and the whole world may be held accountable to God. 20 For "no human being will
be justified in his sight" by deeds prescribed
by the law, for through the law comes the
knowledge of sin.

Textual Notes: Rom 3:1-20

3:1-2: Paul now broaches the question of the value of being a Judean and the advantages of Judean social identity (as he will again in Romans 9). What is the benefit of being a Judean, marked by circumcision? Paul bypasses the circumcision feature and focuses on Judean advantage in having the Law. Most significantly, Judeans have been entrusted with the "the words of God" (Greek: *logia*), that is, the sacred scriptures of Israel.

3:3: The sentence now puns with the Greek word *pistis,* meaning "faith" as well as "trust." The words of God were entrusted (*episteuthēsan*) to Israel, yet if some Israelites were untrusting (*ēpistēsan*), does their untrust (*apistia*) nullify God's trust (*pistis*)?

3:4: Paul answers: "Don't be silly!" Let God prove to be true (trustworthy), even if everyone is a liar (untrustworthy). Paul quotes Ps 50:6 (LXX), which connects to this discussion by the mention of "your words": "So that you may be justified in your words, and prevail in your judging."

3:5: Now Paul takes up the word "justify" (Greek: *dikaiōthēs)* from the Psalm quotation. Paul argues rhetorically: if our unjust deeds (*adikia*) serve to confirm God's justice (*dikaiosynē*), what should we say? The problem for the English reader is that the Greek terms for "justify, unjust deeds, and justice" (listed previously) cover a range of meanings in Paul's social system that are lost in English. *Dikaiosynē* (translated: "justice") means proper interpersonal relations, behaving properly toward God and others. God's justice means God behaving properly in a way that befits God. "Justify" in this context means to find or make acceptable, to approve, to give approbation. "Unjust deeds" means deeds that are inappropriate, unacceptable, not deserving approbation but rejection. So Paul asks: "If our unacceptable behaviors serve to confirm the way God properly behaves, what should we say? That God is behaving improperly when he takes satisfaction (wrath) for our dishonoring God?" Paul specifies that he speaks in a human way: he is using an analogy based on human conduct, specifically the interaction called challenge-riposte with the requirement of satisfaction (wrath) when one dishonors another. **Challenge-Riposte.** If a person does not attempt satisfaction, then one loses honor and is shamed in the estimation of all onlookers! By analogy the same is true of God (and gods).

3:6: Again, Paul answers his rhetorical question with: "Don't be silly!" If God cannot behave properly, honorably, how could God judge the world?

3:7-8: Another facetious, rhetorical question: If through my lying (and untrustworthy behavior), God's truth (and trustworthiness) abound to God's honor, then why am I condemned as one who shames God? In other words: if I dishonor God and God takes satisfaction (wrath) to maintain his honor, then why am I condemned for dishonoring God? After all, I bring honor to God by dishonoring God! Paul ties this silly, circular argument to what he believes some have told the Romans about him, that he teaches "do evil so that good may come." These slanderers are duly condemned.

3:9: Paul now concludes: having the word of God, are we better off? His answer is: not at all, since all Israelites—Judeans and Hellenists—are under the power of sin. As he explains in Rom 5:12, the "sin" in question is a culture of willingness to dishonor or shame God, a willingness to take on God's honor. To prove his point now, he offers a list of scriptural quotations (a practice known in Israelite scribal circles as "stringing pearls"):

3:10: As it is written: "There is no one who is righteous, not even one" (paraphrase of Eccl 7:20).

3:11-12: "There is no one who has understanding, there is no one who seeks God. All have turned aside, together they have become worthless; there is no one who shows kindness, there is not even one" (Ps 14:2-3).

3:13: "Their throats are opened graves; they use their tongues to deceive" (Ps 5:10 LXX); "the venom of vipers is under their lips" (Ps 139:4 LXX).

3:14: "Their mouths are full of cursing and bitterness" (Ps 10:7).

3:15-17: "Their feet are swift to shed blood; ruin and misery are in their paths, and the way of peace they have not known" (Isa 59:7-8).

3:18: "There is no fear of God before their eyes" (Ps 35:2 LXX).

3:19-20: Paul now concludes this segment by noting that the Law of Moses obliges those who are under the Law of Moses, that is, Israelites. The result is that both non-Israelites in their own way and Israelites with the Law of Moses are held accountable to God. Paul applies to Israelites Ps 143:2 (in paraphrase): "no human being will be justified in his sight" by deeds prescribed by the law. "To be justified" means to be acceptable to God, to obtain divine acceptance. The Law of Moses does not produce divine acceptance, as Paul will shortly argue at length. The reason for this is that the Law of Moses triggered awareness among Israelites of the culture of willingness to dishonor and shame God.

VII. Rom 3:21—8:39
The Present Time: Now

This section forms the central element in this letter, as its overall chiastic structure demonstrates. It also contains the sum and substance of Paul's gospel of God that directly or indirectly, patently or latently, forms the leitmotif of all his authentic letters.

After an introduction describing God's new revelation for Israel with proof of the fact (Rom 3:21—4:25), Paul deals with reconciliation with God now available to us (inclusive, Paul and Jesus-group members, 5:1—6:11), then a central description of the new condition of Roman Jesus-group members (6:11—7:25), and finally a description of life with the Spirit available to us (inclusive, Paul and Roman Jesus-group members (8:1-39). These three sections form an A-B-A' chiasm:

A: about us 5:1—6:11
B: about you 6:11—7:25
A': about us 8:1-39

In his gospel of God Paul opens with the proclamation of a new revelation made by the God of Israel. This new revelation of God is a revelation of the righteousness of God. At the outset of Romans, Paul anticipated this topic when he identified the place where one finds this revelation; it is in his gospel of God: "in it [this gospel] the righteousness of God is revealed through faith for faith; as it is written, 'The one who is righteous will live by faith'" (Rom 1:17).

In this passage the word "righteousness" and its cognates receive heavy duty. The English word translates the Greek *dikaiosynē*, a Greek word also translated as "justice," "justification," "piety," and even "religion." All these translations seem to be inaccurate in the context of the behaviors described in the Bible as righteous. Consider the English meanings attached to "righteousness" (the state of moral right or moral justifiability), "justice" (treating each person according to what is his or her due), "justification" (proving right or reasonable), "piety" (the quality of being reverent), and "religion" (a particular system of faith and worship).

In the New Testament documents, the word *dikaiosynē* always describes proper interpersonal behavior. God is righteous because God behaves properly as God toward human beings. Humans are righteous because they behave properly toward other human beings and toward God (this is the theme of the Sermon on the Mount; see Matt 5:17). The question, of course, is what norm does one use to assess what is proper? What is the norm for correctness or appropriateness of behavior? From this perspective, the words "righteousness" and "appropriateness" are quite synonymous.

For first-century Israelites the quality of righteousness essentially encapsulated the privileged and blessed identity that came from being an Israelite. In the Israelite

Greek document called *The Letter of Aristeas* righteousness is what differentiates Israelites from all other non-Israelite outgroups.

> Righteousness is an ascribed honor from God which ennobles a particular identity. It produces a person who is thus righteous and thereby has an identity of a particularly privileged type, characterized by life and blessing. This lines up with what Paul has already said earlier via a quotation from Hab 2:4 at Rom 1:17: "The righteous person by faith will live." Life and blessing are described as characterizing the righteous in the richest OT source we have concerning them—the antithetical proverbs in Proverbs 10–15 where the extent to which righteousness is a way of specifying a privileged identity comes through loud and clear. (Esler 2003:278)

In traditional Israelite perspective, then, righteousness is a privileged identity deriving from divine acceptance due to Israel's ability to act appropriately toward God and toward other humans. In simple terms the word refers to acceptance by God. Paul argues that this privileged identity deriving from divine acceptance was never due to Israel's ability to act appropriately as spelled out in the Law of Moses. Rather, it always derived from divine acceptance of privileged persons who believed in God's activity on their behalf. These persons include, first of all, Israel's original ancestor, the non-Israelite Abraham, and all subsequent Israelites who believed God as Abraham did. Given God's recent revelation of himself in his raising Jesus from the dead, Israelites who believe in God's activity in this event are accepted by God on the basis of their faith in God, just like their non-Israelite ancestor, Abraham.

Introduction to What Has Now Happened—A New Revelation [for Israel] 3:21-30

3:21 But now, apart from law, the righteousness of God has been disclosed, and is attested by the law and the prophets, 22 the righteousness of God through faith in Jesus Christ for all who believe. For there is no distinction, 23 since all have sinned and fall short of the glory of God; 24 they are now justified by his grace as a gift, through the redemption that is in Christ Jesus, 25 whom God put forward as a sacrifice of atonement by his blood, effective through faith. He did this to show his righteousness, because in his divine forbearance he had passed over the sins previously committed; 26 it was to prove at the present time that he himself is righteous and that he justifies the one who has faith in Jesus.

27 Then what becomes of boasting? It is excluded. By what law? By that of works? No, but by the law of faith. 28 For we hold that a person is justified by faith apart from works prescribed by the law. 29 Or is God the God of Jews only? Is he not the God of Gentiles also? Yes, of Gentiles also, 30 since God is one; and he will justify the circumcised on the ground of faith and the uncircumcised through that same faith.

Textual Notes: Rom 3:21-30

3:21-22: Paul opens the section with a time reference ("now") further emphasized in v. 26 ("at the present time"). What is distinctive of this now is that it is marked by the manifestation of God's appropriate activity apart from the Law of Moses. Of course, as Paul will indicate, God's giving of the law of Moses was quite appropriate for previous Israelite generations. But no longer. As a matter of fact, although just recently revealed, this appropriate activity on God's part was actually attested to long ago in Israel's scriptures ("the law and the prophets"). So it is really something ancient, known of old. The righteousness now made known is God's appropriate behavior in raising Jesus from the dead, which endows a new privileged identity upon all who believe in God's appropriate action through their faith in God's having raised Jesus Messiah. Those who believe in God's activity on their behalf are in fact privileged persons who are aware of divine acceptance. That is, they are justified.

3:23-24: Since all among those who believe have previously shamed or dishonored God and therefore have fallen short of the honor due to God, it really does not matter what their previous relation to Judea was. Both Judean Israelites and Greek Israelites dishonored God, but now through their faith in God's raising Jesus, they are accepted by God with his patronal favor, a favor from God that effects the restoration of their status before God (redemption), which takes place in Christ Jesus. The wrath of God announced at the beginning of this letter has been waived thanks to Christ Jesus.

3:24: God's appropriate behavior (righteousness) in this case refers to "the ascription of honor by God to the sinner and, this being a culture in which the announcement of a status or other good on someone by a person in authority is regarded as effectively conferring that status or good, and has the effect of making the person so honored actually righteous. In this setting, to declare righteous and to make righteous are one and the same thing" (Esler 2003:277).

3:25-26: Specifically, God put Christ Jesus forward as a *hilastērion* (in the NRSV, "sacrifice of atonement"). The Greek *hilastērion* has two meanings. As an adjective, it characterizes something intended to reconcile or appease, something propitiatory (Josephus, *Ant.* 16.7.1; 4 Macc 17:22 LXX). As a noun the word may refer to an appeasing gift or offering. But in the Greek version of Israel's scriptures the word is the ordinary LXX translation of the Hebrew *kipporeth*, the covering or lid of the Ark of the Covenant consisting of the lid and the carving of two winged bulls known as cherubim. It was on this lid that sacrificial blood was sprinkled to effect reconciliation with God. The NRSV translation would have the reader believe that God himself put forth Jesus as a sacrifice of atonement to himself! After all, to whom were sacrifices in Israel directed? And here God offers sacrifice to himself. That makes for poor theology and silly sense.

If we understand Paul as referring to the Ark lid, he makes an implicit comparison, in which the crucified Jesus served as a *hilastērion*, as the Ark lid, where blood was sprinkled to effect reconciliation with God. Thus the believer shares in such reconciliation through faith in what God effected in this event, the very crucifixion of Jesus. The purpose of this event was, first, to show forth God's appropriate behavior, since God appropriately waives taking satisfaction for previously occurring deeds that shamed God. This is what sin means. Sin is a claim to worth by standing up to God, by challenging God, by dishonoring God. The later Christian and Islamic introduction to everything people do, "in the name of God . . ." is an avowal, an unwillingness ever to challenge God's honor. To sin is to challenge God's honor by doing something that dishonors God. Obviously the ascription of honor to the sinner has to come from others, namely, other sinners. And a sinner needs other sinners in order to claim the honor of standing up to God. God defending his honor takes away life. There is no other way.

The motive behind this event was to show forth at the present time period that God himself acts appropriately as the deity should and that God considers the person who has faith in the God of Israel who raised Jesus as behaving quite appropriately. Here a believer's acceptability to God derives from faith in God or faith in Jesus. And faith in Jesus always means faith in God, who raised Jesus and made him Messiah and Lord.

3:27: Boasting means taking credit for something that deserves a grant of honor. Honor is a claim to worth that is publicly acknowledged. To boast is to make such a claim to worth. Paul's argument here is that acceptability before God does not derive from any Israelite's claim to worth. Boasting is simply out of the question; it is excluded, for what could the claim to worth rest on? On the Mosaic Law as norm? On fulfilling the specific requirements of the Mosaic Law? Paul denies that doing requirements of the Law gives a person a claim to worth that should be acknowledged by others. Rather, the standard is faith. Faith is the usual high context term referring to faith in God, who raised Jesus from the dead.

3:28: Paul now clearly lays out what his gospel of God implies: that persons are acceptable to God on the basis of their faith in God's raising Jesus and all that implies for Israel, and this quite apart from doing anything prescribed by the Law of Moses.

3:29: In Paul's Jesus groups, the Israelites' insisting on performing the precepts of the law of Moses were notably the Judeans—that is, Israelites from Judea or Israelites who adhered closely to Judean customs. Paul contrasts these with Greeks, meaning Israelites living among non-Israelites who over time have assimilated to local customs and accommodated themselves in the culture of the majority population. Greek meant civilized, and that included Israelite residents in majority non-Israelite populations. So Paul asks, is the God of Israel the God of Judeans only? Is the God of Israel only the God of those who adhere to Judean customs (notably by following the prescriptions of the Mosaic Law?). Is he not also the God of Israelites resident among non-Israelites? Paul's answer is: Of course he is the God of Israelites among non-Israelites as well.

3:30: Therefore, since Israel has its own deity, a single deity (*Shema*, Deut 6:4), that person will ascribe acceptability on the grounds of faith in what God has done in raising Jesus both to those who follow Judean customs, notably circumcision, and those Israelites with unmarked foreskins, on the basis of the same faith. As Paul previously stated, there is no distinction, and this actually upholds the Torah. As proof of his contention, he has recourse to the Torah and offers the case of Abraham, the non-Israelite ancestor of Israelites "according to the flesh."

Proof of the New Righteousness: The Case of Abraham 3:31–4:25

3:31 Do we then overthrow the law by this faith? By no means! On the contrary, we uphold the law.

4:1 What then are we to say was gained by Abraham, our ancestor according to the flesh? 2 For if Abraham was justified by works, he has something to boast about, but not before God. 3 For what does the scripture say? "Abraham believed God, and it was reckoned to him as righteousness." 4 Now to one who works, wages are not reckoned as a gift but as something due. 5 But to one who without works trusts him who justifies the ungodly, such faith is reckoned as righteousness. 6 So also David speaks of the blessedness of those to whom God reckons righteousness apart from works:

7 "Blessed are those whose iniquities
are forgiven,
and whose sins are covered;
8 blessed is the one against whom the
Lord will not reckon sin."

9 Is this blessedness, then, pronounced only on the circumcised, or also on the uncircumcised? We say, "Faith was reckoned to Abraham as righteousness." 10 How then was it reckoned to him? Was it before or after he had been circumcised? It was not after, but before he was circumcised. 11 He received the sign of circumcision as a seal of the righteousness that he had by faith while he was still uncircumcised. The purpose was to make him the ancestor of all who believe without being circumcised and who thus have righteousness reckoned to them, 12 and likewise the ancestor of the circumcised who are not only circumcised but who also follow the example of the faith that our ancestor Abraham had before he was circumcised.

13 For the promise that he would inherit the world did not come to Abraham or to his descendants through the law but through the righteousness of faith. 14 If it is the adherents of the law who are to be the heirs, faith is null and the promise is void. 15 For the law brings wrath; but where there is no law, neither is there violation.

16 For this reason it depends on faith, in order that the promise may rest on grace and be guaranteed to all his descendants, not only to the adherents of the law but also to those who share the faith of Abraham (for he is the father of all of us, 17 as it is written, "I have made you the father of many nations")—in the presence of the God in whom he believed, who gives life to the dead and calls into existence the things that do not exist. 18 Hoping against hope, he believed that he would become "the father of many nations," according to what was said, "So numerous shall your descendants be." 19 He did not weaken in faith when he considered his own body, which was already as good as dead (for he was about a hundred years old), or when he considered the barrenness of Sarah's womb. 20 No distrust made him waver concerning the promise of God, but he grew strong in his faith as he gave glory to God, 21 being fully convinced that God was able to do what he had promised. 22 Therefore his faith "was reckoned to him as righteousness." 23 Now the words, "it was reckoned to him," were written not for his sake alone, 24 but for ours also. It will be reckoned to us who believe in him who raised Jesus our Lord from the dead, 25 who was handed over to death for our trespasses and was raised for our justification.

Textual Notes: Rom 3:31–4:25

In this section Paul takes the case of the patriarch Abraham to prove his thesis: that now we Israelites obtain the approval and acceptance of God through faith in what God has done in raising Jesus from the dead. Such approval and acceptance never really derived from performing the commands of the Law. The experience of Abraham proves this.

3:31: The NRSV rightly translates the word "the faith" here with "this faith," referring to "this faith" about which Paul has just spoken. This faith not only does not render the law ineffective, but actually upholds or firms up the Law of Moses. How can that be? Paul's interpretation of the experience of the patriarch Abraham as described in the Law will prove this. As was customary in Israelite usage, the term "law" (Hebrew: *Torah*) has a fluid range of meanings, covering the whole Old Testament, the section called the Law and the Prophets (from Genesis to 2 Kings), the Law proclaimed by Moses (the Law of Moses), as well as the Ten Commandments (the law proclaimed directly by God). These all formed the written law. To these the Pharisee tradition added an unwritten law consisting of Pharisaic interpretations of the written law.

Works of the law always refers to behaviors prescribed by the Law of Moses. The story of Abraham is found in Genesis, the law understood as consisting of the Law and the Prophets (Genesis to 2 Kings).

4:1: According to the Genesis story Abraham is the genealogical ancestor, the founding personage of subsequent Israelites (and Ishmaelites, normally selectively ignored because of Israelite ethnocentrism). If we read the Genesis account, what are we to say that Abraham unexpectedly discovered?

4:2: Paul presumes all know the story, since he can immediately continue by offering a reason for the implied answer to his question. "For" (Greek: *gar*) nearly always provides a reason for the previous statement. If in fact Abraham, by having fulfilled some precept, won a grant of honor, shown specifically by acceptance and approval by others (hence giving a basis for boasting), Paul emphatically states that these implied others did not include God.

4:3-5: Paul notes that Israel's scripture (which comes from the prophet Moses) says: "Abraham believed God, and it was reckoned to him as righteousness" (Gen 15:6). Because of Abraham's faith in God, God took this faith as basis for ascribing righteousness, that is, approval and acceptance. For persons who perform some work, their recompense is owed to them, not given as a favor. But if one who does not perform any work receives some recompense, that can only be a favor or gift. Abraham, without doing anything, trusted in God, called here "he who justifies the ungodly." "Ungodly" (Greek: *asebēs*) is the opposite of righteous (LXX Proverbs 10–15 frequently). If "righteous" means acclaimed as approved or accepted by God, "ungodly" means assessed as morally unapproved, hence unacceptable by God. He who justifies the ungodly, then, means God who accepts those who are morally unacceptable. In Abraham's case it was his faith in God's promise that won him a grant of acceptance and approval from God.

4:6-8: Paul now turns to Israel's writings, in this case to the prophetic David who spoke of the wonderful situation of those to whom God ascribes acceptance and approval apart from anything they might have done: "Blessed are those whose iniquities are forgiven, and whose sins are covered; blessed is the one against whom the Lord will not reckon sin" (Ps 31:1-2 LXX). In this regard Esler notes: "God's activity in righteousing effects a major change for the individual concerned—from sinner to righteous. In an honor culture, where a person's sense of worth rises or falls on manifestations of external approval, either from the local group or a person in authority, a sinner whom God righteouses will necessarily internalize that act of acceptance and forgiveness" (Esler 2003:188).

4:9-11: Paul now focuses on his main theme here: divine acceptance is not due to what Israelites do but due to what God does and to people's faith in what God does. Thus Paul launches into the argument with the case of Israelite male genital mutilation called "circumcision." By Paul's day, in Judea circumcision is required of all Israelite males by the Law of Moses. **Circumcision.** However, snipping a male's foreskin is not what wins divine approval and acceptance, since the scriptures unequivocally state that Abraham won divine approval and acceptance on the basis of this faith or trust in God who promised an heir to Abraham. It was after God ascribed approval and acceptance that Abraham underwent circumcision. Hence God's approval came before circumcision and apart from it. The first question, then, is why was he circumcised at all? Paul explains that circumcision was a sign (something standing for something else) and served as a seal of his already ascribed divine approval.

4:12: Since, because of his faith in God, he was already ascribed approval and acceptance by God, and since his circumcision was the seal of his approval by God without circumcision, Abraham can now serve as ancestor of all Israelites who are approved by God by their faith in God, whether these males are circumcised or have intact foreskins. Thus even those Israelites who are circumcised can claim Abrahamic lineage, provided that they "follow the example of the faith that our ancestor Abraham had before he was circumcised." What makes one an heir of Abraham is faith like Abraham's.

4:13-15: The promise to Abraham and to his seed (singular; NRSV is simply wrong) to inherit the world was given through God's acceptance due to Abraham's faith in God. Hence it is not Judean Israelites, adherents of the Law of Moses, who are to be heirs, since that would actually nullify Abraham's faith and make God's promise void. A further point: a law system entails divine satisfaction on those who shame God by not observing the law that God prescribes. "Wrath" refers to God's taking satisfaction to defend his honor in face of repeated acts of shame and dishonor (sin) on the part of Israelites. Where there are no prescriptions of law given by God, there is no need to defend God's honor. People who have no commands from God cannot dishonor God by disobeying God's commands.

4:16-17: For this reason, Paul concludes, being an heir of Abraham depends on faith in God and what God is doing, with God's favor central so that God's promise to Abraham's seed (singular) is guaranteed not only to Abraham's seed deriving from the law of Moses but also to Abraham's seed deriving from the faith of Abraham who is the father of all of us. The "us" here pertains to all of us Israelites who have faith in God, who raised Jesus, whether we Israelites follow the Mosaic Law like Judeans or dispense with it like Greeks. That all Israelites in Jesus groups are included is demonstrated by Gen 17:5 (LXX): "I have made you the father of many nations." Paul describes God here as the one "who gives life to the dead and calls into existence the things that do not exist." This description of God fits God's action on behalf of Abraham as well as on behalf of the crucified Jesus.

4:18-21: God promised Abraham numerous progeny. Abraham trusted God in face of the obvious physical impossibility of the realization of the promise, since he was fully convinced that God was about to do what he promised. Hence he grew in faith as he acknowledged God's greatness.

4:22-24: The outcome for Abraham: God gave him a grant of approval. And those who trust in God "who raised Jesus our Lord from the dead" are ascribed a similar grant of approval by God.

4:25: "He was handed over" (the Greek does not have the word "death" as in the NRSV) means that God handed Jesus over, since the passive voice points to God as the agent. Scholars call such usage the "theological passive voice" or "divine passive voice." It is a strategy for talking about God without mentioning the divine name. Paul describes the purposes behind God's handing over and raising Jesus. He was handed over "for our trespasses." The "us" in question are Israelites—Paul and the Roman Israelites—who have trespassed. The word "trespass" means crossing a forbidden boundary, a transgression of some law. Since Israelites had the Law, the trespasses in question refer to Israelite behavior. God raised Jesus (again passive voice) for "our" (Paul's and the Israelites' in Rome) approval or acceptance by the deity. It is faith in God, who raised Jesus, that results in this approval or acceptance.

We (Inclusive: I and You) and Reconciliation 5:1–6:10

We Are Reconciled with God 5:1-11

5:1 Therefore, since we are justified by faith, we have peace with God through our Lord Jesus Christ, 2 through whom we have obtained access to this grace in which we stand; and we boast in our hope of sharing the glory of God. 3 And not only that, but we also boast in our sufferings, knowing that suffering produces endurance, 4 and endurance produces character, and character produces hope, 5 and hope does not disappoint us, because God's love has been poured into our hearts through the Holy Spirit that has been given to us.

6 For while we were still weak, at the right time Christ died for the ungodly. 7 Indeed, rarely will anyone die for a righteous person—though perhaps for a good person someone might actually dare to die. 8 But God proves his love for us in that while we still were sinners Christ died for us. 9 Much more surely then, now that we have been justified by his blood, will we be saved through him from the wrath of God. 10 For if while we were enemies, we were reconciled to God through the death of his Son, much more surely, having been reconciled, will we be saved by his life. 11 But more than that, we even boast in God through our Lord Jesus Christ, through whom we have now received reconciliation.

Textual Notes: Rom 5:1-11

5:1-2: The first conclusion Paul draws ("therefore") is that because we are acceptable to God, approved by God, by faith, we now have peace with God. This observation matches the conclusion to the passage at v. 11: we have received reconciliation. The idea is that God waives the honor-demonstrating satisfaction he is due because of "our" trespasses. As previously noted, this happens through our Lord Jesus Christ, who mediated this favor (NRSV: "grace"). Favor is the gift of a patron. A favor is something a client cannot obtain at a given time or perhaps not even at all. It is this favor that Jesus-group members now have. With it we Jesus-group members have the hope of sharing in God's glory. Glory refers to external features that reveal a person's honor. Boasting means claiming worth or deservingness.

5:3-5: Thanks to our reconciliation with God, Paul notes that he and his Jesus-group fellows can claim worth because of the distress they undergo (see 1 Thess 1:6; 3:3, 7). NRSV translates "distress" (Greek: *thlipsis*) as sufferings. Distress implies an external and usually temporary cause of great physical or mental strain and stress. The distress experienced by the Jesus-group members was the normal result of adopting the innovation proclaimed by Paul in face of those who rejected it in their Israelite communities. Their fellow Israelites, perhaps a local majority, were aggrieved because these Jesus-group members discontinued their Israelite customary behavior and often split with the local Israelite group. Grievance quickly leads to conflict, and this is what distress entailed. **Dispute Process.** Social identity theory suggests "that external opposition and persecution will often encourage members to act in terms of their group membership, so that past suffering, now brought again to mind by Paul, probably strengthened their involvement with, and commitment to, the congregation" (Esler 2001:1203a). In other words, "our distressing experiences" predictably produce endurance, character, and non-disappointing hope because of God's being attached to us as demonstrated by God's giving (passive voice) his power. This power is ascribed to the activity of God's Spirit, usually shown in altered states of consciousness experiences. **Altered States of Consciousness.** We might note that the usual analogy for God's activity, that is "Spirit," concretely refers to wind, and wind, along with fire and water, is a liquid entity, hence pourable. The Spirit can be poured out.

5:6-9: The Hellenistic designation "weak" referred to persons untrained in the customs and amenities of the cultivated strata of society (*HCNT* 673–74). Driven by unwarranted fears, the "weak" behaved irrationally, guided by their dreads rather than by rational knowledge. Paul here identifies the weak with the ungodly and sinners. The dreads of the weak are not due to lack of rational knowledge but due to improper behavior and dishonoring activity relative to God. Such behavior requires God to take satisfaction ("wrath") simply to maintain his honor as Israel's deity. Yet in our "weak" condition, while we were far from "righteous" and "good," Christ died for us. In other words, while our behavior warranted our being killed by God, yet thanks to Jesus' death God waived the required satisfaction, and this enabled us to have continued life. This event demonstrates God's attachment or love for us. As a result, by Jesus' loss of life we somehow find divine acceptance; hence we will be rescued from God's well-warranted taking satisfaction for dishonor.

5:10-11: By shaming God we became enemies of God. Thanks to the death of Jesus, "his Son," God reconciled us to himself; we ceased to be enemies, and friendly relations have been restored. If this is the result of Jesus' death, all the more so will we be rescued from "wrath" through Jesus' resurrection. Paul now takes up the opening theme of boasting (5:2-3), this time in God through our Lord Jesus Christ, through whom we have now received reconciliation (parallel with 5:1: we have received peace).

Why and How of Reconciliation with God 5:12-21

5:12 Therefore, just as sin came into the world through one man, and death came through sin, and so death spread to all because all have sinned— 13 sin was indeed in the world before the law, but sin is not reckoned when there is no law. 14 Yet death exercised dominion from Adam to Moses, even over those whose sins were not like the transgression of Adam, who is a type of the one who was to come.

15 But the free gift is not like the trespass. For if the many died through the one man's trespass, much more surely have the grace of God and the free gift in the grace of the one man, Jesus Christ, abounded for the many. 16 And the free gift is not like the effect of the one man's sin. For the judgment following one trespass brought condemnation, but the free gift following many trespasses brings justification. 17 If, because of the one man's trespass, death exercised dominion through that one, much more surely will those who receive the abundance of grace and the free gift of righteousness exercise dominion in life through the one man, Jesus Christ.

18 Therefore just as one man's trespass led to condemnation for all, so one man's act of righteousness leads to justification and life for all. 19 For just as by the one man's disobedience the many were made sinners, so by the one man's obedience the many will be made righteous. 20 But law came in, with the result that the trespass multiplied; but where sin increased, grace abounded all the more, 21 so that, just as sin exercised dominion in death, so grace might also exercise dominion through justification leading to eternal life through Jesus Christ our Lord.

Textual Notes: Rom 5:12-21

Paul's second conclusion ("therefore") in this section develops the point that life comes through God's favor, just as death came through one human's act of dishonor. This observation matches the conclusion to the passage at v. 21: sin dominates in death; God's favor dominates through divine approval leading to life.

Throughout this passage Paul personifies sin, death, grace, and life. In this he follows the Roman practice of personifying qualities. Many Roman deities were qualities personified (e.g., Victory, Peace, Health, Rome). These impersonal qualities functioned like persons, although for the contemporary Western reader they are not persons. For people in Rome, these values were personified qualities that were effective in human living. They could be prayed to, worshiped, honored with sacrifice, and the like. This leads to problems in translation when dealing with Paul and his personified entities. For example, "sin" means an act of shaming or dishonoring a person, and "sin" entering society acts like a person who claims worth from dishonoring God. Sin personified functions like a personified cultural value of willingness to challenge God's honor. As personification, sin is like a person marked by the quality of being ready and willing to dishonor God. Sin is a societal value because values are qualities. The quality here is enveloped in an attitude of feeling superior to God and God's honor, a willingness to shame God and anybody else, a willingness to stand up to God, a willingness to put oneself over and opposite God. It is willingness to dishonor God. This sort of sin is based on an analogy from human behavior. Humans are often willing to challenge and dishonor another and thus claim worth by dishonoring another.

"Death" is the loss of life; personified death acts like a person seeking to take away life wherever it goes. The culture of willingness to dishonor God results in setting death to work among human beings. For Paul and his reading of Genesis, this state of affairs is due to one human being.

"Trespass," on the other hand, means crossing some line or border or boundary. A "no trespassing" sign means no crossing over some property line or fence. This behavior is used as an analogy for crossing over a boundary or limit set by some directive or law. "Trespass" is synonymous with "transgression." A trespass or transgression will be a sin if it dishonors the person giving the directive or making a law.

5:12: The vocabulary of sin refers to acts of shaming or dishonoring another. The culture of willingness to dishonor God emerged in human society through one human being; v. 15 indicates that Paul has the first earthling, Adam, in mind. Paul, of course, refers to the time when one human being and his helper formed all of society; death affected them and their offspring, since all of them sinned (except Enoch, who was taken into the sky by God; Gen 5:24). With the culture of willingness to dishonor God comes death for human beings. In this way humans have come to the experience of a limited lifespan because all humans at the time have dishonored God.

5:13: As the story in Israel's scriptures demonstrates (Genesis 4–11), the culture of willingness to dishonor God was in society before the time of Moses and the Mosaic Law, even in face of the general principle that "sin is not reckoned when there is no law." This sin, then, is not breaking rules, like trespasses or transgressions against the Mosaic Law. It is an act of challenging God's honor in face of a command directly from God.

5:14: And so apart from Enoch (Gen 5:24), death exercised dominion from Adam to Moses. Death exercised dominion even over those whose acts of dishonoring God were not like the transgression of Adam, since Adam received a command directly from God. For Paul, Adam, the first human being, was a type of the one who was to come, namely, Jesus the Messiah and Lord. A type is a person or thing symbolizing or exemplifying the defining characteristics of something or someone. The first human being exemplified the defining characteristics of Jesus, the one who was to come. Perhaps the most significant defining characteristic of both is that they were first in a long line of descendants. Paul now proceeds to describe what this entailed and how.

5:15: First of all, consider the impact of Adam's focal deed (loss of life for all) and the outcome of Jesus' focal deed (a gift of life from God, presumably for all). God's gift through Jesus is not like the result of Adam's trespass. Paul's reference to "the many" who lost their life thanks to Adam's trespass perhaps derives from a close reading of Genesis 1–10. In that story the fate of humankind has but a single human taken up to God (Enoch; Gen 5:24), while all the rest ultimately are destroyed apart from Noah and his family. On the other hand, "the many" beneficiaries of God's favor through Jesus refers to those who believe in God's raising Jesus from the dead.

In this section the word "favor" (Greek: *charis*; NRSV: "free gift") refers to items given by a patron, items available either not at all or not at the time one needs them. Patrons bestow favors on their clients. In this interaction Jesus functions as mediator or broker between prospective clients and the Patron. God's favor comes to God's client by means of the mediatorial functions of Jesus.

In sum, if because of the first man's sin many lost their lives, how much more will the patronage favor of God and the gift given through that patronage favor in the one man Jesus Christ abound to many?

5:16: And the gift in question is not like what happened because of the one person's challenge to God's honor. The judgment on the one person led to condemnation, but the outcome of God's benefaction following many trespasses leads to divine acceptance and approval.

5:17: If, by means of the one person's trespass, death exercised its dominion through that event, much more surely will those receiving the abundance of patronage favor and the free gift of acceptance by God (Greek: "righteousness") exercise dominion in life through the one man, Jesus Christ.

5:18: Therefore just as through the trespass of one human being the result was the condemnation for all human beings, so through the one human being's divinely approved and accepted action the result is life-giving divine acceptance (literally: "justificationing") for all human beings.

5:19: Just as by one human being's disobedience the many were made willing to dishonor God, so by one human being's obedience the many will be made acceptable to God (literally: righteous).

5:20-21: Now the Torah sneaked into the story so that trespasses might multiply. After all, with the Torah, Israel was given hundreds of precepts. The nonobservance of any of them was a trespass that dishonored God. But where the willingness to dishonor God expanded, God's favor abounded all the more, so that, just as the culture of willingness to dishonor God exercised dominion with loss of life as outcome, so God's patronage favor might also exercise dominion through God' accepting approval (literally: justification) leading to endless life through Jesus Christ our Lord.

Reconciliation Means New Living 6:1-10

6:1 What then are we to say? Should we continue in sin in order that grace may abound? 2 By no means! How can we who died to sin go on living in it? 3 Do you not know that all of us who have been baptized into Christ Jesus were baptized into his death? 4 Therefore we have been buried with him by baptism into death, so that, just as Christ was raised from the dead by the glory of the Father, so we too might walk in newness of life.

5 For if we have been united with him in a death like his, we will certainly be united with him in a resurrection like his. 6 We know that our old self was crucified with him so that the body of sin might be destroyed, and we might no longer be enslaved to sin. 7 For whoever has died is freed from sin. 8 But if we have died with Christ, we believe that we will also live with him. 9 We know that Christ, being raised from the dead, will never die again; death no longer has dominion over him. 10 The death he died, he died to sin, once for all; but the life he lives, he lives to God.

Textual Notes: Rom 6:1-10

As Paul unfolds the new divine revelation given by God in the death and resurrection of Jesus, this passage concludes the section on our (inclusive) reconciliation with God effected through Jesus. Paul now describes the broader significance of this restoration of amicable relations with the God of Israel by contrasting the loss of life characteristic of the period before this reconciliation and the life that must characterize the present situation. His view contrasts the then and the now, the past and the present.

6:1: Previously Paul made the point that where the culture of willingness to shame God existed and people were willing to dishonor God, to sin, even under those circumstances God chose to bestow his favor through Jesus. Now he sets out the rather sarcastic rhetorical question: If, when we dishonored God, God's favor abounded, should we continue to dishonor God? The answer, of course, is the equivalent of: "Don't be silly!" (6:2a).

6:2: What makes the idea so silly is that Jesus-group members have died to sin; they no longer participate in the culture of willingness to dishonor God. If they no longer participate in that culture, how can they continue in it—a patent contradiction! Paul describes this break with the culture of willingness to dishonor God as "death" to sin. The "life" that sin gave and supported has been snuffed out. How was this effected?

6:3: For Paul's Jesus-group members the transition from sin to life was marked by a rite. A rite is a symbolic ritual marking a change of status, a status transformation ritual. The baptismal rite marked a transformation from living in a culture of willingness to dishonor God to living in a culture of active concern for God's honor. **Baptism.** Paul calls this new culture a new life in Christ.

Baptism, an untranslated Greek word, means dipping in a liquid (water, wind, fire were all liquids in first-century perception). In Jesus-group usage, baptism was a symbolic dipping, a rite that conveyed meaning and feeling. As Paul goes on to explain, the meaning of being ritually immersed in water and rising from the water meant being immersed in Jesus' death, being buried with him, of being crucified with him (6:5-6) and rising from the waters transformed into a new life, like the life of Jesus raised by the God of Israel, a life to be realized in new behavior (6:4) and ultimately transformation into a mode of being like that of the resurrected Jesus.

6:6-7: The significance of joining a Jesus group and undergoing the ritual of baptism meant liberation from the culture of willingness to dishonor God, freedom from the old way of living ("the body of sin") to a new way of living marked by concern for God's honor. The payoff eventually is endless living with Christ.

6:9-10: Paul now offers proof for his previous statement. Since Christ Jesus was raised from the dead by the God of Israel, he is henceforth full of life, deathless, beyond the domination of death. He died to the culture of willingness to shame God once for all. Henceforth he lives only concerned for God's honor; "he lives to God."

With these observations Paul concludes his explanation of our (inclusive: Paul and the Romans') reconciliation with the God of Israel through Jesus Christ. He now follows up with a statement directed to Roman Jesus-group members based on his previous reflections on what they have in common.

You Romans 6:11–7:25

Freed from Sin and Slaves to God 6:11-23

6:11 So you also must consider yourselves dead to sin and alive to God in Christ Jesus.

12 Therefore, do not let sin exercise dominion in your mortal bodies, to make you obey their passions. 13 No longer present your members to sin as instruments of wickedness, but present yourselves to God as those who have been brought from death to life, and present your members to God as instruments of righteousness. 14 For sin will have no dominion over you, since you are not under law but under grace.

15 What then? Should we sin because we are not under law but under grace? By no means! 16 Do you not know that if you present yourselves to anyone as obedient slaves, you are slaves of the one whom you obey, either of sin, which leads to death, or of obedience, which leads to righteousness? 17 But thanks be to God that you, having once been slaves of sin, have become obedient from the heart to the form of teaching to which you were entrusted, 18 and that you, having been set free from sin, have become slaves of righteousness. 19 I am speaking in human terms because of your natural limitations. For just as you once presented your members as slaves to impurity and to greater and greater iniquity, so now present your members as slaves to righteousness for sanctification.

20 When you were slaves of sin, you were free in regard to righteousness. 21 So what advantage did you then get from the things of which you now are ashamed? The end of those things is death. 22 But now that you have been freed from sin and enslaved to God, the advantage you get is sanctification. The end is eternal life. 23 For the wages of sin is death, but the free gift of God is eternal life in Christ Jesus our Lord.

Textual Notes: Rom 6:11-23

The very center of this letter runs from Rom 6:11 to 7:25. What marks it off from the rest of the letter is that it is addressed exclusively to "you" (plural), that is, you Roman Jesus-group members. This section opens with a passage describing what Paul believes is typical of these Jesus-group members. He first notes some conclusions that follow from his description of the reconciliation effected by Jesus between Jesus-group members and the God of Israel (6:11-14) and then proceeds to a more extended comparison of their before-and-after situation using the analogy of slavery (6:15-23).

6:11-14: In the previous passage Paul reminds Roman Jesus-group members that they have been brought from the realm of sin/death to life and must therefore act accordingly (6:1-10). They must strive to remain alive to God by staying dead to the culture of willingness to dishonor God. Paul marks off this idea with a parallel statement: "do not let sin exercise kingly rule" (v. 12), "do not let sin have dominion over you" (v. 14). Acceptance of sin's kingly rule is manifested by obedience (v. 12), specifically by engaging one's members as war tools (Greek: *hopla*) fighting for wickedness on behalf of king sin (v. 13). Given that Jesus-group members have been brought from death to life, they ought to engage their members as war tools fighting for what is pleasing to God. This should not be difficult if they make the effort, for they are no longer under the dominion of sin. The culture of willingness to dishonor God no longer exercises its sway on them. In other words, they are no longer under the Law of Moses, given to Moses on Sinai because of Israel's sin (the Golden Calf incident). Rather, they are under the patronage of the God of Israel, who readily bestows his favor.

6:15-23: To describe their situation from another viewpoint, Paul now draws a comparison in terms of the social institution of slavery. The Romans were once enslaved to sin and now have been freed to become slaves of God. As all persons in Paul's society knew, slavery was (and is) an act of dishonor (social death—self or other inflicted) consisting of depriving a person of freedom of decision and action by means of force or enforced solidarity with a view to the social utility of the enslaving agent. As a social institution, slavery was a subset of kinship (domestic slavery) or of politics (political slavery: temple slaves, city slaves, etc.). Paul calls his use of such clear analogies as "speaking in human terms" (6:19).

6:15: Paul opens with a rhetorical question: should we continue to dishonor God because we are no longer bound by Torah rules of trespass but enjoy the favor of God? Again, the answer is "don't be silly." Jesus-group members are in fact no longer under the Law given to obviate future acts of dishonoring God, since through his death Jesus got God to waive the satisfaction provoked by the Golden Calf incident and the Torah regulations intended to prevent any more incidents of that sort. The culture of willingness to dishonor God is not part of their social identity. Rather, they are now in a culture of divine favor. So should they continue to dishonor God? Again, this is a silly question! Paul demonstrates its silliness by drawing an analogy with slavery.

6:16-18: Slaves exist for the social utility of the enslaving agent. If the enslaving agent is sin, the outcome sought by sin is loss of life, death. If the enslaving agent is God and obedience to God, the outcome is righteousness or divine approval and acceptance. Roman Jesus-group members were once slaves to sin. Now, thanks to God, by slave-like obedience to what they have been taught they are liberated from the culture of willingness to dishonor God. Yet they are in turn enslaved to righteousness, that is, divine approval and acceptance. They exist for the social utility of God. The idea here is very Israelite. God freed Israelites in the Exodus from Egyptian slavery in order that Israelites might give slave service to God in God's land. Jesus-group members have been freed from the slavery of sin in order to give slave service to the demands of righteousness, that is, divine approval and acceptance. Such new slave service is possible thanks to God's initiative in raising Jesus from the dead.

6:19-23: Paul draws out his slavery analogy. Jesus-group Romans once employed their abilities on behalf of impurity and wickedness. They gave little thought to Israel's purity rules (impurity) and disregarded the commandments of God (wickedness). Paul does not specify the deviant behavior in question. He is undoubtedly relying on a stereotype of what he knew of Israelites living as minorities in non-Israelite cities. Now these Jesus-group members must employ their abilities on behalf of righteousness and holiness. Righteousness refers to proper interpersonal behavior acceptable to God, while holiness or sanctification means exclusiveness—behavior demonstrating one's exclusive devotedness to God. Slaves serve the social utility of their master. When sin was master, they had to disregard righteousness and do things they are now ashamed of, leading to death. Now that God is master, they are out of sin's control and can behave with exclusivity, leading to endless life. In sum, the payoff of sin is death, while God dispenses his favor of endless life in Christ Jesus our Lord.

Three Examples of Freedom from Legally Controlling Authorities 7:1-25

Paul continues his contrast between the situation of Jesus-group members before Jesus' death and resurrection and their present condition thanks to their faith in God, who raised Jesus from the dead. The before/after situations previously dealt with sin [death]/life, and enslavement to sin/enslavement to God. Now Paul describes the before/after situation in terms of persons under the control of others (husband, slave owner, possessing spirit) who lose their control by their death. A dead husband, a former slave owner, and an exorcised possessing spirit loses their entitlements to control others.

Example 1: The Dead Husband and His Widow 7:1-4

7:1 Do you not know, brothers and sisters—for I am speaking to those who know the law—that the law is binding on a person only during that person's lifetime?
2 Thus a married woman is bound by the law to her husband as long as he lives; but if her husband dies, she is discharged from the law concerning the husband.
3 Accordingly, she will be called an adulteress if she lives with another man while her husband is alive. But if her husband dies, she is free from that law, and if she marries another man, she is not an adulteress.

4 In the same way, my friends, you have died to the law through the body of Christ, so that you may belong to another, to him who has been raised from the dead in order that we may bear fruit for God.

Textual Notes: Rom 7:1-4

7:1: Paul opens with a general legal principle, not clearly translated by the NRSV. The statement, well known to Torah scribes, means "the law is not in force for persons who die." For example, people who now own property no longer own that property from the time they die. Once persons die, all their legal entitlements over persons and goods cease. That this is what Paul means is clear from the following examples.

7:2: A husband's legal entitlements over his wife cease with his death. Take the case of adultery. Adultery means dishonoring a male by having sexual relations with his wife. While the husband is living, a wife's complicity in such sexual relations makes her an adulteress. When the husband dies, the same action with the same person does not make her an adulteress. The social boundaries that embed the wife in her husband have been erased by his death.

7:3: The NRSV's "if she marries another man" is incorrect. The Greek phrase is "if she is with another man." Paul is not interested here about the propriety of sexual intercourse in marriage alone. The example is about adultery and the entitlements of the husband.

7:4: Now Paul applies the analogy to Jesus-group members; Paul calls them "brothers" (not "friends" as in the NRSV). The application makes it clear he is speaking of Israelites previously bound to the Law. For them the Law no longer obliges. They are like the wife whose husband is dead. She, in her own way, is dead to the entitlements that her husband had over her. So, too, Jesus-group members are dead to the Law, freed from the Law's legal entitlements over them through their being in the body of Christ. They are now freed from the Law's legal claims on them, hence free to belong to another. In this case, that other is he who has been raised from the dead by the God of Israel. The goal is that they, with other Jesus-group members, may bear fruit for God, presumably as the freed wife bears fruit for her new husband.

Example 2: The Freed Slave 7:5-14

7:5 While we were living in the flesh, our sinful passions, aroused by the law, were at work in our members to bear fruit for death.
6 But now we are discharged from the law, dead to that which held us captive, so that we are slaves not under the old written code but in the new life of the Spirit.

7 What then should we say? That the law is sin? By no means! Yet, if it had not been for the law, I would not have known sin. I would not have known what it is to covet if the law had not said, "You shall
not covet." 8 But sin, seizing an opportu-
nity in the commandment, produced in me all kinds of covetousness. Apart from
the law sin lies dead. 9 I was once alive
apart from the law, but when the commandment came, sin revived 10 and I died, and the very commandment that promised life
proved to be death to me. 11 For sin, seiz-
ing an opportunity in the commandment, deceived me and through it killed me.
12 So the law is holy, and the commandment is holy and just and good.

13 Did what is good, then, bring death to me? By no means! It was sin, working death in me through what is good, in order that sin might be shown to be sin, and through the commandment might become
sinful beyond measure. 14 For we know that the law is spiritual; but I am of the flesh, sold into slavery under sin.

Textual Notes: Rom 7:5-14

7:5: Paul turns now to reflect on the condition of Jesus-group members in their new life of the Spirit, contrasting it with their previous condition. In this passage he compares that previous condition as one of "slavery under sin" (v. 14), a condition of being held captive as slaves "under the old written code" (v. 6). This analogy considers the Law as a slave owner, with Israelites under the Law as living in the flesh. In what follows, then, to be "in the flesh" means to be in Israel, while to be "in the Spirit" means to be in Christ. Life in Israel under the Law was like life under a slave master, a condition entailing loss of life, the social death that slavery was and is.

7:6: With the demise of the Law and its claims, Jesus-group members are no longer slaves to the old written Law; in effect they are dead to the Law, and so the old slave master is dead as far as they are concerned.

7:7: Another rhetorical question: is the Law the basis of the culture of willingness to dishonor God? Again, Paul's answer is, "Don't be silly!" The Law is not the basis and foundation of the culture of willingness to dishonor God. On the other hand, if the Law did not spell out just what dishonors God, Israelites would not know about those dishonoring behaviors and attitudes. (Just look at the non-Israelites who are not aware of such dishonoring behavior as described earlier in this letter, chapter 1.)

Throughout this passage, Paul personalizes reactions to sin in the various comparisons he uses by putting himself into the scenarios. The word "I" here is the collectivistic self, the ingroup self faced with the Law as slave owner or possessing spirit.

Paul now offers a general example. "Covet" means to desire and take, in effect to steal. In the context of Israel's Law, "to covet" means to desire and take or do something other than what God wants or permits. How would one learn about desiring and taking or doing what God does not want or permit unless the Law said one should not do it?

7:8: In the culture of willingness to dishonor God, the command not to desire or take what God does not want or permit produces all sorts of ideas and behaviors dealing with desiring and taking. If the commands of the Law did not exist, one would not even think of doing what the Law specifies as prohibited. In this sense, apart from the Law sin lies dead.

7:9: Israel was once in that condition, apart from the Law, but when the Law came the culture of willingness to dishonor God was unleashed again. So Israelites died; the commands of the Law brought not life but death.

7:11: Personified sin, like a sly slave trader, seized the opportunity afforded by the Law, deceived the Israelites, and killed them by enslaving them.

7:12: The Law, ostensibly the Law of Moses given by God, is holy, exclusive to God and God's people Israel. Its requirements are equally exclusive to God, appropriate for Israel, and hence good.

7:13: Another rhetorical question: now did this holy Law bring death, enslaving Israel? And again the answer is: "Don't be silly." The problem was the culture of willingness to dishonor God, a culture revealed by Israel's Golden Calf event, the event that triggered the giving of the Law. So the law is holy, and the commandment is holy and just and good. This culture effected loss of life (as with Adam) through the good Law. God's purpose, Paul says, is to reveal the presence of the culture of willingness to dishonor God in all its dimensions.

7:14: While the Law comes from God's spirit, the Israelites who received it were of the flesh, that is, enslaved in a culture of willingness to dishonor God.

Example 3: The Successfully Exorcized 7:15-25

7:15 I do not understand my own actions. For I do not do what I want, but I do the very thing I hate. 16 Now if I do what I do not want, I agree that the law is good. 17 But in fact it is no longer I that do it, but sin that dwells within me. 18 For I know that nothing good dwells within me, that is, in my flesh. I can will what is right, but I cannot do it. 19 For I do not do the good I want, but the evil I do not want is what I do. 20 Now if I do what I do not want, it is no longer I that do it, but sin that dwells within me.

21 So I find it to be a law that when I want to do what is good, evil lies close at hand. 22 For I delight in the law of God in my inmost self, 23 but I see in my members another law at war with the law of my mind, making me captive to the law of sin that dwells in my members. 24 Wretched man that I am! Who will rescue me from this body of death? 25 Thanks be to God through Jesus Christ our Lord!

So then, with my mind I am a slave to the law of God, but with my flesh I am a slave to the law of sin.

Textual Notes: Rom 7:15-25

7:15-16: Paul's third example is that of a person possessed by some spirit or demon. The possessing spirit makes the person do whatever it wants; the possessed person, then, loses control. It is this loss of control by a possessed person that Paul now describes.

7:17-20: In Paul's analogy the possessing agent is sin personified as a possessing spirit or demon. It does not let a person do what the person wants, but what it wants. For Paul Jesus-group members previously lived like persons possessed. Possessed persons no longer do what they wish but what the possessing spirit that dwells within them wishes them to do. Sin works in the same way.

7:21-23: Paul draws out the comparison, noting how possessed persons cannot do the good they want even if "in [their] inmost self" they delight in the law of God, since as persons possessed by sin what they wish is in the power of the controlling, possessing spirit. As possessed persons Jesus-group members previously found it a law that when they wanted to do what is good, the evil possessing spirit was close at hand.

7:24-25: Again, a rhetorical question: as a wretched possessed person, who will exorcize me and free me from the control of sin and what it entails? Paul, of course, knows the answer. Successful exorcism occurs "through Jesus Christ our Lord," thanks to the God of Israel.

7:25b: This verse would have Paul conclude the section with his last analogy: so then I myself do slave service to the Law of God with my mind, but with my flesh, I do slave service to the Law of sin. Yet this statement makes little sense, unless placed before v. 24. On the other hand, some scholars believe it may have been a scribal insertion.

We (Inclusive: I and You) and the Spirit 8:1-39

Living in/with the Spirit 8:1-15

8:1 There is therefore now no condemnation for those who are in Christ Jesus. 2 For the law of the Spirit of life in Christ Jesus has set you free from the law of sin and of death. 3 For God has done what the law, weakened by the flesh, could not do: by sending his own Son in the likeness of sinful flesh, and to deal with sin, he condemned sin in the flesh, 4 so that the just requirement of the law might be fulfilled in us, who walk not according to the flesh but according to the Spirit. 5 For those who live according to the flesh set their minds on the things of the flesh, but those who live according to the Spirit set their minds on the things of the Spirit. 6 To set the mind on the flesh is death, but to set the mind on the Spirit is life and peace. 7 For this reason the mind that is set on the flesh is hostile to God; it does not submit to God's law—indeed it cannot, 8 and those who are in the flesh cannot please God.

9 But you are not in the flesh; you are in the Spirit, since the Spirit of God dwells in you. Anyone who does not have the Spirit of Christ does not belong to him. 10 But if Christ is in you, though the body is dead because of sin, the Spirit is life because of righteousness. 11 If the Spirit of him who raised Jesus from the dead dwells in you, he who raised Christ from the dead will give life to your mortal bodies also through his Spirit that dwells in you.

12 So then, brothers and sisters, we are debtors, not to the flesh, to live according to the flesh— 13 for if you live according to the flesh, you will die; but if by the Spirit you put to death the deeds of the body, you will live. 14 For all who are led by the Spirit of God are children of God. 15 For you did not receive a spirit of slavery to fall back into fear, but you have received a spirit of adoption.

Textual Notes: Rom 8:1-15

After addressing Roman Jesus-group members directly ("you": 6:11—7:25) in the central passage of this section, Paul now includes himself in the "we" as he further lays out his ideology of the Jesus group, comparing "us" with "them." The comparison here labels "us" as those in the spirit, with "them" being those in the flesh. God's Spirit is God's activity, and for Paul this Spirit is a hallmark of Jesus-group members who accept his gospel and have faith in the God of Israel, who raised Jesus from the dead. The contrasting group, the "they," is the flesh. The flesh refers to human beings as weak, as closed to God. In context, the flesh here is Israel opposed to God's revelation in Christ. These are Israelites who reject Paul's gospel and stand firm in the Law of Moses and the sin of the Golden Calf to which it is always connected. To be in the flesh is to be under sin and under the Law, to reject the offer of the spirit and the freedom God offers now through faith.

8:1-2: These two verses might serve as conclusion to the previous section (and be read there) or as introduction to this section. This ambiguous situation is mirrored in the manuscript record of the word "you" (here singular; some manuscripts have plural, and in some it is "me"). They summarize the contrast Paul set out previously: between the sanctions of law wielded by a living person and the demise of those sanctions when the person in question dies. There is now no condemnation for those who are in Christ Jesus because the previously entitled controlling entity is dead. This previously entitled controlling entity was sin and death, whose law obliged persons subject to sin and death. In Christ Jesus, Jesus-group members are now free of the control of sin and death thanks to the entitlements of the living spirit of God. Why this new condition?

8:3-4: This verse ("for") explains the reason for the new condition. It is an axiom in Israel that for God all things are possible. Israel's Law was quite incapable of ameliorating the situation it was intended to deal with; it proved weak, given the state of sinful Israelites. Nevertheless, God sent his Son to persons under the Law, that is, Israel, characterized as "sinful flesh." In this way God dealt with the culture of willingness to dishonor God, condemning this culture in the flesh, that is, among Israelites. God's way of dealing with sin was to condemn it "in the flesh," so that whatever the Law required might be fulfilled in us who elect to conduct ourselves according to God's Spirit and not in the old Israelite way, "according to the flesh."

8:5-9: Paul now presents another extended comparison between the flesh and the Spirit, between living in the old Israelite way and living in the new Jesus-group way. The old Israelite way entails setting one's mind on the things of the flesh (v. 5), which is death (v. 6), hostile to God and unwilling and unable to submit to God's Law (v. 7). In sum, people who live in the traditional Israelite way cannot please the God of Israel. Those in the spirit, in Jesus groups, have God's spirit dwelling "in you [plural]" (v. 9); they set their mind on the things of the Spirit (v. 5), which is life and peace (v. 6). They belong to Christ because of this Spirit (v. 9b).

8:10-11: Even though Jesus-group members die because death is the outcome of the culture of willingness to dishonor God characteristic of present life in Israel, the spirit they have is life because they are approved and accepted by God. Paul's new name for the God of Israel, "he who raised Jesus from the dead," figures prominently here. The Spirit that Jesus groups have is the very Spirit of the God of Israel. And through this same Spirit God will raise Jesus-group members from the dead as well.

8:12-15: Paul now concludes this passage by underscoring that Jesus-group members have no debt to the traditional Israelite way of life, "to live according to the flesh." If they do, they will die, but if they follow the Spirit, they will live. Living in line with God's Spirit makes Jesus-group members adopted children of God, since that Spirit is not one of slavery, entailing fear of the master. The analogy of adoption as a description of the relationship of Jesus-group members to God is a Hellenistic analogy. Traditional Israel (and contemporary Islam) do not have the practice of adoption.

Children of God 8:16-18

8:15b When we cry, "Abba! Father!" 16 it is that very Spirit bearing witness with our spirit that we are children of God, 17 and if children, then heirs, heirs of God and joint heirs with Christ—if, in fact, we suffer with him so that we may also be glorified with him.

18 I consider that the sufferings of this present time are not worth comparing with the glory about to be revealed to us.

Textual Notes: Rom 8:16-18

As throughout his letters, Paul's reference to the Spirit always entails some altered state of consciousness phenomena, often with ensuing behavior. This reference follows from the nature of the analogy of the Spirit. "Spirit" literally means wind, breeze. For people of antiquity the wind was mysterious; no one could predict it, no one knew where it came from, no one knew where it went. Yet when strong enough, all knew the wind was present by means of effects, whether a damaged tree or a dust storm or some equivalent phenomenon ascribed to the activity of the wind. God acting among human beings was considered like the wind. Holy Spirit or God's Spirit always refers to God's activity. **Altered State of Consciousness.**

8:15b-16: These verses describes an altered state of consciousness experience of Jesus groups, as group members cry out "*Abba*" (Aramaic, meaning "O Father!) or "*ho Pater*" (Greek, meaning "O Father"). Paul ascribes this cry to the Spirit of God present at Jesus-group worship and witnessing by the very cry that group members are in fact children of God.

8:17: Thus Paul concludes that if we are children of God, then we are heirs of God's patrimony, joint heirs of Christ. What this entails is that we suffer as he did with a view to our being honored by God (the meaning of "being glorified") through being raised from the dead as Jesus was.

8:18: Still focused on the present, Paul notes that no matter what might befall us, nothing is comparable to the public and visible honor (Greek: glory) to be bestowed by God. Paul considers this honor as forthcoming, to be revealed in us soon.

Children of God: Creation Awaits and We Await 8:19-30

8:19 For the creation waits with eager longing for the revealing of the children of God; 20 for the creation was subjected to futility, not of its own will but by the will of the one who subjected it, in hope 21 that the creation itself will be set free from its bondage to decay and will obtain the freedom of the glory of the children of God. 22 We know that the whole creation has been groaning in labor pains until now; 23 and not only the creation, but we ourselves, who have the first fruits of the Spirit, groan inwardly while we wait for adoption, the redemption of our bodies. 24 For in hope we were saved. Now hope that is seen is not hope. For who hopes for what is seen? 25 But if we hope for what we do not see, we wait for it with patience. 26 Likewise the Spirit helps us in our weakness; for we do not know how to pray as we ought, but that very Spirit intercedes with sighs too deep for words. 27 And God, who searches the heart, knows what is the mind of the Spirit, because the Spirit intercedes for the saints according to the will of God.

28 We know that all things work together for good for those who love God, who are called according to his purpose. 29 For those whom he foreknew he also predestined to be conformed to the image of his Son, in order that he might be the firstborn within a large family. 30 And those whom he predestined he also called; and those whom he called he also justified; and those whom he justified he also glorified.

Textual Notes: Rom 8:19-30

This passage may be surprising for modern readers who confine their religious vision to the human soul or to people in human society. In his vision of the soon to be revealed glorification of Jesus-group members, Paul includes all of God's creation, made subject to sin because of humans. All of creation includes celestial as well as terrestrial entities, since for first-century Mediterraneans, the human environment included entities in the sky as well as on the land. The ancients believed there was mutual influence and impact of these spheres on each other—all created by God.

8:19-21: The word "revealing" is the Greek *apokalypsis*. Perhaps it is significant that the apocalypse or revelation of Jesus-group members in their true, new being as children of God has cosmic repercussions (much like the New Testament book of Revelation, which is about both the celestial and the terrestrial realms). Paul's Israelite tradition raised questions about the outcome of Adam's sin not only for human beings but for all creation. And Paul now addresses the issue in terms of Jesus' resurrection and Jesus-group members' glorification. God's transforming activity embraces all of creation. All creatures are now subject to futility, that is, pointlessness and inadequacy, indicated by death and decay (v. 21), the opposite of immorality and endless life. All creatures, too, were created for the "freedom of the glory of the children of God" (v. 21). This, presumably, is a conclusion Paul draws from the quality and significance of Jesus' being raised by the God of Israel. God's raising Jesus indicates an end to death, both for those who have faith in God and who will share in a glory like that of Jesus and for all creation who will share in some way in that faith. This is a sort of mirror image of the situation prior to the entrance of sin into the world, and with it loss of life for all creation.

Here, hope means abiding confidence and trust in God rooted in personal allegiance to God, which is part and parcel of faith.

8:22-23: That all creation and we ourselves have been groaning in something like labor pains until now is another of Paul's conclusions from the story of Genesis and the positive mirror image in the resurrected Jesus. Thanks to the presence of the Spirit, we enjoy something like the first fruits of a harvest, groaning and awaiting our adoption to be realized with the redemption of ourselves. Redemption means restoration to lost status and honor.

8:24-25: In our abiding confidence in God we have been rescued from the culture of willingness to dishonor God. Our hope is abiding confidence that God will effect for us what has been shown forth in the resurrection of Jesus. This expected reality is not yet apparent to us, so, supported by God's Spirit, we await in confidence God's power.

8:26-27: Paul's description of how the Spirit supports Jesus-group members in their patient and abiding confidence in God again points to altered states of consciousness experiences. In these states Jesus-group members experience the Spirit interceding without words, interceding according to what pleases God. God searches the heart; the Spirit acts and performs. **Three Zones of Personality.**

8:28-30: Paul now makes some inferences on the basis of the after-the-fact predestination perspective common in first-century Israel. This perspective held that one can be sure of God's will after something happens. After one is married, one can be sure God wanted one to be married. After a flood or a storm one can be sure God willed that flood or storm to happen. So, too, the fact that a person belonged to a Jesus group meant that God called that person to become a member of the group.

As Israelite lore had it, all things work together for good for those who love God. To this principle Paul adds that those who love God are those "called according to his purpose." This calling is rooted in Jesus' resurrection. Paul takes an analogy from the common appreciation of the firstborn child. The firstborn child enables all other children from the same womb to be born. The firstborn opens the womb so that all subsequent offspring contained therein like nesting dolls might emerge. Thus the firstborn deserves special respect. Similarly, as the firstborn of the dead, the resurrected Jesus enables all who believe in God's raising him to be conformed to his image (v. 29). And because they actually believe in God's having raised Jesus, Jesus-group members have been foreknown by God and predestined to be called. With their call they have been approved and found acceptable by God (that is, justified), worthy of being honored with their own resurrection from the dead.

Conclusion: God's Role 8:31-39

8:31 What then are we to say about
these things? If God is for us, who is against
us? 32 He who did not withhold his own
Son, but gave him up for all of us, will
he not with him also give us everything
else? 33 Who will bring any charge against
God's elect? It is God who justifies. 34 Who
is to condemn? It is Christ Jesus, who
died, yes, who was raised, who is at the
right hand of God, who indeed intercedes
for us. 35 Who will separate us from the
love of Christ? Will hardship, or distress,
or persecution, or famine, or nakedness,
or peril, or sword? 36 As it is written,

"For your sake we are being killed all
day long;
we are accounted as sheep to be
slaughtered."

37 No, in all these things we are more than
conquerors through him who loved us. 38 For
I am convinced that neither death, nor life,
nor angels, nor rulers, nor things present,
nor things to come, nor powers, 39 nor
height, nor depth, nor anything else in all
creation, will be able to separate us from
the love of God in Christ Jesus our Lord.

Textual Notes: Rom 8:31-39

This passage marks the close of the large central section of the letter to the Romans running from 3:21 to 8:30. The passage deals with the new revelation of the God of Israel presently available to Israelites, as underscored by their reconciliation with God, the Roman Jesus group's own liberation, and their experience of the Spirit.

As this conclusion indicates, Paul along with other early Jesus-group thinkers ascribed the origin of the Jesus movement and the Jesus groups that espoused it to the God of Israel. In somewhat anachronistic terms we might say that according to our ancestors in faith it was the God of Israel who founded Christianity (and not Jesus, Paul, or anyone else). This passage eloquently describes Paul's understanding of the role of God as the founder and abiding supporter of the Jesus movement and its participants.

8:31-34: God demonstrates his concern for and continued support of Jesus-group members by the fact that he gave up his Son for all of us, God's elect (v. 33); hence

God will give us everything else. God himself makes us acceptable and worthy of approbation ("justifies," v. 33). Jesus, who died and was raised, presently intercedes for us at the right hand of God enthroned in the sky. With God for us, who can withstand against us?

8:35: Love means interpersonal attachment revealed in action. The love of Christ here refers to Christ's attachment to all called by God; after all he is the first-born who enables all who follow to participate in God's future raising of the dead. Because he is firstborn and continued intercessor on our behalf, there is nothing to separate us from Christ's attachment to us. Paul lists a range of social conflicts and social pressures that might be brought to bear on Jesus-group members. In spite of these, Christ will be faithful. The scripture quote from Ps 43:23 LXX offers divine approbation for this view.

8:37-39: Now Paul turns to God's attachment to Jesus groups and their members, rooted in Christ Jesus our Lord. While dealing with Christ Jesus' attachment or love, Paul lists social conflicts and calamities. Note that when describing God's attachment or love, Paul's list is cosmic: first, the ultimate human condition, death and life; then a variety of cosmic entities: angels, angelic rulers, controllers of the present and the forthcoming, angelic powers, controllers of the celestial heights or terrestrial depths or any other creature—none of these can deny us access to our loving God in Christ Jesus our Lord. The scenario Paul describes consists of a series of cosmic entities that can actually cut us off from God, either by loss of life or by denial of access as we make our way through the cosmos to the realm of God. These cosmic entities are well known (see Malina and Pilch 2000). Some have as their task to keep creatures away from God, thus protecting God's holiness and majesty (much like palace guards deny access to the king).

VIII. Rom 9:1—11:36 Recalcitrant Israel

Romans 9–11 takes up the topic of Israel once more, a topic previously dealt with in Romans 2–3. In the previous parallel section, Paul dealt with Israel and the Law of Moses, the Ten Commandments, circumcision, and the advantages of the customs of Judea, that is, Judaism. Now Paul treats of Israel in an entirely different perspective. Here he deals with two major questions: First, why haven't all Israelites believed in their God's raising Jesus from the dead? And second, because of Israelite unbelief in this recent revelation of the God of Israel, does that mean that the God of Israel rejects his previously chosen people? In the process of dealing with these questions, Paul sets out his attitudes toward his fellow Israelites with whom he shares common ancestry and a common story. The attitudes that Paul expresses toward the house of Israel here are rooted in both the fact that he is addressing Israelite Jesus-group members who live in a large Israelite enclave in

Rome (so what does Paul think of those Israelite neighbors of theirs?) and the fact that there is a number of non-Israelites who have come to join their Jesus-group ranks (so what does Paul think about non-Israelites ["Gentiles"] in the Jesus gathering?). The fact that Paul has to deal separately with the question of non-Israelites in the Roman Jesus group(s) would indicate that the presence of non-Israelite Jesus-group members is exceptional and anomalous as far as Paul is concerned. Perhaps he was known for avoiding non-Israelites as Jesus-group members. So we ask, what is his attitude to non-Israelite Jesus-group members such as those in the Roman community?

Question 1: Why Haven't All Israelites Believed in Their God's Raising Jesus from the Dead? 9:1—10:4

Paul's Assessment of His Fellow Israelites 9:1-5

9:1 I am speaking the truth in Christ—I am not lying; my conscience confirms it by the Holy Spirit— 2 I have great sorrow and unceasing anguish in my heart. 3 For I could wish that I myself were accursed and cut off from Christ for the sake of my own people, my kindred according to the flesh. 4 They are Israelites, and to them belong the adoption, the glory, the covenants, the giving of the law, the worship, and the promises; 5 to them belong the patriarchs, and from them, according to the flesh, comes the Messiah, who is over all, God blessed forever. Amen.

Textual Notes: Rom 9:1-5

Rom 9:1-5 and 10:1-4 form an inclusion marking off this first section.

9:1-3: Paul gives his word of honor, backed up by a type of self-curse. Both behaviors simply underscore his sincerity relative to Jesus-group members whom he has never met as well as the importance of what he is about to set out. Paul is a collectivistic personality, more concerned with ingroup boundaries and social integrity than with individualistic self-reliance. **Collectivistic Personality.** As a group-oriented, collectivistic personality his career as change agent is rooted in his concern for his fellow Israelites, his people. His admission in these verses is quite to be expected and predictable. After all, Jesus proclaimed theocracy to and for Israelites, to be effected by the God of Israel. That all Israelites did not believe that the God of Israel raised Jesus from the dead provoked a deep, ingroup problem for Paul as well as other New Testament authors.

9:4-5: Now Paul lists the salient characteristics of Israelite collective identity, usually called "ethnicity." Herodotus (8.144.2) defined Hellenic social identity in terms of four features: common blood, common language, common way of life, and common worship. Herodotus excluded common geography or territory since he presumed an immobile population as well as unconcern for outsiders. In Israel these common features were called "ancestral" or "traditional": same ancestors, same language as ancestors used, same ancestral customs, same ancestral worship, and same ancestral land. Ties to ancestral land emerged with the Persian formation of Judea with an "Israel" story during the immigration of elite Judean exiles. In taking natives into exile, conquering nations had no interest in nonelites. They wanted to benefit from the elites. Of course, the categories used to develop a group's social identity are all socially contrived categories used to draw up boundaries and to distinguish "them" from "us." In the ancient Mediterranean, every *ethnos* had a social identity marked by such common ancestral or traditional features that supported its ethnocentrism.

Peoplehood is a form of ingroup social organization in terms of social boundaries. These social boundaries consist of ascribed qualities that are said to inhere in ingroup members, thus marking them off from other groups. What marked off the people Israel over against non-Israelites (called *ta ethnē* or the peoples) were the features listed by Paul: the adoption, the glory, the covenants, the giving of the law, the worship, the promises, the patriarchs, and according to the flesh, the Messiah, Jesus. Interestingly, Paul makes no mention of common language, circumcision, or homeland. Since he deals almost exclusively with Israelites in large non-Israelites population areas, these Israelites were Hellenists, uncircumcised and with no desire to live in Palestine. Such, presumably, was the Roman Jesus group to which Paul writes.

True Israel 9:6-13

9:6 It is not as though the word of God had failed. For not all Israelites truly belong to Israel, 7 and not all of Abraham's children are his true descendants; but "It is through Isaac that descendants shall be named for you." 8 This means that it is not the children of the flesh who are the children of God, but the children of the promise are counted as descendants. 9 For this is what the promise said, "About this time I will return and Sarah shall have a son." 10 Nor is that all; something similar happened to Rebecca when she had conceived children by one husband, our ancestor Isaac. 11 Even before they had been born or had done anything good or bad (so that God's purpose of election might continue, 12 not by works but by his call) she was told, "The elder shall serve the younger." 13 As it is written,

"I have loved Jacob,
but I have hated Esau."

Textual Notes: Rom 9:6-13

Paul's social identity was rooted in the house of Israel (see, e.g., Phil 3:5). He was an Israelite. The considerations in this chapter indicate that Paul underwent a type of group identity dissonance. This sort of dissonance derived from the discrepancy between his attitude toward the innovation he proclaimed and the overt behavior of his fellow Israelites in ignoring or rejecting this innovation. Individuals adopting some innovation as Paul did tend to change their attitudes to make them consonant with the behavior demanded by Jesus-group norms. To make his behavior consonant with his attitudes he had to explain to himself and to others why so many of his ingroup Israelites rejected his gospel and all it entailed. This explanation, in many forms, ran as follows: "For not all Israelites truly belong to Israel, and not all of Abraham's children are his true descendants" (vv. 6-7; a similar view is found in the Synoptics, John, and Revelation). Rather, the opposite is true: those Israelites who believe God's revelation in the death and resurrection of Jesus truly belong to Israel; they are the true descendants of Abraham (a point made clearly in Gal 3:6-18 and taken up again in what follows).

9:6: As Paul now demonstrates, "the word of God" concerning God's promise to Abraham did not fail, since, contrary to popular Israelite belief, Abraham's true descendants are in fact children of the promise. Abraham's children of the flesh are Ishmael and Isaac, but only Isaac is the child of the promise. The same is true with Isaac's children of the flesh, Esau and Jacob. Only Jacob is the child of the promise.

9:7-9: To prove that not all of Abraham's children are his true descendants, Paul cites Gen 21:12: "It is through Isaac that descendants shall be named for you." Isaac is the child of the promise of Gen 21:12: "About this time I will return and Sarah shall have a son."

9:11-12: Paul applies the principle stated in vv. 7-8. What Paul says of Isaac held equally for Jacob: these children of the promise, even "before they had been born or had done anything good or bad," fulfill God's purpose of election by God's call—not by works. Of course the same is true of those called by God to be members of Jesus groups.

9:12-13: Again, he proves his point by citing Gen 25:23: "The elder shall serve the younger," followed by Mal 1:2-3: "I have loved Jacob, but I have hated Esau."

God Elects True Israel Alone 9:14-29

9:14 What then are we to say? Is there
injustice on God's part? By no means!
15 For he says to Moses,

"I will have mercy on whom I have mercy,
and I will have compassion on whom I have compassion."

16 So it depends not on human will or exer-
tion, but on God who shows mercy. 17 For
the scripture says to Pharaoh, "I have raised you up for the very purpose of showing my power in you, so that my name may be proclaimed in all the earth."
18 So then he
has mercy on whomever he chooses, and he hardens the heart of whomever he chooses.

19 You will say to me then, "Why then does he still find fault? For who can resist his will?"
20 But who indeed are you, a human being, to argue with God? Will what is molded say to the one who molds it, "Why have you made me like this?"
21 Has
the potter no right over the clay, to make out of the same lump one object for special use and another for ordinary use?
22 What
if God, desiring to show his wrath and to make known his power, has endured with much patience the objects of wrath that are made for destruction;
23 and what if he has
done so in order to make known the riches of his glory for the objects of mercy, which he has prepared beforehand for glory—
24
including us whom he has called, not from the Jews only but also from the Gentiles?

25 As indeed he says in Hosea,

"Those who were not my people I will call 'my people,'
and her who was not beloved I will call 'beloved.'"

26 "And in the very place where it was said to them, 'You are not my people,'
there they shall be called children of the living God."

27 And Isaiah cries out concerning
Israel, "Though the number of the children of Israel were like the sand of the sea, only a remnant of them will be saved;
28 for the
Lord will execute his sentence on the earth quickly and decisively."
29 And as Isaiah
predicted,

"If the Lord of hosts had not left survivors to us,
we would have fared like Sodom
and been made like Gomorrah."

Textual Notes: Rom 9:14-29

9:14-17: What is the basis for God's choosing one and not another, for calling one and not another? It has nothing to do with human effort or actions, but rather rests on God's choice alone. To demonstrate this point Paul marshals two scriptural passages: Exod 33:19 (cited in v. 15) and Exod 9:16 (cited in v. 17).

9:18: On God hardening the heart, see Exod 7:3, 13-14; 8:19; 9:12; 10:1, 20, 27; 11:10.

9:19-21: If God determines whom he chooses to call and whom not to call, then why can God find fault, since everything happens according to his will anyway? Paul answers this objection with a comparison. God is compared to a potter, and humans are made from clay (as in the creation story in Gen 2:4; see further Isa 29:16; 45:9; Jer 18:1-11; Wis 15:7; Sir 33:13). The potter molds as he wishes, for special use or for ordinary use. The clay has nothing to say about it.

9:22-24: Paul now describes what he believes God is up to. Like an honorable king whose honor has been impugned by "the objects of wrath that are made for destruction," God wishes to take satisfaction ("show his wrath") and make known his power. This will affirm his honor ("make known the riches of his glory") among the "objects of his mercy," which include those whom God has called, namely, Israelites living in Judea and among the non-Israelites.

9:24: God's call goes to all of us Israelites, not only from those resident in Judea, but also from those resident among non-Israelites.

9:25-29: Paul argues that his is a fair assessment, since it was indicated by what God said through his prophets Hosea and Isaiah. Of course Hosea (1:10; 2:23) speaks only of Israelites, now called "my people" and "beloved," indeed "children of the living God." And Isa 10:22-23 stated that only a remnant of Israel responds to God's initiative. In Isa 1:9 the prophet likewise speaks of the survivors of Israel saved from the fate of Sodom and Gomorrah.

Many interpreters read vv. 24-28 as applying to non-Israelites now included in Israelite Jesus groups. But since Paul's activity is among Israelites living among non-Israelites and he does not recruit non-Israelites or have a gospel of God for them, this passage can apply only to Israelite Jesus-group members. His scriptural argument would make sense only to them and their fellow Israelites!

True Israel Is Rooted in Faith 9:30—10:4

9:30 What then are we to say? Gentiles, who did not strive for righteousness, have attained it, that is, righteousness through faith; 31 but Israel, who did strive for the righteousness that is based on the law, did not succeed in fulfilling that law. 32 Why not? Because they did not strive for it on the basis of faith, but as if it were based on works. They have stumbled over the stumbling stone, 33 as it is written,

"See, I am laying in Zion a stone that
will make people stumble,
a rock that will make them
fall,
and whoever believes in him will
not be put to shame."

10:1 Brothers and sisters, my heart's desire and prayer to God for them is that they may be saved. 2 I can testify that they have a zeal for God, but it is not enlightened. 3 For, being ignorant of the righteousness that comes from God, and seeking to establish their own, they have not submitted to God's righteousness. 4 For Christ is the end of the law so that there may be righteousness for everyone who believes.

Textual Notes: Rom 9:30–10:4

9:30-33: Back to the original problem: what is wrong that many in Israel reject the gospel of God? Paul contrasts "peoples [NRSV: "Gentiles"] who did not strive for righteousness" with "Israel who pursued the righteous law" (NRSV paraphrases this). The majority of Israelites outside Palestine and outside the circles of Pharisaic scribalism did not observe the Law with any great devotedness. This nonobservant Israelite group, a group of "peoples [NRSV: "Gentiles"] who did not strive for righteousness" is contrasted with those Israelites who attempted to fulfill the Law. This latter did not succeed in fulfilling the Law because of a lack of faith in God, who raised Jesus from the dead. God has set Jesus as a stumbling block for Zion, yet God is the source of honor. The scriptural quotation in v. 33 combines Isa 28:16; 8:14. Christ as stumbling block is a well-known Jesus-group theme: Matt 21:42; Acts 4:11; 1 Pet 2:6-8.

10:1-3: With all his heart and prayers, Paul wishes for all Israelites to be saved. This salvation, of course, means being saved from God's wrath, shortly to appear. While observant Israelites are zealous for the things of God, they are ignorant of the fact that God's approval and acceptance cannot be acquired by their efforts, but only ascribed by God to those who submit to God's righteousness, through faith in God's revelation in Jesus' death and resurrection. This is, in short, Paul's gospel of the God of Israel.

10:4: The reason for this is that Jesus the Messiah is the goal and purpose of the Torah that those Israelites attempt to observe. The approval and acceptance of God that some Israelites have sought through their Torah observance come from believing in what the God of Israel has done in the death and resurrection of Jesus.

A Description of Law-Observant Israel's Unbelief 10:5-21

The Fault Lies with Israelite Unbelievers, Not with God 10:5-15

10:5 Moses writes concerning the righteousness that comes from the law, that "the person who does these things will live by them." 6 But the righteousness that comes from faith says, "Do not say in your heart, 'Who will ascend into heaven?'" (that is, to bring Christ down) 7 "or 'Who will descend into the abyss?'" (that is, to bring Christ up from the dead). 8 But what does it say?

"The word is near you,
on your lips and in your heart"

(that is, the word of faith that we proclaim); 9 because if you confess with your lips that Jesus is Lord and believe in your heart that God raised him from the dead, you will be saved. 10 For one believes with the heart and so is justified, and one confesses with the mouth and so is saved. 11 The scripture says, "No one who believes in him will be put to shame." 12 For there is no distinction between Jew and Greek; the same Lord is Lord of all and is generous to all who call on him. 13 For, "Everyone who calls on the name of the Lord shall be saved."

14 But how are they to call on one in whom they have not believed? And how are they to believe in one of whom they have never heard? And how are they to hear without someone to proclaim him? 15 And how are they to proclaim him unless they are sent? As it is written, "How beautiful are the feet of those who bring good news!"

Textual Notes: Rom 10:5-15

Paul strings together a number of scriptural passages in order to demonstrate (clearly to Israelites, for whom such an argument has probative value) that Israelite unbelief and rejection of the innovation of the gospel of the God of Israel is the fault of those Israelites, zealous though they be, who strive for divine approval and acceptance on the basis of the Law. That they do so is their own fault, not the fault of God.

10:5: Throughout the passage "righteousness" means divine acceptance and approval. Israelites believed they had such acceptance and approval by reason of belonging to the house of Israel. Their concern was to maintain the exclusivity (holiness) that such divine approval required. The citation of Lev 18:5, "the person who does these things will live by them," is ascribed to Moses, specifying divine approval as coming from the Torah.

10:6-8: Paul now contrasts Torah-based divine approval with faith-based divine approval, citing Deut 30:12-14 (compare Bar 3:29-30): "Do not say in your heart, 'Who will ascend into heaven?'" (that is, to bring Christ down) "or 'Who will descend into the abyss?'" (that is, to bring Christ up from the dead). But what does it say? "The word is near you, on your lips and in your heart" (that is, the word of faith that we proclaim)." The comments in parentheses are Paul's interpretation of the passage. In the context of Deuteronomy, the references to seeking in the sky or in the abyss for the word of God that is nearby refer to God's Law. Paul takes the statements to refer to Israel's Messiah. Of course, the one who brings Christ down and raises him up is the God of Israel. The word we seek is quite present in the gospel of God.

10:9-10: Consequently, all that is necessary for divine acceptance and approval is acceptance of the gospel of God, marked by professing the Lordship of Jesus and belief that God raised Jesus from the dead. The statement is put together in bracketed fashion: lips—heart—heart—mouth. **Three-Zone Personality.** The outcome is being saved, a high context Israelite ingroup term for rescue from God's forthcoming wrath. **Wrath.**

10:11-13: Such belief in the God of Israel will not lead to shame, an important Mediterranean consideration and motive. The citation of Isa 28:16 proves it: "No one who believes in him will be put to shame." "No one" means all who believe, whether Judean Israelites or Hellenistic Israelites. The Lord is Lord of all Israel. All that is necessary is to call upon the Lord. "Name" means person in the first century. Appeal to the Lord results in being saved from God's wrath, as Joel 2:32 demonstrates.

10:14-15: With this passage, Paul explains to the Roman Jesus gatherings what he is up to. He proclaims his gospel of God to his fellow Israelites so they may believe in what the God of Israel has done in the death and resurrection of Jesus and learn about the forthcoming kingdom of God. The concluding statement from Isa 52:7 underscores the value of Paul's activity.

Law Observant Israel's Disobedience 10:16-21

10:16 But not all have obeyed the good news; for Isaiah says, "Lord, who has believed our message?" 17 So faith comes from what is heard, and what is heard comes through the word of Christ.

18 But I ask, have they not heard? Indeed they have; for

"Their voice has gone out to all the earth,
and their words to the ends of the world."

19 Again I ask, did Israel not understand? First Moses says,

"I will make you jealous of those who are not a nation;
with a foolish nation I will make you angry."

20 Then Isaiah is so bold as to say,

"I have been found by those who did not seek me;
I have shown myself to those who did not ask for me."

21 But of Israel he says, "All day long I have held out my hands to a disobedient and contrary people."

Textual Notes: Rom 10:16-21

It seems that in this whole section, Paul is concerned with law-observant Israel who have rejected the gospel of God. He made the distinction between nonobservant and observant Israel previously (9:30-31).

10:16-18: Here Paul presumes Israel's scriptures have already indicated that not all Israel will accept the gospel of God, citing Isa 53:1 to this effect. As he previously noted, faith comes from hearing the gospel of God, called here "the word about Christ." And those observant Israelites have heard this gospel of God, as Ps 18:5 notes: "Their voice has gone out to all the earth, and their words to the ends of the world."

10:19: And they did understand that gospel. To make his point, Paul cites Deut 32:21: "I will make you jealous of those who are not a nation; with a foolish nation I will make you angry." Of course in this context, the foolish people (NRSV: "nation") are nonobservant Israelites. The observant Israelites, rejecters of the gospel of God, will be made jealous. The word translated "make jealous" actually means "to provoke to passionate concern for what is rightfully one's own" (Esler 2003:107–8). Even Isaiah dared to say that Israelite nonobservers of the Law were the ones who found divine approval and acceptance: "I have been found by those who did not seek me; I have shown myself to those who did not ask for me."

10:21: In Paul's high context argument, it was of Torah-observant Israel that God said: "All day long I have held out my hands to a disobedient and contrary people" (Isa 65:2).

Question 2: Has God Rejected Law-Observant Israel? 11:1-36

Has God Rejected Israel? 11:1-12

11:1 I ask, then, has God rejected his people? By no means! I myself am an Israelite, a descendant of Abraham, a member of the tribe of Benjamin. 2 God has not rejected his people whom he foreknew. Do you not know what the scripture says of Elijah, how he pleads with God against Israel? 3 "Lord, they have killed your prophets, they have demolished your altars; I alone am left, and they are seeking

my life." 4 But what is the divine reply to
him? "I have kept for myself seven thousand
who have not bowed the knee to Baal." 5 So
too at the present time there is a remnant,
chosen by grace. 6 But if it is by grace, it is
no longer on the basis of works, otherwise
grace would no longer be grace.
7 What then? Israel failed to obtain
what it was seeking. The elect obtained it,
but the rest were hardened, 8 as it is written
"God gave them a sluggish spirit,
eyes that would not see
and ears that would not hear,
down to this very day."
9 And David says,
"Let their table become a snare and
a trap,
a stumbling block and a retribution for them;
10 let their eyes be darkened so that
they cannot see,
and keep their backs forever bent."
11 So I ask, have they stumbled so
as to fall? By no means! But through
their stumbling salvation has come to the
Gentiles, so as to make Israel jealous. 12
Now if their stumbling means riches for
the world, and if their defeat means riches
for Gentiles, how much more will their
full inclusion mean!

Textual Notes: Rom 11:1-12

11:1: Paul continues his reflections about the relationship of the God of Israel and the Torah-observant Israelites who reject the gospel of God revealed in the death and resurrection of Jesus. This time he raises a rhetorical question as to whether God has rejected his people Israel, and he answers with his usual "Don't be silly!" It is a silly question because Paul is himself an Israelite and has received divine acceptance and approval through faith in the God of Israel, who raised Jesus from the dead. As a type of proof, Paul once more sets out his credentials for his collectivistic group identity. This is the third time he does so in this section (see 9:1-5 and 10:1-2, which form an inclusion to the first part of the section).

11:2: Faithful to his group identity, he notes that "God has not rejected his people" (Ps 94:14), to which he adds, "whom he foreknew." This divine foreknowledge is a theme that has surfaced several times in his letters. Paul can conclude that God has foreknown certain things and events because they have in fact occurred. This is a type of divine foreknowledge that people can know after-the-fact. Paul will now describe God's people, whom God has not rejected since they do in fact accept the innovation of the gospel of God. He makes his point with another string of scriptural "pearls."

11:3-7: He opens his argument with a rather harsh "do you not know . . . ?" When addressed to Torah experts, the phrase is a challenge to honor. Perhaps Paul has some opponents in mind who claimed that because of the way Paul has presented his gospel of God, it is clear that God has rejected his people, specifically the law-observant Israelites who have refused to accept this gospel. He cites an incident in 1 Kgs 19:10-14, in which Elijah pleads with God against the Israelites who oppose him: "Lord, they have killed your prophets, they have demolished your altars; I alone am left, and they are seeking my life." But God replies to the holy man: "I have kept for myself seven thousand who have not bowed the knee to Baal" (1 Kgs 19:18). From this Paul concludes that it was by divine favor (Greek: *charis*, patronage favor) that God chose the remaining faithful ones. God chose them not because of what they did (as the Law-observant Israelites would think), but simply as unowed favor.

11:8: Paul concludes, "What then?" Israelites at the time of Elijah did not obtain what they were seeking, presumably just like Law-observant Israelites now, during Paul's time. But those chosen did obtain what they sought, while those who did not were hardened. The passive voice of this last verb presumes God is the one hardening the faculties of those who opposed Elijah (and Paul). Proof is forthcoming from Israel's scriptures: "God gave them a sluggish spirit, eyes that would not see and ears that would not hear, down to this very day" (Deut 29:4; Isa 29:10). And again: "Let their table become a snare and a trap, a stumbling block and a retribution for them; let their eyes be darkened so that they cannot see, and keep their backs forever bent" (Ps 69:22-23) **Three-Zone Personality.**

11:11: Paul now concludes by explaining his take on why any non-Israelites are in Jesus groups at all. The fact is that these Torah-observant Israelites have stumbled by refusing the gospel of God. But they have not fallen down. Rather, their stumbling has been the occasion for some non-Israelites to be saved from God's forthcoming wrath. **Wrath.** So what are these non-Israelites doing here in Roman Jesus groups? They can only make Law-observant Israel jealous.

As previously noted, the word translated "make jealous" actually means "to provoke to passionate concern for what is rightfully one's own" (Esler 2003:107–8). Faith in the God of Israel, who raised Jesus from the dead, is an experience that in fact belongs to Israelites and not to non-Israelites. That some non-Israelites adopt such faith both in the God of Israel and in God's raising Israel's Messiah Jesus is to provoke among Law-observant Israelites a passionate concern for what is rightfully their own. Non-Israelites have no right to adopt such faith, much less to be thus made acceptable to the God of Israel. But God has let that happen "to make Israel jealous."

11:12: If that benefit to non-Israelites is so great, Paul urges Roman Jesus-group members to imagine what it would be like for Israel if all Israelites believed in the gospel of God.

Non-Israelite Jesus-Group Members in Rome 11:13-24

11:13 Now I am speaking to you Gentiles. Inasmuch then as I am an apostle to the Gentiles, I glorify my ministry 14 in order to make my own people jealous, and thus save some of them. 15 For if their rejection is the reconciliation of the world, what will their acceptance be but life from the dead! 16 If the part of the dough offered as first fruits is holy, then the whole batch is holy; and if the root is holy, then the branches also are holy.

17 But if some of the branches were broken off, and you, a wild olive shoot, were grafted in their place to share the rich root of the olive tree, 18 do not boast over the branches. If you do boast, remember that it is not you that support the root, but the root that supports you. 19 You will say, "Branches were broken off so that I might be grafted in." 20 That is true. They were broken off because of their unbelief, but you stand only through faith. So do not become proud, but stand in awe. 21 For if God did not spare the natural branches, perhaps he will not spare you. 22 Note then the kindness and the severity of God: severity toward those who have fallen, but God's kindness toward you, provided you continue in his kindness; otherwise you also will be cut off. 23 And even those of Israel, if they do not persist in unbelief, will be grafted in, for God has the power to graft them in again. 24 For if you have been cut from what is by nature a wild olive tree and grafted, contrary to nature, into a cultivated olive tree, how much more will these natural branches be grafted back into their own olive tree.

Textual Notes: Rom 11:13-24

11:13: In this passage, Paul for the first time in Romans takes explicit notice of non-Israelite Jesus-group members in the Roman community. As a rule, Paul ignores the presence of such non-Israelite "brothers," since, it seems, he never recruited any non-Israelites. Nevertheless, he knows that they existed in Roman Jesus groups; hence he obviously feels impelled to recategorize the Israelite and non-Israelite subgroups in Rome into a new common ingroup—at least to assuage his social dissonance that triggers the treatment of Israel in this section.

Paul offers his non-Israelite audience an explanation of what he is up to. As change agent sent to Israelites living among non-Israelites, he takes honor from his service if (NRSV "in order to") he can provoke his fellow Israelites to passionate concern for what is rightfully theirs. This is what "provoke to jealousy" means. And what is rightfully theirs is the gospel of the God of Israel, who raised Jesus from the dead. If they accept this gospel, Paul will thus rescue them from the wrath to come. **Wrath.** But some Torah-observant Israelites have rejected the gospel of God, thus occasioning the reconciliation of Israelites and non-Israelites in the Roman Jesus gathering. When those Torah-observant Israelites finally accept the gospel of God, that will mark life for the dead, perhaps the advent of the kingdom of God.

11:16: In this verse Paul reflects upon the situation of non-Israelites in the Jesus group, using Num 14:21, in which the power of a part of dough can make the whole holy. Here the part is believing Israelites, while the whole is the Roman Jesus group. The mention of root and branches takes Paul to another analogy.

11:17-20: The comparison of Israel to a cultivated olive tree is known from Jer 11:16; Hos 14:6. In Paul's comparison, it is the new Israel, Israelites who are in Christ, who form the cultivated olive tree. Non-Israelites in the Roman Jesus group are considered to be like wild olive shoots grafted onto where Israelite branches were broken off in the cultivated olive tree of this Israelite Jesus group. This Israelite Jesus group is the stock that provided support and fertility, not the engrafted branches. Thus ingrafted non-Israelites cannot make honor claims for themselves at the expense of the branches that had been cut off. Instead of arrogance, in view of their situation in the Jesus group, awe is a more appropriate response (see Esler 2003:122).

11:21-23: Paul's contrast between the natural branches (Greek: *kata physin*) and the unnatural engrafted branches is an interesting comparison. The words for "natural" or "according to nature" and "contrary to nature" (v. 24) are the same used in Romans 1 for Paul's assessment of transgressions. Here non-Israelites in Israelite Jesus groups are engrafted "contrary to nature" (Greek: *para physin*), just like the sexual behavior of Romans in Romans 1 is "contrary to nature."

11:24: Grafting was a well-known practice in the ancient Mediterranean. The normal practice was to transplant a wild olive tree and to make it fruitful by grafting on branches from a cultivated olive tree. Paul reverses the image.

> Having chosen to refer to Israel as a cultivated olive tree, in a circumstance where he was seeking to promote the status of Israel and take his non-Judaean addressees down a peg or two, Paul was now in the fortunate position of being able deliberately to diverge from accepted horticultural

> practice in a manner that would be immediately recognized by his eastern Mediterranean audience as a divergence, by describing the branches inserted into the tree as originating from the wild olive. . . . In opting for the wild olive, when he and his readers well knew that its branches did not bear edible fruit, Paul was consciously crafting an image most unflattering to the non-Judeans. (Esler 2003:122)

In sum, Paul has very little good to say about the presence of non-Israelites in Jesus groups. The olive tree in question, the gathering of those in Christ, is always an Israelite olive tree. Paul's judgment in this regard is no different from that of all other New Testament writers. After all, they were first-century Mediterraneans, and ethnocentrism was a hallmark of the people in that region at this period.

Conclusion 11:25-36

11:25 So that you may not claim to be wiser than you are, brothers and sisters, I want you to understand this mystery: a hardening has come upon part of Israel, until the full number of the Gentiles has come in. 26 And so all Israel will be saved; as it is written,

"Out of Zion will come the Deliverer;
he will banish ungodliness from Jacob."
27 "And this is my covenant with them,
when I take away their sins."

28 As regards the gospel they are enemies of God for your sake; but as regards election they are beloved, for the sake of their ancestors; 29 for the gifts and the calling of God are irrevocable. 30 Just as you were once disobedient to God but have now received mercy because of their disobedience, 31 so they have now been disobedient in order that, by the mercy shown to you, they too may now receive mercy. 32 For God has imprisoned all in disobedience so that he may be merciful to all.

33 O the depth of the riches and wisdom and knowledge of God! How unsearchable are his judgments and how inscrutable his ways!

34 "For who has known the mind of the Lord?
Or who has been his counselor?"
35 "Or who has given a gift to him,
to receive a gift in return?"

36 For from him and through him and to him are all things. To him be the glory forever. Amen.

Textual Notes: Rom 11:25-36

11:25: Paul now concludes his consideration of why some Israelites, usually law-observant Israelites, refuse the revelation of the God of Israel in his raising Jesus from the dead. He still has in mind the presence of non-Israelites in Jesus groups. At bottom, Paul says, something mysterious is afoot. "Mystery" is a secret dealing with the divine plan or activity. What God's plan entails is a hardening upon part of Israel. This is the part that has refused the gospel of God. Why has this happened? To enable the full number of non-Israelites to join Jesus groups. When that happens, then all Israel (Paul's concern) will be saved from the forthcoming wrath. Since this wrath of God is soon to come, this number of non-Israelites cannot be very great! **Wrath.**

11:26-27: That all Israel will be saved from the wrath to come is certain from Israel's scriptures. Paul cites Isa 59:20-21: "Out of Zion will come the Deliverer; he will banish ungodliness from Jacob"; Jesus the deliverer will banish ungodliness from Israel. Then he quotes Isa 27:9: "And this is my covenant with them, when I take away their sins." It is Jesus, through his death and resurrection, who takes away sin in Israel.

11:28-29: Again Paul has non-Israelites in mind when he states that it is for their sake that they reject God's gospel, but for the sake of their ancestors, God remains attached to them. This is a conclusion easy for Paul to make from his collectivistic perspective. Israelite ideology is essentially collectivistic, rooted in ancestrism. From the viewpoint of this ancestrism, God's gifts and the calling are irrevocable.

11:30-31: From an Israelite point of view, non-Israelites are all and always sinners. "Gentile sinners" is a fixed phrase. Hence Paul can tell Roman non-Israelite Jesus-group members that they were once "disobedient to God." Again he repeats that their presence in Jesus groups is due essentially to the fact that some Israelites have rejected the gospel of God. In Paul's perspective, the gospel of God is solely for Israelites, and these exist in fixed number in a limited good society. For non-Israelites to find a place in that group, some Israelites had to yield their place, and this they did by their disobedience.

11:32: Just as God has hardened the hearts of those Law-observant Israelites so that they have rejected the gospel of God, so, too, "God has imprisoned all (of them) in disobedience so that he may be merciful to all (of them)." We add "of them" after "all" in this Pauline statement because that is what Paul means in this high context statement. The reference is to the part of Israel that rejects the gospel of God, mentioned at the outset of the passage in v. 25. It is this part of Israel that has now been disobedient (v. 31). (On the other hand, this divine imprisonment might also include the non-Israelites, now shown mercy, and the part of Israelites who reject the Gospel now.)

11:33-35: Paul now weaves his final observation with a tissue of scriptural statements to express wonder at the mystery of God. It reads like a hymn. He opens with the exclamation: "O the depth of the riches and wisdom and knowledge of God! How unsearchable are his judgments and how inscrutable his ways!" He then adds a statement from Isa 40:13: "For who has known the mind of the Lord? Or who has been his counselor?" Then a statement from Job 41:3: "Or who has given a gift to him, to receive a gift in return?"

11:36: This verse, a doxology in praise of God, may have been added by some scribe to round out this short hymn; however see 1 Cor 8:6; Rom 1:25; 9:5; 16:27.

IX. Rom 12:1—13:14
You: Jesus-Group Values

Paul now turns to address the Roman Jesus groups again (note Paul's use of "you" plural) in a chiastic parallel to 2:1-13, where Paul addresses "you" Jesus-group members—Judeans and Hellenists. Romans 12:1—13:14 forms a unit of sorts that Edward Gordon Selwyn (1947:363–466) long ago identified in a number of New Testament documents (1 Thessalonians, Colossians, Ephesians, 1 Peter, James) and called "catechesis." **Pauline Norms.** This unit typically contains a statement of the attitudes characteristic of the new way of Jesus-group living, a description of various social responsibilities, and a concluding reminder of the critical nature of the times, with emphasis on Jesus-group responsibility. The general pattern has the following themes:

- On Jesus-group worship that consists of the proper behaviors of individuals in community (12:1-8)
- Exhortations with maxim-like formulas modeled on and derived from Israel's scriptures (12:9-21)
- The theme of being subject or subordination to authority (13:1-6)
- Exhortation based on the holiness of God (13:7-10)
- Theme of putting off and putting on a demand forms an act of deliberate renunciation to disentangle Jesus-group members from the values and life-style of society at large (13:12-14)

Basic Jesus-Group Analogies: Sacrifice and One Body 12:1-8

12:1 I appeal to you therefore, brothers and sisters, by the mercies of God, to present your bodies as a living sacrifice, holy and acceptable to God, which is your spiritual worship. 2 Do not be conformed to this world, but be transformed by the renewing of your minds, so that you may discern what is the will of God—what is good and acceptable and perfect.

3 For by the grace given to me I say to everyone among you not to think of yourself more highly than you ought to think, but to think with sober judgment, each according to the measure of faith that God has assigned. 4 For as in one body we have many members, and not all the members have the same function, 5 so we, who are many, are one body in Christ, and individually we are members one of another. 6 We have gifts that differ according to the grace given to us: prophecy, in proportion to faith; 7 ministry, in ministering; the teacher, in teaching; 8 the exhorter, in exhortation; the giver, in generosity; the leader, in diligence; the compassionate, in cheerfulness.

Textual Notes: Rom 12:1-8

12:1-2: Paul begins the exhortation section of this letter with mention of worship. Ancient worship was heavily focused on sacrifice. A sacrifice is a ritual in which an offering is rendered humanly irretrievable and ingestible and then directed to some controlling higher personage (usually a deity) by someone lower in social status in order to have some life-effect. There are three dimensions to sacrifice. Something that human beings possess or can ingest (eat or drink) is made unfit for normal human use or as food or drink. Animals are killed; flour or oil are poured out into a fire. These transformed "gifts" are directed to a deity—the second dimension of a sacrifice. Finally, the purpose of sacrificing is to have some life-effect: to preserve life or transform life. Sacrifices are always about life-effects. All ancients knew this.

Paul now urges the Romans to live their lives as though they were a "living sacrifice." The sacrificial gift is themselves (this is what "body" refers to—as in somebody, nobody, meaning persons as a whole). The gift needs to be transformed, here specified in v. 2. The process entails not being conformed to society (that is what "this world" means) and instead being transformed by the renewing of their minds. Their thinking/feeling is to work in a brand-new way so that they discern what is pleasing to God, that is, what is good and acceptable and perfect. This type of worship will produce the effects sought through actual sacrifice, that is life-effects.

12:3: Once more, to explain Jesus-group members' relationship to God and to each other, Paul has recourse to the analogy of God as patron. Here focus is on the patron's favors (Greek: *charis,* Latin: *gratia*; NRSV: "grace"). A favor is something a person needs and cannot acquire or cannot acquire at the time needed. Persons have recourse to patrons for favors. In return, those benefited—clients—develop an attachment to the patron, give the patron grants of honor, and defend the patron's honor when it is attacked by others. On the basis of the favor that God the Patron gave Paul to be prophet/apostle, he believes he is entitled (see Rom 1:5) to exhort others to keep their attitudes and consequent conduct in line with the gospel of God that he proclaims and that other Jesus-group members share with him. He opens his exhortation here by urging his audience not to adopt an attitude of willingness to compete for honors over their fellows ("to think of yourself more highly than you ought to think") but to think within the boundaries of their sense of positive shame and to live according to their group task, ascribed to them by God.

12:4-6: For Paul, all Jesus-group members have a group task ascribed by God, called "charism" (see 1 Corinthians 12). And this group task always works for the well-being of the whole, a typical collectivistic appreciation of the primacy of group integrity over individualistic self-reliance. This feature is obvious in Paul's way of imagining the Jesus group as "one body in Christ and individually . . . members of one another."

12:6-8: As in his treatment of this analogy in 1 Corinthians 12, Paul sets out the range of Jesus-group charisms (gifts) deriving from God's patronage or favor (grace). All of the gifts support the Jesus group in its integrity by supporting individual members in their social ingroup orientation.

Generic Admonitions 12:9-21

12:9 Let love be genuine; hate what is evil, hold fast to what is good; 10 love one another with mutual affection; outdo one another in showing honor. 11 Do not lag in zeal, be ardent in spirit, serve the Lord. 12 Rejoice in hope, be patient in suffering, persevere in prayer. 13 Contribute to the needs of the saints; extend hospitality to strangers.

14 Bless those who persecute you; bless and do not curse them. 15 Rejoice with those who rejoice, weep with those who weep. 16 Live in harmony with one another; do not be haughty, but associate with the lowly; do not claim to be wiser than you are. 17 Do not repay anyone evil for evil, but take thought for what is noble in the sight of all. 18 If it is possible, so far as it depends on you, live peaceably with all. 19 Beloved, never avenge yourselves, but leave room for the wrath of God; for it is written, "Vengeance is mine, I will repay, says the Lord." 20 No, "if your enemies are hungry, feed them; if they are thirsty, give them something to drink; for by doing this you will heap burning coals on their heads." 21 Do not be overcome by evil, but overcome evil with good.

Textual Notes: Rom 12:11-21

12:9-10: With the opening sentence as theme it seems that the whole passage refers to ingroup mutual behavior, not with behavior toward the outgroup. In reading the values that Paul encourages in this passage, we should keep in mind that for first-century Mediterraneans there is no internal state without a corresponding external action. Thus "to love" means to perform actions to or for others that demonstrate one's ingroup belonging and support. "To hate" is to perform actions demonstrating that one disdains and has contempt for someone or something (evil persons and behaviors). At times Paul specifies the corresponding external action he has in mind. The same is true for all the internal states recommended by Paul: each internal state will be identified by some external manifestation.

12:10-11: Love is demonstrated by showing honor toward other Jesus-group members. Verse 11 clearly urges action on behalf of others, further explaining what love means. Jesus-group members are to put out effort and act energetically for others without laziness (NRSV: "do not lag in zeal"), to bubble with activity for others (NRSV: "be ardent in spirit"), and to do slave services to others on behalf of their Master (NRSV: "serve the Lord"). Slavery involves depriving a person of freedom of decision and action by means of force or enforced solidarity with a view to the social utility of the enslaving agent (see 6:15-23 above).

12:12: Now attitudes of individuals: a joyful bearing rooted in trust in God's promises, patience in dealing with conflict, and endurance in prayer.

12:13: Back to activities: support for Jesus-group members (called "saints" or "set apart ones" again). Hospitality refers to taking in strangers and showing them the favor of one's patronage.

12:14: To bless a person is the opposite of cursing a person. A curse is a statement and/or action intended to have negative influence by superhuman means on the welfare or behavior of animate entities (persons, animals, spirits, enspirited beings like winds, seas, etc.), against their will or normal modes of activity. A blessing, similarly, is a statement and/or action intended to have positive influence by superhuman means on the welfare or behavior of animate entities (persons, animals, spirits, enspirited beings like winds, seas, etc.), against their will or normal modes of activity. Paul (like Jesus) urges Jesus-group members to deal with outsiders who instigate conflict by wishing them God's benefactions.

12:15-16: The overriding concern being group attachment or love, Paul urges Jesus-group members to share the same outlook and not nurture thoughts of superiority. Instead they ought to situate themselves with what is "humble." Humility (*tapeinosis*) means remaining in one's ascribed social status, the status proper to oneself, not striving for higher honors or yielding to losses in one's status. Paul's advice in 1 Cor 7:24: "Stay in the state in which you were called" is a statement of such humility. Paul's closing phrase (NRSV: "do not claim to be wiser than you are") is better translated: do not think of yourself as more than you are, that is, stay "humble" as just defined.

12:17-21: This segment is about conflict. The rules of Mediterranean honor in challenge situations require striving for satisfaction if one is dishonored. Assessing what is honorable and dishonorable in a challenge situation is the social task of an audience of onlookers. Paul does not urge Roman Jesus-group members to ignore honor challenges but rather to respond with "what is noble in the sight of all." The audience is still required. And even in face of hostility, in face of conflict initiated by others, Jesus-group members should strive for peace and not think of getting satisfaction (or vengeance; NRSV: "wrath"; there is no "of God" in the Greek text). To make his point, Paul cites Deut 32:35, "Vengeance is mine, I will repay, says the Lord," along with Prov 25:21-22 LXX: "If your enemies are hungry, feed them; if they are thirsty, give them something to drink; for by doing this you will heap burning coals on their heads." "To heap burning coals on their heads" means "to shame them." See "Let burning coals fall upon them" (Ps 140:10) in context; also: "Let no sinner say that he has not sinned; for God will burn coals of fire on the head of him who says: 'I have not sinned before God and his glory'" (4 Ezra 16:53).

12:21: This verse states the same thing in other words: overcome evil people by doing good to them.

If one imagines all of the attitudes listed by Paul as present in a single person, one will envision a typical character portrait, a Jesus-group character formed after the values Paul sets forth. The values or virtues listed are not individual items to be acquired, it seems. Rather they are a configuration intended to design the type of character Jesus-group members should be and expect to see in their fellow group members. The values also serve as norms of expected behavior for ingroup interaction—another dimension of Jesus-group social identity.

Attitude toward Civil Authorities 13:1-6

13:1 Let every person be subject to the governing authorities; for there is no authority except from God, and those authorities that exist have been instituted by God. 2 Therefore whoever resists authority resists what God has appointed, and those who resist will incur judgment. 3 For rulers are not a terror to good conduct, but to bad. Do you wish to have no fear of the authority? Then do what is good, and you will receive its approval; 4 for it is God's servant for your good. But if you do what is wrong, you should be afraid, for the authority does not bear the sword in vain! It is the servant of God to execute wrath on the wrongdoer. 5 Therefore one must be subject, not only because of wrath but also because of conscience. 6 For the same reason you also pay taxes, for the authorities are God's servants, busy with this very thing.

Textual Notes: Rom 13:1-6

The be-subject segment consists of two sections, vv. 1-3 with repetition of the term "authority" (four times) and vv. 4-6 with the phrase "for (the authority) is God's servant" (three times).

13:1: Paul sets out his advice to Jesus-group members concerning their attitudes toward civil authorities. The NRSV "governing" translates the Greek "higher-ranking, superior." It is important not to introduce contemporary ideas of government and government officials. The ranking authorities Paul and his contemporaries know are city officials who obtain their roles in various ways. As a rule these city officials were elite landowners essentially concerned for their own well-being and for that of their clients. Roman emperors considered a significant aspect of their role to be that of patron to client Roman citizens (and "citizen" means a person with rights in a city). Here Paul gives advice concerning civil or city authorities. Clearly his Jesus-group members are not "citizens," since he makes no mention of the fact. This is, perhaps, further indication that there were no Roman non-Israelites in the Jesus groups. All that Paul requires is proper "subjection" or "subordination," which would befit resident foreigners or resident aliens.

The word "authority" (Greek: *exousia*) means the socially recognized entitlement to control the behavior of others. For ancient Mediterraneans, such ability to control the behavior of others was ascribed to interpersonal cosmic forces realized by humans representing those forces. In other words, deities of various sorts, with Zeus at the head, actually controlled the human scene. Those wielding civil authority did so on behalf of those cosmic forces. For Israelites, the actual ultimate cosmic force in question was the God of Israel. Paul presumes this in the principle "there is no authority except from (the) God (of Israel)." Hence civil authorities have their public entitlement from the deity.

13:2: It is very important for the contemporary reader that Paul does not envision post-Enlightenment representative democracy. In this system citizens elect representatives to deal with matters of importance to the citizens. Since authorities in this system get their authority from the voting citizenry and not from God, what Paul advises here is irrelevant. Paul envisions a system of aristocratic empire in the control of elites, with ordinary people—the vast majority—being totally powerless unless they have the assistance of a patron.

Hence, to make sense of Paul, one must imagine an elitist system rooted in political patronage, with ranking officials acquiring ascribed positions (by elite birth, cliques, factions, and the like). Since the positions are ascribed, the process can readily be attributed to God (much like one's birth family or gender may be attributed to God). Paul's advice, then, is not to resist these civil authorities; otherwise condemnation will follow. This, of course, belabors the obvious.

13:3-4: In order not to be terrorized by civil authorities, Paul advises that his Jesus-group members "do good," without specifying what that might entail. Individual wrongdoing leads to "wrath," the word customarily used to describe satisfaction taken for dishonoring or shaming behavior. It would seem that in Paul's view, doing wrong dishonors the civil authorities, who must then get satisfaction for the dishonor in order to maintain their honorable ranking status. The NRSV translation that equates "the authority" with an "it" is inadequate, since it does not take into account the Mediterranean interpersonal assessment of the forces that affect human life. "The authority" is always a "who," an honorable person who requires respect.

13:4-5: Paul considers the authority as a person, as "God's servant for your good" (vv. 4 [twice], 6). One must be subject not only for fear of satisfaction one must pay for dishonor but "because of conscience." Conscience means self-awareness based on and rooted in group awareness, that is, sensitivity, intense scrutiny, and assessment by the group. The image Mediterranean persons have of themselves has to be indistinguishable from the image held and presented to them by their significant others in the family, tribe, village, or city quarter. For Jesus-group members, the significant others now constitute their fellow group members or believers. As Paul frequently urges, a meaningful human existence in the Jesus group depends upon a person's full awareness of what others in the group think and feel about oneself, along with one's living up to that awareness. Not living up to that awareness is a breach of conscience! A Jesus-group member with conscience is a respectable, reputable, and honorable person. Respectability, in this social context, would be the characteristic of a person who needs other people in order to grasp his or her own new identity in Christ. Conscience is a sort of internalization of what these other group members say, do, and think about one, since these others play the role of witness and judge. Their verdicts supply a person with grants of honor necessary for a meaningful, humane existence.

13:6: Taxes in the world of Rome were a form of extortion, since taxes went to elites in power for their own purposes. However, elites needed grants of honor from the populace. To this end they offered benefactions in terms of public works and provided patronage for their clients. While ordinary individuals had no rights to benefactions or patronage, they were obliged to pay taxes to the elites who "protected" them. This sort of paternalism undergirds all of Mediterranean patronage society. Paul describes the ranking elites in the system here as "God's *leitourgoi*," (NRSV: "servants"), that is, administrators for the public good.

Conclusion: Final Admonition and Motivation 13:7-14

13:7 Pay to all what is due them—taxes
to whom taxes are due, revenue to whom
revenue is due, respect to whom respect
is due, honor to whom honor is due.
8 Owe no one anything, except to love
one another; for the one who loves another
has fulfilled the law. 9 The commandments,
"You shall not commit adultery; You shall
not murder; You shall not steal; You shall not
covet"; and any other commandment, are
summed up in this word, "Love your neighbor
as yourself." 10 Love does no wrong to a neighbor; therefore, love is the fulfilling of the law.

11 Besides this, you know what time
it is, how it is now the moment for you to
wake from sleep. For salvation is nearer
to us now than when we became believers;
12 the night is far gone, the day is
near. Let us then lay aside the works
of darkness and put on the armor of
light;
13 let us live honorably as in the
day, not in reveling and drunkenness, not
in debauchery and licentiousness, not in
quarreling and jealousy.
14 Instead, put
on the Lord Jesus Christ, and make no
provision for the flesh, to gratify its desires.

Textual Notes: Rom 13:7-14

13:7-8: This exhortation segment is rooted in the holiness of God, the giver of the Ten Commandments. The mention of taxes in the previous verse leads Paul, it seems, to his concluding theme: do not be interpersonally indebted or obligated. He urges Jesus-group members to be free of social encumbrances by paying their debts of interpersonal obligation. The desired state is to owe nothing to anyone. But for Jesus-group members, such freedom from interpersonal, social obligations is not total, since they are still obliged to God's Ten Commandments, as noted in Romans 1. These can be duly summarized in the demand to love one another (citing Lev 19:18, "Love your neighbor as yourself"). Love means group attachment and the behavior that such attachment requires. Without further specification, the group attachment Paul has in mind is attachment to the Jesus group. Such behavior is what fulfills God's demands in the commandments.

13:11: The reminder of the critical nature of the times segues into the conclusion of the "catechesis pattern" and of Paul's exhortation here.

13:12-14: The conclusion of the pattern offers the contrast of light and darkness, night and day, with the image of taking off (v. 12 here: "lay aside") and putting on (vv. 12 and 14). To live in the day is to live honorably, while living in the night entails revelry, drunkenness, debauchery, licentiousness, quarreling, and jealousy. Such behavior, presumably, is dishonorable and shameful in Jesus groups. Putting on the Lord Jesus Christ entails showing no concern for gratifying self.

X. Rom 14:1—15:13 They (the Weak) and the Torah Commandments

This segment on "they" (the weak) and the Torah Commandments has its chiastic parallel in 1:18-32 where Paul treats of "them," that is, non-Israelites and the Ten Commandments. The Hellenistic designation "weak" referred to persons uneducated in the customs and amenities of the cultivated strata of society (*HCNT* 673–74). Driven by unwarranted fears, the "weak" behaved irrationally, guided by their dreads rather than by rational knowledge. In 1 Corinthians Paul calls some in the Corinthian group "the weak" because they do not really believe in the total impotence and decrepit nature of non-Israelite gods and lords in face of our God and Lord. The weak are Israelites still held in the grip of taboo fears in face of both the alleged powers of non-Israelite deities and the alleged obligatory nature of Mosaic Torah requirements, from circumcision to proscribed and prescribed foods and calendrical times. The weak are simply locked in by their Torah-based dreads and unable to understand and follow the abrogation of Mosaic Torah requirements effected by Jesus' death and resurrection. Those Israelite Jesus-group members who are able to accept the abrogation of Mosaic laws as warranted in Christ are the strong. The strong have assimilated the full ramifications of Paul's gospel of God, perhaps because they previously have accommodated to Hellenistic values and have been enculturated in Israelite life in Rome, with no thought of any return to Judea. In this perspective the weak are Judeans or Judean hopefuls; the strong are Hellenists, willing to await God's inauguration of theocracy in Jerusalem.

This section is marked off by the word "welcome" (Greek: *proslambanomai*) at the beginning and at the end. Paul proceeds as follows:

A The Weak and Their Observances 14:1-6
B Exhortation to the Strong 14:7-13
A' Again, the Weak and Their Observances 14:14-23
B' The Strong and Their Attitudes 15:1-7
C Concluding Admonition 15:8-14

The Weak and Their Observances 14:1-6

14:1 Welcome those who are weak in faith, but not for the purpose of quarreling over opinions. 2 Some believe in eating anything, while the weak eat only vegetables. 3 Those who eat must not despise those who abstain, and those who abstain must not pass judgment on those who eat; for God has welcomed them. 4 Who are you to pass judgment on servants of another? It is before their own lord that they stand or fall. And they will be upheld, for the Lord is able to make them stand.

5 Some judge one day to be better than another, while others judge all days to be alike. Let all be fully convinced in their own minds. 6 Those who observe the day, observe it in honor of the Lord. Also those who eat, eat in honor of the Lord, since they give thanks to God; while those who abstain, abstain in honor of the Lord and give thanks to God.

Textual Notes: Rom 14:1-6

14:1-6: Paul obviously addresses the strong in faith, that is, Israelite Hellenists who have accepted the innovation of the God of Israel raising Jesus as Israel's Messiah soon to return. He commands them to show hospitality to their weak fellow Jesus-group Israelites. "To receive" means to show hospitality, that is, to welcome with respect and honor and provide social and physical support. To demonstrate respect and honor means accepting the peculiar demands and behaviors of the people "received"—hence Paul's demand that the weak not be sniped at concerning their reluctance and hesitancy (NRSV: "opinions"; Greek: *dialogismoi*) in face of the behavior and attitude of the strong. The weak eat only vegetables (v. 3), observe calendric taboos (v. 5), abstain from certain foods (v. 6), and follow Judean purity norms (14:14), and in the end we find out that they insist on circumcision (15:8). His clinching argument is that if they are in the Jesus group, "God has received them" (v. 3), that is, shown them hospitality as patron.

14:4-5: Paul now argues with a comparison based on how people treat the household slaves of others (Greek: *oiketēs*; NRSV: "servant"). Only the master of the slave can command the slave. If others have issues with a slave, they ought take it up with the master and leave the slave alone.

14:6-7: Both weak and strong abstain and eat, respectively, "in honor of the Lord and give thanks to God," and this is what ultimately counts. Paul will return to the subject of abstaining and eating (really the subject of abstainers and eaters) later.

Exhortation to the Strong 14:7-13

14:7 We do not live to ourselves, and we do not die to ourselves. 8 If we live, we live to the Lord, and if we die, we die to the Lord; so then, whether we live or whether we die, we are the Lord's. 9 For to this end Christ died and lived again, so that he might be Lord of both the dead and the living.

10 Why do you pass judgment on your brother or sister? Or you, why do you despise your brother or sister? For we will all stand before the judgment seat of God. 11 For it is written,

"As I live, says the Lord, every knee
shall bow to me,
and every tongue shall give praise
to God."

12 So then, each of us will be accountable to God. 13 Let us therefore no longer pass judgment on one another, but resolve instead never to put a stumbling block or hindrance in the way of another.

Textual Notes: Rom 14:7-13

14:7-9: Paul reminds his fellow Jesus-group members of the collective and communal nature of their fictive kinship group. All are embedded in each other and in Christ. Christ died and lived again and is thereby Lord of all dead and living Jesus-group members. As Lord he alone rightfully has dominion over all. Collectivistic awareness focuses on group integrity and group support. With such awareness, the strong must maintain group integrity and not read anyone out of the group, as though they had lordly entitlements.

14:10-13: With rhetorical questions Paul asks the strong about why they pass judgment on the weak, and treat them like nothing (NRSV: "despise," v. 10). They are not entitled to do so because God alone is judge, a point Paul proves with a quote from sacred scripture (cited freely from Isa 45:23). Hence his final advice is: quit blocking the morally motivated behavior of the weak. In other words, let them alone in what they are doing.

Again, the Weak and Their Observances 14:14-23

14:14 I know and am persuaded in the Lord Jesus that nothing is unclean in itself; but it is unclean for anyone who thinks it unclean. 15 If your brother or sister is being injured by what you eat, you are no longer walking in love. Do not let what you eat cause the ruin of one for whom Christ died. 16 So do not let your good be spoken of as evil. 17 For the kingdom of God is not food and drink but righteousness and peace and joy in the Holy Spirit. 18 The one who thus serves Christ is acceptable to God and has human approval. 19 Let us then pursue what makes for peace and for mutual upbuilding. 20 Do not, for the sake of food, destroy the work of God. Everything is indeed clean, but it is wrong for you to make others fall by what you eat; 21 it is good not to eat meat or drink wine or do anything that makes your brother or sister stumble. 22 The faith that you have, have as your own conviction before God. Blessed are those who have no reason to condemn themselves because of what they approve. 23 But those who have doubts are condemned if they eat, because they do not act from faith; for whatever does not proceed from faith is sin.

Textual Notes: Rom 14:14-23

14:14: Paul just argued that the strong should leave the weak alone. He further clarifies that although he does not agree with the moral convictions and consequent behavior of the weak, they have to be permitted to behave according to those convictions.

14:15: Not only that, but the strong must not cause moral consternation for the weak by acting contrary to those convictions of the weak in their presence. NRSV "to be injured" translates the Greek *lypeo*, meaning to distress, vex. By eating what the weak find abhorrent, the strong cause them distress. Such behavior ("walking") is contrary to the group attachment that is to characterize Jesus-group members. It may lead to the moral ruin of a fellow Jesus-group member.

14:16-18: Hence even though the strong's behavior is in fact good, it will be spoken of as evil because of its effects on the weak. The reason for this is that the forthcoming theocracy is about God's approval and the presence of God's Spirit providing peace and joy, not about food and drink. So do not make an issue of food and drink with the weak and their moral convictions. In this way a strong Jesus-group member does proper slave service to Christ, winning God's commendation and the approval of his fellow Jesus-group members.

14:19-20a: Paul now concludes, urging the strong to work for Jesus-group maintenance and support, and this makes for peace. The Jesus group is the work of God, not to be destroyed because of food. The presupposition in the whole discussion is that the strong are strong because they are flexible, accommodating, capable of giving in to others, compromising, and conciliatory. The weak have none of these qualities—which is what makes them weak. So the strong must yield to the weak and thus maintain the work of God.

14:20b-22: Paul takes up the opening theme of this section, namely that, for Israelite Jesus-group members, everything is clean. And he repeats, the strong must yield to the moral convictions of the weak for the sake of the group, even though the strong's conviction before God is good.

14:23: Many authors take "faith" here to mean "firm persuasion, a certain conscience." Perhaps such a description is too introspective for Paul. It would seem that for Paul, faith here also means faith in what the God of Israel has done through the death and resurrection of Jesus. This event makes the Law of Moses irrelevant, as the strong understand. But the weak, it seems, are still in doubt about the ramifications of what God has done in Christ. They still believe the Law of Moses must be followed as God's law. Hence if their doubts about the significance of the Law of Moses are unresolved and if they eat like the strong, they do not act from faith in the gospel. They act, rather, in obedience to the Mosaic Law. Paul concludes, then, that deviance from the Mosaic Law that does not proceed from faith in the gospel actually dishonors God (it is a sin). The implicit conclusion for the strong is to support the weak in their weakness, since they are Jesus-group members too.

The Strong and Their Attitudes 15:1-7

15:1 We who are strong ought to
put up with the failings of the weak,
and not to please ourselves. 2 Each of us
must please our neighbor for the good
purpose of building up the neighbor. 3
For Christ did not please himself; but,
as it is written, "The insults of those
who insult you have fallen on me." 4 For
whatever was written in former days was
written for our instruction, so that by
steadfastness and by the encouragement of
the scriptures we might have hope. 5 May
the God of steadfastness and encouragement grant you to live in harmony with one
another, in accordance with Christ Jesus,
6 so that together you may with one voice
glorify the God and Father of our Lord
Jesus Christ.

7 Welcome one another, therefore, just
as Christ has welcomed you, for the glory
of God.

Textual Notes: Rom 15:1-7

15:1-3: Once more, Paul urges the strong to accommodate the weak and their moral convictions rather than please themselves. What counts is building up fellow Jesus-group members. The main motive for such behavior should be that that is what Christ did in what he endured in his passion. By undergoing crucifixion, he did not please himself. Proof of this is not a passion account as in the Synoptics or John, but in a scripture quote that explains the meaning of what Jesus underwent (here Ps 69:9).

15:4-5a: After quoting Israel's scriptures Paul explains why we have scriptures at all: for our instruction with a view to endurance and encouragement to maintain hope. The source of this endurance and encouragement is God (not the scriptures).

15:5-6: These verses form a blessing focused on the need for harmony, on one voice in publicly honoring God. To glorify means to give honor by outward manifestations or behavior. Such outward honor will be seen in the strong getting along with and supporting the weak in harmony.

15:7: As with the opening verse of this section, Paul urges hospitality with one another, just as Christ, with a view to God's glory, has shown hospitality to all in the Roman Jesus groups.

Concluding Admonition 15:8-14

15:8 For I tell you that Christ has become a
servant of the circumcised on behalf of the
truth of God in order that he might confirm
the promises given to the patriarchs, 9 and
in order that the Gentiles might glorify
God for his mercy. As it is written,
"Therefore I will confess you among
the Gentiles,
and sing praises to your name";
10 and again he says,
"Rejoice, O Gentiles, with his people";
11 and again,
"Praise the Lord, all you Gentiles,
and let all the peoples praise him";
12 and again Isaiah says,
"The root of Jesse shall come,
the one who rises to rule the Gentiles;
in him the Gentiles shall hope."
13 May the God of hope fill you with all
joy and peace in believing, so that you
may abound in hope by the power of the
Holy Spirit.

14 I myself feel confident about you,
my brothers and sisters, that you yourselves
are full of goodness, filled with all knowledge, and able to instruct one another.

Textual Notes: Rom 15:8-14

15:8-9a: Paul, it seems, cannot let go of the topic of the behavior of the strong toward the weak. Here in this final conclusion to his advice to the strong, he explains the significance of Jesus coming to serve the circumcised (here identified with the weak, and in general with Judeans in the previous parts of the letter). In Paul's judgment Jesus came in the service of the circumcised for two reasons: first, to support the truthfulness of God, since Jesus' coming to Israel realizes God's promises to Israel's ancestors, and second, to fulfill God's covenant debt to Israel, since non-Israelites who see what God has done for Israel will give honor to God. The word "mercy" means paying one's debt of interpersonal obligation. And it is through the covenants with Israel that God incurs a debt of interpersonal obligation with Israel. His sending Jesus Christ to the circumcised fulfills this debt of interpersonal obligation. The non-Israelites get to know about it and applaud God. Paul demonstrates this last point with a series of scriptural quotes.

15:9b: Ps 18:49: God is professed among the Gentiles; this is exactly what Paul does by proclaiming his gospel of God among Israelites living among non-Israelites.

15:10: Deut 32:43 LXX: The Gentiles rejoice with God's people because of what God does for his people, not for the Gentiles.

15:11: Ps 117:1: The verse invites all people to praise the God of Israel.

15:12: Isa 11:10 LXX: Here the Gentiles have hope because they will one day be ruled by the "root of Jesse." Jesus will be Lord of all. There is no mention of these Gentiles believing in God or in God's Messiah.

Commentators frequently consider this series of scriptural quotations as emphasizing the inclusion of non-Israelites (or Gentiles) in Jesus groups. This is a common misunderstanding, perhaps deriving from the inclination to find a role for non-Israelites in Paul's ministry. However, a close reading of those passages indicates that the role of non-Israelites is to applaud what the God of Israel has done for his people—not for non-Israelites. The passages, in Pauline context, reflect Paul's plea for unity between weak and strong in Jesus groups—perhaps like the unity of Israelites and non-Israelites in praising God.

15:13-14: These verses offer another blessing, just as 15:5-6. They offer good wishes for the immediate future: joy and peace with the power of the Spirit (altered state of consciousness experiences) in Roman Jesus groups. Paul is confident in the goodness, knowledge, and abilities of the Romans.

XI. Rom 15:15-32
Conclusion and Travel Plans

5:15 Nevertheless on some points I have
written to you rather boldly by way of
reminder, because of the grace given me
by God 16 to be a minister of Christ Jesus
to the Gentiles in the priestly service
of the gospel of God, so that the offering of the Gentiles may be acceptable,
sanctified by the Holy Spirit. 17 In Christ
Jesus, then, I have reason to boast of my
work for God. 18 For I will not venture to
speak of anything except what Christ has
accomplished through me to win obedience from the Gentiles, by word and deed,
19 by the power of signs and wonders, by
the power of the Spirit of God, so that from
Jerusalem and as far around as Illyricum I
have fully proclaimed the good news of
Christ. 20 Thus I make it my ambition to
proclaim the good news, not where Christ
has already been named, so that I do not
build on someone else's foundation, 21 but
as it is written,

"Those who have never been told of
him shall see,
and those who have never heard of
him shall understand."

22 This is the reason that I have so
often been hindered from coming to you.
23 But now, with no further place for me
in these regions, I desire, as I have for
many years, to come to you 24 when I
go to Spain. For I do hope to see you on
my journey and to be sent on by you,
once I have enjoyed your company for a
little while. 25 At present, however, I am
going to Jerusalem in a ministry to the
saints; 26 for Macedonia and Achaia have
been pleased to share their resources with
the poor among the saints at Jerusalem.
27 They were pleased to do this, and
indeed they owe it to them; for if the
Gentiles have come to share in their spiritual blessings, they ought also to be of
service to them in material things. 28 So,
when I have completed this, and have
delivered to them what has been collected,
I will set out by way of you to Spain; 29 and
I know that when I come to you, I will come
in the fullness of the blessing of Christ.

30 I appeal to you, brothers and sisters,
by our Lord Jesus Christ and by the love of
the Spirit, to join me in earnest prayer to
God on my behalf, 31 that I may be rescued
from the unbelievers in Judea, and that my
ministry to Jerusalem may be acceptable to
the saints, 32 so that by God's will I may
come to you with joy and be refreshed in
your company.

Textual Notes: Rom 15:15-32

This final section provides three explanations that Paul thinks the recipients of his letter deserve. The first is an explanation for why he wrote the way he did, what he included and what he excluded (vv. 15-22). The second is an explanation for why he did not visit Jesus groups in Rome yet, given that he is God's apostle to Israelites living among Gentiles (vv. 23-29). The third is an explanation for why he cannot proceed directly to Rome, but must first go to Jerusalem (vv. 30-32). The first passage is a letter conclusion of sorts; the last two are about travel.

15:15-22: Paul opens, first (vv. 15-18) explaining why he felt bold enough to express himself the way he did in the letter, and then he explains his choice of the topics. He wrote "by way of reminder," presuming, of course, that Roman Jesus groups knew about what he explained to them. In his view he could speak the way he did about what he did because of the patronage favor he received from the God of Israel, who appointed him change agent with the task of proclaiming God's gospel. He now describes his activity with the analogy of priestly Temple service.

Like a Temple priest Paul offers to the God of Israel those Israelites among the Gentiles who have welcomed the innovation he proclaimed. He hopes that his offering of Israelites resident among non-Israelites might be acceptable to the God of Israel. Just as Temple offerings are made exclusive to the deity, so Paul expects these Jesus-group Israelites would be made exclusive to God by God's spirit. Such work on God's behalf is the basis of his boasting.

On the other hand (vv. 18-19) Paul will not mention anything of his own part in the process of innovation communication. His focus is solely upon what the resurrected Jesus did through him among Jesus-group adherents by word and deed. That it was Jesus at work was rather obvious from the power of signs and wonder, the power of God's Spirit, undoubtedly experienced in altered states of consciousness. In v. 19 Paul plainly states that he completed one part of his change-agent task. As he describes it, he already proclaimed the Gospel in non-Israelite regions "from Jerusalem and as far around as Illyricum." This is an important point for what he meant by being an "apostle to the Gentiles." The geographical area he describes makes it rather obvious that he did not reach all non-Israelites in this area in the period of his activity! Realistically, his goal was to proclaim his gospel among Israelites in this region before any other Jesus-group change agent, and he believes he did so.

In the next verse (vv. 20-22) Paul specifies the rationale behind his choice of Israelite groups to approach. He must be the first Jesus-group change agent in any Israelite colony; otherwise he went elsewhere. He offers a scriptural statement from Isa 52:15 as basis for his course of action, which he believes was directed by the God of Israel. And because of his itinerary and rationale, he would not have ventured to Rome previously, since Jesus groups already existed there.

15:23-29: This section opens with a change of focus, to Paul's plans for "now." The section is marked off by the word "Spain," pointing to another region in which he must proclaim the gospel of the God of Israel. There would be very few Israelites in Spain at this time, it seems, yet they too must hear that gospel preparation for the forthcoming kingdom. As Paul explains, however, before he heads to Rome on his way to Spain, he has one more task to complete. That is the task of delivering contributions of Jesus groups from Macedonia and Achaia to the poor waiting in Jerusalem. The rationale he offers for the collection smacks of simony but is typical of antiquity: spiritual goods and material goods were all goods. Reciprocity was basic among ingroup members. It did not matter what one received from another; one must practice generalized reciprocity.

15:30-32: In this third passage Paul indicates he is concerned about two things. First, he expects conflict with Judeans in Jerusalem, since the innovation he proclaims is a cause of alarm for those who reject Jesus as Israel's Messiah to come. Then, he is apprehensive about Jesus groups in Jerusalem, whether they will accept the contributions from him. So he requests Roman Jesus groups to ask God on his behalf that he complete his task and safely move on to Rome.

XII. Rom 15:33
Letter Ending

15:33 The God of peace be with all of you. Amen.

Textual Notes: Rom 15:33

This statement marks the formal ending to Paul's letters. What follows is a sort of appendix.

XIII. Rom 16:1-29
Appendix: Letter of Recommendation for Phoebe and Doxology

Letter of Recommendation for Phoebe and Assorted Greetings 16:1-23

16:1 I commend to you our sister Phoebe, a deacon of the church at Cenchreae, 2 so that you may welcome her in the Lord as is fitting for the saints, and help her in whatever she may require from you, for she has been a benefactor of many and of myself as well.

3 Greet Prisca and Aquila, who work with me in Christ Jesus, 4 and who risked their necks for my life, to whom not only I give thanks, but also all the churches of the Gentiles. 5 Greet also the church in their house. Greet my beloved Epaenetus, who was the first convert in Asia for Christ. 6 Greet Mary, who has worked very hard among you. 7 Greet Andronicus and Junia, my relatives who were in prison with me; they are prominent among the apostles, and they were in Christ before I was. 8 Greet Ampliatus, my beloved in the Lord. 9 Greet Urbanus, our co-worker in Christ, and my beloved Stachys. 10 Greet Apelles, who is approved in Christ. Greet those who belong to the family of Aristobulus. 11 Greet my relative Herodion. Greet those in the Lord who belong to the family of Narcissus. 12 Greet those workers in the Lord, Tryphaena and Tryphosa. Greet the beloved Persis, who has worked hard in the Lord. 13 Greet Rufus, chosen in the Lord; and greet his mother—a mother to me also. 14 Greet Asyncritus, Phlegon, Hermes, Patrobas, Hermas, and the brothers and sisters who are with them. 15 Greet Philologus, Julia, Nereus and his sister, and Olympas, and all the saints who are with them. 16 Greet one another with a holy kiss. All the churches of Christ greet you.

17 I urge you, brothers and sisters, to keep an eye on those who cause dissensions and offenses, in opposition to the teaching that you have learned; avoid them. 18 For such people do not serve our Lord Christ, but their own appetites, and by smooth talk and flattery they deceive the hearts of the simple-minded. 19 For while your obedience is known to all, so that I rejoice over you, I want you to be wise in what is good and guileless in what is evil. 20 The God of peace will shortly crush Satan under your feet. The grace of our Lord Jesus Christ be with you.

21 Timothy, my co-worker, greets you; so do Lucius and Jason and Sosipater, my relatives.

22 I Tertius, the writer of this letter, greet you in the Lord.

23 Gaius, who is host to me and to the whole church, greets you. Erastus, the city treasurer, and our brother Quartus, greet you.

Textual Notes: Rom 16:1-23

This chapter consists of a letter of recommendation (vv. 1-2), a series of greetings to some twenty-six persons (vv. 3-15), an exhortation (vv. 17-20a), a formal letter closing (v. 20b), and a series of greetings from persons who were with Paul (vv. 21-24). A final doxology is also appended (vv. 25-27).

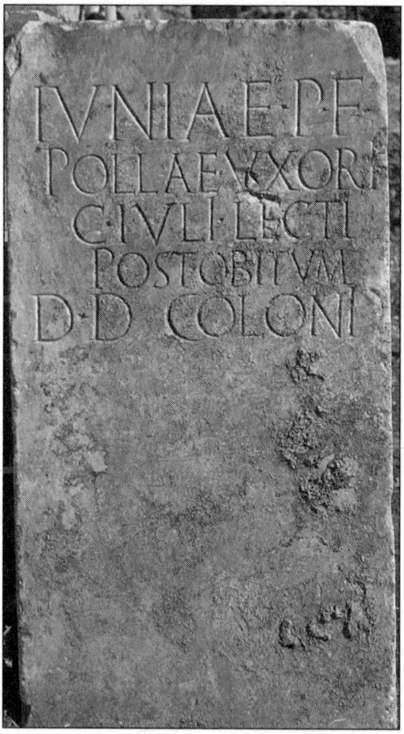

This inscription reads, "To Junia Polla, daughter of Publius, wife of Gaius Julius Lectus. After her death colonists [of Corinth gave this] by decree of the decuriones." The female name "Junia" was fairly common in the Roman period, while the male form "Junias" is not attested; thus, it is likely that Junia in Rom 16:7 was a woman who held an important place among Jesus-group members.

16:1-2: A number of scholars believe this section (chapter 16) has been appended to the letter to the Romans. Many would say it was written to Ephesus, recommending Phoebe to the Ephesians as she is about to undertake a trip to that city. And all the persons listed in vv. 3-13 would be residents of Ephesus, known to Paul who spent some time there, as we know from his own writings (1 Cor 15:32; 1 Cor 16:8, "But I will stay in Ephesus until Pentecost").

This seems quite plausible. In fact, one thing is certain, namely, that Paul did not write a letter of recommendation for Phoebe to the Romans. The problem with imagining such a letter of recommendation written by Paul and directed to the

Romans for a third party is that Paul is not known to the Romans, except perhaps by gossip. On what basis, in the social system of the day, could Paul presume that such a recommendation would be of any value? One who recommends another is like a broker or intermediary. Brokers or intermediaries need to be known to both parties between whom they mediate. For Paul to direct a recommendation for another to a group of persons he did not know would be shameful and socially impossible. The letter to the Romans itself is Paul's own attempt to contact the Roman Jesus group that he did not found and did not know since he never went to Rome (he says). He wishes to travel through Rome to Spain with the assistance of the members of Roman Jesus groups. His letter to the Romans is his own self-recommendation and request for assistance for further travel to Spain.

An informal letter of recommendation has the following pattern: an opening consisting of a request verb plus the name of the person commended; the credentials of the one recommended; and a statement of the desired action (for Paul's letters, see 1 Thess 5:12-13a; 1 Cor 16:15-16, 17-18; Phil 2:29-30; 4:2-3; Phlm 8–9).

16:1: Phoebe was a deacon. A deacon in Hellenistic society was a person who functioned as an agent of a higher-ranking person, either as an intermediary in commercial transactions or as a messenger or diplomat. A deacon was a person in the service of some supervising manager. Paul describes his function at times as that of a deacon. Perhaps a deacon such as Phoebe was a person in the service of the supervisor of the Jesus group in Cenchreae (the seaport of Corinth) or of the Jesus group in general (doing the service of patron, as noted in the next verse).

16:2: Phoebe was a patron (Greek: *prostatis* here; NRSV's "benefactor" translates the Greek *euergetēs*, a word Paul does not use here). Patrons are socially powerful individuals who control resources and use their position to hand out favors to inferiors based on "friendship," personal knowledge, and favoritism. Recipients of a patron's favors are called "clients." Benefactors, on the other hand, were persons of means who generously supported city or village projects with a benefaction (not "favor") for a grant of honor, but without the ongoing interpersonal relationship that patrons have with clients. Phoebe bestowed her patronage on Paul and a number of other Jesus-group members. Hence Paul owes here a debt of gratitude, which he dispenses here, as well as a grant of honor.

"To welcome" is the Greek verb *prosdechomai*, meaning to show hospitality. "Hospitality" refers to accepting and showing patronage favors to a stranger. Since she was a stranger, Phoebe needed this letter of recommendation for people whom Paul knew.

16:3-15: The list of greetings has the following pattern: verb of greeting, name of the greeted person(s), and the credentials of the person(s) greeted. The feature of listing credentials is much like that in the informal recommendation. The twenty-six persons mentioned by name and several implicitly are all commended for their service or work on behalf of other Jesus-group members. Some of the names are well-known slave names, as many commentaries note. However, it would seem that such slaves join Jesus groups along with the master of the household when he became a member.

While we know little about these persons aside from what Paul says, because of the pattern involved in the communication of innovation, the first people to adopt the innovation Paul and those before him disseminated are called "innovators and first adopters." (See **Notes** to 1 Thess 2:13-16.)

16:16: As a rule, one kisses intimate ingroup members as a greeting, specifically those with whom one would eat.

16:17-20: These verses would make no sense addressed to the Roman Jesus gathering, whom Paul did not know except by general reputation. The problem Paul envisions is Jesus-group members who are argumentative and challenge others on the basis of some teaching. Such persons are called "Satan" because they deceive in testing the loyalty to God of group members. What motivates their behavior is that they "serve their belly" (NRSV: "appetites"). As noted relative to Phil 3:19 "belly" (Greek: *koilia*) is the concrete label for the whole body cavity beginning at the throat and ending at the anus. Metaphorically, the word stands for the hidden, innermost recesses of the human body or of the human person. It is the functional equivalent of what we call the heart. As Danker notes, there is often a variation in manuscripts between belly (*koilia*) and heart (*kardia*), for example, at Acts 2:30; Rev 10:9. Since the *koilia* is where the *kardia* is found and since physicians believed the *kardia* was the upper opening of the *koilia*, it was common to consider the *koilia* as the seat of inward life, of feelings and desires—like the *kardia* (Job 15:35; Prov 18:20; 20:27, 30; Sir 19:12; 51:21) (see Danker 2000:550–51). In this metaphorical sense, the "belly" would be equivalent to self-interest or self-centered ambition (as in Phil 3:19). Such self-centered ambition disturbs the peace of the Jesus group in question.

16:21-23: These verses give another list of names, persons sending greetings to the group receiving Paul's letter of recommendation. They offer further indication that this chapter does not belong in the letter to the Romans, since there is no way to tell that anyone in Rome knew these persons, who are presumed to be known to the recipient of the document. Timothy is well known from a number of Paul's letters, while the next three persons are listed as Paul's relatives or mates in some ingroup context. Tertius, the writer, and Quartus are slave names, while Gaius, Paul's host, and Erastus, a city official of sorts, point to the well-placed adopters of innovation mentioned above.

Doxology 16:25-27

16:25 Now to God who is able to strengthen you according to my gospel and the proclamation of Jesus Christ, according to the revelation of the mystery that was kept secret for long ages 26 but is now disclosed, and through the prophetic writings is made known to all the Gentiles, according to the command of the eternal God, to bring about the obedience of faith— 27 to the only wise God, through Jesus Christ, to whom be the glory forever! Amen.

This inscription mentioning "Erastus," dated to the middle of the first century C.E., *likely refers to the city administrator greeted by Paul (Rom 16:23), the only Christian mentioned in the New Testament who is attested by a public inscription. He was probably the man who paid for the paving of this area as part of his civic office.*

Textual Notes: Rom 16:25-27

This doxology is not Paul's usual way of ending a letter. Some scholars say it is included here because of worship use.

16:25-27: This statement praising God perfectly sums up what Paul has been about in his change-agent activity. He ask the God of Israel, the only wise God (v. 27) to strengthen the recipients of the letter (which letter is uncertain) in terms of his proclamation of the gospel of God's raising Jesus from the dead, here called the revelation of a mystery held in silence for long ages.

16:26: The NRSV adopts a word order that departs from the Greek. Literally the statement runs: "but made manifest now through the prophetic writings, made known according to a command of the eternal God for the obedience of the faith among all peoples." The mystery is made manifest and made known by the God of Israel, as the passive voice indicates. The NRSV "to all the Gentiles," refers, of course, to Israelites living among all non-Israelites. This was the scope and goal of Paul's activity.

Philippians

I. Phil 1:1-11
Superscription

1:1-2	**A** About You: Pauline Salutation
1:3-6	**B** About Us (Inclusive): Me and You; Thanksgiving, First Part
1:7-11	About Us (Inclusive): Me and You; Thanksgiving, Second Part

II. Phil 1:12—2:15
Body A: Paul's Prison Circumstances and Its Significance for the Philippians

1:12-22	**C** About Me: Paul's Imprisonment
1:23-28	**B** About Us (Inclusive): Me and You; The Meaning of Paul's Imprisonment for the Philippians
1:29—2:15	**A** About You: Pauline Norms

III. Phil 2:16—3:21
Body B: Ingroup and Outgroup Relations

2:16—3:1a	**B** About Us (Inclusive): Me, You, and Them: Relationships with Timothy and Epaphroditus
3:1b-14	**D** About Us (Exclusive): Me and Them; About Opponents
3:15-21	**B** About Us (Inclusive): Me and You and Them; Warnings against Opponents and Ingroup Conflict

IV. Phil 4:1-23
Concluding Remarks

4:1-9	**A** About You: Pauline Norms
4:10-19	**C** About Me: Acknowledgment for Gifts
4:20-23	**A** About You; Conclusion: Greetings and Blessing

Our first social-scientific reading of this letter indicated a striking alternation of pronouns, very much like in 1 Thessalonians. Sociolinguists tell us that language directed at another person has three dimensions to it: ideational, interpersonal, and modal. The ideational dimension covers the topic of the communication, what one speaks about. The interpersonal dimension looks to whom one speaks, that is, to the statuses and roles of the conversing partners. The modal dimension deals with how the language parts get put together: words, grammar, syntax. The three dimensions, then, deal with the what, who, and how of the linguistic interaction. The three, of course, are fully interconnected, but one or another feature may be highlighted, depending on the situation. The alternating pronouns in this letter focus on the interpersonal. This feature is an indicator of the focus of information exchange intent in the document. The pronoun usage here underscores the author's concern about whom or to whom he was speaking.

The general viewpoint is that Paul wrote to the Philippians while in prison either in Ephesus (rainy season, 55–56 C.E.) or in Rome (about 58–60 C.E.). On the basis of this pronoun usage and coupled with a description of the contents of the passages, we have formulated an outline of the letter as presented above. Furthermore, from a literary point of view, the inclusion formed by 1:1-7 and 4:10-20 confirms this structure. Furthermore, 1:27—2:18 are echoed in 3:2—4:1, so they also belong together.

The letter is usually dated about 56–57 C.E. and said to come from Ephesus.

I. Phil 1:1-11
Superscription

About You: Pauline Salutation 1:1-2

1:1 Paul and Timothy, servants of Christ Jesus,

To all the saints in Christ Jesus who are in Philippi, with the bishops and deacons:

2 Grace to you and peace from God our Father and the Lord Jesus Christ.

Textual Notes: Phil 1:1-2

Hellenistic letters opened with a formula consisting of the name of the sender(s), then the addressee(s) and a greeting. These three elements are called a "superscription" (or prescript). The next element, connecting the superscription with the body of the letter, is called a "thanksgiving." The thanksgiving is a statement of indebtedness to God for something done in the past plus wishes for the proximate future. **Hellenistic Letter.** The letter opening (1:1-7) forms an inclusion with 4:1-19.

1:1: Paul and Timothy, as we learn from Paul's other letters and the third-generation recollections of the book of Acts, were Jesus-group change agents **Change Agent.** Paul uses his Greek name (rather than the Semitic Saul) in all of his letters to Israelites resident among non-Israelites. This is the case with this letter as well. Timothy had a Hellenistic father (Acts 16:1), hence his Greek name. Greek names point to civilized persons. It is important that modern readers of Paul's writings realize that the term "Greek" is not a national or ethnic designation. In the first century C.E. there was no "Greece" in our sense of the word. To be a "Greek" basically meant to be Hellenized, a synonym for "civilized." The opposite of Greek was "barbarian," "uncivilized." Along with a number of values, the common Greek language of the period was the language used by civilized people in the Mediterranean in the first century C.E. **Greeks and Israelites.**

Paul designates himself and Timothy as "slaves" (NRSV: "servants"). Slaves were not simply servants. They were persons socially situated in the social institution called "slavery." Slavery was a symbolic ritual of dishonor (social death—self- or other-inflicted) consisting of depriving a person of freedom of decision and action by means of force or enforced solidarity with a view to the social utility of the enslaving agent. Slavery was a subset of kinship (domestic slavery) or of politics

This panoramic view of Philippi from its akropolis (310 meters above sea level) illustrates the city's relation to its adjacent fertile plains and the mountains to the south and east (in the background).

(political slavery: temple slaves, city slaves, etc.). To be slaves of Jesus Christ meant Paul and Timothy were for the utility of Jesus Christ, who controlled their choices and actions by solidarity—that is, by their commitment to Christ.

1:1: Paul makes no mention of a "church" at Philippi. "Church" (Greek: *ekklēsia*) actually refers to the gathering of the summoned citizenry of a Greco-Roman city (Greek: *polis*). Only cities had citizens in antiquity. The word was also used in the LXX for the gathering of those summoned by the God of Israel in the mythical story of the Exodus. In any case Paul's omission of this designation in favor of "saints" indicates emphasis on the status of the Philippians before God and toward each other rather than on their being constituted by God into a community. "Saints" is not a moral designation but rather points to people set apart by and for God, people exclusively God's (see 2 Cor 1:1; 9:1; 13:12; also 1 Thess 3:13; 1 Cor 1:2; 6:2; 16:1, 15; Rom 1:7). The word emphasizes exclusivity, hence a bounded, centripetal ingroup.

"In Christ Jesus" describes how these saints are set off from other groups. Their group is in Christ Jesus instead of in Israel or any other founding personage. The focus here is on the horizontal—on the ingroup and on the significance of its membership roles. All members are in Christ and constitute (the body of) Christ.

1:2: The greeting here is typical of Paul's letters (Gal 1:3; 1 Cor 1:3; 2 Cor 1:2; Rom 1:7; Phlm 1). The wish for the favor (grace) of the gods or—in Paul's case—of God along with peace is very common in Hellenistic letters. The special feature in the Pauline letters is the assignment of this grace and peace as coming from God our Father and the Lord Jesus Christ. God, of course, is the God of Israel, our patron who provides favor (grace); Jesus Christ in turn is Lord, the person raised by God, now with authority and dominion.

In context the greeting has a vertical dimension, a downward dimension. As always "from God the Father" indicates Paul's perspective as essentially theologically motivated. "Theologically" means God-motivated, with God as the main actor in Jesus-group formation, support, and activity. It is equally important to note that when Paul uses the word "God," he invariably means the God of Israel. After all, he lives in a world where "there are many gods and many lords—yet for us there is one God, the Father, from whom are all things and for whom we exist, and one Lord, Jesus Christ, through whom are all things and through whom we exist" (1 Cor 8:5-6). Paul calls the God of Israel "father," a word deriving from the kinship institution and often used in the kin-like relationship of social superior to inferior called patronage. For Paul, the God of Israel is most often described as "Father" or patron of the gathering summoned by God. **Patronage System.**

The role of "the Lord Jesus Christ" is that of intermediary, of go-between, of broker between God and Paul's Jesus groups. Jesus' titles here are a mixture of Greek and Judean, that is, civilized and barbarian terms. The title "Lord" refers to Jesus as endowed with power, while "Christ" refers to Jesus as Israel's Messiah. (See **Notes** to 1 Thess 1:1.)

Because of the perception that Jesus was with the God of Israel in the sky, to call Jesus "lord" meant that he wielded supreme cosmic dominion, after God (see 2:9-11). Since Paul's gospel is ultimately about a forthcoming Israelite theocracy (its advent is called "the day of Christ," 1:10; 2:16), it is noteworthy that the reigning Roman emperor likewise bore the title "lord." The underlying clash of political-religious ideologies is not far below the surface of social interactions. **Kingdom of God**.

The word "bishop" (Greek: *episkopos*) literally means "supervisor," "supervising manager." Since Paul's Jesus groups looked forward to the forthcoming kingdom of God, the interim supervisory or managerial role in these fictive kin groups was not yet as formally organized as the role requirements in the letters to Timothy and Titus, much less as the political role of bishops after Constantine.

The word "deacon" here is a transliteration of the Greek *diakonos*. In the Hellenistic world the word normally means someone functioning as an agent of a higher-ranking person, either as an intermediary in commercial transactions or as a messenger or diplomat. Perhaps these "deacons" were persons in the service of the supervising manager or of the Jesus group in general.

About Us (Inclusive): Me and You; Thanksgiving, First Part 1:3-6

1:3 I thank my God every time I remember **you**, 4 constantly praying with joy in every one of my prayers for all of **you**, 5 because of **your** sharing in the gospel from the first day until now. 6 I am confident of this, that the one who began a good work among **you** will bring it to completion by the day of Jesus Christ.

Textual Notes: Phil 1:3-6

This is the next section expected in a Hellenistic letter and is usually called a "thanksgiving" (1:3-11). Since, however, "thank you" in Mediterranean culture ends a relationship, it is preferable to understand this as a statement of indebtedness to a benefactor, in this case, God. This segment consists of two parts, the first of which deals with the past to the present and the second with good wishes for the proximate future. 1:3-6 constitute the first part dealing with the past, the present, and a mention of the forthcoming "day of Jesus Christ." The usual best wishes for the proximate future are continued at 1:7-11. **Hellenistic Letter.** While this thanksgiving acknowledges God's benefaction, it is suffused with Paul's feeling of attachment to and solidarity with the Philippians.

1:3-4: "To thank" means to acknowledge with gratitude and indebtedness. What Paul acknowledges is God's activity on behalf of the Philippians, who have shared in his gospel of God from the first day he approached them as change agent until the present. This fills Paul with joy as he prays for the Philippian Jesus-group members. (See **Notes** to 2 Cor 1:10.) **Prayer.**

1:6: Paul expresses his firm hope in God, that is, confident trust that the God of Israel will bring to completion what has begun among the Philippians. This will occur with the forthcoming advent of the kingdom of God, here noted as "the day of Christ Jesus" (1:10; 2:16).

About Us (Inclusive): Me and You; Thanksgiving, Second Part 1:7-11

1:7 It is right for **me** to think this way about all of **you**, because **you** hold **me** in **your** heart, for all of **you** share in God's grace with **me**, both in **my** imprisonment and in the defense and confirmation of the gospel. 8 For God is **my** witness, how **I** long for all of **you** with the compassion of Christ Jesus. 9 And this is **my** prayer, that **your** love may overflow more and more with knowledge and full insight 10 to help **you** to determine what is best, so that in the day of Christ **you** may be pure and blameless, 11 having produced the harvest of righteousness that comes through Jesus Christ for the glory and praise of God.

Textual Notes: Phil 1:7-11

1:7: Paul openly expresses his attachment to and longing for the members of the Philippian Jesus group. In Greek this verse runs as follows: "It is right for me to think this way about all of you, because you hold me in heart, both in my imprisonment and in the defense and confirmation of the gospel, sharing with me in grace all of you." The phrase "all of you" marks off the sentence (and is repeated in v. 8). The Philippian Jesus-group members have known about Paul's imprisonment. Paul does not state who informed them or how they found out. Further, they too have had occasion to defend the gospel of God and to "confirm" it, that is, demonstrate its validity with proofs. The gospel of God for Paul is the event of Jesus' death and God's raising Jesus from the dead with a view to the establishment of a forthcoming kingdom of God in Jerusalem. Paul is a change agent whose task is to proclaim this gospel, thus communicating an innovation inaugurated by the God of Israel for Israelites.

The word "grace" is the Greek *charis* and means the favor bestowed by a patron, something a patron gives that a person needs yet cannot obtain at all or cannot obtain when needed. While Paul does not state it, the presumption is that this favor is given by the God of Israel, as the NRSV adds. This analogy of the God of Israel as patron and bestower of favors is fundamental to the New Testament understanding of God's interaction with human beings. Both Paul and the Philippian Jesus-group members share in this divine favor. All of them shared in the patronage favor. In this very high context letter Paul does not spell out everything that God's favor entails. Everyone knows what he is talking about.

1:8-10: Paul takes an oath with God as witness to make it quite clear that what he says is true and sincere. In prison he longs to be with these people for honest reasons. At the moment, however, he can only ask for God's assistance on their behalf, so that they continue to be attached to each other, growing in knowledge and "full insight." This last phrase is the NRSV version of the Greek word *aisthesis*, which means a feeling for the actual situation at the time. The purpose of the love, knowledge, and insight is to assist the Philippians in determining what is best. The presumption, of course, is that neither Paul nor his fellow Jesus-group members have any inside track or clear plans on how to face the situations that come up in their daily living. The Philippians' choice of action should be made with a view to their proving to be "sun-bright" (NRSV: "pure"; Greek: *eilikrines*) and blameless at the time of the emergence of the kingdom of God, here called "the day of Christ" (also 2:16).

1:11: Righteousness, when referring to human activity, means proper interpersonal behavior. What makes an action or activity "proper" in Jesus groups is divine approval. Paul urges Jesus-group members to produce a harvest of righteous behavior, which can happen through Jesus Christ with a view to giving praise and honor to the God of Israel.

II. Phil 1:12—2:15
Body A: Paul's Prison Circumstances and Its Significance for the Philippians

About Me: Paul's Imprisonment 1:12-22

1:12 **I** want **you** to know, beloved, that what has happened to **me** has actually helped to spread the gospel, 13 so that it has become known throughout the whole imperial guard and to everyone else that **my** imprisonment is for Christ; 14 and most of the brothers and sisters, having been made confident in the Lord by **my** imprisonment, dare to speak the word with greater boldness and without fear.

15 Some proclaim Christ from envy and rivalry, but others from goodwill. 16 These proclaim Christ out of love, knowing that **I** have been put here for the defense of the gospel; 17 the others proclaim Christ out of selfish ambition, not sincerely but intending to increase **my** suffering in **my** imprisonment. 18 What does it matter? Just this, that Christ is proclaimed in every way, whether out of false motives or true; and in that **I** rejoice.

Yes, and **I** will continue to rejoice, 19 for **I** know that through **your** prayers and the help of the Spirit of Jesus Christ this will turn out for **my** deliverance. 20 It is **my** eager expectation and hope that **I** will not be put to shame in any way, but that by **my** speaking with all boldness, Christ will be exalted now as always in **my** body, whether by life or by death. 21 For to **me**, living is Christ and dying is gain. 22 If **I** am to live in the flesh, that means fruitful labor for **me**; and **I** do not know which **I** prefer.

Textual Notes: Phil 1:12-22

1:12: The phrase "I want you to know, brethren" is a disclosure formula used to mark the opening of the body of the letter. Paul informs the Philippians about what he sees as the benefits of his imprisonment. First of all, imprisonment is an act of dishonor (social death) consisting of depriving a person of freedom of movement by means of force or forced confinement with a view to maintaining public order, extortion, or death. Imprisonment is a subset of the political institution and its realization through the military (here called the "praetorian guard"). **Military.** The purpose of imprisonment in antiquity was not punishment but holding a prisoner for some other action—peacekeeping, extortion (paid by family and friends to soldiers), or death. Persons were held in prison in order to maintain public order in face of probable rioting. Such persons might readily be released from prison after some official considered the trigger situation to have passed (this was not a trial, but peacekeeping).

The imprisoned person had to be supported by family and friends, not by jailers. And persons were not imprisoned to be held for a "trial." Furthermore, the purpose of "trials" in antiquity was to dishonor an opponent, not to find for guilt or innocence. If persons were imprisoned after some alleged crime, the presumption was that they were guilty—Romans only imprisoned and subsequently punished the guilty!

Since Paul expected to be released from his chains soon (1:26; 2:24), that meant that he was taken prisoner for purposes of peacekeeping. As often noted in Acts, Paul's fellow Israelites caused near riots in opposition to his proclamation, explanation, and successes in winning over Israelite clients to the innovation he proclaimed. The gospel of God proclaimed by Paul often aggrieved some of his fellow Israelites, and the outcome of their negative response is best described as a conflict. **Dispute Process.**

1:12-13: Paul's opening statement indicates that his being taken prisoner led to the spread of his gospel of God, either through rumor or through direct conversation. People in the Israelite community wondered why he was put in chains, and the story involved his proclamation of the gospel of Jesus' death, God's raising him, and the forthcoming kingdom of God. So all knew he was taken prisoner "for Christ," a shorthand way of saying "for the proclamation of the gospel of the God of Israel."

1:14: Another outcome of his being taken prisoner was that Jesus-group members in the city of his imprisonment (not mentioned in this high context document) grew bold enough to proclaim the gospel of God without fear of outsiders. Since the gospel pertained to what the God of Israel did for Israelites in the death and resurrection of Jesus with a view to the forthcoming kingdom of God, these Jesus-group members took the word to their fellow Israelites.

1:15-17: Paul believed that these Jesus-group members who proclaimed his gospel of God did so either out of good will and love for Paul or out of envy and rivalry with Paul, out of selfish ambition, to aggravate Paul (see 3:2-4, 18-19).

1:18: Paul says he really does not care what their personal motivation might have been, just so information about the innovation he proclaims gets to be known by more and more people. This makes him rejoice: the more Israelites who know the better, and it does not matter how they got to know it.

1:18b-19: And Paul insists that he will continue to rejoice. The reason for this is a citation from Israel's scriptures: "this will turn out for my deliverance" (Greek *sōtēria*; Job 13:16 LXX), specifically through the Philippians' prayers and the assistance of Jesus Christ's spirit. The phrase "prayer and assistance" are clustered as a grammatical unity.

1:20: Paul believes he will not be dishonored. To dishonor a person is to deny his claim to worth. In this case Paul's claim to worth has to do with "speaking with all boldness," a great value in the Hellenistic world. For Paul's opponents to have him silenced would be the great dishonor. As his next comment indicates, this silencing entails death. Hence his conclusion: whether alive or dead, the God of Israel will exalt Christ in Paul's person.

The word "body" (Greek *sōma*) means the self, person, as in English: nobody, somebody, anybody. This self may be the individual self or the collective self (for example, the body of Christ is Jesus himself or the Jesus group). It is not the opposite of "soul" (which also means self, person, as in "don't tell a soul"; it also means life, as in "lose one's soul," meaning to drop dead or die).

The passive voice in the statement "Christ will be exalted" has God as the doer. As a rule, nearly all passive voice statements imply God as doer (for example, Jesus was raised from the dead). Using the passive voice in statements with God as doer was a pious Israelite usage to avoid using the name of the deity. Paul very often sticks to this usage.

1:21-22: A number of authors associate Paul's statements about life or death with ancient philosophical discussions about suicide. It seems that while the wording might be similar, the social system in which the wordings occur are quite different. It is true that all ancients were totally religious in the sense that all believed the deity or deities were part and parcel of society, of the human environment. The provident deity or deities took note of what went on among humans. Most would believe that in some way, in the deity or deities "we live, move and have our being." For Paul and many of his fellow Israelites the significant deity was the God of Israel, provident for God's own and ever ready at hand. And since this God raised Jesus from the dead, those who believe this gospel of the God of Israel presently constitute the body of Christ and are in Christ. Living and dying are simply two aspects of experiencing God and being in Christ. "In the flesh" thus means being presently alive with the obligations and duties present life entails. For Paul to be in the flesh means fruitful labor as change agent of the God of Israel, yet should he die, that would be gain, an advantage, quite profitable for him. This leaves Paul in a state of doubt; he does not know which side to choose (NRSV: "prefer"; Greek: *haireō* = to choose). As his deliberation continues, he will resolve this doubt.

About Us (Inclusive): Me and You; The Meaning of Paul's Imprisonment for the Philippians 1:23-26

1:23 **I** am hard pressed between the two: **my** desire is to depart and be with Christ, for that is far better; 24 but to remain in the flesh is more necessary for **you**. 25 Since **I** am convinced of this, **I** know that **I** will remain and continue with all of **you** for **your** progress and joy in faith, 26 so that **I** may share abundantly in **your** boasting in Christ Jesus when **I** come to **you** again.

Textual Notes: Phil 1:23-26

1:23-25: Paul thus wavers between directly joining Christ or rejoining the Philippians. With Christ he would be in a far better situation awaiting the forthcoming kingdom of God, yet with the Philippians he can facilitate their living out the implications of their acceptance of the gospel of God. He resolves the doubt in favor of the Philippians because "it is more necessary on your account." Choosing "what was necessary" was a noble moral choice in the Hellenistic period.

1:26: This verse indicates Paul's expectation of being released soon. When he gets to see the Philippians again, he will share in their claim to honor in Christ Jesus, undoubtedly because of their way of living. That this is the implied point of honor is indicated by Paul's next observations.

About You: Pauline Norms 1:27–2:15

1:27 Only, live **your** life in a manner worthy of the gospel of Christ, so
that, whether **I** come and see **you** or am
absent and hear about **you**, **I** will know
that **you** are standing firm in one spirit,
striving side by side with one mind for the
faith of the gospel, 28 and are in no way
intimidated by **your** opponents. For them
this is evidence of their destruction, but
of **your** salvation. And this is God's doing.
29 For he has graciously granted **you** the
privilege not only of believing in Christ,
but of suffering for him as well— 30 since
you are having the same struggle that **you**
saw **I** had and now hear that **I** still have.

2:1 If then there is any encouragement in
Christ, any consolation from love, any sharing in the Spirit, any compassion and sympathy, 2 make **my** joy complete: be of the same
mind, having the same love, being in full
accord and of one mind. 3 Do nothing from
selfish ambition or conceit, but in humility
regard others as better than **yourselves**. 4 Let
each of **you** look not to **your** own interests,
but to the interests of others. 5 Let the same
mind be in **you** that was in Christ Jesus,

6 who, though he was in the form of
God,
did not regard equality with God
as some obedient to the point of
death—even thing to be
exploited,
7 but emptied himself,
taking the form of a slave,
being born in human likeness.
And being found in human form,
8 he humbled himself
and became death on a cross.

9 Therefore God also highly exalted
him
and gave him the name
that is above every name,
10 so that at the name of Jesus
every knee should bend,
in heaven and on earth and under
the earth,
11 and every tongue should confess
that Jesus Christ is Lord,
to the glory of God the Father.

12 Therefore, **my** beloved, just as **you**
have always obeyed **me**, not only in **my** presence, but much more now in **my** absence,
work out **your** own salvation with fear and
trembling; 13 for it is God who is at work in
you, enabling **you** both to will and to work
for his good pleasure.

14 Do all things without murmuring
and arguing, 15 so that **you** may be blameless and innocent, children of God without
blemish in the midst of a crooked and perverse generation, in which **you** shine like
stars in the world.

Textual Notes: Phil 1:27–2:15

In this passage, focus on Paul fades into the background as he places renewed focus on the Philippians and their way of living. **Pauline Norms.** Paul offers two models of behavior, each rooted in conflict situations: his own and that of Christ Jesus. Both models have worked because God is at work in their execution. Mention of Paul's "presence or absence" (1:27 and 2:12) blocks off the passage as a unit.

1:27-28: NRSV has "live your life"; here the Greek term is *politeuo*, meaning "live up to your civil (or city) obligations." Paul uses an analogy taken from the public discourse of independent Greco-Roman cities (*poleis*). Philippi at this time was a Roman "colony," meaning an independent city with a population having rights and obligations approved and guaranteed by the central city, Rome. The civil obligations of the Philippian Jesus groups derive from the gospel of God focused on Christ Jesus. The basic requirement for all is unity and harmony: standing firm in one spirit, competing with opponents with one mind shaped by gospel faith. Paul again uses analogies, this time from athletic contests (1:30, NRSV: "struggle";

Greek *agōn*, contest, meet). Here he speaks of standing firm (*stēkō*), competing with competitors (*synathleō*) and opponents (*antikeimenoi*). The Philippians' lack of intimidation is proof to their opponents that these competitors will be destroyed, but for the Philippians, it is proof of their rescue (NRSV: "salvation"). If Paul were consistent with his analogy, he might say "defeat and victory." However, he switches to a military metaphor (destruction and rescue/salvation) to describe the outcome of the contest. In any event, even though the Philippians engage in this contest, the outcome is God's doing.

1:29: The reason for ascribing the outcome of the contest to God is that God has granted the Philippians the patronage favor (NRSV has "privilege," a word lacking in the Greek text) concerning Christ. This favor concerning Christ derives, of course, from the gospel of God concerning Jesus' death and his being raised by God with a view to the forthcoming kingdom of God for Israel. Here Paul underscores two dimensions of this favor concerning Christ: not only to believe "into" him but also to endure conflict (our version of the Greek: *paschein*; NRSV: "suffer") on his behalf. "To suffer or endure conflict for the sake of" is a military metaphor. That Paul has such a military metaphor in mind is indicated by his conclusion to this segment: the Philippians participate in the same sort of contest (NRSV: "struggle"; Greek: *agōn*, contest, competition—a word from athletics) as Paul did and does.

2:1-4: Paul now turns to ingroup behavior. He opens with a description of what he believes is the Philippians' attitude toward him: they encourage him in Christ, console him because of their love for him, share in the spirit, show compassion and sympathy. This, of course, brings him great joy, as previously noted. But to round out his joy, what he wishes to see is a supportive attitude on the part of these Jesus-group members toward each other. As change agent Paul is ever concerned about ingroup social identity. Thus Paul exhorts them, in so many different ways, to ingroup harmony based on mutual support. Members must be of the same mind, same love, full accord, and, again, of one mind. To effect this, of course, they must be humble. Humility means being satisfied with one's status in society, not striving for honor at the expense of others. Selfish ambition and empty claims to honor (NRSV: "conceit") run counter to humility. Practically speaking, ingroup harmony results when Jesus-group members regard others as better than they are and look to the interests of others. Such other-focused thinking and behaving can only result in ingroup harmony and mutual support.

2:5: To make his point again, Paul refers to the thinking and consequent behavior that he believes were evident in Christ Jesus. The NRSV's "mind" (Greek: *phroneō*) is a frequent word in this letter; see 1:7; 2:2 twice; 3:15, 19; 4:2, 10. In the passage that follows, the "mind of Christ" that Paul makes reference to deals with the events, remote and proximate, surrounding Jesus' death.

2:6-11: Most scholars consider this passage to be an early Jesus-group hymn or psalm, deriving from a worship setting. Paul quotes it here because it fits the point he is making, to describe the "mind of Christ." The procedure of citing traditional pieces is not unknown in Paul's letters (e.g., 1 Thess 1:9-10; 1 Cor 15:3-5; Rom 1:3-4; 3:24-25). In Middle Eastern culture the ability to cite traditional pieces appropriately is a mark of honor and an indication of true manliness. This characteristic of manliness is on par with enduring physical punishment without crying.

This passage has three main lines of interpretation. First, there is a christological one that sees a description of the preexistence and incarnation of Jesus in the hymn. Since this description deals with the cosmic nature of the Christ, it is also called an ontological interpretation. Second, there is a kerygmatic interpretation that views the hymn as a salvific proclamation of the true nature of Jesus as Christ, a sort of acclamation of the cosmic Christ. And third, there is an interpretation rooted in the actual context of the Philippian Jesus group at this point. Since Paul is exhorting the Philippians, this interpretation may be called a hortatory one, focused on the thinking and behavior of Jesus of Nazareth as revealed in the traditions about his passion and death. This is a historical interpretation. Given the instructional context in which this pre-Pauline statement is presently found, we opt for the last interpretation.

The passage obviously implies a comparison. Such a comparison has the features of a rhetorical comparison in an encomium. Jesus the Messiah is presented as one who pursued honor by foregoing privilege and status in obedience to God. However the question is, with whom is Jesus being compared? Following John H. Elliott (unpublished paper), we believe the comparison is between Jesus of Nazareth and the first human described in Israel's sacred scriptures, Adam. Such a comparison is well known to Paul (Rom 5:12ff.; 1 Cor 14:49).

2:6: Both Adam and Jesus of Nazareth were in the form of God, as are all human beings (see Gen 1:26, 27; 3:5). While Adam regarded equality with God as something to be sought and taken (see Gen 2:20; 3:5-6, 17, 22), Jesus of Nazareth obviously did not.

2:7-11: The rest of the hymn is based on an understanding of Jesus' death in terms of the death of a righteous Israelite. For first-generation Jesus-group members what primarily required explanation and clarification was the significance of Jesus' death. Because information about Jesus' death was scarce, the general facts, witnessed and assumed, were clarified "according to the Scriptures." And the passages chosen from Israel's scriptures were those dealing with the death of a righteous Israelite. These passages can be found strewn throughout the death accounts in the written Gospels, canonical and noncanonical. The author(s) of this hymn chose passages from Isaiah (Isaiah 45; 52; 53), as did the evangelists.

2:7: "He emptied himself" (see Isa 53:12: "he poured out himself"), "taking the form of a slave" (see Isa 53:11 LXX: "the righteous one, my slave"); "being born in human likeness . . . in human form" (see Isa 52:14: because of his beatings, he looked "beyond human likeness, beyond human form").

2:8: "He humbled himself" (see Isa 53:7: "He was oppressed, and he was afflicted, yet he opened not his mouth; like a lamb that is led to the slaughter, and like a sheep that before its shearers is dumb, so he opened not his mouth"). "And became obedient to the point of death" (see Isa 53:8-9: "By oppression and judgment he was taken away; and as for his generation, who considered that he was cut off out of the land of the living, stricken for the transgression of my people? And they made his grave with the wicked"). "Even death on a cross"—some think Paul added this phrase.

2:9: "Therefore God also highly exalted him" (Isa 52:13: "Behold, my servant shall prosper, he shall be exalted and lifted up, and shall be very high"). "God gave him a name that is above every name": while Isaiah speaks of a portion with the great (see Isa 53:12: "I will allot him a portion with the great"), this hymn puts Jesus above all others. "Name" means person, a person in a role. The verse may be correctly translated: "God gave him a role that is above every other role." And given his role, all intelligent creatures owe him obeisance.

2:10-11: "At the name of Jesus every knee should bend . . . and every tongue shall confess" points to supremacy. Such supremacy was ascribed only to the God of Israel in Israel's scriptures (see Isa 45:23, in which God says, "To me every knee shall bow and every tongue shall swear"). The name "Jesus" now stands for the one raised by God from the dead and exalted by God. Thus Jesus emerges as vice-regent of the God of Israel: he is Lord (see note at 1:2 above), and this honors God the cosmic Patron.

Consider, now, the contrast between Adam and Jesus in this hymn (the chart is from John H. Elliott, unpublished):

Adam	**Christ Jesus**
being in the image of God	being in the image of God
thought equality with God something to be sought	thought equality with God not something to be sought
spurned being God's slave/servant	accepted being God's slave
desiring to be like God (=immortal)	not desiring to be like God (=immortal)
found in human shape or likeness	found in human shape or likeness
he exalted himself	he humbled himself
he was disobedient unto death	he was obedient unto death
he was condemned by God	he was exalted by God and given the status/role of Lord of all

2:12-13: NRSV has "just as you have always obeyed me," but the Greek states, "just as you have always obeyed." There is no "me" in the Greek. Given the context highlighting Jesus' obedience to God, Paul praises the Philippians' obedience to God, both when he is there among them and even more so in his absence. "With fear and trembling" is an Israelite idiom that means "with serious concern" (see Mark 5:33; 1 Cor 2:3; 2 Cor 7:15). "Salvation" means rescue from a difficult situation. Paul does not further specify what difficult situation he has in mind. The context suggests conflict with the outgroup and mutual support in the ingroup. The Philippians are to attend to their salvation with serious concern. The reason for this is that it is God who is at work, giving them the desire to do so, enabling them to carry out the task with the resulting divine good pleasure. In the Israelite tradition as revealed in later writings of Pharisees, human living is entirely the work of the individual human being and entirely the work of God at the same time (see *Avot* 3:6). Paul shares in this Israelite tradition. It is the perspective that stands behind his encouragement here.

2:14-15: Paul concludes with an exhortation that echoes Israelite behavior in the Exodus. Moses' constant complaint to God was that the people continually grumbled and argued in face of God's leading them into the wilderness (Exod 15:24; 16:2, 7 twice, 8 three times, 9, 12; 17:3; Num 14:2, 27 three times, 29, 36; 16:11, 41; 17:5 twice, 10; Deut 1:27; Ps 106:25). That Israelite generation was "no longer his children because of their blemish; they are a crooked and perverse generation" (see Deut 32:5). So Paul urges Philippian Jesus-group members to be blameless and innocent, "unblemished children of God" in the midst of their fellow Israelites, who are "the blemished children of God," "the crooked and perverse generation" that rejects the gospel of God. Among Israelites, these Jesus-group members shine like celestial luminaries (Greek: *phainesthe hōs phōstērēs tou kosmou*). The reference is to Dan 12:3 LXX: "Those who have an intelligent grasp of the situation will shine like the luminaries (*phanousin hōs phōstērēs tou ouranou*) of the sky and those who master my words like the stars of the sky forevermore."

III. Phil 2:16—3:21
Body B: Ingroup and Outgroup Relations

About Us (Inclusive): Me, You, and Them; Relationships with Timothy and Epaphroditus 2:16–3:1a

2:16 It is by **your** holding fast to the word of life that **I** can boast on the day of Christ that **I** did not run in vain or labor in vain. 17 But even if **I** am being poured out as a libation over the sacrifice and the offering of **your** faith, **I** am glad and rejoice with all of **you**— 18 and in the same way **you** also must be glad and rejoice with **me**.

19 **I** hope in the Lord Jesus to send Timothy to **you** soon, so that **I** may be cheered by news of **you**. 20 **I** have no one like him who will be genuinely concerned for **your** welfare. 21 All of them are seeking their own interests, not those of Jesus Christ. 22 But Timothy's worth **you** know, how like a son with a father he has served with **me** in the work of the gospel. 23 **I** hope therefore to send him as soon as **I** see how things go with **me**; 24 and **I** trust in the Lord that **I** will also come soon.

25 Still, **I** think it necessary to send to **you** Epaphroditus—my brother and co-worker and fellow soldier, **your** messenger and minister to **my** need; 26 for he has been longing for all of **you**, and has been distressed because **you** heard that he was ill. 27 He was indeed so ill that he nearly died. But God had mercy on him, and not only on him but on **me** also, so that **I** would not have one sorrow after another. 28 **I** am the more eager to send him, therefore, in order that **you** may rejoice at seeing him again, and that **I** may be less anxious. 29 Welcome him then in the Lord with all joy, and honor such people, 30 because he came close to death for the work of Christ, risking his life to make up for those services that **you** could not give **me**.

3:1a Finally, **my** brothers and sisters, rejoice in the Lord.

Textual Notes: Phil 2:16-30

This passage deals with various ingroup relationships: between Paul and the Philippians (2:16-18); among Paul, Timothy, and the Philippians (2:19-24); and among Paul, Epaphroditus, and the Philippians (2:25-30).

2:16-18: These verses serve as a sort of introduction to what Paul has to say about Timothy and Epaphroditus. His first statement is that he will gain honor on "the day of Christ," when the kingdom of God is inaugurated, on account of the Philippians' adhering to the gospel of God that he proclaimed. Here that gospel of God is called "the word of life," or "the living/life-giving word." By their holding fast to the gospel of God, the Philippians will demonstrate that Paul did not "run in vain" (a metaphor from athletics) or "labor in vain"—both phrases referring to his change-agent activity. He follows this with another analogy, describing his situation in terms of sacrifice: Paul behaves like a libation (that is, an appropriate liquid) that is poured out during a sacrificial action. On the other hand, the faith of the Philippians is like a sacrifice offered by public-spirited citizens. The NRSV "offering" stands for the Greek *leitourgia*, which denotes a public service, including sacrifices, that private citizens performed at their own expense. The purpose of sacrifice is always to have some life-related effect on the deity. The Philippians' behavior causes Paul to be glad and rejoice, and Paul hopes his behavior will have the same effect on the Philippians. The theme of joy, expressed right from the very outset of this letter (1:4), runs through it like a recurrent theme (joy [1:4, 25; 2:2, 29; 4:1]; rejoice [1:18, 19; 2:17, 18, 28; 3:1; 4:4 twice, 10]; glad [2:17, 18]).

2:19-24: Timothy was Paul's change-agent assistant. He is co-sender with Paul of several of the letters (the earliest—1 Thessalonians—along with 2 Corinthians and this one). He often travels on Paul's behalf (see 1 Thess 3:2, 6; 1 Cor 4:17; 16:10), thus assisting in the information exchange relation basic to the change agent's task (v. 19). Paul relates to him like father to son (v. 22), a very close relationship indeed. As an aside, Paul tells of some Jesus-group change agents who seek their own interests and not those of Jesus Christ. What these interests might be, Paul does not say in his usual high context way. More important, Paul believes Timothy is genuinely concerned for the welfare of the Philippians. Hence he does more than transmit information. Rather, his concern would be manifest in his change-agent tasks of diagnosing problems, solidifying the clients' intent to change, stabilizing the membership, and preventing discontinuance. The Philippians know Timothy and his follow-up change-agent activity in the work of the gospel of God. So Paul hopes to send Timothy soon and to follow himself soon after that (vv. 23-24).

2:25-30: From what Paul says of him, Epaphroditus was a Philippian Jesus-group member sent by that group to assist Paul in his imprisonment. As noted previously, people who were imprisoned had to be taken care of by their family and friends (see **Note on Phil 1:12**). Paul praises him as brother, fellow worker, and fellow soldier (a military analogy indicating a conflict situation). Epaphroditus became deathly sick and further distressed because he could not carry out the task that the Philippian Jesus-group membership expected him to carry out on Paul's behalf (v. 26). Paul's description here fully befits the sense of honor of a collectivistic personality. Epaphroditus was concerned, Paul intimates, with the integrity and honor of the Philippian Jesus group. He felt fully obligated in honor to assist Paul on their behalf. Paul ascribes his recovery to God's mercy, God's sense of obligation to those in covenant with him. Paul was thus spared the further pain of dealing with his death (along with that of his own imprisonment). And so he thinks it is necessary to send Epaphroditus back to Philippi, both for Epaphroditus's sake and for the sake of his fellow Jesus-group members in Philippi. Paul urges those Jesus-group members to receive Epaphroditus with joy and acclaim the worth of his service on behalf of the Philippians. He did in fact assist Paul, even though his illness cut short his ability to fulfill that service until Paul's release. What he did was life-threatening for him. It was worthy of honor, and the Philippians should show him that honor. Paul, it seems, had to be explicit in the praise of Epaphroditus and to be so insistent that he be received with honor. The reason for this was the Roman ethos in the city. Philippi was a Roman city with a number of Roman veterans. As just noted, Paul took up the defense of Epaphroditus, who could not stay with Paul until Paul's liberation. This was necessary since in Roman perspective a person who did not fulfill the task assigned him should be held as one who disgraced himself, regardless of circumstances. This scenario is well expressed in the Roman (and Stoic) military perspective that one must stand one's ground to the end, even to death. The Stoic directive ran: *Bonum ex integra causa, malum ex quovis defectu* ("for something to be good, it must be good in entirety; even a slight defect makes it no good").

3:1a: The opening word of this verse in the NRSV is "finally" (Greek: *to loipon*), which has a range of meanings. Unless one wishes to read this verse as the close of the letter, with the following passage as an insertion, it is best to translate the word as "in sum," "so then," "hence." The point is that, in face of all that Paul has said, the appropriate response on the part of the Philippian Jesus-group members is to rejoice.

About Us (Exclusive): Me and Them; About Opponents 3:1b-14

3:1b To write the same things to **you** is not troublesome to **me**, and for **you** it is a safeguard.

2 Beware of the dogs, beware of the evil workers, beware of those who mutilate the flesh! 3 For it is **we** who are the circumcision, who worship in the Spirit of God and boast in Christ Jesus and have no confidence in the flesh—4 even though **I**, too, have reason for confidence in the flesh.

If anyone else has reason to be confident in the flesh, **I** have more: 5 circumcised on the eighth day, a member of the people of Israel, of the tribe of Benjamin, a Hebrew born of Hebrews; as to the law, a Pharisee; 6 as to zeal, a persecutor of the church; as to righteousness under the law, blameless.

7 Yet whatever gains **I** had, these **I** have come to regard as loss because of Christ. 8 More than that, **I** regard everything as loss because of the surpassing value of knowing Christ Jesus **my** Lord. For his sake **I** have suffered the loss of all things, and **I** regard them as rubbish, in order that **I** may gain Christ 9 and be found in him, not having a righteousness of **my** own that comes from the law, but one that comes through faith in Christ, the righteousness from God based on faith. 10 **I** want to know Christ and the power of his resurrection and the sharing of his sufferings by becoming like him in his death, 11 if somehow **I** may attain the resurrection from the dead.

12 Not that **I** have already obtained this or have already reached the goal; but **I** press on to make it **my** own, because Christ Jesus has made **me** his own. 13 Beloved, **I** do not consider that **I** have made it **my** own; but this one thing **I** do: forgetting what lies behind and straining forward to what lies ahead, 14 **I** press on toward the goal for the prize of the heavenly call of God in Christ Jesus.

Textual Notes: Phil 3:1b-14

In the previous passage, Paul took note of those "seeking their own interests, not those of Jesus Christ" (2:21). And at the outset of this letter, he mentioned such Jesus-group operatives who made Paul the target of their opposition (1:15-18). Paul must have set out such an assessment of his opponents for the consideration of the Philippians in some previous letter, since he states that he does so here once more (see 3:1b). With such a description, the conflict between Paul and his opponents (and vice versa) rises to the level of dispute. **Dispute Process.** Again, as in 2 Corinthians, Paul would have these Jesus-group members adjudicate the situation in Paul's favor. To this end Paul once again has recourse to the rhetorical form of encomium (praise) and its comparison feature (*sygkrisis*) **Encomium.** Paul compares himself with those opponents with a view to obtaining a positive adjudication from Philippian Jesus-group members.

3:1b: Paul states that he writes again about this conflict with his opponents basically for the security of his Jesus group in Philippi, yet the comparison that follows indicates he is concerned about having the Philippian Jesus-group members adjudicate in his favor.

3:2: The threefold "beware" emphasizes the safeguard aspect of this description. The opponents are dogs, evil workers, mutilators. Dogs are unclean animals that do not belong within any household. Evil workers will only do negative things for the group. And mutilators (Greek: *katatomē*) seek to castrate (and thus dishonor males and render them permanently unclean for worship). Paul puns here with the Greek words *katatomē* (to cut off entirely) and *peritomē* (to cut around, which is what "circumcise" means), equating castration and circumcision. His reference is to those who insist the Philippians should be following Judean customs if they belong to the Jesus group of the city. **Circumcision.** These designations clearly mark off the opponents as outgroup. Their presence in the Philippian Jesus group is something of which to be wary, for it can only lead to the dissolution of social identity, with the contamination of the ingroup.

3:3: Paul insists that it is Jesus-group membership that provides true circumcision, that is, whatever circumcision is meant to be for Israel. Circumcision was introduced in Judea as a marker of Judean social identity only during the Maccabean period, about 150 B.C.E., when Judea was limited almost only to the city-state of Jerusalem and its environs. For Paul, the true marker of Israelite identity was the experience of the Spirit of God. Membership in the Jesus group enables Israelites to worship in the Spirit of God (an allusion to altered states of consciousness experiences) and to find honor in their being in Christ. This has nothing to do with confidence derived from the flesh. In this context "flesh" refers to genealogical pedigree: a noble birth into an honorable tribe, with a rigorous education and a virtuous life. In this way ascribed honor derives from birth and kingroup membership. It seems that Paul's opponents, by circumcising the Philippians, would restore them to their traditional genealogical pedigree as "true" offspring of Abraham. This need to circumcise indicates the fact that in Paul's day many members of the house of Israel who lived among non-Israelites did not follow the recent Judean practice of circumcision at all.

3:4-6: In line with the comparison that is part of the encomium pattern, Paul compares his "confidence in the flesh" with that of his opponents. "If anyone else has reason to be confident in the flesh, I have more" (v. 4). Following the conventions of a comparison, moreover, he compares his kingroup credentials ("in the flesh") with theirs.

First he tells us of his *genesis,* which consists of mentioning his broader kinship group, clan, and ancestry. His *ethnos* or group of origin is the Israelite people. His family or clan is the tribe of Benjaminite. Regarding his ancestry, he is an observer of traditional kingroup customs; that is what being a Hebrew meant at the time. These traits underscore the quality of his parents. If he was circumcised on the eighth day, then his parents were observant members of the house of Israel, hence honorable people, who socialized him to the customs of his family, clan, and ethnos. Next he tells us of his manner of life (*anastrophē*): "As to the law, a Pharisee" (3:5d). Thus we know of his formation in the strict and honorable tradition of Pharisaic study and practice of "the Law." Then he announces his achievements and deeds: "As to zeal, a persecutor of the church, as to righteousness under the law, blameless" (3:6). He tells us of his life not in terms of chronology but in terms of the traditional virtues or "deeds of the soul." By his own account he epitomizes "righteousness" to the highest degree: "blameless." He was truly loyal to God ("zeal" equates with "devotedness"), even to the point of persecuting the Jesus followers of his generation, and he was "blameless" in regard to his Torah duties to God.

In terms of the rhetorical strategy of a comparison, then, Paul has positioned himself not simply as the equal of those who urge circumcision and other Judean practices ("confidence in the flesh") but as their superior ("I have more . . ."). If praise derives from "the flesh," that is, from a noble birth into an honorable tribe, from a rigorous education, and from a virtuous life, then truly Paul has "more confidence" than they do.

3:7: Although he has a superior Israelite status enabling such "confidence in the flesh," it is interesting to note that Paul does not make this a subject for boasting and honor. Paul changed "on account of Christ." That phrase is a shorthand way of describing God's call imparting to him the gospel of God that Paul would proclaim and the ramifications of Jesus' death and being raised by the God of Israel with a view to the forthcoming Israelite theocracy. In a social system that downgraded personal "change" as ancient Mediterranean society did, this change required explanation. Paul ascribed it to God, who revealed Christ Jesus to him, so now Paul can offer the example of Christ Jesus, who underwent radical personal change by giving up status, privilege, and honor. But he did so in order to carry out God's bidding and so to please God. Paul intimates that his situation directly resembles that of Jesus. He now regards all former "gain" as "loss" because of Christ (3:7). He contrasts himself with those who boast of "confidence in the flesh" by claiming that only the pattern established by Jesus according to the hymn cited at 2:6-11 is what is truly honorable. Jesus had "former" glory but gave it up in obedience to God for the greater glory that God would bestow. Paul, too, had glory in his Israelite way of life as blameless and zealous for the Torah, but he yielded it all at God's behest for the greater glory that comes from conformity to Christ's resurrection (3:10-14). Thus Jesus' "obedience" (2:8) is superior to Paul's old "righteousness" (3:9), which he traded for God's righteousness, which entails "loyalty" (*pistis*).

3:9: Righteousness from God based on faith means divine approval and acceptance based on confidence and loyalty in the God of Israel, who reveals himself in the death and resurrection of Jesus. To know "Christ Jesus my Lord" is of surpassing value, since this knowledge comes from God himself, namely, a revelation by the God of Israel. Consider the elements in Paul's rhetorical comparison:

Opponents	**Paul**
Dogs (unclean), evil workers	[Clean, good]
They do *katatomē* (mutilation).	I and you are *peritomē* (circumcision).
They put stock in the flesh (genealogy).	I and you do not put stock in the flesh. We worship the Spirit and have honor in Christ.
In the flesh, they have genealogical credentials, which they regard as gain.	In the flesh, I have better genealogical credentials, which I regard as loss.
They claim righteousness of their own.	I claim righteousness through faith in Christ.
They claim righteousness from the Law.	I claim righteousness from God.

3:10-11: Jesus arrived at his resurrection from the dead through suffering, as described in the hymn above (2:6-11). Paul's goal is to follow that pattern, a pattern he urged on the Philippian Jesus-group members.

3:12-14: Christ Jesus has made Paul his own through God's call and Paul's subsequent experiences. His goal, that for which he strives, is forthcoming. So the past is of little value. This statement is of great significance, since Israelite Torah-oriented elites lived primarily with their face to the past. The present was a second-order orientation because their social goal was to live up to the past-rooted Torah. As he obeyed God's call, Paul was forced to look primarily to his present task with a view to the forthcoming kingdom of heaven. Forthcoming events became his second-order orientation, and the past was relegated to third place. Here he states that his goal, to use an athletic analogy again, is the prize that comes with a call of God from above (the NRSV "heavenly" is not in the Greek) in Christ Jesus. Using this analogy of a race and its proximate goal further illustrates the fact that for Paul and his fellows, "future" meant "forthcoming." The forthcoming is always rooted in processes already under way in the present; the forthcoming is a process that is believed to exist only because of something already existing in the present. For example, a growing crop points to a forthcoming harvest, a pregnant wife points to a forthcoming baby, the first half of a football game points to a forthcoming second-half conclusion. So, too, with Paul: he is already engaged in a race; the goal is forthcoming (not future). This call of God from above in Christ Jesus is shorthand, again, for the imminent coming of Jesus and the inauguration of the kingdom of God. Such a call was also mentioned in 1 Thess 4:16.

About Us (Inclusive): Me and You and Them; Warnings against Opponents and Ingroup Conflict 3:15-21

3:15 Let those of **us** then who are mature be of the same mind; and if **you** think differently about anything, this too God will reveal to **you**. 16 Only let **us** hold fast to what **we** have attained.

17 Brothers and sisters, join in imitating **me**, and observe those who live according to the example **you** have in **us**. 18 For many live as enemies of the cross of Christ; **I** have often told **you** of them, and now **I** tell **you** even with tears. 19 Their end is destruction; their god is the belly; and their glory is in their shame; their minds are set on earthly things. 20 But **our** citizenship is in heaven, and it is from there that **we** are expecting a Savior, the Lord Jesus Christ. 21 He will transform the body of **our** humiliation that it may be conformed to the body of his glory, by the power that also enables him to make all things subject to himself.

Textual Notes: Phil 3:15-21

3:15-17: Paul opens with an appeal to the mature (NRSV; Greek: *teleoi*). The word *teleios* does in fact mean mature, full grown, complete in development, accomplished in some respect. Paul thus witnesses to Jesus-group members in Philippi who fully fit the norms he envisions for a mature way of living, befitting adherence to Christ. Once more, he turns to the frequent topic of the Philippians' sharing in the same "mind" (see 1:7; 2:2 twice, 5; 3:19; 4:2, 10). The word refers to attitudes of thought and consequent behavior. In 2:6-11 Paul speaks of their having the "mind of Christ," referring to the events, remote and proximate, surrounding Jesus' death. Here Paul asks the Philippians to imitate his behavior as well as that of those who live in this way, yet the cross of Christ is not unconnected to this (v. 18).

3:18: The "many who live as enemies of the cross" would be both fellow Israelites as well as Israelite Judaizers in Philippi. Judaizers were Jesus-group members who insisted that those joining Jesus groups must adopt and practice the requirements of Torah righteousness as spelled out in the customs of Judea. These latter were Paul's opponents. They opposed him out of "envy and rivalry" (1:15), "selfish ambition" (1:17), with confidence in their Israelite genealogy (3:3), and with confidence in righteousness from the Torah (3:9).

3:19: Their end is destruction; their god is the belly; and their glory is in their shame—their minds are set on earthly things. This rhetorical sequence sets their end, their god, their glory, and their minds over against the negatives: destruction, the belly (that is, self-interest), shame, things of earth. The problem word here for most readers might be "belly," equivalent to "self-interest." "Belly" (Greek: *koilia*) is the concrete label for the whole body cavity beginning at the throat and ending at the anus. Metaphorically, the word stands for the hidden, innermost recesses of the human body or of the human person. It is the functional equivalent of what we call the heart. As Danker notes, there is often a variation in manuscripts between belly (*koilia*) and heart (*kardia*), for example, at Acts 2:30; Rev 10:9. Since the *koilia* is where the *kardia* is found and since physicians believed the *kardia* was the upper opening of the *koilia*, it was common to consider the *koilia* as the seat of inward life, of feelings and desires—like the *kardia* (Job 15:35; Prov 18:20; 20:27, 30; Sir 19:12; 51:21) (see Danker 2000:550–51). In this metaphorical sense, the "belly" would be equivalent to self-interest or self-centered ambition (as in 1:17; 2:4, 21).

3:20-21: In the perspective of the Judaizers and Judean Israelites, the practice of Torah righteousness makes one "holy" in the eyes of the God of Israel, a proper Israelite. To use an analogy as Paul does, the practice of Torah righteousness outfits an Israelite with proper Jerusalemite citizenship (recall: only cities had citizens). Jesus-group members are not interested in that sort of citizenship, since their citizenship is "in the sky" (NRSV: "heaven"). It is from some celestial city that they await a savior, the Lord Jesus Christ. "Savior" is a political title usually ascribed to the emperor. Imperial titles included Lord, God, and Savior. Paul now briefly states what he described at length in 1 Corinthians 15. At the coming of the Lord Jesus from the sky, our rescue (Greek: *sōtēria*, salvation) consists of having our humble body transformed into a glorious body like Jesus' by the power of God, that is, the same power of God that enables Christ Jesus to "make all things subject to himself" (see 1 Cor 15:20-28). This passage is a surprising, emphatic, and forceful expression of political religion by one who was imprisoned by the political powers of the time.

This coin (first century C.E.*) probably commemorates the dedication of a temple of the gens Iulia in Corinth. The image of Livia may be a personification of the Salus Augusti—highlighting Augustus's role as savior of the empire. See discussion of "savior" in* **Notes** *to Phil 3:20-21.*

IV. Phil 4:1-23
Concluding Remarks

About You: Pauline Norms 4:1-9

4:1 Therefore, **my** brothers and sisters, whom **I** love and long for, **my** joy and crown, stand firm in the Lord in this way, **my** beloved.

2 **I** urge Euodia and **I** urge Syntyche to be of the same mind in the Lord. 3 Yes, and **I** ask **you** also, **my** loyal companion, help these women, for they have struggled beside **me** in the work of the gospel, together with Clement and the rest of **my** co-workers, whose names are in the book of life.

4 Rejoice in the Lord always; again **I** will say, Rejoice. 5 Let **your** gentleness be known to everyone. The Lord is near. 6 Do not worry about anything, but in everything by prayer and supplication with thanksgiving let **your** requests be made known to God. 7 And the peace of God, which surpasses all understanding, will guard **your** hearts and **your** minds in Christ Jesus.

8 Finally, beloved, whatever is true, whatever is honorable, whatever is just, whatever is pure, whatever is pleasing, whatever is commendable, if there is any excellence and if there is anything worthy of praise, think about these things. 9 Keep on doing the things that **you** have learned and received and heard and seen in **me**, and the God of peace will be with **you**.

Textual Notes: Phil 4:1-9

In this passage Paul exhorts Philippian Jesus-group members as was his custom at the close of his letters. **Pauline Norms.** The focus is on "you" (plural). Of course phrases like "my brothers, my joy and crown, my beloved, "are all ways of saying "you."

4:1: This verse sets out general norms to the Jesus group to persevere in the way they are. Such endurance looks to the proximate coming of the kingdom of God: "The Lord is near" (v. 5b).

4:2-3: There seems to have been a dispute between Evodia and Syntyche, two women of the Philippian Jesus group. Paul urges the women to resolve their conflict by adopting the same "mind," advice that serves as a theme in this letter. Paul frequently mentions women in his Jesus groups (1 Cor 1:11; 16:19; Rom 16:1-15). Since these groups were rather small, there is no reason to deduce that these women were "leaders." At this time every member of Paul's Jesus group was "notable," to each other and to Paul. Nevertheless, because of the status awareness of Mediterraneans, Israelite and non-Israelites, it is probable that these named women were notable for some activity, perhaps as patrons or prophets, "in the work of the gospel."

4:3: The loyal "companion" (Greek: *syzygos*) mentioned here can equally be a person named "Syzygos." Otherwise it is some unnamed person whom Paul urges to act as mediator. Along with Clement now mentioned, other coworkers noted in the letter include Timothy, Epaphroditus, and Titus.

"The book of life" is an analogy based on government registers or rolls. The phrase is known from Israel's scriptures: Exod 32:32; Ps 69:28; Dan 2:1; and cited frequently in Rev 3:5; 13:8; 17:8; 20:12, 15; 21:27. This book of life, dating from the foundation of the world, stands for God's foreknowledge of those who would share in a positive cosmic destiny. For Paul and his Jesus groups, to be enrolled in the book of life is to be entitled to enjoy the forthcoming kingdom of heaven, Israel's forthcoming theocracy.

4:4: Once more Paul sounds the general theme of joy that echoes throughout this letter. (The verb translated "rejoice" [Greek: *chairete*] can also mean "farewell." However, this latter meaning makes no sense here with the adverb "always.")

4:5: Taking note of the proximity of the coming of the kingdom of God, Paul urges the Philippians to forbearance. The NRSV "gentleness" is too psychological for the Greek *epieikesis*: the word means seeking what is equitable by setting aside the demands of justice, a sort of readiness to yield in the face of strict justice, hence our preferred translation: forbearance. What the exhortation means is: don't insist on tit for tat in your interaction with others; be ready to yield. After all the Lord will be here soon anyway!

4:6-7: These verses urge total confidence in God. There is no need to worry. Rather, with the right attitude, make requests known to God in prayer. **Prayer.** The outcome will be the peace of God. Peace usually means the presence of everything that persons need for a meaningful human existence. God's peace will safeguard the heart and mind in Christ Jesus as the Philippians await the coming of the kingdom.

4:8: Paul has no specific directive for the Philippian Jesus-group members. It is really up to them to decide on the direction of their behavior. What should determine the quality of that behavior are characteristics here listed by Paul. Paul lists a sampling of options: what is true or genuine, what is honorable, what is just, what has integrity, what is pleasing to others, what is commendable by others, what has excellence, and what is praiseworthy. They are to keep these qualities in mind when choosing a course of behavior. In sum, if they need some norm, they ought to consider what Paul taught, imparted, and spoke of and how he acted. If they act in this way, they will experience the peace that comes with God's presence.

About Me: Acknowledgment for Gifts 4:10-19

4:10 **I** rejoice in the Lord greatly that now at last **you** have revived **your** concern for **me**; indeed, **you** were concerned for **me**, but had no opportunity to show it. 11 Not that **I** am referring to being in need; for **I** have learned to be content with whatever **I** have. 12 **I** know what it is to have little, and **I** know what it is to have plenty. In any and all circumstances **I** have learned the secret of being well-fed and of going hungry, of having plenty and of being in need. 13 **I** can do all things through him who strengthens **me**. 14 In any case, it was kind of **you** to share **my** distress.

15 You Philippians indeed know that in the early days of the gospel, when **I** left Macedonia, no church shared with **me** in the matter of giving and receiving, except **you** alone. 16 For even when **I** was in Thessalonica, **you** sent **me** help for **my** needs more than once. 17 Not that **I** seek the gift, but **I** seek the profit that accumulates to **your** account. 18 **I** have been paid in full and have more than enough; **I** am fully satisfied, now that **I** have received from Epaphroditus the gifts **you** sent, a fragrant offering, a sacrifice acceptable and pleasing to God. 19 And **my** God will fully satisfy every need of **yours** according to his riches in glory in Christ Jesus.

Textual Notes: Phil 4:10-19

This passage forms a sort of inclusion with 1:1-7 and thus marks off the whole as a unit.

4:10: Paul begins his final description of his own situation with the constant theme of this letter, joy. And he punctuates his statement with another theme of this letter, "to be minded" (Greek: *phroneō*). The phrase "your concern for me" is in Greek "your being minded about me" (*phronein*), and the phrase "you were concerned for me" is in Greek "you were minded" (*ephroneite*). The point he makes is that the Philippians always had him and his welfare in mind, but, as he excuses them, they "had no opportunity to show it" prior to the coming of Epaphroditus.

4:11-13: In his work as change agent Paul does not become a client of any local patrons in Jesus groups. Instead, he would have them be his change-agent clients. To prevent the need for local clientship on his part, Paul always attempted to support himself as a leather tent maker (1 Cor 4:12; 2 Cor 11:7-11; 12:14-15; see Acts 18:3). Becoming a client to some local patron would obligate him to the local patron, and, it seems, Paul did not wish to obligate himself. Instead he would rather put up with all sorts of untoward conditions, including having nothing, going hungry, and being in need (see especially his list of hardships, 2 Cor 6:4-10). The point of enduring such circumstances in the service of proclaiming the gospel of God was to underscore the validity and truthfulness of this gospel. Philosophers likewise listed their hardships in the service of the truth to verify the validity of their doctrine.

4:14: As the case of the Philippians indicates, however, Paul did accept assistance, material and personal, from Jesus groups when he was away from them. The phrase "it was kind of you to share my distress" is a very good translation of a Greek idiom for grateful acknowledgment of a favor or gift. It is not a "thank you," since in Mediterranean society, "thank you" most often means "no more, thank you" and puts an end to reciprocity. If Paul sought to keep his relationship with the Philippians open-ended, he would not thank them in the way a contemporary American might.

4:15-17: Paul recalls his first days as change agent in Macedonia. When he left, presumably for Achaia, only the Philippians expressed reciprocity ("giving and receiving") toward him, and this more than once. Such open-ended reciprocity is called generalized reciprocity. **Reciprocity.** The profit that accumulates to the account of the Philippians presumably is with God, the change agency, who commissioned Paul to his change-agent activity.

4:18: "I have been paid in full" is a phrase used in business: "paid in full," like the idiom "bought with a price," closes the transaction. Paul would say that any reciprocal debt on the part of the Philippians is more than paid in full. They owe him nothing more. He notes that their final gift to him in his imprisonment along with the service of Epaphroditus, likewise sent by them, marks a true high point in their reciprocal interaction. He describes these gifts in terms of an analogy taken from domestic religious behavior, a sacrifice to God. All sacrifices are about life support or life giving. Their gift to Paul surely sustained his life; hence the

In the left foreground the broad steps constitute part of a basilica's monumental staircase, which leads from a semicircular propylon to a terrace. Immediately above and to the right of the propylon entrance, a doorway opens onto a narrow passage leading to a small Roman cistern, venerated by Christians as Paul's prison (Acts 16:17-24). The basilica is located to the north of the Roman Forum in Philippi.

analogy is appropriate. Gifts to Paul, however, were like a sacrifice acceptable and pleasing to God, the giver and sustainer of life.

4:19: Just as the Philippians' gift fully satisfied Paul's needs, so too will God gloriously satisfy their needs, and this according to God's riches in Christ Jesus.

About You; Conclusion: Greetings and Blessing 4:20-23

4:20 To our God and Father be glory forever and ever. Amen.

21 Greet every saint in Christ Jesus. The friends who are with **me** greet **you**.

22 All the saints greet **you**, especially those of the emperor's household.

23 The grace of the Lord Jesus Christ be with **your** spirit.

Textual Notes: Phil 4:20-23

4:20: This letter conclusion acknowledges the honor of the God of Israel, our Patron.

4:21-22: The NRSV "friends" is not in the Greek. The Greek has "brothers." Paul's usual name for fellow Jesus-group members is "saints" (those set apart by God in Christ) and "brothers" (members of our fictive kin group). Mention of the household of Caesar has led commentators traditionally to place Paul's imprisonment in Rome under imperial guard. That would be quite an ascribed honor, even if it meant prison. However, Paul alludes to "saints" in Caesar's household. This "household" was equivalent to our government service. It covered a large number of slaves, freedmen, and soldiers in the imperial administrative apparatus, both in Rome and in the Roman colonies, such as Philippi.

Philemon

I. Phlm 1-3
Superscription

II. Phlm 4-7
Thanksgiving: The Exordium

III. Phlm 8-16
Body of the Letter Part A: Probatio

IV. Phlm 17-22
Body of the Letter Part B: Peroratio

V. Phlm 23-25
Conclusion

This brief letter, dated to about 55–56 C.E., has the hallmarks of high context, Hellenistic personal letters. Unlike Paul's change-agent letters intended to develop and maintain an information exchange relation with Jesus groups, this letter has been written to request a favor in a convincing way. It has the features of deliberative rhetoric, as explained below. As a high context document, little of what was going on then and there between Paul and his addressee(s) is spelled out in it. We are separated by such a broad sweep of time and culture from the communicating persons in their contexts that we must supply quite a bit of information to build a plausible reading scenario.

I. Phlm 1-3
Superscription

1 Paul, a prisoner of Christ Jesus, and Timothy our brother,
To Philemon our dear friend and coworker, 2 to Apphia our sister, to Archippus our fellow soldier, and to the church in your house:
3 Grace to you and peace from God our Father and the Lord Jesus Christ.

Textual Notes: Phlm 1-3

Hellenistic letters opened with a formula consisting of the name of the sender(s), then the addressee(s) and a greeting. The first element is called a "superscription" (or prescript; vv. 1-3). The next element, connecting the superscription with the body of the letter, is called a "thanksgiving" (vv. 4-7). The thanksgiving consists of a statement of gratitude to God for something done in the past, plus wishes for the proximate future. After the thanksgiving there follows the body of the letter (8-22) and a conclusion (23-25). **Hellenistic Letter.**

1: This little letter is one more coauthored by Paul and Timothy, his fellow Jesus-group change agent (see also 1 Thessalonians, 2 Corinthians, Philippians) **Change Agent.** But only Paul presents himself as "prisoner of Christ Jesus." In the letter we find out that Paul is being held as a prisoner, but here he underscores the fact that the one who really holds him as prisoner is Jesus Christ. Paul directs this letter to one Philemon, whom Paul describes as "brother," that is fellow Jesus-group member. The kinship terminology points to Jesus groups as fictive kin groups. **Fictive Kinship.** But more than this, Paul calls Philemon his "beloved and coworker." NRSV translates "beloved" (Greek: *agapētos*) as "friend." "Friend" is often a technical term in Hellenistic Greek, designating one who is a client of some patron. Paul does not use that term here. Rather, he calls Philemon "beloved," a term used for fellow ingroup members, bound by loyalty and solidarity. In the Mediterranean world, past and present, the word is used by both genders of both genders. Paul also calls him "coworker," a term he seems to use for first adopters of the innovation he communicated with his gospel of God.

First adopters as a rule control adequate material and personality resources to absorb the possible failure should the innovation prove unsuccessful. The fact that Philemon owns a house and that he owns a slave such as Onesimus, as we learn later in the letter, indicates that he does have adequate material resources. The usual qualities of first adopters include the ability to understand and apply rather complex knowledge; venturesomeness, that is, a desire for the hazardous, the rash, the daring, the risky; and finally, cosmopoliteness, that is, having contact with outsiders, with more cosmopolite social relationships. **Coworkers: Innovators and First Adopters.** Should one try to imagine Philemon's personal resources, such stereotypical traits would be of utility.

2: Apphia and Archippus, as many commentators have indicated, are family members of Philemon's household, perhaps wife and son. The main reason for ascribing them directly to that household is that, grammatically, Paul greets Philemon, Apphia, Archippus, and the local Jesus group, all of which usually gather in "your" (singular) house. Apphia and Archippus belong to that household, as does Onesimus, whom we soon encounter in the letter.

The NRSV's "church" refers to the gathering of Jesus-group members, summoned by God. ***Ekklēsia* (Gathering).**

3: This is Paul's usual greeting (1 Cor 1:3; 2 Cor 1:2; Gal 1:3; Rom 1:7; Phil 1:2). The wish for the favor (grace) of the gods or—in Paul's case—of God along with peace is very common in Hellenistic letters. The special feature in Pauline letters is the assignment of this grace and peace as coming from God our Father and the Lord Jesus Christ. God, of course, is the God of Israel, our patron who provides favor (grace); Jesus Christ in turn is Lord, the person raised by God, now with authority and dominion.

II. Phlm 4-7
Thanksgiving: The Exordium

Since Paul communicates in the Hellenistic Mediterranean of the first century, and since the rhetorical handbooks are actually based on the social system norms of communication at the time, it is no surprise that patterns of rhetoric are found in Paul's letters. Whether he was trained in rhetoric or learned patterns of communication through socialization, Paul does evidence those patterns in his letters. A cursory reading of the letter to Philemon indicates that Paul seeks to have effect on Philemon in the matter of Philemon's slave, Onesimus. According to rhetorical treatises, the pattern of having effect on person(s) A to take action relative to a problem with person(s) B is called "deliberative rhetoric." The purpose is to have some person or persons take action soon. This is a three-part pattern consisting of an opening gambit to get favor with the person addressed (called the *exordium* in Latin), followed by a request clothed largely in interpersonal appeals (notably to the honor and advantage of the one to whom the appeal is made; called a *probatio*), and then a further restatement of the request with an appeal to the addressee's good will (called the *peroratio*). Paul follows this pattern in this letter.

4 When I remember you in my prayers,
I always thank my God 5 because I hear of
your love for all the saints and your faith
toward the Lord Jesus. 6 I pray that the
sharing of your faith may become effective
when you perceive all the good that we
may do for Christ. 7 I have indeed received
much joy and encouragement from your
love, because the hearts of the saints have
been refreshed through you, my brother.

Textual Notes: Phlm 4-7

The thanksgiving of a Hellenistic letter acknowledges the deity with gratitude, first for something in the past (here vv. 4-5), then for the present and forthcoming

(v. 6). As is usual in an exordium, Paul uses this thanksgiving to gain the benevolence of his addressee, Philemon.

4-5: Paul is moved to acknowledge God's activity in the love and faith of Philemon. The NRSV version should be compared with the original Greek, which runs as follows: "hearing about your love and faith which you have toward the Lord Jesus and for all the saints." "Love" refers to the social value of personal attachment to one's group (family, Jesus group) and to God, which is revealed in one's actions. Philemon's behavior demonstrates that he is personally attached to the Lord Jesus and to all his fellow Jesus-group members, the "saints." Faith refers to the social value of reliability. The value is ascribed to persons as well as to objects and qualities. Relative to persons, faith is reliability in interpersonal relations; it thus takes on the value of enduring personal loyalty, of personal faithfulness. "Works of faith" refers to this bond of faithfulness when revealed in externally, emotionally rooted behavior of loyalty, commitment, and solidarity. Faith toward the Lord Jesus entails enduring personal loyalty revealed in social behavior, manifested in deeds of loyalty and commitment that demonstrate Jesus as Lord.

6: Paul continues by stating the purpose of his prayer now for the future: "so that your [singular] faith-rooted sharing may become effective, known in all the good that is being done among you [plural] because of Christ." The word translated "sharing" is the Greek *koinōnia* (Latin: *societas*) and means partnership, association, partnership contract. Such partnership requires mutual support, material and social. Of course Philemon's partnership with other Jesus-group members is based on his faith in the gospel of God and in Jesus as Lord. The NRSV has "we may do," based on the Greek "among us"; however, many good manuscripts read "among you" (plural). The partnership sharing takes place in Philemon's Jesus group ("you" plural), undoubtedly because of Philemon's active interest and participation ("you" singular).

7: Paul further praises Philemon for the joy and encouragement Paul himself receives from Philemon's love, that is, actions that reveal his attachment to the Jesus group. What he has done is provide rest for or has refreshed the "hearts" of his fellow Jesus-group members. The NRSV's term "heart" is the Greek *splangchna*, meaning concretely the innards, bowels, or intestines, considered as the seat of emotion. Perhaps a better translations would be that Philemon has allayed the anxieties of his fellow Jesus-group members by his activities. This is what gives Paul joy and encouragement. He concludes this exordium with the word "brother" as the final term. The whole point of this exordium is to capture the good will of Philemon for the request that follows.

These manumission inscriptions (circa 200 B.C.E. to 100 C.E.) are found on the terrace wall near the Temple of Apollo at Delphi; they provide the name of the presiding magistrate, the month, and the sale or release to Apollo. If slaves could save enough money and their masters agreed, they could purchase their freedom and then have their new status confirmed by a manumission contract. At Delphi manumission involved selling the slave to Apollo, who then freed him or her after the god was reimbursed.

III. Phlm 8-16
Body of the Letter Part A: Probatio

8 For this reason, though I am bold enough in Christ to command you to do your duty, 9 yet I would rather appeal to you on the basis of love—and I, Paul, do this as an old man, and now also as a prisoner of Christ Jesus. 10 I am appealing to you for my child, Onesimus, whose father I have become during my imprisonment. 11 Formerly he was useless to you, but now he is indeed useful both to you and to me. 12 I am sending him, that is, my own heart, back to you. 13 I wanted to keep him with me, so that he might be of service to me in your place during my imprisonment for the gospel; 14 but I preferred to do nothing without your consent, in order that your good deed might be voluntary and not something forced. 15 Perhaps this is the reason he was separated from you for a while, so that you might have him back forever, 16 no longer as a slave but more than a slave, a beloved brother—especially to me but how much more to you, both in the flesh and in the Lord.

Textual Notes: Phlm 8-16

8-10: Paul now gently broaches his point. He claims he has both the character and the authority to command Philemon to do what he is about to ask, yet he would rather request it based on their relationship of mutual attachment, that is, love. Further, he makes this request from a double situation of weakness: as an old man and as a prisoner of Christ Jesus. With this description of himself and his attitude, Paul sets aside all claims of Mediterranean machismo, all claims of honor based on precedence. He makes his request relying totally on Philemon's benevolence.

10: The point of his request is a person named Onesimus (the Greek name means "useful," "beneficial"). We learn in v. 15 that Onesimus was a slave who belonged to Philemon. Slaves were not simply servants. They were persons embedded in the social institution called "slavery." Slavery was a symbolic ritual of dishonor (social death—self- or other-inflicted) consisting of depriving a person of freedom of decision and action by means of force or enforced solidarity with a view to the social utility of the enslaving agent. Slavery was a subset of kinship (domestic slavery) or of politics (political slavery: temple slaves, city slaves, etc.). **Slavery.** Onesimus was a household slave of Philemon who controlled his slave's freedom of decision and action.

Paul mentions that Onesimus was now "my child to whom I gave birth in prison" (literal translation). Paul does not call himself "father" here. For some reason or other, Onesimus sought out Paul in prison and asked to become a member of the Jesus group. It is highly unlikely that he was a fugitive slave caught and held in the same prison as Paul, since such a fugitive slave would either be killed or be quickly sent back to his owner. Rather it seems that Onesimus had a grievance against his owner and that he sought out Paul to function as mediator. That this is a realistic scenario is rooted in Roman case law about slaves. "This law put stress on intention. A slave was not considered to be a fugitive if he, 'having in mind that his master wished physically to chastise him, left to seek a friend whom he persuaded to plead on his behalf' (*Digesta Iustiniani* 21.1.17.1)" (Duling 2003:214, who cites the instance of Pliny's appeal to Sabinianus for a former slave in *Letters* 9.21).

Onesimus seeks out Paul to mediate between himself and Philemon, based on the presumption that Philemon would find Paul agreeable in this task. Mediation refers to the intervention by a third party, agreed to by both principals, to aid the principals in reaching agreement. The outcome of the procedure is new rules of social interaction mutually consented to by the parties in question. **Dispute Process.**

11-12: Paul now begins to set out his case for Onesimus while punning on his name, "Useful." He sends Onesimus back, undoubtedly with this letter, with great emotional investment in the slave's fortunes. Again the NRSV translates the Greek *splangchna* as "heart" (see v. 7 above).

13: Since Paul states that he wishes to keep Onesimus with him to be of service during his imprisonment for the sake of God, "in your place," the presumption is that Philemon should be there serving Paul. Why? The reason, it seems, is in the partnership or association that Jesus-group members share. Paul mentions this *koinōnia* in v. 6. Persons in *koinōnia* have mutual obligations to assist and support each other relative to the common purpose of the partnership. Paul previously mentioned that Philemon is a coworker, presumably in Paul's change-agent task of proclaiming the gospel of God. And Paul is imprisoned for the gospel of God. The gospel of God is the common purpose of their partnership, requiring both partners to expend their personal and material resources. If a Jesus-group member is imprisoned for the gospel, on the basis of their partnership in the gospel other Jesus-group members would be obliged to support the one imprisoned. This is the point Paul alludes to here.

14: Paul does not wish to presume on Philemon, however. Whatever Philemon decides has to be his free decision; hence Paul seeks his consent.

15: Paul makes a final point to conclude this segment of the letter. The passive "he was separated" indicates God as doer, hence something providential. This separation was short-lived, like an hour compared to forever. Onesimus is now a Jesus-group member. Now Philemon can have him back not as a slave but as more than a slave, that is, as a dear brother both in the flesh and in the Lord. Onesimus was previously a "brother in the flesh," that is, a fellow Israelite. Now, as Jesus-group member, he is "brother in the Lord."

IV. Phlm 17-22
Body of the Letter Part B: Peroratio

17 So if you consider me your partner, welcome him as you would welcome me. 18 If he has wronged you in any way, or owes you anything, charge that to my account. 19 I, Paul, am writing this with my own hand: I will repay it. I say nothing about your owing me even your own self. 20 Yes, brother, let me have this benefit from you in the Lord! Refresh my heart in Christ. 21 Confident of your obedience, I am writing to you, knowing that you will do even more than I say.

22 One thing more—prepare a guest room for me, for I am hoping through your prayers to be restored to you.

Textual Notes: Phlm 17-22

17: The word for partner is Greek *koinōnos*, one sharing in the mutual obligations of *koinōnia* as explained previously. Of course Philemon considers Paul a partner. Hence Paul can ask him to accept Onesimus as he would accept Paul.

18-19: These verses allude to some incident involving Onesimus's actions that gave rise to the grievance against him on the part of Philemon. Paul goes beyond his mediator role in his willingness to cover any costs incurred by Onesimus's behavior. To this effect, he writes his promissory note in his own hand: "I will pay." On the other hand, he does claim that Philemon is similarly indebted to Paul. Just as Onesimus owes Philemon, so too Philemon owes Paul himself. Paul alludes perhaps to his proclamation of the gospel of God, accepted by Philemon.

20: Paul states: "Yes, brother, I would exploit you in the Lord." And once more we have the phrase "refresh the *splangchna*," which means to allay my anxieties in Christ.

21: While Paul does not formally command Philemon, he is confident Philemon will do as he requests, and even more than he asks for. As a final note, Paul expects to visit Philemon and family soon (you plural). He does not expect to be imprisoned much longer.

V. Phlm 23-25
Conclusion

23 Epaphras, my fellow prisoner in Christ Jesus, sends greetings to you, 24 and so do Mark, Aristarchus, Demas, and Luke, my fellow workers.

25 The grace of the Lord Jesus Christ be with your spirit.

Textual Notes: Phlm 23-25

23-24: This concluding notice informs Philemon that Epaphras is imprisoned with Paul. And persons named Mark, Aristarchus, Demas, and Luke have been around, undoubtedly seeing to Paul's needs. They are fellow workers in the gospel, too, like Philemon. Whether any of this list of persons is to be identified with others by that name in the New Testament cannot be certain. It is hard to identify persons on the basis of rather popular first names.

25: The concluding blessing wishes for the favor of the Lord Jesus to be given to your (plural) spirit, undoubtedly the spirit of the Lord manifest in Jesus-group altered states of consciousness experiences in Philemon's house.

Reading Scenarios for the (Authentic) Letters of Paul

Altered States of Consciousness

Anthropologists studying cross-cultural psychology define altered states of consciousness as conditions in which sensations, perceptions, cognition, and emotions are altered. Such states are characterized by changes in sensing, perceiving, thinking, and feeling. When a person is in such a state, the experience modifies the relation of the individual to the self, body, and sense of identity, and the environment of time, space, or other people. One scholar has identified twenty such states of consciousness: dreaming, sleeping, hypnagogic (drowsiness before sleep), hypnopompic (semi-consciousness preceding waking), hyperalert, lethargic, rapture, hysteric, fragmentation, regressive, meditative, trance, reverie, daydreaming, internal scanning, stupor, coma, stored memory, expanded consciousness, and "normal." In trance or in any other altered state of consciousness a person encounters—indeed enters—another level or aspect of reality that is registered physiologically in the brain in the same way "normal" experiences are. Culturally "normal" or consensual reality is that aspect or dimension of reality of which a person is most commonly aware most of the time. Alternate reality describes that dimension of reality in which nonhuman personages such as spirits and/or the deity reside, which human beings from culturally "normal" reality can sometimes visit in ecstatic trance by taking a journey (variously called "sky journey" or "soul loss" and the like), and to which people go when they die. The experience of alternate reality is nonrational but not irrational as claimed by those who do not believe any of these things. From the perspective of these latter persons such experiences would be appropriately described as experiences of nonconsensual reality.

During the centuries before and after Paul, countless persons reported a range of visions and appearances involving celestial entities. Their experiences have to be interpreted within the framework of *their* own culture's consensus reality rather than ours. There is no reason not to take seriously what these persons say of their experiences. Paul ascribes his call by the God of Israel to his change-agent task to an altered state of consciousness experience initiated by God (Gal 1:1, 12). His descriptions of Jesus-group experiences that he ascribes to God's Spirit are all instances of such altered states events, as indicated repeatedly in our commentary. He himself notes his sky journey in which he experienced the ineffable, in

"Paradise" (2 Cor 12:1-7). Paradise in Israelite lore, of course, was the name of the garden of pleasure created by God for the first human beings (Genesis 2). However, by Paul's day this place of blessedness was transposed into the sky (see Luke 23:43), often referred to as the third or highest level of the sky, where the righteous dead dwelt awaiting the resurrection of the dead. Paul himself frequently receives directives from the realm of God (Rom 16:26; 2 Cor 12:8; Gal 2:2). Of course, Paul ascribes the visions of the resurrected Jesus to such altered state experiences (1 Cor 15:5-8). Aside from dreams and angelic appearances, the Synoptics report five main incidents of such visions and/or appearances in the career of Jesus, two by Jesus—at his baptism (Mark 1:9-11//Matt 3:13-17//Luke 3:21-22) and at his being tested as Holy Man (Mark 1:12-13//Matt 4:1-11//Luke 4:1-13)—and three by various disciples: their vision of Jesus walking on the sea of Galilee (Mark 6:45-52//Matt 14:22-33//John 6:16-21); their vision of Jesus transformed (Mark 9:2-10//Matt 17:1-9//Luke 9:28-36); and finally the various resurrection appearances, including the final appearance of Jesus, in God's name, commissioning the apostles to proclaim the gospel of God. In the book of Acts, there is a virtually endless series of episodes depicting altered state of consciousness experiences: 1:1-11 (Ascension of the Risen Jesus); 2:1-4 (descent of spirit), 5-13 (*glossōlalia*); 6:1—8:3 (Stephen 7:55-56); 8:4-40 (Philip); 9:1-9 (Paul); 9:10-19 (Ananias); 9:43—10:8 (Cornelius); 10:9-16 (Peter); 10:17-23 (interpretation of Peter's vision); 10:23-48 (soldier's house in Caesarea: Cornelius repeats; Peter explains; *glossōlalia*; trance experience); 11:1-18 (Peter explains in Jerusalem); 12:5-19 (Peter escapes arrest); 12:13-17 (maid's reaction); 13:1-3 (commission in Antioch), 4-12 (Paul and the curse); 14:1-20 (healing); 16:6-10 (altered state of consciousness experience of Spirit); 18:1-17 (Paul encouraged by the Lord); 18:18—19:4 (*glossōlalia* in Corinth); 20:23 (experience of the Spirit); 22:6-21 (Paul's vision); 23:10-11 (Lord speaks to Paul); 26:9-18 (Paul's vision, again); 27:23-26 (angel tells Paul his destiny) (see Pilch 2004). The whole book of Revelation depends upon the altered state of consciousness experiences of the prophet John (see Malina and Pilch 2000).

Mainstream U.S. culture frowns upon and even denies the human capacity for visions, trances, and experiences of alternate realities. We are very curious about nonrational dimensions of human existence but tend to label all such occurrences as irrational. John Pilch cites the work of Erika Bourguignon, who compiled a sample of 488 societies in all parts of the world, at various levels of technological complexity, and found that 90 percent of these societies evidence "alternate states of consciousness." She concludes: "Societies which do not utilize these states clearly are historical exceptions which need to be explained, rather than the vast majority of societies that do use these states" (cited by Pilch 1993:233). Thus it would be quite anachronistic and ethnocentric to take our post-Enlightenment, post-Industrial Revolution, technologically obsessed society as normative for judging anyone other than ourselves. For most of the world, even today, a report of alternate states of awareness would be considered quite normal.

Cross-cultural comparison suggests that the Gospel authors describe experiences of altered states of awareness. This may be difficult for us to believe because we have been enculturated to be selectively inattentive to such states of awareness except in dreams and under the influence of controlled substances. Pilch (1993:233) has noted:

> The physician-anthropologist Arthur Kleinman offers an explanation for the West's deficiency in this matter. "Only the modern, secular West seems to have blocked individual's access to these otherwise pan-human dimensions of the self." What is the Western problem? The advent of modern science in about the seventeenth century disrupted the bio-psycho-spiritual unity of human consciousness that had existed until then. According to Kleinman, we have developed an "acquired consciousness," whereby we dissociate self and look at self "objectively." Western culture socializes individuals to develop a metaself, a critical observer who monitors and comments on experience. The metaself does not allow the total absorption in lived experience which is the very essence of highly focused ASCs (= alternate states of consciousness). The metaself stands in the way of unreflected, unmediated experience which now becomes distanced.

If we recognize that "objectivity" is simply socially tutored subjectivity, we might be more empathetic with persons of other cultures who report perceptions we find incredible just because they are socially dysfunctional for us. (For more on the subject, see Pilch 2002a, 2002b, 2004.)

Baptism

Baptism is a prophetic symbolic action originally associated with the prophet John the Baptist. **Prophetic Symbolic Action.** The Greek word is usually never translated but simply written in the Latin alphabet. The Greek *baptisma* means dipping in some liquid. In antiquity people used water for purification rituals they undertook by themselves, on their own behalf. Such rituals restored people to some proper state after having stepped out of that state. **Clean and Unclean.** However, John's baptism was not a purification ritual, if only because it required dipping in water by a person other than oneself. John administered baptism as a symbol of the forgiveness of sin among Israelites in preparation for the forthcoming Israelite theocracy. Sin was an act of dishonoring God that, in turn, required divine satisfaction lest God be shamed in the sight of people who knew about the sin. John's baptism, as prophetic symbolic action, effectively removed the expected divine satisfaction. **Wrath.** Jesus groups took up this practice, but now it symbolized new birth into a Jesus group. As Paul explains it, the forgiveness of sin for Jesus-group members took place in the cross of Christ, whose death "for us" waived the requirement of divine satisfaction.

In either case, baptism was an administered ritual dipping by means of which people were brought across social lines into a changed social status. Some recognized status transformation rituals in our society include marriage and taking office. Baptism was such a status transformation ritual symbolizing new birth "in Christ" through which Israelites were brought across the social line separating outsiders from insiders and were transformed from the status of a nonmember to being a member of a Jesus group. With the new birth came a new life marked by the presence of the spirit, usually in altered states of consciousness experiences. **Altered States of Consciousness.** Israelite Jesus-group members looked upon themselves as forming a group of people in Christ, much like old Israel was a group of people in Israel, which is the name of the patriarch Jacob (Gen 32:28). As Paul would have it, they formed "the body of Christ" (see 1 Corinthians 12). Jesus-group baptism was perceived to effect a new birth, a biological or organic analogy for what went on in the process. Since the analogy was biological or organic, the question raised in 1 Corinthians 1–2 was: what was the relationship between the newly baptized person and the one baptizing? Is it like that of a father and child? If so, do the baptizer and the one baptized stand in some sort of ongoing relationship? This perception of the effects of baptism seems to be at issue in the formation of groups in Corinth. At least this is what Paul seems to refer to when he gives thanks to God for not having baptized anyone (with some exceptions). Perception of such relationships resulted in little groups with their own ingroup allegiance. Such sets of persons in Christ, each with its own priorities, would naturally put their own groups first, as people did in the rest of Mediterranean culture. Paul found this disconcerting, since it ruined the Hellenistic ideal of harmony, here the harmony of all in Christ.

Challenge-Riposte

Just as concern about money, paying the bills, or affording something we want to buy is perpetual and pervasive in American society, so was the concern about honor in the world of Paul. **Honor-Shame Societies.** Because honor was a limited good, competition for the scarce resource could be intense. Paul's chief opponents who challenge his honor were the Judaizers mentioned in the letters to the Galatians and the Philippians and the super-apostles mentioned in 2 Corinthians. By attempting to influence and take over Paul's clients, these challengers impugn Paul's honor, insulting him as no decent change agent at all. In this competition the game of challenge-riposte is a central and very public phenomenon, requiring Paul's Jesus-group members to look on and give a grant of honor either to Paul or to his opponents. Ideally challenge-riposte takes place among social equals: to challenge those beneath you on the social scale is to be a bully, while to challenge those above is a failure to know one's proper place. Hence one may presume that the Judaizers and super-apostles were, in Paul's estimation, social equals. Otherwise he would not engage them as he did.

The interaction begins with a challenge (almost any word, gesture, action) that seeks to undermine the honor of another person, who must respond in equal measure or up the ante (and thereby challenge in return). Both positive (gifts, compliments) and negative (insults, dares, public questioning) challenges must be answered to avoid a serious loss of face. In Paul's letters the challenges are negative, with various accusations made against Paul, both personal (his weaknesses, inability to speak in public, and the like) and objective (his dismissal of the Torah in favor of a faith like that of Abraham). In his letters Paul evidences considerable skill at riposte and thereby reveals himself to be an honorable and authoritative change agent of the God of Israel.

Change Agent

A change agent is a person who communicates information about some innovation to some designated receiving group on behalf of some change agency. Such change agents attempt to influence an innovation-decision in a direction deemed desirable by the change agency. Thus the change agent functions as a communication link between two or more social entities, the change agency responsible for the innovation and those to and for whom the innovation is directed. Change agents are usually professionals in that the task of diffusing the innovation in question constitutes a master status and is a full-time occupation.

In the New Testament documents apostles were persons sent with a commission by some commissioning agency. The commission is to proclaim the forthcoming kingdom of God, rooted eventually in God's raising Jesus from the dead. In early Jesus groups the characteristic feature of the change agent role of apostle is that it entails being commissioned by the God of Israel through the mediation of the resurrected Jesus. Of course, in the earliest documents, the letters of Paul, Paul insists on having been commissioned by the God of Israel in his revelation experience of the resurrected Jesus (Gal 1:1, 10-12). In third- and fourth-generation Jesus-group documents, we find mention of such authorization given to the Twelve through the resurrected Jesus (Matt 28:18-20; Acts 1:8).

There are seven tasks that a change agent must undertake. These tasks are traceable in what Paul mentions of his activities in his letters. The first and last tasks take place in that sequence; the other five take place variously and may be repeated: (1) develops need for changes; (2) develops an information exchange relation; (3) diagnoses problems; (4) creates intent to change; (5) translates intent into action; (6) stabilizes and prevents discontinuance; (7) terminates relationship.

1. *Develops need for changes.* A change agent is often initially required to bring awareness or knowledge to persons in some social grouping by pointing out alternatives to existing problems, by dramatizing these problems, and by convincing would-be clients that they are capable of confronting these problems. In collectivistic settings a change agent attempts to influence opinion leaders by emphasizing a broader, forthcoming horizon (thus emphasis on the coming Israelite theocracy and the Age to Come), higher contentment motivation (thus theme of reversal and righteousness through faith), lower fatalism (thus theme of need for change and responsibility), and higher aspirations (in terms of the newly introduced symbol system focused on the presence of the Spirit of the resurrected Jesus). The change agent not only assesses the would-be clients' needs at this stage but also helps to create these needs in a consultive and persuasive manner.

2. *Develops an information exchange relation.* In collectivistic societies would-be clients must accept the change agent before they will accept the innovations he or she promotes (hence the effectiveness of Paul's "all things to all men" in collectivistic Hellenistic society). The "all men" in question, of course, are fellow Israelites of varying ideologies. While initial contact with prospective clients must leave an impression of credibility, trustworthiness, and empathy with their needs and problems, the change agent must maintain an information exchange relationship with those clients to maintain and develop social identity based on the proclaimed innovation. **Social Identity.**

3. *Diagnoses problems.* The change agent is responsible for analyzing his or her clients' problems to point up why existing alternatives do not meet their needs. Thanks to information coming from the Jesus groups he founded, Paul constantly did this, as his letters indicate. In arriving at his diagnostic conclusions, the change agent must view the situation empathetically, from his clients' perspective and not his own. (Such empathy is the ability of an individual to project himself into the role of another; sympathy is the ability of an individual to project another into his own role.) Change-agent empathy is positively related with success in implementing an innovation (provided the change agent is not so empathetic that he completely takes the role of his clients and does not wish to change in the direction desired by the change agency. Such over-empathy would have Paul acquiesce in the acceptance of Israelite Torah obligations insisted upon by Judaizers and practiced by "the weak."

4. *Creates intent to change.* Here the change agent's role is to motivate intent to change. Just like the innovation that the change agent makes known, so too the motives should be client-centered in order to be effective. Hence the repeated insistence on what God has done "for us," that Jesus died "for us," and descriptions of what the forthcoming theocracy holds "for us." Of course, change-agent-centered motivation (e.g., Paul in the apocryphal Acts of Paul and Thecla) and change-agency-centered motivation (for the sake of the survival of "the church," or the Jesus group) are equally possible but in the long run ineffective.

5. *Translates intent into action.* The change agent is after action or behavioral change, not simply intellectual agreement. In essence, the agent works to promote compliance with the program he advocates, but compliance rooted in attitudinal change as well. Paul's exhortation in terms of virtues that would develop Jesus-group character are instances of emphasis upon activity. As a good change agent Paul presents both how-to knowledge (the theme of imitating Paul: 1 Thess 1:6; 2:14; 1 Cor 4:16; 11:1; Phil 3:17) as well as principle (why) knowledge. Here a sort of learning by doing (orthopraxy) precedes orthodoxy. Emphasis on orthodoxy alone prior to the actual innovation-decision to adopt the change leads to "temporizing," hence to no change at all (this is faith without Jesus-group works). On the other hand, emphasis on orthodoxy after orthopraxy, after actual adoption, serves a confirmation function and leads to self-reliance and self-renewal in client behavior (this is Jesus-group works coupled with faith).

6. *Stabilizes and prevents discontinuance.* Here the change agents seek to stabilize the new behavior, especially by directing reinforcing messages to those

who have adopted the change. At this stage, why-knowledge (orthodoxy or faith) and exhortation deriving from why-knowledge serve to allay the dissonance that is bound up with adoption of the new and rejection of the old. Much of what Paul writes to his churches is of this sort, helping to "freeze" new behavior in face of dissonance as well as in face of other change agents.

7. *Terminates relationship.* Paul's goal is to establish local Jesus groups with members who behave according to their new social identity as they await the coming of the Lord Jesus. This is fully in line with the goal of all change agents. "The end goal for any change agent is development of self renewing behavior on the part of his clients. The change agent should seek to put himself out of business by developing his clients' ability to be their own change agents. In other words the change agent must seek to shift the clients from a position of reliance on the change agent to reliance on themselves" (Rogers with Shoemaker 1971:230). It was only traveling apostles such as Paul and his coworkers who had successors (for example, the "bishops and deacons" in Phil 1:1).

By way of conclusion, we might mention that while change agents (including Jesus and Paul) can often foresee the form and social use of the innovation they diffuse, they often simply cannot or do not sense or understand the social meaning of the innovations they introduce. The questions presumably put to Paul in 1 Corinthians all deal with moot social meanings that Paul did not anticipate but that some Corinthians gave to the innovations Paul introduced. "Change agents are especially likely to make this mistake (that is, not anticipate consequences in meaning) when they do not empathize fully with the members of the recipient culture, as in cross-cultural contacts or in other heterophilous situations" (Rogers with Shoemaker 1971:337). Paul was a bridge between the various Israelite stories of his day and the new story of God's raising Jesus with a view to a forthcoming Israelite theocracy. This left him with one foot in the world of polyvalent Israel and another in the world of the gospel of God he proclaimed. His success in linking the change-agency goals with his client system lies at the heart of the process of Jesus-group development. Such a process will be marked largely by attempts at resolving such meaning problems, often with the how-to behavioral knowledge of form and function remaining unfazed.

Circumcision

Many think that in antiquity the main infallible and usable marker distinguishing an Israelite from a non-Israelite was a form of male genital mutilation called circumcision. The reason for this is that many believe that the story of Israel in the Bible is the actual history of Israel. However, the historical fact is that in the Persian empire (fifth century B.C.E.) what was left of historical Israel was Samaria. The new Persian colony of Judea, founded by the Donation of Cyrus (2 Chron 36:22-23) by a handful of returning Persian transferred elites, required a foundation story (the Exile) as well as a set of stories to enable the rather small Persian colonial enclave to establish the antiquity of these immigrants in Judea. This set of stories, composed by elite scribes, resulted in the biblical story of Israel that provided credentials for these new Judeans to claim to be true Israel.

> [By] the third century B.C., Judea proper was a small part of Palestine: it was almost identifiable with the territory of the city of Jerusalem, and as such it was still envisaged by Polybius in the middle of the second century B.C.E. (16, fr.39). Samaria and Galilee were outside it. The Samaritans—or at least those of them who were not entirely Hellenized—had built up a religious center of their own on Mount Gerizim in circumstances which contradictory legends had rendered unrecognizable. A council of laymen and priests under the presidency of the High Priest had a large measure of autonomy in its government of Jerusalem, but the presence of Ptolemaic garrison in the country must be assumed. (Momigliano 1975:88)

The point of this historical excursion is that the Old Testament law about infant circumcision, done on the eighth day after birth (Lev 12:3; a practice retrojected into the story of Gen 17:10-14), is a legend collated by Persian-period Judean scribes. Shaye Cohen, noted American Jewish scholar, has demonstrated that an emphasis on circumcision as a marker distinguishing Israelites from non-Israelites was rather late in Palestine, evidenced only during the Maccabean period, about 150 B.C.E. It took several centuries before the new Judean practice reached Israelite colonies far from Judea. Most Israelites residing among non-Israelite Hellenistic populations would consider the practice barbaric mutilation and would not adopt it.

However, the symbolic genital mutilation practiced at this time was certainly not the removal of the foreskin. The reason for this is that Israelites could have their circumcision normalized. Paul mentions "removing the marks of circumcision" in 1 Cor 7:18. Hellenizing Judeans

> tried to hide their circumcision through *epispasm*, the 'stretching' or 'drawing down' of the remains of the foreskin so that the penis would have the look of an uncircumcised organ. Those who joined the Maccabean state were circumcised as well. Greek historians recounting the Maccabean conquests knew the importance of circumcision to the Maccabees, but over a century had to elapse before outsiders began to associate circumcision with Judaism in the diaspora. The association is documented by one Latin writer in Rome in the second half of the first century B.C.E. (Horace) and by a string of Latin writers from the middle of the first century C.E. to the first quarter of the second century C.E. (Persius, Petronius, Martial, Suetonius, Tacitus, Juvenal). (Cohen 1993:13)

Cohen's research suggests two points. The first is that even the innovation of circumcision practiced in Palestine from about 150 B.C.E. was not identical with circumcision as practiced by Talmudic rabbinism and later Jews. The reason for this is the practice of epispasm, allowing for undoing the mutilation of circumcision. It was only some time after the Bar-Kochba incident, that is, about 150 C.E., that Ben Zakkaist groups of scribes (later called rabbis) introduced the requirement of the removal of the whole foreskin (Hebrew: *peri'ah*), thus preventing the drawing down of the foreskin that allowed for passing in and out of the Israelite community (see Rubin 1989).

The second point is that one cannot presume to non-Israelite identity by reference to lack of circumcision. Many members of the house of Israel were spread around the Mediterranean long before the Maccabean reforms of 150 B.C.E. With the slow rate of information flow in antiquity as well as the high degree of assimilation and accommodation of Israelites in various communities outside of Palestine, many of these Israelites were little concerned with the new trends and customs begun in Judea.

City

In the first-century Mediterranean, large landowners shaped the agenda of daily life for society at large. This sort of arrangement in which the majority of the people lived on the land, controlled by great landowners, is called a ruralized society. These great landowners, the "best people" or "aristocrats," generally had two places of residence. One was a house in the countryside, on the land that provided this elite person with power and wealth. The other was a house built as part of a cluster of such houses of other land-owning elites in a central (or nodal) place, the city. Just as small holders lived in houses clustered together (usually for support and protection) in towns and villages, so too lived the large holders whose secondary housing clusters formed the center of what the ancients called a city (Greek: *polis*; Latin: *civitas*).

The centralized set of social relationships among elites took on spatial dimension by means of territoriality. That is, these elites claimed dominance of their central place and of all the lands and peoples surrounding the central place. This is simply one dimension of the effective collective action that a political institution is. Large numbers of people were required to support the elites and their concerns both in the country and in the city. Resident city support consisted of retainers that constituted the nonelite central place population. Israelites resident in such a city belonged to the retainer status. It was these Israelites who were Paul's target audience.

Thus the first-century Mediterranean *civitas* or *polis* was really a large, ruralized central place in which properly pedigreed "gentlemen farmers/ranchers" displayed and employed their unbelievable wealth in competitions for honor among each other. Largeholders thus found it in their interest to live for a time near other largeholders in central places that likewise provided them with an organized force (the military) to protect their interests from the vast masses of other persons. The elite united to promote and defend their collective honor in face of the outgroup elites in annual rites of war, which, if carried off successfully, brought them more land and/or the produce of that land. They equally participated in the continual, if seasonal, activity of extortion called taxation. Their honor rating rooted in kinship brought them the power that brought them further wealth.

Nevertheless, for elites the city house was a secondary dwelling. It was not a private place like the dwellings of the city nonelite. Rather, the elite city house was multifunctional, a place of constant socializing and economic and sometimes political intercourse, and not simply a place of habitation. For these elites, living together essentially served the purpose of daily challenge-riposte interaction in the pursuit of honor. **Challenge-Riposte.**

Thus a city was a bounded, centralized set of social relationships concerned with effective collective action and expressed spatially in terms of architecture and the arrangement of places. Some general characteristics of cities include the following:

1. Cities always form central nodes within some broader network of social relations. In this sense, cities are central places within some region and cannot be understood without taking the regional network into account.

2. Because they are central nodes, cities are centripetal in the sense that all populations in the region forming a network with some city live with their attention directed to that city. People who live with their face toward a given central place form a general ingroup. In antiquity these people are residents of the city and its attending villages. The outgroup is formed by people whose face looks toward other cities.

3. Since every city is centripetal, a city is a terminal with all roads leading to the terminal from villages and regions in the area. Even other cities are simply part of the surrounding area and connect with the central, ingroup city. What determines whether a city is a final terminal or not is the awareness of the one living in the city. "My city"/"our city" is always a terminal. All others lead to it. This is rooted in the human perception of space and human limitation. In antiquity it is social geography that determines me in my group, that forms the focal node of everything around "us" as opposed to "them." This arrangement helps underscore the boundary between ingroup and outgroup. Our city is always the center of the ingroup. Everything leads to us, including other cities, and it is essentially because it is our city that it is terminal.

4. A city is a way of effectively realizing a range of collective activity by means of some specific arrangement of territoriality. In antiquity territoriality referred to the delimiting of some geographic area in terms of the persons organically related to the area that they define and delimit. In antiquity people thought of themselves and the place they occupied as organically linked. That geographical place was likewise the place where their ancestors dwelt and were buried, and the land itself was often given to them by a deity.

5. Becoming a rightful resident of a city in antiquity was totally unlike modern western territoriality in which simple physical residence can endow persons and groups with civic rights and obligations. In antiquity it was group membership on other than territorial criteria that determined who belonged in a given city, specifically some social relationship with ruling elite and other residents of the city. The

alien or stranger was one who had no social relationship with ruling elites or other city residents.

6. While cities are institutions that primarily seek some effective collective action for some part of their population, the specific focus or social goals of a given city depend on the general social system prevailing at the time. In antiquity the institutions we call economics and religion were embedded in kinship and politics. Hence along with their political functions, often symbolized by the palace and wall, ancient cities likewise pursued political religion and political economy.

7. Political religion means that the roles, goals, and values of the polity serve to articulate and express religion. In theocracies the temple is a replication of the palace, and temple personnel, interactions, and functions follow the pattern of palace personnel, interactions, and functions. If the palace houses a king with a large body of servants, from prime minister to royal slaves running royal farms to feed palace household and army alike, then the temple houses a divine monarch with a large body of servants, from primary major domo (high priest) to temple slaves running temple lands to feed the temple household and staff alike. In other political forms temples are usually the concern of local elite families. In no case are temples directly for the benefit of worshipers, just as palaces are not directly for the benefit of loyal subjects.

The political economy, of course, means that the roles, goals, and values of the polity serve to articulate and express economics. The chief beneficiaries of the economy are central political personages, whether in palace or in temple. The system of taxation and tribute look to the well-being of elites.

8. Given the reality of political religion and political economy and the distinctive features of Greco-Roman and Middle Eastern cities, we might draw up a sort of range of emphases in political institutions of antiquity. With the political institution at the center, and with economics and religion on either end, we might rank the city as a theocracy (at one extreme) or as a port of trade (at the other extreme). Moving toward the center on the theocracy side we have the Middle Eastern city ranging from priestly control to kinship control (royalty), while moving toward the center from the economics side, we have the *polis* or *civitas* in varying degrees: democratic, aristocratic, or monarchic.

9. The populations of cities are stratified. In ancient cities with their political religions, these stratified populations form hierarchies, with superior personages wielding "sacred power" over lesser personages. Injury done to superiors is always some form of "sacrilege." This is what hierarchy implies.

Actual cities of antiquity, such as Rome and Jerusalem or Corinth and Thessalonika, were substantially different from their modern industrial counterparts: 85 percent of the population lived in villages or small towns and were primarily engaged in agriculture. City populations were sharply divided between a small, literate elite that controlled the center of politics, political religion, and political economy, and a large, mostly illiterate nonelite that provided the goods and services the elite required. Since the only real market for most goods and services was the city elite, the labor pool required to provide them was small. Excess population was thus kept out of the cities whenever possible. By modern standards, preindustrial cities were thus quite small.

Elite residences and temples dominated the center of the preindustrial city, often with fortifications of their own. The elites controlled cult, coinage, writing, and taxation for the entire society. At the outer limits of the city lived the poorest occupants, frequently in walled-off sections of the city in which occupational and ethnic groups lived and worked together. (Note that the configuration of an industrial city is just the opposite: the poorest people live in the center, while the richest live in the suburbs.) Outside the city walls lived beggars, prostitutes, persons in undesirable occupations, traders (often wealthy), and landless peasants who drifted toward the city in search of day-laboring opportunities. They required access to the city during the day but were locked out at night. Gates in internal city walls could also be locked at night to prevent access to elite areas for nonelite persons.

Social interaction between various groups living in the cities was kept to a minimum. Like socialized with like. Especially difficult was the position of those living immediately outside the city walls. They were cut off from both elite and nonelite of the city on the one hand and from the protection of a village on the other. In many cities they became the source of continual replenishment of the nonelite, artisan population, needed because of the high death rates among the urban nonelite.

What this description intimates is that Paul's initial Israelite audience was composed of city retainers who lived in an ethnic quarter that had minimal interaction with city elites and largely socialized with each other.

Clean and Unclean: See Purity/Pollution

Clique

For Mediterranean anthropologists, the second most important social institution after the family or kin group in this culture area is the coalition. A coalition is a type of impermanent group gathered for specific purposes over a limited time period. In social-science terminology, it is a fluid, impermanent multidimensional network of relations focused on limited goals. Coalitions characterized both elites and nonelites in the first-century Mediterranean world. In contrast with coalitions stood "corporate groups," such as political parties or closed statuses among elites. Corporate groups were based on enduring principles: for example, birth and marriage (Sadducee party and its priestly basis); birth and political allegiance (Herodians); tested fictive kinship rooted in commitment to a common ideology (the purity fellowship of the Pharisees, community members of Qumran's Essenes).

Corporate groups are rather formal, socially compulsory, and tightly knit. Coalitions are informal, socially elective, and loosely knit. Identifying with a coalition did not override membership or commitments to more fundamental groups such as the family. But membership in a corporate group, such as the Pharisaic movement groups, involved one's family as well. The Jesus groups established by Paul were coalitions. There are a number of different coalition types, such as action sets, cliques, factions, and gangs (other names for coalitions include salon, coterie, entourage, machine, social circle, team, clientele, following, school, and the like; see Boissevain 1974).

A clique is a type of coalition, defined as a collection of people within some larger, encapsulating structure, consisting of distinct parties in temporary alliances for some limited purpose. Specifically, a clique is a coalition whose members associate regularly with each other on the basis of affection (shared commitment, for emotional, expressive reasons) and common interests (for pragmatic, instrumental reasons) and possess a marked sense of identity. In 1 Corinthians 1–3, the sense of identity of Corinthian clique members is indicated by the label "I belong to . . ." Hence the problem Paul addresses in 1 Corinthians is that of clique formation rooted in the social interactions surrounding the ritual introduction of members into the Jesus group of Corinth.

The greater problem with cliques is that they may transform into factions. Factions, too, are a type of coalition specifically formed around some central person who recruits followers for a certain purpose, for a given time. In the Gospels Jesus recruited a faction to assist him in the task of proclaiming the kingdom. In a faction, group members have loyalty to the faction founder, not to each other, and much less to the total coalition membership. Factions share the common goal of the person recruiting the faction. Membership is based on a relationship with that central personage. Thus such cliques and ensuing factions are totally contrary to the "love" and unity that Paul seeks to characterize the Jesus groups he founded. **Love and Hate.**

Collectivistic Personality

In contemporary American culture we consider an individual's psychological makeup to be the key to understanding who a person might be. We see each individual as bounded and unique, a more or less integrated motivational and cognitive universe, a dynamic center of awareness and judgment that is set over against other such individuals and interacts with them. This sort of individualism has been and is extremely rare in the world's cultures and is almost certainly absent from the New Testament.

In the ancient Mediterranean world such a view of the individual did not exist. There every person was understood to be embedded in others and had his or her identity only in relation to these others who formed this fundamental group. For most people this was the family, and it meant that individuals neither acted nor thought of themselves as persons independent of the family group. What one member of the family was, every member of the family was, psychologically as well as every other way. Mediterraneans are what anthropologists call "collectivistic" or group-oriented persons. They are "dyadic" or "other-oriented" people who depend on others to provide them with a sense of who they are. **Love and Hate.**

Consider the chart on the opposite page comparing individualist, weak-group persons (United States) and dyadic, collectivist, or strong-group persons (Mediterranean):

Of course persons enculturated in collectivistic societies are individuals. But there is a difference between the self in collectivistic societies and the self in individualistic societies (see Greenwald and Pratkanis 1984). Anthropologists commonly distinguish three distinctive selves: the privately defined self, the publicly defined self, and the collectively or ingroup defined self (see Rohrbaugh 2002).

(a) The *private self* is what I myself say about my own traits, states, behaviors. Who is it I think I really am in my heart of hearts?

(b) The *public self* consists of what the general group says about me. Who does that range of people with whom I regularly come in contact think I am? What do neighbors, merchants, teachers, and the like say about me? Do I live up to their expectations when I interact with them? And what do I think of all that these people think of me?

(c) The *collective* or *ingroup self* is what the ingroup says about me. Who do my parents say I am? What are their expectations for me? Did my family give me a nickname? What does it say about me? What are the expectations of my grandparents, aunts and uncles, cousins, and brothers and sisters in regard to who I am, how I should behave, what I will be? And what do I think of what these people think of me? What do my friends want me to do, over against what my parents want me to do?

To understand the self in terms of social psychology we need to know the way the defined self emerges in the contrasting collectivist and individualistic cultural types. Consider the following table, in which the enclosed, boxed-in defined selves are expected to match to produce "truth."

Collectivist Culture	**Individualist Culture**
Privately defined self **Ingroup defined self**	**Privately defined self** **Publicly defined self**
Publicly defined self	Ingroup defined self

The types of self appearing in boldface in the above table form a unity in the respective cultures. What this chart makes clear is that in collectivist cultures there is a general conformity between private self and ingroup self. Such people take ingroup self-assessments far more seriously than people in individualist cultures. Moreover, individuals are socialized not to express what they personally think, but to say what their conversation partner or audience needs or wants to hear from the ingroup.

When it comes to dealing with ingroup others, collectivist societies anticipate that individuals will often think one way and speak another. Individuals must keep their private self opinions to themselves, since such individual private opinions

Collectivist Person	**Individualist Person**
1. Much concern about the effect of one's decision upon others (beyond friends and nuclear family).	1. Much concern about the effect of one's decision on one's present standing and future chances.
2. Persons are prepared to share material resources with group members.	2. Those who are not part of the nuclear family are expected to provide their own material resources.
3. Persons are ready to share less tangible resources with group members, for example, giving up some interesting activity for group ends.	3. Generally a person is not expected to and will not share less tangible resources with others, often not even with nuclear family (for example, time to watch weekend football game).
4. Persons are willing to adopt the opinions of others, especially those held in high esteem in the wider group.	4. Persons are expected to form their own opinion on a range of issues, especially politics, religion, and sex. Expert opinion accepted only in law and health, and this only for oneself and nuclear family.
5. Persons are constantly concerned about self-presentation and loss of face, since these reflect upon the group and one's position in the group.	5. Unless others are involved in one's goals, there is little concern about one's impression on others. Embarrassment affects the individual (and at times the nuclear family) but not any group at large.
6. Persons believe, feel, and experience an interconnectedness with the whole group, so that positive and negative behavior redounds to the group.	6. Individualists act as though insulated from others; what they do is not perceived to affect others, and what others do does not affect them.
7. Persons sense themselves to be intimately involved in the life of other group members, to make a contribution to the life of others in the group.	7. The individualist's life is segmented. Persons feel involved in the life of very few people, and when they are, it is in a very specific way (for example, the teacher, the lawyer, etc.).
8. In sum, strong-group people have "concern" for all group members. This is a sense of oneness with other people; a concern is group survival. The root of strong-group feeling is a perception of complex ties and relationships and a tendency to keep other people in mind.	8. In sum, weak-group people have "concern" largely for themselves (and nuclear family, at times). They are insulated from other people, sense themselves independent of and unconnected to others, and tend to think of themselves alone.

are insignificant and quite boring for the most part. Harmony or getting along with ingroup members is valued above all sorts of other concerns. Saying the right thing to maintain harmony is thus far more important than telling what seems to be the truth to the private self. In fact "truth" might be defined here as conformity between what the ingroup thinks about some person, event, or thing, and what the private self believes and knows. Collectivist persons are not expected to have personal opinions, much less to voice their own opinions. It is sufficient and required to hold only those opinions that derive from the social consensus of ingroup members.

In individualist cultures, by contrast, the ingroup self recedes. The public and private selves converge to form a single, "objectively" defined private self. Inconsistency between the public and the private self is understood to be hypocrisy. One must think and say the same thing. Honesty, frankness, and sincerity are more abstract and less interpersonal for individualists. Everyone is expected to have an opinion on everything, and others are supposed to act as though everyone's opinion counted for something.

The way in which the self is defined also determines behavior. The collectivist person represents the ingroup and is presumed to always speaks in its name. It is shameful to tell the truth if it dishonors one's ingroup members or causes them discomfort. It is equally shameful to expect to be told the truth if one is not an ingroup member. Outgroup persons have no right to ingroup truth.

In nonchallenging situations, outgroup persons are almost always told what makes for harmony and what is to be expected. Making a friend feel good by what one has to say is a way of honoring the other, and that is far more important than "telling the truth." Thus in collectivist cultures the privately defined self and the ingroup self tend to coincide. The person speaks in the name of the ingroup in public.

By contrast, individualists as a rule fuse the privately and publicly defined selves. The privately defined self and the publicly defined self tend to coincide. The private self is in fact the acting public self. This is called "objectivity," and individualists value being objective in speech. To lie is to say one thing publicly while thinking another privately. Thus in individualistic cultures a person speaks in his or her own name in public.

In each type of culture, a lie consists of splitting the selves included in the boxes above. Thus an individualistic lie is to think one thing privately and say another publicly. That involves splitting what one knows privately from what one says publicly. To a collectivist, however, a lie involves splitting private and ingroup "truth." In a collectivist culture, one's personal, private knowledge has nothing to do with truth.

The right to the truth and the right to withhold the truth belong to the "man of honor," and to contest these rights is to place a person's honor in jeopardy, to challenge that person. Lying and deception are or can be honorable and legitimate when directed to the outgroup. To lie in order to deceive an outsider, one who has no right to the truth, is honorable. However, to be called a liar by anyone is a great public dishonor. The reason for this is that truth belongs only to one who has a right to it. To lie really means to deny the truth to one who has a right to it, and the right to the truth only exists where respect is due (in the family, to superiors, and not necessarily to inferiors or to equals with whom one competes). Thus to deceive by making something ambiguous or to lie to an outgroup person is to deprive the other of respect, to refuse to show honor, to humiliate another.

A consequence of all this is that ancient collectivistic people did not know each other very well in the way we think most important: psychologically or emotionally. They neither knew nor cared about psychological development and were not introspective. Our comments about the feelings and emotional states of characters in the biblical stories are simply anachronistic projections of our sensibilities onto them. Their concern was how others thought of them (honor), not how they thought of themselves (guilt). Conscience was the accusing voice of others, not an interior voice of guilt (note Paul's comments in 1 Cor 4:1-4). Their question was not the modern one, "Who am I?" Rather, their questions were those asked by Jesus in Mark 8:27-30: "Who do people say that I am?" and "Who do you say that I am?" It is from significant others that such information came, not from oneself. Hence one can understand Paul's insistence on having his ingroup recognize him as an authentic change agent authorized by the God of Israel, and not like the super-apostles of 2 Corinthians or the Judaizers of Galatians.

Conflict

The disputing process consists of three phases: grievance, conflict, dispute. **Dispute Process.** Grievance is individual; a single person or group feels aggrieved by what some aggrieving party says or does. When the aggrieved confronts the person or group causing the grievance, the result is conflict. In terms of this sequence, the conflicts alluded to in Paul's letters began as a rule when local Israelites nurtured a grievance against Paul and the Jesus-group members he recruited. The grievance led to Israelite opposition. Their disagreement with the innovation Paul proclaimed led to the conflict stage.

Aggrieved local Israelites opted for confrontation, as Paul notes. In some unspecified way, they threw down the gauntlet and communicated their resentment or feelings of injustice to the offending parties, their former synagogue members. This is the "persecution" (NRSV; Greek: *thlipsis*) that Paul refers to. There are no details in the document about what fellow Israelites may have done. However, now both parties have become aware that disagreement exists between them. The conflict phase, therefore, is dyadic. It is now the offenders' move. They may escalate or attempt to deescalate the grievance or move to some settlement through coercion or negotiation with the aggrieved party. The general solution of Jesus groups seems to have been simply the avoidance of aggrieved Israelites.

Avoidance means withdrawing from a situation or curtailing or terminating a relationship by leaving, finding new interacting partners, and so on. This way of dealing with conflict might also be called "exiting." It involves no third party, and its outcome is the reduction or termination of social interaction on the basis of unilateral decision. Jesus groups developed social boundaries to avoid interaction with fellow Israelites.

On the other hand, if such interactions continued, this strategy for dealing with conflict is called "lumping it," or the failure of a party to a conflict to press its claim or complaint, ignoring the problem that gave rise to the disagreement, and continuing the relationship with the offending party. Thus "lumping it" means ignoring the issue in dispute and continuing the relationship. Reasons for lumping it include lack of information or access to persons who can help and perception of low gain and high cost (including psychic and social costs and gains). This form of dealing with conflict does not involve any third party. Its expected outcome is continued relations, and it is based on the unilateral decision of the one lumping it.

In Mediterranean society while women, children, and slaves were expected to behave in this fashion, lumping it was certainly no option for an honorable male. Paul is never pictured as acting this way, nor is Jesus (turning the other cheek is not about this sort of behavior).

Coworkers: Innovators and First Adopters

Paul frequently makes reference to his "fellow workers" (Prisca and Aquila, Rom 16:3; Urbanus and Stachys, Rom 16:9; Timothy, Rom 16:21; Titus; 1 Cor 8:23; Philemon, Phlm 1; Mark, Aristarchus, Demas, Luke, Phlm 24; unnamed, 1 Cor 16:16; Phil 4:3). Since these fellow workers were not from the Jerusalem Judean Jesus groups, they came from the groups founded by Paul or other non-Judean Jesus groups. Which clients of such foundations would become coworkers? From the perspective of the process of communicating an innovation, where would these fellow workers fit in? The likely candidates are called innovators and first adopters.

Characteristics of innovators and first adopters include the following. First of all, they must control adequate material and personality resources to absorb the possible failure due to an unsuccessful innovation. Then they need to have the ability to understand and apply rather complex knowledge, and they must have the salient value—venturesomeness, a desire for the hazardous, the rash, the daring, the risky. Finally, innovators and first adopters are cosmopolites; that is, they have contact with outsiders, with more cosmopolite social relationships. If the innovation is mainly functional (affecting how the local social system functions) material resources of these first adopters enable them to absorb the risk of innovation undertaking. When the innovation is restructuring the local social system—for example, establishing a house church—then the material resources of innovators and first adopters get redistributed. That Jesus was after some restructuring innovation is indicated by the tradition of "selling all and following me." The behavior of Jesus-group members who lay their donations at the feet of the apostles, the parade example of Barnabas, who sells his property, as well as Paul's collecting a sort of tithe for the Jerusalem "poor" would indicate a sort of restructuring.

Be that as it may, at least some of the innovators and first adopters of the innovation proclaimed by Paul would have to share in the above qualities to some degree. We would not expect innovators among the local elites nor among the lowest strata of the nonelite, strong-group/high-grid conservative class, since both these groups are usually quite conservative about the status quo. It would be the more cosmopolite and venturesome members of the local Israelite groups who might risk faith in the God of Israel's raising Jesus from the dead at the innovation stage. For Paul's churches, a number of his fellow workers travel, indicating their cosmopolite quality: Prisca and Aquila, Titus, Timothy.

Death and Resurrection

When Paul proclaims that the God of Israel raised Jesus from the dead, he presumes his Israelite audience knows what he is talking about with his reference to resurrection. The term "resurrection" was a technical term in Israel, to be distinguished from the resuscitation of a dead person or reviving a corpse. Resurrection meant the transformation of a dead person into a life marked by a radically different way of being a living human.

The expectation of the resurrection of the dead derived from Persia, undoubtedly part and parcel of the ideology of the Persian scribes responsible for the foundation of Jerusalem and Judea. This feature of Persian belief had its champions in the Judean group that came to be called the Pharisees (perhaps from the Persian word for Persian, "Farsi"). This belief in such a resurrection emerged in ancient Israel about the second century B.C.E. (see Dan 12:2-3; 2 Macc 12:43-46; Wis 4:16; and in subsequent Israelite writings). During the time of Paul, Pharisees believed in such a resurrection, as did the Qumran covenanters; the Sadducees opposed the idea as unscriptural.

Archaeological evidence and later scribal Pharisaic documents disclose to us the meaning of Israelite burial customs among Pharisees at the time of Paul. They regarded death as a lengthy process, not a moment in time. In elite Pharisee circles in Judea, between the last breath and sundown, the body would be laid out on a shelf in a tomb carved into limestone bedrock outside Jerusalem. Mourning rites would commence, continuing throughout the year as the body underwent decomposition. The rotting of the flesh was regarded as painful but also expiatory for the dead person. One's evil deeds were thought to be embedded in the flesh and to dissolve along with it.

After a year, the mourning ritual concluded. In the first century, people thought that the bones retained the personality and that God would use them to support new flesh for the resurrection. After this year of purification and putrefaction, the bones of the deceased were often collected and placed in an ossuary or "bone box," which was in fact a second burial casket. This process was called the *ossilegium*, "the collection of bones." The ossuary was designed like a box for scrolls, just long enough for the thigh bones to be laid in like scroll spindles awaiting a new hide and new inscription by the divine hand. In an alternate image, the bones could also be regarded as loom posts made ready for God to weave a new body. In keeping with these views on the character of resurrection, inkwells and spindle whorls have been found in excavated tombs.

This day of second burial marked the end of the family's mourning and its turn toward the hope of reunion and resurrection. Obviously, then, the disappearance or loss of a body after death would be experienced as a greater calamity than the death itself because the family would be unable to prepare the bones for resurrection.

Legally, even the bones of an executed criminal were supposed to be returned to the family after being held in custody of the Sanhedrin during the year-long period of atoning putrefaction. In effect, capital punishment included the loss of life, the suppression of mourning, and the imposition of supposedly painful but purifying disintegration of the flesh overseen by the court in a special tomb maintained for that purpose. When the flesh was gone, the sentence was completed, the debt was paid, and the bones became eligible for resurrection.

These cultural beliefs and practices provide the context for understanding the claims of the first generations of Jesus' followers about the Resurrected Jesus, then adopted as tradition by second-generation Jesus-group members (see 1 Corinthians 15). In one first-generation view, expressed in the Gospel of John, Jesus dies condemned by the Judean populace, leaders and crowds alike (although at the hands of the Romans). Then a ranking Judean, Joseph of Arimathea, takes his body into custody. It is laid in a separate tomb, to begin to serve the sentence of decay in order to atone for its sins. It is precisely this penal/atonement process that is interrupted if the tomb is suddenly discovered to be empty. To say that Jesus was raised is to say that God overturned the judgment of Israel's chief-priests and the Judean populace, the judgment that Jesus needed to rot to prepare for resurrection. Instead, God supposedly took Jesus directly from last breath to resurrection because there had been no guilt in his flesh. God intervened before the rotting started; hence God overturned the death sentence. The claim that Jesus was raised by God is a claim of divine vindication for the deeds and words of Jesus. Taken in its cultural context, the claim of resurrection for Jesus asserts that his death was wrong and has been overturned by a higher judge. Interestingly, the Gospel of John preserves the first-generation view. For John, Jesus died because of the intransigence of the Judeans, but God rescued and vindicated him because Jesus was in fact the mediator of life itself.

This first-generation understanding of the death of Jesus contrasts sharply with a theological one that emerged among second-generation Jesus-group members like Paul. Jesus' death was considered to be an event that happened "for us," to take away God's wrath, hence to have God waive our previous behavior that dishonored God and required divine satisfaction. **Wrath.** Paul's theology, concerned with the revelation of the activity of the God of Israel in the death and resurrection of Jesus, is heavily rooted in the "for us" dimensions of this double event. Faith in the God of Israel who was responsible for this event results in divine approval and acceptance, that is, righteousness. The objective outcomes include redemption (restoration of social status before God), salvation (rescue from divine wrath), and sanctification (status of ingroup exclusivity, God's own people). In this theological view, Jesus gave himself "for us" quite deliberately because God wanted him dead for the benefit of others.

Third- and fourth-generation Jesus-group authors such as the Synoptics juxtapose the two interpretations of Jesus' death and resurrection in a smooth narrative sequence, with Jesus even predicting three times that he will die and be raised. For these authors, Jesus' resurrection underscores God's vindication of Jesus as well as assures the resurrection of those who believe in this revelation of the God of Israel.

Demons/Demon Possession

In the worldview of first-century Mediterranean people, causality was primarily personal. Every significant effect in a person's or group's life was believed to have been caused by a person, human or other-than-human. Not only was this true at the level of ordinary society, but at the levels of nature and the cosmos as well. Things beyond human control, such as weather, earthquakes, disease, and fertility, were believed to be controlled by other-than-human persons who operated in a cosmic social hierarchy. Each level in the hierarchy could control the ones below:

1. "Our" God, the Most High God
2. "Other" Gods or sons of God or archangels or stars/planets
3. Lower nonhuman persons: angels, spirits, demons
4. Humankind
5. Creatures lower than humankind

The activity of the God of Israel among people is ascribed to God's Spirit, the Holy Spirit. But along with God as unseen, effective agent, there were lesser entities. In Paul the most significant "son of God" (see Job 1) mentioned is Satan, a celestial entity that tests loyalties to God. Satan was a Persian social role, a secret service agent in the service of the Persian kings who tested the loyalties of the king's subjects. In Greek, Satan is translated *diabolos*, "devil," whose social role is not to be confused with that of demons. Demons (these are Greek entities), angels (another social role borrowed from Persia), and spirits (Semitic entities) account for significant effects in a person's life not caused by visible or present human persons. Satan is essentially a tester of loyalty to God, a sort of secret service agent. Originally (see Job 1) Satan was in God's service, but in Israelite lore, this Satan broke away from divine service and began to acquire his own following from among those no longer loyal to the God of Israel. For Satan in Paul's letters, see the commentary at 1 Thess 2:18; 1 Cor 5:5; 7:5; 2 Cor 2:11; 11:14; 12:7; Rom 16:20.

Paul is fully cognizant of the influence of stars and planets (elemental spirits, Gal 4:3, 9), of angels (the Persian/Israelite version of demons: Rom 8:38; 1 Cor 4:9; 6:3; 11:10; 13:1; Gal 2:18; 3:19), and of a hierarchy of angels (archangel, 1 Thess 4:16; principalities, Rom 8:38).

Demons (Greek), angels (Persian), and spirits (Semitic) were thus personified forces that had the power to influence and, at times, control human behavior. Accusations of demon possession were based on the belief that forces beyond human control were causing the effects humans observed. Since evil attacks good, people expected to be assaulted (Luke 13:16). A person accused of demon possession was a person whose behavior (external symptom) was deviant or who was embedded in a matrix of deviant social relationships. Such a deviant situation or behavior required explanation and could be attributed to God (positive) or to evil spirits/demons/angels (dangerous), something the community would be anxious to clarify in order to identify and expel persons who represented a threat.

The only time Paul alludes to such spirit possession is in an analogy in Rom 7:15-25 to explain how sin, the cultural force expressed in the willingness to dishonor God, can take over a person's behavior. And he identifies the entities so effective in non-Israelite sacrifices as demons (1 Cor 10:20-21).

Devolution

It is a common belief of twenty-first century Americans that human society is progressing. Even U.S. biblical fundamentalists who will hear nothing of biological evolution still believe that the United States is the greatest society in the world and getting better and better. This belief in progress, in things getting better and better, is a belief in social evolution. People in antiquity, on the other hand, did not share such a belief. All ancient Mediterranean peoples, it seems, believed the world was running down. The prevailing view was one of devolution and gradual collapse of the cosmos in general and of society in particular (Downing 1995a; 1995b; Ax 1996). A Greek might call this "kakoterology" (= worse-ology).

To call the ancient symbols of this common belief "apocalyptic" and systems of explicating the symbols "eschatology" is simply not useful. We live in a society that has a parallel and equally strong belief in evolution (social and organismic in face of physical entropy) and progress. Should we then call our cultural outlook "scientific" and develop a theological perspective that is "kreittology" (or kreissology or belterology = better-ology)?

The common ancient perception was that both the physical and social environment evidenced devolution, or movement from a greater to a lesser level in quality, character, or vitality; a fall from a higher to a lower level in quality, character, or vitality; a change from a stronger to a weaker level in quality, character, or vitality; an alteration from a certain to a doubtful level in quality, character, or vitality. What people experienced was environmental and social deterioration, degeneration, decadence, and decline. Deterioration generally implies the impairment of value or usefulness. Degeneration stresses physical, intellectual, or especially moral retrogression. Decadence presupposes a reaching and passing the peak of development and implies a turn downward with a consequent loss of vitality or energy. Decline suggests a more markedly downward direction and greater momentum as well as more obvious evidence of deterioration. All Mediterraneans of the first century believed in this sort of devolution. But not all agreed on what would happen when the physical and social systems ran down.

In the time of Paul, members of philosophical schools of Stoics and Epicureans were quite convinced about the devolution of the world. It was attributed to the world's senescence; it was getting too old. The Stoics believed the world would end in conflagration, only to be regenerated. The Epicurean tradition thought the whole world would simply end. And Platonists and Aristotelians thought the world to be eternal, even if slowing down. Philosophical theories of a golden age at creation, followed by a silver age, a bronze age, an iron age, and an age of clay equally point to the running down of the cosmos. (This theory is adopted by the Israelite prophet in Dan 2:30-45: golden, silver, bronze, iron, clay.)

But non-philosophers equally shared this perception. Pliny (*De rerum natura* 7.73) observed, "You can almost see that the stature of the whole human race is decreasing daily, with few men taller than their fathers, as the crucial conflagration which our age is approaching exhausts the fertility of human semen." In Israelite circles as well we learn, "You and your contemporaries are smaller in stature than those who were born before you, and those who come after you will be smaller than you, as if born of a creation which is also aging and passing the strength of [its] youth" (*4 Ezra* 5:51). The document known as *2 Baruch* likewise attests to the fact that "the world is hastening swiftly to its end" (4:26), "for the age has lost its youth and the times begin to grow old" (14:10). Third-generation Jesus-group authors tell of an end in which "after that tribulation, the sun will be darkened, and the moon will not give its light, and stars will be falling from heaven, and the powers in the heavens will be shaken" (Mark 13:24).

In Israelite perspective, while devolution points to some denouement of the present forms of human social and physical experience, yet as the scriptures say, "A generation goes, and a generation comes, but the earth remains for ever" (Eccl 1:4). So the "end of the world" is not the end of the world but the end of present social and physical arrangements. The distinctive feature of Jesus groups is that this devolution concludes with the coming of an Israelite theocracy, the kingdom of God in the Coming Age. When the God of Israel raised Jesus from the dead, Israelite believers knew that the devolutionary process would come to an end with the advent of the kingdom of the God of Israel. The problems raised by life in this devolutionary period deal with the attitudes and behaviors that befit this situation. Paul has this in mind, of course, as he tells the Corinthians, for example, "I mean, brethren, the appointed time has grown very short" (1 Cor 7:29).

Dispute Process

Disputes emerge through a series of stages. At the origin of every dispute is a grievance perceived by a single person or single group. Conflict follows if the aggrieved person or group chooses to confront the person(s) thought to be responsible for the grievance. **Conflict.** In this two-party phase, both are now aware of antagonism. Should the conflict become public, then three parties are actually involved. This three-party stage is called a dispute.

1. Grievance or pre-conflict: The real or imagined circumstances or conditions that one person or group perceives to be unjust and the grounds for resentment or complaint. For instance, in 1 Cor 5:1, Paul sets out a grievance. Since only one party is aware of misconduct, this phase is monadic; any unfolding of a dispute

process depends on steps taken by the offended party. The offended party here is Paul. Of course the implied question is, Why should he be so aggrieved?

2. Conflict: If the offended party opts for confrontation and communicates disapproval, there is resentment or feeling of injustice toward the offending party. Both parties are now aware of antagonism; hence the dispute enters the dyadic phase. The conflict phase is expressed in 1 Cor 5:1b, c. Paul is offended by the behavior of a couple in the community "that is not found even among pagans; for a man is living with his father's wife." The aggrieved Paul then challenges the community's honor with these exclamations: "And you are arrogant! Ought you not rather to mourn?" The further development of the process depends on steps taken by the offender (to escalate or deescalate by coercion or negotiation with the aggrieved party).

3. Dispute: The dispute phase is marked by the escalation of the conflict being made public. A third party (the public: a person or group) is now actively involved, hence a triadic phase. In our text segment this stage is marked by Paul's recommendation that the entire community become aware of the problem: "When you are assembled . . . you are to hand this man over to Satan for the destruction of the flesh" (1 Cor 5:4-5).

All societies have developed procedures that are called into operation when trouble arises (also known as conflict management procedures). The same basic procedural modes are used worldwide in attempts to deal with grievances, conflicts, or disputes: lumping it, avoidance, coercion (conquest), negotiation, mediation, arbitration, adjudication (Nader and Todd 1978:8–11).

Briefly, each procedure can be defined as follows:

a. Lumping it: This is the failure of an aggrieved party to press his claim or complaint, ignoring the problem that gave rise to the disagreement and continuing the relationship with the offending party. Thus lumping it means ignoring the issue in dispute and continuing the relationship. Reasons for lumping it: lack of information or access to persons who can help, perception of low gain and high cost (including psychic and social costs and gains). This form of dealing with conflict does not involve any third party. Its expected outcome is continued relations, and it is based on the unilateral decision of the one lumping it. In Mediterranean society, while women, children, and slaves were expected to behave in this fashion, lumping it was certainly no option for an honorable male. Jesus is never pictured as acting this way (turning the other cheek is not about this sort of behavior). In 1 Corinthians 5, Paul does not act in this way either.

b. Avoidance: This means withdrawing from a situation or curtailing or terminating a relationship by leaving, finding new interacting partners, and so forth. This way of dealing with conflict might also be called "exiting." It involves no third party, and its outcome is the reduction or termination of social interaction on the basis of unilateral decision.

In the story of Jesus Luke's description of Jesus' leaving Nazareth for Capernaum is a prime example of such avoidance (Luke 4:28-30). In Luke's story of Paul, the Apostle was dissuaded from confronting those who had a grievance against him (Acts 19:30-31), so he opted to leave after the uproar had ceased (Acts 20:1).

c. Coercion: This means the threat or actual use of force to resolve a dispute. Conquest is synonymous with such coercion. There is no third party involved in such conflict management. The expected outcome is violent settlement and often aggravation of conflict based on the unilateral decision of the one exerting force. Jesus' death at the hands of significant corporate groups marks the usual way those groups resolved dispute cases. Paul escaped death in Jerusalem when the tribune and soldiers came upon the crowd attempting to kill Paul because of his presumed misbehavior in the Temple (Acts 21:27-32).

d. Negotiation: This is a dyadic arrangement of mutual influence. The two principal parties are the decision makers, and the settlement is one to which both parties agree by mutual persuasion. "They seek not to reach a solution in terms of rules, but to create the rules by which they can organize their relationship with one another" (Gulliver 1973:2–3). Thus while there is no third party involved, the outcome of negotiation is new rules of social interaction mutually consented to. It is therefore a dyadic arrangement. Within the Jesus-movement group, it seems to have been presumed that Jesus' new teaching derived from God through negotiation between God and Jesus. It was Jesus' style of obeying and pleasing God that received divine sanction in the "Listen to him" oracles (Mark 9:7 // Matt 17:5 // Luke 9:35). Paul reports a similar negotiation between himself and the "pillars," James, Cephas, and John (Gal 2:9-10).

e. Mediation: This refers to the intervention by a third party, agreed to by both principals, to aid the principals in reaching agreement. Here a third party is present. The outcome of the procedure is new rules of social interaction mutually consented to. Thus the arrangement is triadic. It seems that all honor-shame interactions based on challenge and riposte are rooted in a form of mediation, for the purpose of such a challenge is to win a grant of honor from the attending onlookers, the crowd or the public. Both challenger and riposter implicitly consent to abide by the decision of the onlookers and are treated accordingly. In 2 Corinthians Paul expects the recipients of his letter to give a grant of honor to him rather than the super-apostles. Yet the judgment of the addressees is really not final but merely ad hoc, until the next challenge.

f. Arbitration: This refers to the intervention by a third party, agreed to by both principals, whose judgment they must agree to accept beforehand. This third party may be human or divine. Thus when both parties agree to perform an ordeal or a divination, or even a duel, and accept the outcome as a decision, the third party in the arbitration is a nonhuman agent. Here, too, some third party is present. The outcome is a decision based on present rules or rules newly formulated by the arbitrator and perceived as binding. This, then, is another triadic arrangement. If the crucifixion of Jesus is looked upon as an ordeal that Jesus must undergo in order to prove his opponents wrong, God's raising him from the dead is a form of arbitration, undoubtedly appreciated as such by persons used to ordeals and duels (for a Torah-sanctioned trial by ordeal, see Num 5:16-28; such arbitration with God as arbiter is also to be found in the drawing of lots, e.g., Acts 1:26). This is Paul's prescription to the Corinthians for resolving their disputes (1 Cor 6:1-7).

g. Adjudication: This refers to the intervention of a third party who has the authority to intervene in a dispute whether the principals wish it or not and the authority to render a decision with the means at his or her disposal and to enforce compliance with that decision. Here a third party is present, and the outcome is an enforced decision based on past and/or present rules. This is a triadic arrangement. The trial of Jesus was a procedure directed at resolving conflict by adjudication. So also are the judgment scenes in parables (e.g., Matt 13:49, in which effectively angels are the judges; Matt 25:31-46, in which the Son of man is judge). In 1 Cor 6:2-3 Paul expects Jesus-group members to have the role of judge (of the "world" and of angels) in the forthcoming theocracy.

The foregoing list indicates that a variety of dispute resolution techniques are attested to in the Bible. What determines which of these seven procedures will be used in a given society and a given case to manage conflict? Variables include:

1. the social position of the disputant in relation to his opponent (social rank, political situation, economic situation, lineage).
2. the social position of both disputants vis-à-vis the helping agent, when one is involved.
3. the goal or aim of those involved: to restore goods, honor; to get satisfaction; to retaliate; to prevent escalation; to disrupt status differences, that is, to challenge; to restate village power and status relationships.

Economics: See Religion, Economics, and Politics

Ekklēsia (Gathering)

The NRSV and nearly all other English translations of the New Testament translate the Greek word *ekklēsia* with the English word "church." While our reading is based on the NRSV, we consistently avoid the word "church" because for the majority of readers "church" refers to a social institution of their twenty-first-century experience, including the buildings in which Christians gather for worship. Because the word has a totally different meaning in the time of Paul, commentators sensitive to cultural context have been translating the word as "Jesus assembly," "Jesus gathering," or as we do here, "Jesus group." It would be inappropriate to insert meanings from our own social experience into the contexts evoked by Paul's letters.

The Greek word *ekklēsia* refers to the gathering or assembly of people called or summoned. In the time of Paul, the word had two related meanings, depending on social context. In a Hellenistic *polis* (city **City**) the word was used to described the gathering or assembly of *politai* (citizens—i.e., property owners with voting entitlements). These persons gathered because they were summoned to deal with matters of significance to the city. The same Hellenistic Greek word was used by the translators of the scriptures of Israel into Greek (LXX, or Septuagint). In this translation, *ekklēsia* translates the Hebrew *qahal* in the story of the mythical Exodus. Both words have a similar meaning, specifically the gathering or assembly of people called by the God of Israel assembled to leave Egypt at the Exodus because they were summoned or called by the God of Israel.

The use of the word *ekklēsia* seems to be well known to Paul and readily understandable by his audiences because of their common Israelite background and knowledge of the Exodus story. The biblical word and its experiential connotations are now applied to Jesus groups. In Paul's viewpoint, the Jesus groups that have gathered or assembled in response to the proclamation of the gospel of God are always considered to have been called by the God of Israel (1 Thess 4:7; Gal 1:6; 5:13; 1 Cor 1:1-2, 9, 24; 7:15, 17, 20-24; Rom 1:6-7; 8:28, 30; 9:24), just like earlier Israel at the Exodus. The goal of this being called is, of course, freedom to serve the God of Israel ("For you were called to freedom," Gal 5:13).

Encomium

An encomium is a speech praising someone. In describing how to write an encomium, ancient rhetoricians instructed pupils to pay attention to important items in a subject's background. Two key items were place of origin and education. Ancient instruction manuals, called *progymnasmata*, provided rules for students learning how to write encomium exercises. In them pupils are told that the very first thing to be praised was place of birth, since being born in an honorable city conveyed honorable status:

> If the city has no distinction, you must inquire whether his nation as a whole is considered brave and valiant, or is devoted to literature or the possession of virtues, like the Greek race, or again is distinguished for law, like the Italian, or is courageous, like the Gauls or Paeonians. You must take a few features from the nation . . . arguing that it is inevitable that a man from such a city or nation should have such characteristics, and that he stands

> out among all his praiseworthy compatriots. (Menander Rhetor, *Treatise II* 369.17–370.10)

The author of Acts tells us that Paul came from Tarsus (Acts 9:11, 39; 11:35; 21:39; 22:3); however, Paul never mentions his place of birth. His self-description intimates a Judean origin (Phil 3:4-5).

The second praiseworthy item on which a fledgling writer is instructed to concentrate in the *progymnasmata* is nurture and training.

> Next comes "nurture." Was he reared in a palace? Were his swaddling clothes robes of purple? Was he from his first growth brought up in the lap of royalty? Or, instead, was he raised up to be emperor as a young man by some felicitous chance? If he does not have any distinguished nurture (as Achilles had with Chiron), discuss his education, observing here: "In addition to what has been said, I wish to describe the quality of his mind." Then you must speak of his love of learning, his quickness, his enthusiasm for study, his easy grasp of what is taught him. If he excels in literature, philosophy, and knowledge of letters, you must praise this. (*Treatise II* 371.17–372.2)

Education was thus important. This concern is evident in Acts 4:13. Peter and John astonish the crowd with their boldness when questioned by authorities, something completely unexpected of uneducated peasants: "Now when they saw the boldness of Peter and John and realized that they were uneducated and ordinary men, they were amazed." The public challenge put to Jesus by the Judeans in John 7:15 shows a similar attitude: "How does this man have such learning, when he has never been taught?"

We mention these points since as Lyons (1985) has shown, the "autobiography" of Paul in Galatians 1–2 follows the template of an encomium. He outlines Gal 1:10—2:21 as follows:

- I. Opening (*prooimion*) 1:10-12—Paul's divine gospel
- II. Lifestyle (*anastrophē*) 1:13-17—Paul's ethos
  - A. 1:13-14—As persecutor of the church
  - B. 1:15-17—As preacher of the gospel
- III. Deeds (*praxeis*) 1:18—2:10—Paul's conduct
  - A. 1:18-20—In Jerusalem
  - B. 1:21-24—In Syria and Cilicia
  - C. 2:1-10—In Jerusalem
- IV. Comparison (*sygkrisis*) 2:11-21—Cephas and Paul
  - A. 2:11-14—Incidental: in Antioch
  - B. 2:15-21—General: Paul and Judean Messianists
- V. Conclusion (*epilogos*) 2:21—Paul does not nullify divine favor

By using the encomium pattern, Paul provides his audience with a shared set of expectations and values. These both constrain and liberate. They constrain because they force Paul and his audience to see Paul only in limited, stereotyped terms, but they liberate because they set forth quite clearly and unequivocally what is required of a person to be a decent human being in that society. And, of course, Paul insists he is such a decent and honorable human being.

By employing the pattern, Paul set out only information of social relevance: birth, manner of life, education, and the like. "Relevance" here refers to the code of honor into which all males were socialized in Paul's world.

It is hardly a minor matter that Paul presented himself as the quintessential collectivistic person, controlled by forces greater than he: (a) God ascribes his role, status, and honor at birth; (b) Paul presents himself in terms of group affiliation, a Pharisee, a member of a specific group; (c) he claims to have learned nothing on his own but to have been taught by another, a truly noble teacher, namely, God; (d) he demonstrated the group virtues of loyalty, faithfulness, and obedience; he sought only the honoring of his patron, not his individual benefit; (e) most importantly, he is ever sensitive to the opinion others have of him—either his detractors, his Galatian audience, or the Jerusalem "pillars." Acknowledgment by the Jerusalem church becomes a matter of the highest importance to this group-oriented person.

In sum, for all of the "independence" claimed for Paul by modern western readers, he presents himself as utterly dependent on group expectations and the controlling hand of forces greater than he—ancestors, groups, God. He was a typically collectivistic personality. In fact, "independence" of any group authorization would have been a major liability to him. **Collectivistic Personality.**

Establishment Violence: See Violence

Evil Eye

Evil eye belief refers to the conviction that certain individuals, animals, demons, or gods have the power of causing some negative effect on any object, animate or inanimate, upon which they may look. Evil eye works voluntarily or involuntarily. The negative effects it can cause are injuries to the life or health of others, to their means of sustenance and livelihood, to their honor and personal fortune.

Basic to this belief was the notion that certain individuals, animals, demons, or gods had the power of injuring or casting a spell upon every object, animate or inanimate, on which their glance fell. Through the power of their eye, which could operate involuntarily as well as intentionally, such evil eye possessors were thought capable of damaging or destroying their unfortunate victims. In fact, though, such negative effects derived not simply from the power of their eye but from the condition of their heart, since eyes and heart worked in tandem. A number of ancient Mediterranean informants have noted how the effects of the evil eye correlate with envy, a quality of the heart. The eye served to express the innermost dispositions, feelings, and desires of the heart. Numerous biblical passages illustrate this connection of eye and heart (Deut 28:65; 1 Kgs 9:3 LXX; Job 30:26-27; 31:1, 7, 9, 26-27; Prov 15:30; 21:4; 44:18; Ps 73(72):7; Isa 6:10; Lam 5:17; Sir 22:19; 1 Cor 2:9). Ephesians 1:18, for instance, speaks of "eyes of the heart" (see also *1 Clem.* 36:2). Jeremiah 22:17 refers to eyes and heart intent on dishonest gain, shedding blood, and practicing oppression and violence. To understand the ancient Mediterranean perspective on the evil eye, consider how they viewed the relationship between light and the eyes.

For the ancient Mediterranean, light was the presence of light, and darkness was the presence of darkness. That is, both light and darkness were positive entities, having no relationship to any source of light or darkness other than themselves. Thus the sun did not "cause" daylight, nor did the moon or stars "cause" light at night. Day and night were simply the structured framework in which the sun and moon operated. Notice that in Genesis the sun, moon, and stars were created after the creation of light and darkness (Gen 1:3-5; 1:14-19). While the sun and moon marked the changing of the seasons, they had no influence on the seasons any more than they influenced day or night. The relative darkness of winter was due to the cloudy sky, not to the low path of the sun. In fact the sun was noted for its warmth rather than its light. Light was present due to the presence of light itself, not the presence of the sun. This meant that the onset of celestial light over the land was the dawn and the coming of celestial darkness over the land was dusk (not sunrise and sunset).

In the story of creation, the creation of light set light itself apart from preexisting darkness, just as the creation of land (earth) set it apart from ever-present water (Genesis 1). Note that light (day) was created before the sun and night before the moon. Dawn (morning) and dusk (evening) occur independently of the sun as well. The presence of light and land (earth) allowed for the coming of earthlings. Earthlings, human and otherwise, are created from earth, animated with the breath of life (Gen 2:7), and endowed with the light of life (Ps 56:14; Job 33:30) or "living light," as opposed to the light of the sky. Thanks to their living light, animate beings can see.

Sight consists of light emanating from the eyes of living beings. Just as the main humanly controlled source of light is fire, so too it is because the eyes are made of fire that humans see. As Jesus says, "The eye is the lamp of the body" (Matt 6:22). Aristotle observed: "Sight (is made) from fire and hearing from air" (*Problems* 31, 960a). "Vision is fire" (*Problems* 31, 959b). "Is it because in shame the eyes are chilled (for shame resides in the eyes), so that they cannot face one?" (*Problems* 31, 957b). The eye emits light that has an active effect upon the objects on which its glance falls. "Man both experiences and produces many effects through his eyes; he is possessed and governed by either pleasure or displeasure exactly in proportion to what he sees," one of Plutarch's dinner guests observes (Plutarch, *Quaestionum convivialium* 5.7, 681A).

Similarly, the Israelite tradition believed God's sky-servants (angels) were made of fire. Hence when they appear to humans, they look like brilliant light. The fact that celestial bodies, such as stars or comets, emanate light means that they are alive. Stars, whether constellated or not, are living animate entities, as all ancients knew. That is why they move while the earth stands still at the center of creation. Since all living beings have light, light and life go hand in hand. In this perspective, all light and life have their origin in the creative work of God alone; they can be handed on by human beings but not created by them.

Envy thus proceeds from the heart through the eyes. The usual suspects thought to harbor evil eye abilities were family enemies, strangers, outsiders, deviants as well as the physically deformed, the disabled, and the blind. Strangers and outsiders were presumed to be envious of the good things locals and insiders enjoyed: the socially deviant (criminals, traitors) were envious of those not caught and labeled as deviants, while the crippled and the blind were envious of those enjoying good health. Resident outgroups were stereotypically believed to be afflicted with the evil eye. Philo stereotypes the Egyptians as an envious and evil-eyed people in his writing against Flaccus: "But the Egyptian," he states, "is by nature an evil eyed person, and the citizens burst with envy and considered that any good fortune to others was misfortune to themselves" (*Flaccus* 29).

This association of evil eye and envy is typical of ancient Mediterraneans. Israelite tradition, for example, is full of warnings against persons with the evil eye. "[The person with] a good eye will be blessed, for he shares his bread with the poor" (Prov 22:9), but "evil is the man with an evil eye; he averts his face and disregards people" (Sir 14:8). "An Evil-eyed man is not satisfied with a portion and mean injustice withers the soul" (Sir 14:9). "An Evil-eyed man begrudges bread and it is lacking at his table" (Sir 14:10; see also Sir 18:18; Tob 4:7, 17). "Remember that an evil eye is a bad thing. What has been created more evil than the eye? It sheds tears from every face" (Sir 31:13). The glance and even the presence of such an individual were to be avoided because he or she was thought to have the power of injuring and destroying with his or her eye. "A fool," says Israelite wisdom, "is ungracious and abusive, and the begrudging gift of an Evil-eyed person makes the eyes dim" (Sir 18:18). "Do not consult with an Evil-eyed man about gratitude or with a merciless man about kindness" (Sir 37:11). "The evil eye of wickedness obscures what is good, and roving desire perverts the innocent mind" (Wis 4:12).

In the Bible envy manifests itself both on the tribal (Gen 26:14; Isa 11:13) and the familial levels (Gen 30:1; 37:11). It is associated with the worldview that prosperity occurs only at the expense of others, hence that the few who prosper are wicked. Their prosperity must have been obtained by social oppression and will be punished by Yahweh in the end (Job 5:2; Ps 37:1; 73:3; Prov 3:31; 23:17; 24:1, 19; 27:4). The situations in which suspicion of an evil eye occurs in the Old Testament vary from famine and the begrudging of food to the starving (Deut 28:53-57) and the sharing and lack of sharing of food in general (Prov 23:1-8; Sir 31:12-31), to the lust after wealth (Prov 28:22), the miserly unwillingness to share with those in need (Deut 15:7-11; Sir 14:3-10; 18:18; Tob 4:1-21), consulting inappropriate counselors for advice (Sir 37:7-15), evil eye fascination at the time of Enoch (Wis 5:10-15), protection of fields with an anti–evil eye device (*Letter of Jeremiah* 69), the control of the evil eye (Tob 4:1-21), and other socially disruptive passions. Further implicit traces of evil eye belief in Old Testament can be found in passages that refer to the envy, hatred, greed, or covetousness of the eye or heart (e.g., Gen 4:5; 30:1; 37:11; Exod 20:17; 1 Sam 2:32; 18:8-9; Ps 73:3; Prov 23:1; Jer 22:17) or to protective amulets (e.g., Judg 8:21, 26; Isa 3:20) customarily used against the evil eye.

In the New Testament, references to the evil eye involved similar social and moral overtones. Jesus himself, according to the Gospels, made mention of the evil eye more than once (Matt 6:22-23; see also Luke 11:34-36; Matt 20:1-16; Mark 7:22). Among the explicit references to the evil eye is Paul's reference in his conflict with his opponents at Galatia: "O foolish Galatians, who has injured you with the evil eye?" (Gal 3:1). This letter contains several indications that Paul had been accused by his detractors of having had an evil eye. Paul defends himself ("You did not shield your eyes from me and my portrayal of the Christ" [Gal 3:1b]; "You did not spit in my presence" [Gal 4:14]; "You would have plucked out your eyes and given them to me" [Gal 4:15]) and counters this charge with an evil eye accusation of his own: "It is not I, but rather my opponents who have the evil eye." "It is they," he implies to his Galatian readers, "and not I who have injured your children (Gal 4:18) with their malignant envy and have caused divisions within your community" (Gal 4:17-18; 5:20, 26). In Galatians we have evidence of the way in which evil eye accusations were employed by rivals to label and publicly discredit their opponents through appeal to the court of public opinion.

Eyes-Heart: See Three-Zone Personality

Fictive Kinship

The household or family provided the early Jesus-group members with one of their basic forms of social identity and cohesion. It is important, therefore, to understand what family meant to ancient people. In the Mediterranean world of antiquity the extended family meant everything. Not only was it the source of one's status in the community, but it also functioned as the primary economic, religious, educational, and social network. However, by the first century of our era, elite acquisition of small holdings reduced extended families to nucleated families. Only larger holding elites maintained traditional extended family patterns. For nonelites, loss of connection to the family meant the loss of these vital networks as well as any connection to the land. Loss of family was the most serious loss one could sustain.

Nevertheless, a surrogate family, what anthropologists call a "fictive kin group," could serve the same functions as a family of biological origin. As we learn from Paul's letters, Jesus-group members, acting as surrogate families, were the locus of his proclamation of the gospel of God. They were brothers and sisters in Christ. Group membership transcended the normal categories of birth, social status, education, wealth, and power, although it did not as readily dismiss categories of gender and race. In the third-generation gospel stories, as well, followers of Jesus were "brothers." For those already detached from their families of origin (for example, non-inheriting sons who go to the city), a surrogate family could become a place of genuine refuge.

Even if they might be interested in an Israelite God's recent revelation, well-connected non-Israelites, particularly among the city elite, would hardly give up their family of origin for the surrogate Jesus-group family, for it would mean breaking ties not only with a larger family but also with the entire social network of which they had been a part. Among Paul's first adopters and innovators in Israelite quarters of Greco-Roman cities, it would seem that whole families joined his Jesus groups, but not always, since some were married to unbelieving Israelites or non-Israelites (1 Cor 7:12-15). For Israelites whose social network would cover largely fellow Israelites, such renewed fictive kinship with fellow Israelites required no radical network break, but it did cause some to be aggrieved, as Paul notes in his letters.

Flesh and Spirit

"Flesh" refers to that part of the animal and human anatomy that is not bone, that is, the soft substance in the body consisting of muscle tissue and fat. Human beings consist of flesh and bone, the soft part with blood in it and the rigid part to which the soft part is attached (Gen 2:23; 29:14). When animals (or humans) die, the flesh quickly rots and dries up, leaving only the bones. Flesh thus is ephemeral, the bones longer lasting. "All flesh is grass," says Isaiah (40:6; cited in 1 Pet 1:16). By analogy, human beings as persons are considered like the flesh component of their being. In this sense, flesh means human beings as weak, transitory, ephemeral entities. As such, human beings are at the opposite side of the comparison with God, who is strong, unchanging, eternal. In a moral sense applied to human beings, humans stand opposed to God, acting in ways that do not please God. "Works or passions of the flesh" refer to any behaviors that do not coincide with the will of God. For Paul these include infractions of the Ten Commandments in several forms (see Gal 5:19-21; **Ten Commandments**).

"Spirit" literally means wind or breeze. Wind had force ranging from the ability to move the leaves on plants and trees to the forceful gales that could knock down trees and buildings under construction. The ancients did not develop effective ways to harness the wind. The type of sails used on boats could just as well capsize the boat as propel it with the wind. Winds were both invisible and unpredictable. As the truism had it, "the wind blows where it wills, and you hear the wind but you do not know whence it comes or whither it goes" (John 3:8). This statement is not a deep scriptural truth but daily practical experience. The wind is invisible and unpredictable. The experience of the wind was used as an analogy to understand the activity of God. A normal analogical way to speak of God acting was to speak of the "Holy Wind," or "Holy Spirit," the Wind of God. Thus for Paul the power of God at work in Jesus groups, thanks to the Lord Jesus, is referred to as God's

Spirit. The presence of this Spirit of God is apparent in the various altered states of consciousness experiences that attended Paul's proclamation of his gospel of God (see 1 Thess 1:5-6; frequently, 1 Corinthians 12). **Altered States of Consciousness.** Thanks to the Spirit (or God's "activity") Jesus-group members are open to God, show support for others by their group attachment (love), and have concern for group integrity (upbuild one another). Thanks to the presence of God acting in ingroup relations, Jesus-group members experience "love, joy, peace, patience, kindness, generosity, faithfulness, gentleness, and self-control" (Gal 5:22-23). There is no law against such things.

Thus with the contrasting pair of flesh and spirit, Paul refers to human beings as weak and human beings as strong thanks to the presence of God acting. God's Spirit is also referred to as the hand of God (1 Pet 5:6) or the finger of God (Luke 11:20). **Three-Zone Personality.**

God: See Many Gods and Many Lords

Greeks and Israelites. See also: Jew and Greek/Judean and Hellenist

People of the Roman Empire among whom Paul traveled were aware of a common set of categories that transcended their own local groupings or lineage. This common set of categories consisted in assessing the inhabitants of the world in terms of "Greek" and "barbarian." Empire-minded people were aware of being part of "the Greco-Roman empire, with its three million and a half square kilometers [as] an island of civilization surrounded by barbarians" (Strabo, *Geography*, end of book 6)" (see Veyne 1993:388). In the perspective of these cosmopolitans (which included Romans and elites of other ethnic groups) all civilized people were "Greeks," while the rest were "barbarians" or some other subset known for something other than their level of humaneness. Israelites, like everyone else, accepted this viewpoint. For example, Philo of Alexandria, when writing of Caesar Augustus's conquests in the Alps and in Illyria, stated how the *princeps*: "had healed the disease common to Greeks and barbarians" (*Embassy to Gaius* 145; *princeps*, transliterated as "prince," means the first among all humans, the principal human being). What in fact had Augustus done? "This is he who reclaimed every state (*polis*) to liberty, who led disorder into order, and brought gentle manners and harmony to all unsociable and brutish nations, who enlarges Greece (*Hellas*) with numerous new Greeces and hellenizes (*aphellenisas*) the outside world (*barbaroi*) in its important regions" (*Embassy to Gaius* 147). Hence it is not surprising that Paul, too, gives a passing nod to "Greeks and Barbarians" (Rom 1:14). In Hellenistic perspective, shared by Roman elites, the barbarians also included Israelites. Josephus notes that, "[Apollonius] says that we [Israelites] are the weakest of all the barbarians, and that this is the reason why we are the only people who have made no improvements in human life" (Josephus, *Against Apion*, II 15). Philo (*On the Life of Moses* II, IV, 15) also includes Israel among the barbarians.

For modern readers, the significant point is that there was no region or nation called Greece in the first-century Mediterranean. Cities like Philippi and Thessalonika were located in Macedonia, while Corinth was located in Achaia. So there were Macedonians and Achaians, but not Greeks. (For Macedonia and Achaia, see 1 Thess 1:7-8; 2 Cor 9:2; Rom 15:26; for Macedonia alone, see 1 Thess 4:10; 1 Cor 16:5; 2 Cor 1:16; 2:13; 7:5; 8:1; 9:4; Phil 4:15; for Achaia alone, see 2 Cor 1:1; 11:10; 1 Cor 16:15.) In the time of Paul, the term "Greek" referred to a social status rather than a geographical origin.

Among "Greeks," it would be difficult to distinguish a Mediterranean Judean from a Mediterranean non-Judean. As Shaye Cohen observes, Israelites and non-Israelites (he confusingly calls them "Jews" and Gentiles) "were corporeally, visually, linguistically, and socially indistinguishable" (Cohen 1999:37). First-century Israelite circumcision was neither an infallible nor a usable marker of Judean or Israelite identity. If there were no genealogical records that would have proven who was an Israelite and who was not, and if the Israelites of antiquity looked like everyone else, spoke like everyone else, were named like everyone else, and supported themselves like everyone else, how did one know an Israelite in antiquity when one saw one? (Cohen 1999:53).

Cohen's observations, based on ancient Mediterranean documents, have little if anything to do with those ninth-century Central Asian converts to Talmud-based Jewishness, the Khazars (also known as Ashkenazi Jews)—people who have what ancient physiognomic authors called "northern" features (see Polemo, *Physiognonomia*, chap. 32; see Malina 1992). These non-Semitic people constitute the vast majority of modern Jews, including Zionist Jews.

Mediterranean Judeans, then, were much like their agonistic neighbors. This, of course, might mask another, more significant set of distinctions. If Israelites were hard to distinguish from non-Israelites, what of ingroup Israelite differences? Would it be equally difficult to distinguish a "true Israelite" from those relegated to the periphery of those who thought they were "true Israelites"? What of those Israelites who found grounds to exclude fellow ethnic groups altogether?

As can be seen from the sources, the house of Israel in the first-century world consisted of quite diverse groupings, with no truly unique cultural features aside from ancestral genealogy traceable in fact to the Persian and Hellenistic periods, but mythologically to one Abraham. Yet there was a configuration of attributes characteristic of Israelites who practice Judaism. Judaism, that is, the customs of Judeans, were heavily rooted in Persian ideology, since Judea was founded by the donation of Cyrus (1 Chron 36:22-23). These customs included endogamy (often called loyalty to family, extended and clan); belief in the God of Israel and in Satan in conflict with this God; belief in the role of angels; belief in predestination; belief in ancestral traditions, which included standards and norms varying in quality and degree from region to region, tribe to tribe, and status to status; adaptability to changing conditions. The integration of many Judeans into non-Israelite cultures due to emigration and colonial settlement, as Cohen intimates, would necessarily dilute many older Israelite cultural values and beliefs, some of which antedated the

Persian period. Not all waves of emigration from Judea had the same definition of who and what is "Israel." What may be accepted as "true Israel" by one group may be Hellenism (= Greek) to another.

Hellenist: See Jew and Greek/Judean and Hellenist

Hellenistic Letter

Paul's letters, aside from Romans and Philemon, are instances of an information exchange relation between Paul and his clients, now his fellow Jesus-group members. While the Thessalonian letter was the first written attempt by Paul to set up such an information exchange relation, with that writing he was not really putting his honor on the line, since Timothy assured him that such a relation would in fact be welcomed. With 1 Corinthians we find Paul in a well-set-up information exchange.

First of all, it is a letter that follows the pattern or structure of a Hellenistic letter: superscription (1–3), thanksgiving (4–7), body (8–22), conclusion (23–25). This letter pattern is a genre of writing, and the letter genre, like all writing genres, derives from some social system behavior. The behavior involved in such private letters follows the behavior of a conversation: initial greeting (based on the status and roles of the conversing partners = superscription), inquiry into well-being (usually quite formulaic, like "how are you? how is the family?" = thanksgiving), then the burden or purpose of the conversation (= body), followed by a departing formula (= conclusion).

Sociolinguists tell us that language directed at another person has three dimensions to it: ideational, interpersonal, and modal. The ideational dimension covers the topic of the communication, what one speaks about. The interpersonal dimension looks to whom one speaks, that is, to the statuses and roles of the conversing partners' status and roles. The modal dimension deals with how the language parts get put together: words, grammar, syntax. The three, then, deal with the what, who, and how of the linguistic interaction. The three, of course, are fully interconnected, but one or another feature may be highlighted, depending on the situation. The choice of emphasis depends upon what effect conversation partners wished to have on each other. With their heavy foregrounding of personal pronouns, the letters to the Thessalonians and to the Philippians communicated emphatic interpersonal overtones. While Romans was essentially about travel arrangements, the way Paul drew ingroup and outgroup boundaries throughout the structure of the document points to his goal of including himself within the Roman ingroup prior to his visit. The letter to Philemon, essentially a letter of request, likewise emphasizes the interpersonal dimension of language.

Holy Man

While they are not labeled as such, Elijah and Elisha were typical prophets and holy men (1 Kings 17—2 Kings 13). In the Synoptics, Jesus is called a holy man of

God by a possessing spirit (Mark 1:24; Luke 4:34; see John 6:69). The reports of Paul's so-called conversion (and presumed name change, Acts 13:9) likewise point to Paul's call to be a holy man and prophet.

A holy man is a person who has direct contact or communication with the realm of God by means of altered states of consciousness. **Altered States of Consciousness.** The activity of holy men usually is directed to the benefit of people in their society. Such persons heal the sick, exorcize the possessed, and know what is going on in the unseen realm of spirits, demons, and angels. In their encounter with spirits, holy men can interact with them without fear of being possessed. They can travel through the spirit/demon world, and they can readily make contact with the realm of God.

All cultures identify a holy man or woman ("shaman") characterized by two things: easy access to the realm of the deity and the ability to broker gifts (information, healing) from that realm to this world. There is sufficient information reported by Paul (Gal 1:15-16; 1 Cor 15:8-9; 2 Cor 4:6; Phil 3:12) and Luke (Acts 9:3-19; 22:6-16; 26:12-18) to rank Paul in this category.

Six common elements surface in the process of becoming a holy person, alluded to by Paul:

1. A spirit contacts the candidate to possess or adopt him. In retrospect, Paul believed such adoption happened to him after his conception (Gal 1:15). Allusions to Isaiah (49:1) and Jeremiah (1:5) align him with prophetic ministry.
2. Identification of the possessing or adopting spirit: God of Israel (Rom 1:1; see also 1 Cor 1:1; 2 Cor 1:1; Gal 1:1).
3. Acquisition of ritual skills: from his heritage as a Pharisee (Phil 3:5-6).
4. Tutelage by both a spirit and a real-life teacher(s). Paul attributes his instruction mainly to God (Gal 1:11, 15-16). Other indications: Spirit (Acts 13:2); real-life teachers: Cephas (Gal 1:18: perhaps ritual skills of inducing and interpreting altered states of consciousness, healing, casting out evil spirits), Ananias (Acts 9:10, 19), and Barnabas (Acts 9:27).
5. Growing familiarity with the possessing or adopting spirit: 2 Cor 12:7 (57 C.E., twenty-three years after Paul's call in 34 C.E.).
6. Ongoing trance experiences: 2 Cor 12:7; *glossōlalia* (1 Cor 14:8); sky journeys (2 Cor 12:1-4).

While it is difficult to offer an all-embracing definition of a holy man, there is a series of typical characteristics. All holy persons have the first five:

1. The holy man has direct contact or communication with spirits. For Paul this is mainly the God of Israel but also other spirits in the divine realm (1 Thess 2:4; Gal 1:16, see also 1:12; 1 Thess 4:15; Gal 2:2). (Spirit of God for Paul: 1 Cor 2:10, 13).
2. Control of or power over the spirit. Paul is never actually controlled by any spirits, but does attribute some reversals to Satan, an Israelite-

specific personification of a hostile force testing loyalty to God (1 Thess 2:18; 2 Cor 12:7; compare Exod 15:26). However, he performed signs among Corinthians (2 Cor 12:12; Rom 15:19—healing as well as casting out spirit).

3. Control of the altered state of consciousness experience through which the holy man contacts the unseen world. Paul has *glossōlalia* (1 Cor 14:18), which need interpretation (1 Cor 14:13).
4. A holy man possesses a this-worldly focus on the material world. His gifts are for the benefit of the group he serves. Such is the case with the charismata listed in 1 Corinthians 12, especially vv. 6 and 7.
5. A holy man often takes sky journeys ("soul flight") to the realm of God and throughout that realm; for example, Paul mentions such a trip fourteen years earlier than 2 Corinthians: 2 Cor 12:2, hence circa 43 C.E.
6. A holy man does not fear spirits in encountering them. This characteristic is not explicitly mentioned, but see 2 Cor 12:12, Rom 15:19.
7. Memory. Holy man remembers trance experiences (see 2 Corinthians 12).
8. Healing is a major focus. Acts mentions more than Paul does (2 Cor 12:12; Rom 15:19).

Honor-Shame Societies

People in all human societies use sanctions during the early enculturation of children to gain compliance. These sanctions include guilt, shame, and anxiety. While all humans can experience all three of these sanctions, cultural groups emphasize one or the other. Unlike our western, guilt-sanctioned society, Mediterranean societies of the first century (as in the traditional societies of that region today) had shame as the pivotal sanction for noncompliance. The proof of the absence of shame was honor. The pivotal social value of honor kept the sanction of shame in abeyance. Concern for honor permeated every aspect of public life in the Mediterranean world. Honor was the fundamental value. It was the core, the heart, the soul. Philo speaks of "wealth, fame, official posts, honors and everything of that sort with which the majority of mankind are busy" (*Worse* 122). He complains that "fame and honor are a most precarious possession, tossed about on the reckless tempers and flighty words of careless men" (*Abr.* 264). And note Romans 12:10, in which Paul admonishes Jesus-group members to outdo one another in showing honor, thereby acknowledging the value placed on honor among Jesus-group members as well.

Simply stated, honor was public reputation. It was name or place. It was one's status or standing in the community together with the public recognition of it. Public recognition was all-important. To claim honor that was not publicly recognized was to play the fool. To grasp more honor than the public would allow was to be a greedy thief. To hang on to what honor one had was essential to life itself.

It was likewise a relative matter in which one claimed to excel over others, to be superior. It thus implied a claim to entitlements on the basis of social precedence.

As a result, honor and shame were forms of social evaluation in which both men and women were constantly compelled to assess their own conduct and that of their fellows in relation to each other. The vocabulary of praise and blame could therefore function as a social sanction on moral behavior. It was perpetuated by a network of evaluation, the gossip network, which created an informal but effective mechanism of social control.

Honor was likewise a limited good—related to control of scarce resources including land, crops, livestock, political clout, and female sexuality. Being a limited good, honor gained was always honor taken from another. Legitimate honor that was publicly recognized opened doors to patrons; honor withheld cut off access to the resources patrons could bestow. In a very pervasive way, then, honor determined dress, mannerisms, gestures, vocation, posture, who could eat with whom, who sat at what places at a meal, who could open a conversation, who had the right to speak, and who was accorded an audience. It served as the prime indicator of social place (precedence) and provided the essential map for persons to interact with superiors, inferiors, and equals in socially prescribed or appropriate ways.

In ancient Greek and Latin literature, honor was at the center of a wide network of related values: power, wealth, magnanimity, personal loyalty, precedence, sense of shame, fame or reputation, courage, and excellence. It is no surprise, therefore, to find that the vocabulary of honor and shame is pervasive in the literature of antiquity. Josephus spoke of honors bestowed by Caesar, Vespasian, David, Saul, Jonathan, Augustus, Claudius, and the city of Athens (*War* 1.194; 1.199; 1.358; 1.396; 1.607; 3.408; *Life* 423; *Ant.* 7.117; 6.168; 6.251; 13.102; 14.152; 19.292). He told of the honor that belonged to consuls, governors, priests, village judges, and prophets (*War* 4.149; 7.82; *Ant.* 4.215; 10.92; 11.309; 15.217). Philo spoke often of honor, glory, fame, high reputations, being adorned with honors and public offices, noble birth, the desire for glory, honor in the present, and a good name for the future (*Migr.* 172; *Alleg. Interp.* 3.87; *Worse* 33; 157; *Post.* 112; *Abr.* 185; 263). In his *Roman Questions* 13, par. 267A (*Moralia* IV, 25), Plutarch noted that the Latin word "honor" is "glory," "respect," or "honor" in Greek. These were also the Greek words used to translate the Hebrew word for "glory" in the pre-Christian Greek translation of the Hebrew Bible, the Septuagint (LXX). English versions of the Bible often translated all these words with "glory." Thus "honor" and "glory" referred to the same reality, that is, the public acknowledgment of one's worth or social value.

Honor could be ascribed or acquired. Ascribed honor derived from birth: being born into an honorable family makes one honorable in the eyes of the entire community. By contrast, acquired honor was the result of skill in the never-ending game of challenge and response. Not only did one have to win to gain it, but one had to do so in public because the whole community had to acknowledge the gain. To claim honor that the community did not recognize was to play the fool. Since honor was a limited good, if one person won honor, someone else lost. Envy was thus institutionalized and subjected anyone seeking to outdo his or her neighbors to hostile gossip and the pressure to share. **Evil Eye.**

Challenges to one's honor could be positive or negative. Giving a gift was a positive challenge and required reciprocation in kind. An insult was a negative challenge that likewise could not be ignored. The game of challenge and response was deadly serious and could literally be a matter of life and death. It had to be played in every area of life, and every person in a village watched to see how each family defended and maintained its position. **Challenge-Riposte.**

Since the honor of one's family determined potential marriage partners as well as with whom one could do business, what functions one could attend, where one could live, and even what religious role one could play, family honor had to be defended at all costs. The smallest slight or injury had to be avenged, or honor would be permanently lost. Moreover, because the family was the basic unit in traditional societies rather than the individual, having a "flushed face" (*wajh* in Arabic, meaning a "face blushing due to being shamed"), as Middle Eastern villagers call it, could destroy the well-being of an entire kin group.

It is also important not to misunderstand the notion of "shame." One could "be shamed," and this referred to the state of publicly known loss of honor. This was negative shame. Being "thrown into outer darkness, where there will be weeping and gnashing of teeth" (Matt 8:12; 13:42; 13:50; 22:12; 24:51; 25:30; Luke 13:28; see Acts 7:54), describes a reaction of persons who have been publicly shamed or dishonored.

By contrast, to "have shame" meant to have proper concern about one's honor. This was positive shame. It can be understood as sensitivity for one's own reputation (honor) or the reputation of one's family. It was sensitivity to the opinions of others and was therefore a highly desirable quality. To lack this positive shame was to be "shameless" (compare the modern Hebrew term "chutzpah," the Israeli core value and national virtue; the word is often translated "arrogance," but means "shamelessness," that is, without positive shame or concern for honor).

Women usually played this positive shame role in agrarian societies, meaning they were the ones expected to have this sensitivity in a special way and to teach it to their children. People without shame, without this necessary sensitivity to what was going on, made fools of themselves in public. Note the lament in Job 14:21 that a family's "children come to honor and they do not know it, they are brought low, and it goes unnoticed."

Perceiving status was as important as having it. Certain people, such as prostitutes, innkeepers, and actors, among others, were considered irreversibly shameless in antiquity because their occupations loudly announced that they did not possess this sensitivity for their honor. They did not respect the boundaries or norms of the honor system and thus threatened social chaos.

Of special importance was the sexual honor of a woman. While male honor was flexible and could sometimes be regained, female honor was absolute and once lost was gone forever. It was the emotional-conceptual counterpart of virginity. Any sexual offense on a woman's part, however slight, would destroy not only her own honor but that of all males in her paternal kin group as well. Significantly, the order of those expected to defend (to the death) the honor of younger women, even married ones, ran: brother(s), husband, father. For older married women, the son or sons were the primary defenders of honor.

Israelite: See Greeks and Israelites; Jew and Greek/Judean and Hellenist

Jew and Greek/Judean and Hellenist

Since words, like language itself, have their meanings from social systems, Bible translators and interpreters are essentially anachronistic when they assert that the New Testament Greek word "*Ioudaios*" means Jew and that "*Ioudaismos*" means Judaism in the sense of Jewishness. Actually "*Ioudaios*" means of or pertaining to Judea; "*Ioudaismos*" means the behavior typical of and particular to those from Judea. "Jewishness" and those espousing it, "Jews," are a post-fifth-century phenomenon at the base of the Jewish tradition, with its Talmud and rabbinical structure. The fact that people known as Jews today have their kinship religion rooted in the Babylonian Talmud would indicate that this form of religion dates back to the Babylonian Talmud, the fifth century C.E.

In Israelite usage, the terms "Judean and Greek" form a general binary division of the house of Israel, like the Hebrew-Hellenist division in Acts 6. (For "Judeans and Greeks," see Rom 1:16; 2:9, 10; 3:9; 10:12; see also 1 Cor 1:24 and passim; Gal 3:28; Col 3:11. This perspective is likewise evidenced in the narratives of Acts—Acts 14:1; 18:4; 19:10, 17; 20:21.) "Greek" was the general designation for "civilized," living in a Hellenistic way. The opposite of "Greek" was "barbarian." In this collocation as used by Paul, "Judeans" refers to Israelites resident in Judea, Galilee, Perea, and nearby cities with high Israelite population (Antioch, Damascus, Alexandria). Similarly, for an Israelite "Greeks" were Israelites in Roman Hellenistic cities with low Israelite populations.

Consider the many ways Israelites might describe themselves. In Paul's self-description, note the Israelite groups to which the terms point (Phil 3:5; see also Rom 11:1; see Malina and Neyrey 1996):

Hebrew: referred to pious observer of Israelite traditions, with due respect for Israel's ancestral patriarchs, hence all their offspring (also a modern Italian word for Jews).

Israelite: pointed to the offspring of the genealogical line of Jacob/Israel and of his "twelve" sons; "Israel" is the name of a people (generic ethnicity; a people). It was the New Testament, Mishnaic, Talmudic name for a people whom Romans and Diaspora Israelites called "Judeans."

Benjamin: pointed to specific tribal grouping in idealized twelve-tribe system.

The attributes "Hebrew," "Israelite," and "of the tribe of Benjamin" all point to ancestry, ancestral lineage.

Pharisee: indicated membership in a political religious elective association focused on core values of consumption (tithing, clothing), commensality (food rules), and cohabitation (marriage rules); an instrumental group concerned with

Israelite political religion. Members divided their Israelite world into *haberim* and *'am ha-'aretz*. The *haberim* were companions who could consume, share table, and cohabit with each other. They formed fictive political groups (*haburoth*) concerned with the effective implementation of Torah, Israel's political-religious charter. For Pharisees, *'am ha-'aretz* were "natives, people of the land," fellow Israelites who did not practice the ancestral customs assiduously or at all. "Pharisee" is a reference to ancestral customs.

Judean: name for people dwelling in the territorial region called Judea, where the Temple of the God of Israel was located; it also referred to people who followed the ancestral customs of Israel as practiced in Judea; emigré Judeans, that is, emigré Israelites. "Judean" refers to ancestral place of origin.

Dispersion: (Greek: *diaspora*) was a collective term for emigré Israelites who one day were expected to return to Judea. Once expectations of return waned, emigrés were simply immigrants or resident aliens. The coming of Jesus as Israel's Messiah would refocus attention of Jesus groups (but not Israelite unbelievers) on these emigrés and their return. See, for example, James 1:1, "James, a servant of God and of the Lord Jesus Christ, To the twelve tribes in the Dispersion"; also 1 Pet 1:1, "Peter, an apostle of Jesus Christ, To the exiles of the Dispersion in Pontus, Galatia, Cappadocia, Asia, and Bithynia, etc." (see Elliott 2000:313–14). "Dispersion" refers to an ancestral group outside its ancestral place of origin.

Greek: meant civilized, a characteristic of any person who spoke Hellenistic Greek, followed Hellenistic customs, and shared Hellenistic values and ideals. The reason why "Greek" referred to a status rather than a people was that there was no "Greece" in the first-century Mediterranean. Cities like Philippi and Thessalonika were located in Macedonia (for Macedonia, see 1 Thess 4:10; 1 Cor 16:5; 2 Cor 1:16; 2:13; 7:5; 8:1; 9:4; Phil 4:15), while Corinth was located in Achaia (for Achaia, see 2 Cor 1:1; 11:10; 1 Cor 16:15). So there were Macedonians and Achaians, but not Greeks (for both Macedonia and Achaia, see 1 Thess 1:7-8; 2 Cor 9:2; Rom 15:26). In the time of Paul, the term "Greek" referred to a social status rather than geographical origin. Greek meant the opposite of barbarian. **Greeks and Israelites.** "There is ample evidence to show that the Romans of the Republic and later were usually content with the term *Graecus* to denote both ethnic Greeks and Hellenized peoples of non-Greek origin" (Petrochilos 1974:18). There really were no Greek ethnics in the first century. What Petrochilos calls an "ethnic" Greek was a person from a specific city (e.g., Athenian) or region (e.g., Macedonian) from where Hellenism derived. But in the first century there were no "Greeks" in any ethnic (same Greek ancestry), nationalistic, or political sense. Thus the term "Greek" in Israelite contexts was an Israelite ingroup generic designation for Israelite residents outside Judea in Hellenistic areas. (Note John 7:35: "The Judeans said to one another, "Where does this man intend to go that we shall not find him? Does he intend to go to the Dispersion among the Greeks and teach the Greeks?") Among Israelites, "Greek" refers to Hellenized ancestral group members or ancestral groups located in Hellenized *poleis*.

Outside Judea, non-Israelite Hellenistic peoples called all Israelites "Judeans," a term emigré Israelites likewise used of themselves! Thus "Judean and Greek" served as an Israelite self-designation for Israelites resident in Judea and Israelites resident outside Judea who were "Greek," speaking Hellenistic Greek, practicing Hellenistic customs, and sharing Hellenistic values and ideals.

Consequently, when used by an Israelite like Paul, a set of categories such as "neither Judean nor Greek, slave nor free, male nor female" (Gal 3:28) are all ingroup categories; they provided a division of persons to be found within Israel and now to be found in Jesus groups. Since meaning in language derives from social systems, Paul's ethnocentric attitudes and social location within Israelite groups provide no linguistic or semantic evidence that this categorization has to do with non-Israelites (also known as "Gentiles"). Paul's ethnocentrism precludes social systemic concern for "Gentiles."

To appreciate these social line drawings and the stereotypes they entail, one must adopt the point of view of the speaker and the way he or she marks off the world. For Paul the world is either Israelite or non-Israelite, with many category divisions within Israel. Not so among non-Israelites, who are all of a piece: "they," or "Gentile sinners." Not only are peoples and groups divided into Israelite and non-Israelite, but also the region or territory in which these people were found had similar boundaries. The reason for this is that people were considered part of the land and influenced by the sky above. The land, water, and air, the environment of human groups, were as much part of self-understanding and self-definition as personality is for us. The value of air, waters, and places for ethnic qualities was common knowledge among elites and points of honor among nonelites as well (Hippocrates, *Airs, Waters, Places*; Strabo, *Geography*; see Aujac 1966:270–73). First-century people were not much interested in personality. Personality could change, and first-century people despised change. No one ever "converted" in the first century (on conversion, see Nock 1933; however they do adopt innovations—see Malina and Neyrey 1996; Rogers 1995). And even when change happened, the ancients were often selectively inattentive to it in favor of ongoing similarity.

In summary, from the perspective of the members of the house of Israel who described the activities of the God of Israel in the activities and discourses of the Israelite Messiah, Jesus of Nazareth, the map of social groups changes labels depending on where the speaker/writer is located. The following charts illustrate these results:

From an Israelite Perspective when inside Judea, Galilee, or Perea

speaking with	individually	collectively
ingroup persons	Judeans, Galileans, Pereans	House of Israel
outgroup persons	Romans, Corinthians, Philippians, etc.	The People (other than Israel), *ta ethnē*, Everyone Else

From an Israelite Perspective when outside Judea, Galilee, or Perea

speaking with	about the ingroup	about the outgroup
fellow Israelites	general name is Israel, broken down into Judeans (barbarians) and Hellenes (Greeks) or territory names.	general name is Gentiles or the people (other than Israel)
non-Israelites (Everyone Else)	Judeans	specific non-Israelite group names: Romans, Corinthians, etc.

For the outgroup the name for Israelites regardless of provenance was "Judean." It is significant to note that at the time there was in fact no Israelite community that could acquiesce to the title of the one "true Israel." As we see from New Testament authors, the title was still negotiable (see arguments in Matthew for true Israel; in Rom 2:28-29 "true Judeans"; Rom 9:6 "true Israel"; Gal 6:16 "Israel of God"; Rev 2:9; 3:9 "true Judeans"). Thus Jesus groups took the label "(true) Israel" and "(true) Judeans" to themselves. Since all Jesus-group members at the time were Israelites, is this co-opting of the generic name "Israel" or "Judean" a kind of supersessionism? The fact is the Pharisee elites or scribes were organized by Johannan Ben Zakkai only after the destruction of Jerusalem, when Jesus groups already existed quite independently of Jerusalem. Jesus groups were Israel awaiting the theocracy proclaimed by Jesus. Later Ben Zakkaist groups were Israel awaiting the restoration of the Temple. While Jesus groups were earlier in time and some of their number laid claim to being true Israel, it is historically false to consider Jesus groups as the "younger brother" of "older brother" Ben Zakkaism. Jesus groups were in historical fact older. If anything, Ben Zakkaist scribal Pharisees, whose opinions formed the collection known as the Mishna, sought to co-opt Israelite identity, and this they eventually did with the rise of Christendom and the rabbinization of non–Jesus-group Israelites.

Judean: See Jew and Greek/Judean and Hellenist

Kingdom of God

The phrase "kingdom of God" often has the form "kingdom of heaven." The reason for this is that the word "God" was not to be used in Judean circles; instead the surrogate name for God, "heaven," was used. Both "kingdom of God" and "kingdom of heaven" mean the same thing. For Americans the meaning of the word "kingdom" is difficult to appreciate since Americans have no experience of kings and kingship. There are no individual human rights or democratic choices in a kingdom. A kingdom refers to the population found in a territory under the authority of some central person called a king. A king, by reason of his personal status, is lord and master of all persons and things within his territory. The king owns everyone and everything in the kingdom and can dispose of them as he wishes. Residents within the kingdom are expected to treat the king as lord and master. A "king of kings" would be lord and master even of other kings and embrace dominion of all other kingdoms.

A lord (Greek: *kyrios*; Latin: *dominus*; Semitic: *adon* or *baal*) is a Hellenistic word referring to a person having the most complete power over persons and things. The lord is the absolute owner of all persons and things in his domain. He is a person who has the power to dispose of persons and things as he likes and who holds this power by a title recognized as valid (either by ad hoc force, custom, or law). This power is lordship (Greek: *kyriotēs*, Latin: *dominium*). The lord was entitled to use any thing or person that was his, to enjoy all their products or properties, and to consume entirely whatever was capable of consumption. Because of the perception that Jesus was with the God of Israel in the sky, to call Jesus "lord" meant that he wielded supreme cosmic dominion, after God. Significantly, in Paul's letter to the Jesus group in Thessalonika, the title "lord" is the main title for Jesus, used twenty-four times (1:3, 6, 8; 2:15, 19; 3:11, 12, 13; 4:3, 15, 16, 17; 5:9, 23, 27, 28; without article, 1:1; 4:6, 15, 17; 5:2; and in the phrase "in the Lord," 3:8; 4:1; 5:12). Paul mentions the kingdom of God as something well known to his audience (1 Thess 2:12; Gal 5:21; 1 Cor 4:20; 6:9-10; 15:24, 50; Rom 14:17).

Love and Hate

First-century Mediterranean persons were collectivistic personalities. They quickly learned that a meaningful human existence required total reliance on the groups in which they found themselves embedded. Most important were the kin group, the village group, the neighborhood, and/or the factions one might join. In various ways these groups provided a person with a sense of self, with a conscience (always external to the individual in honor-shame societies), and with a sense of identity. Such first-century Mediterranean persons always needed others to know who they were and to support or restrain their choices of behavior. The group, in other words, was an *external* conscience. Because of this, "true" or enlightened behavior would always match what the group valued.

An important result of such group orientation was an anti-introspective way of being. Persons had little concern for things psychological. What we would call "psychological states" were usually ascribed to spirits, good and bad. It follows that in such cultural arrangements words referring to internal states always connote a corresponding external expression as well. For example, the term "to know" always involved some experience of the object known. "To covet" always involved the attempt to take what one desired (hence the word is best translated "to steal"). **Ten Commandments.**

Two words nearly always assigned to *internal* states in our society are "love" and "hate." To understand what they meant in the first-century Mediterranean world, however, it is necessary to recognize both their group orientation and their corresponding *external* expression. The term "love," for example, is best translated "group attachment" or "attachment to some person." To "love" the light is to be attached to the enlightened group. There may or may not be affection, but it is the inward feeling of attachment, along with the outward behavior bound up with such attachment, that love entails. So naturally those who love, or are attached to the group, do what the group values.

Correspondingly, "hate" would mean "dis-attachment," "nonattachment," or "indifference." Indifference is perhaps the strongest negative attitude that one can entertain in Mediterranean interpersonal relations (see, e.g., Rev 3:16). Once again, there may or may not be feelings of repulsion. But it is the inward feeling of nonattachment, along with the outward behavior bound up with not being attached to a group (and the persons who are part of that group), that hate entails. To hate the light would thus be to be dis-attached from the enlightened group or to be attached to an outside group and to behave accordingly. Those who "hate the light" (John 3:20) thus do what the enlightened group considers evil.

Since "to hate" is the same as "to dis-attach oneself from a group," one can describe departure from one's family "for the sake of Jesus and the Gospel" as either "hating" one's father, mother, wife, children, etc. (Luke 14:26), not loving "father or mother more than me" (Matt 10:37), "leaving everything" (Matt 19:27; Mark 10:28), or, more precisely, leaving one's "house" (Luke 18:28). Paul's famous triad in 1 Cor 13:13 (faith, hope, love) might be best translated: "personal loyalty, enduring trust in another, group attachment," and, of course, the greatest of these is group attachment.

From a historical and social point of view, it is important to note that in the ancient world, love extended only to other members of the ingroup, not to those outside the group. This holds for the "Golden Rule" (Lev 19:18: "You shall love your neighbor as yourself," borrowed from Mesopotamian tradition), in this context one's "neighbor" is a fellow Israelite, an ingroup person. In Israel's traditions from the time of Jesus, for example, we read about Isaac's final words to Esau and Jacob, as follows: "Be loving of your brothers as a man loves himself, with each man seeking for his brother what is good for him . . . loving each other as themselves" (*Jub.* 36:4-5). This sentiment is also apparent in Jesus Messiah groups: 1 Thess 4:9; Rom 13:9; Gal 5:14; Mark 12:31; the well-known parable of the Good Samaritan in Luke 10:29-37 simply extends Israel's ingroup to include Samaritans.

Many Gods and Many Lords

There is a general cognitive principle that states that all theology is analogy. This means that human beings can describe the deity, "God," the ultimate "All" of the universe, by comparisons with some dimension of human experience, since the only thing human beings know immediately and directly is the human. Knowledge of everything else, including puppies, guppies, and molecules, is by analogy with the human.

Hence for a fundamental perspective about God to permeate a society, there has to be some social structure to serve as analogy for articulating that perspective. For example, take a society with the social structure of "lordship" and the social role of "lord." A first-century Mediterranean "lord" is a male with total authority over and control of all persons, animals, and objects within his purview. To call the God of Israel "Lord," as frequently occurs in the Greek version of the Hebrew Bible, requires the existence and experience of the role of "lord." Given the social reality labeled by the word, "lord" can now serve as meaningful analogy for what the God of Israel might be like. The same is true of the word "lord" applied to the resurrected Jesus.

In the Hebrew Scriptures, ancient Israelites found a theological image of God rooted in the social structure of monarchy, especially Persian monarchy. While the Persian monarch might be king of kings, there were many other kings. Israelite kings in the period before and during the New Testament period were confined to a single ethnic group or region. The image of God as king based on that experience was one of henotheism rather than monotheism. Henotheism means "one-God-ism," while monotheism means "only-one-God-ism." Henotheism refers to loyalty to one God from among a large number of gods, like loyalty to one king from a large number of kings. It means each ethnic group or even each subgroup gave allegiance to its own supreme God, while not denying the existence of other groups and their gods. The king of Israel is one king among many other kings, so too the God of Israel is one God among the many Gods of other nations. The label "chosen people," in turn, replicates a henotheistic conception of God: one God with preeminence over other gods with one people with preeminence over other peoples. In this case, the God of Israel is named YHWH or Elohim or Adonai (Lord) YHWH/Elohim. The commandment "You shall have no other gods before me" (Exod 20:3; Deut 5:7) insists on precedence and preeminence for the God of Israel, not uniqueness. Similarly, the creed of Israel underscored this henotheism in a polytheistic world: "Hear, O Israel, the Lord *our* God is one Lord; and you shall love the Lord *your* God with all your heart and with all your soul and with all your might!" (Deut 6:4-5; Matt 22:37; Luke 10:27). Paul, in turn, states: "Indeed, even though there may be so-called gods in heaven or on earth—as in fact there are many "gods" and many "lords"—yet for us there is one God, the Father, from whom are all things and for whom we exist, and one Lord, Jesus Christ, through whom are all things and through whom we exist" (1 Cor 8:5-6).

Perhaps the first social structure to serve as an analogy for a monotheistic God was the Persian Empire. The Persian monarch as king of kings might serve as an analogy for a supreme God among other gods. Monotheism, both as a practical political-religious orientation and as an abstract philosophical system, came to permeate the awareness of some Middle Eastern persons through a monarchy that embraced the whole known world. The first monarchy to have this impact on the ancient world seems to have been the Persian. Like Zoroaster, Israel's prophets, too, were helped to see the oneness and uniqueness of God thanks to the Persian experience. With the collapse of the Persian Empire and with the Greek "catholic" experience of Alexander, the result was an eventual fragmentation that left only another set of "henotheistic" monarchies and a reversion to henotheism.

From Israel's postexilic period on, there was no social structure to serve as an analogy for a monotheistic God until the Roman Empire gradually emerged at the beginning of the first century C.E. This empire eventually came to serve as the all-embracing social structure in the circum-Mediterranean. And the individual control of the whole known world by a single emperor could serve as an analogy for a monotheistic deity. At the time the Jesus movement emerged, it is difficult to say whether its context was traditional Israelite henotheism or some incipient monotheism. The former seems historically more likely. In second-generation Paul the gospel of God revealed to him was the gospel of the God of Israel, who raised Israel's Messiah from the dead with a view to a forthcoming Israelite theocracy. And in third-generation Matthew, Jesus' final edict to "make disciples of all nations" in context means Israelites dwelling among all nations (Matt 28:16-20). This is similar to fourth-generation Luke, where at the close of the Gospel we read of Jesus explaining Israel's henotheistic scriptures dealing with the God of Moses and the prophets: "Repentance and the forgiveness of sin" against the God of Israel are for those in covenant with that God (Luke 24:44-49). In the book of Acts Luke notes how this discipleship spread among Israelites living amid all nations, "to the ends of the earth." Yet Luke also notes how God calls non-Israelites (Acts 13:46ff.) who seek out Jesus groups, to the dismay of some Jesus-group members.

The profound significance of the spread of faith in Jesus as Israel's Messiah designated by the God of Israel in the first century is intimately bound up with the eventual realization of monotheism. With the diffusion of Jesus groups in the Roman Empire, with the proclamation of Jesus (Christ) as unique mediator, "the man Christ Jesus," and with the proclamation of one God in the Roman imperial setting (see 1 Tim 2:5), monotheistic Jesus-group traditions begin to develop. By the time of Emperor Constantine (early fourth century), this monotheism was perhaps the radical way in which the Christian tradition differed from that other development of Israelite Yahwism, the traditional henotheism that eventually took the shape of Jewish kinship religion (fifth century C.E.).

Meals

Meals in antiquity were what anthropologists call "ceremonies." Unlike "rituals," which confirm a change of status, ceremonies are regular, predictable events in which roles and statuses in a community are affirmed or legitimated. In other words, the microcosm of the meal is parallel to the macrocosm of everyday social relations.

Though meals could include people of varying social ranks, normally that did not occur except under special circumstances (for example, in some Roman clubs called *collegia*). Since eating together implied sharing a common set of ideas and values, and frequently a common social position as well, to understand meals in antiquity it is important to ask:

Who eats with whom?	*How is it prepared?*
Who sits where?	*What utensils are used?*
What does one eat?	*When does one eat?*
Where does one eat?	*What talk is appropriate?*
Who does what?	*When does one eat what course?*

Answering such questions tells us much about the social relations a meal affirms.

There is much evidence from Hellenistic sources of the importance of such matters. Old Testament food regulations are also well known, as are the provisions for ritual purity required when eating. From the later rabbinic period we learn that people formed devotional societies (*haburoth*) that came together for table fellowship and vows of piety. In order to avoid pollution they would not accept an invitation from ordinary people (the *'am ha-'aretz*, literally "people of the land"). Such people could not be trusted to provide tithed food. If they invited such a person to their own home, they required the guest to put on a ritually clean garment that the host provided (*m. Demai* 2, 2–3).

In a similar fashion, Roman sources describe meals at which guests of different social rank are seated in different rooms and even served different food and wine depending on their social status (Martial, *Epigrams*, I, 20; III, 60; Juvenal, *Satires* V; Pliny, *Letters* II, 6). Here we cite this last-named passage from Pliny the Younger. In it he offers criticism of socially discriminatory meal practices.

> It would be a long story, and of no importance, were I to recount too particularly by what accident I (who am not fond at all of society) supped lately with a person, who in his own opinion lives in splendor combined with economy; but according to mine, in a sordid but expensive manner. Some very elegant dishes were served up to himself and a few more of the company; while those that were placed before the rest were cheap and paltry. He had apportioned in small flagons three different sorts of wine; but you are not to suppose it was that the guests might take their choice: on the contrary, that they might not choose at all. One was for himself and me; the next for his friends of a lower order (for you must know, he measures out his friendship according to the degrees of quality); and the third for his own freed-men and mine. One who sat next to me took notice of this, and asked me if I approved of it. "Not at all," I told him. "Pray, then," said he, "what is your method on such occasions?" "Mine," I returned, "is to give all my company the same fare; for when I make an invitation, it is to sup, not to be censoring. Every man whom I have placed on an equality with myself by admitting him to my table, I treat as an equal in all particulars." "Even

> freed-men?" he asked. "Even them, " I said; "for on those occasions I regard them not as freed-men, but boon companions." "This must put you to great expense," says he. I assured him not at all; and on his asking how that could be, I said, "Why you must know my freedmen do not drink the same wine I do—but I drink what they do." (Pliny the Younger, *Letters* II, 6)

Sharing in common meals among Jesus-group members proved to be a source of conflict. First of all, there is the principle known to Israelites about "how unlawful it is for a Judean to associate with or to visit any one of another nation" (Acts 10:28). Jesus-group members in Jerusalem espoused this principle. After Peter's encounter with Cornelius, presumably a non-Israelite, we read: "So when Peter went up to Jerusalem, the circumcision party criticized him, saying, 'Why did you go to uncircumcised men and eat with them?'" (Acts 11:2-3). Paul makes significant mention of problems raised by behavior at meals, especially given the fact that Jesus-group members gathered together to celebrate the Lord's supper. The sharing of the bread and cup of the Lord's supper would be quite a problem for the weak Judeans averse to table fellowship with the strong Greeks (see Gal 2:12-14; Esler 1998:93–116 on mixed table fellowship). Similarly, for all who are one in Christ, that some dined sumptuously while others had relatively nothing would be a grave breach of ingroup solidarity (1 Cor 11:17-22). A further problem would be raised in the minds of the weak by Jesus-group Greeks dining with non-Israelites (1 Cor 8:1-13). Paul would have people put their entitlements aside for the benefit of an inclusive table fellowship for all in the one body of Christ (1 Cor 8:13 and the argument in 1 Corinthians 9).

The Military

The first-century Mediterranean world was a ruralized society. A ruralized society is one in which great landowners set the agenda for the empire on the basis of their interests, values, and concerns. A number of traditional features typical of ruralized society punctuated life in the cities that Paul visited: physical violence, a sense of no control and little responsibility, endless challenges to honor with public humiliation. "Roman society demanded an uncomfortable mixture of pervasive deference to superiors and openly aggressive brutishness to inferiors, not just slaves. It was a world of deference and condescension, of curt commands and pervasive threats" (Hopkins 1998:210–11). If our modern cities produce industrial products and information technology, what cities in antiquity essentially produced was power sanctioned by force, and what Rome attained was a monopoly on power sanctioned by force. The concrete, physical face of this power that Rome produced in such abundance was the Roman army.

The army was a social institution forming a subset of the overarching political institution. In the Roman system the political institution was called an empire, that, is a commander-in-chiefdom. The Roman emperor or *imperator* was essentially a commander in chief of the Romans, since that is what *imperator* means. A commander in chief exists only within an army context. Rome, in sum, was a sort of militarized state in which elites got their status by participating in and excelling in the military before they joined the commander in chief's counseling body, the senate, or other elite orders.

In the time of Paul, if anyone knew about Rome and Romans throughout the Roman commander-in-chiefdom, it was through the presence of the Roman military. As a social institution the army was a social institution that inhered in the political institution. The army was a system of symbols that acted to establish powerful, pervasive, and long-lasting moods and motivations in people, formulating conceptions of power expended for collective action and clothing these conceptions with such an aura of factuality that the moods and motivations were perceived to be uniquely realistic.

As a system of symbols, the military consisted of a set of interrelated parts arrayed in hierarchical structure. Symbols are signs that denote meaning with feeling. As in all institutions, symbols adhere in persons, groups, things, time, space, and God. Hence there were military persons in ranks, from emperor to ordinary foot soldier; military groups ranging from army to squads, military things including weapons, arms, clothing; military time, notably war, raids, occupation; and deities that support the military and their activities.

Military symbols are attached to persons and objects invested with power. Power is a more generalized or abstract symbol that has effect on others because it is sanctioned by physical force. The military deals with power clothed with an aura of factuality. The appurtenances of the military—uniforms and arms—are meant to reveal power and the force that can be applied to sanction power.

The purpose of the Roman military was to defend Rome's honor and to provide security for its citizenry. At least this is what ancient apologists always claimed and perhaps believed. From a modern perspective, however, it is rather obvious that the Roman military in the service of Roman elites was a power syndicate, like modern organized crime. It was founded entirely on fear: its function was to provide protection, occasionally genuine but more usually spurious protection from itself. It produced neither goods nor services yet extorted goods and services from people in the empire for the benefit of Roman elites. As it was based on violence, it was highly unstable. Individual emperors would come and go, but the system itself continued with very little basic change over long periods.

For modern organized crime to prosper, it needs close ties to the body politic. In the Roman world, the Roman commander-in-chiefdom was the official body politic. It had the protection and risk minimization that only the political system could offer. And for people in the Roman empire, this system was the will of God (see Rom 13:1-7).

Opinion Leaders

An opinion leader is a person who informally influences the attitudes or overt behavior of people in a group in some desired way with some relative frequency.

All somewhat enduring groups have one or more opinion leaders. In the context of a group's exposure to some innovation, such as Paul's gospel of God, opinion leaders in the local Israelite community who accept Paul's gospel will confirm their own innovation decision and that of others either by fostering obedience to what that innovation entails or by allaying dissonance. Local Israelite opinion leaders opposed to the innovation presented by Paul would deter other Israelites from deciding in favor of the innovation, and if others still decided in favor, they would attempt to dissuade them from the decision they had made.

Such opinion leaders normally possess some formal sanctioning ability, although they have no formal power. What that means is that opinion leaders are not *the* recognized authority in the group. They hold their influential position in the group because they represent the group's norms and values. That means Jesus-group opinion leaders were perceived to represent Jesus-group norms and values. They held this position of leadership only so long as they were responsive to the wishes of their followers or so long as their followers perceived them to be responsive. By conforming to Pauline norms, Jesus-group leaders provided a valuable service to the group by acting as a living model of the norms for Paul's followers. **Pauline Norms.** Opinion leaders have to conform to the most valued norms of the group as a minimum condition of maintaining their leadership.

In the context of Paul's communication of the innovation of the gospel of God, how can a local Israelite opinion leader in Paul's initial audience be perceived as most conforming to Israelite norms while leading in the adoption of new ideas? In a social context of Israelite minorities living in majority non-Israelite societies, Israelite opinion leaders will be more open to innovation than opinion leaders living in populations of Israelite majorities. While opinion leaders in collectivistic societies are no more or less competent than the people in their groups, the qualities sought in collectivistic opinion leadership are social competencies like gregariousness, sociability, interpersonal competence, age, and higher (and more useful) status. Thus technical competence is not even considered.

Characteristics of opinion leaders include: (a) they are not too far ahead of the average individual in the system in innovativeness; (b) they serve as a role model for other members of the group; (c) they are respected by their peers; (d) they are the embodiment of successful and discreet use of new ideas; (e) they know that they must continue to earn the esteem (or reputation) of their colleagues if their position in the group is to be maintained. Presumably, the "bishops" (Greek: *episkopoi*, supervisors) mentioned by Paul at Philippi were such opinion leaders in Jesus groups. Perhaps the persons noted as Paul's coworkers in Rom 16:21ff. were likewise opinion leaders in Ephesus. **Coworkers: Innovators and First Adopters.**

Patronage System

Patron-client systems are socially fixed relations of generalized reciprocity between social unequals in which a lower-status person in need (called a "client") has his or her needs met by having recourse for favors to a higher-status, well-situated person (called a "patron"). By being granted the favor, the client implicitly promises to pay back the patron whenever and however the patron determines. By granting the favor, the patron, in turn, implicitly promises to be open for further requests at unspecified later times. Such open-ended relations of generalized reciprocity are typical of the relation between the head of a family and his dependents: wife, children, and slaves. By entering a patron-client arrangement, the client relates to his patron as to a superior and more powerful kinsman, while the patron sees to his clients as to his dependents. **Reciprocity.**

Patron-client relations existed throughout the Mediterranean; we will examine the Roman version of the system as an example. From the earliest years of the Roman Republic, the people who settled on the hills along the Tiber included in their families freeborn retainers called "clients." These clients tended flocks, produced a variety of needed goods, and helped farm the land. In return they were afforded the protection and largesse of their patrician patrons. Such clients had no political rights and were considered inferior to citizens, though they did share in the increase of herds or goods they helped to produce. The mutual obligations between patron and client were considered sacred and often became hereditary. Virgil tells of special punishments in the underworld for patrons who defrauded clients (*Aeneid* VI, 60). Great houses boasted of the number of their clients and sought to increase them from generation to generation.

By the late years of the republic the flood of conquered peoples had overwhelmed the formal institution of patronage among the Romans. A large population torn from previous patronage relations now sought similar ties with the great Roman patrician families. Consequently, patronage spread rapidly into the outer reaches of the Roman world, even if in a much less structured form. By the early years of the empire, especially in the provinces, we hear of the newly rich competing for the honor and status considered to derive from a long train of client dependents. These were mostly the urban poor or village peasants who sought favors from those who controlled the economic and political resources of the society.

In his Epigrams Martial gives us many of the details of a Roman client's life. In the more formalized institution in Rome itself, the first duty of a client was the *salutatio*—the early morning call at the patron's house. Proper dress was important. At this meeting clients could be called upon to serve the patron's needs and thereby eat up much of the day. Menial duties were expected, though public praise of the patron was considered fundamental. In return, clients were due one meal a day and might receive a variety of other petty favors. Humiliation of clients was frequent, and little recourse was available. Patrons who provided more were considered gracious.

As the Roman style of patronage behavior spread to provinces such as Syria (Palestine), its formal and hereditary character changed. The newly rich, seeking to aggrandize family position, competed to add dependent clients. Formal, mutual obligations degenerated into petty favor seeking and manipulation. Clients competed for patrons just as patrons competed for clients in an often desperate struggle to gain economic or political advantage.

A second institution that complemented the patronage system was the *hospitium*, the relation of host and guest. Such covenants were only between social equals and were often formalized in contractual agreements for mutual aid and protection that became hereditary. So long as a party remained in the city of the host, protection, legal assistance, lodging, medical services, and even an honorable burial were his due. Tokens of friendship and obligation were exchanged that sealed the contractual arrangement and could be used to identify parties to such covenants who had never met (for example, descendants). Such agreements were considered sacred in the highest degree.

Patrons, then, were powerful individuals who controlled resources and were expected to use their positions to hand out favors to inferiors based on "friendship," personal knowledge, and favoritism. Benefactor patrons were expected to generously support city, village, or client. The Roman emperor related to major public officials this way, and they in turn related to those beneath them in similar fashion. Cities related to towns and towns to villages in the same way. A pervasive social network of patron-client relations thus arose in which connections meant everything. Having few connections was shameful.

Brokers mediated between patrons above and clients below. First-order resources—land, jobs, goods, funds, and power—were all controlled by patrons. Second-order resources—strategic contact with or access to patrons—were controlled by brokers who mediate the goods and services a patron has to offer. City officials served as brokers of imperial resources. Holy men or prophets could also act as brokers on occasion. In the Gospels Jesus often acts as the broker for God, the one through whom clients obtain access to God's favor. An example is Matt 8:13, in which Jesus acts as broker to bring the benefits of the Patron (God) to the centurion's servant.

Clients were those dependent on the largesse of patrons or brokers to survive and do well in their society. They owed loyalty and public acknowledgment of honor in return. Patronage was voluntary but ideally lifelong. Having only one patron to whom one owed total loyalty had been the pattern in Rome from the earliest times. But in the more chaotic competition for clients and patrons in the outlying provinces, playing patrons off against each other became commonplace. Note that according to Matthew and Luke, one cannot be client of both God and the wealth acquisition system (Matt 6:24; Luke 16:13).

While clients boasted of being "friends" of their patrons (for example, Pilate as a "friend of Caesar," John 19:12), friends were normally social equals, and having few friends was likewise shameful. Bound by reciprocal relations, friends were obligated to help each other on an ongoing basis, whereas patrons (or brokers) were not. Patrons had to be cultivated, including the God of Israel. Divine worship, the service of God, entailed such patronage cultivation.

In the letters of Paul, the language of grace is the language of patronage. The Greek word *charis*, translated in the NRSV as "grace," refers to the favor given by a patron. God is the ultimate patron whose resources are graciously given. By proclaiming the gospel of God about the God of Israel raising Jesus from the dead with a view to an emerging kingdom of God, Paul in effect is announcing a forthcoming theocracy for Israel along with the ready presence of divine patronage. In Paul's proclamation, Jesus is broker or mediator of God's patronage and proceeds to broker the favor of God through the Spirit of God.

Pauline Norms

Norms are a feature of social reality, not of personal or individual reality. It is only because individuals belong to groups of some sort that they experience norms. Consequently, to understand norms, one must begin with an understanding of groups, of what holds groups together and of what makes them distinctive. A group is a collection of human beings gathering for some purpose. This gathering may be short-term and ephemeral, like waiting for a bus, or long-term, like people in a family. What is typical of all groups is that they develop an ideology. An ideology is a set range of values, attitudes, and behaviors shared by people in a group both to direct the expectations of persons within a group as well as to mark the group off from non–group members and groups. Thus ideology has intragroup and intergroup dimensions. The articulation of the values, attitudes, and behaviors required within a group and toward outsiders is called a norm. Norms might be described as statements of the acceptable range of values, attitudes, or behaviors that are to characterize a typical group member. Such norms deal either with intragroup expectations for members toward each other (or toward the group as a whole) or with intergroup orientations, how to deal with non–group members and their groups.

Ideologies not only are held by group members but hold group members. Ideologies hold groups together. Individual members follow ideologies both cognitively and emotionally; they make satisfying sense. As a rule, ideologies hold persons. They are implicit, unsaid, unexpressed, and undefended; group members "know" how to behave. But when the ideology of a group has to be expressed and explained to group members, this indicates that some new members have joined the group and have not learned to be held by the ideology or that the group is in a process of radical change or dissolution.

Paul frequently sets out norms for his churches, notably in the exhortation segments toward the close of his letters (and even in his letter to the Romans, when he deals with the Roman Jesus groups and their values in 12:1—13:14 and the "they" who observe Torah commandments in 14:1—15:13). When we read the norms set out by Paul, specifically when he contrasts "all" the other Jesus groups held by the norms he proposes, this indicates that the new groups he founded are having difficulties with the ideological implications of the gospel of God that Paul proclaims. These norms must be in place to stabilize the social identity of the Jesus group in question. As change agent Paul must consolidate group members, make their intent firm, and stabilize the acceptance of the innovation. To this end, he articulates dimensions of the Jesus-group ideologies held in all the other Jesus groups (1 Cor 7:17; 14:33; 15:1, 3; Gal 6:16; see also Gal 1:9; 1 Cor 11:23; 2 Cor 11:14; Phil 4:14).

This dimension of Paul's activity belongs to a storming period of group formation with the intent of norming—forming stable norms. **Small-Group Development.**

Pharisaic Ideology

In the social sciences the term "ideology" refers to the set of values, beliefs, attitudes, assumptions, and modes of perception and assessment, normally held unawares, that a group develops in order to make sense of its experiences and to mark itself off from other groups. Ideology reflects the interests and concerns of a group at a given time in its history. As a mode of (un)conscious perception and assessment, ideology includes criteria interpreting reality and legitimating conduct.

The ideology of the Pharisees was rooted in the perception of holy community (see Jeremias 1969:246–67). The term "holy" refers to Pharisaic purity claims, that members of their group are set apart by the God of Israel as an exclusive group. They sought to extend this sense of exclusivity to all Israelites. They assumed Israel, set apart by God as a holy and exclusive people, should be acknowledged as such by political authorities. Since Israel was apart and above Everyone Else (our translation of the Greek *ethnē*: peoples, people other than Israel), Everyone Else was simply inferior and potentially harmful. Pharisees devised roles and strategies that insured their gaining power over Everyone Else in the event that governments were not forthcoming in elevating and exempting Israelites from the customs and laws that governed Everyone Else. Thus they created the expectation that Israelites are entitled to the privileges and power of their unique status yet exempt from the hostility and alienation that such entitlements inevitably elicited from Everyone Else. In the Israelite perspective such hostility merely confirmed the malevolence and inferiority of Everyone Else, who secretly recognized the superiority of the Israelites, and the legitimacy of their boundless sense of entitlement and exemptions.

Among Pharisee beliefs we find: a supreme God who is the Creator; an evil power opposed to God; the kingdom of righteousness versus the kingdom of Satan or evil; the existence of the Holy Spirit and diverse strata of angels; the belief that God created this world for a purpose, that in its present state it will have an end, and that this end will be heralded by the coming of a cosmic Savior, who will help to bring it about; the existence of heaven and hell, with an individual judgment to decide the fate of each person at death; the belief that at the end of time there will be a resurrection of the dead and a last judgment, with annihilation of the wicked, and thereafter the kingdom of God will emerge on earth, and the righteous will be raised from the dead to enter God's kingdom as into a garden (like Eden) and be happy there in the presence of God forever, immortal in body as well as soul. All these beliefs are Persian (as well as the words "Satan" and "paradise"). It seems that the roots of Pharisaic ideology lie in the Zoroastrian views of the elites of the Persian empire who set up "Israel" in the kingdom of Yahud (known as Juda and Judea) in sixth-century Israel (Mills 1913; 1977). The name "Pharisee" may derive from Parsi or Farsi, as the Persians were known. A number of features of Pharisaic ideology, of course, put them at odds with other and earlier Yahweh worshiping groups, such as the Sadducees and Essenes. It also put them in conflict with nascent Jesus groups, whose behavior they thought was blasphemous—insulting to the God of Israel. As a good Pharisee Paul persecuted Jesus-group members in defense of the honor of the God of Israel.

Political Religion: See Religion, Economics, and Politics

Porneia

The Greek word *porneia* is difficult to translate into English because of all the presuppositions any translation might evoke in a modern reader. It is often translated "fornication," but in antiquity it refers to anything but what we would call fornication, that is, sexual intercourse between unmarried persons. The reason for this is that in the first-century social systems the sexual union of an unmarried male and an unmarried female was not considered "sinful" because it was not prohibited by law. People could and did elope. There was no marriage ceremony governed by the state or by the church. Marriage was a private affair in the hands of families (not individuals) contracted between families for their offspring. The usual instance of marriage was the contractual bonding off of teenagers by their families. They were bound off in marriage. Marriage outside of a family context was rather difficult, if not impossible, because people without families had no one to bond off for them or they were not capable of contracts (if they were slaves). The best translation for *porneia* is "deviant sexual behavior." What was deviant would have to be spelled out. In Israel such deviant sexual behavior included all the prohibitions listed in Leviticus 18—notably marriage in forbidden degrees and transgressions of adultery prohibitions along with behaviors considered typical of non-Israelites. Forbidden marriage degrees is the *porneia* problem in 1 Corinthians 5–6.

Prayer

Prayer is a socially meaningful symbolic act of communication directed to persons perceived as somehow supporting, maintaining, and controlling the order of existence of the one praying. It is performed for the purpose of getting results from or within the interaction of communication. Thus the object of prayer is a person in charge. The activity of prayer is essentially communication. The purpose of prayer is always to get results. And prayer is always social, that is, rooted in the behaviors of some cultural group.

Humans pray to each other all the time. This human activity of attempting to have effect on those who control and can help them is applied by analogy to God. Prayer to God, religious prayer, is directed to the one ultimately in charge of the total order of existence. Not only the activity of prayer but the prayer forms directed to God derive by analogy from prayer forms to those in control of the various orders of existence in which human beings find themselves (for example, parents, rulers, economic superiors of all sorts). Just as people speak to others with a view to having effect, so too people pray to have effect.

Like other types of language, prayer can be:

1. Instrumental ("I want . . ."): prayer to obtain goods and services to satisfy individual and communal material and social needs (prayers of petition for oneself and/or others)
2. Regulatory ("Do as I tell you"): prayers to control the activity of God, to command God to order people and things about on behalf of the one praying (another type of petition, but with the presumption that the one praying is superior to God)
3. Interactional ("me and you"): prayers to maintain emotional ties with God, to get along with God, to continue interpersonal relations (prayers of adoration, of simple presence, of examining the course of a day before and with God)
4. Self-focused ("Here I come; here I am"): prayers that identify the self (individual or social) to God and express the self to God (prayers of contrition, of humility, of boasting, of superiority over others)
5. Heuristic ("tell me why"): prayer that explores the world of God and God's workings within us individually and/or in our group (meditative prayer, perceptions of the spirit in prayer)
6. Imaginative ("Let's pretend"; "What if"): prayer to create an environment of one's own with God (prayer in tongues, prayers read or recited in languages unknown to the person reading or reciting them)
7. Informative ("I have something to tell you"): prayers that communicate new information (prayers of acknowledgment, of thanksgiving for favors received)

Paul frequently mentions prayer, notably instrumental prayer (1 Thess 3:10; 5:17, 25; 2 Cor 1:11; 9:14; 13:7, 9; Phil 1:4, 9, 19). God's spirit helps Jesus-group members in their praying (Rom 8:26; 15:30). But Paul finds imaginative prayer, even if a gift of the spirit, to be of little value for the Jesus group that meets to pray together (1 Cor 14:13-15). And just as there are suitable ways to dress when one approaches another human to have effect, the same is true in Jesus-group praying (1 Cor 11:4-5, 13).

Prophetic Symbolic Action

A symbolic prophetic action consists in literary genres of the description of some symbolic action (usually commanded by God) performed by a prophet, followed by words that clarify the meaning of the action. A symbolic action is an action that conveys meaning and feeling and invariably effects what it symbolizes (see Fohrer 1952 for a fuller explanation and many examples). For example, in Ezekiel 5 God commands the prophet to cut off and divide some of the hair on his head and face; the described fate of this hair will be the fate of the Jerusalemites ("Thus says the

Lord God: This is Jerusalem" [Ezek 5:5]), before whom he performs the symbolic action. The fulfillment of that prophetic action is equally described there.

The two prophetic symbolic actions mentioned in Paul's writings are Baptism and the Lord's supper. **Baptism.** Paul does not describe what actually happened at Baptism, but he does describe its significance; it means sharing in Christ' death (Rom 6:3), putting on Christ (Gal 3:27), and being incorporated into one body, the body of Christ (1 Cor 12:13). As for the Lord's supper, Paul hands down a tradition similar to that of the Synoptic Gospels (1 Cor 11:23-25).

In terms of the pattern of prophetic symbolic action, in the Lord's supper the action is eating bread and drinking a cup of wine. The first action is explained as Jesus' body, Jesus himself given or "broken for us." The cup, a symbol of one's fate intended by God, is covenant blood poured out "for us." The separation of self from blood, the locus of life, indicates death in a covenant context. In effect this prophetic symbolic action proclaims the meaning of Jesus' death "for us." In Paul's tradition, Jesus himself requested that this prophetic symbolic action be repeated "in remembrance of me." It is a continued memorial of Jesus, what he did in instituting a new covenant, and his dying "for us," yet there is more, since participation in the Lord's supper is itself a symbolic action that proclaims the Lord's death with a view to his proximate coming (1 Cor 11:26).

Purity/Pollution

Human meaning-building is a process of socially contriving lines in the shapeless stuff of the human environment, thus producing definition, socially shared meaning. Human groups draw lines through and around time (the social times of childhood, adulthood, old age) and space (the social spaces called your house and your neighbor's, or called the United States and Mexico). They also mark off persons with social roles and statuses, things with norms of ownership, and God as a unique being controlling the whole human scene.

Human beings the world over are born into systems of lines that mark off, delimit, and define nearly all significant human experiences. Not only do people define and delimit, but they also invest the marked-off areas (persons, things, places, events) with feeling, with value. Line drawing of this sort enables people to define their various experiences so as to situate themselves and others and everything and everyone that they might come into contact with, as well as to evaluate and feel about those experiences on the basis of where they are located within the lines. Thus the set of social lines people learn through enculturation provides a sort of socially shared map that helps and compels people to situate persons, things, places, and events. Line making normally results in a special social emphasis on the boundaries, since clear boundaries mean clear definition, meaning, and feeling, while blurred boundaries lead to ambiguous perceptions and reactions.

The set of social lines in question provide systems of meaning. Such systems of meaning consist of imaginary lines drawn around and through self, others, nature, time, and space. These lines determine where people, actions, and things belong.

When something is out of place as determined by the prevailing system of meaning, that something is considered wrong, deviant, senseless, dirty.

Dirt is matter out of place. When people clean their houses or cars, they simply rearrange matter, returning it to its proper place. The perception of dirt and the behavior called "cleaning" both point to the existence of some system according to which there is a proper place for everything. This system of place is one indication of the existence of a larger system for making sense out of human living.

One traditional way of talking about such an overall system of meaning is called the purity system, the system of pure (in place) and impure (out of place), clean (in place) and unclean (out of place). Pure and impure, clean and unclean, can be predicated of persons, groups, things, times, and places. Such purity distinctions embody the core values of a society and thereby provide clarity of meaning, direction of activity, and consistency for social behavior. What accords with these values and their structural expression in a purity system is considered "pure," and what does not is viewed as "polluted."

Hence "pollution," like dirt, refers to someone out of place, to what does not belong or to what inheres in something where it should not be. Purity systems thus provide maps designating social definitions or bounded categories in which everything and everybody either fits and is considered clean or does not and is regarded as defiled. As such, these socially contrived maps provide boundaries that fit over individuals, over groups, over the environment, over time, and over space. Everyone enculturated in the society knows these boundaries; hence they also know when behavior is "out of bounds." Cleaning, or "purification," refers to the process of returning matter (or persons) to its proper place.

The Judean society of Paul's day provided many such maps, articulated largely in later Pharisaic writings. There were maps of (1) time, which specified rules for the Sabbath, when to say the *Shema*, and when circumcision should be performed; (2) places, spelling out what could be done in the various precincts of the Temple or where the scapegoat was to be sent on the Day of Atonement; (3) persons, designating whom one could marry, touch, or eat with, who could divorce, who could enter the various spaces in the Temple and Temple courtyards, and who could hold certain offices or perform certain actions; (4) things, clarifying what was considered clean or unclean, could be offered in sacrifice or allowed contact with the body; (5) meals, determining what could be eaten, how it was to be grown, prepared, or slaughtered, in what vessels it could be served, when and where it could be eaten and with whom it could be shared; and (6) "others," that is, whoever and whatever could pollute by contact. Consider the following maps, taken from third-century C.E. Israelite scribal documents. First a map of times:

Map of Times
m. Moed

1. *Shabbat* and *Erubim*	Sabbath
2. *Pesachim*	Feast of Passover
3. *Yoma*	Day of Atonement
4. *Sukkoth*	Feast of Tabernacles
5. *Yom Tov*	Festival Days
6. *Rosh ha-Shana*	Feast of New Year
7. *Taanith*	Days of Fasting
8. *Megillah*	Feast of Purim
9. *Moed Katan*	Mid-Festival Days

Now a map of uncleannesses:

Map of Uncleanness
m. Kelim 1,3

1. There are things that convey uncleanness by contact (for example, a dead creeping thing, male semen).
2. They are exceeded by carrion. . . .
3. They are exceeded by him that has a connection with a menstruant. . . .
4. They are exceeded by the issue of him that has a flux, by his spittle, his semen, and his urine. . . .
5. They are exceeded by the uncleanness of what is ridden upon by him that has a flux.
6. The uncleanness of what is ridden upon by him that has a flux is exceeded by what he lies upon. . . .
7. The uncleanness of what he lies upon is exceeded by the uncleanness of him that has a flux. . . .

Paul assessed all of these lines as useless. The only purity lines he accepted were those delineated by the requirements of the Ten Commandments. **Ten Commandments.** Because he dismissed the other purity demands of the law of Moses, he ran into constant conflict with Judaizers, Jesus-group members who insisted that Jesus' death and resurrection did not faze the obligatory nature of the law of Moses for group members (see the superlative apostles of 2 Cor 11:5; 12:11; and those who wish Israelites of the Diaspora to be circumcised and to observe the Mosaic law, noted throughout Galatians). By disregarding these Judean maps, Paul asserted a clear rejection of Judean conceptions controlling purity relations both within Jesus groups and with those outside.

Reciprocity

Reciprocity is a type of social exchange, typical of small-scale social groups (for example, villages or neighborhoods in cities), involving back-and-forth exchanges that generally followed one of three patterns:

1. Generalized reciprocity: open sharing based on generosity or need. Return was often postponed or forgotten. Such reciprocity characterizes family relations and those with whom one has fictive kin relationships, for example, friends, fellow members of associations.
2. Balanced reciprocity: exchange based on symmetrical concern for the interests of both parties. Here return was expected in equal measure. Such reciprocity characterizes business relations or relations with known persons who are not in any kin or fictive kin relationship.
3. Negative reciprocity: based on the interests of only one party who expected to gain without having to compensate in return. It characterizes relations with strangers, enemies, and unknown persons.

At the other end of the spectrum of social exchange relations there was redistribution. Redistributive relations were typical of the large-scale agrarian societies of antiquity (Egypt, Palestine, Rome). They involved pooling resources in a central storehouse (usually via taxation and tribute) under the control of a hierarchical elite that could then redistribute them through the mechanisms of politics and elite kinship. Redistribution relations are always asymmetrical and primarily benefit those in control. Taxes went to elites. The Temple system of first-century Judea functioned as a system of redistributive relations.

Religion, Economics, and Politics

In the twenty-first century, Europeans and Americans generally believe there are four basic social institutions: kinship, economics, politics, and religion. These are conceived as separate social institutions, and people make arguments about keeping them separate. However, in the world of the New Testament, people attended to only two institutions as distinctive: kinship and politics. (After all, separation of "church" and state and the conceptualization of economics as a separate institution are eighteenth-century C.E. phenomena.) In the New Testament period, neither religion nor economics had a separate institutional existence, and neither was conceived of as a system on its own, with a special theory of practice and a distinctive mode of organization. Both were inextricably intertwined with the kinship and political systems.

Economics was rooted in the family, which was both the producing and the consuming unit of antiquity (unlike the modern industrial society, in which the family is normally a consuming unit but not a producing one); hence there was a family economy. There was also a political economy in the sense that political organizations were used to control the flow and distribution of goods, especially luxury and temple goods and war materials. But nowhere do we meet the terminology of an economic "system" in the modern sense. There is no language implying abstract concepts of market, monetary system, or fiscal theory. Economics is "embedded," meaning that economic goals, production, roles, employment, organization, and systems of distribution are governed by political and kinship considerations, not "economic" ones.

Ancient Mediterranean religion likewise had no separate, institutional existence in the modern sense. It was rather an overarching system of meaning that unified political and kinship systems (including their economic aspects) into an ideological whole. It served to legitimate and articulate (or de-legitimate and criticize) the patterns of both politics and family. Its language was drawn from both kinship relations (father, son, brother, sister, virgin, child, honor, praise, forgiveness, etc.) and politics (king, kingdom, princes of this world, powers, covenant, law, etc.) rather than a discrete realm called religion. Religion was "embedded," meaning that religious goals, behavior, roles, employment, organization, and systems of worship were governed by political and kinship considerations, not "religious" ones. There could be domestic religion run by "family" personnel and/or political religion run by "political" personnel, but no religion in a separate, abstract sense run by purely "religious" personnel. The temple was never a religious institution somehow separate from political institutions, nor was worship ever separate from what one did in the home. Religion was the meaning one gave to the way the two fundamental systems, politics and kinship, were put into practice.

In trying to understand the meaning of Paul's statement about being subject to the governing authorities (Rom 13:1-6) it would be anachronistic to read back into the statement the modern idea of the separation of church and state. In such an anachronistic interpretation, Paul would be exhorting Roman Jesus-group members to obedience to governing authorities. It is important to note that Paul does not refer to these "Romans" as citizens. This is another indication that they were Israelite resident aliens. Further, the governing authorities in question would be local officials who came into contact with residents of their city quarter. Paul notes that these city officials are "the servant of God to execute wrath on the wrongdoer" (Rom 13:4). **Wrath.** The mention of wrath points to a context of challenge-riposte, a context in which disobedience to authority is a dishonor for which those in authority must get satisfaction, that is, wrath.

What this means is that the relationship of subject to official is an interpersonal one in which disobedience personally dishonors the official. The reason for this is that ancient Rome elites did not have an idea of juridical relations among various peoples. Instead Roman statesmen dealt with other peoples in terms of good faith based on the analogy of patron-client relations. Rome was patron, not holder of an empire; it wanted persons to behave like clients. To behave otherwise was to be a rebel, an outlaw. Paul exhorted Roman Jesus-group members to be good clients and show honor to their patrons. **Patronage.**

Righteousness

In traditional Israelite perspective, "righteousness" referred to a privileged identity deriving from divine acceptance due to Israel's ability to act appropriately toward God and toward other humans. In simple terms, the word refers to acceptance and approval by God. Paul argues that this privileged identity deriving from divine acceptance was never due to Israel's ability to act appropriately as spelled out in the law of Moses. Acting appropriately is what "works" means. The ability to act appropriately always derived from the divine acceptance of privileged persons who believed in God's activity on their behalf. This belief is what "faith" means.

Such divinely accepted and approved persons include, first of all, Israel's original ancestor, the non-Israelite Abraham, and all subsequent Israelites who believed in God as Abraham did. Given God's recent revelation of himself in his raising Jesus from the dead, Israelites who believe in God's activity in this event are accepted by God on the basis of their faith in God, just like their non-Israelite ancestor of Israel, Abraham, who was accepted and approved by God without the law of Moses.

Paul's argument about who is and who is not righteous derives from his ingroup argument with fellow Israelites. His point is that only those Israelites who believe in God's raising Jesus from the dead and a forthcoming theocracy for Israel are righteous. Such faith in what the God of Israel has recently accomplished is the true basis of divine acceptability and approval, that is, of righteousness.

Sacred/Profane

Human beings feel closely attached to those persons, places, and things that they feel are exclusively theirs. Such a bond of exclusivity causes feelings of pain when the persons, places, or things to which persons are attached are violated. This feeling of exclusive attachment is called a feeling of the "sacred," of what is holy to a person. And the feeling of concern that persons have for what is exclusive to them is called "jealousy." This human experience toward what is exclusive to persons is applied by analogy to God. Just as humans have their holy persons, places, and things, so God, too, is said to have holy persons, places, and things about which God is jealous (that is, protective).

Thus the sacred is that which is set apart as exclusive to or for some person. It includes persons, places, things, and times that are symbolized or filled with some sort of set-apartness that we and others recognize. The sacred is what is mine as opposed to what is yours or theirs, what is ours as opposed to what is yours or theirs. (In our culture, it might be no one's, since we believe in all goods being limitless, but in the first-century world, there is nothing that is no one's—all goods are limited and distributed.) Some common synonyms for the sacred include "holy," "saint," and "sacral." We feel jealous about our sacred persons, places, and things.

The opposite of the sacred is the profane, the unholy, the non-sacred. The profane is that which is not set apart to or for some person in any exclusive way, that which might be everybody's and nobody's in particular to varying degrees. Thus the words "sacred" and "profane" describe a human relationship of varying degrees of exclusivity relative to some person or thing (and we include time, space, and goods under "thing"). For example, to say that human life is sacred is to point out that human life is set apart and exclusive among the forms of life we might encounter and therefore that it should be treated differently from animal life. Again, to say that sex is sacred means that human sexual encounters are set apart and exclusive among the various forms of sexual encounters we might know and therefore that human sexual encounters are unlike and not to be treated as animal copulations. These examples derive from a comparison of the human with the animal domain and indicate belief in the exclusivity of the human. To profane human life and behavior is to treat them just like animal life and behavior.

Of course, exclusivity or set-apartness can take place in different dimensions: between mine and yours, between ours and theirs, and between the human and the nonhuman. **Purity/Pollution.** The Pharisees of Paul's background sought to maintain group exclusivity or holiness specifically by avoiding all mixtures. The result was a sort of centripetal focus on group exclusivity. Obviously, other distinctions can be drawn, and perhaps the set of social boundaries our society tends to focus on (or ignore) are those that mark off the area of persons, things, and events set apart by or for or to God. We often refer to this area as *the* sacred, *the* holy, *the* sacral. We speak of God's holy people—a group of people set apart by or for God or God's service; God's holy name—God's person symbolized by some specific name and belonging to a category that is fully unlike and not to be treated as any human name or person. We also talk of sacrifice, a word that literally means to make (*-fice*) sacred or holy (*sacri-*), hence, to set apart to or for God, the nation, the family, or some other person. The word "sanctify" means much the same thing. "Holy" and "exclusive" are quite synonymous.

Perhaps the outstanding usage of the term "holy" relative to God is the ascribing of God's activity to the Holy Spirit (1 Thess 1:5, 6; 4:8; Rom 1:2; 5:5; 9:1; 14:17; 15:13, 16, 19; 1 Cor 12:3; 2 Cor 6:6; 13:14). The commandments of God are holy (Rom 7:12), as is the dough offered as first fruits (11:16). If the root is holy, so are the branches (Rom 11:16). And just as the Jesus group forms a temple of God's Spirit (1 Cor 3:17; 6:19), so too the behavior of Jesus-group members is a living sacrifice, holy to God (Rom 12:1). God's will is that Jesus-group members remain exclusively God's (that is the meaning of sanctification: 1 Thess 4:3; 1 Cor 1:30; Rom 6:19, 22). Finally, Paul notes that Jesus-group members manifest their ingroup attachment by greeting one another with a "holy kiss" (1 Thess 5:26; 1 Cor 16:20; 2 Cor 13:12; Rom 16:16).

Salvation

Salvation means rescue from some difficult situation. The rescuer in question is called a "savior." As a rule, in antiquity the title was bestowed on persons and deities whose actions benefited a great number of people. For this reason benefaction on behalf of the public was seen as salvation, especially if the public were in some notable difficulty. In Greco-Roman sources, the title of "savior" was used of gods such as Zeus, Asclepius, Isis, and Serapis as well as of great philosophers and leaders of various ranks. In the Greek version of Israel's scriptures, God is called a "savior" (for example, Isa 45:15, 21), and so are humans (Othniel and Ehud in Judg 3:9, 15). Philo calls the God of Israel "savior of the world" (*Spec. Laws* 2.198) as well as "savior of all" (*Unchangeable* 156).

A whole list of Roman emperors receive similar titles: Julius Caesar, Claudius, and Hadrian are called "savior of the inhabited world," while Hadrian is called "savior of the world." Augustus is titled "savior of the civilized ['Greeks'] and of the whole inhabited world"; both Augustus and Tiberius are lauded as "benefactor and savior of the whole world"; Nero and Titus are called "savior and benefactor of the inhabited world"; Vespasian is called "savior and benefactor of the world." Trajan receives the titles of "savior of the whole world" and "savior and benefactor of the whole world."

Thus the title "savior" is empty—it has no connotation concerning what people have been or have to be saved from. "Benefactor" at least intimates something given to the people for their well-being. Paul alludes to Jesus as Savior only once (Phil 3:20), in a context of salvation coming from the sky. Reference to the "day of salvation" (2 Cor 6:2) looks to the coming of the Israelite theocracy, the kingdom of heaven, which, of course, is when Jesus ushers in the salvation bound up with his death and resurrection (Rom 13:11). This salvation is open to people with faith in the God of Israel who effected the raising of Jesus (Rom 1:16). Jesus-group members contribute to this coming salvation by their conduct (1 Thess 5:8; Phil 2:12; 2 Cor 7:10). The title "savior of the world" is found in the New Testament only twice: in John 4:40-42 on the lips of some Samaritans and in 1 John 4:14. This usage is much like Paul's in that in Johannine anti-language, the "world" is John's name for Israel. However, if John is read as straight language, then the title sounds much like the one given to Roman emperors.

Slavery

Slavery is a symbolic ritual of dishonor (social death—self or other inflicted) consisting of depriving a person of freedom of decision and action by means of force or enforced solidarity with a view to the social utility of the enslaving agent. As a social institution or a fixed form of social life, slavery was a subset of kinship (domestic slavery) or of politics (political slavery: temple slaves, city slaves, etc.). Domestic slavery was concerned with the social utility of the kin group, while political slavery sought the social utility of the political elites. What both had in common was that they deprived the slave of freedom of decision and action.

It is important to see that the Greco-Roman domestic and political economies were in many respects slave economies. Slaves, not machines, did the heavy labor, and this made possible the leisure, thus the culture, of the free. Slavery was an accepted institution throughout the Mediterranean.

Most studies of slavery in Greco-Roman antiquity suggest that it was not the same as slavery in the pre–Civil War period of the United States. Ancient slavery was not based on race, for example. One could become a slave by being born into slavery, being captured in war, falling into debt, selling oneself (or family members) into slavery, or being "rescued" from infant exposure and then raised as a slave. Slaves did not constitute a separate social or economic "class." Rather, the status of a slave was based on the status of the master. Indeed, a slave's status was often higher than a free person's status. Moreover, poorer folk sometimes had slaves; even slaves sometimes had slaves! Many slaves, especially those enslaved as a result of war, were more educated than their masters, and they were often encouraged to continue their education in order to benefit their masters. Many slaves held very responsible positions, such as teachers, doctors, accountants, secretaries, and property managers. Caesar's household included responsible slave positions, indeed quite powerful positions. Slaves could also accumulate property and wealth and buy their freedom, although they normally remained indebted to their former masters, who became their patrons. Female slaves were sometimes set free by their male masters to marry them. Finally, most slaves in Greco-Roman society could expect to be emancipated by the age of thirty, from which masters normally benefited economically. The previous observations relate mainly to domestic or household slaves. Since honor was the focal value of Mediterranean society, slavery was always bad, since it thoroughly deprived a person of honor.

Slaves also worked on plantations and alongside persons condemned to death by working in mines or rowing galley ships. Their life was harsh and brutal. Slaves were property (like animals) and did not enjoy the same legal status as free persons. For example, they were sometimes beaten or molested; as witnesses in court they could, in contrast to free Roman citizens, be tortured to obtain testimony. Slaves were not legally married, their families were sometimes broken up, and disreputable masters sometimes sexually abused female and young male slaves. Fugitive slaves had to be returned, and debts were to be paid to their owners by anyone who harbored them. Israelites did not normally enslave other Israelites—when they did, Israelite law limited the time to six years—because their own slavery in Egypt was deeply embedded in their ritual consciousness (e.g., Passover ritual). Nonetheless, Israelite law permitted slavery, and Israelites sometimes had non-Israelite slaves as well. To be sure, there were slave rebellions in the second and first centuries B.C.E., but they were usually led by prisoner-of-war slaves who wanted to go home or make slaves of their masters, not abolish the institution of slavery itself. Like his contemporaries, Paul accepted slavery as an institution and did not seek to abolish it.

Small-Group Development

Once some segment of a local Israelite association adopted the innovation proclaimed by Paul, adopters inevitably formed a small group (Paul called these groups *ekklēsiai* or "churches" ***Ekklēsia* [Gathering]**). Small groups go through a process entailing a number of stages of development. This process has been verified by cross-cultural studies (the work of Tuckman 1965, corroborated by Moreland and Levine 1988). The value of this developmental model is that it can situate the condition of the Jesus groups to which Paul wrote.

Small groups are of two types, task-oriented groups and social activity groups. Task-oriented groups consist of members recruited to perform a task. The faction recruited by Jesus was a group with a task to perform. The task activity of this group is articulated in the Synoptic tradition in the so-called mission charge: to proclaim God's forthcoming theocracy, to require Israelites to get their affairs in order to this end, and to heal those in need of healing (see Mark 6:1-11; Matt 10:1-23; Luke 9:1-6). Social activity groups consist of members whose association focuses on mutual support, mutual concern, and mutual experiences that further group integrity. Both types of small groups proceed sequentially through the following stages, conveniently set in rhythmic form: forming, storming, norming, performing, and adjourning. If difficulties or circumstances change at any stage, group members may always revert to some previous stage, a sort of feedback loop process:

Group Development

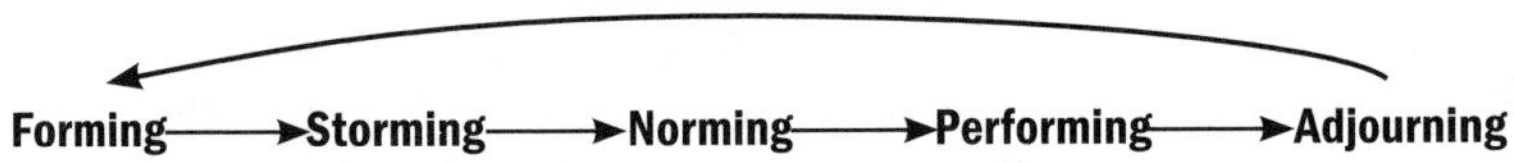

(Tuckman 1965; Moreland and Levine 1988)

Each stage is marked by verifiably predictable behavior. Here we consider Paul's social activity groups.

1. *Forming*: The forming stage is the period when the group is constituted, thanks to Paul's proclamation of the gospel of God in Israelite associations. These Jesus groups, or churches, were social activity groups. They responded to the Israelite innovation launched by the God of Israel: God sent favor to Israel through Jesus' being raised and thus proclaimed him as Israel's Messiah and Lord. God would soon "redeem" Israel through Jesus, restoring the honor of fellow Israelites who see God working in Jesus' being raised. During the forming stage, synagogue members were invited by a change agent such as Paul to constitute a local Jesus group and give their loyalty to that group and its members. Of course there were other Jesus-group change agents at work as well, for example, Apollo (mentioned in 1 Cor 3:1-9) and the Judaizers of Galatians. The forming stage develops group dependence.

At this stage, group members are predictably anxious and uncertain about belonging to the group. They exhibit typically cautious behavior. Members cautiously try to ascertain whether the group will meet the needs the change agent said it would—thus, for example, the questions of those Jesus-group members dying before the Israelite theocracy is launched (1 Thess 4:13-18). The behavior of group members toward each other is tentative; commitment to the group is low—hence Paul's concern about mutual loyalty (that is what "love" means) in the group (1 Thess 4:1-12).

2. *Storming*: At the storming stage, group joiners jockey for position and ease into interpersonal stances. Social activity group members form grievances against each other and often against the change agent or designated leader; this leads to conflict, with group members arguing with each other and heaping criticism on the leader.

Group members become more assertive, and cliques form to change the group to satisfy expected needs. Resentment and hostilities erupt among group members with differing expectations. Members attempt to persuade the others to adopt group goals that will fulfill their own aspirations. All of Paul's letters give evidence of the storming stage, whether it be business fraud in Thessalonika (e.g., 1 Thess 4:6), conflict in Corinth (e.g., 1 Cor 1:11-18), rejection of Paul's advice (Gal 5:2-8), or conflict with outsiders in Philippi (Phil 1:29-30). The behavior of group members toward one another is assertive, and their commitment to the group is higher than it was before.

3. *Norming*: The norming stage is marked by interpersonal conflict resolution in favor of mutually agreed upon patterns of behavior. In social activity groups such as Paul's Jesus groups, this stage is one of growing cohesion. Group members begin to feel more positive about their membership in their particular group. Norming involves group members in the attempt to resolve earlier conflicts, often by negotiating clearer guidelines for group behavior. The exhortation segments of Paul's letters look to such norming (1 Thess 5:12-22; 1 Cor 13:1—14:1; 2 Cor 13:11-13; Phil 2:1-11; 4:4-9; Gal 6:1-6).

4. *Performing*: In the performing stage group participants carry out the program for which the group was assembled. Social activity groups move into the performing stage by role taking. Members take social roles that make the group more rewarding to all. They work together cooperatively to achieve mutual goals. There is little, if any, evidence from Paul's letters for a performing stage in Paul's Jesus groups. The problems addressed by Paul look exclusively to storming and norming. However, third-generation documents in the Pauline tradition (Ephesians, Timothy, Titus) present organizational advice concerning group leadership that bears witness to the existence of these roles in these Jesus groups at the turn of the century.

5. *Adjourning*: With adjourning, group members gradually disengage from social support groups in a way that reflects their efforts to cope with the approaching end of the group. It seems that in third-generation Pauline groups there is an implicit storming and norming going on, triggered by the fact that the theocracy proclaimed in Paul's gospel of God did not materialize. The destruction of Jerusalem in 70 C.E. marked the non-arrival of any kingdom of God/heaven in Israel such as that expected by Paul. Hopes for a coming kingdom were put in abeyance in favor of the performing roles described in third-generation Pauline writ-

ings. Thus with the growing dimming of any forthcoming redemption of Israel, a feedback loop enters the process with new norming and subsequent performing, as described implicitly and telescopically in the final sections of Matthew and Luke. The new norms point to a shift from political concerns about a coming Israelite kingdom of God/heaven, to fictive kinship concerns emphasizing group loyalty, with abiding if transformed emphasis on the ritual of Baptism and the main group ceremony, the common meal. Thus in the development of Jesus groups founded by Paul, the adjournment of these associations signaled by the non-appearance of an Israelite theocracy loops back to renewed norming and performing as witnessed in third-generation Pauline group documents. The trigger event for this looping back would be some events in Judea that would preclude any "coming of the kingdom." What these events were is unclear.

We might note in conclusion, with Moreland and Levine (1988:164), that "most theories of group socialization implicitly assume that the group is in the performing stage of development." This of course is the situation in studies of Paul's letters and the associations to which he writes. Paul's letters look to storming and norming situations for the most part and are studied by scholars in performing (or adjourning) phases. Furthermore, the documents are used in churches that are in the performing stage themselves. Inattention to this state of affairs can lead to some distortion due to a sort of mental Doppler effect, with the contrast between churches in performance and Paul's letters addressed to storming and norming.

Social Identity

Social identity results in an individual's perception of belonging to a social ingroup (for example, the house of Israel, a kin group, a Jesus group, an "ethnic" group). It is the outcome of a process whereby an individual patterns thoughts, feelings, and actions after the thoughts, feelings, and actions attributed to significant group members and has incorporated these as a mental image. When a group of people share a social identity, they constitute an ingroup (as opposed to others who do not share that identity, an outgroup). An ingroup is a collection of individuals who perceive themselves to be members of the same social category (cognitive dimension), share some emotional involvement in this common definition of themselves (affective dimension), and achieve some degree of social consensus about the evaluation of their group and of their membership in it (evaluative dimension).

Ingroups develop sets of norms or values used to direct the behavior of members of the group toward each other as well as toward outsiders. **Pauline Norms.** Paul frequently sets forth various norms of this sort and encourages group members to put them into practice. Very often later scholars extract these norms from both the letter context and the social context and propose a "Pauline morality." It is far more accurate to consider these norms as ingroup norms. If people lived according to those norms, they would develop what the ancients called "character" typical of group members.

While it is true that individuals joining groups formed a social identity, these individuals always retained an individual identity, even as collectivistic selves. **Collectivistic Personality.** Individual identity may be described as the individual self.

> The self here is defined as all the statements a person makes that include the word "I," "me," "mine," and "myself." This definition means that all aspects of social motivation are included in the self. Attitudes (e.g. I like . . .), beliefs (e.g. X has attribute X in my view), intentions (e.g. I plan to do . . .), norms (my ingroup expects me to do . . .), roles (my ingroup expects people who hold this position to do . . .), and values (e.g. I feel that . . . is very important), are aspects of the self. The self is coterminous with the body in individualist cultures and in some of the collectivist cultures. However, it can be related to a group the way a hand is related to the person whose hand it is. The latter conception is found in collectivist cultures, where the self overlaps with a group, such as family or tribe. (Triandis 1990)

Individual identity differs from culture to culture. Individual identity thus runs along a range from individualistic to collectivistic. In individualistic societies, the focus is on individual self-reliance. In collectivistic societies, the focus is on group integrity.

For social identity, individual identity is equally significant because in individualistic societies individuals belong to many groups and offer total allegiance to none of them. In collectivistic societies individuals belong to very few groups and offer rather full allegiance to the very few groups to which they belong.

Son of God

In first-century Hellenism the title "son of God" was rather common. To determine the meaning of this title, it seems best to begin with a linguistic observation befitting the Semitic cultures of the time. A phrase such as "son of X" means "having the qualities of X." Thus "son of man" would mean having the qualities of "man," hence human. "Son of the day" means having the quality of the day, hence full of light, morally upright. And "son of hair" means hairy or hoary. In this vein, "son of God" would mean "having the quality of God," hence divine, divine-like. In a singular henotheistic context (Deut 6:4: Israel's God is One), it is important to note that "son of X" could hardly mean "having the essence of X." In other words, "son of X" forms are adjectival forms, pointing to a significant, extremely notable quality, as, for instance, Jesus' reference to James and John as "Sons of Thunder" in Mark 3:17.

In Israel's scriptures, the phrase designates angels and human beings (Gen 6:1-4; Pss 29:1; 82:6), the people Israel (Exod 4:22-23; Jer 31:9; Hos 11:1; see Matt 2:15) and kings (2 Sam 7:14; 1 Chron 7:12-14; 22:10).

However, in the world of Paul it is important to note that the title "son of God" was common and publicly applied to Roman emperors—for example, inscriptions to "Tiberius Caesar, the August God, the son of the God Augustus, emperor, most great high priest, etc." (*OGIS* 583) or "Tiberius Caesar, the son of the God Augustus, the grandson of the God Julius, August personage, most great high priest, etc." (*OGIS* 471). This made perfect sense since, as the dictum had it: "The king is the last of the gods as a whole, but the first of human beings" (vol. 3; fragment XXIV, 3, in Nock and Festugière 1946–1954:53). Then, too, non-kings might also be recognized as gods. Consider the report in Acts 14:11-12: "And when the crowds saw what Paul had done, they lifted up their voices, saying in Lycaonian, 'The gods have come down to us in the likeness of men!' Barnabas they called Zeus, and Paul, because he was the chief speaker, they called Hermes."

In the Synoptics the people Israel was called God's son (Matt 2:15, citing Hos 11:1). Jesus frequently designated people "sons of God" (Matt 5:9, peacemakers; Matt 5:40//Luke 6:35, those who do not hate enemies; Luke 20:36, the dead now with God). Outside Israel, Roman emperors were designated sons of God, as were Hellenistic holy men. **Holy Man.** Thus the title designates persons in some special relationship with God as well as those who perform deeds of divine quality.

The Gospel of Mark designates Jesus "son of God" (Mark 1:1) in its very first line, while the title is taken up by a Roman centurion at Jesus' crucifixion as he stood in awe of the way Jesus died: "Truly this man was a son of God" (Mark 15:39//Matt 27:54). Throughout the Synoptics we find the designation "son of God" as the basis for the claim that Jesus was an Israelite holy man, authorized by the God of Israel: the celestial voice at Jesus' baptism directed to Jesus himself (Mark 1:11//Luke 3:22, "You are my beloved Son"; Matt 3:17, "This is my beloved Son"); the acknowledgment of unclean spirits successfully challenged by Jesus (Mark 3:11//Luke 4:41, "Son of God"; Mark 5:7//Luke 5:7, "Son of the Most High God"; Matt 8:29, "Son of God"; Mark 1:24//Luke 4:34, "Holy One of God"); and God's acknowledgment of Jesus directed to his core disciples (Mark 9:7//Matt 17:5//Luke 9:35, "my Son, the Beloved"). Eventually this designation becomes the central charge against Jesus: being the Messiah, "the son of the Blessed One" (Mark 14:61; Matt 26:63 has "Messiah son of God," while Luke 22:67 has only "the Messiah").

Paul too calls Jesus-group members "sons of God" (Gal 3:26; Rom 8:14). But his reference to Jesus as God's Son (Gal 2:20; 2 Cor 1:19; Rom 1:4; and frequently) is undoubtedly rooted in some of the aforementioned. With his focus on Jesus' being raised by the God of Israel, however, it was that event that revealed the specific quality of Jesus as God's Son. He is not simply "son," like other Israelites or even like the emperors, rather he is "Lord." In honor-shame societies it is always assumed that one will act in accord with his publicly recognized honor rating. Highborn persons are expected to lead in public, and their status provides legitimacy for doing so. A lowborn person is not expected to lead in public, and when that happens, some explanation must be found. Jesus' death on the cross points to his lowborn social status, yet his being "son of god in power" (Rom 1:4) must be explained by some extraordinary event or circumstance, and this was the resurrection effected by the

God of Israel. In speaking of Jesus as Son, Paul never identifies Jesus with the God of Israel; he never makes the types of statements found in the Gospel of John and its anti-language descriptions.

Ten Commandments

During the time of Jesus and the Gospel authors, Israelites were forbidden to recite the Ten Commandments. Josephus reports (about 90 C.E.) that in the Israel of his day, just as it was forbidden to utter the Tetragrammaton—YHWH, the most sacred name of the God of Israel—so, too, it was forbidden to utter the "Ten Words" given on Sinai to Israel. While these are the very Ten Words "which Moses has left inscribed on the two tablets," yet "these words it is not permitted us to state explicitly, to the letter." Nevertheless, Josephus indicates their "power" (*Ant.* 3.90 LCL). After all, these very words, "the Ten Commandments which God himself gave to his people without employing the agency of any prophet or interpreter" (Philo, *Spec. Laws* III, 2, 7), were the direct words of the God of Israel himself, hence full of power. They were taboo words that must not be repeated verbatim. But they could be *written* verbatim. Since these words were put in *tephilin* (prayer boxes) and *mezuzoth* (on doorposts) by no command of God (unlike the *Shema* of Deut 6:4ff.), it seems their presence there, "to the letter," was to serve as apotropaic or prophylactic devices to ward off hostile power, the evil eye, and the like.

While it was forbidden to recite the Ten Words in the exact wording and order as found in the Torah passage recounting the Sinai incident, yet first-century Israelites did not refrain from quoting them. They simply disguised them or reordered them. In the Synoptic tradition, for example, Jesus offers a listing to the greedy young man as follows: "You shall not kill, You shall not commit adultery, You shall not steal, You shall not bear false witness, Honor your father and mother, and You shall love your neighbor as yourself" (Matt 19:18-19; Mark 10:19 omits love of neighbor as does Luke 18:20, who inverts adultery and killing).

There are further truncated listings. For example, in the Sermon on the Mount, the antitheses (Matt 5:21-36) cover five of the Ten Commandments. In the list of evils proceeding from the heart, Mark 7:21-22 has three parallel categories with five of the ten, plus pride and foolishness, that is, placing other gods before God and idolatry. Matthew 15:19 has a list of six (or seven or five), but these are the last five of a listing, just like in the antitheses in the Sermon on the Mount: (1) murder, (2) adultery, fornication, (3) theft, (4) false witness, (5) slander.

Then Rom 1:29-32, in turn, is another disguised version. After demonstrating how God is dishonored by non-Israelites because of their "unnatural" sexual behavior, contrary to Israel's conventions and customs revealed in the Torah, Paul goes on to list typical non-Israelite wickedness that likewise dishonors God, presenting an alternate listing of the Ten Commandments, as follows: "The were filled with all manner of wickedness: (1) evil, covetousness, (2) malice, envy, (3) murder, strife, (4) deceit, malignity, (5) gossips, slanderers, (6) haters of God, (7) insolent, haughty, (8) boastful inventors of evil, disobedient to parents, (9) foolish, faithless, (10) heartless, ruthless" (Rom 1:29-32).

We find the same procedure in the lists in 1 Cor 6:9-11 and 1 Tim 1:9-11. These lists collocate males who lie with males as with a woman (*arsenokoitai*) and those taking the woman's place (*malakoi*) with adulterers. (Philo does the same thing [*Spec. Laws* 3]; they impugn the honor of the male.)

What is distinctive of Israel is that all breaches of the Ten Commandments, aside from coveting (that is, stealing property), require the death penalty. While in the Israelite tradition guilty persons alone are to be killed, not members of their family (Deut 24:16: "every man shall be put to death for his own sin").

Idolatry: Those serving and worshiping other gods (Deut 17:7) as well as false prophets (Deut 13:5) are to be put to death.

Blasphemy: Blasphemers of the name of the YHWH shall be put to death (Lev 24:16).

Temple Defilement: In Exod 19:12 going up Mount Sinai or touching the border of it while Moses was up there required the death penalty of the offender. The same rules were then applied to the Tent (and Temple: the altar and what is within the veil), where God dwelt in Israel (Num 1:51; 3:10; 18:7).

Sabbath Observance: Infractions of the Sabbath require the death penalty for the offender (Exod 31:14-15; 35:2; Num 15:35).

Parents: The death penalty is required of anyone who strikes father or mother or who curses father or mother (Exod 21:15, 17; Lev 20:9); this is also the fate of a recalcitrant son disobedient to parents (Deut 21:21).

Adultery: The death penalty is commanded for adulterer and adulteress (Deut 22:22), consenting betrothed woman and another man (Deut 22:24), rapist of unconsenting betrothed woman (Deut 22:25), a wife without tokens of virginity (Deut 22:21).

Murder: "Whoever strikes a man so that he dies shall be put to death" (Exod 21:12); also Num 35:16-21: murderers must be put to death. Specifically, "the avenger of blood shall put the murderer to death, when he meets him," for in Israel "you shall accept no ransom for the life of a murderer, who is guilty of death; but he shall be put to death" (Num 35:31; also Lev 24:17; 24:21). The owner of an ox known to kill must also be killed if the ox kills again (Exod 21:29); one disobedient to a priest-judge's judgment in a homicide case likewise gets the death penalty (Deut 17:12).

Kidnappers must be put to death (Exod 21:16; Deut 24:7).

False witnesses are to be put to death (Deut 19:19).

What about non-Israelites who transgress the Ten Commandments? This is not a concern in the Synoptics, yet as Paul describes it in Romans, outside Israel such transgressions are dealt with by God.

Three-Zone Personality

Whereas some philosophically oriented persons in the Greco-Roman world thought of the human person in terms of body and soul, the Mediterranean world traditionally thought in terms of what anthropologists have called "zones of interaction" with the world around. Three such zones make up the human person, and all appear repeatedly in the Gospels:

1. The zone of emotion-fused thought includes will, intellect, judgment, personality, and feeling all rolled together. It is the activity of the eyes and heart (sight, insight, understanding, choosing, loving, thinking, valuing, etc.).
2. The zone of self-expressive speech includes communication, particularly that which is self-revealing. It is listening and responding. It is the activity of the mouth, ears, tongue, lips, throat, and teeth (speaking, hearing, singing, swearing, cursing, listening, eloquence, silence, crying, etc.).
3. The zone of purposeful action is the zone of external behavior or interaction with the environment. It is the activity of the hands, feet, fingers, and legs (walking, sitting, standing, touching, accomplishing, etc.).

Human activity can be described in terms of any particular zone or all three.

Paul refers to the heart as equivalent to the mind (Phil 4:7); he mentions two zones (eyes-heart and mouth-ear zones) in the course of an argument (Rom 11:8-10), and he cites all three in an unknown scriptural quote that states, "What no eye has seen, nor ear heard, nor the heart of man conceived, what God has prepared for those who love him" (1 Cor 2:9: the three zones here are eyes—ears—heart—hands/feet or doing), and in his famous description of the body of Christ (1 Cor 12:14-21). When a writer refers to all three zones, we can assume comment is being made about complete human experience.

While Paul includes a section in nearly all of his letters exhorting his audiences to action (hands/feet), it is especially in the Corinthian correspondence and Romans that he focuses on the eyes-heart (1 Cor 2:9; 4:5; 7:37; 14:25; 2 Cor 1:22; 2:4; 3:2-3; 4:6; 5:12; 6:11, 13; 7:2-3, 15; Rom 2:5, 15, 29; 5:5; 6:17; 8:27; 9:2, 18; 10:6-10). This is not very surprising, since as change agent he seeks to create the intent to change perspectives and to stabilize and prevent discontinuance of the innovation he has proclaimed. Both these features, of course, are eyes-heart concerns.

Violence

Violence is about coercing others in a way that social norms do not endorse. Paul's letters frequently allude to instances of persons, visible and invisible, doing or planning violence toward him, usually in the name of the status quo. The use of violence here has as its ostensible purpose to maintain established values. Paul himself used violence in an attempt to control the behavior of Jesus-group members (Gal 1:23). He tells us that his fellow Israelites *lashed* him five times, that he was *beaten* with rods three times and *stoned* once (2 Cor 11:12). He knew of Jesus-group members suffering violence at the hands of Judeans as Jesus did (1 Thess 2:14), and he himself was leery of Judean "unbelievers" (Rom 15:31). As for invisible opponents, Paul was thwarted in his plan to visit the Thessalonians by Satan (1 Thess 2:18). It seems Satan too opposed some in Ephesus (Rom 16:20), as he did Paul himself (2 Cor 12:7).

The book of Acts is full of such incidents: the *arrest* of Peter and John (Acts 4:3), *violence* by unseen agents to Ananias and Sapphira (Acts 5:5, 10), the *arrest* of the apostles out of jealousy (Acts 5:18), the council's desire *to kill* them (Acts 6:33), the vigilante treatment of Stephen by a provoked crowd (Acts 7:54-60), and the like.

Instances of coercion and violence are evidenced throughout the Synoptic narratives. In Mark, after his baptism Jesus is *forced* into the wilderness by the spirit (Mark 1:12//Matt. 4:11//Luke 4:1). And soon after Jesus *drives out* an unseen, unclean spirit from a possessed man in the synagogue of Capernaum (Mark 1:25-26//Luke 4:35). The incident implies that unclean and unseen spirits can do violence to humans and that some humans know how to control them. Then, after the healing of the man with the withered hand, "the Pharisees went out, and immediately held counsel with the Herodians against him, how *to destroy* him" (Mark 3:6//Matt. 9:14//Luke 6:11). Soon after that notice, as crowds gathered so that Jesus and his core group could not even eat, "when his family heard it, they went out *to seize* him, for people were saying, "He is beside himself" (Mark 3:21). Luke, in turn, reports of Jesus' fellow villagers, "When they heard this, all in the synagogue were filled with wrath. And they *rose up and put him out* of the city, and led him to the brow of the hill on which their city was built, that they might *throw him down* headlong" (Luke 4:28-29). On a whim Herod Antipas could *seize* John the Baptist (Mark 6:17//Matt. 14:3//Luke 3:20). Jesus himself felt free to trespass over presumably well-established social boundaries when "he entered the Temple and began to *drive out* those who sold and those who bought in the Temple, and he overturned the tables of the money-changers and the seats of those who sold pigeons. He would not allow any one to carry anything through the Temple" (Mark 11:15-16//Matt. 21:12//Luke 19:45). Jesus' close followers would retaliate for shameless inhospitality with fire from the sky (Luke 9:54). As Mark notes, even legitimate authorities (high priests in the Temple area) held back in face of the possibility of *violence* against themselves: "And they tried to arrest him, but feared the multitude, for they perceived that he had told the parable against them; so they left him and went away" (Mark 12:12//Matt. 21:46//Luke 20:19). Yet Mark would have us believe that the authorities continued in their resolve: "And the chief priests and the scribes were seeking how to *arrest him* by stealth, and *kill him* for they said, 'Not during the feast lest there be a tumult of the people'" (Mark 14:1-2//Matt. 26:4//Luke 22:2). Finally, a crowd came and forcibly *seized* Jesus (Mark 14:43-52//Matt. 26:47-56//Luke 22:47-53).

Finally, when we get to the letter to the Hebrews, we are asked to focus on blood and gore (Heb 9:7—10:20; 12:4, 24; 13:11-12, 20). This is a community that regales in sacrifice and the endurance of pain. Even God is said to use pain as a "fatherly" device for his sons: "do not regard lightly the discipline of the Lord, nor lose courage when you are punished by him. For the Lord disciplines him whom he loves, and chastises every son whom he receives. It is for discipline that you have to endure. God is treating you as sons; for what son is there whom his father does not discipline?" (Heb 12:5-7).

By any reading, first-century Israelite societies, like their Roman and Greek counterparts, were violent societies, with frequent public violence and unsure and explosive crowd reaction. Ordinary persons did not have any rights. There was no universalism in the sense that all human beings were equally human, bearing common human endowments, common human rights independent of individual ethnic origin and social status. Tolerance was an idea whose time would come some 1,700 years later! Furthermore, the idea of a plurality of nations endowed with equal rights in the forum of nations was totally absent, since there were no "nations" as yet. Neither ancient Israelites nor ancient Athenians nor ancient Romans had any idea of juridical relations among broader ethnic groups. In the first century C.E., Roman statesmen dealt with other ethnic groups in terms of good faith based on patron-client relationships. In Roman perception, Rome was a patron, not a holder of an empire; it wanted persons to behave like clients. To behave otherwise was to be a rebel, an outlaw. Neither persons nor ethnic groups had what we would call "rights."

What modern readers often interpret as rights is political entitlement. For example, Roman citizens had preeminence in the *oikoumene* (the inhabited world). To dishonor one Roman was to dishonor, hence challenge, Rome itself. Consequently Roman citizens were always to be treated honorably by non-citizens; they were not to be flogged publicly, nor were they answerable to any tribunal but that of their own Caesar. Such were the ramifications of the customary values of honor and shame. Since persons and ethnic groups had no rights in our sense, any modern reader's perception of "oppression" in the first-century Mediterranean world would be quite anachronistic.

In short, the Mediterranean world was a violent world, and the Israelite tradition hallowed such violence. Philo, an Israelite Hellenistic philosopher of Alexandria, clearly explains this tradition:

> But if any members of the nation betray the honor of the One, they should suffer the utmost penalties. . . . All who have zeal for virtue should be permitted to exact the penalties offhand and with no delay, without bringing the offender before jury or council, or any kind of magistrate at all, and give full scope to the feelings which possess them, that hatred of evil and love of God which urges them to inflict punishment without mercy on the impious. They should think that the occasion has made them councilors, jurymen, governors, members of assembly, accusers, witnesses, laws, people,

> everything in fact, so that without fear or hindrance they may champion respect for God in full security. (*Spec. Laws* I, 54)

Later, he adds:

> Further if anyone cloaking himself under the name and guise of a prophet and claiming to be possessed by inspiration lead us on to the worship of the gods recognized in the different cities, we ought not to listen to him and be deceived by the name of prophet. For such a one is no prophet, but an impostor, since his oracles and pronouncement are falsehoods invented by himself. And if a brother or son or daughter or wife or a housemaster or a friend, however true, of anyone else who seems to be kindly disposed, urge us to a like course, bidding us fraternize with the multitude, resort to their Temples and join in their libations and sacrifices, we must punish him as a public and general enemy, taking little thought for the ties which bind us to him; and we must send round a report of his proposals to all lovers of piety, who will rush with a speed which brooks no delay to take vengeance on the unholy man, and deem it a religious duty to seek his death. For we should have one tie of affinity, one accepted sign of goodwill, namely the willingness to serve God and that our every word and deed promotes the cause of piety. But as for these kinships . . . let them all be cast aside if they do not seek earnestly the same goal, namely the honor of God, which is the indissoluble bond of all the affection which makes us one. (*Spec. Laws* I, 315–17)

Of course he is simply restating the biblical warrant for establishment violence set out in the book of Deuteronomy (13:5, 12; 17:2-6, 7, 12; 19:19; 21:21; 22:7, 21-24).

Wrath

In the context of challenge and riposte (**Challenge-Riposte**), the term "wrath" indicates that part of the riposte of the one challenged consisting in taking satisfaction for some dishonoring behavior. Honorable persons who are challenged must respond to the challenge. This response or riposte entails obtaining satisfaction for the dishonor done by the challenger. The "wrath of God" in the context of Israel's story refers to God's taking satisfaction to defend his honor in face of repeated acts of shame and dishonor (sin) on the part of Israelites. According to Paul's gospel of God, those called by the God of Israel comprise both Judean and Hellenistic Israelites, for whom Jesus crucified is God's power to offset the wrath of God and God's wisdom pointing to a way of meaningful human living (1 Cor 1:24-25). The cross as the power of God refers to Jesus crucified on the cross. Since power means the ability to produce some effect backed by a sanction of force, here the effect in question is that of disengaging and releasing persons from God's wrath. The outcome is redemption. Redemption means the restoration of family or group honor, and it is this honor that Jesus restores through his dying "for us" and thus allaying the threat of God's just wrath.

Bibliography

Aujac, Germaine. 1966. *Strabon et la science de son temps: Le sciences du monde.* Paris: Belle Lettres.

Aune, David E. 1997. *Revelation.* Vol. 1. WBC 52. Dallas: Word.

Ax, Wolfram. 1996. "Quattuor Linguae Latinae Aetates. Neue Forschungen zur Geschichte der Begriffe 'Goldene' und 'Silberne' Latinität." *Hermes* 124:220–40.

Baldwin, C. S. 1928. *Medieval Rhetoric and Poetic.* New York: Macmillan.

Barclay, John M. G. 1996. *Jews in the Mediterranean Diaspora: From Alexander to Trajan (323 BCE—117 CE).* Berkeley: University of California Press.

Barker, Margaret. 1992. *The Great Angel: A Study of Israel's Second God.* Louisville: Westminster/John Knox.

Bartchy, S. Scott. 1992. "Philemon, Epistle to." In *Anchor Bible Dictionary,* ed. David Noel Freedman, 5:305–10. New York: Doubleday, 1992.

Betz, Hans Dieter. 1979. *Galatians: A Commentary on Paul's Letter to the Churches in Galatia.* Hermeneia. Philadelphia: Fortress.

Blass, F., and A. Debrunner. 1961. *A Greek Grammar of the New Testament and Other Early Christian Literature.* Trans. and ed. Robert W. Funk. Chicago: University of Chicago Press.

Bodson, Liliane. 1982. "La notion de race animale chez les zoologistes et les agronomes dans l'antiquité." *Bulletin de la société d'ethnozootechnie* No. 29:7-14.

Boissevain, Jeremy. 1974. *Friends of Friends: Networks, Manipulators, and Coalitions.* New York: St. Martin's.

Boring, M. Eugene, Klaus Berger, and Carsten Colpe, eds. 1995. *Hellenistic Commentary to the New Testament.* Nashville: Abingdon.

Butts, James R. 1986. *The Progymnasmata of Theon: A New Text with Translation and Commentary.* Ph.D. Diss., Claremont Graduate School.

Cohen, Shaye. 1999. *The Beginnings of Jewishness: Boundaries, Varieties, Uncertainties.* Hellenistic Culture and Society 31. Berkeley: University of California Press.

———. 1993. "'Those Who Say They Are Jews and Are Not': How Do You Know a Jew in Antiquity When You See One?" In *Diasporas in Antiquity,* ed. Shaye Cohen and Ernest Frerichs, 1–46. Brown Judaic Studies 288. Atlanta: Scholars.

Craffert, Pieter F. 1989. "Paul's Damascus Experience as Reflected in Galatians 1: Call or Conversion?" *Scriptura* 29:36–47.

———. 1993. "The Pauline Movement and First-Century Judaism: A Framework for Transforming the Issues." *Neotestamentica* 27:233–62.

Danker, Frederick W., ed. 2000. *A Greek-English Lexicon of the New Testament and Other Early Christian Literature by Walter Bauer.* 3rd ed. Chicago: University of Chicago Press.

Davidson, Maxwell J. 1992. *Angels at Qumran: a Comparative Study of 1 Enoch 1-36, 72-108 and Sectarian Writings from Qumran*. Sheffield: JSOT.

Derrett, J. Duncan M. 1977. "The Disposal of Virgins." In idem, *Studies in the New Testament*, Vol. 1: *Glimpses of the Legal and Social Presuppositions of the Authors*, 185–92. Leiden: Brill.

Destro, Adriana, and Mauro Pesce. 1998. "Self, Identity, and Body in Paul and John." In *Self, Soul and Body in Religious Experience*, ed. A. I. Baumgarten, J. Assmann, and G. G. Stroumsa, 184–97. SHR 78. Leiden: Brill.

Downing, F. Gerald. 1995a. "Common Strands in Pagan, Jewish and Christian Eschatologies in the First Century." *Theologische Zeitschrift* 51:196–211.

———. 1995b. "Cosmic Eschatology in the First Century: 'Pagan,' Jewish and Christian." *L'antiquité classique* 64:99–109.

Duling, Dennis C. 2003. *The New Testament: History, Literature and Social Context*. 4th ed. Belmont, Calif.: Thomson/Wadsworth.

Dunn, James D. G. 1985. "Once More—Gal 1:18 *Historēsai Kēphan*; In Reply to Ottfried Hofius." *Zeitschrift für die Neutestamentliche Wissenschaft* 76:138–39.

Elliott, John H. 1990. "Paul, Galatians, and the Evil Eye." *Currents in Theology and Mission* 17:262–73.

———. 2000. *1 Peter: A New Translation with Introduction and Commentary*. AB 37B. New York: Doubleday.

———. 2003. "Elders As Honored Household Heads and Not Holders of 'Office' in Earliest Christianity." *BTB* 33:77–82.

Esler, Philip F. 1992. "Glossolalia and the Admission of Gentiles into the Early Christian Community." *BTB* 22:136–42.

———. 1995a. "Making and Breaking an Agreement Mediterranean Style: A New Reading of Galatians 2.1-14." *BibInt* 3:285–314.

———, ed. 1995b. *Modelling Early Christianity: Social Scientific Studies of the New Testament in Its Context*. London: Routledge.

———. 1996. "Group Boundaries and Intergroup Conflict in Galatians: A New Reading of Gal. 5:13—6:10." In *Ethnicity and the Bible*, ed. Mark Brett, 215–40. BibIntSer 19. Leiden: Brill.

———. 1997. "Family Imagery and Christian Identity in Gal. 5.13—6.10." In *Constructing Early Christian Families: Family as Social Reality and Metaphor*, ed. Halvor Moxnes, 121–49. London: Routledge.

———. 1998. *Galatians*. New Testament Readings. New York: Routledge.

———. 2001. "1 Thessalonians." In *Oxford Bible Commentary*, ed. John Barton and John Muddiman, 1199–212. Oxford: Oxford University Press.

———. 2003a. "Ancient Oleiculture and Ethnic Differentiation: The Meaning of the Olive-Tree Image in Romans 11." *JSNT* 26:103–12.

———. 2003b. *Conflict and Identity in Romans: The Social Setting of Paul's Letter*. Minneapolis: Fortress.

———. 2003c. "Social Identity, the Virtues, and the Good Life: A New Approach to Romans 12:1—15:13." *BTB* 33:61–63.

———. 2004a. "Paul and Stoicism: Romans 12 as a Test Case." *NTS* 50:106–24.

——. 2004b. "The Sodom Tradition in Romans 1:18-32." *BTB* 34:4–16.

Fohrer, Georg. 1952. "Die Gattung der Berichte über symbolishes Handlungen der Propheten." *Zeitschrift für die alttestamentliche Wissenschaft* 64:101–20.

Ford, Josephine Massingberd. 1964. "Levirate Marriage in St. Paul." *NTS* 10:361–65.

——. 1965. "St. Paul the Philogamist." *NTS* 11:326–48.

——. 1966a. "The First Epistle to the Corinthians or the First Epistle to the Hebrews?" *CBQ* 28:402–16.

——. 1966b. "The Meaning of Virgin." *NTS* 12:293–99.

Gieschen, Charles A. 1998. *Angelomorphic Christology: Antecedents and Early Evidence.* Arbeiten zur Geschichte des antiken Judentums und des Urchristentums 42. Leiden: Brill.

Gooch, Peter D. 1993. *Dangerous Food: 1 Corinthians 8–10 in Its Context.* Studies in Christianity and Judaism 5. Waterloo, Ont.: Wilfred Laurier University Press.

Goodman, Felicitas D. 1972. *Speaking in Tongues: A Cross-Cultural Study of Glossolalia.* Chicago: University of Chicago Press.

——. 1973. "Glossolalia and Hallucination in Pentecostal Congregations." *Psychiatria Clinica* 6:97–103.

——. 2001. *Maya Apocalypse: Seventeen Years with the Women of a Yucatan Village.* Bloomington: University of Indiana Press.

Greenwald, A. G., and Pratkanis A. R. 1984. "The Self." In *Handbook of Social Cognition*, ed. R. S. Wyler and T. K. Srull Wyler, vol. 3, 129–78. Hillsdale, N.J.: Erlbaum.

Gulliver, P. H. 1979. *Disputes and Negotiations: A Cross-Cultural Perspective.* Studies on Law and Social Control. New York: Academic.

Harris, Harold A. 1972. *Sport in Greece and Rome.* Ithaca, N.Y.: Cornell University Press.

Harvey, Graham. 1996. *The True Israel: Uses of the Names Jew, Hebrew and Israel in Ancient Jewish and Early Christian Literature.* Arbeiten zur Geschichte des antiken Judentums und des Urchristentums 35. Leiden: Brill.

Hopkins, Keith. 1998. "Christian Number and Its Implications." *Journal of Early Christian Studies* 6:185–226.

Jeremias, Joachim. 1969. *Jerusalem in the Time of Jesus: An Investigation into Economic and Social Conditions during the New Testament Period.* Trans. F. H. Cave and C. H. Cave. Philadelphia: Fortress.

Jewett, Robert. 1993. "Tenement Churches and Communal Meals in the Early Church: The Implications of a Form-Critical Analysis of 2 Thessalonians 3:10." *Biblical Research* 38:23–42.

Joubert, Stephan. 2000. *Paul as Benefactor: Reciprocity, Strategy and Theological Reflection in Paul's Collection.* WUNT 124. Tübingen: Mohr/Siebeck.

Kant, Laurence H. 1987. "Jewish Inscriptions in Greek and Latin." In *ANRW* 2.20.2:617–713.

Kennedy, Charles A. 1987. "The Cult of the Dead in Corinth." In *Love and Death in the Ancient Near East: Essays in Honor of Marvin H. Pope*, ed. John H. Marks and Robert M. Good, 227–36. Guilford, Conn.: Four Quarters.

———. 1994. "The Semantic Field of the Term 'Idolatry.'" In *Uncovering Ancient Stones: Essays in Memory of H. Neil Richardson*, ed. Lewis M. Hopfe, 193–204. Winona Lake, Ind.: Eisenbrauns.

Koester, Craig R. 1990. "'The Savior of the World' (John 4:42)." *JBL* 109:665–80.

Lampe, Peter. 2004. *From Paul to Valentinus: Christians at Rome in the First Two Centuries.* Trans. Michael Steinhauser. Ed. Marshall D. Johnson. Minneapolis: Fortress.

Lutz, Cora E. 1947. *Musonius Rufus: "The Roman Socrates."* New Haven: Yale University Press. Reprinted from *Yale Classical Studies* 10.

Lyons, George. 1985. *Pauline Autobiography: Toward a New Understanding.* SBL Dissertation Series 73. Atlanta: Scholars.

Malina, Bruce J. 1969. "Some Observations on the Origin of Sin in Judaism and in St. Paul." *CBQ* 31:18–34.

———. 1981. "The Apostle Paul and Law: Prolegomena for a Hermeneutic." *Creighton Law Review* 14:1305–39.

———. 1986. "'Religion' in the World of Paul." *BTB* 16:92–101.

———. 1992. "Is There a Circum-Mediterranean Person? Looking for Stereotypes." *BTB* 22:66–87.

———. 1994a. "Establishment Violence in the New Testament World." *Scriptura* 51:51–78.

———. 1994b. "Religion in the Imagined New Testament World." *Scriptura* 51:1–26.

———. 1995a. "Early Christian Groups: Using Small Group Formation Theory to Explain Christian Organizations." In Esler 1995b:96–113.

———. 1995b. "Power, Pain and Personhood: Asceticism in the Ancient Mediterranean World." In *Asceticism: Proceedings of the First International Congress on Asceticism*, ed. Vincent L. Wimbush and R. Valantasis, 162–77. New York: Oxford University Press.

———. 2001. *The New Testament World: Insights from Cultural Anthropology.* 3rd ed. Louisville: Westminster John Knox.

———, 2005. "From the Jesus Faction to the Synoptic Gospels. The Synoptic Gospels as Third Generation Phenomena." In *Kontexte der Schrift, Bd. 2: Kultur, Politik, Religion, Sprache-Text—Für Wolfgang Stegemann zum 60. Geburtstag*, ed. Christian Strecker. 61–74. Kohlhammer: Stuttgart.

———, and Jerome H. Neyrey. 1996. *Portraits of Paul: An Archaeology of Ancient Personality.* Louisville: Westminster John Knox.

———, and John J. Pilch. 2000. *Social-Science Commentary on the Book of Revelation.* Minneapolis: Fortress.

———, and Richard L. Rohrbaugh. 1998. *Social-Science Commentary on the Gospel of John.* Minneapolis: Fortress.

———, and Richard L. Rohrbaugh. 2003. *Social-Science Commentary on the Synoptic Gospels.* 2nd ed. Minneapolis: Fortress.

Mills, Lawrence. 1913. *Our Own Religion in Ancient Persia.* Chicago: Open Court.

——. 1977. *Zarathustra, Philo, The Achaemenids and Israel.* New York: AMS. Reprints from 1903–1906.

Momigliano, Arnaldo 1975. *Alien Wisdom: The Limits of Hellenization.* Cambridge: Cambridge University Press.

Moreland, Richard L., and John M. Levine. 1988. "Group Dynamics Over Time: Development and Socialization in Small Groups." In *The Social Psychology of Time: New Perspectives*, edited by Joseph E. McGrath, 151–81. Newbury Park, Calif.: Sage.

Murphy-O'Connor, Jerome. 1996. *Paul: A Critical Life.* Oxford: Clarendon Press.

Nader, Laura, and Harry F. Todd Jr. 1978. "Introduction." In *The Disputing Process—Law in Ten Societies*, ed. Laura Nader and Harry F. Todd Jr., 1–40. New York: Columbia University Press.

Neufeld, Dietmar. 2000. "Acts of Admonition and Rebuke: A Speech-Act Approach to I Corinthians 6:1-11." *BibInt* 8:375–99.

Neyrey, Jerome H. 1986a. "Body Language in 1 Corinthians: The Use of Anthropological Models for Understanding Paul and His Opponents." *Semeia* 35:129–70.

——. 1986b. "Witchcraft Accusations in 2 Cor 10–13: Paul in Social Science Perspective." *Listening* 21:160–70.

——. 1988. "Bewitched in Galatia: Paul in Social Science Perspective." *CBQ* 50:72–100.

——. 1990. *Paul in Other Words: A Cultural Reading of His Letters.* Louisville: Westminster John Knox.

——. 2004. *Render to God: New Testament Understandings of the Divine.* Minneapolis: Fortress.

Nock, Arthur Danby. 1933. *Conversion: The Old and the New in Religion from Alexander the Great to Augustine of Hippo.* London: Oxford University Press.

Nock, Arthur Danby, ed., and A. J. Festugière, trans. 1946–1954. *Corpus hermeticum.* 4 vols. Collection des universités de France. Paris: Belles Lettres.

Oakman, Douglas E. 2002. "Money in the Moral Universe of the New Testament." In Stegemann, Malina, and Theissen 2002:335–48.

O'Donnell, James J. 1974. "The Demise of Paganism." *Traditio* 35:45–88.

Osiek, Carolyn, and David L. Balch. 1997. *Families in the New Testament World: Households and House Churches.* Louisville: Westminster John Knox.

Osiek, Carolyn, and Margaret Y. MacDonald, with Janet H. Tulloch. 2005. *A Woman's Place: House Churches in Earliest Christianity.* Minneapolis: Fortress.

Petrochilos, Nicholas. 1974. *Roman Attitudes to the Greeks.* Athens: National and Capodistrian University of Athens, Faculty of Arts.

Pilch, John J. 1983. *Galatians and Romans.* Collegeville Bible Commentary 6. Collegeville, Minn.: Liturgical.

——. 1991. *Introducing the Cultural Context of the New Testament.* Hear the Word, vol. 2. New York: Paulist.

——. 1993. "Visions in Revelation and Alternate Consciousness: A Perspective from Cultural Anthropology." *Listening* 28:231–44.

——. 1995. "The Transfiguration of Jesus: An Experience of Alternate Reality." In Esler 1995b:47–64.
——. 1997. "Psychological and Psychoanalytical Approaches to Interpreting the Bible in Social-Scientific Context." *BTB* 27:112–16.
——. 1998. "Appearances of the Risen Jesus in Cultural Context: Experiences of Alternate Reality." *BTB* 28: 52–60.
——. 1999. *The Cultural Dictionary of the Bible*. Collegeville, Minn.: Liturgical.
——. 2000. *Healing in the New Testament: Insights from Medical and Mediterranean Anthropology*. Minneapolis: Fortress.
——, ed. 2001. *Social Scientific Models for Interpreting the Bible: Essays by the Context Group in Honor of Bruce J. Malina*. BibIntSer 53. Leiden: Brill.
——. 2002a. "Paul's Ecstatic Trance Experience near Damascus in Acts of the Apostles." HTS 58:690–707.
——. 2002b. "Altered States of Consciousness in the Synoptics." In Stegemann, Malina, and Theissen 2002:103–15.
——. 2002c. "A Window into the Biblical World: No Thank You!" *The Bible Today* 40.1:49–53.
——. 2003. "Paul's Call to Be an Apostle." *Analecta Cracoviensia* 35:221–30.
——. 2004. *Visions and Healing in Acts of the Apostles: How the Early Believers Experienced God*. Collegeville, Minn.: Liturgical.
——. 2005. "Paul's Call to Be a Holy Man (Apostle): In His Own Words and In Other Words." *HvTSt* 65:371–83.
——, and Bruce J. Malina, eds. 1998. *Handbook of Biblical Social Values*. Peabody, Mass.: Hendrickson.
Rogers, Everett M. 1995. *Diffusion of Innovations*. 4th ed. New York: Free Press.
——, with F. F. Shoemaker. 1971. *Communication of Innovations: A Cross-Cultural Approach*. 2nd ed. New York: Free Press.
Rohrbaugh, Richard L., ed. 1996. *The Social Sciences and New Testament Interpretation*. Peabody, Mass.: Hendrickson.
——. 2001. "Gossip in the New Testament." In Pilch 2001:239–59.
——. 2002. "Ethnocentrism and Historical Questions about Jesus." In Stegemann, Malina, and Theissen 2002:27–44.
Rubin, N. 1989. "On Drawing Down the Prepuce and Incision of the Foreskin—*Peri'ah*." *Zion* 54:105–17 (in Hebrew).
Sanford, A. J., and S. C. Garrod. 1981. *Understanding Written Language: Explorations of Comprehension Beyond the Sentence*. New York: Wiley.
Scott, Alan. 1991. *Origen and the Life of the Stars: A History of an Idea*. Oxford Early Christian Studies. Oxford: Clarendon.
Selwyn, Edward Gordon. 1947. *The First Epistle of St. Peter: The Greek Text with Introduction, Notes, and Essays*. 2nd ed. New York: St. Martin's.
Smith, Jay E. 2001. "Another Look at 4Q416 2 ii.21, a Critical Parallel to First Thessalonians 4:4." *CBQ* 63:499–504.

Stegemann, Ekkehard W., and Wolfgang Stegemann. 1999. *The Jesus Movement: A Social History of Its First Century*. Trans. O. C. Dean Jr. Minneapolis: Fortress.

Stegemann, Wolfgang, Bruce J. Malina, and Gerd Theissen, eds. 2002. *The Social Setting of Jesus and the Gospels*. Minneapolis: Fortress.

Taylor, Nicholas H. 2002. "Who Persecuted the Thessalonian Christians?" HTS 58:784–801.

Triandis, Harry C. 1990. "Cross-Cultural Studies of Individualism and Collectivism." In *Nebraska Symposium on Motivation 1989*, ed. Richard A. Dienstbier et al., 41–133. Lincoln: University of Nebraska Press.

Tuckman, B. W. 1965. "Developmental Sequence in Small Groups." *Psychological Bulletin* 63:384–99.

Van der Horst, P. W. 1979. "Der Schatten im Hellenistischen Volksglauben." In *Studies in Hellenistic Religions*, ed. M. J. Vermaseren, 27–36. Etudes preliminaires aux religions orientales dans l'empire romain 78. Leiden: Brill.

Veyne, Paul. 1993. "*Humanitas*: Romans and Non-Romans." In *The Romans*, ed. Andrea Giardina, 342–69. Trans. Lydia G. Cochrane. Chicago: University of Chicago Press. Italian ed. 1989.

Walbank, F. W. 2002. "The Problem of Greek Nationality." In *Greek and Barbarians*, ed. Thomas Harrison, 234–56. Routledge: New York.

White, Richard J., ed. and trans. 1975. *The Interpretation of Dreams (Oneirocritica) by Artemidorus*. Torrance, Calif.: Original Books.

Zerwick, Maximiliano. 1966. *Graecitas Biblica Novi Testamenti Exemplis Illustratur*. 5th ed. Rome: Pontificio Instituto Biblico.

List of Reading Scenarios

Altered States of Consciousness
Baptism
Challenge-Riposte
Change Agent
Circumcision
City
Clean and Unclean: See Purity/Pollution
Clique
Collectivistic Personality
Conflict
Coworkers: Innovators and First Adopters
Death and Resurrection
Demons/Demon Possession
Devolution
Dispute Process
Economics: See Religion, Economics, and Politics
Ekklēsia (Gathering)
Encomium
Establishment Violence: See Violence
Evil Eye
Eyes-Heart: See Three-Zone Personality
Fictive Kinship
Flesh and Spirit
God: See Many Gods and Many Lords
Greeks and Israelites See also Jew and Greek/Judean and Hellenist)
Hellenist: See Jew and Greek/ Judean and Hellenist
Hellenistic Letter
Holy Man
Honor-Shame Societies
Israelite: See Greeks and Israelites; Jew and Greek/Judean and Hellenist
Jew and Greek/Judean and Hellenist
Judean: See Jew and Greek/ Judean and Hellenist
Kingdom of God
Love and Hate
Many Gods and Many Lords
Meals
The Military
Opinion Leaders
Patronage System
Pauline Norms
Pharisaic Ideology
Political Religion: See Religion, Economics, and Politics
Porneia
Prayer
Prophetic Symbolic Action
Purity/Pollution
Reciprocity
Religion, Economics, and Politics
Righteousness
Sacred/Profane
Salvation
Slavery
Small-Group Development
Social Identity
Son of God
Ten Commandments
Three-Zone Personality
Violence
Wrath